INSTRUCTOR'S MANUAL TO ACCOMPANY

Literature for Composition

Essays, Fiction, Poetry, and Drama

SEVENTH EDITION

Edited by

Sylvan Barnet
Tufts University

William Burto
University of Massachusetts at Lowell

William E. Cain
Wellesley College

New York   Boston   San Francisco
London   Toronto   Sydney   Tokyo   Singapore   Madrid
Mexico City   Munich   Paris   Cape Town   Hong Kong   Montreal

Acquisitions Editor: Erika Berg
Senior Supplements Editor: Donna Campion
Electronic Page Makeup: Dianne Hall

> This work is protected by United States copyright laws and is provided solely for the use of instructors in teaching their courses and assessing student learning. Dissemination or sale of any part of this work (including on the World Wide Web) will destroy the integrity of the work and is not permitted. The work and materials from it should never be made available to students except by instructors using the accompanying text in their classes. All recipients of this work are expected to abide by these restrictions and to honor the intended pedagogical purposes and the needs of other instructors who rely on these materials.

Instructor's Handbook to Accompany *Literature for Composition: Essays, Fiction, Poetry, and Drama*, Seventh Edition, by Sylvan Barnet, William Burto, and William E. Cain.

Copyright © 2005 Pearson Education, Inc.

All rights reserved. No part of this book may be reproduced, stored in a retrieval system, or transmitted in any form or by any means, electronic, mechanical, photocopying, recording, or otherwise, without the prior written permission of the publisher. Printed in the United States.

ISBN: 0-321-27721-X

1 2 3 4 5 6 7 8 9 10—PBT—07 06 05 04

Contents

Preface   xv
Using the CD-ROM   xvii
Using the "Short Views"   xix
The First Day   1

PART I Getting Started: From Response to Argument

CHAPTER 1   THE WRITER AS READER   4
KATE CHOPIN Ripe Figs   4

CHAPTER 2   THE READER AS WRITER   6
KATE CHOPIN The Story of an Hour   6
KATE CHOPIN Désirée's Baby   7
KATE CHOPIN The Storm   8
TOBIAS WOLFF Powder   10

CHAPTER 3   READING LITERATURE CLOSELY: EXPLICATION   12
LANGSTON HUGHES Harlem   12
WILLIAM SHAKESPEARE Sonnet 73 ("That time of year thou mayst in me behold")   13
JOHN DONNE Holy Sonnet XIV ("Batter my heart, three-personed God")   14
WILLIAM BLAKE London   15
EMILY BRONTË Spellbound   16

LI-YOUNG LEE I Ask My Mother to Sing   18
RANDALL JARRELL The Death of the Ball Turret Gunner   18

CHAPTER 4 READING LITERATURE CLOSELY: ANALYSIS   20

Suggestions for Further Reading   20
ANONYMOUS The Judgment of Solomon   21
LUKE The Parable of the Prodigal Son   23
JAMES THURBER The Secret Life of Walter Mitty   25
APHRA BEHN Song: Love Armed   27
EDGAR ALLAN POE The Cask of Amontillado   27
GUY DE MAUPASSANT The Necklace   28
KATHERINE ANNE PORTER The Jilting of Granny Weatherall   32
JOSÉ ARMAS El Tonto del Barrio   34
LESLIE MARMON SILKO The Man to Send Rain Clouds   36
ROBERT FROST Come In   38
ELIZABETH BISHOP Filling Station   38
ROBERT HERRICK To the Virgins, to Make Much of Time   39
LYN LIFSHIN My Mother and the Bed   40
MARTÍN ESPADA Bully   40

CHAPTER 5 OTHER KINDS OF WRITING ABOUT LITERATURE   42

WILLIAM BLAKE The Tyger   42
X. J. KENNEDY For Allen Ginsberg   43
WILLIAM BUTLER YEATS Annunciation, Leda and the Swan [1924],
   Leda and the Swan [1933]   44
MONA VAN DUYN Leda   49
WILLIAM CARLOS WILLIAMS This Is Just to Say   50

CHAPTER 6 READING AND WRITING ABOUT VISUAL CULTURE   53

LOU JACOBS JR. What Qualities Does a Good Photograph Have?   53
   AN AMERICAN PICTURE ALBUM: TEN IMAGES   54
      GRANT WOOD American Gothic   54
      GORDON PARKS American Gothic   55
      LEWIS W. HINE Singer Power Machine Sewing Group   56
      ALBERT BRESNIK Amelia Earhart   58
      LEWIS W. HINE Icarus, Empire State Building, 1930   59
      ERNEST C. WITHERS "No White People Allowed in Zoo Today"   60
      ALON REININGER Pledging Allegiance   62

ANONYMOUS Marilyn Monroe 63
ANONYMOUS Charlotte Perkins Gilman at a Suffrage Rally 64
NEIL ARMSTRONG Buzz Aldrin on the Moon 65

PART II Up Close: Thinking Critically about Literary Works and Literary Forms

CHAPTER 7 CRITICAL THINKING: ASKING QUESTIONS AND MAKING COMPARISONS 68

WILLIAM NOTMAN Sitting Bull and Buffalo Bill 68
E. E. CUMMINGS Buffalo Bill's 71
EMILY DICKINSON I felt a Funeral, in my Brain; I felt a Cleaving in my Mind— ; The Dust behind I strove to join 74
WILLIAM BUTLER YEATS The Wild Swans at Coole 77
GWENDOLYN BROOKS We Real Cool 78
ANDREW HUDGINS The Wild Swans Skip School 79
ANONYMOUS The Silver Swan 80

CHAPTER 8 READING AND WRITING ABOUT ESSAYS 82

BRENT STAPLES Black Men and Public Space 82
LANGSTON HUGHES Salvation 83
LAURA VANDERKAM Hookups Starve the Soul 84
AMY TAN fish cheeks 84

CHAPTER 9 READING AND WRITING ABOUT FICTION 86

GRACE PALEY Samuel 86
ANTON CHEKHOV Misery 87
EUDORA WELTY A Worn Path 90
OSCAR CASARES Yolanda 91

CHAPTER 10 THINKING AND WRITING CRITICALLY ABOUT SHORT STORIES: TWO CASE STUDIES 93

FLANNERY O'CONNOR A Good Man Is Hard to Find 93
FLANNERY O'CONNOR Revelation 94
JOHN UPDIKE A & P 96
JOHN UPDIKE Pygmalion 97
JOHN UPDIKE The Rumor 99
JOHN UPDIKE Oliver's Evolution 101

CHAPTER 11 FICTION INTO FILM   103

JOYCE CAROL OATES Where Are You Going, Where Have You Been?   103

CHAPTER 12 READING AND WRITING ABOUT DRAMA   106

SOPHOCLES Antigone   106
AUGUST WILSON Fences   107

CHAPTER 13 THINKING CRITICALLY ABOUT DRAMA   110

TENNESSEE WILLIAMS The Glass Menagerie   110

CHAPTER 14 READING AND WRITING ABOUT POETRY   112

EMILY DICKINSON Wild Nights—Wild Nights   112
WILLIAM SHAKESPEARE Sonnet 146 ("Poor soul, the center of my sinful earth")   114
ROBERT FROST The Telephone   114
WILLIAM SHAKESPEARE Sonnet 130 ("My mistress' eyes are nothing like the sun")   116
DANA GIOIA Money   117
ROBERT FROST The Hardship of Accounting   118
EDMUND WALLER Song (Go, Lovely Rose)   118
WILLIAM BLAKE The Sick Rose   119
LINDA PASTAN Jump Cabling   119
ROBERT HERRICK Upon Julia's Clothes   120
CHRISTINA ROSSETTI In an Artist's Studio   120
BILLY COLLINS Sonnet   121
ROBERT BROWNING My Last Duchess   123
E. E. CUMMINGS anyone lived in a pretty how town   123
SYLVIA PLATH Daddy   124
LOUISE ERDRICH Indian Boarding School: The Runaways   125
ETHERIDGE KNIGHT For Malcolm, a Year After   126
BASHO An Old Pond   129
THOMAS HARDY Neutral Tones   132
WILLIAM BUTLER YEATS Sailing to Byzantium   133
JAMES WRIGHT Lying in a Hammock at William Duffy's Farm in Pine Island, Minnesota   135
ANONYMOUS Deep River   136
WILLIAM CARLOS WILLIAMS The Red Wheelbarrow   137
WALT WHITMAN A Noiseless Patient Spider   138
THOMAS HARDY The Photograph   139

CHAPTER 15 **THINKING CRITICALLY ABOUT POETRY** **141**
    A CASEBOOK ON EMILY DICKINSON 141
        I heard a Fly buzz—when I died— 141
        The Soul selects her own Society 142
        These are the days when Birds come back 143
        Papa above! 143
        There's a certain Slant of light 144
        This World is not Conclusion 146
        I got so I could hear his name— 148
        Those—dying, then 149
        Apparently with no surprise 149
        Tell all the Truth but tell it slant 150
W. C. HANDY St. Louis Blues 151
BESSIE SMITH Thinking Blues 152
ROBERT JOHNSON Walkin' Blues 154
PAUL LAURENCE DUNBAR Blue 155
W. H. AUDEN Funeral Blues 157
LANGSTON HUGHES Too Blue 158
JOHNNY CASH Folsom Prison Blues 159
MERLE HAGGARD Workin' Man Blues 160
LINDA PASTAN Mini Blues 162
ALLEN GINSBERG Father Death Blues 163
CHARLES WRIGHT Laguna Blues 165
SHERMAN ALEXIE Reservation Blues 167
JANE FLANDERS Van Gogh's Bed 169
WILLIAM CARLOS WILLIAMS The Great Figure 170
ADRIENNE RICH Mourning Picture 172
CATHY SONG Beauty and Sadness 174
MARY JO SALTER The Rebirth of Venus 175
ANNE SEXTON The Starry Night 176
W. H. AUDEN Musée des Beaux Arts 178
X. J. KENNEDY Nude Descending a Staircase 179
GREG PAPE American Flamingo 181
CARL PHILLIPS Luncheon on the Grass 183
JOHN UPDIKE Before the Mirror 186
WISLAWA SZYMBORSKA Brueghel's Two Monkeys 188

PART III Standing Back: Arguing Interpretations and Evaluations, and Understanding Critical Strategies

CHAPTER 16 ARGUING AN INTERPRETATION   192

ROBERT FROST Stopping by Woods on a Snowy Evening   192
JOHN MILTON When I Consider How My Light Is Spent   193
ROBERT FROST Mending Wall   193
WILLIAM WORDSWORTH A Slumber Did My Spirit Seal   194
T. S. ELIOT The Love Song of J. Alfred Prufrock   196
JOHN KEATS Ode on a Grecian Urn   197

CHAPTER 17 ARGUING AN EVALUATION   201

MATTHEW ARNOLD Dover Beach   201
ANTHONY HECHT The Dover Bitch   203
ROBERT FROST Design   204
IRA GERSHWIN The Man That Got Away   205
KATHERINE MANSFIELD Miss Brill   205

CHAPTER 18 WRITING ABOUT LITERATURE: AN OVERVIEW OF CRITICAL STRATEGIES   208

Suggestions for Further Reading   208

PART IV A Thematic Anthology

CHAPTER 19 JOURNEYS   214

JOAN DIDION On Going Home   214
MONTESQUIEU (Charles de Secondat, Baron de la Brède) Persian Letters   214
TONI CADE BAMBARA The Lesson   215
BOBBIE ANN MASON Shiloh   217
ANONYMOUS JAPANESE FOLK TALE The Mountain-Climber   219
JOHN KEATS On First Looking into Chapman's Homer   221
PERCY BYSSHE SHELLEY Ozymandias   222
ALFRED, LORD TENNYSON Ulysses   223
CARL SANDBURG Limited   224

COUNTEE CULLEN Incident 226
WILLIAM STAFFORD Traveling Through the Dark 227
ROBERT FROST The Pasture 228
WENDELL BERRY Stay Home 231
ADRIENNE RICH Diving into the Wreck 231
DEREK WALCOTT A Far Cry from Africa 232
SHERMAN ALEXIE On the Amtrak from Boston to New York City 233
CHRISTINA ROSSETTI Uphill 234
EMILY DICKINSON Because I could not stop for Death 234

CHAPTER 20   LOVE AND HATE   236

SEI SHŌNAGON A Lover's Departure 236
JUDITH ORTIZ COFER I Fell in Love, or My Hormones Awakened 237
ERNEST HEMINGWAY Cat in the Rain 237
WILLIAM FAULKNER A Rose for Emily 239
ZORA NEALE HURSTON Sweat 241
BEL KAUFMAN Sunday in the Park 243
RAYMOND CARVER Mine, Little Things 245
RAYMOND CARVER What We Talk about When We Talk about Love 249
RAYMOND CARVER Cathedral 251
MICHAEL GERBER AND JONATHAN SCHWARZ What We Talk about When We Talk about Doughnuts 254
ANONYMOUS Western Wind 255
CHRISTOPHER MARLOWE Come Live with Me and Be My Love 256
SIR WALTER RALEIGH The Nymph's Reply to the Shepherd 256
JOHN DONNE The Bait 256
WILLIAM SHAKESPEARE Sonnet 29 ("When, in disgrace with Fortune and men's eyes") 257
WILLIAM SHAKESPEARE Sonnet 116 ("Let me not to the marriage of true minds") 259
JOHN DONNE A Valediction: Forbidding Mourning 259
ANDREW MARVELL To His Coy Mistress 260
WILLIAM BLAKE The Garden of Love 261
WILLIAM BLAKE A Poison Tree 262
WALT WHITMAN When I Heard at the Close of the Day 263
WALT WHITMAN I Saw in Louisiana a Live-Oak Growing 264
EDNA ST. VINCENT MILLAY Love Is Not All: It Is Not Meat nor Drink 265
ROBERT FROST The Silken Tent 265
ADRIENNE RICH Novella 266

ADRIENNE RICH XI.   267
ROBERT PACK The Frog Prince   267
JOSEPH BRODSKY Love Song   269
NIKKI GIOVANNI Love in Place   270
CAROL MUSKE Chivalry   270
KITTY TSUI A Chinese Banquet   271
TERRENCE McNALLY Andre's Mother   273

CHAPTER 21 MAKING MEN AND WOMEN   276

STEVEN DOLOFF The Opposite Sex   276
GRETEL EHRLICH About Men   277
CHARLOTTE PERKINS GILMAN The Yellow Wallpaper   278
RICHARD WRIGHT The Man Who Was Almost a Man   281
GLORIA NAYLOR The Two   283
ALICE MUNRO Boys and Girls   284
ANONYMOUS NURSERY RHYME What Are Little Boys Made Of   286
ANONYMOUS Higamus, Hogamus   286
DOROTHY PARKER General Review of the Sex Situation   287
RITA DOVE Daystar   287
ROBERT HAYDEN Those Winter Sundays   288
THEODORE ROETHKE My Papa's Waltz   289
SHARON OLDS Rites of Passage   289
FRANK O'HARA Homosexuality   290
TESS GALLAGHER I Stop Writing the Poem   294
JULIA ALVAREZ Woman's Work   296
MARGE PIERCY Barbie Doll   297
HENRIK IBSEN A Doll's House   298

CHAPTER 22 INNOCENCE AND EXPERIENCE   301

MAYA ANGELOU Graduation   301
NATHANIEL HAWTHORNE Young Goodman Brown   302
JAMES JOYCE Araby   304
LANGSTON HUGHES One Friday Morning   307
ISAAC BASHEVIS SINGER The Son from America   308
WILLIAM BLAKE Infant Joy   309
WILLIAM BLAKE Infant Sorrow   310
WILLIAM BLAKE The Echoing Green   311
GERARD MANLEY HOPKINS Spring and Fall: To a Young Child   312
A. E. HOUSMAN When I Was One-and-Twenty   313

E. E. CUMMINGS in Just-   313
LOUISE GLÜCK The School Children   314
LOUISE GLÜCK Gretel in Darkness   315
WILLIAM SHAKESPEARE Hamlet   315
A Note on Staging Scenes in the Classroom   316
A Note on Writing a Review   318
Scene-by-Scene Commentary   319

CHAPTER 23 STUDYING AMERICA IN CRISIS: RESPONDING TO LITERATURE OF THE CIVIL WAR, THE GREAT DEPRESSION, THE VIETNAM WAR, AND SEPTEMBER 11, 2001   355

JEFFERSON DAVIS Inaugural Address   355
MARY BOYKIN MILLER CHESNUT November 28, 1861   358
ABRAHAM LINCOLN Address at the Dedication of the Gettysburg National Cemetery   359
MARTHA LIGGAN Dear Madam   361
W. E. B. DU BOIS The Lesson for Americans   363
AMBROSE BIERCE A Horseman in the Sky   365
STEPHEN CRANE An Episode of War   367
DANIEL DECATUR EMMETT Dixie's Land   369
JULIA WARD HOWE Battle Hymn of the Republic   370
HERMAN MELVILLE The March into Virginia   371
HERMAN MELVILLE DuPont's Round Fight   373
HERMAN MELVILLE Shiloh   374
SIDNEY LANIER The Dying Words of Jackson   375
ANONYMOUS Women at the Grave of Stonewall Jackson   377
WALT WHITMAN Reconciliation   378
WALT WHITMAN Vigil Strange I Kept on the Field One Night   378
ANDREW HUDGINS At Chancellorsville   380
STUDS TERKEL Interviews   382
TILLIE OLSEN I Stand Here Ironing   385
E. Y. HARBURG Brother, Can You Spare a Dime?   387
ANONYMOUS My God, How the Money Rolls In   390
ALFRED HAYES Joe Hill   391
LANGSTON HUGHES Out of Work   392
DAVID WAGONER Hooverville   393
MOLLY IVINS A Short Story about the Vietnam War Memorial   394
TIM O'BRIEN The Things They Carried   395
YUSEF KOMUNYAKAA Facing It   398
MAYA LIN Vietnam Veterans Memorial   399
JOHN UPDIKE Talk of the Town: September 11, 2001   401

MICHAEL KINSLEY How to Live a Rational Life   402
CATHARINE R. STIMPSON Staffing   405
BILLY COLLINS The Names   407
DEBORAH GARRISON September Poem   410

CHAPTER 24   IDENTITY IN AMERICA   411

THOMAS JEFFERSON The Declaration of Independence   411
ANNA LISA RAYA It's Hard Enough Being Me   413
ANDREW LAM Who Will Light Incense When Mother's Gone?   414
AMY TAN Two Kinds   415
ALICE WALKER Everyday Use   417
KATHERINE MIN Courting a Monk   418
EMMA LAZARUS The New Colossus   422
TSENG KWONG CHI Statue of Liberty, New York City   425
THOMAS BAILEY ALDRICH The Unguarded Gates   426
JOSEPH BRUCHAC III Ellis Island   428
ANONYMOUS The Registry Room, Ellis Island, ca. 1912   429
ANONYMOUS Slavic Women Arrive at Ellis Island in the Winter of 1910   429
EDWIN ARLINGTON ROBINSON Richard Cory   430
AURORA LEVINS MORALES Child of the Americas   430
GLORIA ANZALDÚA To Live in the Borderlands Means You   431
JIMMY SANTIAGO BACA So Mexicans Are Taking Jobs from Americans   432
LANGSTON HUGHES Theme for English B   433
PAT PARKER For the white person who wants to know how to be my friend   433
MITSUYE YAMADA To the Lady   434
DOROTHEA LANGE Grandfather and Grandchildren Awaiting Evacuation Bus   436
LUIS VALDEZ Los Vendidos   437
   CASE STUDY: WRITING ABOUT AMERICAN INDIAN IDENTITY   438
      ANONYMOUS ARAPAHO My Children, When at First I Liked the Whites   440
      ANONYMOUS ARAPAHO Father, Have Pity on Me   440
      JAMES MOONEY Ghost Dance   442
      LYDIA HOWARD HUNTLEY SIGOURNEY The Indian's Welcome to the Pilgrim Fathers   443
      ROBERT FROST The Vanishing Red   444
      EDWARD S. CURTIS The Vanishing Race   446
      WENDY ROSE Three Thousand Dollar Death Song   449
      NILA NORTHSUN Moving Camp Too Far   450
      JAMES LUNA The Artifact Piece   451

CHAPTER 25 LAW AND DISORDER 453

HENRY DAVID THOREAU *From* "Civil Disobedience" 453
GEORGE ORWELL A Hanging 455
ZORA NEALE HURSTON A Conflict of Interest 458
MARTIN LUTHER KING JR. Letter from Birmingham Jail 460
AESOP A Lion and Other Animals Go Hunting 461
A Note on Fables, Parables, and Oher Moral Stories 461
JOHN The Woman Taken in Adultery 462
ANONYMOUS Three Hasidic Tales 463
FRANZ KAFKA Before the Law 465
ELIZABETH BISHOP The Hanging of the Mouse 467
URSULA K. LE GUIN The Ones Who Walk Away from Omelas 469
WILLIAM FAULKNER Barn Burning 470
JAMES ALAN MCPHERSON An Act of Prostitution 472
RALPH ELLISON Battle Royal 473
GORDON PARKS Ralph Ellison 475
BOOKER T. WASHINGTON Atlanta Exposition Address 476
CHARLES KECK The Booker T. Washington Memorial 478
W. E. B. DU BOIS Of Our Spiritual Strivings 480
ANONYMOUS Birmingham Jail 480
A. E. HOUSMAN The Carpenter's Son 480
A. E. HOUSMAN Eight O'Clock 482
A. E. HOUSMAN Oh who is that young sinner 482
A. E. HOUSMAN The laws of God, the laws of man 484
EDGAR LEE MASTERS Judge Selah Lively 485
CLAUDE MCKAY If We Must Die 489
JIMMY SANTIAGO BACA Cloudy Day 491
SUSAN GLASPELL Trifles 494

APPENDIX C NEW APPROACHES TO THE RESEARCH PAPER: LITERATURE, HISTORY, AND THE WORLD WIDE WEB 496

MITSUYE YAMADA The Question of Loyalty 496
DAVID MURA An Argument: On 1942 497

INDEX OF AUTHORS AND TITLES 499

Preface

Our title, *Literature for Composition,* announces the aim of this seventh edition, and our preface to the book clearly, we hope, explains the organization. We want to repeat that the first seven chapters offer a good deal of advice about writing, and the next eight are a mini-anthology arranged by genre—four chapters with genres (essays, fiction, drama, poetry), and other chapters with casebooks (on Flannery O'Connor, John Updike, Emily Dickinson, and the Blues) and a discussion of film and fiction. Next are chapters on arguing interpretations and arguing evaluations, plus an overview of critical positions. The rest of the book (except for the appendices) is devoted to a thematic anthology. Several of the thematic chapters include casebooks.

We have tried to choose works of literature that will interest students in a composition class, and we have suggested topics for essays in the book and in this handbook. Some of these topics are the sort that are common in literature courses—"The function of religious imagery in 'Araby,'" for example, or "To what extent is Nora [in *A Doll's House*] a victim, and to what extent is she herself at fault for her way of life?" Such topics need no defense; they help to bring the student into close contact with the work of literature, and they help to develop analytic powers.

But we have also included some topics that invite students to try their hands at imaginative writing: for instance, "Write a dialogue—approximately two double-spaced typed pages—setting forth a chance encounter between Torvald and Nora five years after the end of Ibsen's play." Such an assignment will, if nothing else, give students some idea of the difficulty of writing dialogue; but of course it will do much more, for again, it will require them to think about the play itself, especially if the instructor cautions them that their dialogue ought to be rooted in Ibsen's play.

Still other suggested topics in this handbook, however, use the work of literature as a point of departure for expository or persuasive essays. For instance, for an essay that takes off from Grace Paley's "Samuel," we ask:

If you had been on the train, would you have pulled the emergency cord? Why, or why not?

We have just said that such topics use the literary work as a point of departure; we do not mean that the work gets left behind. A good essay will be based on a close reading of the text, but it will also allow the student to develop an argument on an issue larger than the work. Moreover, such topics as those on the Declaration of Independence can easily be made into small-scale research papers if the instructor wishes to teach research methods. In the text, three appendices on "Research Papers" provide information about documentation and about electronic sources.

In this handbook we discuss, in varying degrees of detail, every literary selection that we reprint, except for a handful that are discussed extensively within the text itself. We also offer in this handbook additional Topics for Critical Thinking and Writing on many of the works. Unfortunately, however, assignments that work well for one instructor may not work well for another, and even an assignment that works well at nine o'clock may not work well at ten. Still, over the years we have had good luck with the selections we include and with the writing assignments given in the text and in this handbook. We will be most grateful to any instructors who write to us to suggest additional topics. If there is a seventh edition of the book, we will try to include such suggestions, giving credit to the contributors.

Note: We provide bibliography for most of the authors included in this handbook, but we do not repeat this information in the case of authors for whom we have more than one selection. You will find the bibliography the first time that the author is discussed.

ACKNOWLEDGMENTS

We cannot adequately express our indebtedness to Sharon Buehrig and to Dianne Hall, whose sharp eyes and inquiring minds caused us to revise many passages in this handbook.

Using the CD-ROM

LITERATURE: THE CRAFT OF ARGUMENT

Additional resources for you and your students can be found on *Literature: The Craft of Argument*, the CD-ROM that accompanies *Literature for Composition*. These resources include interactive readings of literary texts and media explorations. The interactive readings contain annotations and response questions that prompt students to write about the texts they are studying. Students can save their responses to the prompt questions on their personal computers. Media explorations provide audio or video clips of materials from the book or background information about works and writers. The *Literature for Composition* Companion Website at <http://www.ablongman.com/barnet> also provides response questions keyed to the media explorations. Students can answer questions on the Website and print out their work or e-mail their responses to themselves or their instructor. There are a number of ways that you might use the CD-ROM resources in your class.

 Extend Class Discussions

You can use the CD-ROM materials as an extension of class activities. You might partially discuss a text in class, then ask students to continue their explorations of the work outside of class by responding to the questions in an interactive reading. Similarly, you might cover a text by an author in class, then assign an alternate text for students to investigate on their own using the CD-ROM. Students could also use the media explorations on the CD-ROM to extend their work with the texts under study. You might assign media explorations that provide background information about a writer or text as a way of reinforcing or problematizing in-class activities.

Prepare for In-Class Activities

An alternate approach might use the interactive readings and media explorations as a way of preparing students for in-class activities. Asking students to compose responses to an interactive reading before class can serve as a brainstorming activity. Students may find it easier to participate in or deepen class discussions as a result of having already written about the materials. Assigning supplemental multimedia materials can also streamline classroom logistics. Students can listen to lengthier audio or video clips at their convenience before class meets.

 ## Integrate Material Directly into the Classroom

Depending on the resources available at your institution, you also may be able to use the CD-ROM to extend in-class activities. If students have access to computers in the classroom, you can ask them to conduct an interactive reading during class. These readings and the writing they generate could either facilitate preliminary thinking before an in-class activity or be used to reflect on and solidify some of the work that has taken place during a class. You also may be able to use a single computer to integrate media explorations into a class. On a simple level, you might play an audio clip in class so that students could hear the reading of a poem. You could also project multimedia materials to facilitate close readings of nontextual elements in class or to provide information contained in video clips.

Ultimately, you will most likely achieve the best effect by blending these possibilities. For instance, you might ask students to respond to an interactive reading outside of class but to come to class prepared to share and discuss their responses. You might have students conduct an interactive reading, then ask them to turn their saved responses into a more formal composition. You might combine in-class activities with other teaching goals such as facilitating group work, asking students to collaborate in developing responses to interactive readings. Think of ways that writing about literature will benefit your students and that the interactive readings might facilitate the process. Imagine how the multimedia CD-ROM materials can supplement thinking about authors or texts. Begin by considering these possibilities and you should be able to develop creative ways of using *Literature: The Craft of Argument* both in and out of class.

Using the "Short Views"

Each thematic section of *Literature for Composition* begins with a group of brief statements entitled "Short Views." These range from epigrammatic sentences to a few paragraphs. Often the views are controversial, and sometimes we juxtapose contrasting views.

Short Views can be used in a variety of ways to stimulate writing—and to call to the attention of students some of the characteristics of effective prose. We have found it useful to start a class hour by asking students to take turns reading aloud the Short Views from the unit they are working on. We have noticed how few students nowadays can read aloud with any comfort, probably because they have seldom been asked to read aloud or have had anyone read to them. Reading aloud is a good way to learn to pay attention to the text—the beginning, of course, of thinking critically about it. Having Short Views read aloud also lets the instructor see which ones create a response from the class, a question, a look of puzzlement, a laugh, a groan. Any one of these responses is a good place to start a discussion. "What is it here that makes you laugh?" "Is there something here you don't understand? Or are you saying that you disagree? Try to slow down your reaction and see if you can explain it."

Each group of Short Views is followed by specific questions on the theme, but here are two writing assignments that can be applied to Short Views on any of the thematic topics.

1. Select a quotation that especially appeals to you, and make it the focus of an essay of about 500 words.
2. Take two of these passages—perhaps one that you especially like and one that you think is wrong-headed—and write a dialogue of about 500 words in which the two authors converse. They may each try to convince the other, or they may find that to some degree they share views and they may

then work out a statement that both can accept. If you do take the first position—that one writer is on the correct track but the other is utterly mistaken—do try to be fair to the view that you think is mistaken. (As an experiment in critical thinking, imagine that you accept it, and make the best case for it that you possibly can.)

The First Day

When you meet your students on the first day of classes, in addition to the usual business of taking attendance and reviewing the syllabus, you may want to spend a few minutes describing *Literature for Composition*. Explain how this book will enable the students to fulfill the goals of the course. Your students have purchased the book, and they will be spending lots of time working with it; they will benefit from hearing from you why you have chosen it and about the features in it that will help them to improve their writing.

On the first day, we also give the students some advice about other resources upon which they should draw. These are obvious enough: a good dictionary and a thesaurus. But we recommend that you be more specific. Bring to class the dictionary and the thesaurus that you keep on your own desk. One of us in fact carries to each and every class a dictionary he especially admires: *The American Heritage Dictionary of the English Language,* third edition (1996); he places the dictionary, open and ready for reference, on his desk in the classroom, alongside his copy of *Literature for Composition.*

This, we know, may seem heavy-handed. But we think the teacher needs to provide a model for the students; if you urge the students to use the dictionary to check on the meanings of words and to expand their vocabularies, show them that you do this yourself—that it is a natural part of studying literature and becoming a skillful writer.

It is tempting on this first day or during the first week to identify for students many other books and Internet resources to which they can turn. But be careful not to give students more than they can handle or absorb, especially if you are teaching first-year students in the first semester of college, who tend to feel overwhelmed anyway. We also increasingly find that many of our students are non-native speakers; indeed, it is not unusual for us to encounter students for whom English is their third language.[1] We try to keep this point in mind,

---

[1] One of the best students one of us has ever taught began her college career by writing her papers first in Vietnamese, then translating them into French, and, finally, into the English version she handed in.

even as we set a high standard for these students and all of the others. There will be plenty of opportunities, as the semester unfolds, to outline the elements of a research paper and the relevant print and electronic sources for them. At the outset, keep the focus on the resources that *Literature for Composition* itself contains from one chapter to the next, and on the value derived from regular use of the dictionary and the thesaurus.

The only exception we make to this rule is when we are teaching a course, or a section of a course, designed for English majors, say, in the second semester of the first year or the first semester of the second. In these cases, we highlight two basic tools of the trade:

- *The Oxford Companion to American Literature,* 6th edition, ed. James D. Hart and Phillip W. Leininger (1995).
- *The Oxford Companion to English Literature,* rev. ed., ed. Margaret Drabble (1998).

Students who know that they will be majoring in English enjoy hearing about the reference books that matter in particular for them. We suggest that you bring your own copies of these books to class. You might even make copies of an entry or two so that the students can see for themselves how the information in such books can prove useful to them in interpreting literature and writing about it.

PART I
Getting Started
From Response to Argument

1

The Writer as Reader

KATE CHOPIN
Ripe Figs (p. 3)

This story teaches marvelously. Some stories supposedly teach well because the instructor can have the pleasure of showing students all sorts of things that they missed, but unfortunately stories of that kind may, by convincing students that literature has deep meanings that they don't see, turn students away from literature. "Ripe Figs" teaches well because it is a first-rate piece that is easily accessible.

Elaine Gardiner discusses it fully in an essay in *Modern Fiction Studies* 28:3 (1982), reprinted in Harold Bloom's collection of essays *Kate Chopin* (1987), pp. 83–87. Gardiner's essay is admirable, but instructors will be interested to find that their students will make pretty much the same points that Gardiner makes. Gardiner emphasizes three of Chopin's techniques: her use of *contrasts*, *natural imagery*, and *cyclical plotting*.

The chief contrast is between Maman-Nainaine and Babette, that is, age versus youth, patience versus impatience, experience versus innocence, staidness versus exuberance. Thus, Chopin tells us that "Maman-Nainaine sat down in her stately way," whereas Babette is "restless as a hummingbird" and dances. Other contrasts are spring and summer, summer and fall, figs and chrysanthemums.

Speaking of natural imagery, Gardiner says, "Not only are journeys planned according to when figs ripen and chrysanthemums bloom, but places are defined by what they produce; thus, Bayou-Lafourche, for Maman-Nainaine, is the place 'where the sugar cane grows.'" Gardiner calls attention to the references to the leaves, the rain, and the branches of the fig tree, but of course she emphasizes the ripening of the figs (from "little hard, green marbles" to "purple figs, fringed around with their rich green leaves") and the flowering of the chrysanthemums. The contrasts in natural imagery, Gardiner says, "ultimately convey and emphasize continuity and stability."

Turning to cyclical plotting—common in Chopin—Gardiner says, "With the ripening of the figs in the summertime begins the next period of waiting, the continuance of the cycle, both of nature and of the characters' lives. . . . The reader finishes the sketch anticipating the movements to follow—movements directed by the seasons, by natural happenings, by the cyclical patterns of these people's lives."

Our classes on Chopin's stories are always successful. Students find her work subtle and intriguing and enjoy writing their first critical essays for the course about them. For this reason, we make sure to take a few moments to encourage students to read—on their own—*more* of her stories and her novel *The Awakening*. *The Awakening and Selected Stores,* ed. Sandra M. Gilbert (1984), is a good, inexpensive paperback edition you can recommend. Your best students may not need prodding of this kind, but many students do need to be reminded that a rich world of books awaits them outside the classroom, beyond the list on the syllabus.

Dated, but still useful, are the sections on Chopin in Marlene Springer, *Edith Wharton and Kate Chopin: A Reference Guide* (1976). Per Seyersted has written a cogent, well-paced biography (1969); Emily Toth has written another—more recent and more detailed (1990). In addition to the collection edited by Harold Bloom that we noted above, we have also benefited from the range of work included in *Kate Chopin Reconsidered: Beyond the Bayou,* ed. Lynda S. Boren and Sara deSaussure Davis (1992), and *Critical Essays on Kate Chopin,* ed. Alice Hall Petry (1996).

2

The Reader as Writer

KATE CHOPIN
The Story of an Hour (p. 13)

The first sentence of the story proves to be essential to the end, though during the middle of the story the initial care to protect Mrs. Mallard from the "sad message" seems almost comic. Students may assume, too easily, that Mrs. Mallard's "storm of grief" is hypocritical. They may not notice that the renewal after the first shock is stimulated by the renewal of life around her ("the tops of trees . . . were all aquiver with the new spring of life") and that before she achieves a new life, Mrs. Mallard first goes through a sort of death and then tries to resist renewal: Her expression "indicated a suspension of intelligent thought," she felt something "creeping out of the sky," and she tried to "beat it back with her will," but she soon finds herself "drinking the elixir of life through that open window," and her thoughts turn to "spring days, and summer days." Implicit in the story is the idea that her life as a wife—which she had thought was happy—was in fact a life of repression or subjugation, and the awareness comes to her only at this late stage. The story has two surprises: the change from grief to joy proves not to be the whole story, for we get the second surprise, the husband's return and Mrs. Mallard's death. The last line ("the doctors . . . said she had died . . . of joy that kills") is doubly ironic: The doctors wrongly assume that she was overjoyed to find that her husband was alive, but they were not wholly wrong in guessing that her last day of life brought her great joy.

In a sense, moreover, the doctors are right (though not in the sense they mean) in saying that she "died of heart disease." That is, if we take the "heart" in a metaphorical sense to refer to love and marriage, we can say that the loss of her new freedom from her marriage is unbearable. This is not to say (though many students do say it) that her marriage was miserable. The text explicitly says "she had loved him—sometimes." The previous paragraph in the story nicely calls attention to a certain aspect of love—a satisfying giving of the self—and yet also to a most unpleasant yielding to force: "There would be no one to live for her during those coming years; she would live for herself. There would be no powerful will bending her in that blind persistence with which men and women believe they have a right to impose a private will upon a fellow-creature."

A biographical observation: Chopin's husband died in 1882, and her mother died in 1885. In 1894 in an entry in her diary she connected the two losses with her growth: "If it were possible for my husband and my mother to come back to earth, I feel that I would unhesitatingly give up every thing that has come into my life since they left it and join my existence again with theirs. To do that, I would have to forget the past ten years of my growth—my real growth."

Topic for Critical Thinking and Writing

Chopin does not tell us if Mrs. Mallard's death is due to joy at seeing her husband alive, guilt for feeling "free," shock at the awareness that her freedom is lost, or something else. Should the author have made the matter clear? Why, or why not?

KATE CHOPIN
Désirée's Baby (p. 30)

Students tend to differ in their responses to this story, and in particular to the ending. In the final lines, Armand learns that his own mother "belongs to the race that is cursed with the brand of slavery." The point is that he carries within himself the traces of the "black" race that he found intolerable in his wife, whom he has exiled from his presence and who, apparently, commits suicide along with their child.

But what exactly is it that Armand learns? Is he learning with a shock something he never suspected or, instead, something he sensed was true (or might have been true) all along? Some students contend that the letter from his mother that Armand reads stuns him with its sudden, shocking disclosure, whereas others maintain that he really knew the truth all along or that he may not have known the truth for sure but likely suspected it.

We tend to start the class, then, by asking the students for their responses to the ending of the story. And we have always found some version of this sharp difference in interpretation to emerge from the opening discussion. There is of course a risk in keying the structure of the class to a debate; sometimes the positions can become too polarized, too rigidly upheld. The way to avoid this is to keep pressing the students to connect their positions to details in the language, moments in the story's unfolding narrative. As the students talk about the ending, ask them to explain where, earlier in the story, they find evidence that supports their interpretation.

On the one hand, this reminder spurs the students to seek evidence for their statements about the text: they must return to the text and its organizations of language. On the other hand, this close attention to passages usually complicates the polarized terms of the debate, making the story more complex and harder to simplify.

Notice, for example, the detail about Armand that Chopin gives halfway through: "And the very spirit of Satan seemed suddenly to take hold of him in his dealings with the slaves." This is the kind of detail that is worth lingering over. Does Armand begin to act cruelly because of his rising anger at his wife and child? Or, somewhat differently, because he knows on some level that he cannot deny the truth about who he is—the truth that his mother's letter will later confirm?

In her biography of Chopin (1990), Emily Toth states that "Désirée's husband, Armand, has a relationship with the slave La Blanche." We are not sure that the text sustains this intriguing idea, but it's a useful comment to mention in class, for it returns the students once more to the text, leading them to focus on a key passage in order to test whether they agree with Toth or not. Students are frequently unsure about how to make use of secondary sources in their own analytical essays, and an example like this one, which a student could cite for agreement or disagreement and *work with*, can be instructive to them.

We might mention a couple of assignments that have gone over well for Chopin's story. On occasion we have asked students to "complete the story": Write a new final paragraph that presents Armand's reaction to his mother's letter. Sometimes we have also assigned a student to present an oral report on the term "miscegenation," which derives from the title of a faked anonymous pamphlet written during the Civil War. The authors, David Goodman Croly and George Wakeman, were Democratic newspapermen, and their pamphlet (which they pretended had been written by a member of the Republican Party) was designed to discredit Abraham Lincoln and his fellow Republicans by revealing that they favored interracial marriages—which was untrue. The student might be directed to dictionaries and encyclopedias and, for more detail, to George M. Fredrickson, *The Black Image in the White Mind: The Debate on the Afro-American Character and Destiny, 1817–1914* (1971), which includes an insightful account of how the term "miscegenation" arose and gained prominence.

KATE CHOPIN
The Storm (p. 34)

Chopin wrote this story in 1898 but never tried to publish it, presumably because she knew it would be unacceptable to the taste of the age. "The Storm" uses the same characters as an earlier story, "The 'Cadian Ball," in which Alcée is about to run away with Calixta when Clarisse captures him as a husband.

Here are our tentative responses to the topics for discussion and writing in the text.

On the characters of Calixta and Bobinôt. In Part I, Bobinôt buys a can of shrimp because Calixta is fond of shrimp. Our own impression is that this detail is provided chiefly to show Bobinôt's interest in pleasing his wife, but Per Seyersted, in *Kate Chopin*, finds a darker meaning. Seyersted suggests (p. 223) that shrimp "may represent a conscious allusion to the potency often denoted by sea foods." (To the best of our knowledge, this potency is attributed only to oysters, but perhaps we lead sheltered lives.) At the beginning of Part II Calixta is "sewing furiously on a sewing machine," and so readers gather that she is a highly industrious woman, presumably a more-than-usually diligent housekeeper. The excuses Bobinôt frames on the way home (Part III) suggest that he is somewhat intimidated by his "overscrupulous housewife." Calixta is genuinely concerned about the welfare of her somewhat simple husband and of her child. The affair with Alcée by no means indicates that she is promiscuous or, for that matter, unhappy with her family. We don't think her expressions of solicitude for the somewhat childlike Bobinôt are insincere. We are even inclined to think that perhaps her encounter with Alcée has heightened her concern for her husband. (At least, to use the language of reader-response criticism, this is the way we "naturalize"—make sense out of—the gap or blank in the narrative.)

Alcée's letter to his wife suggests that he thinks his affair with Calixta may go on for a while, but we take it that the affair is, like the storm (which gives its title to the story), a passing affair. It comes about unexpectedly and "naturally": Alcée at first takes refuge on the gallery, with no thought of entering the house, but because the gallery does not afford shelter, Calixta invites him in, and then a lightning bolt drives her (backward) into his arms. The experience is thoroughly satisfying, and it engenders no regrets, but presumably it will be treasured rather than repeated, despite Alcée's thoughts when he writes his letter.

Clarisse's response. By telling us, in Part V, that Clarisse is delighted at the thought of staying a month longer in Biloxi, Chopin diminishes any blame that a reader might attach to Alcée. That is, although Alcée is unfaithful to his wife, we see that his wife doesn't regret his absence: "Their intimate conjugal life was something which she was more than willing to forego for a while."

Is the story cynical? We don't think so, since cynicism involves a mocking or sneering attitude, whereas in this story Chopin regards her characters affectionately. Blame is diminished not only by Clarisse's letter but by other means. We learn that at an earlier time, when Calixta was a virgin, Alcée's "honor forbade him to prevail." And, again, by associating the affair with the storm, Chopin implies that this moment of passion is in accord with nature. Notice also that the language becomes metaphoric during the scene of passion. For instance, Calixta's "lips were as red and as moist as pomegranate seed," and her "passion . . . was like a white flame," suggesting that the characters are transported to a strange (though natural) world. There is, of course, the implication that people are less virtuous than they seem to be, but again, Chopin scarcely seems to gloat over this fact. Rather, she suggests that the world is a fairly pleasant place in which there is enough happiness to go all around. "So the storm passed and everyone was happy." There is no need to imagine further episodes in which, for instance, Calixta and Alcée deceive Bobinôt; nor is there any need to imagine further episodes in which Calixta and Alcée regret their moment of passion.

Two additional points can be made. First, there seems to be a suggestion of class distinction between Calixta and Alcée, though both are Creoles. Calixta uses some French terms, and her speech includes such expressions as "An' Bibi? he ain't wet? Ain't hurt?" Similarly Bobinôt's language, though it does not include any French terms, departs from standard English. On the other hand, Alcée speaks only standard English. Possibly, however, the distinctions in language are also based, at least partly based, on gender as well as class; Calixta speaks the language of an uneducated woman largely confined to her home, whereas Alcée—a man who presumably deals with men in a larger society— speaks the language of the Anglo world. But if gender is relevant, how can one account for the fact that Bobinôt's language resembles Calixta's, and Clarisse's resembles Alcée's? A tentative answer: Bobinôt, like Calixta, lives in a very limited world, whereas Clarisse is a woman of the world. We see Clarisse only at the end of the story, and there we hear her only through the voice of the narrator, but an expression such as "The society was agreeable" suggests that her language (as might be expected from a woman rich enough to take a long vacation) resembles her husband's, not Calixta's.

TOBIAS WOLFF
Powder (p. 38)

The first paragraph provides the necessary background. The parents are separated, the mother is sensible, and the father is irresponsible—but even at this stage one may wonder if perhaps there isn't something especially engaging about a father who sneaks his young son into a nightclub in order to see Thelonious Monk.

The father's irresponsibility is underlined in the second paragraph. He promised to get the boy home to the mother for Christmas Eve dinner, but "he observed some quality [in the snow] that made it necessary for us to get in one last run. We got in several last runs." The father tries to be reassuring at the diner, but the boy, a worrier, is distressed. He's a strange kid, as he himself knows, someone who bothers "teachers for homework assignments far ahead of their due dates" so he can make up schedules. But with a father like his, and a mother who clearly is not sympathetic to the father's adventurous (or childish?) enthusiasms, who can blame the boy? And though the boy in his orderliness is his mother's son, the last paragraph of the story validates the father. Although the father is "bankrupt of honor," the ride (or the boy's experience of the ride) is something so special that it is "impossible to describe. Except maybe to say this: if you haven't driven fresh powder, you haven't driven."

One detail may escape some readers. When the father makes a phone call from the diner, the boy quite reasonably thinks the father must be calling the mother, but this man-child in fact is calling the police, with some sort of bull that causes the officer to drive away and thus gives the father a chance to put aside the barrier and drive home. The evidence? After making the call, the father stares through the window, down the road, and says, "Come on, come on." (He is impatiently waiting for the result of his call.) As soon as the trooper's car passes the window, the father hurries the boy out of the diner. When the boy asks the father where the policeman may have gone, the father ignores the question.

"Bankrupt of honor," yes, and one can easily imagine the impossibility of being married to such a man. But the father desperately wants to keep the family intact, and he wants to get the boy home for dinner with the mother in an effort to buy "a little more time," though we are not surprised to learn that the mother decides "to make the split final."

Wolff's stories have been published in two excellent collections: *Back in the World* (1985) and *The Night in Question* (1996). He has also written a somber, disturbing book about his childhood in the 1950s, *This Boy's Life: A Memoir* (1989), and an excellent book about his experiences in Vietnam, *In Pharaoh's Army: Memories of the Lost War* (1994).

3

Reading Literature Closely: Explication

LANGSTON HUGHES
Harlem (p. 47)

In the eight lines enclosed within the frame (that is, between the first and next-to-last lines) we get four possibilities: The Dream may "dry up," "fester," "crust and sugar over," or "sag." Each of these is set forth with a simile, for example, "dry up / like a raisin in the sun." By the way, the third of these, "crust up and sugar over—like a syrupy sweet," probably describes a dream that has turned into smiling Uncle Tomism. Similes can be effective, and these *are* effective, but in the final line Hughes states the last possibility ("Or does it explode?") directly and briefly, without an amplification. The effect is, more or less, to suggest that the fancy (or pretty) talk stops. The explosion is too serious to be treated in a literary way. But, of course, the word "explode," applied to a dream, is itself figurative. That is, the last line is as "literary" or "poetical" as the earlier lines, but it is a slightly different sort of poetry.

A word about the rhymes: notice that although the poem does use rhyme, it does not use a couplet until the last two lines. The effect of the couplet ("load" / "explode") is that the poem ends with a bang. Of course, when one reads the poem in a book, one sees where the poem ends—though a reader may be surprised to find the forceful rhyme—but an audience hearing the poem recited is surely taken off-guard. The explosion is unexpected (especially in the context of the two previous lines about a sagging, heavy load) and powerful.

There is an excellent two-volume biography of Hughes by Arnold Rampersad (vol. 1, 1986; vol. 2, 1988); another good resource is Thomas A. Mikolyzk, *Langston Hughes: A Bio-Bibliography* (1990). The short stories have been edited by Akiba Sullivan Harper (1996). But most of the scholarly books focus on the poetry, rather than on the fiction. The best points of departure for studying this writer are two recent collections: *Langston Hughes: Critical Perspectives Past and Present* (1993), ed. Henry Louise Gates, Jr., and

K. A. Appiah, and *Langston Hughes: The Man, The Art, and His Continuing Influence* (1995), ed. C. J. Trotman.

A "Voices and Visions" videocassette of Langston Hughes is available from Longman Publishers.

Topic for Critical Thinking and Writing

One might keep the first line where it is, and then rearrange the other stanzas—for instance, putting lines 2–8 after 9–11. Which version (Hughes's or the one just mentioned) do you prefer? Why?

WILLIAM SHAKESPEARE
Sonnet 73 ("That time of year thou mayst in me behold") (p. 56)

Shakespeare's 154 sonnets were published in 1609, although it is thought that most of them were composed in the middle 1590s, around the time *Romeo and Juliet* and *A Midsummer Night's Dream* were written. Francis Meres spoke of Shakespeare's "sugared sonnets" in 1598, and two were published in an anthology in 1599. The order of the sonnets is probably not Shakespeare's, but there are two large divisions (with some inconsistent interruptions). Sonnets 1–126 seem to be addressed to, or concerned with, a handsome, aristocratic young man who is urged to marry and thus to propagate his beauty and become immortal. Sonnets 127–152 are chiefly concerned with a promiscuous dark woman who seduces a friend, at least for a while.

Wordsworth thought the poems were autobiographical ("With this key Shakespeare unlocked his heart"), to which Browning replied, "If so, the less Shakespeare he." Scholars have not convincingly identified the friend or the lady, and the whole thing may be as fictional as *Hamlet*. Certainly it *sounds* like autobiography, but this is only to say that Shakespeare is a writer who sounds convincing. The chief argument that the poems really may be autobiographical is that the insistence that the friend marry is so odd a theme. As C. S. Lewis says in *English Literature in the Sixteenth Century,* what man (except a potential father-in-law) cares if another man gets married? One other point: Do the poems addressed to the beautiful friend suggest a homosexual interest? Certainly they suggest a *passionate* interest, but it doesn't seem to be erotic. Sonnet 20, a bawdy and witty poem, expressly denies any interest in the friend's body. It seems reasonable to say that what the speaker of the sonnets wants from the friend is not sex but love.

Of the many studies, we are partial to Stephen Booth, *An Essay on Shakespeare's Sonnets* (1969), and to his edition of the sonnets (1977), which prints both the facsimile of the first edition and a modernized text, along with extremely detailed commentaries. For a fuller discussion of each sonnet, see Helen Vendler, *The Art of Shakespeare's Sonnets* (1997), which also prints a facsimile of each sonnet.

Sonnet 73 is chiefly a meditation on growing old, though the couplet relates this topic to the theme of love that is the subject of many of Shakespeare's sonnets. All three quatrains, in varying degrees, glance at increasing coldness and darkness, and each successive quatrain is concerned with a briefer period. In the first, the human life is compared to a year; in the second, to a day; in the third, to a few hours. In the first quatrain, there is a further comparison: the boughs of the autumnal trees are compared (in "bare ruined choirs") to the churches that had fallen into decay after England broke with Rome. ("Sweet birds" refers primarily to the feathered creatures that recently sang in the boughs, but it also glances at choristers in the choirs.) Note, too, that it is reasonable to perceive, faintly, a resemblance between the shaking boughs and a trembling old person. The first quatrain, then, is rich in suggestions of ruined beauty and destroyed spirituality.

The second quatrain, by speaking of night as "Death's second self," explicitly introduces death into the poem. The third quatrain personifies the fire, speaking of its "youth" (i.e., the earlier minutes or hours of the blaze) and its "deathbed," and in its reference to ashes it introduces a common idea of the decayed body. (The idea, of course, is that the last embers lie on the ashes, which were the "youth" or earlier hours of the fire, and these ashes now help to extinguish the embers.) The year will renew itself, and the day will renew itself, but the firewood is utterly destroyed. In the final line the speaker is reduced to "that," not even "me."

JOHN DONNE

Holy Sonnet XIV ("Batter my heart, three-personed God") (p. 57)

"Batter my heart" has been discussed several times in *Explicator* (March 1953, Item 31: December 1953, Item 18; April 1954, Item 36; October 1956, Item 2). In *College English* 24: (January 1963): 299–302, John Parrish summarized these discussions, rejecting the idea that in the first quatrain, especially in lines 2 and 4, God is compared to a tinker mending a damaged pewter vessel, and offering his own reading. All these are conveniently reprinted in the *Norton Critical Edition of John Donne's Poetry*, ed. A.L. Clements.

Our own winnowings from these essays follow. Although the first line introduces the "three-personed God," it is impossible to associate each quatrain with only one of the three persons. Still, the idea of the trinity is carried out in several ways: "knock, breathe, shine" becomes "break, blow, burn." And there are three chief conceits: God as a tinker repairing the speaker, damaged by sin; the speaker as a town usurped by satanic forces; God as a forceful lover who must ravish the sinful speaker; or (lest one get uneasy at the thought that Donne presents himself as a woman) God as a lover who must fully possess the speaker's soul (the soul is customarily regarded as female). "O'erthrow" in the first quatrain, in line 3, leads to the image of the besieged town in the second quatrain; "untrue" at the end of the second quatrain leads (because it can refer to marital infidelity) to the conceit of the lover in the third quatrain; and "ravish" in the final line can take us back to "heart" in the first line of the poem.

A useful, relatively long explication by M. T. Wanninger appeared in *Explicator* (December 1969), Item 37. M. H. Abrams, *Natural Supernaturalism*, 50–51, points out that in "Batter my heart" Donne draws on Revelation 21:5 ("Behold, I make all things new"), and that "the ultimate marriage with the Bridegroom, represented as the rape of the longingly reluctant soul" draws on "commonplaces of Christian devotion."

For a lively, provocative study, we recommend John Carey, *John Donne: Life, Mind, and Art* (1981). For an example of a New Historicist approach, see Arthur Marotti, *John Donne, Coterie Poet* (1986). We should note that we often consult editions of Donne's writings that include annotations and commentaries: *The Songs and Sonnets*, ed. Theodore Redpath (rev. ed., 1983); *John Donne's Poetry*, ed. A. L. Clements (rev. ed., 1992); and *John Donne: The Complete English Poems*, ed. A. J. Smith (1971). See also Robert H. Ray, *A John Donne Companion* (1990).

Topic for Critical Thinking and Writing

How do you feel about an observation made in *Explicator* (Spring 1980), to the effect that "no end" (line 6) is an anagram for "Donne"? What is the point? According to the author of the note, "This anagram is, I think, another of the many ingenious samples of Donne's playing upon his name for poetic effect." Is this reading helpful? Why? Why not?

WILLIAM BLAKE
London (p. 57)

"London," from *Songs of Experience*, is a denunciation of the mind-forged manacles, that is, of manmade repressive situations, not a denunciation of cities and a glorification of rural life. The church assists in exploitation by promises of an eternal reward, the monarchy slaughters men for private gain, and marriage drives the unmarried (or the unsatisfactorily married) to harlots. "Chartered" (2)—not merely mapped but also licensed—is perhaps almost acceptable for streets, but that the river, an image of freedom, should also be chartered is unnatural and intolerable. As the poem develops, it is evident that children are licensed (as chimney sweeps), soldiers are licensed (to kill and to be killed), and harlots are licensed (bought and sold). E. D. Hirsch, Jr., in *Innocence and Experience* (1964), suggests that there is a further meaning: the English were proud of their "chartered liberties," rights guaranteed by Magna Carta, but "these chartered liberties are chartered slaveries." For "ban" in line 7 Hirsch offers four references: a summons to arms (king), a formal denunciation or curse (church), a proclamation of marriage, and a prohibition (king, church, marriage).

A few additional points: The church is "blackening" because (1) it is covered with the soot of an industrial (mechanistic) society; (2) it is spiritually corrupt; and (3) it corrupts people. The chimney sweeper's cry appalls the church because the cry is a reproach, and "appalls" hints at "pall" (suggestive of the dead church) and at its literal meaning, "to make pale," that is, the hypocritical church is a whited sepulcher. In line 14, "the youthful Harlot's curse" may be a cry (thus linked with the infant's cry, the chimney sweeper's cry, and the soldier's sigh), or it may be the disease that afflicts her and is communicated to others. In *Poetry and Repression* (1976), Harold Bloom offers the astounding suggestion that "the harlot's curse is not, as various interpreters have said, venereal disease, but is indeed what 'curse' came to mean in the vernacular after Blake and still means now: menstruation, the natural cycle in the human female. . . . [Blake knows that one] curse or ban or natural fact (menstruation) blasts or scatters another natural fact, the tearlessness of the newborn infant."

In an earlier version, "dirty" stood in lines 1 and 2 instead of "chartered," and "smites" instead of "blights" in line 16.

For an analysis of several readings of "London," see Susan R. Suleiman and Inge Crosman, *The Reader in the Text* (1980). Also important is an essay by E. P. Thompson in *Interpreting Blake,* ed. Michael Phillips (1978).

Thompson has also written a richly contextualized study of Blake: *Witness Against the Beast: William Blake and The Moral Law* (1993). We also enjoyed the vividly written biography of Blake by Peter Ackroyd (1996).

Emily Brontë
Spellbound (p. 58)

We first came across this poem in *The New Oxford Book of English Verse,* ed. Helen Gardner (1972), where it is given the title "Spellbound," though we have since seen it printed without this title as well. Here is a good place to begin: ask the students what it means to be "spellbound" and how this word creates in us a set of associations—about enchantment, fascination—that in the poem itself Brontë seeks to capitalize upon and develop. You can return to a version of this question after you have reached the end of the poem. How much does the poem benefit from this title? Would the poem change, for better or worse, if it were printed not with this title, but (as it sometimes is) with the opening line as the title?

Another good question for the class: Where is the speaker? More precisely, is she outside, with the night "darkening" around her and the winds blowing? Or is she—less likely, but still possible—inside, looking outward on a wintry scene from which she cannot break free? Or—another possibility—is the description of the scene not something that is happening "outside" the speaker but, rather, the expression of something within her: this is how she feels—in the dark, cold, alone.

When we pitch the discussion in this way, we are trying to prompt the students to perceive that a description is not only *that,* but it is also a means through which a writer can dramatize the temperament and personality of a speaker. What counts is not just the description in its own terms but also the description as it serves to reveal to us the speaker's thoughts and feelings. The point is perhaps an obvious one, but we have found that it needs to be made explicitly and demonstrated to the students through examples.

Still another question: What is it that has overtaken the speaker? It is more than a little hard to say. She gives us some indication—"a tyrant spell has bound me." "Tyrant" tells us that the spell is oppressive, harsh, and cruel; and "bound" suggests the physical force of the spell, as if it had literally tied down the speaker. But what about the spell itself? What does it consist of, and from where has it come?

Brontë does not explain or clarify the nature of the spell. It is present, and it is powerful—so powerful that the storm's intense power cannot shake the speaker free from it.

The spell seems terrible and terrifying, but not entirely. It is one thing for you or I to say, "I cannot go," which implies that a force is holding us back, and another thing to say, as does the speaker in the final line, "I will not" go, which intimates that the choice is one's own. Perhaps, one suspects, the speaker will not go because she needs to discover what this spell is about.

"Drear" is a curious word. *The American Heritage Dictionary* defines it simply as "dreary," which is unhelpful. *Webster's Third New International Dictionary* is better: cheerless and depressing; uninteresting and dull. The *Oxford English Dictionary* weighs in with dreariness, sadness, gloom. But how then does this word fit in the poem? Is the speaker saying: no matter how cheerless and gloomy the scene is around me, I will not, cannot, go from it—the spell is too powerful? Maybe, but one might have expected to find here a different, stronger phrase: "But no great fear can move me." As poetry, this revision may not be appealing, but it has the virtue of naming the speaker's predicament more directly.

It could be that the modern dictionaries we consulted are not the right ones for this word. When our curiosity led us to Samuel Johnson's *Dictionary of the English Language* (4th ed., 1773), we found that he includes for "drear" the meaning "dread, terror." This would give the forcefulness to the line that we might otherwise assume is oddly missing from it. And it seems likely that Brontë's own sense of the word would be close to or the same as Johnson's.

"Spellbound" is an alluring, yet mysterious, poem—it has a spellbinding power itself. The speaker tells us that something intense is happening to her, but she leaves unstated its exact source or cause. We can probe and speculate, but this speaker remains distant from us even as she tells us that paralysis has overtaken her. Unless, that is, we are drawn to say that this speaker is not addressing us at all but, rapt as she is, is speaking solely to herself.

For students interested in reading more of Brontë's poetry, *The Poems of Emily Brontë*, ed. Derek Roper with Edward Chitham (1995), is recommended. Chitham has also written a good biography: *A Life of Emily Brontë* (1987). For the study of the Brontë family, there is a superb, richly detailed biography: Juliet Barker, *The Brontës* (1994). Barker also edited *The Brontës: A Life in Letters* (1997), an illuminating selection of the family's correspondence.

LI-YOUNG LEE
I Ask My Mother to Sing (p. 59)

Singing is infectious; the speaker asks his mother to sing, and his grandmother joins her. The reference to the deceased father—who would have joined in too if he had been there—adds a note of pathos and thus anticipates the second stanza, where we learn that the song is about the land of the speaker's ancestors, a land he has never seen.

The song apparently is joyful (picnickers—though admittedly the picnic is dispelled by rain), but since it is about a lost world it is also sorrowful (the women begin to cry). Yet, even singing about sorrow provides the singer with joy, or, we might say, the making of a work of art (here, singing a song) is pleasurable even when the content is sorrowful. One way of mastering sorrow, of course, is to turn it into art.

Students who enjoy "I Ask My Mother to Sing" might be directed to Lee's collections of poems, *Rose* (1986) and *The City in Which I Love You* (1990).

RANDALL JARRELL
The Death of the Ball Turret Gunner (p. 60)

We reprint here a good explication, by a student, Juan Alonso.

> Reading the first line aloud, one pauses slightly after "sleep," dividing the line in half. The halves make a sharp contrast. The point of transition in this line is "I fell," a helpless movement from the mother to the State, from sleep to the State. The mother and the State make an evident contrast, and so do "sleep" and "the State," which resemble each other in their first sound and in their position at the end of a half-line but which have such different associations, for sleep is comforting and "the State" is associated with totalitarianism. ("The country" or "the land" might be comforting and nourishing but "the State" has no such warm suggestions.) We will soon see in the poem that life in the "belly" of the state is mindless and cold, a death-like life which ends with sudden and terrible death. A mother, even in her "sleep," naturally protects and nourishes the child in her warm womb; the State unnaturally cramps the man in its icy belly. He "hunched in its belly" until his "wet fur froze." We gather from the title that "its" refers not only to the State but also the airplane in whose womb-like ball turret he led his confined existence and died. Given the title, the fur probably literally refers to the fur lining of the jackets that fliers wore in World War II, and it also suggests the animal-like existence he led while confined by this unfeeling foster parent, the State-airplane.
>
> His unnatural existence is further emphasized by the fact that, in the airplane, he was "Six miles from earth." From such an existence, far from

the "dream of life" that people hope for, and still hunched in the turret like a baby in the womb, he was born again, that is, he awoke to (or became aware of) not a rich fulfillment of the dream but a horrible reality that is like a nightmare. "Woke to black flak" imitates, in its rattling k's at the end of words, the sound of gunfire that simultaneously awakened and killed him. His awakening or birth is to nightmarish reality and death. It is not surprising, but it is certainly horrifying, that in this world of an impersonal State that numbs and destroys life, his body is flushed out of the turret with a hose. That this is the third horrible release: the first was from the mother into the State; the second was from the belly of the State into the belly of the airplane; and now in shreds from the belly of the airplane into nothing. That this life-history is told flatly, with no note of protest, increases the horror. The simplicity of the last line more effectively brings out the horror of the experience than an anguished cry or an angry protest could do.

Jarrell is a splendid critic, whose likes and dislikes are illuminating: See *Poetry and the Age* (1953) and *Kipling, Auden, and Co.* (1980). *The Complete Poems* (1969) is available, but for students, *The Selected Poems* (1991), is a preferable point of entry. William Pritchard, *Randall Jarrell: A Literary Life* (1990), is helpful.

Jarrell reads and discusses the poem on Caedman cassette SWC 1363.

4

Reading Literature Closely: Analysis

Suggestions for Further Reading

Subsequent chapters will cite a fair number of recent titles relevant to this chapter, but for a start a reader might first turn to an old but readable, humane, and still useful introduction, David Daiches, *A Study of Literature* (1948). Another book of the same generation, and still a useful introduction, is a businesslike survey of theories of literature by René Wellek and Austin Warren, *Theory of Literature*, 2nd ed. (1956). For a fairly recent, readable study, see Gerald Graff, *Professing Literature: An Institutional History* (1987).

Some basic reference works should be mentioned. C. Hugh Holman and William Harmon have written an introductory dictionary of movements, critical terms, literary periods, and genres: *A Handbook to Literature,* 7th ed. (1996). For fuller discussions of critical terms, see Wendell V. Harris, *Dictionary of Concepts in Literary Criticism and Theory* (1992), which devotes several pages to each concept (for instance, "author," "context," "evaluation," "feminist literary criticism," "narrative") and gives a useful reading list for each entry.

Fairly similar to Harris's book are Irene Makaryk, ed., *Encyclopedia of Contemporary Literary Theory: Approaches, Scholars, Terms* (1993), and Michael Groden and Martin Kreiswirth, ed., *The Johns Hopkins Guide to Literary Theory and Criticism* (1994). *The Johns Hopkins Guide,* though it includes substantial entries on individual critics as well as on critical schools, is occasionally disappointing in the readability of some of its essays and especially in its coverage, since it does not include critical terms other than names of schools of criticism. Despite its title, it does not have entries for "theory" or for "criticism," nor does it have entries for such words as "canon" and "evaluation." In coverage (and also in the quality of many entries) it is inferior to an extremely valuable work with a misleadingly narrow title, *The New Princeton Encyclopedia of Poetry and Poetics,* ed. Alex Preminger and T. V. F. Brogan (1993). Although *The New Princeton Encyclopedia* does not include terms that are unique to drama or fiction, it does include generous, lucid entries (with suggestions for further reading) on such terms as "allegory," "criticism," "canon," "irony," "sincerity," "theory," and "unity," and the long entries on "poetics," "poetry," and "poetry, theories of" are in many respects entries on "literature."

See also *A Dictionary of Cultural and Critical Theory,* ed. Michael Payne (1996).

For a collection of essays on the canon, see *Canons,* ed. Robert von Hallberg (1984); see also an essay by Robert Scholes, "Canonicity and Textuality," in *Introduction to Scholarship in Modern Languages and Literatures,* ed. Joseph Gibaldi, 2nd ed. (1992), pp. 238–258. Gibaldi's collection includes essays on related topics, for instance literary theory (by Jonathan Culler) and cultural studies (by David Bathrick).

ANONYMOUS
The Judgment of Solomon (p. 62)

The story is told chiefly to emphasize Solomon's wisdom, or, more specifically, to indicate that "the wisdom of God was in him, to do judgment" (3:28), but we include the story here because it seems to us to be a moving tale of a mother's love and (a lesser reason, but a respectable one) because it relates to Raymond Carver's "Mine" and "Little Things," included later in Chapter 20 ("Love and Hate").

The Biblical story is, in a way, a sort of early detective story. There is a death, a conflict in the testimony of the two witnesses, and a solution by a shrewd outsider. We say "shrewd" because although any of us could have reached the correct judgment after the two women had responded to Solomon's proposal to divide the child, few of us would have been shrewd enough to have devised the situation that led each woman to declare what she really was.

Consider Solomon's predicament. There seems to be nothing that distinguishes the two claimants. There came before him "two women, that were harlots." Until late in the story—that is, up to the time that Solomon suggests dividing the child—they are described only as "the one woman," "the other woman," "the one," "the other." The reader, like Solomon, has nothing to go on, since neither of the witnesses is known to be morally superior, and since there are no other witnesses. Solomon's inspired wisdom, then, is to set up a situation in which each claimant will reveal her true nature—the mother will reveal her love, and the culprit will reveal her hard heart.

Instructors interested in discussing the literary structure of the story may want to call attention to the nice way in which the author takes the cry of the true mother (in which she gives up her suit), "Give her the living child, and in no wise slay it," and then puts these identical words, without change, into Solomon's mouth as his final judgment, though of course the meaning of "her" shifts from (in the first case) the liar to (in Solomon's sentence) the true mother. This exact repetition of a sentence is, of course, especially appropriate in a story about two seemingly indistinguishable women and about a proposal to divide an infant into two.

We have already mentioned that it is important for the two women to be, in effect, indistinguishable, but why did the author make them harlots? We can offer a few guesses: (a) the story demands that there be no witnesses, and by making the women harlots the author thus disposed of husbands, parents, and siblings who might otherwise be expected to live with the women; (b) the author wishes to show that Solomon's justice extended to all, not only to respectable folk; and (c) the author wished to dispel or at least to complicate the stereotype of the harlot as thoroughly disreputable by calling to mind another—overriding—stereotype of the mother as motivated by overwhelming maternal love.

One other point: the basic motif of two women fighting over an infant, and the true mother revealing her identity by rejecting a proposal that will kill the infant, is found in many cultures. For instance, in an Indian Jataka story (a story of the lives of the Buddha before he reached his final incarnation as the Historical Buddha, Siddhartha), a mother brought her child to a river bank, where a she-demon claimed it as her own. The two brought the case to the Buddha-to-be, who ordered the women to engage in a tug-of-war with the child in the center, but the mother yielded her claim rather than destroy the child. See E. B. Cowell and W. H. D. Rouse, *Jataka Stories*, 6 (1912), p. 163.

For a strong feminist reading—a reading very much against the grain of the traditional interpretation that Solomon's deep wisdom solved a difficult problem—see Anne C. Dailey, "The Judgment of Women," in *Out of the Garden*, ed. Christina Buchmann and Celina Spiegel (1994). We quote a few extracts; you may want to try them out with your students.

> Shouldn't we question Solomon's responsibility for raising the sword in the first place? Had he not called for the sword, the other woman might never have expressed her seemingly violent impulse.... (p. 147)

> But does the second woman really *choose* to have the child killed? Maybe she would have picked up the sword and slain the child with her own hands, but we certainly do not know that. All we know is that she says, "Cut him up." Her response may have represented many things besides a heartless desire to see the child killed: futility, hopelessness, anger, or perhaps a disbelief that Solomon would follow through on his murderous threat.... (p. 147)

> The institutional violence that the two women confront in the sword of Solomon mirrors the violence that women face in their everyday lives. Women are expected to back down, negotiate, settle, and accept arbitrary assaults of men at home, on the street, and in the workplace. They are expected to respond with the self-sacrifice of the first prostitute. And when they do not, when they defiantly transgress the laws of men, women must endure, Eve-like, the punishment meted out to them.... (p. 148)

Blind faith in the correctness of Solomon's judgment can be maintained only because we hear so little from the women. When the sword is raised and the command given to divide the child, the women know that they have but moments to plead their case. Their speech is uttered in a fearful rush, a female cry in the face of seemingly arbitrary male violence. Had Solomon recognized that the women's initial responses were incomplete, had he desired to *know* these women rather than to judge them immediately according to a preconceived ideal, then, had he been truly wise, he would have listened with a patient ear to all they had to say. . . . (p. 148)

Solomon succeeds in resolving the dispute over the child in a swift and expedient manner, but he fails to comprehend the cost in human terms of doing so. By judging the women on the basis of a few frantic words, he erases the fullness and complexity of their lives. (pp. 148–149)

LUKE

The Parable of the Prodigal Son (p. 66)

A bibliographic note about parables may be useful. In the *Encyclopedia Britannica,* in a relatively long article entitled "Fable, Parable, Allegory," fable and parable are defined as "short, simple forms of naive allegory," and yet a few paragraphs later the article says, "The rhetorical appeal of a parable is directed primarily toward an elite, in that a final core of its truth is known only to an inner circle, however simple its narrative may appear on the surface. . . ." Perhaps, then, a parable is not a "naive allegory." Two other passages from the article are especially interesting: "The Aesopian fables emphasize the social interaction of human beings," whereas "parables do not analyze social systems so much as they remind the listener of his beliefs." That may not always be true, but it is worth thinking about.

The traditional title of this story is unfortunate, since it makes the second half of the story (the father's dealings with the older brother) superfluous. Joachim Jeremias, in *The Parables of Jesus,* rev. ed. (1972), suggests that the work should be called "The Parable of the Father's Love."

Here is a way to provoke thoughtful discussion of the parable. Roger Seamon, in "The Story of the Moral: The Function of Thematizing in Literary Criticism," *Journal of Aesthetics and Art Criticism* 47 (1989): 229–236, offers an unusual way of thinking about this parable. He summarizes his approach as follows:

I want to reverse the traditional and common sense view that stories convey, illustrate, prove or emotionally support themes. Morals and themes, I argue, convey to audiences what story is to be made out of sentences. The story flows, so to speak, from theme, rather than the theme following from the story. (p. 230)

He goes on to suggest an experiment. "Imagine," he says, that instead of reading a story that traditionally is called "The Prodigal Son,"

> we were to find the same set of sentences in another book under the title "The Prodigal Father," and at the end we found the following moral: "waste not your heart on the unworthy, lest you lose the love of the righteous." We now go back and re-read the sentences, and we find that *we are now reading a different story*. In the new story the father's giving the son money is wrong.

Seamon goes on to say that in *this* story the son's confession is "a way of evading responsibility for his error," and that the father is as prodigal with his love as he was with his property. In this version (remember: the sentences are identical, but the title is different), Seamon claims, "The story concludes with the father happily returning to his error. The absence of poetic justice at the end is meant to arouse our indignation" (p. 232).

It's interesting to hear students respond to this view. Of course Seamon's title, "The Prodigal Father," is merely his own invention, but the conventional title ("The Prodigal Son") has no compelling authority. The question is this: Once we apply Seamon's title, do we read the story the way he suggests—that is, do we see the father as blameworthy and the stay-at-home son as justified? If not, why not? Again, Seamon's point is that although the common-sense view holds that the story yields a moral, in fact the reverse is true: the moral (i.e., the theme we have in mind) yields the story. For Seamon, "A thematic statement conveys information about how the critic constructs the *nature and motivations of the characters, [and] the value of their actions* . . ." (p. 233). True, but can't we add that the skilled critic, i.e., reader, is in large measure guided by the author who knows (again, at least in large measure) how to control the reader's response? Seamon apparently takes a different view, for he holds that "the sentences used to project the events are not, in themselves, sufficient to tell us how we are to characterize or evaluate what is going on." Our response to Seamon is of no importance; what is important is to get students to think about why they do or do not accept the view that the story might be entitled "The Prodigal Father."

We spend some time in class teaching this parable because we find the artistry admirable—and also because the story is profound. One small but telling artistic detail may be noted here, a detail mentioned by Joachim Jeremias, who points out that the elder son, speaking to his father, "omits the address"; we had never noticed this, but now it seems obvious, and surely it is revealing that when the younger son addresses his father he says, "Father," and that when the father addresses the older son he says, "Son." The older son's lack of address, then, speaks volumes: he refuses to see himself as bound by family ties of love—a position evident also when, talking to his father, he identifies the prodigal not as "my brother" but as "this thy son." The story is (among many other things) an admirable example of work in which a storyteller guides an audience into having certain responses.

It's also worthwhile in class to spend some time cautioning against a too--vigorous attempt to find meaning in every detail. (Professionals as well as students sometimes don't know when to leave well enough alone. For instance, a writer in *Studies in Short Fiction* 23 (1986), talking about Updike's "A & P," says that Queenie's pink bathing suit "suggests the emerging desires competing with chastity." But come to think of it, this statement isn't surprising, considering what has been said about the pink ribbon in "Young Goodman Brown." One writer, for instance, says it symbolizes feminine passion, and another says it symbolizes a state between the scarlet of total depravity and the white of innocence.)

To illustrate the danger of pressing too hard, you might mention medieval allegorizations of the story. The gist of these is this: the older brother represents the Pharisees and teachers who resented the conversion of the Gentiles. Thus the fact that the older brother was in the fields when the prodigal returned was taken as standing for the remoteness of the Pharisees and the teachers from the grace of God. The younger brother, according to medieval interpretations, represents the Gentiles, who wandered in illusions and who served the devil (the owner of the swine) by tending the devil's demons (the swine). The pods that the prodigal ate represent either the vices (which cannot satisfy) or pagan literature (again, unsatisfying). The father represents God the Father; his going forth to meet the prodigal stands for the Incarnation; his falling on the neck of the prodigal stands for the mild yoke that Christ places on the neck of his followers (Matthew 11:29–30). The music the older brother hears represents the praise of God, and the feast of the fatted calf represents the Eucharist. A great deal more of this sort of thing can be found in Stephen L. Wailes, *Medieval Allegories of Jesus' Parables* (pp. 236–245). The point should already be clear. On the other hand, it's also worth mentioning that the medieval interpreters of the parable at least paid it the compliment of taking it seriously. Odd as the interpretations now seem, they were the result of an admirable love of the word, and surely such an excess is preferable to indifference.

Is the parable an allegory? No, and yes. Certainly it does not have the detailed system of correspondences that one associates with allegory. Moreover, since the prodigal says, "Father, I have sinned against heaven and . . . thee," the father cannot be said to represent heaven, i.e., God. And yet, as Jeremias says (p. 131):

> The parable describes with touching simplicity what God is like, his goodness, his grace, his boundless mercy, his abounding love.

Need a reader believe in God or in the divinity of Jesus in order to value this story? The point is surely worth discussing in class. Most students will agree that such belief is not necessary, and from here one can go on to discuss stories as ways of imaginatively entering alien worlds.

JAMES THURBER
The Secret Life of Walter Mitty (p. 77)

Class discussion may begin with an examination of the point at which it is apparent that this story is comic. Anyone who knows Thurber's name will of course expect comedy, but not every student has heard of him. The first two sentences do not (on first reading) reveal themselves as comic, though in hindsight one sees that at least the first sentence is from the world of inferior adventure stories. An alert reader may become suspicious of the third sentence with its "full-dress uniform" and its "heavily braided white cap pulled down rakishly over one cold gray eye." Suspicions are confirmed with "ta-pocketa-pocketa-pocketa-*pocketa-pocketa*"; the ludicrous "eight-engined Navy hydroplane" and the cliché about the Old Man make the comedy unmistakable.

Instructors may find it useful to introduce the concept of pathos and to lead the class in a discussion of the relation of the pathetic to the tragic and the comic. Here, of course, Mitty's daydreams are comic; we may pity him because of his weakness, but we can only laugh at his daydreams, which (1) are so greatly in contrast with the actual event, and (2) are so indebted to bad movies and pulp magazines.

Brooks and Warren provide an interpretation of the story in various editions of *Understanding Fiction;* Charles S. Holmes's *The Clocks of Colombus* (1972) is a useful study of Thurber. Carl Sundell examines the structure of the story (e.g., it begins and ends with Mitty dreaming) [*English Journal* 56 (1967): 1284–1287]. James Ellis [*English Journal* 54 (1965): 310–313] points out that Mitty's fantasies are made even more fantastic by various bits of misinformation. For example, Mitty the sea captain calls for "full strength in No. 3 turret," mistakenly thinking that the turrets move the ship; the surgeon nonsensically speaks of obstreosis (primarily a disease of cattle and pigs) of the ductal tract and thinks coreopsis (a flower) is a disease; the marksman refers to a 50.80-caliber pistol (its diameter would be more than four feet); the pilot speaks of von Richtman but means von Richthofen.

One other study of the story should be mentioned, Ann Ferguson Manx's in *Studies in Short Fiction* 19 (1982): 315–357. This essay is a vigorous defense of Mrs. Mitty, who is usually thought of as a nag. Manx argues that Mitty's fantasies are not provoked by Mrs. Mitty's naggings. Rather, Mitty is a hopeless fantasist, and it's a good thing for him that he has Mrs. Mitty to see that he wears his galoshes, doesn't drive too fast, and so on. Manx writes: "If we think seriously about what life with a man like Mitty would be like, Mrs. Mitty seems responsible and concerned." Perhaps the best thing is not to "think seriously" about what living with Walter Mitty would be like.

For a well-annotated selection of Thurber's work, along with a detailed chronology of his life, see *James Thurber: Writings and Drawings* (Library of America, 1996). See also Charles Shiveley Holmes, *The Clocks of Columbus: The Literary Career of James Thurber* (1972), and Robert Emmet Long, *James Thurber* (1988).

Topics for Critical Thinking and Writing

1. In a paragraph, characterize Mrs. Mitty.
2. In an essay of 500 words, evaluate the view that Mrs. Mitty is exactly the sort of woman Walter Mitty needs.

APHRA BEHN
Song: Love Armed (p. 90)

Although the allegory may at first seem unfamiliar to relatively inexperienced readers, if you ask students whether they have ever heard of any connections between love and war, they will quickly come up with phrases such as "the battle of the sexes" and "all is fair in love and war," and someone will mention that Cupid is armed with a bow and arrows. And although we don't want to push this delightful poem too far in the direction of realism, probably many students will find Behn's characterization of love as "tyrannic" quite intelligible.

It happens, however, that what especially interests us about the poem is the issue we raise in our first question: Why do people enjoy songs about unhappy love? Because it gives us a chance to impose form onto suffering and thus implies a kind of mastery over suffering? In any case, many students will be familiar with the motif and will be able to offer explanations accounting for the pleasure they take in the material.

Aphra Behn was not only a poet but also a playwright and novelist, and when teaching her poetry, we often take note of her powerful narrative of slavery and colonization, *Oroonoko* (c. 1688). On this work, which has received much attention recently, see Katharine M. Rogers, "Fact and Fiction in Aphra Behn's *Oroonoko*," *Studies in the Novel* 20 (Spring 1988), 1–15. See also George Woodcock, *The Incomparable Aphra* (1948; rpt. as *Aphra Behn: The English Sappho*, 1989), and Angeline Goreau, *Reconstructing Aphra* (1980).

EDGAR ALLAN POE
The Cask of Amontillado (p. 96)

Because many students will have read this story in high school, it can be used effectively as the first assignment. They will start with some ideas about it, and at the end of the class discussion they will probably see that they didn't know everything about the story. It may be good to begin a class discussion by asking the students to characterize the narrator. The opening paragraph itself, if read aloud in class, ought to provide enough for them to see that the speaker is probably paranoid and given to a monstrous sort of reasoning, though, of course, at the start of the story we cannot be absolutely certain that Fortunato has not indeed heaped a "thousand injuries" on him. (In this paragraph, notice too the word "impunity," which we later learn is part of the family motto.) When we meet Fortunato, we are convinced that though the narrator's enemy is something of a fool, he is not the monster that the narrator thinks he is. And so the words at the end of the story, fifty years later, must have an ironic tone, for though *in pace requiescat* can apply to Fortunato, they cannot apply to the speaker, who is still talking (on his deathbed, to a priest?) of his vengeance on the unfortunate Fortunato.

The story is full of other little ironies, conscious on the part of Montresor, unconscious on the part of Fortunato:

- The narrator is courteous but murderous.
- The time is one of festivity but a murder is being planned.
- The festival of disguise corresponds to the narrator's disguise of his feelings.
- Fortunato thinks he is festively *disguised* as a fool, but he is a fool.
- He says he will not die of a cough, and the narrator assures him that he is right.
- Fortunato is a Freemason, and when he asks the narrator for the secret sign of a brother, the narrator boldly, playfully, outrageously shows him the mason's trowel that he will soon use to wall Fortunato up.

But what to make of all this? It has been the fashion, for at least a few decades, to say that Poe's situations and themes speak to our anxieties, our fear of being buried alive, our fear of disintegration of the self, and so on. Maybe. Maybe, too, there is something to Marie Bonaparte's interpretation. She sees the journey through the tunnel to the crypt as an entry into the womb; the narrator is killing his father (Fortunato) and possessing his mother. And maybe, too, there is something to Daniel Hoffman's assertion in *Poe Poe Poe Poe Poe Poe Poe* (223) that Montresor and Fortunato are doubles: "When Montresor leads Fortunato down into the farthest vault of his family's wine-cellar, into a catacomb of human bones, is he not . . . conducting his double thither? My treasure, my fortune, down into the bowels of the earth, a charnel-house of bones." Maybe.

In addition to Hoffman's book (1972), we can recommend Kenneth Silverman's fine biography, *Edgar Allan Poe: Mournful and Never-Ending Remembrance* (1991).

A videocassette of Edgar Allan Poe's "The Cask of Amontillado" is available from Longman Publishers.

GUY DE MAUPASSANT
The Necklace (p. 101)

This story apparently remains a favorite among instructors and students, though perhaps because (at least for many readers) it is a story they love to hate. When we typed "Maupassant necklace" into a search engine, a couple of student essays came up, including one by someone—presumably an undergraduate—named Gregory Weston. His essay ends thus:

> I earlier compared "The Necklace" with "Cinderella," but the story reminds me more of the myth of Icaris [*sic*]. Mathilde wanted more then [*sic*] what was given to her and used her natural talents to get what she

aspired to. She did, and her only crime was trying to fly high. Maupassant delights in melting her wings, and then cheapens her fall with his "ironic twist" at the end. Why someone would write such a vicious and cynical story is beyond me.

Why someone would post such an essay is beyond us, but, come to think of it, instructors might well start a class discussion by distributing copies of this paragraph and inviting comment. Does Mathilde "use her natural talents" to get what she aspires to? Does Maupassant "delight" in reducing her? Is the story "vicious and cynical"?

A second essay that we found on the Internet is an anonymous piece entitled "Diamonds and Paste: A Marxist Reading of Guy de Maupassant's 'The Necklace.'" There is absolutely nothing Marxist about it, other than that it talks about "class distinction," "the social ladder," and "different economic classes." That is, it reveals no understanding of Marxist views of the role of the artist in bourgeois society or of class relationships. Here is the final paragraph:

> This story illustrates the different perspectives on value that are created by different economic classes. Value is viewed differently by different classes because of their different perspectives. The couple in the story would not have had to go into so much debt if they had simply realised that the necklace might not have much monetary value. Their social class made them believe that only expensive things are valuable and this brought them down.

Are we to understand that only lower-middle-class people "believe that only expensive things are valuable" and that, for instance, Mme. Loisel's rich friend holds a different view?

We confess that "The Necklace" is not our favorite Maupassant story, but we do think it is far richer than these two essayists indicate. Yes, the heart of the story is the ironic twist, the idea that the couple engaged in ten years of needless drudgery, that a moment or two of humiliating confession would have spared them a decade of slavery. But Maupassant is convincing in his swift characterization, for instance in the husband's "triumphant air" (paragraph 7) when he presents the invitation to his wife, in the wife's unexpected (but to us natural) expression of "disdain" (11), in the husband's embarrassment that he had not thought about what she might wear to the affair (15–18), in the wife's "intoxication" at the ball (54) and then her shame as she leaves, dressed in the "modest wraps of common life" rather than in the furs of the other women (55). We might notice, too, Maupassant's unsentimental (is it cynical—or merely realistic?) statement that her years of drudgery coarsened her ("she went to the fruiterer, the grocer, the butcher, her basket on her arm, bargaining, insulted, defending her miserable money sou by sou").

All these skillful touches of characterization raise the story to a level far above a merely ironic anecdote. Notice, too, how Maupassant darkens the tale when the couple leaves the ball, first by the wife's thoughts about her wraps, then by the difficulty they have in finding a cab. From here on, things go downhill swiftly. In class one might talk about the ways in which Maupassant from the very beginning prepares for the outcome. For instance, the very first paragraph speaks of "destiny," more specifically of "a mistake of destiny." Admittedly a reader does not put much weight on this phrase at first but on rereading, it takes on significance. There is something odd, something almost unnatural or freakish, Maupassant suggests, in the fact that this pretty, charming girl was born into the class she finds herself. Further in this paragraph we are told that "she let herself be married to a little clerk," that is, she seems to have no will of her own; her fate is settled for her. And surely we all realize that although we feel we are acting freely, chance plays an enormous part in our lives: had we gone to a different college, we might well now have a different spouse, and we might be engaged in a different career. And (unless we smoke cigarettes) we do not choose to fall ill or to die the way we will die. And—nagging thought—had our parents not met (an act that was not of our doing), we would not be here, thinking these thoughts. For the most part we *feel* as though our actions are free—we may think we are the captain of our fate, the master of our soul—but most of us probably recognize that in many ways we are puppets. A good deal of proverbial wisdom holds this view: Man proposes, God disposes; *che sarà sarà* (what will be will be); *ça ira* (it will go its own way—supposedly said by Benjamin Franklin about the American Revolution, when he was in Paris in 1776–1777).

Our point is, in brief, that Maupassant's characterization is convincing (the people behave plausibly) and that the overarching idea is scarcely shocking: our mistakes, sometimes rooted in a combination of our character and bad luck, can be catastrophic. If Mme. Loisel out of pride borrows jewelry, loses it, and later makes the mistake of not admitting that she has lost it, all three actions are entirely intelligible to us—we might do exactly what she has done. As for disastrous mistakes, well, if we haven't made them ourselves, we know of other people who have. Further, even as we say, "Why *of course* X *should* have done such-and-such," we realize that X (for whatever reasons) couldn't have done it, or perhaps didn't do it because there seemed to be no need to do it at the time.

Still, it might be worth asking students whether they do indeed find the story "cruel." One could ask them, even more generally, what it means for an author to treat his or her characters cruelly.

What's behind this question is a common fact of the students' experiences as readers—that characters in novels and stories can take on for them and, for that matter, for us a life of their own, a life that we feel keenly interested in and that—so compelling does the illusion seem—we believe that the writer himself or herself should not interfere with. The character is, on the one hand, the writer's creation, yet, on the other hand, enters into the reader's imagination as more than that, as an independent person rather than as something that the writer controls. There is a magic and mystery in the creation of a literary character that teachers are sometimes hesitant to admit to, but that they, and certainly their students, respond to when caught up in the story of, for example, Emma Woodhouse, Jane Eyre, or Anna Karenina.

Thus, when a writer seems to us to be imposing an unfair fate on a character we care about, a fate that the character does not deserve or that is not in keeping with his or her nature or that makes the character no more than a victim, we may be led to protest that the author or story is a cruel one. Again, this touches on a dimension of the students' experiences as readers, and perhaps the analysis of "The Necklace" can invite some discussion of it.

A few words about the questions that we ask in the text:

Question 1. What do we learn about Mme. Loisel in the early part of the story, and what is the reader's response to the narrator's generalization about women in the second paragraph? All generalizations are suspect (including even William Blake's assertion that "To generalize is to be an idiot"), but we find something attractive in the narrator's comment that "Natural fineness, instinct for what is elegant, suppleness of wit, are the sole hierarchy," and in his comment that lowborn women may thus be the equals of great ladies. In this period, with very few exceptions women had no way of rising, other perhaps than by selling their bodies, and so we take Maupassant to be asserting that even though a woman may be of low status, she may indeed be the mental equivalent of "the very greatest ladies."

Question 2. Is she "justly punished for her vanity and pride"? We don't think so. Yes, she shows traces of vanity and pride, but what kind of justice requires that vanity be sentenced to ten years at hard labor?

Question 3. Is "heroism" the appropriate word? We are glad that Maupassant used this word. Up to now, Mme. Loisel has exhibited petulance, vanity, and some other less-than-attractive qualities, though she has certainly not been villainous. Now, confronted with adversity, we are heartened to see her accept responsibility: "She took her part, moreover, all of a sudden, with heroism. That dreadful debt must be paid. She would pay it." And so she begins a decade of hard work, in which she comes to know "the horrible existence of the needy." Notice that Maupassant does not sentimentalize her behavior. Her heroic willingness to pay for the necklace does not mean that she becomes noble-minded. Rather, the reverse is true, as we indicated when we quoted the passage that tells us she harangued the fruiterers, the grocer, the butcher. Suffering doesn't ennoble, it harshens (or at least it usually does). But surely readers are able to see something heroic—however mistaken, however ironic—in her struggle.

Question 4. How well does the story fit with Maupassant's comment on the aim of a writer? In the text we isolate three issues: the purpose of fiction ("to make us understand the hidden meaning of events"); the assertion that fiction gives the reader a "personal view"; and the assertion that readers should be moved but should not be aware that the writer has foisted a personal view on them, i.e., the writer's purpose and artistry should be inconspicuous. We have already indicated that we think Maupassant's highly anecdotal story does imply a view of life, a revelation of "the hidden meaning of events," and it does indeed seem that Maupassant's "personal view" was that we have little control over our destiny. Finally, we think that the work has been constructed so skillfully that—despite the outrageous irony—the reader cannot say, "Oh, no; people do not behave this way. Maupassant, like the writer of a soap opera, is inventing crazy improbabilities and crazy inconsistencies in the characters merely to create a gripping story." In our view, the characters are sketched convincingly, and the plot is plausible enough. People *are* sometimes motivated by vanity, and they *do* lose things, and they *do* conceal embarrassing truths. For us, the behavior of Mme. Loisel and her husband is entirely believable.

In our view, the great improbability is that the Loisels could somehow find a real diamond necklace that was so similar to the paste necklace that the owner, Mme. Forestier, would not notice the difference. Curiously, we don't recall a student ever bringing up this point—further proof, of course, that Maupassant has done his work very well.

KATHERINE ANNE PORTER
The Jilting of Granny Weatherall (p. 108)

Students do not always understand that there are two narratives here: one of a woman's dying hour and another of the past that floods her mind. The old lady, a tough Southerner or Southwesterner with an intense love of life, has "weathered all," even a jilting; she had expected a groom, George, and was publicly disappointed when he failed to show up. Now, at her death, again a priest is in the house, and again she is disappointed or "jilted": The bridegroom (Christ) fails to appear. (It surely is worthwhile to call attention to the parable of the wise and foolish virgins, in Matthew 25:1–13, where the bridegroom does appear, but the foolish virgins miss him.) The first jilting could in some measure be overcome, but the second is unendurable.

Porter gives us the stream of Granny's consciousness, and if we are not always perfectly clear about details (did Hapsy die in childbirth?), we are nevertheless grateful for the revelation of an unfamiliar state of consciousness.

Exactly who is Hapsy? We assume that Hapsy was her last child, "the one she really wanted," and that is why Hapsy plays such an important role in Granny's consciousness. Presumably she had at last come to love her husband. (On this point, it is relevant to mention, too, that one of her sons is named George—presumably for the man who jilted her—and the other son is not named John, for his father, but Jimmy.) But other readers interpret Hapsy differently. Among the interpretations that we find far-fetched are (1) Hapsy was a black friend and midwife who secretly delivered Ellen of an illegitimate child, but George learned of this and therefore jilted Ellen, and (2) Hapsy was Ellen's illegitimate child, fathered by George, and George then jilted her.

Also, who is the "he" who, at the first jilting, "cursed like a sailor's parrot and said, "I'll kill him for you'"? Among the answers usually given are: her father, a brother, the man she later married. Probably the question can't be answered authoritatively. And who is the driver of the cart, whom she recognizes "by his hands"?

These details probably do not affect the overall interpretation of the story. To return to a larger matter, what interpretation of the story makes the most sense? What happens if we consider the story chiefly in the light of the Parable of the Ten Virgins? "The Jilting of Granny Weatherall" has engendered considerable comment in books on Porter, in journals, and especially in the instructors' manuals that accompany textbooks, but it is probably fair to say that the story is usually interpreted as setting forth the picture of an admirable—even heroic—woman who finds, at the end of her life, that there is no God, or, more specifically, that Christ the Bridegroom does not come to her. That is, putting aside the matter of the author's own beliefs (and putting the whole matter rather crudely) the story shows us an energetic woman who at the end of her life learns that she lives in a godless world.

This is the way we have long seen the story, and we still have a strong attachment to that view, but a rereading of the parable (Matthew 25:1–13), may raise some doubt:

1. Then shall the kingdom of heaven be likened unto ten virgins, which took their lamps, and went forth to meet the bridegroom.
2. And five of them were wise, and five were foolish.
3. They that were foolish took their lamps, and took no oil with them.
4. But the wise took oil in their vessels with their lamps.
5. While the bridegroom tarried, they all slumbered and slept.
6. And at midnight there was a cry made, Behold, the bridegroom cometh; go ye out to meet him.
7. Then all those virgins arose, and trimmed their lamps.
8. And the foolish said unto the wise, Give us of your oil; for our lamps are gone out.
9. But the wise answered, saying, Not so; lest there be not enough for us and you: but go ye rather to them that sell, and buy for yourselves.
10. And while they went to buy, the bridegroom came; and they that were ready went in with him to the marriage: and the door was shut.
11. Afterward came also the other virgins, saying, Lord, Lord, open to us.
12. But he answered and said, Verily I say unto you, I know you not.
13. Watch therefore, for ye know neither the day nor the hour wherein the son of man cometh.

Before we learned (chiefly from Wimsatt and Beardsley) of "the Intentional Fallacy," we might have studied Porter's letters, prefaces, and other stories in an effort to ascertain her view of the parable—we still might try to do so, but if we do we will be frustrated since Porter apparently did not comment on the parable, except in this story. Nor does the fact that she had a Catholic education tell us much about what she made of the parable. It appears that to understand the story we can do nothing more than read the story, and perhaps read the parable.

Matthew's final line, "Watch [i.e. remain awake] therefore, for ye know neither the day nor the hour wherein the son of man cometh," somewhat confuses the point of the parable, since the wise virgins as well as the foolish virgins slept, but the point nevertheless is very clear: the foolish virgins—foolish because they were shortsighted—overlooked the possibility of the bridegroom's delay. The bridegroom may come unexpectedly.

Can one (or should one) interpret the story in the light of the evident meaning of the parable? If one interprets it thus, the point or theme might be roughly stated along these lines: Granny, despite all of her apparently commendable worldly activity—ministering to the sick, keeping the farm in good repair, etc.—is (in a spiritual sense) improvident. The second bridegroom does not appear at the moment that she expects him, and she therefore despairs and abandons her belief:

> For the second time there was no sign. Again no bridegroom and the priest in the house. She could not remember any other sorrow because this grief wiped them all away. Oh, no, there's nothing more cruel than this—I'll never forgive it. She stretched herself with a deep breath and blew out the light.

One might almost say Granny Weatherall is guilty of the sort of hubris shown by some of Flannery O'Connor's characters, who think (for example) that because they wear clean clothing (the grandmother in "A Good Man Is Hard To Find") or hose down their pigs (Mrs. Turpin in "Revelation") they will be saved. Some support for this reading can be found in this passage:

> Granny felt easy about her soul. . . . She had her secret comfortable understanding with a few favored saints.

However, another way of looking at the story is to emphasize the point that, although at the end she is deeply disappointed, she remains active; she blows out the light. Against this, David C. Estes argues [*Studies in Short Fiction* 22 (1953)], "Her final act . . . reveals the ironic futility of all that has kept her so busy."

The interpretation that she is hubristic is offered very tentatively, and certainly not as one that gives *the* meaning of the story. But a reading of the parable is bound to call into question the usual view that "The Jilting of Granny Weatherall" is a story about a strong woman's perception that her faith is delusive.

For biography: Joan Givner, *Katherine Anne Porter: A Life* (1982). Critical interpretation is provided by: Jane K. DeMouy, *Katherine Anne Porter's Women: The Eye of Her Fiction* (1983); Robert H. Brinkmeyer, Jr., *Katherine Anne Porter's Artistic Development* (1993); and Janis P. Stout, *Katherine Anne Porter: A Sense of the Times* (1995).

José Armas
El Tonto del Barrio (p. 114)

If you have any Spanish-speaking students in your class, or even students whose acquaintance with Spanish does not go beyond a few years of high school study, you might ask them how they would translate the title. We thought of glossing

"El Tonto" as "The Fool" or "The Idiot," but "Fool" is a bit old-fashioned and "Idiot"—as Armas suggested to us—is too strong. Armas's own suggestion, "Dummy," strikes us as exactly right.

While one is reading the story, say through the first one-third, it may seem to be chiefly a character sketch of Romero and a sketch of the community in which he lives, but then come two sentences that mark a turning point:

> Romero kept the sidewalks clean and the barrio looked after him. It was a contract that worked well for a long time.

"Worked well *for a long time*" implies that something happened that broke the contract, and we are promptly introduced to the disruptive element:

> Then, when Seferino, Barelas' oldest son, graduated from high school he went to work in the barber shop for the summer. Seferino was a conscientious and sensitive young man and it wasn't long before he took notice of Romero and came to feel sorry for him.

In the light of what happens next, some readers may think that the narrator (or the author?) is being ironic, even sarcastic, when he characterizes Seferino as "conscientious and sensitive," but Seferino really is conscientious and sensitive. He just isn't mature, or wise in the ways of the barrio, and (an important point) isn't able to understand that not everyone feels as he does. Thus, when he argues with his father he says, "How would you like to do what he does and be treated in the same way?" That's a reasonable position (we all know that we should do unto others as we would have others do unto us)—but Barelas's answer is wiser than Seferino's question: "I'm not Romero." Further, and this may seem to be a paradox, Barelas is not only wise enough to know that he is not Romero, but he is also wise enough to know (as Seferino does not) *why* Romero sweeps the sidewalks: "He sweeps the sidewalks because he wants something to do, not because he wants money."

Although the conflict between Seferino and Romero is the obvious conflict, the conflict (though that is almost too strong a word) between Seferino and Barelas is worth discussing in class. (The question in the text about Barelas's character is one way of approaching it.) This conflict is amusingly resolved when the well-meaning Seferino disappears into Harvard, thus sparing us a potentially embarrassing or painful scene in which the boy acknowledges his error. Indeed, instead of emphasizing the conflict between Barelas and his son, we get a scene in which Barelas—whose son has caused Romero to misbehave—is pitted against the rest of the community, which now seeks to confine Romero. And although Barelas again is on the right side, in one tiny detail he reveals that he too has been rattled, we might even say corrupted, by his son's well-intentioned plan. When one of the men of the barrio says, "What if [Romero] hurts . . . ?" Barelas interrupts: "He's not going to hurt anyone." Tino replies: "No, Barelas, I was going to say, what if he hurts himself?" It's a lovely touch, showing that Barelas (who is right about so much) can be mistaken, and, more important, showing that even though the community wants to lock Romero up, it is concerned chiefly for Romero's well-being.

These comments are obvious, and perhaps a bit too solemn, since the story has a good deal of delightful humor in it. (One can ask the class what it finds *amusing* in the story.) A favorite passage is the bit recounting how Romero, after breaking with Seferino, at first simply skipped the barber shop in his sweeping, but then refined his action and pushed all of the trash from elsewhere in front of the barber shop.

Topic for Critical Thinking and Writing

The story is about Romero, but almost as interestingly it is about Seferino. We can fairly easily guess what will happen to Romero in the next few years. What would you guess will happen to Seferino? Will his Harvard education lead to his increasing alienation from his community? (Our own response is yes, in the short run, but—since he is a bright and sensitive youth and he has a wise father—we can hope that in the long run he will learn to appreciate and to cherish the ways of the barrio.)

LESLIE MARMON SILKO
The Man to Send Rain Clouds (p. 120)

The church—especially perhaps the Roman Catholic Church—has often adapted itself to the old ways and beliefs of new converts, sometimes by retaining the old holidays and holy places but adapting them and dedicating them to the new religion. For instance, although the date of Jesus's birth is not known, from the fourth century it was celebrated late in December, displacing pagan festivals of new birth (e.g., the Roman *Saturnalia,* which celebrated the sowing of the crops on December 15–17, and the feast of the *Natalis Solis Invicti,* celebrating the renewal of the sun a week later).

Practices of this sort have facilitated conversion, but from the church's point of view the danger may be that the new believers retain too much faith in the old beliefs. In Silko's story the priest has every reason to doubt that his parishioners have fully accepted Christianity. The unnamed priest—he's just "the priest" or "the young priest," not anyone with a personal identity, so far as the other characters in the story are concerned—is kind and well meaning, and he is even willing to bend the rules a bit, but he knows that he does not have the confidence of the people. He is disturbed that they didn't think the Last Rites and a funeral Mass were necessary, and he is not at all certain that they have given up their pagan ways: "He looked at the red blanket, not sure that Teofilo was so small, wondering if it wasn't some perverse Indian trick—something they did in March to ensure a good harvest. . . ." He is wrong in suspecting that Teofilo (the name means "beloved of God," from the Greek *theos* = God, and *philos* = loving) is not in front of him, but he is right in suspecting that a "trick" is being played, since the reader knows that the holy water is wanted not to assist Teofilo to get to the Christian heaven but to bring rain for the crops. In Part One we hear Leon say, "Send us rain clouds, Grandfather"; in Part Three we hear Louise express the hope that the priest will sprinkle water so Teofilo "won't be thirsty"; and at the very end of the story we hear that Leon "felt good because it was finished, and he was happy about the sprinkling of the holy water; now the old man could send them big thunderclouds for sure."

We aren't quite sure about what to make of the passage in which the water, disappearing as soon as it is sprinkled on the grave, "reminded" the priest of something, but the passage is given some emphasis and surely it is important. Our sense is that the priest vaguely intuits an archetypal mystery, something older and more inclusive than the Roman Catholic ritual he engages in.

During most of the story the narrator neither editorializes nor enters the minds of the characters; we are not told that the characters are reverential, and (for the most part) we are not allowed to hear their thoughts. Rather, we see them perform ceremonies with dignity, and, because the point of view is chiefly objective, we draw our own conclusions. Possibly, too, by keeping outside of the minds of the characters the narrator helps to convey the traditional paleface idea that Native Americans are inscrutable people, people of few words. Certainly Leon hoards words when, responding to the priest's admonition not to let Teofilo stay at the sheep camp alone, he says, "No, he won't do that any more now." But we do get into the priest's mind, notably in the passage in which he suspects trickery, and we get into Leon's mind at the end of the story when, in what almost seems like a thunderstorm of information, we are told his thoughts about the water.

Because the narrator, like the characters, is taciturn, some readers may think that Leon and his companions are callous. "After all," one student said, "don't they first round up the sheep before attending to the burial rites? And why don't they weep?" Class discussion can usually bring out the dignity of the proceedings here, and some students may be able to provide specific details about burial customs unfamiliar to other members of the class.

We do not know if the different colors of paint—white, blue, yellow, and green—have specific meanings, but perhaps blue suggests the sky and the water, yellow suggests corn meal, and green suggests vegetation. White is a fairly widespread sign of purity, but we have not been able to find out how Pueblo people regard it. (If you know about these things, we'll be most appreciative if you write to us, in care of the publisher.)

Silko has written two novels: *Ceremony* (1977) and *Almanac of the Dead* (1991). Short stories and prose poems are included in *Storyteller* (1981). Per Syersted has written a cogent introduction, *Leslie Marmon Silko* (1980), but it needs to be updated. For additional commentary, see Alan R. Veile, *Four Indian Masters* (1982). For students working on the stories, we recommend Helen Jaskoski, *Leslie Marmon Silko: A Study of the Short Fiction* (1998).

ROBERT FROST
Come In (p. 124)

Most students will already be familiar with Frost's "Stopping by Woods on a Snowy Evening," so you may want to ask them to reread that poem (it is in Chapter 16) and to write a comparison.

The dark woods of "Come In" are as seductive as the woods of "Stopping by Woods," and in "Come In," as in the earlier poem, Frost powerfully represents their attractiveness. The sound of the thrush in the wood prompts the speaker to say in the second line "hark," a word with archaic—and can we say religious?—connotations (cf. "Hark the herald angels sing, / Glory to the newborn king"). In line 13 "the pillared dark" sees the trees as columns, giving the woods the stateliness of a majestic building, perhaps a Greek temple. As we already mentioned, all of this is immensely seductive, as is the wood in "Stopping by Woods on a Snowy Evening," but in "Come In," as in the earlier work, Frost, though fully appreciative of the dark beauty, resists yielding to it: "But no, I was out for stars." And then, in a typically Frostian way, the speaker not only brings himself back to earth, so to speak, but cuts himself down, sees himself as the mere human being that he is, moving in a natural world that, far from trying to entrap him, is sublimely indifferent to him:

> But no, I was out for stars:
> I would not come in.
> I meant not even if asked,
> And I hadn't been.

ELIZABETH BISHOP
Filling Station (p. 125)

We hope that we are not being sexist pigs (doubtless something that sexist pigs often say) when we say that we hear a woman's voice in "Oh, but it is dirty!" (It's a good idea to ask students to read this line aloud—and, indeed, to read the entire poem aloud.) We even hear a woman's voice, though less obviously, in "Be careful with that match!" (One can ask students if they hear a woman's voice. If they do, it can be interesting to ask them to alter the line to something a man might say—perhaps, "Watch out with that match" or some such thing.) Other words that seem to us to indicate a female speaker: "saucy" (describing the sons, in line 10), "all quite thoroughly dirty" (13), "comfy" (20, though here perhaps the speaker is consciously using the diction of the woman who may live at the gas station), "Why, oh why; the doily?" (30), and the knowledgeable remarks about embroidery in lines 30–33.

The somewhat snobbish tone of the first stanza is moderated in the third, when the speaker begins to take an interest in the *life* of this station, and if snobbery continues in the fourth and fifth stanzas (21–30), it is also moderated by the speaker's interest in the technique of the doily. In the last stanza there is a bit of snide humor in "Somebody waters the plant, / or oils it, maybe," but clearly by now the speaker is won over. However coarse the taste of the owners, they have tried to add a bit of order and a bit of beauty to life—not only to their own lives, but to the lives of passersby. The cans that spell out ESSO of course advertise a product, but they speak "softly" (38), their "so-so-so" serving to soothe the drivers of "high-strung automobiles," as a groom might soothe a horse or a mother her fretful baby. "Somebody loves us," the poet ends, referring most obviously to the owners of the filling station, but surely the reference is also larger, perhaps even unobtrusively hinting at the existence of a loving God. The close attention to detail, for which Bishop is widely known, is in fact loaded with moral value. Students might be invited to think of the poem partly in terms of Frost's comment (later in the text) about a poem as "a clarification of life . . . [and] a momentary stay against confusion."

The movement in this poem from the rather prim and disapproving opening line, through the sympathetic union with what she observes—achieved especially when the speaker, taken out of herself by her rapt attention to the embroidery—and finally to the larger or more generous view reminds us of a comment about her poetry in one of Bishop's letters. The arts, Bishop says, begin in observation. "Dreams, works of art, . . . unexpected moments of empathy . . . , catch a peripheral vision of whatever it is one can never really see full-face but that seems enormously important. . . . What one seems to want in art, in experiencing it, is the same thing that is necessary for its creation, a self-forgetful, perfectly useless concentration" (quoted by Helen McNeil in *Voices and Visions* (1987), ed. Helen Vendler, p. 395).

Students who value Bishop might be advised to turn to her *Complete Poems 1927–1979* (1983). Her *Collected Prose* (1984) and *Letters* (1994) are also stimulating—excellent sources for studying this important poet. Also rewarding: *Conversations with Elizabeth Bishop*, ed. George Monteiro (1996), and Gary Fountain, *Remembering Elizabeth Bishop: An Oral Biography* (1994).

ROBERT HERRICK
To the Virgins, to Make Much of Time (p. 126)

On Herrick's "To the Virgins," see E. M. W. Tillyard in *The Metaphysicals and Milton* (1956); Tillyard argues effectively that in "To the Virgins," "the trend of the poem is urgency, touched with reflection."

This wonderful lyric seems ideally suited to introduce students to matters of persona and tone. We have found that when asked, "Who is speaking?" most students will answer, "A man." (Possibly some offer this opinion simply because a man wrote this poem.) A few will say that a woman is the speaker, and we have found it interesting to ask them why. (Those who say that a woman is the speaker usually suggest that she is unmarried and is speaking regretfully.)

Almost all students hear the voice of an older person, though they cannot always say why. Similarly, although a few students find the speaker aggressively offering unsolicited advice, most hear a friendly voice. True, the first and last stanzas begin with imperatives ("Gather ye rosebuds," "Then be not coy"), but most students hear in "Old Time," "a-flying," and "a-getting" an engaging old-codgerliness. They may hear, too, even a touch of elderly loquacity in the explanation of a fairly obvious figure: "The glorious lamp of heaven, the sun."

One other point about Herrick's poem: The shift to "you" in the last stanza (from the earlier "ye") gives the moral great emphasis.

The *carpe diem* motif allows the poem to be related easily to Marvell's "Coy Mistress." What is especially interesting, however, is the difference in tone, even though the poems share both a motif and a structure—the logical argument.

Is the poem offensive to women? Some of our students have found it so. Our hope is that readers will be able to read the poem not so much as advice to women to submit passively to marriage, but rather as advice (which can apply to males as well as to females) "to make much of time." Against "dying" and "setting," we can "gather," "smile," and "run."

John Press (1961) and Roger B. Rollin (1966) have written good introductions to Herrick's life and work.

Lyn Lifshin
My Mother and the Bed (p. 127)

Students enjoy this poem, and classroom discussion may be animated, especially concerning the second question in the text, which asks if bitterness overshadows geniality.

Our first question, concerning the unexpected extra spaces in the poem, calls attention to the need to pay close attention to—to enjoy—the physical appearance of the poem. Of course readers of this book will see Pastan's "Jump Cabling" in Chapter 14, a poem whose meaning is partly conveyed by its appearance on the page, but it is useful to remind students to consider the physical appearance of every poem. Long lines convey a feeling different from short lines, and the breaks between stanzas can say a lot. True, we should read poems aloud, if possible, but we should also look at them closely—"hear with eyes," in Shakespeare's words—and take their appearance seriously.

Martín Espada
Bully (p. 128)

The editors of *Literature for Composition* belong to a generation that was taught, in grade school and in high school, that Teddy Roosevelt was a hero. Some of his words entered the classroom, just as half a century later some of the words of John Kennedy—notably the Inaugural Address—entered the classroom. In school we heard such Rooseveltisms as "I wish to preach, not the doctrine of ignoble ease, but the doctrine of the strenuous life" (1899), "In life, as in a football game, the principle to follow is: Hit the line hard" (1901), and "There is no room in this country for hyphenated Americanism. . . . The one absolutely certain way of bringing this nation to ruin, of preventing all possibility of its continuing to be a nation at all, would be to permit it to become a tangle of squabbling nationalities" (1915). In the fifth question in the text, we quote yet another (in)famous remark, expressing the opinion that all immigrants should be required to learn English within five years. Persons who doubt that Roosevelt was regarded as one of America's greatest heroes need only call to mind Mount Rushmore National Memorial, in South Dakota, where an enormous bust of Roosevelt, along with busts of Washington, Jefferson, and Lincoln, is carved. Although the sculptures (visible for some sixty miles) were not finished until the 1950s, the monument was dedicated in 1927, and in effect it represents the values of the 1920s.

In our third question, we ask about the word "bully," as an adjective and as a noun. Roosevelt used the adjective, meaning "excellent," in a famous comment, to the effect that the presidency is a "bully pulpit." But given Roosevelt's enthusiasm for military action, in particular for the Spanish-American War (a war whose name somehow omits the efforts of the Cuban patriots who fought for independence), it is hard not to think of the other and more common meaning of the word. Certainly in this poem entitled "Bully," where it is said of Roosevelt that "each fist [is] lonely for a sabre," the image that comes across is of someone who pushes other people around. A century ago Roosevelt stormed San Juan with his Rough Riders, but today Puerto Rican children invade Roosevelt School (line 11). The end of the poem, with its reference to Roosevelt's "Victorian mustache / and monocle," present a hopelessly outdated and somewhat comic figure who contrasts with the vitality of the "Spanish-singing children."

5

Other Kinds of Writing about Literature

WILLIAM BLAKE
The Tyger (p. 138)

E. D. Hirsch, Jr., in *Innocence and Experience* (1964), Harold Bloom, in *The Visionary Company* (1961), and Hazard Adams, in *William Blake* (1980), discuss "The Tyger." Also of interest are Martin K. Nurmi, "Blake's Revisions of 'The Tyger,'" *PMLA* 71 (September 1956): 669–685, and Harold Bloom, *Blake's Apocalypse* (1970). See also, for a collection of essays and extracts from books, *William Blake: The Tyger,* ed. Winston Weathers.

In the course of arguing on behalf of reader-response criticism, Stanley Fish, in *Is There a Text in This Class?* (1980), has some fun calling attention to the diversity of opinions. He points out that in *Encounter* (June 1954), Kathleen Raine published an essay entitled "Who Made the Tyger?" She argued that because for Blake the tiger is "the beast that sustains its own life at the expense of its fellow-creatures," the answer to the big question ("Did he who made the Lamb make thee?") is, in Raine's words, "beyond all possible doubt, No." Fish points out that Raine, as part of her argument, insists that Blake always uses the word "forest" with reference "to the natural, 'fallen' world." Fish then calls attention to E. D. Hirsch's reading, in *Innocence and Experience*, in which Hirsch argues that "forest" suggests "tall straight forms, a world that for all its terror has the orderliness of the tiger's stripes or Blake's perfectly balanced verses." In short, for Hirsch "The Tyger" is "a poem that celebrates the holiness of tigerness." Hirsch also argues that Blake satirizes the single-mindedness of the Lamb.

We find all of this very baffling. We are not specialists in Blake, but it seems to us that both poems celebrate rather than satirize or in any way condemn their subjects. In "The Lamb" (such is our critical innocence), innocence is celebrated; in "The Tyger," energy is celebrated.

In "The Tyger" the animal is "burning bright" because of its fiery eyes (line 6) and presumably because of its orange stripes, also flame-like. (Since the tiger is imagined as being created in a smithy, the poem also includes other images of fire in such words as "forge" and "furnace.")

Blake's question in effect is this: Was the tiger created in hell ("distant deeps") or in heaven ("skies")—and by Satan or by God? Blake hammers these questions into our minds, but it seems to us that Blake clearly implies an answer: The creator is "immortal," daring, "dread," and—most important—creative. In traditional Christian thinking, then, the answer is that God created the tiger.

Lines 17–18 ("When the stars threw down their spears / And watered heaven with their tears") have engendered much commentary. Possibly the lines allude to the war in heaven in Milton's *Paradise Lost*, and Blake's gist might be paraphrased thus: "When the rebel angels cast down their spears in defeat, did the triumphant God smile at his success, i.e., what were God's feelings when he had to be tiger-like to an aspect of his own creation?" This makes sense to us, but we admit that, strictly speaking, in *Paradise Lost* the rebellious angels never do "cast down their spears," i.e., never surrender.

One last comment. Harold Bloom probably understands Blake as well as anyone else alive. In *The Oxford Anthology of English Literature* (1973) he gives this footnote, which we can't quite bring ourselves to believe. You may want to think about it and to try it out on your students.

> However the poem is interpreted, the reader should be wary of identifying the poem's chanter with Blake, who did not react with awe or fear to any natural phenomenon whatsoever.
>
> Blake probably had considerable satirical intention in this lyric, as a juxtaposition of his verbal description of the Tyger with his illustration seems to suggest. [The illustration shows an unimpressive beast.] The poem's speaker, though a man of considerable imagination (quite possibly a poet like William Cowper), is at work terrifying himself with a monster of his own creation. Though Blake may mean us to regard the poem's questions as unanswerable, he himself would have answered by saying that the "immortal hand or eye" belonged only to Man, who makes both Tyger and Lamb. In "the forests of the night," or mental darkness, Man makes the Tyger, but in the open vision of day Man makes the Lamb.

X. J. KENNEDY
For Allen Ginsberg (p. 139)

This poem is a multi-leveled tribute. It is Kennedy's tribute to Ginsberg; Kennedy's tribute to William Blake, a poet whom Ginsberg esteemed and whose poem "The Tyger" Kennedy echoes; and Kennedy's tribute, one might suggest, to his own poetic prowess, as he seizes upon Blake's vivid words and adapts their rhythm into witty, exuberant praise of a poet whom Kennedy admired.

Blake's poem begins: "Tyger! Tyger! burning bright." Kennedy keeps the second part of the line but changes the first into "Ginsberg, Ginsberg," which, as one of our students noted, may lead readers to see Ginsberg in the image of the fearsome, fierce tiger: Blake's tiger has become Kennedy's Ginsberg. This is not what we would visualize as the appropriate animal for the peace-loving Ginsberg, but it is in tune with the fun-making spirit of the poem.

Kennedy clearly took a good deal of pleasure in composing this playful elegy. The pun in the phrase "*Queen* of Maytime" gets at the festive frolics in which the radical Ginsberg delighted and also alludes to his homosexuality (as does the earlier word "Queer"). Kennedy took pleasure too, we are sure, in the double alliterative phrases "foe of fascist" and "bane of bomb" in line 10.

Kennedy changes the rhythm of the poem at line 14. There is a significant pause after "What a catch for Death," which may be Kennedy's way of dramatizing his (and our own) recognition that the vital, wild Ginsberg is dead—that the person whom Kennedy has been making so present and real has departed from us, and that all we retain are memories of Ginsberg's antics.

It intrigues us that Kennedy focuses almost exclusively on Ginsberg the merry-making prankster and social critic. He mentions the fact that Ginsberg was a foe to "proper poets," but he does not compliment Ginsberg *as* a poet. What have we lost with Ginsberg's death? "Glee and sweetness, freaky light." That's a fine and noble line of sentiment, but different from lamenting the departure from us of a great poet. It strikes us that "For Allen Ginsberg" pays tribute to Ginsberg the personality even as it may also imply Kennedy's assessment of Ginsberg the poet. At the least it raises the possibility that Ginsberg will endure because of who he was rather than because of the poetry he wrote.

Students will enjoy Barry Miles, *Ginsberg: A Biography* (1989). Another good source is Carolyn Cassady, *Off the Road: My Years with Cassady, Kerouac, and Ginsberg* (1990). Somewhat dated, but still interesting, is *Allen Verbatim: Lectures on Poetry, Politics, Consciousness,* ed. Gordon Ball (1974). There are also a number of Websites devoted to Ginsberg, the best of which is *Welcome to Allen Ginsberg: Shadow Changes into Bone* <http://www.ginzy.com/>; this site is especially useful for its links to interviews.

WILLIAM BUTLER YEATS
Annunciation, Leda and the Swan [1924], Leda and the Swan [1933] (p. 140)

Before we briefly talk about the differences among the three versions, we want to say something about rape in mythology and in art and literature.

Probably twenty years ago most people would have taught this poem without fretting about the possibility that Yeats is insufficiently concerned about the victim of the rape. Indeed, amazing though it sounds, discussions of the story of Leda—we are not talking about Yeats's poem, but about the legend—commonly did *not* use the word "rape." A standard handbook of mythology on our shelves,

Michael Grant and John Hazel's *Gods and Mortals in Classical Mythology* (1973)—a book that announces it is a "Merriam-Webster Reference Book"—tells the reader that "Zeus seduced Leda" (p. 423). This book and virtually all others of the same sort, in speaking of Zeus's assaults on Leda, Io, Europa, and others (usually female, but don't forget Ganymede), use a variety of euphemisms: He "made love" to them, he "seduced" them, he "pursued" them, he "took" them. Occasionally the books will say that he "abducted" X or Y or Z, but only very rarely that he "raped" someone. (The same euphemisms are used of rapes committed by other gods: Hades "took" Persephone, and Apollo "pursued" Daphne.) Consider Richard J. Finneran's astounding note on "Leda and the Swan" in his valuable edition of *The Poems of W. B. Yeats* (1983): "In classical mythology, the god Zeus comes to the mortal Leda in the form of a swan" (p. 652). Comparably sanitized (and preposterous) language is used by the editors of *The Norton Anthology*, 7th ed. (2000), in their footnote to the poem: "In Greek mythology Zeus visited Leda in the form of a swan" (vol. 2, p. 2110).

The authors of the handbooks were perhaps being cautious—they knew that their books would be in school libraries—but, like Finneran, they were also simply reflecting the thought of the period. Speaking a bit broadly we can say that from the Renaissance onward much of the violence of the ancient myths has been reduced. For instance, in Leonardo's *Leda and the Swan* (the original painting is lost, but a copy exists), Leda stands, caressing the swan's neck while she smiles and gazes at two eggs on the ground, from each of which has emerged a pair of twins. Admittedly a swan for a father is a bit odd, but on the whole the picture shows a happy family. In Michelangelo's lost painting (again, copies exist and Yeats in fact owned a photographic reproduction of a copy), a recumbent and apparently relaxed Leda is kissed by a swan. As Diane Wolfthal points out in *Images of Rape* (1999), even paintings that do show more violence, such as Titian's *Rape of Europa* and Giambologna's *Rape of the Sabine Women,* were likely to be discussed in terms of color and composition. The emphasis, Wolfthal rightly says, was on the genius of the male artist, not on the emotions of the depicted women.

It's hard to speak authoritatively concerning the ancient view of rape (for one thing, "the ancient view" covers several centuries and, for a second, such evidence as there is is not entirely coherent), but it does seem as though these rapes (including Zeus's rape of Ganymede) were presented from the god's point of view: a human being was done the great honor of being brought into the realm of the gods, of being united with a god. Whether one can present this idea convincingly in class is a question; it may be of a piece with the quaint idea that whites conferred a blessing on black Africans by enslaving them and thereby freeing them from idolatry.

There is a further difficulty. Students may say that Yeats is saying that women don't mind (and perhaps even enjoy) being raped. After all, in line 6 in all three versions he speaks of Leda's "loosening thighs." We can only suggest that Yeats is speaking about one particular mythological episode, not about rape in general or women in general. We do not want to minimize the violence of the poem. Yeats emphasizes the violence, as one can see by comparing the opening lines. In the first version we get "Now can the swooping godhead have his will," which is fairly strong but is weak compared to the second version, "A rush, a sudden wheel, and hovering still / The bird descends." Even this opening, however, is mild compared with the shocking violence of the final version: "A sudden blow." And in the fifth line of each version, Yeats speaks of Leda's "terrified" fingers that seek to push the bird away from her.

How to help students to see that Yeats is not condoning rape and is not saying that Leda participated in her own violation? The attack is sudden—Leda is taken so unawares that she can scarcely resist. All three versions ask a question, "How can those terrified vague fingers push / The feathered glory from her loosening thighs?" But the question is rhetorical; the only possible answer is that her fingers cannot push the swan away, since the attack was unforeseen and the bird's grip is firm. Caught (in the final version) between the "beating" wings of the first line and the "beating" heart of the eighth line, i.e., locked within the octave, her "loosening thighs" yield to "the feathered glory" and to "that white rush." With the "shudder in the loins" Zeus and Leda generate Helen and the Trojan War and the death of Agamemnon.

Still, even though Leda is presented as a victim, and Zeus is not the rapist lurking in the park but a supernatural power, students may have difficulty seeing the poem as something more than a presentation of a rape. Here is an approach that we have been thinking about and that we may conceivably try out in the classroom the next time we teach the poem. (But by the time that you read this, we may have abandoned the idea.) St. Paul in Acts 9:3–8 speaks of his sudden vision of Jesus, and in 2 Corinthians 12:2 he says he was "caught up to the third heaven," i.e., taken into paradise. Paul's enforced visit to paradise is commonly spoken of as "The Rapture of Paul," *rapture* here being defined as "the transportation of a person, especially to heaven." The word, which can also mean "the state of being transported by a lofty emotion," comes from the same Latin word that gives us *rape*. The Latin word also gives us *rapt* (in a state of deep delight or absorption). Now, we are not saying that because the Latin *rapere* (to seize) is at the root of several English words, and some of these words have favorable meanings, all of them therefore must have favorable meanings. Rather, we are saying that the rape of Leda may somewhat resemble the rapture of Paul, where a mortal suddenly, violently, encountered divinity. So shattering was Paul's vision of Jesus that he became temporarily blind, and for three days he neither ate nor drank. Caravaggio's great painting, circa 1601, is relevant. Whereas earlier painters had usually shown Jesus descending through the clouds, surrounded by angels, Caravaggio shows us Paul on his back on the ground. The experience of encountering Jesus has knocked him off his horse and now, sprawled on his back, his legs spread and his arms helplessly outstretched, the divine light strikes his body. At this point we may recall Yeats's comment, printed in our headnote in the text: "Then I thought, 'Nothing is now possible but some movement, or birth from above, preceded by some violent annunciation.'" When God or a god makes use of a mortal, things are not easy for the mortal.

Yeats's use of "annunciation" reminds us that he associated the beginning of a new age with the combination of the divine and the bestial; in "The Magi," for instance, Yeats speaks of "The uncontrollable mystery on the bestial floor," and in "The Second Coming" he asks, "And what rough beast, its hour come round at last, / Slouches towards Bethlehem to be born?"

If you have read thus far, you have been patient, but we are still not ready to comment on the drafts. We want to mention that much has been published on pictorial sources for the poem. Neither Leonardo's nor Michelangelo's picture of Leda is especially close to the poem; indeed the Leonardo, with its standing Leda who caresses the swan, is very far from the poem. These pictures, and several others, are reproduced in Giorgio Melchiori, *The Whole Mystery of Art* (1960). In the *Times Literary Supplement* for July 20, 1962, p. 532, Charles Madge published a bas relief of the rape, exhibited in the British Museum—a favorite haunt of Yeats's—and published an illustration of it with his article. (It is also published in the first volume of Elie Faure's *History of Art*, English translation 1920, which Yeats owned.) Madge points out that in ancient art there seem to have been two traditions, one showing Leda "recumbent and acquiescent" and the other showing her "standing and . . . being taken by force." The British Museum relief is of the second type: the swan is pressing his bill against the standing Leda's neck, forcing her face against his breast, and he has encircled her legs with his feet. Interestingly, whereas the first version of the poem specifies that the swan has "bowed her face upon his breast," as in the relief, by the final version this detail has been replaced by "He holds her helpless breast upon his breast." Madge points out that the relief is not consistent with the "stretched body" mentioned later in the poem, but he says, quite reasonably, "Perhaps the poet has carried the scene a stage farther in his imagination to a point where the girl has been forced backwards on to the ground."

We don't doubt that Yeats could have seen (and probably did see) the British Museum sculpture, but we think that another source is equally likely. Charles B. Gullans, in an article in *TLS*, November 9, 1962, p. 864, reproduces a bookplate showing Leda and the swan, a woodcut, that Yeats's friend T. Sturge Moore designed for A. G. B. Russell. It was first published in *Modern Woodcutters, No. 3: T. Sturge Moore* (1921). Moore had designed bookplates for Yeats and for Yeats's father, so it is easy to believe that Yeats was familiar with the bookplate his friend designed for another friend. In this image Leda's face is not exactly bowed upon the breast of the swan (as in line 4 of the first version), but the swan's neck encircles Leda's neck, and her "helpless thighs" (draft, line 2) are certainly "Pressed / By the webbed toes" (lines 2–3). Last words about visual sources for the poem: Yeats probably was familiar with all of the images mentioned, and with others, but there is no reason to believe that any one image played an especially significant role.

Incidentally, for a rich range of uses of the story in literature and in art, see the entry on Leda in *The Oxford Guide to Classical Mythology* (1993).

Now for some comments on the three versions. The opening quatrain gave Yeats the most trouble ("nothing so difficult as a beginning," Byron said, and all writers know) and dissatisfied him the most. The relatively slow opening of the first version ("Now can the swooping godhead have his will") in the second version is greatly speeded up: "A rush, a sudden wheel, and hovering still / The bird descends"). Notice, too, that the explicit reference to the "godhead" disappears, perhaps because Yeats came to think it was too inflated and in any case unnecessary. The "helpless thighs" of the second line become "frail thighs" in the second version, and simply "thighs" in the final version because, perhaps, Yeats came to feel that the contrast between "frail thighs" and "all-powerful bill" was too obvious. It is not until the final version that we get "the staggering girl" (line 2) and "helpless breast." That is, Yeats deletes the relatively sentimental word "frail," and so far as Leda goes, he tells us only that she is "staggering" and that the swan "holds her helpless breast upon his breast." "The webbed toes" of the third line in the first version remain in the second, but in the final version they are replaced by the much more evocative "dark webs" which suggest mystery ("dark") and entrapment ("web"). Part of the mystery is that "A shudder in the loins"—a very brief action—can engender a tragic history of humanly unimaginable but inevitable painful and yet glorious consequences ("The broken wall, the burning roof and tower / And Agamemnon dead"), and part of the mystery is in the poet's unanswered question ("Did she put on his knowledge with his power . . . ?"). The two earlier questions in the poem were rhetorical: "How can those terrified vague fingers push / The feathered glory from her loosening thighs?" and "And how can body, laid in that white rush, / But feel the strange heart beating where it lies!" The question that ends the poem, however, is unanswerable. If pressed for an answer, we would say, first, "No, she did not acquire Zeus's knowledge. Why would the victim of a sexual assault learn anything about the future?" And yet the very fact that Yeats raises the question, so different from the earlier rhetorical questions, makes us modify this response and makes us entertain the possibility that somehow Leda did understand that this astounding union would have astounding consequences. We may say of this question what Sir Thomas Browne said of other mysteries: "What song the Sirens sang, or what name Achilles assumed when he hid himself among women, though puzzling questions, are not beyond all conjecture." Conjecture, yes; decisive answer, no.

In short, the second version extensively rewrites the first four lines of the poem but retains the rest except for some changes in punctuation and for a revision of line 12. In the draft, line 12 is "Did nothing pass before her in the air?"; in the second version it becomes "Did she put on his knowledge with his power . . . ?", and this revision is retained in the final version. Interestingly, the off-rhyme of "up" and "drop" in lines 11 and 14, indicating Zeus's post-coital weariness or indifference now that he has finished using Leda, was present even in the first version. Speaking of the last line, notice, too, that in all three versions "beak" is used, and "bill" is used in the third line of each version. Why the change (putting aside the matter of rhyme)? We take "beak" to be more menacing than "bill," and so our guess is that Yeats wanted to suggest, even after the culmination of the act that Alexander Pope called "the fierce embrace," the violent character of the god.

If the glimpse of Zeus's mental condition at the end of the poem was present even in the first version, so too was the *absence* of any inner presentation of Zeus in the octave. For the most part we get what seems to be an objective view of the episode, though in speaking of Leda's "terrified vague fingers" (line 5 in all versions) we do get into Leda's mind, and we also see things from her point of view in "that white rush" and perhaps even in "The feathered glory," though this last expression celebrates Zeus. Still, the impression on the whole is objective—first a report of a past event in the present tense, and then, at the very end, a distancing of the event by putting it into the past ("Did she" and "could let her drop") and by asking a mysterious question.

A final point. Yeats, an endless reviser of his work, in the 1908 edition of his *Collected Works* urged his readers not to search for his unpublished material.

> Accursed who brings to light of day
> The writings I have thrown away!
> But blessed be he that stirs them not
> And lets the kind worm take the lot.

But he didn't reprint the lines after 1908, perhaps because he thought they were not worth printing, or perhaps because he had changed his mind.

See *W. B. Yeats: The Poems*, 2nd ed., ed. Richard J. Finneran (1997), vol. 1 of *The Collected Works of W. B. Yeats*; this volume includes detailed "explanatory notes" for each poem. Biographies include A. Norman Jeffares, *W. B. Yeats: A New Biography* (1988), and R. F. Foster, *W. B. Yeats: A Life, The Apprentice Mage 1865–1914* (1997). Two rewarding books for students, A. Norman Jeffares, *A New Commentary on the Poems of W. B. Yeats* (1984), and *Critical Essays on W. B. Yeats*, ed. Richard J. Finneran (1986). Still useful, too, are two books by Richard Ellmann, *Yeats: The Man and the Masks* (1948) and *The Identity of Yeats* (1954). Some students might be interested in examining the *Variorum Edition* of Yeats's poems, ed. P. Allt and R. K. Allspach (1957).

Mona Van Duyn
Leda (p. 142)

Mona Van Duyn makes her response to William Butler Yeats's "Leda and the Swan" all the more direct by choosing two lines from Yeats's poem as her epigraph. By italicizing them, she dramatizes the fact that it is this question in particular that her speaker will engage and explore.

As the questions we present in our Topics for Critical Thinking and Writing may indicate, this is a poem that we work through line by line with the students. We prompt them to notice, for example, the shifts in point of view in it. The poem begins with the scene as it appears to the swan, but then moves to the perspective of Leda herself. There is also a movement back and forth from the details of the scene to the speaker's general observations about the behavior of men in love and the place that women occupy in "men's stories."

We also emphasize the various shifts of tone. It is sometimes direct and close to conversational—"He knew, for one thing, what he was"—and yet it is also formal and distanced— "collecting these rare pictures of himself was his life." There's also the deliberately jarring effect of the first line of the second stanza and the satiric thrust of the reference to the "smaller man with a beaky nose," which is cast at both Leda and the man, and maybe by implication a little at Zeus/swan too.

We think that the specific treatment of point of view and tone in the poem helps the students to see and work toward Van Duyn's response to and critique of Yeats. His poem has a powerful forward momentum, aggressive and unstoppable, whereas Van Duyn's has a slower, more reflective pace, suited to her purpose of making us reconsider, reinterpret, the telling of the myth that Yeats has so grandly—some would say, infamously—presented.

One of us teaches at a women's college, and in his experience, students nearly always take a vigorous dislike to Yeats's poem, which in their judgment glorifies rape. These women students much prefer Van Duyn's poem because its speaker makes clear her awareness of the parts that women are obliged to play in "men's stories."

At the same time, however, we think it is important to stretch the responses of both men and women students to these two poems. As we discuss them in the classroom, we find it useful to inquire into the strengths and limitations of the poetic work in them that both Yeats and Van Duyn have done. We think it is a good thing for students to feel drawn to debate the merits of these poems and to make up their minds one way or another about them (and about which one is better). But here, as always, we don't want the students to state their judgments too quickly, without a real and considered testing (and questioning) of their initial responses.

For discussions of Van Duyn's work, see Lorrie Goldensohn, "Mona Van Duyn and the Politics of Love," *Ploughshares* 4:3 (1978): 31–44; Judith Hall, "Strangers May Run: The Nation's First Woman Poet Laureate," *The Antioch Review* 52 (Winter 1994), 141–146; and Michael Burns, ed., *Discovery and Reminiscence: Essays on the Poetry of Mona Van Duyn* (1998).

WILLIAM CARLOS WILLIAMS
This Is Just to Say (p. 144)

In a way this is a hard poem to discuss with students because it is so simple-seeming—the statement of an action and an apology for it—and thus apparently it offers little for the class to delve into and comment on. But in another way, "This Is Just to Say" is an easy poem to discuss, for it leads inevitably to the remark (or the complaint) from many in the room that "this isn't a poem."

Often we start the class by asking, provokingly, "Why is this a good poem?" Usually there is a pause because few students have been thinking about "This Is Just to Say" in these terms. There might be a volunteer or two who will risk saying that he or she admires the poem for its humor or its accessibility (the implication being that poetry most of the time is not accessible!). But things perk up when we ask, "Do any of you think this is a bad poem?" Hands shoot into the air, some students saying that yes, indeed, this is a bad poem and others contending that it's bad because it isn't a poem.

In our view, it does not much matter whether or not the students become convinced, as a result of the discussion, that "This Is Just to Say" is a poem (and a good poem) after all. The great value of this poem is that it gets students thinking about what a poem is, and, even more, what might make the difference between a good poem and a bad one.

We devote some of our time in the class to asking the students to write out the text in their notebooks as a single sentence, which we then compare to Williams's poem, with its line breaks and stanzas. But we also invite the students to rewrite the sentence in other forms, as a single stanza, for example, with different line breaks. What we are attempting to do is to spur the students to perceive that Williams did not simply rewrite a prose sentence into *this* form, but, rather, that he had many different forms he might have chosen and that he experimented with before he finally settled on *this* one. The students can then begin to recognize the decision making that the writing of "This Is Just to Say" entailed. It seems so simple, but in fact to write this poem took a lot of care and craft—some hard thinking—that the clarity and directness of the final version deliberately refrain from announcing. It seems so inevitable that the poem would be *this* way! And that's the point: to write a poem so natural, so laden with the factual, that some, even many, readers will conclude that it's "not a poem." And yet it is profoundly artificial, very much something that Williams has made. In a sense the complaints about "This Is Just to Say" really imply that Williams succeeded in what he was aiming to accomplish.

We enjoy having another kind of fun with this poem. When students say that there is "nothing there," that "not much is happening," we like to press them to consider the subtle and elusive drama of relationship that Williams evokes. Does the speaker eat the plums first (an understandable thing to do if one is hungry) and only then realize that "you" might have been saving them? Or does the speaker know from the start that the "you" who is addressed was probably saving the plums but goes ahead and eats them anyway? That would be a mean thing to do; why might the speaker do something like that? And why "probably"? Does this word suggest that the speaker is leaving himself some wiggle-room ("Well, I wasn't sure you were saving them")? And at what time is all of this happening? The middle of the night? Just before breakfast? And how much stock should we place in the speaker's request for forgiveness: Does he mean it or not?

Paul Mariani's biography, *William Carlos Williams: A New World Naked* (1990), is excellent for scholars and teachers, but it is too big, too detailed, for beginning students. The shorter book by Reed Whittemore, *William Carlos Williams: Poet from Jersey* (1975), is a better choice for them. Good critical studies include James E. Breslin, *William Carlos Williams: An American Artist* (1970); Stephen Cushman, *William Carlos Williams and the Meanings of Measure* (1985); and Barry Ahearn, *William Carlos Williams and Alterity: The Early Poetry* (1994). For lively commentary on Williams and other poets, students might enjoy Randall Jarrell's essays and reviews in *Poetry and the Age* (1953) and *The Third Book of Criticism* (1969).

For articles pertinent to "This Is Just to Say," see Patrick Moore, "Cubist Prosody: William Carlos Williams and the Conventions of Verse Lineation," *Philological Quarterly* 65 (Fall 1986): 515–536; George P. Castellito, "A Taste of Fruit: The Extended Hand in William Carlos Williams and Imaginative Distance in Wallace Stevens," *Papers on Language & Literature* 28 (Fall 1992): 442–450; and David H. Grubb, "The Silences of William Carlos Williams," *Critical Quarterly* 39 (Summer 1997). For interesting biographical background, we recommend Ann Fisher-Wirth, "The Allocations of Desire: 'This Is Just to Say' and Flossie Williams's 'Reply'," *William Carlos Williams Review* 22:22 (Fall 1996): 47–56.

6

Reading and Writing about Visual Culture

Lou Jacobs Jr.
What Qualities Does a Good Photograph Have? (p. 173)

Although the first word of Jacobs's first paragraph might have been "None," the title leads a reader to expect that Jacobs will indeed name some qualities, and he does. He believes there are "criteria" (paragraph 2) for judging photographs (works of art, we might say), although in paragraph 4 he grants that judging photographs includes a "subjective" element. His compromise position is that "There is enough agreement in the tastes of a variety of people to make certain standards general and valid" (4).

Jacobs, a journalist writing in a newspaper, is not a philosopher trying to set forth an air-tight case in *Journal of Aesthetics and Art Criticism,* and it would be inappropriate to press him very hard concerning the meaning of key terms, such as *enough agreement, taste, general,* and *valid.* His words are clear enough to ordinary readers, and they make considerable sense. Most of us probably are of two minds when it comes to matters of aesthetic judgment: With half of our mind we say *De gustibus non est diputandum*—well, we probably say it in English, "There's no disputing about tastes"—and with the other half we say, "Of course I know what is good and what is bad. What is more, I can explain why this movie is better than that, or this novel is better than that." If we recommend a movie to a friend and then she tells us that she didn't care for it at all, we are likely to say things like, "What didn't you like about it?" and "Didn't you think the characters were interesting, and weren't the settings beautiful? And the dialogue! It was so witty!" That is, we do *not* assume that a film (or a play, or—can we say a photograph?) is like a dish of ice cream. If someone says she prefers vanilla to chocolate, we *don't* ask her why she has this preference. We assume, in this instance, that there is no disputing tastes. But, again, with works of art (films, photographs, novels, etc.) most of us do try to give reasons for our responses, which implies that there are standards. These standards may not be universal (probably few people think that African sculpture, Impressionist painting, and American Indian beadwork can all be judged by the same criteria); they may be limited to what has recently been called an interpretive community. Half a dozen teachers of composition may disagree about which essay (out of a hundred) gets first prize in an essay competition, but they will probably agree, with very few exceptions, about which five essays are the strongest candidates for first prize, and they will also agree about which essays are in the top quarter and about which are in the bottom quarter. Similarly, a panel of judges at a photography exhibition will share most values and will agree in their evaluations of most of the works in the exhibition. Different final judgments will often boil down to differences in the weight allotted to one criterion or another—just as they usually do in evaluating figure skating, automobiles, candidates for admission to college or to graduate school, and candidates for jobs.

So much by way of background. In teaching Jacobs's essay, you may want to ask students if, given the limitations of space, Jacobs has made clear his criteria. If more space had been available, doubtless he would have included two images for each criterion, one image showing a photograph lacking in the quality under discussion (say, "human interest"), the other showing a photograph strong in this quality. Our own feeling is that Jacobs is pretty vague about his first quality, "Impact," but pretty clear about the others.

Topics for Critical Thinking and Writing

1. If you think Jacobs omits some important criteria, write a response (350–500 words) to his essay.
2. If you think that it is impossible to evaluate rationally the qualities of photographs, set forth your reasons in an essay of 250 words.
3. Suppose someone were to say to you that Ansel Adams's *Moonrise, Hernandez, NM* with its small glowing crosses in a vast landscape is a sentimental picture and therefore not of high quality. What would be your written response?
4. If you think Jacobs makes sense, discuss two of the pictures in *Literature for Composition,* using some or all of his criteria.

AN AMERICAN PICTURE ALBUM: TEN IMAGES

GRANT WOOD
American Gothic (p. 178)

The pose in this painting (1930) is frontal, like those in an amateur's snapshot of the family, and the faces display the seriousness of ordinary people who are uneasy at the attention being paid to them but who are doing their best to rise to the occasion. The man stares fixedly at the "camera"; his rectitude will not allow him to put on an act. The woman (deferentially standing a bit behind her husband, of course) is a trifle more compliant, softening the pose by turning her head slightly. Both figures convey strength and honesty. They are utterly harmonious with each other, with their work and their clothing and their Carpenter Gothic home: the shape of the pitchfork (a reminder of life lived close to the soil) reappears in the man's coveralls, in the house's windows and siding, and (less emphatically) in the lower part of the man's face and in the rickrack of the woman's apron. A variation of the pattern on the apron reappears in the upper window. The meticulous detail in the painting tells us not only of the scrupulous effort that these two people exert but also of the painter's admiration for their way of life. By the way, Wood intended the figures to be a father and his spinster daughter (the pitchfork was supposed to be a threat to suitors), but no one ever sees it this way.

For a brilliant discussion of the technology behind the picture—the construction of the house, the origin of the bib-overall and of the bamboo sunscreen at the left, and other details—see Guy Davenport's essay, "The Geography of the Imagination" (1981), in his book with that title. Virtually all commentators on the picture point out its resemblance (in pose and in meticulous finish) to Flemish painting, for example, to van Eyck's double portrait of the Arnolfini, but so far as we know, only Davenport points out the resemblance to Egyptian sculpture of pharaohs and their wives. For an essay emphasizing American sources of the painting (photography, fiction, etc.), see Wanda Corn's essay in *Art, the Ape of Nature* (1981), edited by Moshe Barasch and Lucy Freeman.

GORDON PARKS
American Gothic (p. 179)

Gordon Parks (b. 1912), best known as a photographer for *Life* magazine, is also a musician and a composer, a novelist, a screenwriter, and a memoirist.

Before we talk about his *American Gothic*, a few comments on portraiture may be useful. A good many painted portraits, and perhaps most photographic portraits, have been commissioned by the sitter; of these, one can safely conjecture that vanity was the moving force. Still, the traditional justification for portraiture was that the pictures not only paid tribute to great achievements—almost always by males—but also served to inspire us lesser folk. Vasari, in *Lives of the Painters* (1568) puts it thus:

> To what other end did the ancients place the images of their great men in public places, with laudatory inscriptions, except to kindle those who come after to virtue and glory!

Customarily we think that a portrait (a) should resemble the sitter and (b) should reveal the sitter's personality—it should, in brief (the theory goes) catch not only facial features but also spiritual or psychological traits such as piety or determination or artistic interests or whatever. Even if a modern photographic portrait is made in the photographer's studio, with the subject seated on a posing stool, head in front of a seamless background, it probably seeks to convey the sitter's charm or dignity. More often (or at least more often in pictures that hold our attention) the subject is placed in a relevant environment and perhaps holds some object—art historians call these objects *attributes*—that helps to convey status and personality (the professor in a book-lined study, suggesting a lifetime of high thinking; the student in a dormitory room with a poster of Einstein and several other posters of rock stars, suggesting a range of lively interests).

Although Parks's *American Gothic* (1942), a photograph of Ella Watson taken in Washington, D.C., in 1942, at first glance seems to be a portrait, it is not a portrait, if a portrait is supposed to convey an inner life, the *essential* person. Rather, it embodies the photographer's comment on the life that blacks lead (or led) in a society dominated by whites. Under the joking echo of Grant Wood's painting we hear Parks's indignant voice saying that in the nation's capital, the home of countless portraits of politicians and jurists holding books or pens or eyeglasses, the attributes that best identify the black are the broom and the mop.

Of course all portraits, photographs no less than paintings, are false. The photographer poses the subject; or even if the subject is caught unawares, the photographer chooses the angle of the shot and may crop the print. As photographers say, they don't *take* pictures, they *make* them. Here, Parks has obviously posed the subject. The subject has been constrained, so to speak, into a particular pose, just as (Parks must have felt) blacks have been constrained into certain roles in American society. The twofold absurdity conveyed by the picture—a photographer giving us an image that mimics one of America's most famous paintings, and a black woman posing with a broom and a mop against a background consisting of the American flag—immediately indicates that this image is not the rendition of a personality but rather is a statement about a social order.

Although Parks's subject is not one of Vasari's "great men," she does seem possessed of a dignity that, given the circumstances, is not only impressive but is amazing. And (to continue with Vasari) we can guess that Parks's motive is indeed to "kindle those who [see the image] to virtue"; they would (he may have hoped) be moved not in the usual way of emulating the subject, but in another way; they might be moved to indignation, or at least to some self-questioning.

LEWIS W. HINE
Singer Power Machine Sewing Group (p. 180)

We give a few biographical facts about Hine in our discussion of another photo, *Sky Boy* (p. 59 of this manual). Briefly, his early photos documented abuses of labor, especially children working in mills, canneries, and sweatshops, but his last important series, on the Empire State Building (1930–1931), showed the (male) worker as hero. Hine regarded himself as a reformer, not an artist; for him, the camera was a useful sociological tool.

But as everyone now knows, the camera aestheticizes, that is, it pictorializes, prettifies, beautifies what it reports. A scene that in real life would cause pain—let's say the corpse of a soldier—when photographed can become beautiful. Again, Hine would have been distressed if someone had said that in his photos of children working ten-hour days he was an artist, producing beautiful images, but the fact is that the images are attractive to look at. If you look at a book of 153 photos by Hine called *Women at Work* (1981)—Hine never imagined this book, which was compiled after his death—we think you will agree that many of the pictures are attractive to look at, and that whatever reforming zeal originally motivated Hine is irrelevant. For one thing, the conditions that he depicts have changed. But even in their day the pictures must have been attractive, and Hine seems to have been moved as much by a desire to celebrate workers as a desire to reform their working conditions. Many of the pictures show individual women, some of them smiling, taking pride in their work at a telephone or a typewriter or a loom. In the case of images of a worker at a loom, the threads themselves make an interesting pattern—in one photo, for instance (p. 84 in *Women at Work*) , the woman is photographed standing behind the horizontal strings of warp, and in another (p. 89) a smartly coiffed young woman is painting attractive floral designs for textiles. No sign of oppression here, though in fact the workers may have been paid a pittance.

The picture that we reproduce, *Singer Power Machine Sewing Group*, taken in 1936 or 1937, in many ways looks back to the earlier pictures of sweatshops, with oppressed woman confronting heaps of fabric. And we do not mean to minimize the unpleasant conditions under which these Singer women worked. Nor do we overlook the fact that the workers at the machines are women, whereas the supervisor at the right foreground is a man. At the same time, to return to a point we made near the beginning of this discussion, the photograph aestheticizes the scene: we are looking at quaintly dressed folk ordered by geometry. "*Appalling*," we half mutter, when we think of the close quarters, the tedious work, the low pay, the long hours; "*Interesting*" we half say when we contemplate the arrangement of bodies, the pattern of light and dark, the clutter and yet the overall elegance.

Certainly this picture does not celebrate the woman worker in a way analogous to Hines's celebration of the male worker in *Sky Boy;* we can scarcely expect that sort of image of a factory worker. True, Amelia Earhart (see below) was seen as heroic, but unlike most women she was celebrated for her individuality. Women as a class were thought of as good (or bad) wives and mothers, helpful secretaries, and—here we get to this photograph—dutiful hands in factories. Interchangeable, taken for granted, but at least in Hine's view deserving of attention. Hine would have been puzzled and hurt by Susan Sontag's assertions, in *On Photography* (1990), that "There is an aggression implicit in every use of the camera" (p. 7) and "To photograph people is to violate them" (p. 14).

Albert Bresnik
Amelia Earhart (p. 180)

Amelia Earhart (1898–1937) was the first woman to fly across the Atlantic (1928), but she was a passenger, not the pilot, because she had no experience with multi-engine planes or with flying by instruments. The flight was essentially a publicity stunt for a newspaper publisher, so her official title—very good for publicity purposes—was "commander of the flight." Later in 1928 she flew solo from the Atlantic to the Pacific coast, and in 1932 (exactly five years after Lindbergh's famous flight to Paris) she flew solo across the Atlantic, from Newfoundland to Ireland (1932). She was named Outstanding Woman of the Year, an award that she accepted on behalf of "all women." In response to an article asking if she could bake a cake, she said:

> I accept these awards on behalf of the cake bakers and all of those other women who can do some things quite as important, if not more important, than flying, as well as in the name of women flying today.

In 1935 she became the first person to fly solo from Honolulu to California—ten men had died attempting this flight. In 1937 she attempted, with a navigator, to fly around the world but her plane disappeared between New Guinea and Howland Island. Nothing further is known about her disappearance, but improbable theories abound: she was on a spy mission authorized by President Roosevelt; she deliberately dove the plane into the Pacific; she was captured by the Japanese, and collaborated with them; she landed on a Pacific island and lived the rest of her life there with a fisherman.

During her attempt to circumnavigate the world she regularly sent letters to her husband, and these were posthumously published in a book, *Last Flight* (1937). The book concludes with this note:

> Please know I am quite aware of the hazards. . . . I want to do it because I want to do it. Women must try to do things as men have tried. When they fail their failure must be but a challenge to others.

Our photo of Amelia Earhart shows her, appropriately solo, with what art historians call an *attribute*, that is, something closely associated with her. Painted monarchs hold a scepter, scholars hold a book, noblemen have large dogs at their feet and their ladies hold lap dogs. But of course this photograph does *not* have the feel of a portrait painting, does not have the feel of a photograph that seeks to be art. Rather, it looks like a snapshot of someone posing for a picture. We can almost hear the photographer saying, "Move a little to the left, and put your hand on your hip; fine; now say 'cheese.'" The photo, with the figure routinely placed in the center, looks like a thousand other photos of a family member or a friend, unusual only in that the smiling figure stands in front of an airplane instead of in front of a baby carriage or a house. And it also looks like countless advertisements from the 1930s, showing a smiling woman standing in front of the new washing machine that her thoughtful husband has bought for her.

But the photo is of *Amelia Earhart,* and she is standing in front of an *airplane.* However ordinary, however dated such a picture seems today, it shows a heroic woman who showed the world that a woman could do things that most men (and perhaps women too?) thought only a few men could do.

LEWIS W. HINE
Icarus, Empire State Building, 1930 (p. 181)

Lewis W. Hine (1874–1940), a giant in the field of social documentary photography, made his mark in the first two decades of the twentieth century with pictures of exploited workers and child laborers. Hine had studied sociology at the University of Chicago, New York University, and Columbia University, and he used the camera as an instrument in his role as social reformer. In fact, he called his work *Social Photography*; the term *documentary photography* was not coined until later, in the 1930s, on the model of the term *documentary film.* In short, for Hine, photography was a means of documenting his work as a reformer, not a means of self-expression or of creating beautiful images. Nevertheless, one of his comments about his goals does go beyond the vision of a social reformer:

> There are two things I wanted to do. I wanted to show the things that had to be corrected. I wanted to show the things that had to be appreciated.

Icarus (1930), originally called *Sky Boy,* shows something Hine wants us to appreciate. Although it was taken during the Great Depression, it was not part of his reforming effort. (For the most part, his photographs of social protest were taken in the first two decades of the twentieth century, when he worked for the National Child Labor Committee.) This picture is part of a series that documented the construction of the Empire State Building, a series that showed the dignity and the heroism of the American worker. Inevitably the workers were male—we talked about Hine's images of female workers when we discussed another photo in our album, *Singer Power Machine Sewing Group*—and Hine emphasizes their skill and their courage. Sometimes he shows us a small team of workers, for instance, three men riveting, but in the present image we get a single handsome, virile worker engaged in a dangerous job, a hero monumentally silhouetted against the sky. These images are not portraits; rather, they are celebrations of American creativity. The sky boy is almost god-like, and indeed a number of Hine's images from this series show well-muscled men (some are shirtless) in poses that remind a viewer of ancient Greek statues.

Sky Boy appears in Hine's only book, *Men at Work* (1932), where it faces the title page and thus serves as an introduction. In the foreword, headed "The Spirit of Industry," Hine sets forth his theme:

> This is a book of Men at Work; men of courage, skill, daring and imagination. Cities do not build themselves, machines cannot make machines, unless back of them all are the brains and toil of men. We call this the Machine Age. But the more machines we use the more do we need real men to make and direct them.
>
> I have toiled in many industries and associated with thousands of workers. I have brought some of them here to meet you. Some of them are heroes; all of them persons it is a privilege to know. I will take you into the heart of modern industry where machines and skyscrapers are being made, where the character of the men is being put into the motors, the airplanes, the dynamos upon which the life and happiness of millions of us depend.
>
> Then the more you see of modern machines, the more may you, too, respect the men who make them and manipulate them.

In *Men at Work* Hine's caption for this figure (beneath the title of the image) runs thus: "One of the first men to swing out a quarter of a mile above New York City, helping to build a skyscraper." In later years, at some point he decided to call the image *Icarus*. The copy owned by the Metropolitan Museum has, inscribed in ink on the mount, "Icarus: High Up on Empire State Building." Ordinarily in reprinting material one uses the author's latest version, and so perhaps we ought to use Hine's revised title. But sometimes an author revises for the worse—most readers believe, for example, that Keats's changes in "La Belle Dame" are not improvements. What to do? Should the editor be bound to the principle that the last revision is what counts, i.e., the version to be reprinted is the version that the author last tinkered with? Our own sense is that *Icarus* is a most unfitting title. The photograph clearly celebrates the American worker's achievements, whereas the story of Icarus sets forth a story of hubris and failure. (His father, Daedalus, flew a middle course between sea and sun, and flew safely, but Icarus soared too near the sun, the wax holding the feathers to the framework melted, and he drowned.) You may want to ask your students to discuss the two titles and the ways in which a title shapes a viewer's response to an image. By the way, when the Metropolitan Museum exhibited the photograph in 2001, the label summarized the story of Icarus and then said, "The optimism of this image suggests that it was not Icarus's folly but his youth and his ability to fly that prompted Hine's title." (Our thanks to Maria Morris Hambourg and Lisa Hostetler of the Metropolitan Museum for this information.)

Ernest C. Withers
"No White People Allowed in Zoo Today" (p. 182)

First some background. In 1896 the Supreme Court held, in *Plessy v. Ferguson*, that segregated facilities were legal, under the idea of "separate but equal." This meant that in the South there were white schools, hospitals, cemeteries, swimming pools, libraries, and restaurants, and there were drinking fountains and restrooms that were off-limits to African Americans. Movies, too, were segregated (blacks were confined to the balcony) and so were buses (blacks sat in the rear). Of course, one could argue that whites, too, were segregated, were equally restricted—they could not sit in the balconies of movie theaters, for instance, or in the rear of buses—but somehow this argument does not sound very convincing. In fact, it sounds very much like Anatole France's wry observation: "The law, in its majestic equality, forbids the rich as well as the poor to sleep under bridges, to beg in the streets, and to steal bread."

By the end of World War II, some two million African Americans had left the South for the North and the West, and they were beginning to get political power. In 1947 baseball, allegedly the national pastime, finally was integrated when Jackie Robinson joined the Brooklyn Dodgers, but (unbelievable though it sounds) the armed forces in this country were still segregated. In 1948 President Truman issued an executive desegregating them, but he allowed the order to remain unenforced until the need for men in the Korean War (1950) compelled the top brass to comply. In 1950, in *McLawrin v. Oklahoma,* the Supreme Court ruled that a state university could not segregate students, and (also in 1950) in *Sweatt v. Painter* the Court ruled that the creation of an inferior school in order to keep African Americans out of the University of Texas Law School violated the rights of African Americans. The great step toward desegregation occurred in 1954, in *Brown v. Board of Education,* when the Court, unanimously overturning the fifty-eight-year-old precedent of *Plessy,* ruled that "Separate educational facilities are inherently unequal" and therefore violate the equal protection clause of the 14th Amendment. Nevertheless, in 1956 the University of Alabama refused to admit a black student, and in 1957 Governor Orval Faubus of Arkansas sent the National Guard troops to block the enrollment of nine African American students at Central High School in Little Rock, claiming that their presence would cause public disorder. Faubus did soon allow the students to enter, but he also withdraw the National Guard, leaving the students to face angry whites. When television coverage revealed the disgraceful scene to the entire nation, President Eisenhower was forced to send soldiers to protect the students, but he made the point that he acted not to further integration but to preserve order. As late as 1963 Governor George Wallace of Alabama in his inaugural address proclaimed, "Segregation now, segregation tomorrow and segregation forever."

A sad history. But we confess that we find something comic in *"No White People Allowed in Zoo Today."* We can't quite put our fingers on the source of the comedy, but perhaps it is that ordinarily one would expect "No Colored People Allowed." Such a sentiment would be horrid, but it was widespread and it was so commonly accepted that it would hardly be noticed, except by black people, and they didn't count. Maybe, too, some of the humor is in the fact that the photograph includes a sign that, quite reasonably, says, "Bicycles, Cars, Dogs Not Allowed in the Zoo." Well, that makes sense. But "No White People"? Perhaps, too, some of the comedy resides in the fact that we are talking about a zoo, a place where strange species are on display. Lots of different types behind the bars, but only one type—white or black but not both—can look at them. But, gee, one can hardly expect the city to have two zoos with identical birds and beasts, one for whites and one for blacks—separate but equal—so it makes sense, in a crazy, comic way, to open the zoo on certain days to whites and on other days to blacks.

What can we make of this? Can we understand it? Can we understand it any more than we can understand slavery? How could people have behaved thus? We can understand the economic forces at work, but can we ever really get into the minds of the slave owners or of the people who insisted that whites and blacks could not simultaneously visit a zoo? Perhaps we must take refuge in a remark by an English author, L. P. Hartley: "The past is a foreign country; they do things differently there."

ALON REININGER
Pledging Allegiance (p. 183)

Probably the two most famous remarks about the nature of the American people are almost one, since they both use the image of melting. In 1782 J. Hector St. John Crèvecoeur said, "Here [in America] individuals of all nations are melted into a new race of men, whose labors and posterity will one day cause great changes in the world." And in 1908 Israel Zangwill said, "America is . . . the great melting pot, where all the races of Europe are melting and re-forming." We can regret that Zangwill mentioned only Europe, but the quotation nevertheless remains memorable and it contains a good deal of truth. Even today, when there is an enormous emphasis on preserving ethnic identity, almost everyone agrees that in the United States the children of immigrants are quickly assimilated, and as for the grandchildren, well, they retain a fondness for some of the food they ate in their childhood, but their native language is English and indeed English is the only language for most of them.

It is easy to wave the flag, and it is also easy to think that flag-wavers must be excessively sentimental or excessively militant or both, but a display of the flag may reveal love, courage, and dedication to lofty ideals, especially a dedication to the ideals of democracy. For many new citizens, holding an American flag and reciting the pledge of allegiance at the naturalization ceremony is one of the most important moments of their lives, a moment that may be compared only with the choice of a lifetime partner or the birth of a child. This picture happens to show more men than women, but in other respects it is fairly representative—representative of the variety of ethnic types (the older man at the left probably is Middle Eastern, the younger man at the right is Asian, and the woman in the center may be Latina) and representative of the deep emotion that the new citizens feel. Election posters show the candidate in a three-quarter view, head slightly tilted upward as though envisioning the future, eyes dreamy, and lips slightly parted—stock stuff, signs assuring the voter that the candidate is both idealistic and energetic—but here these same signs are, well, sincere.

ANONYMOUS
Marilyn Monroe (p. 184)

Described by one observer as "a phenomenon of nature, like Niagara Falls and the Grand Canyon," and by another as "the meteor of show business," the American actress and international sex symbol Marilyn Monroe was born Norma Jean Mortenson in June 1926, in Los Angeles, and died in the same city in August 1962. She was, and remains, a fascinating, ultimately tragic figure, akin perhaps to Elvis Presley, striking and glamorous, yet lost and lonely, and in that combination she is compelling for students of cultural history and charismatic for legions of followers and fans.

Norma Jean's mother was mentally ill and was often confined to an asylum; her father abandoned his wife and daughter, and later, in her teenage years, Norma Jean discovered that Mortenson probably was not her father after all. As a child, she was bounced from one set of foster parents to another and also lived for a period in an orphanage. She married an aircraft factory worker in 1942, but they divorced after the war. Her first success came as a photographer's model, which led to a contract in 1946 with Twentieth Century Fox, for which she took the name Marilyn Monroe. She made some forgettable films and continued to pose for photographers (including a nude pinup for a calendar that's now a collector's item), finally achieving a breakthrough in 1950 when she performed a minor role in the crime film *The Asphalt Jungle* that caught the attention of moviegoers across the country, who deluged Monroe with fan mail.

Monroe's career moved forward in the early 1950s, finally taking off with her appearances in *Gentlemen Prefer Blondes* (1953), *How to Marry a Millionaire* (1953), and *There's No Business Like Show Business* (1954). She was an international star and celebrity, and her fame increased in 1954 when she married the baseball legend Joe DiMaggio. The marriage was a disaster, and the two divorced within a year, a breakup that was connected to Monroe's discontent with the limits of the sexpot roles she had been playing. She studied acting with Lee and Paula Strasberg at the Actors Studio in New York City, and her gifts as a comic actress showed themselves eye-catchingly in *The Seven-Year Itch* (1955) and *Bus Stop* (1956).

In 1956 Monroe married the acclaimed playwright Arthur Miller and for a time stopped appearing in films. But her work in *Some Like It Hot* (1959) was well received, and it was followed by another solid performance in *The Misfits* (1961), written by Miller, whom she had divorced in 1960. Restless, frightened, unstable, Monroe died in her home in Los Angeles in 1962 from an overdose of barbiturates.

Promoted at first as ditzy and maybe downright dumb, Monroe in her prime projected an image of intense, sultry sexuality combined with vulnerability, and her uncanny blend of innocence and experience gave her an extraordinary power. Audiences perhaps sensed, as part of her appeal, that she both inhabited and resisted her role as a sex symbol. As she herself remarked: "A sex symbol becomes a thing. I hate being a thing." The vulnerability was no pose; she was abused and exploited by powerful, wealthy, predatory men (President Kennedy and his brother Robert were among those who had affairs with her) and by the Hollywood system—a dimension of her anguished life that Joyce Carol Oates brilliantly explores in her sprawling, devastating novel *Blonde* (2000).

When working in the classroom with this photograph, taken near the end of Monroe's life, we invite the students to describe how they interpret and respond to Monroe's facial expression. To us, that's the most striking element of the photograph. There's the blonde hair, the naked body, the seductive lips, but even more, something haunted, possibly ravaged, in Monroe's look. The eyebrows and eyelids are heavy, weighing down the face. And her hand behind her head feels as if she were thrusting herself toward us, conveying the burdensome duty of stardom.

It was said of Monroe that "the camera loved her," a comment that bears witness both to her mesmerizing appeal and her own imprisonment in the iconic sexual role, endlessly repeated before countless cameras, that she and Hollywood imposed on herself.

For biography and background, see Carl Rollyson, *Marilyn Monroe: A Life of the Actress* (1986), and Randall Riese and Neal Hitchens, *The Unabridged Marilyn: Her Life from A–Z* (1987).

ANONYMOUS
Charlotte Perkins Gilman at a Suffrage Rally (p. 184)

Charlotte Perkins Gilman (1860–1935) today is known chiefly for "The Yellow Wallpaper" (we include it in *Literature for Composition*), but in her lifetime she was known not for short fiction but for her abundant writing on economics and for her advocacy—in publications and in public assemblies—of women's suffrage.

The first response to this photograph, by students and maybe by all of us, probably is a smile: how quaint it all seems, the serious-faced women wearing big hats and funny dresses. All photographs of any age evoke nostalgia, pathos, a sense that this scene—even if only a scene from a year ago—was real, was felt on real pulses, and now is irretrievably gone. When the writer of this page sees a photo of, say, thirty or forty years ago, maybe a photo by Diane Arbus or Cartier-Bresson, he has the curious hang-up of wondering whether any of the people frozen in the image might still be alive, and, if so, how their lives might differ from the lives depicted in the image. Or take the present photograph, from the early twentieth century: certainly no one in the picture is alive today, but the writer's deceased parents might have been among those who heard Gilman speak, and even if they never heard (or heard of) Gilman, they surely heard one of her colleagues earnestly argue on behalf of giving the vote to women. Photos—fossils of deceased ancient moments—have this ability to make us daydream, to make us think of vanished days.

If photographs evoke pathos, they are also likely, because the costumes seem so unreasonable, so outlandish, so unlike the allegedly sensible and rational clothing with which we adorn ourselves, to seem a bit comic. But in fact there was nothing comic about the long battle to win the vote for women, a battle that perhaps first became evident at Seneca Falls in 1848 and that did not end until 1920, when two-thirds of the states ratified the 19th Amendment, which Congress had passed in 1919. The women in this photograph, serious and a bit funny looking, were still some years short of winning the vote, but it was primarily their seriousness, coupled with the achievements of women as nurses and factory workers during World War I, that at last, more than seventy years after Seneca Falls, brought about a condition that today we take for granted. Gilman is not so evidently a heroic figure as Hine's *Sky Boy* (p. 57) backed by the heavens or Armstrong's *Buzz Aldrin* (see below), whose feet are planted on a heavenly body and whose head extends into the heavens, but she earned a place in the American pantheon.

NEIL ARMSTRONG
Buzz Aldrin on the Moon (p. 185)

It would be hard to find another picture that so effectively catches the tentative gestures of a visitor to an alien world and that also catches the contrast between the visitor—all gussied up—and the forbidding landscape. And yet, if one just squints a bit, the astronaut melts beautifully into his blotchy environment. Well, almost; the head, or rather the helmet, insists on poking above the horizon and into the heavens.

Reflected in the visor we can see pieces of scientific equipment and also (in the center) the photographer, Neil Armstrong.

On earth, President Nixon characterized the adventure as "the greatest moment in history since the Creation." In a telephone call to the moon he told the astronauts, "Because of what you have done, the heavens have become a part of man's world. And as you talk to us from the Sea of Tranquility, it inspires us to double our efforts to bring peace and tranquility to earth." According to Norman Mailer, who describes the exploit in *Of a Fire on the Moon* (1970), "On earth, a handful of young scientists were screaming, 'Stop wasting time with flags and presidents—collect some rocks!'" (p. 406).

Part II

Up Close

Thinking Critically about Literary Works and Literary Forms

7

Critical Thinking: Asking Questions and Making Comparisons

William Notman
Sitting Bull and Buffalo Bill (p. 191)

The picture is discussed at some length in the text but we can add a few points, chiefly about Sitting Bull's flowing feather war bonnet—but before we get there, we will talk about General Custer and about scalping.

On July 7, 1876, George Armstrong Custer, as part of a campaign against the Sioux, attacked a Sioux and Cheyenne encampment at the Little Bighorn valley in Montana. (Sitting Bull was a Sioux leader, but he did not participate in this battle.) Custer, who divided his regiment into three parts, lead one part (some 200 men) himself, but he had disastrously underestimated his foe; all of the men in his party were killed, and many were scalped. Curiously, Custer himself apparently was not scalped, a fact (if it is a fact) that has caused much comment. One explanation is that his foes left him unscalped as a tribute to his courage. Another explanation is that the man known as Long Hair was by now balding, and his scalp would scarcely have been worth exhibiting.

Buffalo Bill was some hundreds of miles away from the Little Bighorn at the time of the battle, but he inserted himself into his representation of the battle in his immensely popular *Buffalo Bill's Wild West*. L. G. Moses, in *Wild West Shows and the Images of American Indians* (1996), reports that in this spectacle Custer, played by a cowboy who was six feet, five inches tall, was the last to succumb to the Show Indians (that's what they were called):

> After a pause so the audience could ruminate upon the tableau made deafening by the silence, Cody would gallop into the arena at the head of his cowboy command, react to the carnage he beheld upon the battle-

field, and sweep his hat from his head in respect for the fallen soldiers. As the garden's [i.e., Madison Square Garden, in New York] lights dimmed, a spotlight trained on Cody. The words *Too Late* were projected on the cyclorama behind him. Buffalo Bill, scouting for the Fifth Cavalry on June 25, 1876, was actually hundreds of miles away from the valley of the Little Bighorn. In the arena, however, he shamelessly created the impression that, with better timing, he could have saved the day. (pp. 34–35)

Moses, following several sources, in a note (p. 290) points out that in this reenactment of Custer's last stand, at least Bill had stopped presenting himself as the avenger of Custer. Three weeks after Custer's last stand, there occurred a less memorable fight, the Battle of War Bonnet Creek. In this encounter Buffalo Bill claimed—apparently truthfully, since eyewitnesses corroborated him—to have scalped an Indian, announcing that the scalp was "The First Scalp for Custer." (Whether the Indian was Yellow Hand, a Cheyenne leader, as Bill claimed, is less certain.) In his *Wild West* he later displayed the scalp as well as Yellow Hand's war bonnet, shield, gun, belt, and scabbard. A painting by Robert Lindneux, *First Scalp for Custer* (1928), now in the Buffalo Bill Historical Center and reproduced in many books on the West, has given the episode visual currency. Bill's reenactment of Custer's defeat, then, does seem elegiac rather than vengeful.

Susette La Flesche, a native of the Omaha tribe, seems to have been the first person reported as asserting that scalping was a white man's practice later adopted by Indians. (We derive this information, and the other information in this paragraph, from James L. Roark, et al., *The American Promise: A History of the United States* [1998], pp. 664–665.) In 1879 La Flesche said that the whites in the eighteenth century introduced scalping, paying a bounty for each scalp, and the Indians ultimately retaliated in kind. Vine Deloria in *Custer Died for Your Sins* (1969) repeats the charge. But the evidence does not seem to support La Flesche and Deloria. The earliest reference to scalping is Jacques Cartier's report (1535) of finding "skins of five men's heads, stretched on hoops, like parchment." In subsequent decades there are many comparable reports—all by whites, of course, since the Indians did not have a system of writing. But there are also archaeological excavations that, we are told, clearly indicate that scalping was practiced in Pre-Columbian times. By the eighteenth century, however, it is certain that some whites were offering bounties for Indian scalps.

Buffalo Bill apparently did dress in fancy attire (a *vaquero* suit of black velvet with scarlet trim) at the Battle of War Bonnet Creek, and so he probably was telling the truth when he appeared in the *Wild West* and claimed to be wearing the very clothes he wore when he scalped the Indian. But did Indians wear elaborate eagle feather bonnets with long feather trailers into battle? Some early nineteenth-century paintings do indeed show embattled Indians wearing such headdresses, but the paintings may not be entirely accurate. This type of bonnet was used by the Plains Indians, but only by the highest-ranking men, and only on ceremonial occasions or sometimes in battle. Today, however, when we think of Indians we almost inevitably think of these feathered headdresses. It seems that *Buffalo Bill's Wild West* was largely responsible for the popular idea that most Indians wore bonnets; his show established in the popular mind the stock images of Indian life (warbonnets, tipis), and other tribes found that they had to adopt Plains customs if they were to be accepted as Indians by the general white public.

A final comment on Buffalo Bill. Despite his reputation as an Indian fighter, he seems to have been well ahead of most whites when it came to racial tolerance. All of the evidence indicates that he was much concerned that the Indians with his *Wild West* be treated fairly. Further, he employed African Americans, notably in his recreation of Teddy Roosevelt's attack on San Juan Hill, an episode that he used in 1898 in place of "Custer's Last Fight." (That's what he called the Custer episode; it was restored to the *Wild West* program in 1905.) The advertising spoke of the daring of "white, red, and black soldiers," which is more than Roosevelt himself did, since Roosevelt spoke slightingly of the black regiments. Of course Buffalo Bill talked about "civilizing" Indians, and he assumed that Indian cultures could not survive in a competitive world, and thus by our standards he was racist, but Social Darwinism was virtually universal at the time.

Bibliographic note: There is plenty of material (much of it with wonderful pictures) for students to read, if you want to assign a research paper on Buffalo Bill or Sitting Bull or both. In addition to L. G. Moses's *Wild West Shows* (1996), mentioned above, good places to begin are Harry Blackman Sell and Victor Weybright, *Buffalo Bill and the Wild West* (1955); Don Russell, *The Lives and Legends of Buffalo Bill* (1960); Don Russell, *The Wild West or, A History of the Wild West Shows* (1970); *Buffalo Bill and the Wild West* (1981; a well-illustrated exhibition catalog with essays by various hands, including Vine Deloria Jr. and Leslie A. Fiedler); Richard Slotkin, *The Myth of the Frontier in Twentieth-Century America* (1992); Joseph A. Manziona, "*I Am Looking to the North for My Life*": *Sitting Bull, 1876–1881* (1991); and Robert M. Utley, *The Life and Times of Sitting Bull* (1993). Also of great interest is a longish essay by Jane Tompkins, "At the Buffalo Bill Museum—June 1988," *South Atlantic Quarterly* 89:3 (Summer 1990). Tompkins's essay, in a fairly colloquial style, is highly readable but it is long and subtle, and therefore we decided against including it in the present chapter. Briefly, it presents Buffalo Bill in a highly sympathetic light.

For a vivid, detailed account of the momentous battle at Little Bighorn, we recommend Evan S. Connell, *Son of the Morning Star* (1984). Two other recent books are also stimulating: Robert Marshall Utley, *Cavalier in Buckskin: George Armstrong Custer and the Western Military Frontier* (1988), and Brian W. Dippie, *Custer's Last Stand: The Anatomy of an American Myth* (1994). Through her lectures and writings, Custer's widow played an important role in building up the story of Custer as a grand military hero; her activities are described in Shirley A. Leckie, *Elizabeth Bacon Custer and the Making of a Myth* (1993).

E. E. CUMMINGS
Buffalo Bill's (p. 193)

Here are responses to the questions that we pose in the text.

1. *The speaker's attitude.* We take the speaker to be an adult remembering his youthful enthusiasm for Buffalo Bill. The language is of course adult ("defunct," "stallion," "blueeyed boy") but the enthusiasm seems boyish, especially in line 6 where the words for the six clay pigeons are run together and the line ends with "justlikethat." Perhaps "Mister Death" (line 11) is also a boyish term. We do *not* find satire either in the speaker's voice or in the poet, a point we will discuss in a moment.
2. *Run-on words in line 6.* We assume that by running the words together Cummings indicates the continuous rhythm of the shooting, i.e., Buffalo Bill's action is uninterrupted. We might almost say that the word applied to the horse, "watersmooth," applies also to Buffalo Bill. Oddly, however, when Cummings reads the poem (a 1976 Caedmon release, *Collected Poetry 1920–40 and Prose*) he does *not* read "onetwothreefourfive" rapidly.
3. *The spacing.* Cummings was certainly interested in the appearance of the poem on the page, and he probably also thought that the appearance would offer guidance to a reader. We do not take seriously the arrowhead that one reader has pointed out—we think the poem is about Buffalo Bill's accomplishments, not about a weapon used by Indians—but we do find some aspects of the lineation significant. Buffalo Bill, Jesus, and Mister Death each get an entire line, and each of these lines is in a prominent place—the first line, the line set at the farthest right, and the last line. As we see it, by putting "defunct" on a line by itself, Cummings emphasizes the death; the poem then expands, in stages, to the long sixth line ("and break onetwothreefourfive pigeonsjustlikethat"); "Jesus" might have been put flush left, but instead it is put at the right, giving it lots of space before it, perhaps indicating a hushed moment that culminates in an ejaculation. (We talk more about "Jesus" in our response to the sixth question.)
4. *Mister Death.* Perhaps the expression suggests that the speaker is a child; in any case, in its context ("how do you like your blueeyed boy?") we think it indicates that the speaker feels he can talk easily, almost cheekily, with Death. What answer might Death give? Since we do not think Cummings is satirizing Buffalo Bill, we imagine that Death would reply along these lines: "He *is* terrific, isn't he? I wish I had more people like him."
5. *Defunct (line 2).* This fancy word for "dead" has engendered much comment, always to the effect that it debunks Buffalo Bill. For instance, Louis Budd writes, in *Explicator* 11 (1953), item 55: "Bill has not undergone a tragic crisis, he has not passed through a spiritual ordeal; he simply has ceased operating, liquidated like a bank or a poorly-placed filling sta-

tion." Since we don't find other evidence that Cummings is debunking Bill, we reject this reading of the word. Our own view, which we offer only tentatively, is that Cummings is using, by way of tribute, the somewhat pretentious language of the showman. That is, the opening words might be spoken by a ringmaster (incidentally, in the program for *Buffalo Bill's Wild West*, the ringmaster is called "the Orator"), who might have said something like this: "Ladies and gentlemen, it is my sad duty to announce to this distinguished assembly that Buffalo Bill, who has so often amazed and astounded us with his unparalleled equestrian feats, is defunct." Although the word consists of only two syllables, it is a "big" word in the sense that it is unusual, and it is derived from a Latin word *de,* an intensive, and *fungi,* to discharge. Probably its most famous use in literature is Othello's assertion that "the young affects"—the passions— are in him "defunct" (1.3.259), in a speech that includes such terms as "proper satisfaction" and "speculative and officed instrument." Conceivably, too, Cummings has in mind not only *deceased* but also *discharged,* like a gun that has fired its shot. But we realize that these positions cannot be demonstrated conclusively.

6. *Jesus (line 7).* The fact that Jesus, like Buffalo Bill and Mister Death, is given a line to himself has caused some readers to see Jesus as an important figure in the poem. Robert Wegner, in *The Poetry and Prose of E. E. Cummings* (1965), says that the word "Jesus . . . by reason of its position in the poem introduces a new subject as a correlative to that of Buffalo Bill" (p. 96). Wegner continues: "Christ [like Buffalo Bill] also is a figure embedded in myth and legend, also a type of hero, cherished as a symbol but unheeded in practice and hence for all practical purposes in disrepute" (p. 96). Earl J. Dias in *CEA Critic* 29:3 (Dec 1966) sees a contrast between Jesus and Buffalo Bill: "Of the two types of individualism implied in the poem—the man of war and the man of peace—I submit that the latter is more akin to Cummings's basic ideas revealed throughout the body of his writing" (p. 7). With some embarrassment—in our naiveté we had never conceived of such notions when we thought about the poem—we must say that these statements seem far fetched, wrongheaded. We take "Jesus" to be an expletive, an utterance indicating strong admiration for Buffalo Bill, and that's all—and that's a great deal. Having said this, we should go on to add that Jane Tompkins has an interesting comment in her essay, "At the Buffalo Bill Museum," *South Atlantic Quarterly,* Summer 1990. Calling attention to a poster of Buffalo Bill that says *"Je viens,"* she says that these are the words of a "savior" (see her paragraph 48), and she goes on to say that Buffalo Bill "comes in the guise of a redeemer." Here she might seem to be going too far, but in fact she clarifies this comment by saying that Buffalo Bill comes as "someone who will save us, who will through his own actions do something for us that we cannot. He will lift us above our lives, out of the daily grind, into something larger than ourselves." We don't find this view excessive.

7. *The manuscript.* In our question we call attention to only one line omitted from the finished poem, but other passages are also worth discussion. Our own guess is that Cummings decided to drop this line because he decided to concentrate on Buffalo Bill's amazing achievements, not on his appearance. What counts is not what his hair and face looked like but what he could *do.* Similarly, we imagine that the emphasis on Buffalo Bill caused Cummings to drop the "indian" and the "Comanche brave" from the final version. It's a one-man show.
8. *Is the poem satiric?* We have already indicated that we think it shows admiration, and nothing but admiration, for Buffalo Bill's skill. (We are reminded, perhaps irrelevantly, of Hopkins's praise, in "The Windhover," of "the achieve of, the mastery of the thing.") We do not think that the poem in any way judges Bill's personality or morality; it says nothing about his treatment of Indians—or, for that matter, his treatment of buffalo. (Incidentally, notice that the final version omits the draft's "Comanche" and "indian." If these had remained in the poem, we suppose one might conceivably make a case (very weak, but a case) that in Bill's world, Indians are reduced to "the Other," but, again, this poem is about Bill's ability, not about his use or abuse of others.

Among the astounding comments that we have encountered is Rushworth M. Kidder's discussion, in his *E. E. Cummings: An Introduction to the Poetry* (1979). In the course of suggesting that the poem is concerned with "heroic deeds" reduced to "circus stunts" and "the glib and the fraudulent," Kidder says, "This performer, after all, merely broke clay pigeons instead of Indians" (p. 28). Is it possible that we would regard Bill as a greater hero if Cummings showed him killing Indians? As for the expression "Mister Death," which we have already glanced at, we do *not* think that it is intended to ridicule death (and most definitions of satire include the idea that the speaker ridicules the subject). Admittedly it takes the terror out of death—death here is no skeleton wielding a scythe—but it does not ridicule death. It domesticates him, makes him a part of daily life, but we don't see satire here. In any case, how can one satirize death—as opposed to satirizing, say, a neurotic fear of death? There are poems, of course, that diminish death, notably John Donne's "Death, be not proud," and Shakespeare's Sonnet 146 ("Poor soul, the center of my sinful earth"), but we would not say that these poems satirize death; rather, they mock persons who do not understand the limitations of death.

The two quotations that we give at the end: The first is from David Ray, in *College English* 23 (Jan 1962): 289. In this article Ray also says (you may want to use this quotation as a topic for discussion) that the poet gives us "his adult's awareness that Bill was, historically, a fraud" (p. 289). The second quotation is from Dias's article in *CEA Critic* 29:3 (Dec 1966): 7. Our preceding comments indicate that we strongly disagree with both interpretations.

EMILY DICKINSON

I felt a Funeral, in my Brain; I felt a Cleaving in my Mind—; The Dust behind I strove to join (p. 198)

Thomas H. Johnson prints these lines as a separate poem (#992), though he indicates that the lines are really a variant of stanza 2 of "I felt a Cleaving in my Mind" (#937). R. W. Franklin agrees, so much so that he maintains that "The Dust . . ." should not be printed as a separate poem at all.

One good way, then, to begin is to ask the students, "Does 'The Dust behind I strove to join' stand on its own, or does it make sense only when it is read as a possible stanza 2 of "I felt a Cleaving . . . ?"

Sometimes we have stated this question at greater length, and to good effect, in a four-step writing assignment:

1. Please write an analysis of "The Dust behind I strove to join," on the assumption that it is a separate poem.
2. Now, substitute "The Dust . . ." for the current second stanza of "I felt a Cleaving . . . ," and give your analysis of the poem in that form.
3. In which way does "The Dust . . ." work better, as its own poem or as a second stanza for "I felt a Cleaving . . . ?"
4. Does "I felt a Cleaving . . ." strike you as more effective with the second stanza it now has, or do you think it is more effective with the variant stanza that Dickinson herself seems to have rejected?

The problem with most criticism of Dicksonson's poetry is that critics typically approach it from the outside in. They focus first on facts (or reports and rumors and legends) about Dickinson, or on historical contexts, or on philosophical ideas and themes about identity and the self, and then proceed to interpret the poems accordingly. On one level this makes good sense; we want to learn as much as we can about the life and times, and about the abiding themes, of a writer, in order to extend and enrich our understanding of his or her work. But the risk of this procedure is that it forces Dickinson's language to conform to ideas and themes that in fact she intends to resist, challenge, and explore. When we read the poems intensively, the striking thing about them is that it is difficult to make them fit into any one pattern or theme.

For the teacher, especially in an introductory course, it is hazardous, in our view, to set out biographical and historical contexts or a dominant idea or theme before turning to the poems themselves. The students find Dickinson a very hard poet to begin with. If you suggest to them that there is a big, controlling idea they must first know about, or biographical and historical facts they must be aware of as they get underway, they will feel frustrated. They will conclude that they cannot really appreciate the poems because they will never know enough about Dickinson, her era, and so on.

The better approach, we think, is to turn immediately to the poems. Sometimes we have said at the outset of the discussion, "All of you probably have heard something about Dickinson's reclusive life, family, and history—all of these are interesting. But let's experiment today. Let's see what we can make of the poems on our own and discover together what kind of portrait of Dickinson as a poet emerges from them."

With "I felt a Funeral, in my Brain," move through it carefully, asking the students to hear and feel the language, registering its meanings as Dickinson moves from one line to the next.

You'll want the students, for example, to note that the poem begins with "I." This is the point of departure, the sign that *this* voice is speaking, and that she is addressing us—or that we are overhearing her. "I felt a Funeral" is an intriguing phrase, not what we expect. *See* a funeral: that is something we are familiar with, that we can understand. But how does one *feel* a funeral? Dickinson is organizing her language to make us ask the question and imagine what it's like to *feel*, not see or watch or attend, a funeral.

The comma after "Funeral" makes us pause. Dickinson is giving us a moment to picture the funeral. But no sooner do the scenes form than the next phrase, "in my Brain," complicates them. It's not a funeral that we conceive of but one that the speaker imagines in *her* brain. It is a funeral, one might say, that takes place internally. It is not out there, but inside, an event on the landscape of her mind.

"And Mourners": Who are they? At whose funeral are they mourning? "To and fro"—such a curious phrase, a phrase with a bit of a playful rhythm that we often find used about children as they gambol, "to and fro." It's a phrase that makes an uneasy combination with the funeral and the mourners, and it is that disconcerting feeling that Dickinson wants.

"Treading" is a harder, more severe word. Its general meaning is to walk on, over, or along. But it means, more precisely, to press beneath the feet, trample; to crush or injure, to subdue harshly or cruelly. Dickinson uses the word twice, for greater impact, so that there is no missing its point and power. The mourners press their way back and forth, relentlessly—maybe one should even say, punitively.

"That Sense was breaking through"—a complex line, which is (as Dickinson intends) difficult to pin down to a single meaning. Is the speaker saying that finally she began to make sense of what the funeral was about? Or is she saying that the mourners finally began to make *their* sense known to her? The line has an agonizing import—the sense breaking through, like a wound in the skin. But this feeling that the line gives us is combined with the more positive cast that we frequently assign to a phrase like this one: "I thought for a long time about the matter, and at last it made sense to me—the breakthrough that I was hoping for came."

These comments on the first stanza are meant to show how you can work inductively on the poem in the classroom. It is a demanding experience for the students, but we have found it to be very productive. This kind of close scrutiny enables the students to perceive the astonishing unusualness of Dickinson's writing; they can see, hear, and feel what makes this poet special. The challenge for you as a teacher is to acknowledge that Dickinson is difficult even as you convey to the students why she is intensely interesting.

When you focus on this poem, or on others by Dickinson, you can launch the analysis yourself. But turn after a line or two to the students. Get them involved; get them *inside* the poem.

We want to add: keep your eye on the clock. You need to work carefully, deliberately. But make sure that the class has a good rhythm. If the pace becomes too slow, the students will begin to feel bogged down, as if they were in the midst of an exercise rather than engaged with a rich and stimulating, if hard and disquieting, poem.

Recently we taught this poem in an introductory course, a seminar for first-year students that emphasized weekly essays and oral reports. For the first part of class, we worked as a group on the text of "I felt a Funeral, in my Brain" as it is printed in *The Complete Poems of Emily Dickinson,* ed. Thomas H. Johnson (1957). This is the text as we know it today, the one that all of the introductory and American literature anthologies use when they print it. We then distributed to the class a packet of materials, which we have included in our book for your students to work with:

1. The poem as it appears in Dickinson's own hand—the manuscript version.
2. The poem as it appeared in *Poems by Emily Dickinson,* third series, ed. Mabel Loomis Todd (1896)—the first published version of the poem.
3. Two more poems, from Johnson's edition: "I felt a Cleaving in my Mind" and "The Dust behind I strove to join."

We divided the class of sixteen students into four groups. One separated off to examine and talk together about the manuscript; another discussed Todd's edition; and the other two were assigned one of the short poems from Johnson's edition. The question we asked was, "What does the manuscript or poem tell you about the poem we have been studying today?" After about fifteen to twenty minutes of discussion among themselves, the students then reassembled and the groups reported on their discoveries.

The subsequent general discussion went well. One group commented, for example, on Dickinson's change in line 10 of the manuscript, where she crossed out "Brain" and substituted "Soul." They noted too that this kind of revision differs from the more puzzling one at the end, where Dickinson seems to have written two concluding lines and not made a choice between them. Was Johnson right, they wondered, in omitting the final line of the manuscript from the poem? What led him to decide that the manuscript should be changed into the version that he prints?

Similarly, another group wondered why Todd not only made minor changes throughout, but, more boldly still, cut the entire last stanza. How does the poem affect us without the final stanza? Why, furthermore, might the final stanza in the manuscript have impelled Todd to conclude that it did not belong, that the poem would be better without it?

In their own way, the other two Dickinson poems also helped to reveal and dramatize the distinctiveness of "I felt a Funeral, in my Brain." As the students pointed out, "I felt a Cleaving in my Mind" has a different force. "Cleaving" is one thing, "Funeral" is another. "Cleaving" comes from a verb that means to pierce or penetrate, or to split or cut with a sharp instrument. Not an event, not a funeral, but an action, a cutting, wounding, rending action. Nor is "Mind" the same as "Brain." As one student remarked, we might have expected the line of the second poem to read: "I felt a Cleaving in my Brain," because a person's brain is something tangible, something that can suffer a disease, something that a doctor can operate on or a scientist dissect. The mind: we know it is there and can talk about how it works, but can we *see* a person's mind in the way we can see and analyze the brain?

When our students finish their study of Dickinson, we hope they will be interested enough to want to read more about her and the biographical, historical, religious, literary, and philosophical contexts that bear upon her writing. We do not mean to confine the students to the poems alone, and no more than that. But if students are to get anywhere with Dickinson, they will need to feel they can make something of the poetry on their own. Our task as teachers is to make these hard poems accessible—literary works that students will believe they have the capacity to read, struggle with, profit from, and, yes, enjoy.

For our purposes, the two best resources for studying Dickinson and becoming intimate with her as a writer are *The Poems of Emily Dickinson,* 3 vols., ed. Thomas H. Johnson (1955), and *The Poems of Emily Dickinson: Variorum Edition,* 3 vols., ed. R. W. Franklin (1998). These scholarly works meticulously examine the manuscript and variant readings for each and every poem.

WILLIAM BUTLER YEATS
The Wild Swans at Coole (p. 202)

In "Posthumous Impresario," *The New Criterion* 19:1 (September 2000), Eric Ormsby makes a point about the opening lines that is helpful for getting discussion started:

> In "The Wild Swans at Coole," Yeats initially wrote, "The woods are in their autumn colour/ But the lake waters are low. . . ." He then revised this to read, "The trees are in their autumn foliage/ The water in the lake is low" and later still, "The trees are in their autumn foliage/ The woodland paths are dry." It was only after four or five such revisions that he hit upon: "The trees are in their autumn beauty,/ The woodland paths are dry. . . ." Why did Yeats first choose "colour" and then change it to "foliage" and then settle on "beauty?" Through a study of such revisions, students are obliged to recognize that words have weight and cadence, and that one word may be distinctly superior to another in a given place.

See, more generally, Herbert J. Levine, "Teaching the Versions of 'The Wild Swans at Coole,'" *Yeats: An Annual of Critical and Textual Studies* 13 (1995): 72–80.

The poem, and the revisions to it that Yeats made, have also been examined in the context of Yeats's love for Maud Gonne (1865–1953), the Irish journalist and political campaigner whom Yeats loved and wanted to wed but who rejected his proposals of marriage. In "'Freeing the Swans': Yeats's Exorcism of Maud Gonne," *ELH* 48:2 (Summer 1981), 411–426, Levine "traces the story of how Maud Gonne came to be associated in Yeats's mind with the consummately beautiful image of the swan, and how Yeats finally learned to release the nine-and-fifty swans at Coole from his private obsession, freeing them and all later swans in his poetry to become universal symbols for his readers" (p. 411). Levine notes that in the version of the poem we have printed, a revision of the first version of 1916, there is a new final stanza (lines 25–30). This final stanza, he explains,

> opens *after* the invidious comparisons between Yeats's heart and the swans have been drawn. The swans' flight is no longer aborted by Yeats's heartache or by his retreat to the past when he "Trod with a lighter tread." Instead, our attention is focused on two possibilities that are hinted at, but virtually denied in the first version: that the poet can awake to a future without the swans and that the swans can "Delight men's eyes" other than Yeats. With this deliberate and important revision, Yeats began to liberate himself from the obsessive burden of the past, and, what's more, to include us in that symbolic act of liberation. (p. 420)

Levine's observation can, we think, be taken further. Perhaps the key word in the poem is "mysterious," which means "simultaneously arousing wonder and inquisitiveness, and eluding explanation or comprehension." The swans are beautiful, but in themselves they do not mean what the speaker had taken them in the past to mean—that they were pairs of lovers, with one exception (the fifty-ninth), which represented Maud Gonne, whom Yeats would (he hoped) one day marry. The swans are separate from the speaker, beautiful yet mysterious (they inhabit a world of their own), and he and others can take pleasure in them without feeling that they function as reminders, as embodiments, of personal loss.

The speaker's earlier relationship to the swans was, in truth, both evocative and self-indulgent, and the final movement of the poem (in this version) is powerful and affecting because the speaker is now moving beyond that earlier stage of wounded self-regard.

Good biographies include A. Norman Jeffares, *W. B. Yeats: A New Biography* (1989), and R. F. Foster, *W. B. Yeats: A Life* (1977). See also A. Norman Jeffares, *A New Commentary on the Poems of W. B. Yeats*, 2nd ed. (1984).

GWENDOLYN BROOKS
We Real Cool (p. 203)

The unusual arrangement of the lines, putting what ordinarily would be the first syllable of the second line at the end of the first line, and so on, of course emphasizes the "we"—and therefore emphasizes the absence of "we" in the final line, which consists only of "Die soon," the "we" having been extinguished. The disappearance of the "we" is especially striking in a poem in which the "we" is so pleased with itself.

By emphasis we don't necessarily mean a heavy stress on the word. An emphasis can be gained by the slightest of pauses (even though the word is not followed by a comma or a shift in tone). In *Report from Part One* (1972), Brooks comments on this poem:

> The ending WEs in "We Real Cool" are tiny, wispy, weakly argumentative "Kilroy-is-here" announcements. The boys have no accented sense of themselves, yet they are aware of a semidefined personal importance. Say the "we" softly. (p. 185)

"We" presumably refers to a gang of seven confident pool players, but if seven is traditionally a lucky number, it brings these people no luck. The subtitle allows one to infer that at the Golden Shovel they are digging their own graves.

ANDREW HUDGINS
The Wild Swans Skip School (p. 204)

The Topics for Critical Thinking and Writing suggest the approach to this poem that we take, and we have found, the one time we taught it, that students enjoyed it with little prompting from us.

But you might seek to make a more general point or two about Hudgins's poem, which our fourth Topic implies. His poem makes sense only because of the prior existence of the poems by Yeats and Brooks, which Hudgins brings surprisingly and entertainingly together through his parodic echoes of both. Hudgins knows that many readers of poetry are familiar with these two poems, in large measure because the poems have been anthologized and reprinted so often—in books like the one that your students are using this semester.

"The Wild Swans Skip School" thus is an original work, yet it is entirely dependent on the works by the two other poets that preceded it, that give it the interest and pleasure it offers. Hudgins's poem is made from two previous poems, and in this respect it shows, with special (indeed extreme!) vividness, that poets work with literary tradition, with the poems (and literary conventions) that they have studied and absorbed, and then can make fertile use of in both serious and comic ways.

Hudgins's most recent book of poems is *Babylon in a Jar: New Poems* (1998). We also recommend *The Glass Anvil* (1997), in which Hudgins explores a range of topics, including language, autobiography, religion, racism, and Southern literature.

ANONYMOUS
The Silver Swan (p. 206)

This poem—really a song—may or may not be by Gibbons. It is an adaptation of an Italian song, and Gibbons certainly wrote the music, but the lyrics probably are anonymous.

You may want to get into the poem by talking with the class about songs, i.e., about poems that are set to music. We include some in the book in addition to "The Silver Swan"—"Western Wind," "The Titanic," "Deep River," "The Man That Got Away," "Birmingham Jail"—and it is a good thing to remind students that poems are not merely ink on paper; they are sounds in air, often accompanied by music. If in class you use the word "lyric," you might remind students that this word—derived from the name of an instrument—suggests the close connection between song and the kind of poetry they are most familiar with. For all of the classroom talk about the "speaking tone of voice," a singing voice is often faintly heard, in the meter and in the rhyme. Ezra Pound somewhere says, "Poetry withers and dries out when it leaves music, or at least imagined music, too far behind it. Poets who are not interested in music are, or become, bad poets."

The meter and the rhymes of "The Silver Swan," as well as the fact that each line divides pretty strongly into two halves, make the work "musical," but there are plenty of additional subtleties. In the first line, for instance, one notices—or at least unconsciously senses—the play of sounds in "silver" and "living," and in the third line the assonance in "leaning" and "reedy" sticks in the mind.

The silver swan is not quite the bird "of hammered gold and gold enameling" that Yeats wants to become in "Sailing to Byzantium," but it certainly is something more than a smelly swan. After all, Gibbons's "silver swan" (let's assume he is the author) could have been white, or snow white; indeed, the Italian song which was his source speaks of "Il dolce e bianco cigno" (the sweet white swan). But "silver" makes it unusual, mysterious, and precious. Presumably this silver bird has been floating around on a lake, silent as is the way with swans, and now, at its death, it sings.

Traditionally a swan's song is a final beautiful accomplishment, and the accomplishment of a silver swan might be expected to be exceptionally beautiful. "Unlocked," in "Unlocked her silent throat," suggests that something precious, hitherto kept under lock and key, will at last be revealed. Further, deathbed utterances are traditionally thought to be wise and true, even inspired (cf the dying John of Gaunt, in *Richard II*, who says, "Methinks I am a prophet new inspired"). You might ask students if they are familiar with any famous last words. Among the famous ones that come to our mind are a Confederate soldier's comment, "Tell my father I died with my face to the enemy," Darwin's "I am not in the least afraid to die," Goethe's "More light" (though we have read that what he really said was "Open the shutter, so that more light can come in"), and Thoreau's alleged comment when a friend or relative at his deathbed asked if he could see the next world, "One world at a time."

What precious song—what melodious message—will the all-but-supernatural silver swan reveal at its death, reveal while it is "leaning"—a word that in this context suggests both weakness (a need for support) and urgency (it is pressing toward the land, delivering its message to any who will listen)? The first line is traditional enough: "Farewell, all joys, Oh death, come close mine eyes," so the important truth will have to be in the second (final) line. This line comes (we think) as a shock, for it comes from the realm of satire, not of lyric: "More geese than swans now live, more fools than wise." So death comes to the swan as a release (that's good), and we are left with its wisdom: we live surrounded by fools. Although the swan's words are something of a put-down, implying that the reader probably is a fool, each listener-reader can fortunately (if vainly, in two senses of the word) assume that he or she is one of the wise.

Why swans were thought to sing beautifully at death remains a mystery, just as mysterious as why geese are thought to be especially foolish. (Cf. such expressions as "Don't be a goose," and Macbeth's angry comment to a confused, inarticulate servant, "Where got'st thou that goose look?") In fact, the chief differences between swans and geese are in the color and in the longer necks of swans.

8

Reading and Writing about Essays

BRENT STAPLES
Black Men and Public Space (p. 210)

Although Staples's marvelous first sentence speaks of his "first victim," and his second paragraph speaks of "that first encounter," he doesn't begin his essay with the chronologically earliest event of his narrative. Rather, he begins with an experience that revealed to him the fear he evokes in others and also revealed how that fear alienates and endangers him. He begins, in other words, with an account that dramatizes the focus of his essay. After recounting other incidents that revealed to him that a black male is an object of fear not only to white females but also (at least in some circumstances) to everyone "black, white, male, or female," he goes back in time to explain why at the age of twenty-two he was unaware of the effect he would have on others and then forward again to explain how the "first" experiences altered his behavior. The structure of the essay, beginning in the middle of things and containing a flashback, works so well it may appear artless; it's often useful in a composition class to ask some obvious questions to reveal the writer's options, as well as his decisions and their effects: Where does Staples begin his essay? Why does he begin there? Why not begin with his account of "coming of age" in Chester, Pennsylvania? and so on.

In addition to admiring the effective organization of the essay, we admire the deftness of Staples's language. We've already referred to the electrifying first sentence: "My first victim was a woman—white, well dressed, probably in her early twenties." (The next sentences even heighten the suspense.) We admire too Staples's rigor and his self-assurance as a writer, which enables him to describe himself as others might see him, as a "youngish black man—a broad six feet two inches with a beard and billowing hair, both hands shoved into the pockets of a bulky military jacket." There's a touch of humor in that description, certainly no self-pity. The self-assurance also allows him to acknowledge that there is some basis in fact for pedestrians' fear of black males (paragraph 6) while at the same time characterizing himself as "a softy who is scarcely able to take a knife to a raw chicken" (paragraph 2) and as "timid, but a survivor" (paragraph 9). Other virtues of his prose: the vivid imagery (for example, the memorable *"thunk, thunk, thunk, thunk"* of the car door locks in paragraph 3), the succinct summaries ("being perceived as dangerous is a hazard in itself" in paragraph 2), and the often wry humor ("bear country" in paragraph 12).

Perhaps most of all we admire Staples's restraint. Given the topic and the experiences he recounts (including the loss of a brother to street violence), Staples does not pull out the organ stops of rage to which, we might think, he is entitled. He leaves us instead with the "bright, sunny" warbling of Vivaldi's *Four Seasons* and a refreshing and important contribution to "New York mugging literature."

Staples is the author of *Parallel Time: Growing Up in Black and White* (1994), a vivid, often disturbing memoir of his childhood, college and university studies, and successful career as a journalist, which has led to his membership on the editorial board of *The New York Times*.

Topics for Critical Thinking and Writing

1. Write an essay of approximately 1,000 words explaining how you learned that your behavior and intentions were being misinterpreted and what you did to alter others' perceptions of you. (An example: a woman or girl whose behavior was being misread as sexually responsive or even aggressive.)
2. Write a narrative essay (approximately 1,000 words) on "coming of age," focusing on a particular lesson you learned from encounters with others.

LANGSTON HUGHES
Salvation (p. 219)

Most instructors who used the earlier editions of this book taught several of the stories in "Innocence and Experience." Hughes's essay can serve as an excellent introduction to that chapter.

Hughes, of course, is writing as an adult, but the simplicity of many of his sentences ("But not really saved. It happened like this") and of much of his diction ("there was a big revival") is appropriate to a boy not yet thirteen. This is not really the speech of a youngster ("escorted" in the first paragraph, "dire" in the third, "work-gnarled" in the fourth), but on the whole the style evokes the child's state of mind; we might say that we are chiefly conscious of the youthful subject rather than of the mature writer. But a very artful and adult ironic writing pervades the piece. Notice, for instance, the deflating effect that the last, brief sentence of paragraph 3 has upon the slightly longer previous sentence: "And some of them jumped up and went to Jesus right away. But most of us just sat there." And, of course, the contrast between the hypocritical, grinning Westley (who surely did not cry that night) and the narrator effectively emphasizes Hughes's sense of isolation. If the story is, on the surface, amusing, it is also finally serious and moving.

LAURA VANDERKAM
Hookups Starve the Soul (p. 221)

Vanderkam announces her thesis in her title, a device common in writings published in newspapers or large-circulation magazines. In essays of this sort, the goal is to be as simple and direct—and challenging—as possible. Thus, although "starve" is metaphoric, it cannot puzzle even the most casual reader. Still, the essay is by no means artless. Vanderkam skillfully gives us dialogue and specific examples, and she is fully aware of her audience, as, for instance, in paragraph 5, which begins "Lest you think college students are all libertines," and paragraph 7, where she says, "I hear the traditionalists clucking."

She also knows the value of citing an authority and letting the reader hear another voice, so in paragraph 10 she quotes David Brooks. And she also knows that an occasional literary allusion can be helpful, so she mentions Scarlett O'Hara, Juliet, Lady Chatterley, and (more risky) Dmitry and Ivan Karamazov. In short, we think the essay is effectively written; instructors can go through it paragraph by paragraph, helping students to see that argumentative prose can be clear, simple, and engaging—qualities they should aim for in their own essays.

AMY TAN
fish cheeks (p. 223)

We think it is a fact that many young people are ashamed of their parents, and they are especially ashamed if the parents are not native-born Americans, which is to say if they speak with an accent, eat foods that are not commonly found outside of the ethnic community, have distinctive table manners, etc. Amy Tan emphasizes her youthful embarrassment by speaking of the "shabby Chinese Christmas" and the "noisy Chinese relatives." The comments on the food, too—the "slimy rock cod," the tofu that looks like "rubbery white sponges," the squid that "resembled bicycle tires"—are ways of conveying her unhappiness with her heritage; these merely reenforce the message of the first paragraph, with its admiration for the "blond-haired boy" and the wish for "a slim new American nose." Many of your foreign-born students will know very well what Tan is talking about.

The mother's message is twofold: (1) The dinner she prepares, though it embarrasses Amy, in fact consists of the foods that Amy is especially fond of, i.e., it tells Amy that her inside (so to speak) is Chinese; (2) the Christmas present, the tweed miniskirt, is Amy's American outside. Yes, the mother says, be American on the outside, but also be proud to be Chinese on the inside. There is nothing shameful about liking Chinese foods or eating in a Chinese manner. "You only shame," the mother says in her imperfect English, "is be ashame." In the final paragraph the writer indicates that she understands the message: Although in the fifth paragraph Tan tells us that she "wanted to disappear" when her "father poked his chopsticks just below the fish eye and plucked out the soft meat," she now understands that the menu was lovingly chosen, to give Amy her favorite foods and also to teach her a lesson.

In addition to her best-known book, *The Joy Luck Club* (1989), Tan is the author of *The Kitchen God's Wife* (1991), *The Hundred Secret Senses* (1995), and *The Bonesetter's Daughter* (2001). Tan has written two books for children, *The Moon Lady* (1992) and *SAGWA, the Chinese Siamese Cat* (1994). For further study, consult E. D. Huntley, *Amy Tan: A Critical Companion* (1998).

9

Reading and Writing about Fiction

GRACE PALEY
Samuel (p. 225)

"All those ballsy American stories," Grace Paley has said of much of the American canon, "had nothing to say to me." Is she, then, a feminist writer? She denies it, insisting that she is something rather different, "a feminist and a writer." Some instructors may wish to have a class consider in what ways, if any, "Samuel" is the work of a feminist.

There is a particularly female insight in the last two paragraphs of "Samuel" which (though the second of these mentions Samuel's father) focus on Samuel's mother. The first of these paragraphs emphasizes the mother's agony when she learns of her son's death; the final paragraph, describing a later time, emphasizes a grief that is less visible or audible but that is perhaps even more painful, for this grief is stimulated by the sight of her newborn baby: "Never again will a boy exactly like Samuel be known."

Interestingly, the narrator (can we say the female author?) conveys a good deal of enthusiasm for what some people might regard as offensive *macho* displays of jiggling on the subway, riding the tail of a speeding truck, and hopping on the tops of trucks. Paley makes these actions sympathetic partly by implying that they take real skill, partly by implying that the show-off performing kids usually turn out to be very decent guys (one daredevil has graduated from high school, is married, holds a responsible job, and is going to night school), and partly by mildly discrediting those who oppose them. Thus one lady who disapproves of the jigglers thinks, "Their mothers never know where they are," but the narrator immediately assures us that the mothers of these boys *did* know where they were, and, moreover, the boys had been engaged in the thoroughly respectable activity of visiting a "missile exhibit on Fourteenth street."

Like this woman, the man who pulls the alarm cord is somewhat discredited: he is "one of the men whose boyhood had been more watchful than brave." Although it's no disgrace for a boy to be "watchful," the sentence probably guides most readers to feel some scorn for the man who (so to speak) was never a boy. Many readers will feel that although the man "walked in a citizenly way" to pull the cord, he is motivated less by an impulse of good citizenship than (though probably he doesn't know it) by resentment, by irritation that these children are experiencing a joy that he never experienced in his childhood. On the other hand, Paley does not present him as a villain, and the story is not chiefly concerned with his guilt. By the end of the story, readers are probably so taken up with the mother's grief that they scarcely remember the man.

Although "Samuel" resembles a fable in that it is fairly brief, is narrated in an apparently simple manner, and concludes with a message, it differs significantly from a fable. Most obviously, it does not use the beasts, gods, and inanimate objects that fables commonly use. In fact, however, these are not essential in fables. More significantly, the characters in "Samuel" are more complicated, since the noisy boys are treated sympathetically and the apparently respectable adults are treated ironically. Finally, where the fable traditionally utters or implies a hard-headed, worldly wise (and often faintly cynical) message, the message uttered at the end of "Samuel" arouses the reader's deepest sympathy.

Students will enjoy reading the selections in Paley's *Collected Stories* (1994). Critical studies include Jacqueline Taylor, *Grace Paley: Illuminating the Dark Lives* (1990), and Victoria Aarons, "Talking Lives: Storytelling and Renewal in Grace Paley's Short Fiction," *Studies in American Jewish Literature* 9:1 (Spring 1990): 30–35. The best secondary source is Judith Arcana, *Grace Paley's Life Stories: A Literary Biography* (1993). See also *Conversations with Grace Paley*, ed. Gerhard Bach and Blaine Hall (1997), which collects interviews from 1978 to 1995, and Paley's *Just As I Thought* (1998), which includes three decades of her essays, reviews, and lectures; the essays on Isaac Babel and Donald Barthelme are especially worth reading.

Topics for Critical Thinking and Writing

1. If you had been on the train, would you have pulled the emergency cord? Why, or why not?
2. Write a journalist's account (250–300 words) of the accidental death of a boy named Samuel. Use whatever details Paley provides, but feel free to invent what you need for an authentic news story.

ANTON CHEKHOV
Misery (p. 238)

Like all good stories, this one can be taught in many ways. Since we teach it near the beginning of the course, we tend to emphasize two things: the artistry of the story and the reader's response, especially the reader's response to the ending. But first we want to mention that plot is given little emphasis. The cabman encounters several passengers, but these encounters do not generate happenings—actions—in the obvious or usual sense, though of course they are in fact carefully arranged and lead to the final action when Iona speaks to the mare. Second, we want to mention that we believe that writers usually express their values in the whole of the story, not in a detachable quotation or in a statement that a reader may formulate as a theme. Chekhov himself made a relevant comment to an editor: "You rebuke me for objectivity, calling it indifference to good and evil, absence of ideals and ideas, etc. You would have me say, in depicting horse thieves, that stealing horses is evil. But then, that has been known for a long while, even without me. Let jurors judge them, for my business is only to show them as they are."

By "the artistry," we mean chiefly the restrained presentation of what could be a highly sentimental action. Chekhov does not turn Iona into a saint, and he does not turn the other characters into villains. The passengers are unsympathetic, true, but chiefly they are busy with their own affairs, or they are drunk. (One of the drunks is a hunchback, and although we feel that he behaves badly toward Iona, we feel also that nature has behaved badly toward him.) Second, Chekhov does not simply tell us that the world is indifferent to Iona; rather, he takes care to *show* the indifference before we get the explicit statement that Iona searched in vain for a sympathetic hearer. Third, it seems to us that the episodes are carefully arranged. First we get the officer, who, despite his initial brusqueness, makes a little joke, and it is this joke that apparently encourages Iona to speak. The officer displays polite interest—he asks of what the boy died—and Iona turns to respond, but the passenger immediately (and not totally unreasonably) prefers the driver to keep his eyes on the road. Next we get the drunks, who can hardly be expected to comprehend Iona's suffering. All of this precedes the first explicit statement that Iona searches the crowd for a single listener. Next, in an extremely brief episode (we don't need much of a scene, since we are already convinced that Iona cannot find an audience) the house-porter dismisses him, and finally, again in a very brief scene, even a fellow cabman—presumably exhausted from work—falls asleep while Iona is talking. But again Chekhov refrains from comment and simply shows us Iona going to tend his horse. At this point Iona does not intend to speak to the animal, but the sight of the horse provokes a bit of friendly talk ("Are you munching"?), and this naturally leads to a further bit of talk, now about the son, couched in terms suited to that horse—and this, in turn, opens the floodgates.

So far as responses go, all readers will have their own, but for what it's worth, we want to report that we find the ending not so much painful as comforting. The tension is relieved; Iona finds an audience after all, and if the thought of a man telling his grief to his horse has pathos, it also has its warmth. It seems to us to be especially satisfying, but we will have to explain our position somewhat indirectly. First, we will talk about attempts to state the theme of the story.

We sometimes ask students to state the theme. Of the responses we have received, "Suffering is incommunicable, but the sufferer must find an outlet" is the closest to our response. That is, we are inclined to think that the reason Iona cannot tell his story to the officer or to any other person is that grief of this sort cannot be communicated. It isolates the grief-stricken person. One notices in the story how much physical effort goes into Iona's early efforts to communicate with people. As a cabman, of course, he is in front of his passengers, and he has to turn to address his audience. At first his lips move but words do not come out, and when he does speak, it is "with an effort." Near the end of "Misery," just before he goes to the stable, Iona thinks about how the story of his son's death must be told:

> He wants to talk of it properly, with deliberation. He wants to tell how his son was taken ill, how he suffered, what he said before he died, how he died. He wants to describe the funeral and how he went to the hospital to get his son's clothes. He still has his daughter Anisya in the country. And he wants to talk about her too. Yes, he has plenty to talk about.

Now, we are all decent people—not at all like the brusque officer or the drunken passengers or the indifferent house-porter or the sleepy young cabman—but which of us could endure to hear Iona's story? Which of us really could provide the audience that he needs? Which of us could refrain from interrupting him with well-intended but inadequate mutterings of sympathy, reassurances, and facile pity? Iona's grief is so deeply felt that it isolates him from other human beings, just as the indifference of other beings isolates them from him. Overpowering grief of this sort sets one apart from others. We hope we are not showing our insensitivity when we say that the mare is the only audience that can let Iona tell his story, in all its detail, exactly as he needs to tell it. And that is why we think that, in a way, this deeply moving story has a happy ending.

Chekhov once said that the aim of serious literature is "truth, unconditional and honest." He stated, too, that, in his estimation, "the artist should be, not the judge of his characters and their conversations, but only an unbiased witness." Both of these observations can prove useful in opening up the story for discussion. Ask students to point to moments in the text where Chekhov's intentions for his art are realized.

Much of the best scholarship focuses on Chekhov's plays, but for the stories (and for sensitive treatments of his central themes) we can recommend the discussions in D. Rayfield, *Chekhov: The Evolution of His Art* (1975); Beverly Hahn, *Chekhov: A Study of the Major Stories and Plays* (1977); and *Chekhov: New Perspectives*, ed. René Wellek and N. D. Wellek (1984).

For biography, the standard work is still Ernest J. Simmons, *Chekhov: A Biography* (1962). But Ronald Hingley, *A New Life of Anton Chekhov* (1976), is also worth consulting. The most recent biography is Donald Rayfield, *Anton Chekhov: A Life* (1998); he is excellent on the sources of the stories and plays, and he draws a complex portrait of a troubled, sometimes cruel and detached man, but he does not deal with the texts themselves as works of art.

Students can be encouraged to seek out an excellent selection of stories, supplemented by critical essays: *Anton Chekhov's Short Stories: Texts of the Stories, Backgrounds, Criticism*, ed. Ralph E. Matlaw (1975).

Eudora Welty
A Worn Path (p. 242)

In an essay in the *Georgia Review* (Winter 1979), Eudora Welty (speaking mainly of her first story, "The Death of a Traveling Salesman") says that her characters "rise most often from the present," but her plots are indebted to "the myths and fairy tales I steeped myself in as a young reader.... By the time I was writing stories I drew on them as casually as I drew on the daily newspaper or the remarks of my neighbors."

Clearly "A Worn Path" draws on the myth of the phoenix, the golden bird that periodically consumes itself in flames so that it, rising from the ashes, may be renewed. Phoenix Jackson renews her ancient body on each visit to the doctor's remote office. The chief clues: the woman's name ("Phoenix"), the story's early description of her (her stick makes a sound "like the chirping of a solitary little bird"; "a golden color ran underneath, and the two knobs of her cheeks were illuminated by a yellow burning under the dark"), a reference to cyclic time ("I bound to go to town, mister. The time come around"—and the time is Christmas, i.e., a time of renewal), her "ceremonial stiffness" in the doctor's office, and finally, the words "Phoenix rose carefully."

The myth is wonderfully supported by details, details that are strictly irrelevant (e.g., Phoenix's deception of the hunter, which nets her a nickel, and her cadging of a nickel's worth of pennies from the nurse) but that make the character unsentimental and thoroughly convincing.

A writer in *Studies in Short Fiction* 14 (1977): 288–290, assuming that the boy is dead, argues: "The journey to Natchez . . . becomes a psychological necessity for Phoenix, her only way of coping with her loss and her isolation. . . . Having at first made the journey to save the life of her grandson, she now follows the worn path each Christmas season to save herself" (p. 289). On the other hand, not all of the criticism of the story is on this level. For a good discussion, see Alfred Appel, *A Season of Dreams: The Fiction of Eudora Welty* (1965).

Because Welty is one of our favorite writers, we have often used *The Collected Stories of Eudora Welty* (1980) as the basis for an introduction to writing a research paper. We work together in class on one or two stories—for example, "A Worn Path"—and then each student selects a story of his or her own for study and some library research. We place two copies of the *Collected Stories* on reserve for this purpose; and recently we have been able to add the Welty volumes in the Library of America series: *Stories, Essays, and Memoir* (1998) and *Complete Novels* (1998).

Of the books devoted to Welty's stories, we recommend Peter Schmidt, *The Heart of the Story: Eudora Welty's Short Fiction* (1991), and Carol Ann Johnston, *Eudora Welty: A Study of the Short Fiction* (1997).

For a wider range of secondary materials, you and your students can profit from these resources:

The Eudora Welty Newsletter (published twice a year, beginning in Winter 1977). Stays up-to-date with coverage of primary and secondary sources.

McDonald, Jr., W. U. "An Unworn Path: Bibliographical and Textual Scholarship on Eudora Welty." *Southern Quarterly* 20 (Summer 1982): 101–108.

McHaney, Pearl Amelia. "A Eudora Welty Checklist, 1973–1986." In *Welty: A Life in Literature,* ed. Albert J. Devlin. Jackson: UP of Mississippi, 1987. 266–302. See Polk.

Polk, Noel. "A Eudora Welty Checklist." *Mississippi Quarterly* 26 (Fall 1973): 663–693. Lists both primary and secondary sources. Rpt. in *Welty: A Life in Literature,* ed. Albert J. Devlin. Jackson: UP of Mississippi, 1987. 238–265. See McHaney.

Swearingen, Bethany C. *Eudora Welty: A Critical Bibliography, 1936–1958.* Jackson: UP of Mississippi, 1984. A good resource, but note that its coverage ends in 1958.

Thompson, Victor H. *Eudora Welty: A Reference Guide.* Boston: G. K. Hall, 1976. Covers secondary studies from 1936 to 1975.

Some students, we have found, are already familiar with Welty's evocative memoir *One Writer's Beginnings* (1984). *Conversations with Eudora Welty,* ed. Peggy W. Prenshaw (1984), and Welty's *The Eye of the Story: Selected Essays and Reviews* (1978) are also illuminating about her artistic aims, techniques, and influences.

Topics for Critical Thinking and Writing

1. Is the story sentimental? (We'd say no, for several reasons: Phoenix, though old and—at moments—mentally failing, is dignified and never self-pitying; the writer, letting Phoenix tell her own story, never asks us to pity Phoenix; Phoenix exhibits both a sense of humor and a sense of self-reliance, and on those occasions when she needs help she exhibits no embarrassment. Her theft of the nickel and her shrewdness in getting the nurse to give her another nickel instead of "a few pennies" also, as mentioned a moment ago, help to keep her from being the sentimental old lady of Norman Rockwell pictures.)
2. Write a character sketch (250–300 words) of some old person whom you know. If possible, reveal the personality by showing him or her engaged in some characteristic activity.

Oscar Casares
Yolanda (p. 247)

The story is told in the first-person, a common enough device especially in stories about the transition from innocence to experience (cf. Updike's "A & P") but in this instance the narrator's voice is an engaging combination of the mature man that he now is and the boy that he was at the time of the episode. In the first paragraph, he is all adult:

> When I can't sleep at night I think of Yolanda Castro. She was a woman who lived next door to us one summer when I was growing up. I've never told Maggie about her because it's not something she'd appreciate knowing. Trust me. Tonight, like most nights, she fell asleep before I was even done brushing my teeth. And now all I can hear are little snores. Sometimes she even talks to herself, shouts out other people's names, and then in the morning says she can't remember any of it. Either way, I let her go on sleeping. She's over on her side of the bed. It's right where she ought to be. This thing with Yolanda doesn't really concern her.

There is plenty to discuss here—not merely the narrator's sense that Maggie would not "appreciate" knowing about the attractive Yolanda who spent some time in bed with him but also his report that (a) Maggie falls asleep even before he gets into bed at night, and (b) Maggie has her own life in dreams, when she calls out names that she later (when awake) claims she can't remember. Presumably Maggie, like the narrator, has her own secrets, and the narrator has enough sense not to pry. Live and let live: "She's over on her side of the bed. It's right where she ought to be. This thing with Yolanda doesn't really concern her."

Although the story concerns infidelity and violence, the treatment is somewhat comic, occasionally almost farcical, with such details as a drunken driver who runs over "the Baby Jesus that was still lying in the manger," Frank with forearms "like Popeye's," a Jehovah Witness who tries to give Frank a pamphlet, Frank knocked off balance when "his head hit the clothesline," and of course Yolanda pressing her breasts against the boy's back—and how he "never turned around and always regretted it."

What might have been a tender initiation into sexuality is, at least as we see it, here presented as a comic story of a missed opportunity and a golden memory. Notice, however, that Casares does not sentimentalize Yolanda: In the next-to-last paragraph the reader learns that she has been having an affair with an assistant manager, that she is pregnant, and that "she'd been taking money out of the register and was about to be caught." (Presumably the bonuses that in paragraph 19 she claimed had been given to her are in fact dollars she has taken out of the till. The brutal Frank was right to wonder where her money came from.) But, as the narrator says in the last sentence of the next-to-last paragraph, "that's not the part of the story I like to remember." What he likes to remember is set forth in the final paragraph, which more or less summarizes the gist of what the innocent-eye narrator told us, the experience of being with Yolanda, safe, though now romanticized into a vision wherein they are "riding off to some faraway place on an Appaloosa." No need to tell his wife Maggie about this private world, and she, we recall from the first paragraph, has her own private world too.

10

Thinking and Writing Critically about Short Stories: Two Case Studies

FLANNERY O'CONNOR
A Good Man Is Hard to Find (p. 255)

In the early part of this story the grandmother is quite as hateful as the rest of the family—though students do not always see at first that her vapid comments, her moral clichés, and her desire to be thought "a lady" are offensive in their own way. Her comment, "People are certainly not nice like they used to be," can be used to convince students of her mindlessness and lack of charity.

The Misfit, like Jesus, was "buried alive"; he believes that "Jesus thrown everything off balance," and he finds no satisfaction in life (i.e., his life without grace). Life is either a meaningless thing in which all pleasure is lawful (and, ironically, all pleasure turns to ashes), or it derives its only meaning from following Jesus. The Misfit, though he does not follow Jesus, at least sees that the materialistic view of life is deficient. Confronted by the suffering of The Misfit, the nagging and shallow grandmother suddenly achieves a breakthrough and is moved by love. She had earlier recognized The Misfit ("'You're The Misfit!' she said. 'I recognized you at once'"), and now she has a further recognition of him as "one of her own children," that is, a suffering fellow human. Faced with death, she suddenly becomes aware of her responsibility: her head clears for an instant and she says, "You're one of my own children." This statement is not merely an attempt to dissuade The Misfit from killing her; contrast it with her earlier attempts, when, for example, she says, "I know you come from nice people! Pray! Jesus, you ought not to shoot a lady. I'll give you all the money I've got." Rather, at last her head is "cleared." This moment of grace transfigures her and causes her death. The Misfit is right when he says, "She would of been a good woman if it had been somebody there to shoot her every minute of her life."

On the "moment of grace" in O'Connor's fiction, see *College English* 27 (December 1965): 235–239, and R. M. Vande Kiefte in *Sewanee Review* 70 (1968): 337–356. Vande Kiefte notes that the description of the dead grandmother ("her legs crossed under her like a child's and her face smiling up at the cloudless sky") suggests that death has jolted the grandmother out of her mere secular decency into the truth of eternal reality. See also Martha Stephens, *The Question of Flannery O'Connor* (1973).

For Flannery O'Connor's comments on this story, see our text. In her collected letters, entitled *The Habit of Being* (1979), O'Connor says (letter to John Gawkes, Dec. 26, 1959) that she is interested in "the moment when you know that Grace has been offered and accepted—such as the moment when the Grandmother realizes The Misfit is one of her own children" (p. 367).

The best place to begin is with the volume on O'Connor in the Library of America series (1988); it includes her novels and stories and a selection of her letters and essays. Students might next turn to Robert E. Golden and Mary E. Sullivan, *Flannery O'Connor and Caroline Gordon: A Reference Guide* (1977), and *Critical Essays on Flannery O'Connor*, ed. Melvin J. Friedman and Beverly Lyon Clark (1985). Of the many critical studies, we value in particular Josephine Hendin, *The World of Flannery O'Connor* (1970); Carol Shloss, *Flannery O'Connor's Dark Comedies: The Limits of Inference* (1980); and Robert H. Brinkmeyer, *The Art and Vision of Flannery O'Connor* (1989).

Topics for Critical Thinking and Writing

1. Explain the significance of the title.
2. Interpret and evaluate The Misfit's comment on the grandmother: "She would of been a good woman if it had been somebody there to shoot her every minute of her life."
3. O'Connor reported that once, when she read aloud "A Good Man Is Hard to Find," one of her hearers said that "it was a shame someone with so much talent should look on life as a horror story." Two questions: What evidence of O'Connor's "talent" do you see in the story, and does the story suggest that O'Connor looked on life as a horror story?
4. What are the values of the members of the family?
5. Flannery O'Connor, a Roman Catholic, wrote, "I see from the standpoint of Christian orthodoxy. This means that for me the meaning of life is centered in our Redemption by Christ and what I see in the world I see in relation to that." In the light of this statement, and drawing on "A Good Man Is Hard to Find," explain what O'Connor saw in the world.

FLANNERY O'CONNOR
Revelation (p. 266)

This story, like "A Good Man Is Hard to Find," is concerned with a moment of grace, which most obviously begins when Mary Grace hurls a hook at Mrs.

Turpin—an action somewhat parallel to The Misfit's assault on the grandmother. The doctor's office contains a collection of wretched human beings whose physical illnesses mirror their spiritual condition. There is abundant comedy ("The nurse ran in, then out, then in again"), but these people are treated sympathetically too. Mrs. Turpin's pitiful snobbery—especially her desperate effort to rank people in the eyes of God—is comic and horrible, but it at least reveals an uneasiness beneath her complacency, an uneasiness that finally compares well with the monumental hatred that characterizes Mary Grace. Yet Mary Grace, a pimply girl, is a messenger of grace. And so when the blow comes (from a book nicely called *Human Development*), it is not in vain. The girl's accusation ("Go back to hell where you came from, you old wart hog") strikes home, and later, among the pigs that Mrs. Turpin so solicitously cleans, the message produces a revelation, a revelation that forces upon her an awareness of the inadequacy of "virtue" (her horrible concept of respectability) as she has known it. Virtue is of as little value to fallen humanity as a hosing-down is to a pig; in her vision she sees that even virtue or respectability is burned away in the movement toward heaven.

On the one hand, some students have difficulty seeing that Mrs. Turpin is not simply a stuffy hypocrite; on the other, some students have difficulty seeing that her respectability is woefully inadequate and must be replaced by a deeper sympathy. But perhaps students have the greatest difficulty in reconciling the comic aspects of the story with its spiritual depth, and here the instructor can probably not do much more than read some passages and hope for the best.

In O'Connor's writings the sun is a common symbol for God. Here, the light of the sun transforms the hogs, so that they appear to "pant with a secret life," a parallel to the infusion of grace into Mrs. Turpin, which causes her to see the worthlessness of her earlier "respectable" values.

The story is deeply indebted to the Book of Revelation, traditionally attributed to St. John the Evangelist and probably written at the end of the first century A.D. (A revelation is, etymologically, an "unveiling," just as an apocalypse is, in Greek, an unveiling. What is unveiled in the Book of Revelation is the future.) Numerous details in O'Connor's story pick up details in the biblical account: O'Connor's "red glow" in the sky echoes the fiery heaven of Revelation; the "watery snake" that briefly appears in the air echoes the water-spewing "serpent" of Revelation (12:15), and even the "seven long-snouted bristling shoats" echo the numerous references to seven (angels, churches, seals, stars) in Revelation. But the details should not be pressed too hard; what matters most is the apocalyptic vision of the oppressed rejoicing and shouting hallelujah at the throne of God.

The story is not difficult, and no published discussions of it are essential reading, though it is of course discussed in books on O'Connor and in general comments on her work, such as A. R. Coulthard, "From Sermon to Parable: Four Conversion Stories by Flannery O'Connor," *American Literature* 55 (1983): 55–71. Two essays devoted entirely to "Revelation" are "'Revelation' and the Book of Job" by Diane Rolmedo, *Renascence* 30 (1978): 78–90, and

Larve Love Slone's "The Rhetoric of the Seer: Eye Imagery in Flannery O'Connor's 'Revelation,'" *Studies in Short Fiction* 25 (1988): 135–145.

Topics for Critical Thinking and Writing

1. Why does Mary Grace attack Mrs. Turpin?
2. Characterize Mrs. Turpin before her revelation. Did your attitude toward her change at the end of the story?
3. The two chief settings are a doctor's waiting room and a "pig parlor." Can these settings reasonably be called "symbolic"? If so, symbolic of what?
4. When Mrs. Turpin goes toward the pig parlor, she has "the look of a woman going single-handed, weaponless, into battle." Once there, she dismisses Claud, uses the hose as a weapon against the pigs, and talks to herself "in a low fierce voice." What is she battling, besides the pigs?

JOHN UPDIKE
A & P (p. 285)

It may be useful for students to characterize the narrator and see if occasionally Updike slips. Is "crescent" in the third sentence too apt a word for a speaker who a moment later says, "She gives me a little snort," and "If she'd been born at the right time they would have burned her over in Salem"? If this is a slip, it is more than compensated for by the numerous expressions that are just right.

"A & P" is a first-person story, and in its way is about growing up. Invite students to characterize the narrator as precisely as possible. Many will notice his hope that the girls will observe his heroic pose, and some will notice, too, his admission that he doesn't want to hurt his parents. His belief (echoing Lengel's) that he will "feel this for the rest of his life" is also adolescent. But his assertion of the girls' innocence is attractive and brave.

Some readers have wondered why Sammy quits. Nothing in the story suggests that he is a political rebel or that he is a troubled adolescent who uses the episode in the A & P as a cover for some sort of adolescent emotional problem. An extremely odd article in *Studies in Short Fiction*, 23 (1986): 321–323, which seeks to connect Updike's story with Hawthorne's "Young Goodman Brown," says that "Sammy's sudden quitting is not only a way of attracting the girls' attention but also a way of punishing himself for lustful thoughts." Surely this is nonsense, even further off the mark than the same author's assertion that Queenie's pink bathing suit "suggests the emerging desires competing with chastity" (p. 322). Sammy quits because he wants to make a gesture on behalf of these pretty girls, who in appearance and in spirit (when challenged, they assert themselves) are superior to the "sheep" and to the tedious Lengel. Of course Sammy hopes his gesture will be noticed, but in any case the gesture is sincere.

What sort of fellow is Sammy? Is he a male chauvinist pig? An idealist? A self-satisfied deluded adolescent? Someone who thinks he is knowledgeable but who is too quick to judge some people as sheep? Maybe all of the above, in varying degrees. Certainly his remark that the mind of a girl is "a little buzz, like a bee in a glass jar," is outrageous—but later he empathizes with the girls, seeing them not as mindless and not as mere sex objects but as human beings who are being bullied. If we smile a bit at his self-dramatization ("I felt how hard this world was going to be to me hereafter"), we nevertheless find him endowed with a sensitivity that is noticeably absent in Lengel.

Helpful studies of Updike include George W. Hunt, *John Updike and the Three Great Secret Things: Sex, Religion, and Art* (1980); *Critical Essays on John Updike*, ed. William R. McNaughton (1982); Donald J. Greiner, *John Updike's Novels* (1984); and Julie Newman, *John Updike* (1988).

Students will likely be familiar with Updike's name; some will have seen the film version of his novel, *The Witches of Eastwick* (1984). But because he has written so much, students may be unsure what by Updike they should read. For starters, we recommend the early novel, *Rabbit, Run* (1960), and the short story collections, *Pigeon Feathers* (1962) and *Problems* (1979).

Topics for Critical Thinking and Writing

1. Sammy: comic yet heroic?
2. What kind of person do you think he is?

JOHN UPDIKE
Pygmalion (p. 291)

We think this story will cause no difficulty. There are few if any words (other than the title, perhaps) that will stop a reader, and no unfathomable actions. In fact, if the story does cause a difficulty, it may be that some students will think it is too simple. "Nothing happens, except that at the end the woman falls asleep" may be the response of some students. In fact, however, there is a good deal of "action" in the Aristotelian sense, not physical action but mental action, mental changes. Further, a sort of action takes place in the reader's mind, as the reader increasingly comes to understand Pygmalion and his wives.

But first a word about the title. Pygmalion, a king of Cyprus who was displeased with all of the women around him, either sculpted or commissioned an ivory image of an ideally beautiful woman. (In Ovid's *Metamorphoses* 10, he carved the image himself.) When the image was complete, he fell in love with it, brought it gifts, spoke to it, embraced and kissed it, and placed it on his bed. Venus, pitying him, endowed the image with life.

What is the relevance of the myth to Updike's story? Like the mythical Pygmalion, Updike's Pygmalion creates—or thinks he creates—an ideal woman. Here is part of paragraph 11:

> He laughed and laughed, entranced to see his bride arrive at what he conceived to be a proper womanliness—a plastic, alert sensitivity to the human environment, a susceptible responsiveness tugged this way and that by the currents of Nature herself.

(Incidentally, some students may misinterpret "plastic," not knowing its primary sense of "capable of being shaped or formed." Today this sense of the word is chiefly used in connection with sculpture, so perhaps Updike is having a bit of fun hoping that his readers hear the allusion to this form of art.) But the paragraph then adds a sentence that marks this Pygmalion as different from the classical figure. Updike says of his man, "He could not know the world . . . unless a woman translated it for him."

The story is rich in irony. In the first paragraph we are told that what Pygmalion liked about his first wife (Marguerite) "was her gift of mimicry"—we get a sample, with her imitation of his mistress—and what he liked about his mistress (Gwen, soon to become his second wife) "was her liveliness in bed." Further, we are told in this paragraph that "what he disliked about his first wife was the way she would ask to have her back rubbed and then, under his laboring hands, night after night, fall asleep." As early as paragraphs 5 and 6 we see Pygmalion, now married to the lively-in-bed Gwen, retreating from Gwen's sexuality ("'It's awfully late,' he warned her. 'Oh, come on,' she said"). In the final paragraph he offers to rub her back, and he finds that the formerly lively Gwen "night after night . . . fell asleep."

Moreover, once this lively mistress, now a wife who falls asleep when he rubs her back, retains a "small something in her that was all her own." In short, his effort to turn a woman into a toy of his own, and into his interpreter of the world, fails. Even the mimicry that he demands of her because his first wife had entertained him with it no longer entertains. It turns out that this second wife has views that are decidedly her own. Pygmalion apparently accepted his first wife's view of life ("Marguerite met [the hostess's brother] once a few years ago and she was struck by what a pompous nitwit he was"), but Gwen maintains her own view. More precisely, although she is willing to go a bit of the way to accommodate Pygmalion ("Sensing with feminine intuition that he expected more, she might add, 'Harmless. Maybe a little stuffy'"), but when he presses Gwen to accept Marguerite's view of the hostess's brother (and therefore now presumably Pygmalion's own view) she firmly draws the line: "I thought he was perfectly pleasant. . . . He had a *lot* to say about tax shelters." Given this display of independence, we are not surprised a moment later to read, in paragraphs 8 and 9, that Gwen strongly disagrees with Pygmalion about Marguerite's second husband, Marvin. Pygmalion found him "perfectly pleasant, in what could have been an awkward encounter," but Gwen continues to diminish Marvin by mimicking him. We never meet Marvin and therefore we cannot tell whether Pygmalion or Gwen is the more perceptive, but probably most readers will assume that Gwen is, since Pygmalion by now is seen as something of a nerd—something, indeed, of the "pompous nitwit" that he sees elsewhere.

As we just mentioned, in the final paragraph, Gwen not only falls asleep while Pygmalion rubs her back, just as Marguerite did, but she also possesses a "small something in her that was all her own." Incidentally, Updike's typescript is interesting here, as indeed throughout the story. Apparently he first typed "that in her which was all her own," then revised it to "that something in her which was all her own," and then further revised the passage to "that small something in her which was all her own." At some point he revised, in pencil, "all her own" to "all herself," but the printed version reverts to "all her own."

Because, as we read the story, a somewhat self-satisfied stuffy man is put down by the two women whom he has sought to shape, it is our hunch that women may enjoy it more than men.

Note: Some students might enjoy exploring other representations, in art and literature, of the Pygmalion myth. Many painters and sculptors, including Bronzino, Veronese, Boucher, Daumier, and Rodin, have depicted Pygmalion, usually with Galatea (the name of the statue). Reversing the outcome, the Surrealist painter Paul Delvaux, in his "Pygmalion" (1939), shows a woman embracing a male statue. In literature, George Bernard Shaw's *Pygmalion* (1912) is the best-known example. Few students will have read it, but many will be familiar with Lerner and Loewe's musical *My Fair Lady*, which was based upon it. *My Fair Lady* was first performed in New York City in March 1956 and later, in 1964, made into a highly successful film. Worth taking a look at is Charles A. Berst, *Pygmalion: Shaw's Spin on Myth and Cinderella* (1995).

JOHN UPDIKE
The Rumor (p. 294)

One might almost have thought that the emergence of the gay liberation movement had put an end to all talk about "latent" homosexuality, but it hasn't; indeed, although sexual identity is much talked about, it remains at least as mysterious as ever.

One of the interesting things about "The Rumor" is that it is about sex and yet it has very little sexual action in it. We hear that Sharon had sex with Frank when she was sixteen, that they "made love just two nights ago," that Frank had a "flurry of adulterous womanizing," and (about a third of the way through the story) that Frank, after the rumor has changed everything, engages in "pushing more brusquely than was his style at her increasing sexual unwillingness," but that's pretty much it, as far as sexual activity goes. Yet the story glances at a wide spectrum of sexual activity. We can begin with heterosexuality:

1. Frank and Sharon married partly as a way of getting out of Cincinnati. ("Their early sex had been difficult for her; she had submitted to his advances out of a larger, more social, rather idealistic attraction. She knew that together they would have the strength to get out of Cincinnati and, singly or married to others, they would stay.")

2. Frank has had adulterous heterosexual affairs—but after the rumor has reached his ears, he wonders if these were not really a manifestation of his homosexuality.

As for homosexuality:

1. The unambiguous homosexuality of Walton Forney and Jojo, and of others who make up "the queer side" of the art world.
2. The part of Frank's nature that, as he now sees it, is homosexual. Here too we find a spectrum. Probably some of Frank's speculations strikes a reader as tenuous (e.g., his belief that his attraction to "stoical men" had a homosexual component). The passage about the golfing trip in Bermuda, however, is more convincing; Frank "had felt his heart make many curious motions, among them the heaving, all-but-impossible effort women's hearts make in overcoming men's heavy grayness and achieving—a rainbow born of drizzle—love." Finally, at the end of the story, it seems clear that Frank's interest in Jojo, which he characterizes as "Hellenic fellowship," is a mixture of the physical ("that silvery line of a scar . . . lean long muscles . . . white skin") and the intellectual and paternal (Jojo now seems "unexpectedly intelligent," and someone who "needed direction").

Is Frank a homosexual? Any answer would of course have to say what homosexuality is, or, more precisely, would have to say what it means to be a homosexual. It's our sense of the story that as the rumor persists, Frank finds in himself things that seem to confirm it, that is, he begins to take his identity from the identity ascribed to him. He now looks back on various episodes and sees in them a homosexual slant which cannot quite be disproved, though it cannot be proved either, for example, the idea that his adulterous affairs were an attempt to deny his essential homosexuality.

The first half of the story pretty clearly establishes Frank—or seems to establish him—as heterosexual, though even here there are some ambiguous notes. For instance, when he first denies that he has a lover, he does so "too calmly." We take the comment to reflect Sharon's perception, but it comes from the omniscient narrator and therefore can at least be conceived as an authoritative comment. Similarly, Frank's hostile comment about gays—"You know how gays are. Malicious. Mischievous"—sounds like the unambiguous comment of a straight male; yet of course it can be taken as a reflection of Frank's insecurity, a disparaging comment made by someone unsure of his own masculinity. (By the way, the comment is *Frank's,* not—as some students may think—Updike's.)

The idea that gays are "malicious" probably is fairly common among straight men; what is especially interesting in this story is that Updike goes on to use the words "malice" and "maliciousness" in connection with Frank's behavior: "Frank sensed her discomfort and took a certain malicious pleasure in it," and Sharon's belief in the rumor "justified a certain maliciousness" on Frank's part. So, again, we get Frank taking his identity from society's view; if (at least in Frank's view) gays are malicious, Frank—now rumored to be gay—

will be malicious. In any case, the first half of the story is largely devoted to setting forth the rumor and to giving evidence of Frank's heterosexuality, and the second half of the story is largely devoted to Frank's perception (creation?) of himself as a homosexual. Whereas in the first half of the story, his denial increased his wife's belief in the truth of the rumor and indeed the very "outrageousness" of the rumor paradoxically served to confirm her suspicions, now, in the second half we find a new belief (Frank's) based, it may seem to most readers, on evidence almost equally insubstantial. In the first half she spied on him, looking for tiny clues (e.g., his response to a waiter) and interpreting them in one way, and in the second half he spies on himself, equally attentive to tiny clues, and equally seeing the evidence only one way.

Does Updike take a stand on the nature/nurture argument about gender identity? We don't think so (and we certainly don't think a writer of fiction need do so), but he does force the issue into a reader's mind. Frank himself sometimes seems to incline to the "nature" view, for instance when he thinks of himself as someone likely to be a homosexual because he is a man "slight of build, with artistic interests," but at other times he senses that what he is depends on who is around him: "Depending on which man he was standing with, Frank felt large and straight and sonorous, or, as with Wes, gracile and flighty."

A word about some of the questions we ask in the text. Question 1: The point of view in the first paragraph is omniscient (we are told about the feelings of both characters). Question 2: As we have already said, in "Frank said, too calmly," the reader enters into Sharon's mind, that is, here (and in some other passages early in the story) the "central intelligence" is Sharon. Question 3: Here (and in much of the second half of the story) we get into Frank's mind, "annoyingly, infuriatingly" (his response to her action).

JOHN UPDIKE
Oliver's Evolution (p. 302)

Because our fourth question in the text invites students to evaluate a comment about parenting, we may be guilty of turning attention away from Updike's story and to the issue in the outside world with which the story is concerned. On the whole in our teaching we try to keep attention focused on the literary work. Yes, literature is connected with life, but the job that we like to do is to talk in detail about how particular works of literature achieve their meaning and why they make the impression that they do; we try not to use literary works as mere jumping-off points for a discussion of love or death or (in this case) parenting or whatever. Still, we recognize that it is sometimes acceptable and even appropriate to stand back from the work and to think about its connection with the world around us.

The narrative of Oliver's early life, for all its matter-of-factness, is harrowing (corrective casts on his feet, his stomach pumped, his face blue from a near-drowning, his defective eye, and so on), not least because "He was the least complaining of their children" (paragraph 3). A few apparently flat statements in fact convey wry humor ("the friendly men who appeared to take her mother out," the broken arm that resulted either from "falling down the frat stairs, or leaping, by another account of the confused incident, from a girl's dormitory window") but, again, for the most part the narrative proceeds almost mechanically, unrelieved by dialogue or by expansive description.

It proceeds, in fact, steadily, relentlessly, in the spirit of the title, "Oliver's Evolution." It just keeps going ("the teeth grew firm again"), but it takes a twist in the fifth paragraph, where we are told that Oliver married (no surprise), and that the girl "was as accident-prone as he" (again no surprise) and that "she looked up to him" (big surprise). Oliver, now loaded with responsibilities, begins to function effectively: "What we expect of others, they endeavor to provide." In evolutionary terms, or let's say in creative evolutionary terms, the circumstances demand a certain kind of response and the creature responds appropriately. The story ends, then, with Oliver having evolved into "a protector of the weak."

As Updike reports the story of Oliver's evolution, it all seems inevitable, a sort of up-from-the-apes narrative, each stage leading to the next, as inevitably or at least as easily as the word "Oliver" leads to the word "Evolution."

11

Fiction into Film

If you want to know if there is a film adaptation of a story, just go to <http://us.imdb.com/> for the International Movie Database. On the left side of this site you will see a search line, where you can search by title.

Among available films are:

Ambrose Bierce, "An Occurrence at Owl Creek Bridge" (27 minutes, black and white, 1962). Distributed by Festival Films and Video Yesteryear.
Raymond Carver, "What We Talk about When We Talk about Love" (movie title: *Short Cuts;* 189 minutes, color, 1993). Distributed by Columbia Tristar Home Video.
William Faulkner, "A Rose for Emily" (27 minutes, color, 1983). Distributed by Pyramid Film & Video and The Video Catalog.
Mary E. Wilkins Freeman, "The Revolt of 'Mother'" (60 minutes, color, 1988). Distributed by Karol Video and Monterey Home Video.
Charlotte Perkins Gilman, "The Yellow Wallpaper" (30 minutes, color, 1994). Distributed by Pyramid Film & Video.
Nathaniel Hawthorne, "Young Goodman Brown" (30 minutes, color, 1972). Distributed by Pyramid Film & Video.
Shirley Jackson, "The Lottery" (18 minutes, color, 1969). Distributed by Britannica Films.
Guy de Maupassant, "The Necklace" (20 minutes, color, 1981). Distributed by Britannica Films and Knowledge Unlimited, Inc.
Eudora Welty, "A Worn Path" (30 minutes, color, 1994). Distributed by Pyramid Film & Video.

JOYCE CAROL OATES
Where Are You Going, Where Have You Been? (p. 318)

The title seems to be derived from Judges 19.17 ("So the old man said, 'Where are you going, and where do you come from?'"), a point made in a rather strained discussion of the story in *Explicator* (Summer 1982).

Tom Quirk, in *Studies in Short Fiction* 18 (1981): 413–19, pointed out that the story derives from newspaper and magazine accounts (especially one in *Life*, March 4, 1966) of the activities of a psychopath known as "The Pied Piper of Tucson," who drove a gold-colored car and seduced and sometimes murdered teenage girls in the Tucson area. Because he was short, he stuffed his boots with rags and flattened tin cans, which caused him to walk unsteadily. Oates herself has confirmed, on various occasions, her use of this material (e.g., *New York Times*, March 23, 1986).

According to Oates, in an early draft of her story "Death and the Maiden" (she is fond of a type of fiction that she calls "realistic allegory"), "the story was minutely detailed yet clearly an allegory of the fatal attractions of death (or the devil). An innocent young girl is seduced by way of her own vanity: She mistakes death for erotic romance of a particularly American/trashy sort." The story went through several drafts. Oates has said she was especially influenced by Bob Dylan's song, "It's All Over Now, Baby Blue." One line of Dylan's song ("The vagabond who's standing at your door") is clearly related to the story, and note that in the story itself Connie wishes "it were all over."

In speaking of the revisions, Oates writes that "the charismatic mass murderer drops into the background and his innocent victim, a 15-year-old, moves into the foreground. She becomes the true protagonist of the tale. . . . There is no suggestion in the published story that Arnold Friend has seduced and murdered other girls, or even that he necessarily intends to murder Connie." Oates goes on to explain that her interest is chiefly in Connie, who "is shallow, vain, silly, hopeful, doomed—perhaps as I saw, and still see, myself?—but capable nonetheless of an unexpected gesture of heroism at the story's end. . . . We don't know the nature of her sacrifice [to protect her family from Arnold], only that she is generous enough to make it." Instructors who are interested in discussing the intentional fallacy (and is it a fallacy?) will find, if they use this passage, that students have strong feelings on the topic.

The story has abundant affinities with the anonymous ballad called "The Demon Lover." The demon lover has "music on every hand," and Connie "was hearing music in her head"; later, Arnold and Ellie listen to the same radio station in the car that Connie listens to in the house; the demon lover's ship has "masts o' the beaten gold," and Arnold's car is "painted gold."

The second sentence tells us that Connie "had a quick nervous giggling habit of craning her neck to glance into mirrors." Her mother attributes it to vanity, and indeed Connie does think she is pretty, but a more important cause is insecurity. Connie's fear that she has no identity sometimes issues in her a wish that "she herself were dead and it were all over with." "Everything about her had two sides," which again suggests an incoherent personality.

Arnold Friend has a hawklike nose, thick black lashes, an ability to see what is going on in remote places, a curious (lame) foot, a taste for strange bargains, incantatory speech, an enchanted subordinate, and a charismatic personality; all in all he is a sort of diabolical figure who can possess Connie, partly because he shows her an enormous concern that no one else has shown her. (The possession—"I'll come inside you, where it's all secret"—is possession of her mind as well as of her body.) Notice, too, that like a traditional evil spirit, Arnold Friend cannot cross the threshold uninvited.

The dedication to Dylan has provoked considerable comment. Marie Urbanski, in *Studies in Short Fiction* 15 (1978): 200–03, thinks it is pejorative, arguing that Dylan made music "almost religious in dimension among youth." Tom Quirk, on the other hand, says it is "honorific because the history and effect of Bob Dylan's music had been to draw youth away from the romantic promises and frantic strains of a brand of music sung by Buddy Holly, Chuck Berry, Elvis Presley, and others." A. H. Petry, in *Studies in Short Fiction* 25 (1988), 155–57, follows Quirk and goes on to argue that Ellie is meant to suggest Elvis Presley (lock of hair on forehead, sideburns, etc.). According to Petry, Oates is seeking "to warn against the dangerous illusions and vacuousness" generated by Elvis's music, in contrast to Bob Dylan's.

Perhaps the most astounding comment is by Mike Tierce and John Michael Crafton (*Studies in Short Fiction* 22 [1985]: 219–24). Tierce and Crafton argue that Arnold Friend, the mysterious visitor, is not satanic but rather a savior, and that he is (as his hair, hawklike nose, unshaved face, and short stature suggest) an image of Bob Dylan. Arnold's visit, in their view, is a fantasy of Connie's "overheated imagination," and it enables her to free herself "from the sense of confinement she feels in her father's house. . . . She broadens her horizons to include the 'vast sunlit reaches of the land' all around her."

Many readers find resemblances between the fiction of Oates and Flannery O'Connor, but in an interview in *Commonweal* (Dec. 5, 1969), Oates said that although she at first thought her fiction was indebted to Flannery O'Connor, she came to see that in O'Connor there is always a religious dimension whereas in her own fiction "there is only the natural world."

The story has been made into a film called *Smooth Talk* (Spectra Films, 1986).

For further study of this story, we recommend the casebook *"Where Are You Going, Where Have You Been?"*, ed. Elaine Showalter (1994). For biography, see Greg Johnson, *Invisible Writer: A Biography of Joyce Carol Oates* (1998). A good critical overview is Johnson's *Understanding Joyce Carol Oates* (1987). Other helpful resources include *Critical Essays on Joyce Carol Oates*, ed. Linda W. Wagner (1979), and Francine Lercangee, *Joyce Carol Oates: An Annotated Bibliography* (1986). Oates is best known for her fiction, but her criticism is worth reading as well. See, for example, *Contraries: Essays* (1981) and *The Profane Art: Essays and Reviews* (1983).

12

Reading and Writing about Drama

SOPHOCLES
Antigone (p. 347)

On *Antigone*, consult two books by H. D. F. Kitto, *Greek Tragedy* (1978), and especially *Form and Meaning in Drama* (1964). See also D. W. Lucas, *The Greek Tragic Poets* (1959); Cedric H. Whitman, *Sophocles* (1951); and R. P. Winnington-Ingram, *Sophocles* (1980). Hegel's view, most often known through A. C. Bradley's essay on Hegel in Bradley's *Oxford Lectures* (1963) (and reprinted in *Hegel on Tragedy* [1975], ed. Anne and Henry Paolucci), claims that both sides are right and that both are also wrong because they assert they are exclusively right. (For a long anti-Hegelian reading, see Brian Vickers, *Toward Greek Tragedy* (1979), which insists that Creon is brutal and Antigone is thoroughly admirable.) Bradley says, "In this catastrophe neither the right of the family nor that of the state is denied; what is denied is the absoluteness of the claim of each."

Most subsequent commentators take sides and either see Creon as a tragic hero (a headstrong girl forces him to act, and action proves ruinous, not only to her but to him) or see Antigone as a tragic heroine (a young woman does what she must and is destroyed for doing it). The critical conflict shows no sign of terminating. Mostly we get assertions, such as D. W. Lucas's "There is no doubt that in the eyes of Sophocles Creon is wrong and Antigone right," and Cedric Whitman's "Antigone's famous stubbornness, . . . the fault for which she has been so roundly reproved, is really moral fortitude." One of the most perceptive remarks on *Antigone* is by William Arrowsmith, in *Tulane Drama Review* 3 (March 1959): 135, where he says that Antigone, "trying to uphold a principle beyond her own, or human, power to uphold, gradually empties that principle in action, and then, cut off from her humanity by her dreadful heroism, rediscovers herself and love in the loneliness of her death." He suggests, too, that the play insists on "not the opposition between Antigone and Creon, but [on] the family resemblance which joins them in a common doom."

John Ferguson, in *A Companion to Greek Tragedy* (1972), offers a fairly brief, commonsensical, scene-by-scene commentary on the play. Toward the end he argues that Hegel was utterly wrong in his view that both Creon and Antigone are right. Ferguson points out that Creon "behaves as a tyrant" and that Creon's law "is disastrous for the state." And Antigone is "wrong," Ferguson says, because although her "view of the situation is the true one," as a woman it was her duty to obey Creon. The play is about Antigone's *hubris*, and therefore it is properly titled.

For an excellent extended discussion of the play, see Helene P. Foley, *Female Acts in Greek Tragedy* (2001).

Topics for Critical Thinking and Writing

1. What stage business would you invent for Creon or Antigone at three points in the play?
2. In an essay of 500 words, compare and contrast Antigone and Ismene. In your discussion consider whether Ismene is overly cautious and whether Antigone is overly cold in her rejection of Ismene.
3. Characterize Haimon, considering not only his polite and even loving plea when he urged Creon to change his mind but also his later despair and suicide. In what way is he like his father and also (in other ways) like Antigone?

AUGUST WILSON
Fences (p. 374)

Some background (taken from our *Types of Drama*) on the history of blacks in the American theatre may be of use. In the 1940s and 1950s black playwrights faced the difficult problem of deciding what audience they were writing for—an audience of blacks or of whites? The difficulty was compounded by the fact that although there were a number of black theatre groups—for example, the American Negro Theatre (founded by blacks in 1940)—there was not a large enough black theatre-going public to make such groups commercially successful. In fact, although the original ideal of the American Negro Theatre was "to portray Negro life . . . honestly," within a few years it was doing plays by white writers, such as Thornton Wilder's *Our Town* (not only by a white but about whites) and Philip Yordan's *Anna Lucasta* (by a white, and originally about a Polish working-class family, but transformed into a play about a black family). Further, the aim of such groups usually was in large measure to employ black actors and theater technicians; some of the most talented of these, including Harry Belafonte, Sidney Poitier, and Ruby Dee, then went on to enter the mainstream of white theatre, on Broadway or—a short step—in Hollywood. Meanwhile, such writers as James Baldwin and Lorraine Hansberry, though writing about black life, wrote plays that were directed at least as much at whites as at blacks. That is, their plays were in large measure attempts to force whites to look at what they had done to blacks.

In the mid-1960s, however, the most talented black dramatists, including LeRoi Jones (Imamu Amiri Baraka) and Ed Bullins, largely turned their backs on white audiences and in effect wrote plays aimed at showing blacks that *they*—not their white oppressors—must change, must cease to accept the myths that whites had created. Today, however, strongly revolutionary plays by and about blacks have difficulty getting a hearing. Instead, the newest black writers seem to be concerned less with raising the consciousness of blacks than with depicting black life and with letting both blacks and whites respond aesthetically rather than politically. Baraka has attributed the change to a desire by many blacks to become assimilated in today's society, and surely there is much to his view. One might also say, however, that black dramatists may for other reasons have come to assume that the business of drama is not to preach but to show, and that a profound, honest depiction—in a traditional, realistic dramatic form—of things as they are, or in Wilson's play, things as they were in the 1950s—will touch audiences whatever their color. "Part of the reason I wrote *Fences*," Wilson has said, "was to illuminate that generation, which shielded its children from all of the indignities they went through."

This is not to say, of course, that *Fences* is a play about people who just happen to be black. The Polish family of *Anna Lucasta* could easily be converted to a black family (though perhaps blacks may feel that there is something unconvincing about this family), but Troy Maxson's family cannot be whitewashed. The play is very much about persons who are what they are because they are blacks living in an unjust society run by whites. We are not allowed to forget this. Troy is a baseball player who was too old to join a white team when the major leagues began to hire blacks. (The first black player to play in the major leagues was Jackie Robinson, whom the Brooklyn Dodgers hired in 1947. Robinson retired in 1956, a year before the time in which *Fences* is chiefly set.) For Troy's friend, Bono, "Troy just came along too early;" but Troy pungently replies, "There ought not never have been no time called too early." Blacks of Troy's day were expected to subscribe to American ideals—for instance, to serve in the army in time of war—but they were also expected to sit in the back of the bus and to accept the fact that they were barred from decent jobs. Wilson shows us the scars that such treatment left. Troy is no paragon. Although he has a deep sense of responsibility to his family, his behavior toward them is deeply flawed; he oppresses his son Cory, he is unfaithful to his wife, Rose, and he exploits his brother Gabriel.

Wilson, as we have seen, calls attention to racism in baseball, and he indicates that Troy turned to crime because he could not earn money. But Wilson does not allow *Fences* to become a prolonged protest against white oppression—though one can never quite forget that Troy insists on a high personal ideal in a world that has cheated him. The interest in the play is in Troy as a human being, or, rather, in all of the characters as human beings rather than as representatives of white victimization. As Troy sees it, by preventing Cory from engaging in athletics—the career that frustrated Troy—he is helping rather than oppressing Cory: "I don't want him to be like me. I want him to move as far from me as he can." But Wilson also makes it clear that Troy has other (very human) motives, of which Troy perhaps is unaware.

A note on the word "black": The play is set in 1957 and (the last scene) 1965, before "black" and "African American" were the words commonly applied to persons of African descent. The blacks in the play speak of "coloreds" and of "niggers." "Black" did not become the preferred word until the late 1960s. For instance, the question was still open in November 1967, when *Ebony* magazine asked its readers whether "Negro" should be replaced by "black" or "Afro-American". The results of polls at that time chiefly suggested that "Afro-American" was the preferred choice, but "black" nevertheless became the established term until about 1988, when "African American" began to displace "black".

A 30-minute videocassette of Bill Moyers' interview with August Wilson is available from Longman Publishers.

There are two good studies: Kim Pereira, *August Wilson and the African-American Odyssey* (1995), and Sandra Garrett Shannon, *The Dramatic Vision of August Wilson* (1995). For an excellent collection of essays on *Fences* and Wilson's other plays: *May All Your Fences Have Gates: Essays on the Drama of August Wilson,* ed. Alan Nadel (1994). Also helpful is *August Wilson: A Casebook,* ed. Marilyn Elkins (1994).

13
Thinking Critically about Drama

TENNESSEE WILLIAMS
The Glass Menagerie (p. 421)

The books on Williams that have appeared so far are disappointing. The best general survey is Henry Popkin's article in *Tulane Drama Review* 4 (Spring 1960): 45–64; also useful is Gordon Rogoff, in *Tulane Drama Review* 10 (Summer 1966): 78–92. For a comparison between the play and earlier versions, see Lester A. Beaurline, *Modern Drama* 8 (1965): 142–149. For a discussion of Christian references and motifs (e.g., Amanda's candelabrum, which was damaged when lightning struck the church), see Roger B. Stein, in *Western Humanities Review* 18 (Spring 1964): 141–153, reprinted in *Tennessee Williams* (1977), ed. Stephen S. Stanton. Stein suggests that the play shows us a world in which Christianity has been replaced by materialism.

Perhaps the two points that students find most difficult to understand are that Amanda is both tragic *and* comic (see the comments below, on the first suggested topic for writing), and that Tom's quest for reality has about it something of adolescent romanticism. Tom comes under the influence of his father (who ran away from his responsibilities), and he depends heavily on Hollywood movies. This brings up another point: it is obvious that Amanda, Laura, and Tom cherish illusions, but students sometimes do not see that Williams suggests that all members of society depended in some measure on the illusions afforded by movies, magazine fiction, liquor, dance halls, sex, and other things that "flooded the world with brief, deceptive rainbows," while the real world of Berchtesgaden, moving toward World War II, was for a while scarcely seen. If Amanda, Laura, and Tom are outsiders living partly on illusions, so is everyone else, including Jim, whose identification with the myth of science may strike most viewers as hopelessly out of touch with reality.

The Glass Menagerie has twice been filmed, most recently in 1987, directed by Paul Newman. Newman followed Williams's sequence of scenes, and he kept almost all the dialogue, yet the film strikes us as unsuccessful. Why? Probably this "memory play" needs to be somewhat distanced, framed by a proscenium. Further, the film's abundant close-ups seem wrong—they make the play too energetic, too aggressive. Such are our impressions; instructors who rent the film (Cineplex Odeon) can ask students to set forth their own impressions—in writing.

Delma Eugene Presley has written a stimulating monograph on this play: *The Glass Menagerie: An American Memory* (1990). The standard biography has been written by Donald Spoto (1985), but it will be eclipsed by the biography that Lyle Leverich has begun—the first volume is *Tom: The Unknown Tennessee Williams* (1995). There are two helpful surveys: Felicia Hardison Londre, *Tennessee Williams* (1979), and Signi Lenea Falk, *Tennessee Williams*, 2nd ed. (1978). Students will find useful essays on Williams's career as a dramatist in *The Cambridge Companion to Tennessee Williams*, ed. Matthew C. Roudane (1997).

Topics for Critical Thinking and Writing

1. Discuss comedy in *The Glass Menagerie*. (Students should be cautioned that comedy need not be "relief." It can help to modify the tragic aspects, or rather, to define a special kind of tragedy. A few moments spent on the Porter scene in *Macbeth*—with which almost all students are familiar—will probably help to make clear the fact that comedy may be integral.)
2. Compare the function of Tom with the function of the Chorus in *Oedipus*. (Williams calls his play a "memory play." What we see is supposed to be the narrator's memory—not the dramatist's representation—of what happened. Strictly speaking, the narrator is necessarily unreliable in the scene between Laura and Jim, for he was not present, but as Williams explains in the "Production Notes," what counts is not what happened but what the narrator remembers as having happened or, more exactly, the narrator's response to happenings.)
3. What cinematic techniques are used in *The Glass Menagerie*? (Among these are fade-ins and fade-outs; projected titles, reminiscent of titles in silent films; the final "interior pantomime" of Laura and Amanda, enacted while Tom addresses the audience, resembles by its silence a scene from silent films, or a scene in a talking film in which the sound track gives a narrator's voice instead of dramatic dialogue. By the way, it should be noted that Williams, when young, like Tom, often attended movies, and that this play was adapted from Williams's rejected screenplay, *The Gentleman Caller*, itself derived from one of Williams's short stories.) Topics 3 and 4 in the text are ways of getting at the importance of unrealistic settings and techniques in this "memory play."
4. Compare the play with the earlier Williams short story, "Portrait of a Girl in Class," in *One Arm and Other Stories* (1948).

14

Reading and Writing about Poetry

Emily Dickinson
Wild Nights—Wild Nights (p. 474)

A reader tends to think of Emily Dickinson as the speaker of "Wild Nights" and therefore is perhaps shocked by the last stanza, in which a woman apparently takes on the phallic role of a ship mooring in a harbor. But perhaps the poem is spoken by a man. (In one of her poems the speaker says, "I am a rural man," in another the speaker refers to "my brown cigar," and in "A narrow fellow in the Grass" the speaker identifies himself as male in lines 11–12.)

Possibly we are superficial readers, but we don't attach to "Might I but moor—Tonight— / In Thee!" the strong sexual associations that several critics have commented on. Some but not all assume that the image suggests male penetration. Albert Gelpi, in *The Tenth Muse* (1975), pp. 242–243, says that "the sexual roles are blurred." He adds, "Something more subtle than an inversion of sexual roles is at work here, and the point is not that Emily Dickinson was homosexual, as Rebecca Patterson and John Cody have argued," but he doesn't clarify the point. (Patterson's discussion is in *The Riddle of Emily Dickinson* [1951]; Cody's is in *After Great Pain* [1971].) Paula Bennett, in *My Life a Loaded Gun* (1986), drawing on a discussion by L. Faderman, seems to reject the idea of a male speaker. She says that "the imagery of the poem, with its emphasis on entering rather than being entered, is . . . far more appropriate for one woman's experience of another than for a woman's experience with a man" (p. 61). Christine Miller too insists that the speaker is a woman. In *Feminist Critics Read Emily Dickinson*, ed. Suzanne Juhasz (1983), Miller says that the speaker is a woman but she adds that "The woman is the ship that seeks to 'moor—Tonight— / In Thee!'—an activity more representative of male than of female social behavior" (p. 137). Our own simple view: a reader need not find an image of penetration in "moor"; rather, we think that in this poem the word suggests a longed-for security.

Is the poem sentimental? We don't think so, chiefly because it is brief, controlled, and (in "Tonight") it does not claim too much.

In *Explicator* 25 (January 1967), Item 44, James T. Connelly pointed out that in letter No. 332 (T. H. Johnson's edition, *Letters,* II, 463), Dickinson writes, "Dying is a wild Night and a new road." Looking at the poem in the light of this letter, Connelly concludes that "to die is to experience a wild night on a turbulent, surging sea. Only by plunging into this uncharted sea of Death can one at last reach the port of rest and calm. The poem, thus considered, is an apparent death wish: a personification and apostrophe to Death whose presence and company are paradoxically exhilarating luxury." We are unconvinced, partly because the poem speaks not of "a wild night" but of "Wild Nights," and we cannot see how the plural form lends itself to this reading.

When we teach a poem by Dickinson, we always start with two books by Joseph Duchac: *The Poems of Emily Dickinson: An Annotated Guide to Commentary Published in English, 1890–1977* (1979), and *The Poems of Emily Dickinson: An Annotated Guide to Commentary Published in English, 1978–1989* (1993). Duchac skillfully summarizes and quotes from a wide range of critical discussions of each of the poems, and he thereby provides students with a feeling for the variety of critical approaches to Dickinson that scholars have taken.

Dozens of books focus in whole or in part on Dickinson. The standard biography is Richard B. Sewall, *The Life of Emily Dickinson,* 2 vols. (1974). In our view, the best critical study (which includes a good deal of biographical and cultural context) has been written by Cynthia Griffin Wolff: *Emily Dickinson* (1986). The problem for students is that both of these studies are very long and densely detailed. They might do better with a brief overview: Helen McNeil, *Emily Dickinson* (1986). And some might benefit as well from consulting *An Emily Dickinson Encyclopedia* (1998).

We need to report that in general our students have not gained much from perusing lengthy critical and scholarly discussions of Dickinson. They seem to get better results when they read and think carefully about the poems on their own, without the confusion that being exposed to many over-ingenious, unduly ideological, or highly theoretical analyses all too easily produces. Remember, too, that even as you focus on specific words, phrases, and images, you should also highlight the effect on the reader of the poem as a whole. As our comments in this manual make clear, we are great believers in the value of attending to local details. But for Dickinson, one must be wary of turning each poem into a series of puzzles. If you take the poem apart, fine: this is an important part of the critical process. But then put it back together. Ask the students, for example:

- What's it like to read this poem?
- How did you feel about this poem when you were in the midst of it, and then when you were done?
- What makes reading Dickinson so different from reading other poets you know?

Give the students a chance to say and explain what's on their minds. An open and honest discussion and debate about Dickinson will do much to make her seem vivid, accessible, immediate, rather than a remote author who designed impossibly "hard" poems that we must pry into until at last (if we are lucky) we discover their secrets.

WILLIAM SHAKESPEARE
Sonnet 146 ("Poor soul, the center of my sinful earth") (p. 476)

This poem is engagingly discussed in an old book, Edward Hubler's *The Sense of Shakespeare's Sonnets* (1952). Instructors who want more rigorous discussions should turn to Helen Vendler, *The Art of Shakespeare's Sonnets* (1997) and to Michael West's article in *Shakespeare Quarterly* 25 (Winter 1974): 109–22.

See also an article by Charles A. Huttar, "The Christian Basis of Shakespeare's Sonnet 146," *Shakespeare Quarterly* 19 (Autumn 1968): 355–65, which rejects a reading that the poem ironically argues that spiritual health is achieved by bodily subjugation. The rejected reading holds that the advice that the soul exploit the body must be ironic, since if it were not ironic, the soul would be guilty of simony, the sin of buying (or attempting to buy) salvation. According to this ironic reading, the poet really is pleading for the life of the body against a rigorous asceticism which glorifies the spirit at the expense of the body. But Huttar argues (by citing Biblical sources and Christian commentaries) that the poem argues in behalf of the traditional Christian doctrine that the soul should be the master of the body; the body (which must in any case die) should not be allowed to cause the soul to "pine." The poem, Huttar says, is close to Jesus's words in Matthew 6.20: "Lay up for yourself treasures in heaven, where neither moth nor rust cloth corrupt, and where thieves do not break through and steal."

ROBERT FROST
The Telephone (p. 477)

A student of ours, Jane Takayanagi, wrote an entry in a journal that we think is worth reprinting. In our opinion she is right in seeing that a quarrel has precipitated the speaker's walk ("When I was just as far as I could walk / From here today"), but it is hard to convince someone who doesn't sense it. In any case, here is the entry from her journal:

> As the poem goes on, we learn that the man wants to be with the woman, but it starts by telling us that he walked as far away from her as he could. He doesn't say why, but I think from the way the woman speaks later in the poem, they had a fight and he walked out. Then, when he stopped to rest,

he thought he heard her voice. He really means that he was thinking of her and he was hoping she was thinking of him. So he returns, and he tells her he heard her calling him, but he pretends he heard her call him through a flower on their window sill. He can't admit that *he* was thinking about her.

This seems very realistic to me; when someone feels a bit ashamed, it's sometimes hard to admit that you were wrong, and you want the other person to tell you that things are OK anyhow. And judging from line 7, when he says "Don't say I didn't," it seems that she is going to interrupt him by denying it. She is still angry, or maybe she doesn't want to make up too quickly. But he wants to pretend that *she* called him back so when he says, "Do you remember what it was you said?" she won't admit that she *was* thinking of him, and she says, "First tell me what it was you thought you heard." She's testing him a little. So he goes on, with the business about flowers as telephones, and he says "someone" called him. He understands that she doesn't want to be pushed into forgiving him, so he backs off. Then she is willing to admit that she did think about him, but still she doesn't quite admit it. She is too proud to say openly that she wants him back but does say, "I *may* have thought as much." And then, since they both have preserved their dignity and also have admitted that they care about the other, he can say, "Well, so I came."

Two other (small) points: (1) Why in line 11 does Frost speak of having "driven a bee away"? We think that maybe in a tiny way it shows the speaker's willingness to exert himself and to face danger. It's a miniature ordeal, a test of his mettle. (2) In line 17 the speaker says, "I heard it as I bowed." Of course "bowed" rhymes with "aloud," but putting aside the need for a rhyme, surely the phrase is better than, say, "I heard it as I stood," since it conveys a gesture of humility.

Students always enjoy the time we spend on Frost's poetry, in part because most of them are already familiar with a number of Frost poems from their high school English courses. Perhaps for this reason, students seem able to respond well to, and make good use of, critical writing on Frost. The students have responses of their own to begin with; they can work with a new idea or insight, or reject it, and they do not see the criticism as preventing them from knowing their own views about the poem.

The point of departure for a student's work on Frost should be the *Collected Poems, Prose, and Plays* (1995), in the Library of America series. The standard biography has been written by Lawrance Thompson (3 vols., 1966–1976), but for students a better choice is William H. Pritchard, *Frost: A Literary Life Reconsidered* (1984; 2nd ed., 1993). Insightful critical studies include Reuben A. Brower, *The Poetry of Robert Frost* (1963), and Richard Poirier, *Robert Frost: The Work of Knowing* (1977). The best recent book on Frost: Mark Richardson, *The Ordeal of Robert Frost: The Poet and His Poetics* (1997). Your students will also benefit from Mordecai Marcus, *The Poems of Robert Frost: An Explication* (1991), which explicates each of the 355 poems in *The Poetry of Robert Frost* (1969), ed. Edward Connery Lathem. See also *Critical Essays on Robert Frost*, ed. Philip L. Gerber (1982), and *Robert Frost: Centennial Essays*, 3 vols. (1974–1978).

We don't think it is a good idea simply to assign critical essays to students. Even when they are reading about a poet whom they know a little about, students at an introductory level need some guidance from you. We therefore explain to them first why it is both helpful and important to read criticism—that it sharpens our knowledge, gives us (at its best) examples of attentive reading, and provides us with responses, ideas, and arguments against which we can test our own. In a word, we suggest to students that they use criticism not in order to learn *what* to think, but, rather, *how* to think more clearly and complicatedly themselves. "When you read criticism," we say to our students, "you enter into the ongoing critical conversation about (for example) Frost." "As in any conversation," we add, "you are not obliged to agree with all or any of the voices that you hear: you listen, learn, respond, and work your way toward your own conclusions."

Students will gain even more from criticism if you give them some exercises and writing assignments. When you are studying Frost, or Blake, or Dickinson, or some other poet whom critics have written about well, select one or two critical selections—perhaps, for instance, one of Poirier's explications of a Frost poem. Ask the class to answer these questions:

- What is the critic's main argument about this poem?
- Which details in the poem's language does the critic cite and examine to support his or her argument?
- Which aspects of the poem does this critic help you to understand more clearly?
- Do you interpret the poem differently? Do you think that this critic misreads the poem as a whole or misunderstands parts of it?

WILLIAM SHAKESPEARE
Sonnet 130 ("My mistress' eyes are nothing like the sun") (p. 482)

Students enjoy what seems to be Shakespeare's genial dismissal of metaphoric poetry in favor of reality, but of course Shakespeare uses comparable metaphors in his other writing. Although here he says (to take only the first line) that his "mistress' eyes are nothing like the sun," in Sonnet 18 he speaks of the sun as "the eye of heaven," and in Sonnet 49 he speaks of "that sun, thine eye." All this is only to say that Shakespeare can satirize himself as well as other poets, and that the house of poetry has many mansions, including not only the Petrarchan sonnet but also satires of Petrarchan sonnets, or, to put the matter slightly differently, poetry can include love poetry (this poem is an example) and satires of love poetry (this poem is an example).

In the Oxford Shakespeare's *Complete Sonnets and Poems* (2002), Colin Burrow makes the nice point that the first word of the sonnet, "My," is "given a proud emphasis to distinguish the poet's mistress from the majority of Elizabethan sonneteer's mistresses" (640). And the interest and pleasure of the poem as a whole develop from the speaker's comparisons and contrasts. Some critics have said that Sonnet 130 should not be taken too seriously. Stephen Booth, for example, in *Shakespeare's Sonnets* (1977), finds it "a winsome trifle," "easily distorted into a solemn critical statement about sonnet conventions." Booth agrees that the poem "does gently mock the thoughtless, mechanical application of the standard Petrarchan metaphors," but he adds "the speaker's clown act in taking hyperbolic metaphors literally appears to have no target and no aim" (452, 54). Helen Vendler, in *The Art of Shakespeare's Sonnets* (1997), offers in our view a more balanced, supple response (see 556–58). She observes about the final lines: "His beloved, the speaker ends by saying, is *as rare as* anyone else's, the more so since the other women are actively *mis*represented (*belied*) in their sycophants' verses" (557).

DANA GIOIA
Money (p. 483)

It's our guess that only two terms may be unfamiliar to most of your students, "rhino" (money), a term that is chiefly British and whose origin is unknown, and "Ginnie Maes," the plural of Ginnie Mae, the nickname of the Government National Mortgage Association.

The pleasure that we take in this poem is partly the pleasure one takes in catalogs—an old device, at least as old as the catalog of ships in Homer—and partly the pleasure of reveling in variety. Who would have thought there were so many terms for money?

But of course there is a further pleasure; even in this short playful poem there is a sort of plot, or at least a mild shift in the speaking tone of voice. The poem begins merely by enunciating nouns that mean money ("Money, the long green, / cash, stash, rhino, jack / or just plain dough"). That is, the first stanza simply gives us nouns; it simply names something, though in an entertaining way (notice the rhyme in the second line). In the second stanza we get verbs and sentences ("Chock it up, fork it over"). In the third stanza the voice gets more excited ("To be made of it! To have it / to burn!"), and in the fourth and fifth stanzas the voice becomes more meditative, reflective, philosophic ("It greases the palm, feathers a nest"). The final stanza continues the philosophizing, and rather wittily brings together the idea of filthy lucre ("You don't know where it's been") with the idea that money is nevertheless something we hold dearly ("you put it where your mouth is"), and it then picks up the idea of "mouth" by ending with the grand truth about money: "it talks."

Here are two additional wise remarks about money:

"Money is like muck; not good except it be spread" (Francis Bacon, *Essays*)

"You can be young without money but you can't be old without it" (Tennessee Williams, *Cat on a Hot Tin Roof*)

ROBERT FROST
The Hardship of Accounting (p. 484)

We don't want to put too much weight on this small bit of light verse, but we do think it is engaging, and we think it sneaks under the wire and counts as poetry, whereas "Thirty days hath September" is verse, not poetry. Our point is this: Anything that rhymes is verse (as opposed to prose); poetry may rhyme or it may not (blank verse, free verse), but—as a work of literature—poetry brings us into an imagined world, taking us up (at least for a moment) into its own world. "Thirty days" has the grand virtues of being true, being memorable, and being very useful, but it doesn't take us into a new world, it doesn't enlarge our horizons. Frost's little poem, in our view, does enlarge our minds.

"The Hardship of Accounting" begins with a dry, unpromising title, but almost immediately we hear an engaging voice. The avuncular speaker, commanding our attention, seems to be pointing his finger at us: "Never ask of money spent / Where the spender thinks it went." Probably most of us are ready to agree even now; we have been asked the question more than once, and we squirmed while thinking of an answer. The speaker now amplifies his position, explaining *why* we should not demand to know where the money went:

> Nobody was ever meant
> To remember or invent
> What he did with every cent.

The wonderful moment in the poem comes with the word "invent," where Frost mercifully tells us that we should not have to invent an explanation (as in this sad world we sometimes do) that accounts for the missing money. OK, OK, so I am a stamp collector (or an orchid breeder, or the buyer of a new pair of shoes, or whatever) and I spent a lot more on this stamp (or orchid, or shoes, or whatever) than I should have, but, well, do I have to tell you that, do I have to justify my extravagance? In our view, the little drama or confrontation that is conjured up by the line about remembering—or *inventing!*—the little glimpse of imagined domestic conflict, is what makes these lines not merely verse but poetry.

EDMUND WALLER
Song (Go, lovely rose) (p. 485)

Students may already have encountered Herrick's "To the Virgins, to Make Much of Time" in Chapter 4, and if they read the poem that immediately follows Waller's they will encounter Blake's "The Sick Rose." In combination, these offer plenty of opportunity to discuss symbolism—though we hasten to add that the real point of assigning these poems is not to talk about symbolism but to read some wonderful poems.

In line 2, "wastes" is perhaps more potent than many students at first find it, for the word implies not simply squandering but destroying as in, for example, "to lay waste a city," and "cancer wasted her body." The modern slang usage, "to kill," conveys the old meaning.

WILLIAM BLAKE
The Sick Rose (p. 486)

"The Sick Rose" has been much interpreted, usually along the lines given in the text. (See Reuben Brower, *The Fields of Light* [1962] and Rosenthal and Smith, *Exploring Poetry* [1955].) But E. D. Hirsch Jr., in *Innocence and Experience* (1975), argues that "The rose is being satirized by Blake as well as being infected by the worm. Part of the rose's sickness is her ignorance of her disease. Her ignorance is her spiritual disease because in accepting 'dark secret love' she has unknowingly repressed and perverted her instinctive life, her 'bed of crimson joy.'" Hirsch argues his point for a couple of pages.

We especially like Helen Vendler's comment on this poem in her introduction to *The Harvard Book of Contemporary American Poetry* (1985):

> The world of the poem is analogous to the existential world, but not identical with it. In a famous created world of Blake's, for instance, there is a rose doomed to mortal illness by the love of a flying worm who is invisible. We do not experience such a poem by moving it piecemeal into our world deciding what the rose "symbolizes" and what the worm "stands for." On the contrary, we must move ourselves in to its ambience, into a world in which a dismayed man can converse with his beloved rose and thrust upon her, in his anguished jealousy, diagnosis and fatal prognosis in one sentence.... After living in Blake's world for the space of eight lines, we return to our own world, haunted and accused.

Allen Ginsberg has "tuned" the poem (MGM Records FTS-3083).

LINDA PASTAN
Jump Cabling (p. 486)

The physical appearance of a poem on the page is always important. As anthologists, we are unhappy that we must add line numbers, and that a poem sometimes begins near the bottom of a right-hand page so that most of the poem is invisible at the start. With Pastan's poem, the appearance is especially important. True, if "Jump Cabling" is read aloud, something of the physical appearance can be conveyed (1) by pausing, to indicate the space between the two columns—the space between the two cars or the two people—and (2) by not pausing when one reads the final line; still, this is a poem that must be seen as well as heard.

We take the poem to be about what it explicitly says it is, but obviously the journey together will include bodily contact. The words *touched, intimate workings, underneath*—and we can include *lifted the hood*— add a strong sexual element.

In the past we have recommended Pastan's *PM/AM: New and Selected Poems* (1982), but it has now been superseded by *Carnival Evening: New and Selected Poems, 1968–1998* (1998).

ROBERT HERRICK
Upon Julia's Clothes (p. 488)

A good deal has been published on this tiny poem. Much of what has been published seems odd to us, for instance, an argument that in the first stanza Julia is clothed but in the second is imagined as nude ("free" is alleged to describe her body, not her clothes), or that the first stanza describes her from the front, the second from the rear.

One of our students, Stan Wylie, seems to us to have written a far better discussion of the poem. We print it in the book.

Other things, of course, might be said about this poem. For instance, Wylie says nothing about the changes in the meter and their contributions to the poem. Nor does he say anything about the sounds of any of the words (he might have commented on the long vowels in "sweetly flows" and shown how the effect would have been different if instead of "sweetly flows" Herrick had written "sweetly flits," and he might have commented on the spondees in "Then, then" and "O, how" and the almost-spondees in "Next, when," "each way free," and "that glittering"), but such topics might be material for another essay.

Probably few students will become devotees of Herrick's poetry, but for the rare soul who might, there is a helpful survey, Roger B. Rollin, *Robert Herrick* (1966), and a good collection of essays, *"Trust to Good Verses": Herrick Tercentenary Essays,* ed. Roger B. Rollin and J. Max Patrick (1978). The standard edition of the poetry has been edited by L. C. Martin (1956).

CHRISTINA ROSSETTI
In an Artist's Studio (p. 491)

The octave seems devoted to the "nameless girl," who appears again and again as "A queen" and as "A saint, an angel." Although her "loveliness" is mentioned, a reader may sense that the woman herself is stifled, for she is "hidden," seen in a "mirror," and characterized as "nameless." Furthermore, "every canvas means / The same one meaning, neither more nor less," a passage suggesting not only her limitations but also those of the painter. That is, the painter apparently keeps repeating himself, a trait that in the nineteenth century, as well as in our times, suggests some sort of dehumanization.

In the sestet further attention is paid to the artist, who (vampire-like?) "feeds upon her face." Still, the emphasis probably is on the woman, who is further dehumanized by being deprived of her own identity. Once she was "joyful" and full of "hope," but now, transformed by his imagination into works of art, she is not a creature of flesh and blood with her own identity but is an image that "fills his dream."

Having said all this, we want to mention that we have heard students and colleagues argue a very different reading: the artist relentlessly pursues his idea, nourished by the "loveliness" and the "kind eyes" of the woman. Still, we stubbornly think that this reading overestimates the nobility of the artist and underestimates the woman's loss of identity.

Feminist literary theory and criticism have renewed and enriched the study of Christina Rossetti's work. The major achievement of this new scholarship is *The Complete Poems of Christina Rossetti; A Variorum Edition*, 3 vols., ed. Rebecca W. Crump (1979–1990). There are two good biographies, written by Kathleen Jones (1991) and Jan Marsh (1995). The best critical studies are Dolores Rosenblum, *Christina Rossetti: The Poetry of Endurance* (1986), and Antony H. Harrison, *Christina Rossetti in Context* (1988). Also valuable: Rebecca W. Crump, *Christina Rossetti: A Reference Guide* (1976). You might also direct students to Virginia Woolf's essay "I Am Christina Rossetti," in *The Second Common Reader* (1932).

BILLY COLLINS
Sonnet (p. 502)

This poem will cause students no difficulty, and we think they will greatly enjoy it. Collins does introduce talk about the difficulties of writing a sonnet—he even dares to compare the poet's burden to Christ's via dolorosa—but the tone is easy-going from start to finish. In our view, the comparison of the fourteen stages in Christ's journey to the fourteen lines of the sonnet is a bit of self-mockery rather than blasphemy, though of course other readers may disagree with our easy assessment.

We especially like the ninth line, where the Petrarchan sonnet regularly takes a "turn"; Collins's language suggests that the "little ship" of line 3 has become a speeding car, and the rhetorical "turn" becomes physical: "But hang on here while we make the turn." In line 10 he assures us that "all will be resolved" (we are confident that indeed it will be, as it is in any successful sonnet), and by the end of the poem Laura invites Petrarch into bed. Presumably the "crazy medieval tights" are removed, along with the eccentric behavior, just as the "storm-tossed seas" of line 3 have been weathered, and we are in the comfortable, ordinary world where people "at last [go] to bed."

The amazing thing about this sonnet—often overlooked by students—is that it does *not* employ rhyme. Surely Collins is playing a little joke on his readers.

Collins is very popular—sales of his books have broken all records for poetry—and many critics and poets have spoken highly about his work.

> Billy Collins writes lovely poems—lovely in a way almost nobody's since Roethke's are. Limpid, gently and consistently startling, more serious than they seem, they describe all the worlds that are and were and some others besides.
> —John Updike

> Billy Collins is an American original—a metaphysical poet with a funny bone and a sly, questioning intelligence. He is an ironist of the void, and his poems—witty, playful and beautifully formed—bump up against the deepest human mysteries.
> —Edward Hirsch

> Billy Collins's poems are graceful, ironic, smart, and full of feeling. Sometimes wrongfully described as a defense against feeling, irony is, in fact, a deeply mixed feeling. In poems as good as Collins's, it is a mirror in which we see ourselves not by reflecting in lazy categories, but perhaps as experience sees us, and certainly as we imagine ourselves.
> —William Matthews

Source for these quotations: http://www.contemporarypoetry.com/dialect/biographies/collins.html.

Some critics, and some of his fellow-poets, however, find his style and approach unchallenging. Consider, for example, this passage from an essay on Collins by the poet-critic Jeredith Merrin, "Art Over Easy," *The Southern Review* 38:1 (Winter 2002):

> The big draw here, for both writers and readers, is that Collins makes it all look more than easy; a breeze. Collins might be dubbed, in fact, Our Laureate of Easiness.... The problem, though, with an esthetic of easiness—though it might at first seem the right homespun riposte to Continentally influenced modernist difficulty—is that it condescends to readers and tries to pass off as unhighfalutin' honesty what are in fact downright untruths. This is a writer who takes you for a walk on the mild side. What you already know on earth, he assures you, is all you need to know.

Students, especially in an introductory course, often find poetry "hard," and we think it is a good idea to raise this issue with them and explore it. And it helps if you can key the discussion to a specific literary work, like this poem (which we admire) by Collins. Is the poem easy? Is it too easy? What makes one poem easier than another? Should poetry be "hard," and what exactly does this term mean? What are some examples of "hard" poems in other chapters of this book? Is the hardness a matter of the language, or of the thoughts and feelings that the poet describes, or both?

Here are two more quotations to keep in mind as the discussion proceeds. Gerard Manley Hopkins says that poetry is "speech framed . . . to be heard for its own sake and interest even and above its interest of meaning." For his part, T. S. Eliot suggests that "poetry communicates before it is understood."

ROBERT BROWNING
My Last Duchess (p. 505)

Robert Langbaum has an old but still good analysis of "My Last Duchess" in *The Poetry of Experience* (1957). On this poem, see also Laurence Perrine, *PMLA* 74 (March 1959): 157–159. W. J. T. Mitchell, in "Representation," in *Critical Terms for Literary Study* (1969), ed. Frank Lentricchia and Thomas McLaughlin, discusses the poem at some length. One of his points: "Just as the duke seems to hypnotize the envoy, Browning seems to paralyze the reader's normal judgment by his virtuosic representation of villainy. His poem holds us in its grip, condemning in advance all our attempts to control it by interpretation. . . ."

It may be mentioned here that although every poem has a "voice," not every poem needs to be a Browningesque dramatic monologue giving the reader a strong sense of place and audience. No one would criticize Marvell's "To His Coy Mistress" on the grounds that the "lady" addressed in line 2 gives place (in at least some degree) to a larger audience—let us say, a general audience—when we get to "But at my back I always hear / Time's winged chariot hurrying near."

Biographies include William Irvine and Park Honan, *The Book, the Ring, and the Poet* (1974), and Clyde de L. Ryals, *The Life of Robert Browning: A Critical Biography* (1993). The best critical discussion of "My Last Duchess" is still, we think, the one by Robert Langbaum. Though there are many books and articles on Browning, we have found few that have proven rewarding to us, and students likely will find even these hard to benefit from. Of the recent studies, the most helpful are Herbert F. Tucker, *Browning's Beginnings: The Art of Disclosure* (1980), and Loy Martin, *Browning's Dramatic Monologues and the Post-Romantic Subject* (1985). When you teach Browning, be sure to read the poems aloud in class—it would not hurt if you practiced beforehand, in order to sense where the emphasis and pacing fall. The students need to hear the sharp, subtle, self-revealing turns of voice in these poems.

E. E. CUMMINGS
anyone lived in a pretty how town (p. 507)

It can be useful to ask students to put into the usual order (so far as one can) the words of the first two stanzas and then to ask students why Cummings's version is more effective. Here are a few rough glosses: line 4: "danced his did" = lived intensely (versus the "someones" who in line 18 "did their dance," that is, unenthusiastically went through motions that might have been ecstatic); line 7: "they sowed their isn't they reaped their same" gives us the little-minded or small-minded who, unlike "anyone," are unloving and therefore receiving nothing; line 8: "sun moon stars rain" = day after day; line 10: "down they forgot as up they grew" implies a mental diminution that accompanies growing up; line 17: "someones," that is, adults, people who think they are somebody; line 25: "anyone died," that is, the child matured and stopped loving (and became dead as the other adults). The last two stanzas imply that although children grow into "Women and men" (line 33), the seasons continue the same. (This reading is heavily indebted to R. C. Walsh, *Explicator* 22 no. 9 [May 1964], Item 72. For a more complicated reading, see D. L. Clark, *Lyric Resonance* (1972), pp. 187–194.)

Like Robert Frost, E. E. Cummings is frequently read in high school English courses, and his work gets a lively response from students in our introductory literature and composition courses. From time to time, in fact, we find a student who owns the *Complete Poems, 1904–62,* ed. George L. Firmage (1991) and who may even have purchased the standard biography, written by Richard S. Kennedy (1979; rpt. 1994). Still valuable is Norman Friedman, *E. E. Cummings: The Art of the Poetry* (1960). But you might prefer to direct students to a more recent introduction: Richard S. Kennedy, *E. E. Cummings Revisited* (1994).

SYLVIA PLATH
Daddy (p. 509)

C. B. Cox and A. R. Jones point out, in *Critical Quarterly* 6 (Summer 1964): 107–122, that literature has always been interested in perverse states of mind (Greek and Roman interest in the irrational; Elizabethan interest in melancholy, jealousy, madness, etc., and Browning's dramatic monologues). The "fine frenzy" of the poet himself (in the words of Shakespeare's Theseus), once associated with inspiration and even divinity, in the twentieth century links the poet with the psychotic personality. And apparently a sensitive (poetic) mind can make only a deranged response in a deranged world. Plath's "Daddy" begins with simple repetitions that evoke the world of the nursery rhyme (and yet also of the witches in *Macbeth*, who say, "I'll do, I'll do, and I'll do"). The opening line also connects with the suggestion of the marriage service ("And I said I do") in line 67. The speaker sees herself as tormented yet also as desiring the pain inflicted by her father/love ("Every woman adores a Fascist"). She recognizes that by accepting the need for love she exposes herself to violence. The speaker's identification of herself with Jews and the evocation of "Dachau, Auschwitz, Belsen" suggest some identity between the heroine's tortured mind and the age's. Death, Cox and Jones go on to say, is the only release from a world that denies love and life. The "Daddy" of the poem is father, Germany, fatherland, and—life itself, which surrounds the speaker and which the speaker rejects.

In *Commentary* (July 1974 and October 1974), there is an exchange of letters on the appropriateness of Plath's use of Nazi imagery in a poem about her father. Roger Hoffman, in the July issue, argues that the imagery is valid because in a child's mind an authoritarian father is fearsome. Irving Howe, in October (pp. 9–12), replies that this argument is inadequate ground "for invoking the father as a Nazi." The speaker of the poem is not a child, Howe says, but "the grown-up writer, Sylvia Plath." He goes on: the "unwarranted fusion of child's response and grown-ups' references makes for either melodrama or self-pity." Howe also rejects Carole Stone's argument (July) that the images are acceptable because "one individual's psyche [can] approximate the suffering of a people." Howe replies that the victims of the concentration camps didn't merely "suffer"; they were methodically destroyed. He questions the appropriateness of using images of the camps to evoke personal traumas. There is, he says, a lack of "congruence" between the object and the image, "a failure in judgement."

Of the many studies of Plath's life and work, we recommend two: Anne Stevenson, *Bitter Fame: A Life of Sylvia Plath* (1989), and Jacqueline Rose, *The Haunting of Sylvia Plath* (1992). Janet Malcolm, *The Silent Woman: Sylvia Plath & Ted Hughes* (1994), which examines Plath, Hughes, and the biographers who have written about them, is absorbing from beginning to end. We have sometimes supervised students working on a topic or theme in Plath's *Collected Poems,* ed. Ted Hughes (1981; rpt. 1992). In addition, they can now turn to Hughes's own poems about Plath: *Birthday Letters* (1998).

A "Voices and Visions" videocassette of Sylvia Plath is available from Longman Publishers.

Topic for Critical Thinking and Writing

The speaker expresses her hatred for her father by identifying him with the Nazis, herself with the Jews. Is it irresponsible for a poet to compare her sense of torment with that of Jews who were gassed in Dachau, Auschwitz, and Belsen?

LOUISE ERDRICH
Indian Boarding School: The Runaways (p. 511)

The speaker is one of the "runaways." From the title and the first two lines ("Home's the place we head for in our sleep / Boxcars stumbling north in dreams") we know that the speaker dreams of running away from school and probably *has* run away, more than once. Calling the railway lines "old lacerations that we love" announces at once what the rest of the poem recalls: the runaways, having been captured by the sheriff (line 12) and taken back to school, are physically punished. The image of punishment is repeated in

"Riding scars" (line 7), "it hurts / to be here" (lines 10–11), and the concluding lines of the first stanza:

> The highway doesn't rock, it only hums
> like a wing of long insults. The worn-down welts
> of ancient punishment lead back and forth.

The "ancient punishment" refers to the punishment of the runaways but it may also recall the punishment meted out by whites who laid down the railroad tracks as they gradually subdued the Native Americans. "Home" is not described in the poem, but making "Home's" the first syllable, rather than "Home is," accentuates it.

Erdrich's books of poetry include *Jacklight* (1984) and *Baptism of Fire* (1989). Of her fictional works, we still value her first one, *Love Medicine* (1984), the most, though her story collection *Tales of Burning Love* (1996) is also well worth reading. *Conversations with Louise Erdrich and Michael Dorris,* ed. Nancy Feyl Chavkin and Allan Chavkin (1994), is an illuminating source for students. There is not much critical commentary on Erdrich's writing, except for reviews and a few essays in journals. Students can turn to Louis Owens, *Other Destinies: The American Indian Novel* (1992), and Marya Mae Ryan, *Gender and Community: Womanist and Feminist Perspectives in the Fiction of Toni Morrison, Amy Tan, Sandra Cisneros, and Louise Erdrich* (1995). But neither offers much help on Erdrich's poetry.

Topic for Critical Thinking and Writing

In a paragraph, describe a place you "head for in [your] sleep." Or, describe "shameful work" that you were given, which you did not deserve, or did. (If you are lucky, you can use a color as Erdrich uses green as "the color you would think shame was" in lines 17–18.)

ETHERIDGE KNIGHT
For Malcolm, a Year After (p. 513)

We like to remind students that careful reading is the result of being attentive—of paying attention to the meanings, movements, and rhythms of the words on the page. And we often add that everything in a poem is worth paying attention to, from the title to the final line.

Knight's poem is a good case in point, for its interest begins with the title. The title states the occasion, the purpose: this poem is written for Malcolm, for the African-American leader assassinated in 1965. But more than that: it is a poem written a year after the event, which leads the reader to believe that this poem will be more reflective, more deliberative, than a poem that had been written in the immediate aftermath of Malcolm's killing. Possibly, the reader might assume, it will not be a bitter or angry poem, or, if it is in part, that those feelings will be blended with others that are more measured, more controlled.

The title also raises questions: Has the speaker written about Malcolm before, making this new poem another installment in his exploration of Malcolm's life and death? Or has he waited until now to write, and if so, what kind of special burden or opportunity becomes available to him, having waited as he has for a year to pass?

Stanzas 1 and 2 both begin with a verb about art and writing—"compose." The poem as a whole is both about Malcolm and, as much or more, about the act of writing a poem about him. At first hearing, the opening line might seem directed to the reader—"this is your task to perform; do it this way." But quickly it is made clear that the speaker is addressing himself: "this is what you should do." The poem is in a sense a prelude to a poem for Malcolm.

Notice, too, that the title says "For Malcolm," while the first line says "for Red," Malcolm's nickname during his earlier years as a criminal and prisoner. A small-seeming detail, perhaps, but you might ask the students what are the differences between the two names, and why Knight makes the shift from one to another that he does.

The verbs in the poem are noteworthy in, for example, the lines:

Or they might boil and break the dam.
Or they might boil and overflow
And drench me, drown me, drive me mad.

Here, Knight may be echoing some well-known lines from one of John Donne's Holy Sonnets:

BATTER my heart, three person'd God; for, you
As yet but knocke, breathe, breathe, shine, and seeke to mend;
That I may rise, and stand, o'erthrow mee, and bend
Your force, to breake, blowe, burn and make me new.

See also Shakespeare's Sonnet XV:

When I consider every thing that grows
Holds in perfection but a little moment,
That this huge stage presenteth nought but shows
Whereon the stars in secret influence comment;
When I perceive that men as plants increase,
Cheered and check'd e'en by the self-same sky,
Vaunt in their youthful sap, at height decrease,
And wear their brave state out of memory;
Then the conceit of this inconstant stay
Sets you most rich in youth before my sight,
Where wasteful Time debateth with Decay,
To change your day of youth to sullied night;
And, all in war with Time for love of you,
As he takes from you, I engraft you new.

Knight is, in a sense, making the opposite claim from Shakespeare. Shakespeare's writing will keep alive the beloved, fighting against the decay that time causes, whereas Knight states that the verse he (or anyone else) will compose for Malcolm "will die." Poems die, just as all men die. "But not the memory of him," Knight affirms.

These final lines, however, are a bit of a puzzle. Everything will pass away, but not the "memory" of Malcolm X. No, that's not quite right: it is not the memory, but the "anger" that will endure. The memory is the anger. But the tone of the final lines does not sound angry; the tone is more that of resignation, almost of defeat. It is conceivable that the use of the term "anger" could carry a potent charge, akin to Langston Hughes's final word in his poem "Dream Deferred." But the force and fear and threat that Hughes puts into the tone is not there (not for us at any rate) in Knight's poem. You might ask the students how they "hear" these final lines, and how they would characterize the tone.

Of course the key turn in the poem that Knight intends is that the "anger" referred to in the final line reaches back to the "angry words" described in the first stanza: Knight, ultimately, concludes that no poem for Malcolm is possible: no poem could hope to channel and contain the anger felt on the day of his death and that lingers a year after.

Because Knight himself spent a number of years in prison and in rehab programs, it is tempting to associate the fact of imprisonment in his life, and the many images of and references to prison in his poetry, to the thrust of this poem, which is about trying to give a kind of imprisoning form to angry feelings. But this formal prison will not work, the speaker suggests: the feelings are too strong to be held in check, kept back; they demand release, they break free and always will.

Knight is less familiar to contemporary readers than are, for example, Langston Hughes and Gwendolyn Brooks, but in the 1960s and 1970s he was a powerful voice and influence. "His work was hailed by black writers and critics as another excellent example of the powerful truth of blackness in art," comments Shirley Lumpkin in *The Dictionary of Literary Biography, Volume 41: Afro-American Poets Since 1955* (1985). "His work became important in Afro-American poetry and poetics and in the strain of Anglo-American poetry descended from Walt Whitman."

Much of Knight's prison poetry, according to Patricia Liggins Hill in "The Violent Space: The Function of the New Black Aesthetic in Etheridge Knight's Prison Poetry," *Black American Literature Forum* 14:3 (Autumn 1980), 115–121, "focuses on imprisonment as a form of contemporary enslavement and looks for ways in which one can be free despite incarceration." And, again, this impulse toward freedom is implied in "For Malcolm, a Year After," when the speaker contends that no verse form or structure can control "the anger of that day."

For more on Knight, we recommend "Etheridge Knight—Portrait," a special feature in the journal of *Callaloo* 19:4 (1996).

Included in this issue is a good essay by Jean Anaporte-Easton, "Etheridge Knight, Poet and Prisoner: An Introduction." She notes, in a passage that might spur students to read more of this poet's disturbing work:

Much of Knight's finished writing seems to have taken place while he was in prison or during stays in jail or rehabilitation centers. Furthermore, it was in prison that he first defined himself as a poet. From the poems available to us now, over half of those Knight published, and the majority of his best poems, were written by 1973. He had been out of prison only five years and had spent at least a year of that time in jail and drug and alcohol rehab programs. Just as a prison with ribbon wire and chain-link fences might be easier to deal with than the invisible prison of cultural assumptions and values, so might it be easier to confront and cope with the finite emptiness of solitary confinement than an infinite interior emptiness. (pp. 941–942)

BASHO
An Old Pond (p. 515)

Basho's poem has engendered an enormous body of commentary in Japanese and more than enough in English. It is not unusual to find someone arguing that the "ancient pond" is the enduring spiritual world, and the frog that jumps in is the material, transient world; or the ancient pond is the body of traditional literature (today we would say the canon), and the frog is the new writer. And so on.

Here is the poem (originally published in 1686) in transliterated Japanese, with a literal English translation next to it:

Furu ike ya	old pond place
Kawazu tobikomu	frog jumps
Mizu no oto	water's sound

The *ya* in the first line, a suffix often added to a noun, is used to denote a place. Thus, the word for *fish* is *sakana*, but a fish store is *sakanaya*. In the third line, *no* is a possessive, something like our *'s*, which turns (for instance) water into *water's* (here, *the water's sound,* or *the sound of water*).

Next, six versions we have collected. One difficulty, it will immediately be recognized, is that the original has more syllables than a close translation will have. *Frog* is one syllable, but the Japanese *kawazu* is three; similarly, *jumps* is one syllable, but *tobikomu* is four. Translators have tended to pad their poems by adding an *ah* here or there.

You may want to write two or more of these on the board and invite students to discuss the differences.

1. The old pond, ah!
   A frog jumps in:
   The water's sound.

2. There, in the old pond—
   A frog has just jumped in
   With a splash of water.

3. The ancient pond—
   A frog jumps in,
   The sound of water.

4. A frog
   Jumping into the ancient pond.
   Splash.

5. Ah, the ancient pond.
   A frog makes the plunge.
   The sound of water.

6. An old pond.
   A frog jumps in—
   Plop!

The translator of this last version justifies *plop*—which might seem too crude or whimsical—on the grounds that it is onomatopoeic, and that the Japanese *oto* (= sound) is closer to *plop* than are such words as *splash* or *sound*.

The wittiest translation that we have come across is by D. J. Enright, in *Old Men and Comets* (1994). It preserves the 5-7-5 count:

An ancient bayou
A batrachian flops in—
Sound of H$_2$O.

And, for good measure, here are two responses to Basho, by the Zen priest Sengai (1750–1837):

1. An old pond;
   Basho jumps in,
   The sound of water!

2. If there were a pond around here
   I would jump in
   And let him hear the splash.

The haiku in our text, along with the editorial comment, is enough to give students an idea of the form and to allow them to write their own haiku. We have found that most students enjoy—because they can achieve at least a decent degree of success—writing haiku.

For collections of haiku, with substantial commentaries, see Harold G. Henderson, *An Introduction to Haiku* (1958), and Kenneth Yasuda, *The Japanese Haiku* (1957). For a shorter but still moderately detailed history of the form, see the article on haiku in *The Kodansha Encyclopedia of Japan* (1983). We summarize the last part of the Kodansha article, "On Writing Haiku in English." As you will see in a moment, the author takes us through several versions of a haiku. You may want to write the first version on the board, discuss it, and then move on to the second, and so on.

The author begins by saying what a haiku does: "When a haiku is successful, it endows our lives with freshness and new wonder and reveals the charm and profundity of all truly simple things." Almost any subject is possible, from the stars on a stormy night to a heron in the evening breeze. He gives as an example (in the traditional 5-7-5 syllable pattern) a roadside encounter:

Meeting on the road,
we chat leisurely awhile
and go on our ways.

"The problem with this verse," he says, "is that it tells us something but evokes nothing. It is flat and one-dimensional. What is needed, among other things, is a sharper 'cutting' (usually indicated by a colon or dash) after either the first or the second line," thus:

> A roadside meeting:
> we chat leisurely awhile
> and go on our ways.

But there still is not enough of a cutting here; there is no imaginative distance between the two elements. Another try:

> A baby's crying:
> we chat leisurely awhile
> and go on our ways.

Here, however, the distance between the two parts is too great. One would have to be deaf or cruel to chat while a baby cries. The two images don't somehow connect. The next version:

> A peaceful country:
> we chat leisurely awhile
> and go on our ways.

Not bad; the peaceful country provides a grand background for this pleasant encounter between two friendly people; or, to put it the other way around, the encounter between the two people "crystallizes the abstract notion of a peaceful country."

The two parts of the poem, then, must be remote to a degree and yet must somehow connect, and each must enhance the other. Further, in the traditional Japanese haiku there must be a seasonal theme. When does a leisurely chat occur? Probably not in winter (too cold to stand chatting); nor does spring (the author says) seem right for this sort of talk, since spring is the time for "the fresh encounters of the young." Autumn? No, "Autumn is too suggestive of reflective maturity and eventual partings." Only summer is right:

> Another hot day
> we chat leisurely awhile
> and go on our ways.

But the author of the article says the word "leisurely" is wrong here; one wouldn't chat in a leisurely fashion on a hot day. A summer chat is characterized not by leisureliness but by "involuntary lethargy." The final version:

> Another hot day:
> yawning "good-bye" and "take care"
> we go on our ways.

The author's final judgment of this work: "Not a haiku masterpiece, but not discreditable for a first try."

THOMAS HARDY
Neutral Tones (p. 516)

Brooks, Purser, and Warren, in *An Approach to Literature*, astutely point out that the first stanza is conversational and somewhat slow, for the speaker is trying to recollect all of the details. Notice especially the dash at the start of the fourth line, making the line itself seem to be an afterthought. In contrast, the last stanza is firm, emphasized by alliteration ("lessons . . . lover," "wrings with wrong").

The gray leaves of the last line of the first stanza recur in the last line of the last stanza, but now there is no sense of an afterthought; rather, each item (face, sun, tree, leaves) seems firmly in place. Still, one does not want to minimize the effect of lifelessness—the white sun, the "starving sod," the gray leaves (doubtless there is a pun on "ash"), the numbed looks, and the dull words exchanged. Hardy tells us almost nothing about the conversation, and nothing at all about why this love failed, but of course that is part of the point. The point is the lifelessness of the encounter, and (in the end) of subsequent encounters with others. No explanation for the decay is given, unless in "the God-curst sun" we hear a suggestion that God is, for some unstated reason, hostile.

By the way, line 8 puzzles many readers. We paraphrase it thus: "[We exchanged a few words] about which of the two of us lost the more [i.e., suffered the more greatly from] our love affair."

Samuel Hynes, in *The Pattern of Hardy's Poetry* (1961), identifies "Neutral Tones" as a poem written in Hardy's "most characteristic style: the plain but not quite colloquial language, the hard, particular, colorless images, the slightly odd stanza-form, the dramatic handling of the occasion, the refusal to resolve the issue" (136). There are a number of good studies of Hardy's poetry, including James Richardson, Jr., *Thomas Hardy: The Poetry of Necessity* (1977); Dennis Taylor, *Hardy's Poetry, 1860–1928* (1981); and William E. Buckler, *The Poetry of Thomas Hardy: A Study in Art and Ideas* (1983). But for "Neutral Tones" and other poems akin to it in the Hardy canon, we continue to find stimulating a cogent comment made long ago by James Granville Southworth in *The Poetry of Thomas Hardy* (1947):

> [Hardy] saw that, in marriages of less than true minds, those moments are more frequent than one willingly admits, when following the marital act a man does not have enough emotional reserve to sustain the projection of his beloved as he had done before. At such a time man sees—or thinks he sees—the woman with his mind and not with his heart, and the sight is not pleasant. (47)

WILLIAM BUTLER YEATS
Sailing to Byzantium (p. 517)

It is worth showing students a few images from Byzantium, especially mosaics since Yeats speaks of "the gold mosaic of a wall" (line 18). In these mosaics showing holy figures, the background does not depict a landscape or even a heaven with clouds; rather, the background is uniformly gold, in order to symbolize the uniform, unchanging nature of God. And the gold itself of course symbolizes preciousness. The standard college histories of the survey of art, such as H.W. Janson's *History of Art* (2001), Marilyn Stokstad's *Art History* (1999), or Honour and Flemings's *The Visual Arts* (1999), include a few appropriate reproductions. We suggest that the day before you teach the poem you ask your students if any of them are taking a survey course in art, and if some are, ask them to bring the text to class. This way you can have several books circulating among students, as opposed to a single copy that you might yourself bring. But you may also want to bring a copy of *The Glory of Byzantium* (1997), the catalog of a great exhibition that was held at the Metropolitan Museum of Art. Most of the objects illustrated in this catalog of course are not mosaics, but even smaller works such as ivories and the covers of Bibles will convey a good idea of Byzantine art.

Byzantium, originally a Greek trading station, was rebuilt by Constantine, who in 330 renamed it Constantinople and dedicated it to the Christian God. The most important city of the Roman empire in the East, Constantinople became the cultural center of the Christianized Roman world. But in the early Renaissance, Byzantine art—because of its lack of interest in naturalism—fell into disrepute: Byzantine figures, swathed in heavy drapery, reveal almost nothing of the body (except for representations of Christ on the cross), and their postures are usually static. An important medium, mosaic—lightweight squares of colored glass set into cement—hardly lends itself to naturalism. In short, to the unsympathetic eye, Byzantine figures seem lifeless, unable to move or to feel. But for the aging Yeats (he wrote the poem when he was sixty-one), seeking an alternative for a failing body, Byzantine art, with its other-worldly images, provided intimations of immortality. He had seen Byzantine mosaics in Ravenna in 1907, but not until his visit to Palermo in 1924 did Byzantine culture come to have great meaning for him.

The poem: Students will not have much difficulty in drawing up lists of contrasts between (to put it bluntly) youth and age, transience and permanence, the body and the mind, the flesh and the soul. Examples:

"birds in the trees"	a bird of "hammered gold" on "a golden bough"
"fish, flesh, or fowl"	"sages standing in God's holy fire"
"those dying generations"	"once out of nature"
"whatever is begotten, born, and dies"	"monuments of unaging intellect"
"that sensual music"	"singing-masters of my soul"

"dying animal" "artifice of eternity"
"the young in one another's arms" "an aged man"
"That is no country" "Byzantium"

That is, Yeats establishes a contrast between, on the one hand, Ireland (with its "salmon falls," line 3), which stands for the natural world, the cycle of birth and death, and, on the other hand, Byzantium, which stands for permanence.

The first stanza is largely devoted to presenting a memorable image of the natural world, the world of youth and of fertility. This world will be disparaged, but Yeats also lets us see its appeal, as in "The young in one another's arms, birds in the trees," "The salmon falls, the mackerel-crowded seas." But even as he shows us the attractive, sensuous world, he reminds us of its transience: "birds in the trees / —Those dying generations at their song. . . ." And the stanza ends with a sharp put-down:

Caught in that sensual music all neglect
Monuments of unaging intellect.

The second stanza, devoted to the intellectual and spiritual life, contrasts the physical world—now concisely symbolized as "an aged man," who is a mere "tattered coat upon a stick" (a scarecrow)—with the "monuments" that were introduced at the end of the first stanza. We are now told that the aged man, or, more precisely, his "soul," must "sing" (a contrast with the song of the dying birds of the first stanza), and that the soul learns to sing by "studying / Monuments of its own magnificence." And, the speaker tells us, this is why he has come to "the holy city of Byzantium." The poet was, so to speak, trying to prepare himself for his final examination. In *A New Commentary on the Poems of W. B. Yeats* (1984), A. Norman Jeffares quotes (p. 213) a statement Yeats composed in 1931 for a broadcast of his poems:

Now I am trying to write about the state of my soul, for it is right for an old man to make his soul, and some of my thoughts upon that subject I have put into a poem called "Sailing to Byzantium." When Irishmen were illuminating the Book of Kells [in the eighth century] and making the jewelled croziers in the National Museum, Byzantium was the centre of European civilisation and the source of its spiritual philosophy, so I symbolise the search for the spiritual life by a journey to that city.

The third stanza introduces art and associates it with the wisdom that the soul acquires. Notice, however, that the mosaic is introduced merely as a comparison: the sages are "standing in God's holy fire / *As* in the gold mosaic of a wall."

The fourth stanza combines the permanence of art (the golden bird on a golden bough) with the transient stuff of "nature" (line 25), which is in fact the subject of most art. And whereas the first stanza showed "Fish, flesh, or fowl" caught up in the richness of the present, this final stanza takes us into a fuller world, a world of what is "past, or passing, or to come." Are we wrong in thinking that this poem, about human weakness, human blindness, also celebrates human achievements—and that one of these achievements is the poem itself?

Bibliographic note: The literature on this poem is enormous. A classic piece is Elder Olson's essay in *University Review* 8 (Spring 1942): 209–219, reprinted in *The Permanence of Yeats* (1971), ed. James Hall and Martin Steinman. Less readable, but highly impressive, are Curtis Bradford's study of Yeats's interest in Byzantium and of the manuscripts, in *PMLA* 75 (1960): 110–125, reprinted in *Yeats* (1963), ed. John Unterecker, and Jon Stallworthy's discussion of the manuscripts in *Between the Lines* (1963). For a hostile discussion of the poem see Yvor Winters, *Forms of Discovery* (1967).

For further background and context, students might consult "The Byzantine Gallery of Art," an exhibition on the Internet sponsored by the Royal Ontario Museum: <http:/www.rom.on.ca/galleries/byzantine/>.

JAMES WRIGHT

Lying in a Hammock at William Duffy's Farm in Pine Island, Minnesota (p. 519)

It seems to us that the title is somewhat paradoxical, in its implication of utter relaxation and apartness—lying *in* a hammock, *at* someone's farm, *on* an island—and (on the other hand) the almost pedantic or fussy specification of the locale. And we find the rest of the poem paradoxical too.

The speaker's eye ranges. He takes in the view above (a natural starting place for someone lying in a hammock), then looks "Down the ravine," then "to my right," and then, at the end, up again ("I lean back"), when he observes the chicken hawk. In a sense he ends where he began, but meanwhile he has explored (or at least surveyed) a good deal. He has, from his sleep-like condition in the hammock, begun by seeing a bronze-colored butterfly "Asleep," then has heard the distant cowbells, and has seen "The droppings of last year's horses" (so we get some extension into time as well as into space), and then glances again at the skies. This exploration—all from the hammock—is marked by keen yet imaginative observations.

Let's go back a moment, to the first perception, the "bronze butterfly / Asleep." The poet is describing the color, but the effect is paradoxical, giving the reader a fragile insect made of an enduring material. From perceptions of colors ("bronze," "black," "green") we go to aural perceptions ("the cowbells follow one another") and then back to visual perceptions (the horse droppings, now "golden stones"). In all of this beauty there is a keen sense of isolation—the cows and horses are not present, and even the chicken hawk is looking for home. Now, "as the evening darkens," the speaker has an epiphany, uttered in the final line.

The final line probably comes to the reader as a shock, and perhaps the reader is uncertain about how to take it. Is the speaker kidding? Or is he saying, in dead seriousness, all creatures except me seem to have their place in a marvelously beautiful, peaceful nature, whereas I am not even in my own home? Our own impression is that, whatever he says, *we* feel that he has not wasted his life, since he has so interestingly recorded his perceptions.

For further study of Wright, see *Collected Prose,* ed. Anne Wright (1983), and *Above the River: The Complete Poems,* with an introduction by Donald Hall (1990). The best critical discussions can be found in *The Pure Clear Word: Essays on the Poetry of James Wright,* ed. Dave Smith (1982). Also recommended: Kevin Stein, *James Wright: The Poetry of a Grown Man* (1989), and Andrew Elkins, *The Poetry of James Wright* (1991).

ANONYMOUS
Deep River (p. 520)

The introductory note in the text mentions that one of the chief themes is the desire for release, and that this theme is often set forth with imagery from the Hebrew Bible, but some additional points should be mentioned. Most of what follows here is derived from Albert J. Raboteau, *Slave Religion* (1978).

Although the passages about release undoubtedly refer to the release from slavery, the songs should not be taken only as disguised statements about secular life. Many slaves—like at least some of their masters—believed that the Bible was the book of the acts of God, which is to say that they "believed that the supernatural continually impinged on the natural, that divine action constantly took place within the lives of men, in the past, present, and future" (Raboteau, p. 250).

Raboteau makes a second very important point:

> Identification with the children of Israel was, of course, a significant theme for white Americans, too. From the beginnings of colonization, white Christians had identified the journey across the Atlantic to the New World as the exodus of a new Israel from the bondage of Europe into the promised land of milk and honey. For the black Christian, as Vincent Harding has observed [in *The Religious Situation* (1968), ed. Donald R. Cutter], the imagery was reversed: the Middle Passage had brought his people to Egypt land, where they suffered bondage under Pharaoh. White Christians saw themselves as a new Israel; slaves identified themselves as the old. (pp. 250–251)

Instructors who have time for some additional reading may wish to consult—for a survey of scholarship on the topic—John White, "Veiled Testimony: Negro Spirituals and the Slave Experience," in *Journal of American Studies* 17 (1983): 251–263. White is especially concerned with adjudicating between those who see spirituals (of the type that we reprint) as highly revolutionary and, on the other hand, those who see the songs as in effect serving the cause of the masters, since the songs seem to suggest that suffering in this world is transient and that God will later reward the sufferers. (As an example of this second view, White quotes E. Franklin Frazier, an African-American scholar who in *The Negro Church in America* [1964] rejected "the efforts of Negro intellectuals . . . encouraged by white radicals, to invest the spirituals with a revolutionary meaning.")

Other recommended works (in addition to Raboteau and White): John Lovell, *Black Song: The Forge and the Flame* (1972); James H. Cone, *The Spirituals and the Blues* (1972); and Lawrence Levine, *Black Culture and Black Consciousness* (1977).

Obviously this song (like all oral literature) really ought to be heard, not simply read. Many excellent recordings are available, but if you are lucky you may find a student who will give a live performance in class.

WILLIAM CARLOS WILLIAMS
The Red Wheelbarrow (p. 521)

Roy Harvey Pearce, in *The Continuity of American Poetry* (1961), (p. 339), regards William Carlos Williams's "The Red Wheelbarrow" as sentimental (but of some value) and says that what depends is the poet: "He assures himself that he is what he is by virtue of his power to collocate such objects into sharply annotated images like these." Charles Altieri, in *PMLA* 91 (1976): 111, suggests that although the items are stripped of associations, "No poem in English is more metonymic. Three objects evoke a mode of life in the sparsest, most succinct manner possible. The poverty of detail, like that in the rural paintings of Andrew Wyeth, at once intensifies the starkness of rural life and exemplifies it." Altieri also points out that in each of the last three stanzas, the first line "depends" on the second, for the word that ends each first line is often a noun ("wheel," "rain," "white"), but in the poem turns out to be an adjective. Thus the reader's mind "is made to hover over details until its waiting is rewarded, not only within the stanza, but also as each independent stanza emerges to fill out this waiting and to move us beyond details to a complex sense of a total life contained in these objects." John Hollander (*Vision and Resonance* [1975], p. 111) suggests that cutting "wheelbarrow" and "rainwater" (with no hyphens to indicate that "rain" and "wheel" are parts of the compounds) helps to convey what the poem is about: seeing the constituents of things in the freshness of light after rain.

Two older studies remain useful: Linda Wagner, *The Poems of William Carlos Williams* (1964), and James E. Breslin, *William Carlos Williams: An American Artist* (1970). Paul Mariani's biography, *William Carlos Williams: A New World Naked* (1981), is detailed and definitive, but for students, Reed Whittemore's *William Carlos Williams: Poet from Jersey* (1975) might be a better place to start.

A "Voices and Visions" videocassette of William Carlos Williams is available from Longman Publishers.

WALT WHITMAN
A Noiseless Patient Spider (p. 522)

Whitman's "A Noiseless Patient Spider" is in free verse, though in fact the poem is not terribly "free"; each stanza has five lines, helping to establish the similitude of spider and soul, and the first line of each stanza is relatively short, the other lines being longer, helping to establish the idea of "venturing, throwing." The near-rhyme at the end helps to tie up the poem, as though finally the bridge is at least tentatively "form'd," the "anchor" holding, but the fact is that the action is not yet complete, the soul is not yet anchored. A discussion of this poem will also necessarily get into Whitman's use of figurative language. Implicitly, the speaker's soul is a noiseless, patient spider, "ceaselessly musing, ceaselessly venturing," building a "bridge" in the vastness (i.e., uniting the present with eternity—or are the filaments that the soul flings poems that unite mankind?).

In addition to the biographies by Gay Wilson Allen (1967) and Justin Kaplan (1980), we admire Paul Zweig's sensitively written study, *Walt Whitman: The Making of the Poet* (1984). A brisk, informative overview of the period can be found in David S. Reynolds, *Walt Whitman's America: A Cultural Biography* (1995). Harold Bloom's chapter, "Walt Whitman as Center of the American Canon," in his book, *The Western Canon* (1994), is also stimulating, though students unfamiliar with the culture and canon wars may lack the context to perceive Bloom's polemical aims here.

Another excellent resource is *Walt Whitman: An Encyclopedia,* J. R. LeMaster and Donald D. Kummings (1998).

Topics for Critical Thinking and Writing

1. In about 250 words describe some animal, plant, or object that can be taken as a symbol of some aspect of your personality or experience.
2. The text gives Whitman's final version (1871) of "A Noiseless Patient Spider." Here is Whitman's draft, written some ten years earlier. You may want to distribute this version and ask students to compare the two poems and evaluate them.

The Soul, Reaching, Throwing Out for Love

The soul, reaching, throwing out for love,
As the spider, from some little promontory, throwing out filament after
    filament, tirelessly out of itself, that one at least may catch and form
    a link, a bridge, a connection
O I saw one passing along, saying hardly a word—yet full of love I
    detected him, by certain signs
O eyes wishfully turning! O silent eyes!
For then I thought of you o'er the world,

> O latent oceans, fathomless oceans of love!
> O waiting oceans of love! yearning and fervid! and of you sweet souls
>   perhaps in the future delicious and long:
> But Death, unknown on the earth—ungiven, dark here, unspoken, never
>   born:
> You fathomless latent souls of love—you pent and unknown oceans of love!

A "Voices and Visions" videocassette of Walt Whitman is available from Longman Publishers.

THOMAS HARDY
The Photograph (p. 522)

As we see it, the plot or drama—the story, so to speak—in this poem takes place in the speaker's mind. The poem begins with a brief but relatively detailed and therefore painful description of the fire consuming the photograph, or rather, to take the words of the poem, not so much a photograph, a mere piece of paper with an image on it, but the very thing that is represented, "the delicate bosom's defenceless round" (line 5), "her breasts, and mouth, and hair" (10).

The effect on the speaker is far greater than he had anticipated it would be. He cries out and averts his eyes (line 6), and yet he is also "compelled to heed" and so he "again looked furtivewise" (line 9). In line 19 he tells us that he had put the picture into the fire "in a casual clearance of life's arrears," a mere moment of cleaning up, or, to take the word *arrears* seriously, of discharging old debts. But the sight of the image being consumed by fire causes him an unanticipated pain; it is as though he is burning the woman herself, and not until the card is an "ashen ghost" can he stop feeling her pain.

The last two stanzas tell us a little, but only a very little, about the speaker's relation to the woman: He knew her long ago, but he does not know if she is dead or alive. Still, at the moment of burning the photograph his feeling for her is so strong that he almost feels he is burning the woman herself. In the last stanza, beginning with "Well," he comforts himself that if she is alive she knows nothing of what he has just done, and if she is dead she is equally ignorant, but "Yet—yet" (23), how can he be sure: Possibly if she is alive she did feel something, and if she is in heaven, well, maybe she was looking down on him, and his action provoked her to "shake her head," a gesture that we take to suggest a sort of forgiving superiority, a gesture that in effect says, "Oh, there is that foolish boy, he's at it again, hurting people (including himself), he just doesn't know what he is doing."

Presumably all readers will agree that the photograph is of a person with whom the speaker was romantically involved, rather than, say, of an aunt. The emphasis on the picture's "delicate bosom" and "breasts, and mouth, and hair" seem to us decisive on this question. Inevitably scholars have tried to identify the subject of the photograph, but the best they have come up with is the conjecture that the subject was Tryphena Sparks, to whom Hardy had been engaged but whom he apparently never again saw after he married another woman.

We want to return briefly to the central point of the poem, the pain that the destruction of an image can cause. Yes, an image is only an image, but there is enough of some sense of primitive magic in us that we sometimes endow images and other inanimate things with life. E. H. Gombrich, in *The Story of Art,* 12th edition, makes the point almost too forcefully:

> Suppose we take a picture of our favourite champion from today's paper—would we enjoy taking a needle and poking out the eyes? Would we feel as indifferent about it as if we poked a hole anywhere else in the paper? I do not think so. (20)

If Gombrich is right, and we are certain that he is, you may want to invite students to comment on this passage. In any case, we take the poem to be rooted in this sort of response, and the plot of the poem moves from the poet's initial unawareness through his painful awakening (with a relapse when he tries to assure himself that the woman did not feel anything) to his final sense ("Yet—yet") that indeed she may be aware, and if she is in heaven she may be smiling at his continuing shallowness, or, we might say, his merely mortal condition.

15

Thinking Critically about Poetry

A CASEBOOK ON EMILY DICKINSON

Joseph Duchac has edited two useful guides to Dickinson criticism: *The Poems of Emily Dickinson: An Annotated Guide to Commentary Published in English, 1890–1977* (1979) and *The Poems of Emily Dickinson: An Annotated Guide to Commentary Published in English, 1978–1989* (1993).

A "Voices and Visions" videocassette of Emily Dickinson is available from Longman Publishers.

Note: Elsewhere in the text we include other poems by Dickinson ("I felt a Cleaving," "I felt a Funeral," "I'm nobody," "The Dust behind," "Wild Nights"), and these are discussed in this manual at the appropriate places, except for "I'm nobody" and "Wild Nights," which are extensively discussed in the text.

EMILY DICKINSON
I heard a Fly buzz—when I died— (p. 526)

Dickinson's poem juxtaposes some conventional religious images ("that last Onset," "the King," "What portion of me be / Assignable") with the buzz of a fly, rather than with, say, choirs of angels, and so, as Charles R. Anderson suggests in *Emily Dickinson's Poetry* (1960), "The King witnessed in his power is physical death, not God." Should one go further and suggest that Death-as-fly equals putrefaction?

The last line of the poem ("I could not see to see") especially has attracted attention. Gerhard Friedrich (*Explicator* 13 [April 1955], Item 35) paraphrases it thus: "Waylaid by irrelevant, tangible, finite objects of little importance, I was no longer capable of that deeper perception which would clearly reveal to me the infinite spiritual reality." The fall into skepticism, Friedrich says, demonstrates the inadequacy of the earlier pseudostoicism. John Ciardi took issue with this interpretation and suggested (*Explicator* 14 [January 1956], Item 22) that the fly is "the last kiss of the world, the last buzz from life," reflecting "Emily's tremendous attachment to the physical world"; the final line, in his view, simply means, "And then there was no more of me, and nothing to see with."

The Todd-Higginson editions gave "round my form" for "in the Room" (line 2), "The eyes beside" for "The Eyes around" (line 5), "sure" for "firm" (line 6), "witnessed in his power" for "witnessed—in the Room" (line 8), and "What portion of me I / Could make assignable—and then" for "What portion of me be / Assignable—and then it was" (lines 10–11). It is worth discussing with students the differences these changes make.

EMILY DICKINSON
The Soul selects her own Society (p. 526)

Richard Sewall, in *Voices and Visions* (1987), ed. Helen Vendler, calls this poem Dickinson's "most famous 'choice' poem" (p. 72), and indeed he leaves the choice of its subject to the reader; it may be read as concerned with the choice of a lover, or a friend, or a kind of spiritual life. Even without being certain of the subject of this poem, one can sense how the form contributes to meaning. The even-numbered lines are shorter than the odd-numbered lines that precede them, and each even-numbered line ends emphatically with a monosyllable, thus contrasting with the previous lines' feminine endings. And in the final stanza the short lines are even shorter (a mere two syllables each); the tight-lipped speaker leaves no doubt about the determination of the soul which has made a choice and now rejects all other suppliants, however noble. But details remain uncertain, and critics have not been so tight-lipped.

W. C. Jumper, in *Explicator* 29 (September 1970), Item 5, suggests that the soul (feminine because Latin *anima* is feminine) has a "divine Majority" because Thoreau had said in *The Duty of Civil Disobedience* that "any man more right than his neighbors, constitutes a majority of one." Jumper points out that the second stanza makes ironic use of two folktales, "The Querulous Princess" and "The King and the Beggar Maid." In the first of these tales, the wooers arrive in chariots, but the winner of her hand is he who will bow his head to enter through a low gate; in the second tale, the king kneels before a beggar maid and wins her. In "The Soul Selects" the soul rejects two such humble wooers, having already made her choice.

The word "Valves" in the penultimate line has especially disconcerted critics. *Explicator* 25 (April 1967), Item 8, suggests that it is connected with "Door" in line 2 via two old meanings: (1) the leaves of a double or folding door and (2) the halves of the shell of a bivalve such as an oyster, which closes its valve when disturbed and thus remains "like Stone." Sewall takes "Valves" to refer to a double door and says that "the line simply dramatizes further the action of line two" (p. 73).

EMILY DICKINSON
These are the days when Birds come back (p. 528)

The time is Indian summer, that is, a day that seems summery but is late, hence it is a sort of sophistry of mistake or fraud. (By the way, it is not true that birds, deceived by Indian summer, return.) Lines 10–11 introduce religious imagery ("ranks of seed their witness bear," and the pun on alter-altar, which suggests a communion scene), anticipating the more overt religious images in the next two stanzas.

Some readers take the poem to suggest that just as the season can be deceptive, communion too can be deceptive or illusory. Other readers see the poem moving the other way: from the illusory season, which evokes nostalgic thoughts, to the real or firm joys of Christian immortality. Charles Anderson, in *Emily Dickinson's Poetry* (1960), gives a substantive analysis. He suggests that the season's ambiguity provokes the question, "Does it symbolize death or immortality?" and he answers that Dickinson does not give an answer but gives us "warring images poised in ironic tension."

Topics for Critical Thinking and Writing

1. What season or weather is being talked about? Why does Dickinson use the words "mistake" (line 6) and "fraud" and "cheat" (line 7)?
2. Explain the pun on "altered" in line 11.
3. Take the first three stanzas as a group and summarize them in a sentence or two. Do the same for the last three. Then, in a sentence or two, state the relationship between these two halves of the poem.
4. Why "a child" in line 15?

EMILY DICKINSON
Papa above! (p. 528)

At one extreme, we have encountered readers who find the poem a bitter protest masquerading as a prayer, a scathing attack on the anthropomorphic God of Judaism and Christianity; at the other extreme we have encountered readers who find nothing but piety in the poem, albeit piety in a very Dickinsonian idiom, a piety rooted in affection for God's creatures, even the mouse or rat. Our own view is somewhere in the middle; we hear genial—even affectionate—satire of anthropomorphism, and we also hear acceptance of the strange government of the world. Chiefly, we think, the poem expresses—again, in a characteristically Dickinsonian way—the "primal sense of awe" that Charles R. Anderson commented on.

"Papa above" begins with a domesticated version of the beginning of the Lord's Prayer (Matthew 6:9–13, "Our Father who art in heaven"; Luke 11:2–4,

"Father"). In "Regard a Mouse O'erpowered by the Cat" we hear a solemn (and perhaps a wondering) voice, although we grant that one might hear some comedy in the let-down. That is, a reader who expects, after the invocation of the deity, something like "Regard the sufferings of mortals," or some such thing, is surprised to find that the speaker calls attention to a mouse. Or if the reader expects something that continues the idea of the Lord's Prayer, the shift from the expected "Give us this day our daily bread" to a picture of a mouse overpowered by the claws or jaws of a cat is indeed shocking, first because of the implied violence, and second because of the ironic contrasts between the meal Jesus spoke of and the meal Dickinson shows.

In the next two lines ("Reserve within thy kingdom / A 'Mansion for the Rat!'") we hear primarily a serious if not a solemn voice, though others hear mockery in the juxtaposition of "Mansion" and "Rat." In any case, there is surely a reference to the comforting words Jesus offered to his disciples (John 14:2) when he assured them of reunion in heaven: "In my Father's house are many mansions." But a heavenly mansion (dwelling place) for a rat? We are by no means convinced that Dickinson must have abhorred mice and rats, and that therefore "A 'Mansion for the Rat'" must be ironic. As we see it, the poem thus suggests that the mouse (or rat), destroyed at the moment, has its place in the enduring heavenly scheme. Again, some readers take this to be so evidently absurd or so disgusting that they believe Dickinson is satirizing the idea of a divinely governed universe; others find a tolerant pantheism.

The first two lines of the second stanza get us almost into a Walt Disney world of cute animals—here the mouse is "Snug" and it is able to "nibble all the day"—but in the final two lines the camera draws sharply back from the domestic scene and gives us a world of immense space and time, a world indifferent to ("unsuspecting" of) the mouse (and by implication indifferent to all of us). If there is any satire here, we think it is of persons who believe the "Cycles" are concerned with their existence, but we do not take these lines to be the fierce condemnation of the Judeo-Christian God that some readers take them to be.

The poem raises enough difficulties in itself, but you may want to ask students to compare it with Frost's "Design" (also in the text). Is Frost's "Design" a sort of restatement of Dickinson's "Papa above"? Or is Frost's poem something of a reply?

EMILY DICKINSON
There's a certain Slant of light (p. 528)

The poem seems difficult to us, and any questions about it therefore lead to difficulties, but perhaps our fifth question, below, on the rhyme scheme is fairly straightforward. Some students may recognize that metrically the poem is close to the "common meter" or "common measure" (abbreviated C. M. in hymnals) of a hymn. (C. M. can be defined thus: stanzas of four lines, the first and third in iambic tetrameter, the second and fourth in iambic trimeter, rhyming *abcb* or *abab.*) In fact, no two stanzas in the poem are metrically identical (if we count the syllables of the first line of each stanza, we find seven, six or seven, six, and eight), but despite such variations, the meter and especially the rhyme scheme (*abab*) seem regular. The second and fourth lines of each stanza have five syllables, and these lines end with exact rhymes, though the first and third lines of each stanza rely less on rhyme than on consonance. The regularity of the rhyme scheme, especially in such short lines, is something of a tour de force, and (because it suggests a highly ordered world) it might seem more suited to a neat little poem with a comforting theme than to the poem Dickinson has given us. Further, since the meter and some of the rhymes might occur in a hymn ("Despair," "Air"; "breath," "Death"), there is an ironic contrast between the form (a hymn, that is, a poem celebrating God's goodness) and the content of the poem.

But what, in fact, is the content? And what is the "certain Slant of light" that, perceived on "Winter Afternoons," makes "Shadows—hold their breath"? No two readers seem to agree on the details, but perhaps we can offer a few inoffensive comments. Like Hopkins, Dickinson sees a divinity behind phenomena, but her nature-suffused-with-divinity differed greatly from his. "There's a certain Slant of light" begins with "light," which might suggest life and eternal happiness (think of Newman's "Lead, kindly light"), but it soon becomes darker and ends with "the look of Death." The ending is not really a surprise, however, since the "certain Slant of light" is seen on "Winter Afternoons," that is, a season when the year may be said to be dying and when light is relatively scarce and a time of day when light will soon disappear.

This "Slant of light," we are told, "Oppresses, like the Heft / Of Cathedral Tunes." Surely "Oppresses" comes as a surprise. Probably most of us think that cathedral tunes (even funeral music) exalt the spirit rather than oppress it, and so most of us might have written something like, "That elevates, like the Lift / Of Cathedral Tunes." But of course most of us couldn't have written even this, since we would not have had the imagination to think of light in aural terms ("Tunes") and in terms of weight ("Heft").

In any case, a certain appearance in nature induces in the poet a sensation that requires such words as "Oppresses," "Hurt," "Despair," "affliction," "Shadows," and "Death." These words might appear in a traditional hymn, but, if so, the hymn would move toward the idea that God helps us to triumph over these adversities. Dickinson, however, apparently is saying that on these wintry afternoons the slant of light shining in the air gives us a "Heavenly Hurt," that is, it moves us to a painful consciousness of God and nature, and to a sense of isolation. In the final stanza presumably we are back to the "Winter Afternoons" of the first. Projecting herself into the surrounding world, the speaker personifies nature: "the Landscape listens"—but hears nothing further. (By the way, "listens" to or for what? A "Slant of light"? Again, as in the earlier comparison of light to "Cathedral Tunes," Dickinson uses synesthesia.) If during the moment when one perceives the light or "listens" there is no further insight, and certainly no amelioration of the "Heavenly Hurt," when "it goes" there is an intensification of despair, since one is left with "the look of Death."

146   Chapter 15: Thinking Critically about Poetry

Is Dickinson evoking an image of the remote stare of a corpse? And is she suggesting that this stare corresponds to the paralyzed mental condition of those who have perceived the "Slant of light"?

Earlier in this brief discussion we contrasted Hopkins with Dickinson. But, as Charles R. Anderson points out in *Emily Dickinson's Poetry* (1960), there is a connection between the two. The perception in this poem resembles Margaret's perception in "Spring and Fall," where the child senses "the blight man was born for."

Topics for Critical Thinking and Writing

1. In the first stanza, what kind or kinds of music does "Cathedral Tunes" suggest? In what ways might they (and the light to which they are compared) be oppressive?
2. In the second stanza, the effect on us of the light is further described. Try to paraphrase Dickinson's lines or interpret them. Compare your paraphrase or interpretation with that of a classmate or someone else who has read the poem. Are your interpretations similar? If not, can you account for some of the differences?
3. In the third stanza, how would you interpret "None may teach it"? Is the idea "No one can instruct (or tame) the light to be different"? Or "No one can teach us what we learn from the light"? Or do you have a different reading of this line?
4. "Death" is the last word of the poem. Rereading the poem, how early (and in what words or images) is a "death" suggested or foreshadowed?
5. Describe the rhyme scheme. Then, a more difficult business, try to describe the effect of the rhyme scheme. Does it work with or against the theme, or meaning, of the poem?
6. What is the relationship in the poem between the light as one might experience it in New England on a winter afternoon and the experience of despair? To put it crudely, does the light itself cause despair, or does Dickinson see the light as an image or metaphor for human despair? And how is despair related to death?
7. Overall, how would you describe the tone of the poem? Anguished? Serene? Resigned?

EMILY DICKINSON
This World is not Conclusion (p. 529)

First, a brief comment about Dickinson and religion. She clearly was not fond of the patriarchal deity of the Hebrew Bible. "Burglar! Banker—Father," she wrote of this deity, and in a note to Thomas Wentworth Higginson she says that the members of her family, except for herself, "address an Eclipse every morning—whom they call their Father." She seems to have been amused by preachers. She said, of one, that "the subject of perdition seemed to please him somehow." Still, in the words of Charles R. Anderson, in *Emily Dickinson's Poetry* (1960), no reader can doubt that she "faced creation with a primal sense of awe" (p. 17). And, as Anderson and everyone else points out, the Bible was "one of her chief sources of imagery" (p. 18).

Now for "This World is not Conclusion." The first two lines sound like the beginning of a hymn ("Conclusion" presumably means "ending," not "inference drawn"). The poem is not divided into stanzas by white spaces, but clearly it moves in units of four lines. The first four lines assert that although a world beyond our own is (like music) invisible, we strongly sense it. "Positive" in line 4 perhaps refers both to our conviction that it exists and also to its goodness.

Line 5 introduces a complication: "It beckons, and it baffles." Although the rest of the stanza (i.e., lines 6–8) seems to affirm the initial confident (positive) assertion, it also raises doubts in the reader, since it dismisses "Philosophy" and "Sagacity," and it characterizes life (or is it death?) as a "Riddle."

Lines 9–12 seem more positive. They remind us that although human experience "puzzles Scholars," martyrs have given their lives to affirm religious faith, to affirm (in the words of the first line) that "This World is not Conclusion."

Lines 13–16, however, present "Faith" in a somewhat less heroic light: "Faith slips—and laughs, and rallies—Blushes, if any see." Surely this is in a much lower key than "Men have borne / Contempt of Generations," a couple of lines earlier. The enduring power of Faith is still affirmed (Faith "rallies"), but in "slips" and "Blushes, if any see" we seem to be presented with a rather adolescent world. Further, the last two lines of the stanza (15–16) similarly diminish Faith, showing it clutching after "a twig of Evidence," and inquiring of a "Vane" (a weathervane, a most unstable thing). Perhaps, too, "Vane" hints at emptiness, insubstantiality (Latin, *vanitas*).

The final four lines at first seem more affirmative. They begin with a strong assertion that calls up a picture of a vigorously gesticulating preacher, and they reintroduce imagery of music (now "Strong Hallelujahs roll"), but these lines at the same time are unconvincing or, rather, almost comic. A reader may find in the preacher's abundant gestures a lack of genuine conviction. (One thinks of the marginal note in the politician's speech: "Argument weak; shout here.") The "Strong Hallelujahs" may strike a reader as less potent than the "Music" that was "positive" in lines 3–4. Are the gestures and the hallelujahs "Narcotics" that don't quite work, that is, that don't quite convince us of the pious forthright assertion that "This World is not Conclusion"? Yet the poem ends with the word "soul"; if "Much Gesture, from the Pulpit" reveals a preacher who is not wholly convincing, we nevertheless cannot therefore lapse into the belief that this world is conclusion. Something "nibbles at the soul."

Topics for Critical Thinking and Writing

1. Given the context of the first two lines, what do you think "Conclusion" means in the first line?

2. Although white spaces here are not used to divide the poem into stanzas, the poem seems to be constructed in units of four lines each. Summarize each four-line unit in a sentence or two.
3. Compare your summaries with those of a classmate. If you substantially disagree, reread the poem to see if, on reflection, one or the other of you seems in closer touch with the poem. Or does the poem (or some part of it) allow for two very different interpretations?
4. In the first four lines the speaker seems (to use a word from line 4) quite "positive." Do some or all of the following stanzas seem less positive? If so, which—and what makes you say so?
5. How do you understand "Much Gesture, from the Pulpit" (line 17)? Would you agree with a reader who said that the line suggests a *lack* of deep conviction? Explain.

EMILY DICKINSON
I got so I could hear his name— (p. 529)

This poem is not as well known as others, but we think it is one of Dickinson's best, and it is one that students find very powerful. They respond to it and are especially eager to probe its complexities because they feel the immediacy of its subject. It is something that has happened to them—or that they fear might happen. One of our students in an American literature class said, "This is exactly what it feels like to have your heart broken."

The poem does express *that,* but it is also about somehow trying to recover from the pain. What measures might be taken to overcome a devastating loss? Dickinson is stunningly effective, we believe, in noting the physical closeness that the persons in her poem shared, and the wrenching experience of their separation—"all our Sinews tore." The detail about the letters is very powerful as well, for it describes precisely the terrible way we return to memories, to signs of the beloved's presence, when what we want is to get beyond them.

This is, then, a poem about feeling and confronting pain and seeking a means of self-control. In the final three stanzas, the speaker turns to God—though notice the distancing effect of "I think, they call it 'God'." Perhaps this higher force, outside the wounded self, might be able to heal it. Students find the last stanza somewhat obscure, and we agree. But the main thrust is clear enough: the speaker is uncertain whether any power exists that might aid her, and, if there is, whether this power would ever care about the pain felt by just one person. A good question to ask is how much or how little closure takes place in the final line. Does the speaker reconstitute, at least partially, her shattered self through the process of articulating and working through, cathartically, her pain? Or is the poem the record of a pain that persists, that the speaker cannot find a remedy for?

Dickinson has legions of admirers, but in our experience, many students have trouble with her intense, gnomic, highly condensed verse. This, again, is a poem to which students do feel connected, and it is valuable as a point of entry into the study of Dickinson's life and work. See Richard B. Sewall, *The Life of Emily Dickinson* (2 vols., 1974), and Cynthia Griffin Wolff, *Emily Dickinson* (1986).

Two charged, self-dramatizing comments by Dickinson on herself, both from undated letters to the critic, editor, and journalist, Thomas Wentworth Higginson: "I had no portrait, now, but am small, like the Wren, and my Hair is bold, like the chesnut Bur, and my eyes, like the Sherry in the Glass, that the guest leaves"; and "I had no monarch in my life, and cannot rule myself; and when I try to organize, my little force explodes and leaves me bare and charred."

EMILY DICKINSON
Those—dying, then (p. 530)

The faith of her ancestors is, Dickinson apparently feels, no longer possible, but it serves to enrich behavior. An *ignis fatuus* (a phosphorescent light—caused by gases emitted by rotting organic matter—that hovers over a swamp) presumably resembles, however weakly, the beautiful flames of heaven and the demonic flames of hell. It is only a will-o'-the-wisp, but at least it is *something*. The image of amputation is shocking, but it can be paralleled in the Bible, for example, by "and if thy right eye offend thee, pluck it out, and cast it from thee. . . . and if thy right hand offend thee, cut it off, and cast it from thee" (Matthew 5:29–30).

Topics for Critical Thinking and Writing

1. In a sentence or two, state the point of the poem.
2. Is the image in line 4 in poor taste? Explain.
3. What is an *ignis fatuus*? In what ways does it connect visually with traditional images of hell and heaven?

EMILY DICKINSON
Apparently with no surprise (p. 530)

As in most nature poems, nature is humanized—but with a difference. If a flower is Wordsworthian in being at "play," the frost is not: it is a "blonde Assassin"; blonde because it is white, and the fact that this color is usually associated with innocence makes the personification the more shocking. (See Frost's white spider in "Design," in our text). Note, too, that "at its play" can go with the frost as well as with the flower, in which case the frost is only playing but happens to play too vigorously with a destructive (but unlamented) result. And still more shocking, at least on first reading, is the fact that God (like the sun) approves. God stands behind the world, approving of the accidental destruction of beauty and joy. One could, by agile philosophizing, justify the necessary destruction of beauty and joy—but the "accidental" destruction? The sun, as usual, measured off the days, but mysteriously withheld its warmth and allowed the frost to do its work. The flower, the sun, God, all seem indifferent; only human beings are shocked.

"Apparently," of course, has two almost opposed meanings: (1) evidently, clearly; (2) seemingly (but not really), as in "The magician apparently vanished into thin air." So the lack of surprise and the impassivity of the sun and the approval of God *may* be unreal; maybe this is just the way things look or seem, not the way things really are. After all, it is only apparent (seemingly), not real, that flowers are "happy" and that they "play."

Topics for Critical Thinking and Writing

1. What is the implication of the action described in lines 1–3?
2. Why is the frost's power called "accidental"?
3. Why is the assassin called "blonde"? What does this word contribute to the poem?
4. Is the last line shocking? Explain.

EMILY DICKINSON
Tell all the Truth but tell it slant (p. 531)

A student once brought up, by way of comparison, Polonius's words:

> And thus do we of wisdom and of reach,
> With windlasses and with assays of bias,
> By indirections find directions out. (*Hamlet* 2.1.64–66)

The last line especially seems to have affinities with Dickinson's first line, but the thrust of the two passages is fundamentally different. Polonius, worried about the behavior of his son Laertes, is sending Reynaldo to find out if Laertes has been misbehaving. He tells Reynaldo to slander Laertes, to see if Reynaldo's hearers deny the charges. Polonius thus is advocating deceit, whereas Dickinson is saying that because truth is too bright for our "infirm Delight," if we want to communicate, we must use indirection.

For Dickinson, the truth *is* splendid—it does "dazzle"—but we can perceive this splendor only after we have become accustomed to it, and we arrive at this condition "gradually."

The word "slant" nicely plays against "Circuit," and on rereading it may be taken to anticipate the word "lightning," which is often represented by a diagonal line. In any case, one of the charms of the poem is the homely comparison in lines 5–6, where the need to tell the truth "slant" is compared to offering "explanation kind" to children who presumably have been frightened by lightning. Telling the truth "slant" or "in Circuit" is not an attempt to deceive but to be "kind."

An extant draft of the poem shows that Dickinson contemplated two possible changes, "bold" for "bright" in line 3, and "moderately" for "gradually" in line 7.

W. C. HANDY
St. Louis Blues (p. 538)

There is some dispute about the original date of "St. Louis Blues," one of the first and best-known blues and jazz songs: It has been termed "the *Hamlet* of jazz music." We have given the date 1914 in the text, but others have proposed earlier and later dates. Part of the issue (or problem) here is that "St. Louis Blues" builds upon an earlier song, "Jogo Blues" ("jogo" is a slang term for an African-American), which in turn is based on an even earlier blues tune or riff. Blues songs develop from other blues songs and sections of songs, and in a sense it can even be misleading to speak of a "blues song" because each singer or performer gives it his or her own stamp—which means altering the music a lot or a little, and doing the same (or more) to the lyrics.

Blues singers pretty much take this fact for granted: It is one of the conventions of their art. But it can seem strange and even frustrating to others. Influenced by jazz and blues, Frank Sinatra, especially during his concerts, frequently made changes in the words of Pop and Broadway songs. This drove many of the composers crazy: They wanted Sinatra to sing the lyrics they had written, staying faithful (one might say) to the words on the page of the song chart. But a blues singer usually views the words on the page not as *the* song, but, instead, as one version of the song: He or she might stick very close to these words, or adjust and modify them a bit, or else take them as a point of departure for some new lyrics.

W. C. Handy said he wrote "St. Louis Blues" after an accidental encounter with a woman on the streets of New Orleans, Louisiana, who, grief-stricken about her separation from her husband, was crying out, "Ma man's got a heart like a rock cast in de sea"—a line that Handy included directly in the song.

When we first heard "St. Louis Blues," and before we knew the words well, we misinterpreted it: We took the title to mean that the song deals with a relationship or an incident in the city of St. Louis. But as the song makes clear, "St. Louis" is the home-city of the woman who has taken away the husband or lover whose absence the speaker laments.

There are some striking details in the language that you can explore with students. Notice, for instance, the intensity of the verb, "I *hate*," used twice in the first stanza. Notice, too, that the St. Louis woman has a "diamond ring": This is the only thing we are told about her. We know nothing about her looks, age, clothing, etc., except for the fact that she has a diamond ring. It may be a gift from the wandering, unfaithful lover; it may function on a symbolic level to spotlight the glamour and sparkle of the St. Louis woman; and it may also intimate a flaw in the male lover, who is easily bewitched by alluring appearances. Perhaps, in addition, the diamond looks forward to the "rock cast in the sea," the simile that the speaker uses to characterize the hard-heartedness of the man. A large, flashy diamond is often described as being as "big as a rock" (e.g., "Did you see the size of the rock she had on her finger?").

You can do some productive study of the language of the final stanza in particular. There are two similes here, and with your students you can focus on the first—why a "school boy," and why his "pie?"—and then on the second as complementing and extending the first—why a colonel, and why from Kentucky, and why this special drink? In this fashion, you can help to show students how a simile functions, and then how another functions in relation to it: What makes the second similar to, yet different from, the first? And, then, with the two similes and their meanings and implications in place, you can explore how the final line of the stanza (and the poem) operates.

The point of the final line, of course, is that it could easily be the opposite, and perhaps, we might say, even *should* be the opposite. Why *should* this speaker love the man who has deserted her? And even if she still loves him, should she vow to be loyal to him forever (until the day she dies), given his bad treatment of her? You and I might want to exclaim, "Good riddance! Let him go! He'll regret it!" But that's not how the blues behaves. The blues are not that easy; they are more complex, and ultimately more human.

Within the blues context, abandoned lovers are often, to be sure, distraught and angry. Sometimes they swear vengeance and entertain thoughts of mayhem and murder. But they never stop loving the man or woman they feel angry towards. No one in a blues song, it seems, can shed his or her love: The speaker of "St. Louis Blues" declares she will go to her grave loving the man who has walked away from her. And this is not just a sign of weakness, but of strength as well. She possesses the virtue of constancy that her man lacks; she is wounded and ravaged but she vows she will not do to him (or to his memory) what he has done to her.

There is nobility and integrity in the speaker that, if we are a true devotee of the blues, we will esteem. This is a woman very much worth loving, and one would not want to bet against her: Some day, perhaps, her man will return to her, chastened and wiser.

For further reading: W. C. Handy, *Father of the Blues: An Autobiography*, ed. Arna Bontemps (1941; rpt. 1991).

BESSIE SMITH
Thinking Blues (p. 540)

The mood or atmosphere of the music of blues songs often veils from us how complex their lyrics are. "Thinking Blues" is a good example, and after you listen to it (see details on recordings below), you might turn the class's attention to it as a poem, as a sequence of words on the page.

The first stanza creates an impression, an expectation really, that the song then subverts. Smith begins by inviting the reader—let's say reader because we are considering this song as a poem—to join her in "thinking" about someone who has treated her "nice and kind." The point seems to be that the "thousand things" are good things—good thoughts about this kindly person, presumably the speaker's lover.

Soon enough, however, perhaps as soon as the first line of stanza two, it becomes clear that this speaker has been mistreated: it's an "old letter" she is reading (the type of letter, she says, that the reader is doubtless familiar with too), a token or memento of a relationship that has faded or failed.

We need to interject a point here: When we are in the midst of the blues experience, we likely will hear in the first stanza the signs of trouble already. When there's a reference to someone "nice and kind," the emphasis, nearly always in the blues, is that the person is *not* like that now. He or she once was, but not anymore. That's something that the blues bears witness to: It is a means through which the blues singer or poet affirms a connection to members of the audience, who *know* themselves from their own experiences what the speaker describes and is living through.

Smith's speaker declares she has a bad case of the blues: She is in pain, and alone. She still thinks of "that man" (he is a specific man indeed) as *her* man. "I wanna be": The phrase does not complete itself; it is left hanging, as though the speaker cannot bring herself to voice that she still desires someone she does not have, and maybe never will have again.

The "you" of the third stanza is different from the "you" of stanzas one and two. Literally and figuratively, the speaker is seeking to return to her lover's company. She cannot believe his willful refusal to abide by her request to be with him again. "Request" in fact is a misleading term. It's more of a desperate appeal; she knocks on her door and he refuses to heed her at all.

Note: On her recording, Smith stretches out the phrase "knocking on your door," especially the "knocking," to dramatize that it's repeated and prolonged.

"Drive" her away: That's an intriguing choice of term. It suggests force, determination. The former lover may be tired of her pleas and wishes to be rid of her. She, for her part, is insistent, intense. Perhaps, too, there is more than a flash of lingering feeling *for* her in him; he doesn't want her anymore, but there is feeling *in him* for her yet: he has to push her away, casting her aside because (in his view) she is no good for him any longer.

"Have you got the nerve": The speaker uses this phrase three times, with a mix of anger and incredulity. "Reap what you sow" is a reference to Galatians 6:7: ". . . for whatsoever a man soweth, that shall he also reap." One gloss on this New Testament passage states: "According as we behave ourselves now, so will our account be in the great day of judgment." Another maintains: "This proverb about sowing and reaping is a nearly universal maxim warning that actions have consequences." Smith's speaker thus may be implying that the lover will one day be on the receiving end of the cruel behavior he is now showing toward the speaker herself. Or, more generally, the point perhaps is that the speaker will be judged—by God? By the hand of Fate?—for his heartless conduct. There may be another possibility: the speaker could be saying, "You made me pregnant (you sowed me with your seed), and now you have a responsibility to me and your child that's on the way."

The final stanza is anguished: The speaker tells her lover that all she asks is a chance, a "trying out." She is beseeching him: "You don't have to say you will take me back. I'm not asking for that. All I'm asking for is a chance. I know I can show you how good to you I can be." This is the only remedy through which the speaker avers she can be relieved of the "thinking blues," the thoughts that plague her. Now, we realize, looking back to stanza one, that the "thousand things" are in truth one big thing, all of the thoughts one wrenching thought.

For a brief biography: Elaine Feinstein, *Bessie Smith* (1985). For more detail: Chris Albertson, *Bessie* (rev. ed., 2003); Albertson is very informative about Smith's early years, and he also provides much valuable material from interviews. See also: Edward Brooks, *The Bessie Smith Companion: A Critical and Detailed Appreciation of the Recordings* (1982). "Thinking Blues" is included on: *Bessie Smith, 1927–1928* (Melodie Jazz Classic, 1996); and *Bessie Smith: The Complete Recordings*, vol. 3 (Legacy/Columbia, 1992).

ROBERT JOHNSON
Walkin' Blues (p. 541)

It's a brilliant touch: giving the lover a name, Bernice, which instantly makes her special, individuating her. Johnson may not have known it, but "Bernice" has a Greek origin, "brings victory," which fits very well (and painfully) the woman who has conquered the speaker's heart and soul.

One of the striking things about the blues is that when you have them they are immediately and always *there*; they hit the moment you wake up. The speaker is disoriented ("feelin' 'round"), lost, alienated, and devastated: His woman has gone, which means that for him "everything" is gone.

This aspect of "Walkin' Blues" sometimes vexes students: The speaker claims that his woman has mistreated him, so why is he so upset? Why should he be distraught about such a cruel person's departure? We reply: But he loves her, and (in more than one sense) is crazy about her. That's why he has the blues, because his merged feelings of love and anger do not allow him to do anything as neatly efficient as cast aside the woman's memory.

Notice that Johnson embeds in his song the fact that some people do indeed fail to understand his plight. They insist that the "worried blues" that affect him are not so bad. But they're wrong: These are the worst feelings he has ever had.

This is one of the curious and complex features of the blues. When someone sings the blues, we know what he or she means; unless we are very fortunate, we've suffered from such blues too. But, paradoxically, we are inclined to think that the pain someone else suffers is really not *that* bad after all. Maybe there's some hyperbole, some feelings that are in excess of the facts of the situation. We understand and sympathize but then are quick to offer good and sensible advice, or we engage in some emotional rebuking and cheerleading ("stop feeling sorry for yourself; she wasn't any good for you, and you need to get a grip on yourself . . .").

We're reminded here of William James's reflections in *The Varieties of Religious Experience* (1902) on the suffering of the sick soul. James says that we on the outside invariably come forward with smart suggestions and fine pieces of advice, all of which seems eminently reasonable and right to us. But, he adds, to the soul who is sick, what we are recommending comes across as utterly impossible. To the person in pain, we seem not to know in the slightest what we are talking about, not to know how absurd it is to propose such things.

Each of us can feel another's blues, but only each of us alone can know the depths of our own blues—how far down they go.

Johnson's reference to the woman's "Elgin movement" may imply her cool elegance. It may also intimate something cold and mechanical about her: she inspires great passion and desire in him, but she is unaffected herself. If she had been affected, then she would not have left him. There's a sense as well of her deftness as a manipulator. She "breaks in on a dollar" wherever she goes: She knows how to use her wiles and prompt men to spend their money on her: she cannot be resisted. And if she came the speaker's way right now, he would fall for her (and fast!) all over again.

Note: In his detailed, informative study, *Escaping the Delta: Robert Johnson and the Invention of the Blues* (2004), Elijah Wald argues that white musicians and listeners have romanticized and idealized Robert Johnson. He claims that Johnson was a minor figure in his own era, less original than Son House and Skip James, and less popular among black audiences than were Lonnie Johnson, Peetie Wheatstraw, Kokomo Arnold, and others. Wald's book is fascinating, but we think he overstates his case. Perhaps the key point is not that later generations of musicians misinterpreted Johnson, but, rather, that his work powerfully affected them and influenced their styles, compositions, and recordings. Their lack of knowledge about his roots matters less than the impact of his music on their own, and on their appreciation of the depth of the blues experience. A similar study, but not as polemical, is: Barry Lee Pearson and Bill McCulloch, *Robert Johnson: Lost and Found* (2003).

PAUL LAURENCE DUNBAR
Blue (p. 542)

We know teachers who shy away from poems and stories that are written in, or that include, dialect. For them, reading and discussing such works in the classroom is awkward, and runs the risk of upsetting students. This is a reasonable concern to bear in mind—which is why we recommend that you follow the sequence of Topics for this selection that we prepared. But in our own experience—perhaps we are simply lucky—no problems have arisen. We enjoy works in dialect; we find them to be interesting, sometimes entertaining, and always illuminating. We like hearing and responding to a wide variety of voices.

When we begin any selection featuring dialect, we note to students that many authors, white and African American, have made use of forms of dialect—Mark Twain, Zora Neale Hurston, and Richard Wright, for example. It is one of their resources as writers, and, as the critic Stanley Crouch has said, "dialect" of many kinds is a large fact of American experience as well as of American literature. As Crouch says, the range and richness of American speech, with all of its dialects, helps to dramatize the meaning of the United States as a democracy and American culture as a democratic enterprise. Some scholars, including Werner Sollors, Marc Shell, and Lawrence Rosenwald, developing this insight, have come to identify American literature as a "multilingual" literature: American authors from the colonial era forward have written in many dialects and, indeed, in many languages besides English.

"Blue" is a wonderful poem, evoking the blend of sadness and happiness, pain and pleasure, that blues poems and songs express. The speaker feels glum, lowdown, dispirited: he's no good. But even as he utters these low and lonely feelings, his language shows sparks of humor and playfulness: the raindrops, for instance, are akin to players of the kettle drum, and the "rain-crow" is chuckling (ask your students how "chuckling" differs from "laughing") as the storm approaches.

"Delight" marks the turn in Dunbar's poem, for the next line is addressed to his wife. He may feel sick and blue, but he directs his wife and children and Uncle Isaac and Aunt Hannah to join him, and he tells his wife to bring in his banjo. It's time for music, and for the vigorously rhythmic music that banjo-playing is associated with.

Dunbar's speaker is, he insists, "blue," but the details and tones of his language suggest that being blue means, yes, being blue but also *resisting* being blue. Blues poems and songs are sad, melancholy, wounded, and, at the same time, they ward off, contain, and thereby control the worst damage that such bruised and bitter feelings could cause. Dunbar's "Blue," even more, concludes with the speaker proposing an explicit remedy. No more time for talking. It's time for music, and with members of immediate and extended family.

Once you have commented on the final lines, ask the class, "Why is (or was) the speaker 'blue' to begin with?" There are hints—e. g., maybe the rainy weather means no work and hence no money for the speaker and his family. But feeling blue is also a feeling that comes from nowhere, or (one could say instead) that is always there, or at least that is always ready to make its presence felt. One of the great blues songs opens, "Good morning blues / Blues how do you do?" The implication is that feeling blue or being blue, starts first thing in the morning. It's there, and of course we should be aware of it—and be prepared to deal with it.

For further study: *The Paul Laurence Dunbar Reader: A Selection of the Best of Paul Laurence Dunbar's Poetry and Prose*, ed. Jay Martin and Gossie H. Hudson (1975); and *The Collected Poetry of Paul Laurence Dunbar*, ed. Joanne M. Braxton (1993). Dated but still useful is Addison Gayle, *Oak and Ivy: A Biography of Paul Laurence Dunbar* (1971). See also: *The Multilingual Anthology of American Literature: A Reader of Original Texts with English Translations*, ed. Marc Shell and Werner Sollors (2000).

W. H. AUDEN
Funeral Blues (p. 544)

Even students who have little familiarity with traditional literature will enjoy the poem, but readers familiar with traditional elegies (such as "Lycidas") will especially enjoy it, since it is a modern version of the classical pastoral elegy. From the days of the Greek Sicilian poet Theocritus, the pastoral elegy called upon all nature to mourn for the deceased shepherd; the poet ordered the trees to shed their leaves, the streams to stop flowing, etc., all in order to express proper grief for the great loss that the speaker had experienced in the death of his beloved.

Auden wryly introduces into this form the paraphernalia of our world—clocks, telephones, airplanes, and so on—and yet keeps the basic motifs of the original. A phrase such as "let the mourners come" (4) might occur in almost any classical elegy (from Theocritus to Milton or Matthew Arnold), where customarily there is a procession of mourners. Next we would expect to hear something about the depth of their expression of grief—perhaps the heavens would reverberate with their cry. In Auden's poem, however, the invocation to mourners is followed by "Let aeroplanes circle moaning overhead / Scribbling on the sky the message He Is Dead."

But we do not take the poem as merely a joke, or as lacking in feeling. Yes, it uses hyperbole and it has comic elements, but it also seems to us to effectively express the emotions of a grieving lover, someone who—though of course knowing better—nevertheless feels that the beloved is the moon and sun, someone who might reasonably say that the beloved was "my North, my South, my East and West,/My working week and my Sunday rest." Incidentally, the poem is recited in the film *Four Weddings and a Funeral*. It aroused much favorable comment—so much that the publisher promptly issued a little book with this poem and a few others by Auden, and announced on the cover that the book contained the poem from the film.

There are a number of books on Auden that can be brought to the attention of students. The best biography so far is Humphrey Carpenter, *W. H. Auden: A Biography* (1981). For social and historical context, see Samuel Hynes, *The Auden Generation: Literature and Politics in England in the 1930s* (1976). On the poetry: Monroe K. Spears, *The Poetry of W. H. Auden* (1963); and Edward Mendelson, *Early Auden* (1981).

Langston Hughes
Too Blue (p. 545)

Notice in the first line that Langston Hughes does not use commas in the phrase "those sad old weary blues." You might ask students to consider the difference between the phrase rendered this way and the phrase with punctuation: "sad, old, weary blues." Using commas would slow down the pace a little: One could make a case for why this might be in keeping with the meaning of the poem as a whole. But it would also make each of the adjectives more discrete, separated off from one another, than Hughes wants to be the case here. The point about the blues that afflict this speaker is that they are, all at once, *sad and old and weary*. Not three feelings (I'm sad, and old, and weary), but one feeling (I'm sad old weary). If these were separate, perhaps the speaker would be less blue than he is: he could look at and maybe get some control over each one. But his blues are a blend or combination: it's no wonder he is blue, indeed *too* blue.

Of course part of the reality of being blue is that one always feels too blue. Or so some would propose: Feeling blue is feeling very burdened, and weighted down, more than one can handle. On the other hand, the best blues singers and poets are also capable of making fine, subtle distinctions: Not every experience produces exactly the same level or depth of blue-ness.

Hughes's speaker seems deeply blue—to the point of asking in the second stanza whether he should kill himself. There are plenty of examples of violence in blues songs, including murder and suicide. But it's also true that feeling suicidal is very much of a blues feeling: it's not that the speaker really intends to do away with himself, but it's important to him to express that he feels *that* bad. A typical blues song or poem is not a suicide note, not a good-bye. It's an expression of or, rather, a confrontation with anguish and suffering: Everyone has the blues (you only *think* you don't), and everyone must learn to cope with the blues. Which perhaps suggests why Ralph Ellison, author of *Invisible Man* (1952), described the blues as "existential"—"involved in or vital to the shaping of an individual's self-chosen mode of existence and moral stance with respect to the rest of the world."

Although Hughes's speaker is blue, he also hears himself and comments *back* on himself. He wonders whether one bullet would be enough. And as soon as he says *that*, he adds in a way that's both glum and wry, that his hard head probably would require two bullets. This is something of a triumph over suicidal feelings: the speaker is blue, yet stubborn, and maybe there's an intimation there of his resiliency. The blues singer is a survivor, vulnerable, yes, but someone who endures.

The final stanza evokes this doubleness with both simplicity and precision. The speaker is so blue that he cannot even look for the bullet and gun he needs to kill himself. He sure does feel blue! But the very blue-ness that produces thoughts of suicide also prevents suicide: the speaker's feelings lead him to imagine extreme remedies and, simultaneously, as he expresses these feelings in the blues mode, he protects himself. The blues are his foe, his omnipresent shadow, and voicing the blues is his salvation.

For biography: Arnold Rampersad, *The Life of Langston Hughes*, 2 vols. (1986, 1988; 2nd ed., 2002). Critical studies include: Onwuchekwa Jemie, *Langston Hughes: An Introduction to the Poetry* (1976); R. Baxter Miller, *The Art and Imagination of Langston Hughes* (1989); and *Langston Hughes: Critical Perspectives Past And Present*, ed. Henry Louis Gates, Jr. and K. A. Appiah. See also Hans Ostrom, *A Langston Hughes Encyclopedia* (2002).

JOHNNY CASH
Folsom Prison Blues (p. 546)

Once you begin listening to the blues, you'll encounter many songs that deal with the experiences of someone who is in prison, or who has been in prison, or who is on the way to prison. Many jazz musicians and blues and country-blues performers, including Johnny Cash, have run astray of the law and have spent time in prison. (Later in the book, in Chapter 25 ["Law and Disorder"], we reprint an anonymous song, "Birmingham Jail.")

And the reality is that the United States has long had a very large prison population. As the *New York Times* recently noted (6/24/04),

> thirteen million Americans have been convicted of felonies and spent time in prison—more than the population of Greece. And they tend to return to prison again and again. Of the 650,000 inmates who will be released in 2004, two-thirds will be back behind bars within a few years. The operating expenses for state prisons alone is around $30 billion a year. . . .

In the year 2004 (as we write this entry) there are approximately 2.03 million people behind bars, which amounts to 701 per 100,000 population. Of the total number of persons imprisoned throughout the world, one-quarter of them are in the United States.

Violent, dangerous people are sent to prison. Sometimes innocent persons are wrongly sent there as well. And both kinds appear in the blues. Prisons are places of confinement, and the singers and poets of the blues often feel trapped, hemmed in, their freedom taken away as they live under the rough hand of authority. There's a coldness, hardness, and despair associated with the prison that finds a natural home in the blues—just as one could say that the mood of the blues would make singers and poets inevitably turn to the literal and figurative meanings of the prison.

The speaker of "Folsom Prison Blues" begins by referring to the sound of a train—trains are everywhere in the blues, too. He is a long-time prisoner, and the fact that he hasn't seen the sunshine implies he is a very serious offender—someone who is not even allowed exercise in the yard. Indeed we learn in stanza two that the speaker killed a man, and not for any desperate need, or through a terrible accident: He killed the man because he wanted to watch him die.

One wonders why the speaker hangs his head and cries. Perhaps he feels guilt for having so cruelly taken another's life. Although he may be crying because he knows he is stuck in prison, possibly (one suspects) with a life-sentence.

We might mention in passing that in a way this speaker is fortunate. Quite a few blues and country-blues songs deal with the fate of inmates sentenced to death. Cash's "25 Minutes to Go," for example, included on *At Folsom Prison* (1968; reissued 1999), is narrated by a man recounting the final minutes of life before his execution: The song ends as he dies. (If you do introduce this song, you may want students to compare it with A. E. Housman's "Eight O'Clock" [in Chapter 25], a poem about a prisoner's last thoughts).

The third stanza seems to dramatize the speaker's resentment of the rich and privileged. Presumably they have always enjoyed the good fortune denied to him. They are indifferent to his fate; they know nothing about him. Possibly on the edges of these lines is the implication that they have done their own share of bad deeds ("corporate crime," perhaps?), but, as a bluesman knows, it's only the poor, lowly, and down-on-their-luck folks whom the law catches and punishes. But the resentment never quite emerges with full force, and that's because the speaker here acknowledges his own wrongdoing: He has gotten what he deserves for his crime. It's not their wealth, but their sheer mobility, the movement, of the people on the train that "tortures" him. If he gained his freedom, he would "move" far from Folsom, but of course the thrust of the song is that this speaker is going nowhere. He killed a man, justice was done, and thus he does not even have the bitter consolation of knowing he has been mistreated. Tomorrow he'll be singing this same doleful tune again.

Bill Miller, *Cash: An American Man* (2004), provides a good overview through photographs, letters, and an interview with Cash that took place three weeks before his death. *Cash* (2004), a special tribute book by *Rolling Stone Magazine*, includes many recollections, commentaries by Bob Dylan, Merle Haggard, Emmylou Harris, Tom Petty, Sheryl Crow, and others, as well as essays. See also *Cash: An Autobiography* (rpt. 2003).

MERLE HAGGARD
Workin' Man Blues (p. 548)

"Workin' (sometimes printed as "Working") Man Blues" is one of Merle Haggard's most widely played and acclaimed songs. Indeed it's one of the best-known of all country-music songs, listed in a recent poll as #13 among "the top 500 country hits of all time." In his entire body of work, Haggard seeks to be direct and accessible, noting in an interview (2001) that the melody "has to be appealing—you can't forget it's a song"—and emphasizing that the subject must be "easily understood in all languages": It must have "some emotion" and "a real reason for being there." In his autobiography, *Merle Haggard's My House of Memories: For the Record* (1999), he makes a similar point, defining the "art called country music" as "emotion set to rhythm." (That's a topic worth discussing: Are certain rhythms suggestive of certain emotions?)

There's a brisk pace and a jaunty movement to the melody of "Workin' Man Blues," but the "emotion" of the lyrics is rough and raw. Haggard gives us a speaker who is a little wild but who is finally a responsible father and family man, and a proud worker. The speaker has "nine kids," which perhaps testifies to something less than good sense. Haggard could have given us basically the same portrait, but of a father with, say, three kids, which to us on the outside might sound more reasonable, more sensible. But instead Haggard wanted a big family—a family, we would wonder, that might be too big. And the "nine kids" might lead us also to consider, if not the first time through then certainly the second or the third, about the plight of the speaker's wife: What kind of blues might *she* sing, with nine children to care for and a husband away all day at his job, a job that barely enables the family to make ends meet?

This speaker is a manual laborer: He works with his hands, and with a crew. He is dutiful, determined; he pays attention to his own job ("I keep my nose on the grindstone") and doesn't make trouble. As the song shows, he likes a good time but watches himself (he drinks a "little" beer) and does not challenge authority. It is very important to him to know and affirm, twice, that he *earns* his living; he is not, nor will he ever be, a recipient of welfare, someone who relies on a handout.

Haggard reveals, however, that this hardworking family man isn't contented. He may not drink a lot of beer, but part of each day's ritual, it seems, is a stop at the tavern, a place located between the world of work (where one's nose must be kept close to the grindstone) and the world of family (where there is a wife and nine kids to feed and clothe and provide a home for). The speaker dreams about escaping from the life he leads—a life in which he is trapped, with too many "bills" and not enough money to get on top of them. But he has some grit, a moral code: He drinks his beer and imagines a getaway, but then back to work he goes—the kids need shoes.

Notice that through most of the song, Haggard has written "sing" the blues, but toward the end, he also uses the word "cry." He didn't have to do that. But he wanted the shift in tone and perspective that "cry" gives. This is a working *man*, but one who cries, which in this context is not perhaps a "manly" thing to do. Would he ever "cry" when among the other workers on his crew? Maybe, but we doubt it. The "cry" is a deft stroke of characterization on Haggard's part, dramatizing the speaker's near-despair, with a current of self-pity, and yet a self-pity that takes us closer to the speaker. It's a very tough existence: This speaker has earned the right to some self-pity.

"Workin' Man Blues" operates all the more powerfully because of the range and depth of experiences that it—deliberately—does not engage. There's not a jot of detail here about fun, leisure, vacationing, work that might be truly fulfilling, real pleasure with the family on the weekends, or much else. There's sex (the "nine kids" do not appear by magic), but nothing about love. That's all part of someone else's world, a life that this speaker does not inhabit. He feels highly responsible for his wife and family, but one wants to say that he is too hard-pressed and over-burdened (and physically worn out) to enjoy their company. When the workday is over, he heads to the tavern, where he relaxes for a time after work and readies himself for the trip home. It's a grim future that this speaker has ahead of him, and he knows it: "I'll be working long as my two hands are fit to use."

This is one timeless feature of the blues—a situation that is desperate and, from more than one angle, bleak and even awful, yet within this situation there is a figure who persists, a Sisyphus hero of the over-worked working class. Haggard's speaker would wish from us a measure of sympathy, but no charity and no condescension. There's a desperate dignity in his conception of himself, as he wages his struggle against madness, against the "chaos" that, as blues performers have said, threatens to overwhelm us.

For further study: *Merle Haggard: Poet of the Common Man: The Lyrics*, ed. Don Cusic (2001). See also Cecelia Tichi, *High Lonesome: The American Culture of Country Music* (1994), which connects country music and country-blues to central themes in American literature and art. Tichi links Merle Haggard, Hank Williams, Emmylou Harris, and other country stars to Ralph Waldo Emerson, Mark Twain, Edward Hopper, and many more.

LINDA PASTAN
Mini Blues (p. 549)

Through her choice of title, Linda Pastan relates her poem to the tradition of blues songs and poems even as she acknowledges that it is a "mini" blues. It is a miniature—only ten lines long, and the lines are very short.

Pastan starts with the simile "Like a dinghy," and you'll find that some of your students may be unclear about what a "dinghy" is. Many will know it's a small boat, and that's sufficient, but you could offer a bit of additional detail. "Dinghy" derives from a Sanskrit word that means trough or tub, and the original sense is a rowboat or sailboat carrying passengers or cargo off the coasts of India, especially in sheltered waters around the peninsula. More generally, it has come to mean any small boat propelled by oars, sails, or motors, and such a boat, when it's not in operation, is often attached to the end of a larger vessel that tows it.

With line two, Pastan connects this simile to herself. She is like a dinghy, and that is because she always lags behind. "Lag" means to stay or fall behind, to fail to keep up, to move slowly **or** hang back. It can also mean to delay or procrastinate, which implies that the speaker's situation may be due to choice rather than necessity. The first impact of the simile is, we think, that the speaker has this condition *imposed* on her: that is how she was made, what her lot in life is. But there is too the implication that she wishes to lag behind, to stay somewhat distant from another who is stronger, more powerful.

A "wake" is the track left by a ship or other body in the water, but there may be another sense to the word, placed significantly at the end of the line—and at the end of the opening four-line unit: "wake" as the watch held over a dead body prior to burial. Possibly we are pushing the word too far, but this poem is about a kind of death-in-life, about a person who is not vitally present to herself or others. So perhaps hearing a deathly reverberation in "wake" may not be excessive after all.

"Or" marks the shift in "Mini Blues," and here you might invite students to explore how "or" functions. Pastan writes "or" in order to suggest that these are two conceptions of who the speaker is: The first is defined through a simile, while the second is rendered by a short ("mini") story. Ask the students how the second part of the poem builds on the first while adding something to the first, as though the speaker were not satisfied that what she said in lines 1–4 has really caught the hard truth of her condition.

The real "blues" spirit emerges in the final lines: It is often the case in blues that the speaker or singer is called forth, is beckoned to, only to encounter disappointment. Things don't work out: Things don't turn out as one had hoped. We glean from Pastan's poem that this speaker is stuck: The same experience happens over and over again ("always"). The speaker, one might propose, is always facing the sorrow of second-hand status, of an invitation that turns out to be a rejection. But "Mini Blues," in line with so many blues poems and songs, is also a portrait of a speaker who keeps coming back for more. She's hopeful, and then disillusioned. But she still keeps following the bigger boat, she keeps answering the foghorn's call. That's bad, that's good, and it's this good/bad rhythm that blues is made of.

Life is full of good and bad, and bad and good. According to the blues tradition, that's where we are, and who we are: we find courage and dignity in our persistent seeking and hoping in the face of pain.

The best point of departure for studying Pastan is her *Carnival Evening: New and Selected Poems, 1968–1998* (1998). For secondary sources: *Dictionary of Literary Biography, Volume 5: American Poets Since World War II*, first series, ed. Donald J. Greiner (1980), 158–163.

ALLEN GINSBERG
Father Death Blues (p. 550)

We know a number of poems that, like "Father Death Blues," deal with the death of a father. A famous example that comes to mind is Dylan Thomas's "Do Not Go Gentle into That Good Night." Sharon Olds's "The Race" is another we admire. But offhand we could not recall any poem, besides Ginsberg's, in which an address is made to "*Father* Death." Nor have we been able to locate one in the Poetry anthologies we have on our bookshelves. This leads us to suggest that you might begin discussion by asking why Ginsberg portrays Death *as* a "Father": What kinds of connotations does the word "father" evoke? And how might Ginsberg be making use of them?

Note that the tone in the first stanza is jaunty ("Hey"), even disrespectful. We were, and are, a little unsure of where the Father actually is: Is the speaker moving toward him, or away from him? The speaker says he is "flying home," but is Father Death there, or someplace else?

"Flying Home," by the way, is the title of a wonderful jazz tune, made famous by the Benny Goodman Quartet and Sextet in the late 1930s. The African-American writer Ralph Ellison used "Flying Home" as the title for one of his first short stories, published in 1944.

But we need to say a word or two about Ginsberg's parents, for this bears directly on the poem. Second-generation Russian-Jewish immigrants, very much on the political Left, they were interested in Marxism and other radical ideas and movements. When Ginsberg was a child, his mother, Naomi (Levy) Ginsberg (b. 1895), suffered serious mental illness and was institutionalized, and eventually a lobotomy was performed on her. She died in 1956. Louis Ginsberg (b. 1895), a teacher and a poet, was known for his playful way with words and sayings: "Is life worth living? It depends on the liver," and "I've got no axiom to grind." He died in 1976, and his death is reflected in "Father Death Blues."

Sometimes we have seen "Father Death Blues" printed with this line at the end: July 8, 1976 (Over Lake Michigan). This connects the poem all the more specifically to the place and time of its composition, almost immediately after Ginsberg learned of his father's death. As Ginsberg noted, "Father Death Blues" is both a poem and a song:

> "Father Death Blues" was written within 20 hours of hearing of my father's passing. A message from my Tibetan meditation teacher the Ven. Chögyam Trungpa, Rinpoche, said: "I extend my thought that your father enter Dharmakaya. Please let him go, and continue your celebration." I was on the plane home with my harmonium on my lap and wrote it word for word, note for note. . . . One of the rare occasions when both words and music—the vowels and their tones and pitch—were conceived simultaneously in the depth of feeling, realization of death. The voice on it is a voice located in the heart area, that is, it resonates in the breast . . . I never consciously actualized that voice in poem or song of my own until "Father Death Blues." Physical energy diminishes as you get older, but supposedly there's a deepening of wisdom. It seems to me "Father Death Blues" has as much weight and will be as lasting as anything I've done.

Note: Dharmakaya is "the experience of the transcendence of form of the five senses . . . the true nature of the Buddha, which is identical with reality, the essential laws of the universe. . . . the experience is timeless, permanent, devoid of characteristics and free from duality. It is the spiritual body of the buddhas, their true nature, which all buddhas have in common. The Dharmakaya stands for the fundamental truth of emptiness (*shunyata*), the experience of reality or enlightenment."

A few more brief definitions, for terms in the poem:

Buddha: The Sanskrit *buddha* means "awakened, enlightened, from *bodhati*, he awakes, understands.

Gautama, known as the Historical Buddha, d. 483 B.C.E. Gautama (also known as *Shakyamuni* or *Sakyamuni*, literally "Sage of the Shaka clan," and as Siddhartha) was the Indian philosopher who founded Buddhism.

Dharma: a) The natural order or law that underlies the universe; b) Ideal truth especially as taught by Buddha.

Sangha: A Buddhist religious community or monastic order.

For some additional comments about Buddhism, see our discussions of Katherine Min's "Courting a Monk" (this manual, p. 418) and of an anonymous Japanese folktale, "The Mountain-Climber" (this manual, p. 219).

What Ginsberg is doing in this poem is combining Western and Eastern traditions, singing, one might say, the Buddha blues, in order to express his feelings of loss, grief, and *acceptance*—in relation to the specific death of his father and to the sheer omnipresent fact of death in general. The blues note is in the awareness of death, and in the condition of pain in which life is lived: "suffering is what was born." It's death that releases persons from pain, so that the tears we shed are signs of sorrow but also of gratitude—a welcome of the emptying out of pain from our souls.

Walt Whitman's "Song of Myself" (1855) is an influence on "Father Death Blues" as well—Whitman and William Blake were the poets whom Ginsberg cherished the most. As Whitman proposes at one point in his poem, "All goes onward and outward, nothing collapses, / And to die is different from what any one supposed, and luckier." Perhaps this passage intimates something of what Ginsberg means at the end, when he professes that his heart is "still." It is "still" because of his awareness and embrace of Whitman's (and Buddha's) insights and lessons: He is at holy peace with himself. And this awareness foreshadows the stilling of the heart that will transpire at his death, which is where "time" is taking him, as it does all of us.

Biographies include: Barry Miles, *Ginsberg: A Biography* (1989); and Graham Caveney, *Screaming with Joy: The Life of Allen Ginsberg* (1999). See also: James Campbell, *This is the Beat Generation: New York, San Francisco, Paris* (2001). Also illuminating: *Spontaneous Mind: Selected Interviews, 1958–1996, Allen Ginsberg*, ed. David Carter (2001). For critical interpretation: *On the Poetry of Allen Ginsberg*, ed. Lewis Hyde (1984); and John Lardas, *The Bop Apocalypse: The Religious Visions of Kerouac, Ginsberg, and Burroughs* (2001).

CHARLES WRIGHT
Laguna Blues (p. 551)

As we mention in the first of our Topics, Laguna Beach is a beautiful resort area in Orange County, California, and we suspect that part of Wright's strategy (and point) is to move against this fact: He is in a great spot, but he feels blue. Such an incongruity is very much in the line of the blues: When you are feeling low, it does not matter where you are. And in truth if you are feeling low, a nice place will make you feel even worse. Others are enjoying themselves; they look wonderful, in a very pleasant and pleasing setting. Meanwhile, you are glum and melancholy, and why should *that* be? The reason is, you have the blues, as Wright does here.

Before we proceed further, a couple of pedagogical points.

1. It's a battle that never ends, but we keep trying to urge students to look up the meanings of words. It's one thing to know what a word means in general, and another to know what it means in its specific senses—which in turns dramatizes the aims of the writer in using *this* word rather than another in the work he or she has composed. In the case of "Laguna Blues," you might stress to the students that in order to enjoy the poem fully, they should know what a "thermal" is: ("a rising body of warm air"). And they should also be aware of what "trundle" means: when used as a transitive verb, it means "to propel by causing to rotate"; a related, older usage is "to cause to revolve." "Castor beans" and "pepper plant": It might be a good idea to define (and picture) these too.

2. You might also explore the repetition of the line "Whatever it is, it bothers me all the time," with which Wright closes each stanza. Students often view repetition as saying the same thing: They do not grasp the fact that each repetition is a repetition with a difference. When Wright repeats this line in stanzas two and three, each is intended to mark a stage in the poem's movement. The line has one meaning, or range of meanings, the first time we hear it, but it then acquires a related, though different and usually richer, range of meanings the second time, and even more so the third time. Repetition, for a writer, is a means for building up and developing connotations and effects. Ask your students: How does our understanding of the line "Whatever it is, it bothers me all the time" change each time that we hear it? And you might want to stress *hear it*, so the class can feel the impact of the line both as words and sounds.

"Laguna Blues" is also a good poem for working with the class on literal and figurative uses of language. "Saturday afternoon" establishes the day of the week and the time of day, and the reference to the "white pages" seems to imply that the speaker is reading a book that flutters in the breeze. But "cut loose from the heart" has a different thrust—the visceral ache or pain of something, or someone, no longer loved. The phrase is unsettling, a surprise if not a shock. Possibly "dust threads" prepares for it in some way, but we think that this phrase appears to the reader to follow from and be connected to the falling of the white pages. And, looking ahead, notice that you can invite the students later on to comment on why the pages are "white" in line two and then "black" in line twelve.

"Edge of the world": We should not pass by this phrase in line one. The reader may take the phrase literally, especially if he or she knows that Laguna Beach is on the West coast. But maybe, if not on the first reading, then likely on the second, "edge of the world" implies something precarious, fragile, unnerving: it is disquieting to feel "on edge," and if we are on the edge of something we might fall off.

In this context, we have benefited from some observations by the poet-critic Edward Hirsch, in an essay on Wright in *The Columbia History of American Poetry* (1993). He speaks of Wright's "metaphysical search for spiritual meaning," and he adds, "Wright has defined a radiant metaphysics of absence and aspiration, of the longed-for presence of the divine." Hirsch indicates that this "metaphysics of absence" is expressed with a special clarity and intensity in *The World of the Ten Thousand Things: Poems 1980–1990*, the collection in which "Laguna Blues" appears. We agree: there is a strong sense of "absence" in this poem—the speaker gropes for "whatever it is" that bothers him, and without let-up ("all the time"). But the accent or note of "aspiration" is not quite present in this poem: The emphasis is on what is not there.

Though maybe not entirely: Perhaps the fact of the poem's existence bears witness to Wright's aspiration to find out what it is that nettles and discomforts him, to locate the burr on his consciousness. Here, we may find the blues tone of Wright's poem, the voicing of a discontented condition whose origins are unknown, but a condition that *has* to be voiced, put into words and inquired into.

We have to be careful about pushing Wright's poem too far. But the expression of low and empty feelings is important in the blues tradition. It hurts to face pain; but it is also good to face pain: You feel better when you know and acknowledge that you feel bad. This is why Billie Holiday, for example, sings in one of her best songs that she is "so glad to be unhappy." And it's why Louis Armstrong, when he sings the great tune "I Got It Bad, and That Ain't Good," changes the final line, as the song ends, to "I got it bad, and it sure is good."

For further study, we recommend: Charles Wright, *Halflife: Improvisations and Interviews, 1977–87* (1988); and *The Point Where All Things Meet: Essays on Charles Wright*, ed. Tom Andrews (1995).

SHERMAN ALEXIE
Reservation Blues (p. 552)

Perhaps the key point to make is Sherman Alexie's use of the blues tradition—a tradition that developed from African-American sources—to express his feelings as a Native American living (i. e., trapped) on a reservation.

The poem itself is not difficult: It has many of the elements that one encounters everywhere in blues songs and poems—the loneliness, the lowdown mood, the sense of worthlessness. There are tears, and there is no one who understands the speaker's plight. The speaker is hungry, in a literal sense—he has nothing to eat—but he is hungry in another sense as well, hungry for fulfillment as a person, hungry for the chance to find an opportunity to make his life better. Life hems him in, denying him choices, giving him no freedom.

The familiar phrases and feelings of "Reservation Blues" are very much part of Alexie's point: He seeks to locate his poem in the blues tradition, and to gain the emotional authority and the history, that it offers. Paradoxically, the speaker may become less lonely, less isolated, by aligning himself with other blues poets and singers. Alexie sees himself in the blues that he reads and hears, and thus it becomes natural (one is tempted to say, inevitable) for him, as a writer and a Native American with wounds, to voice the blues himself.

As Melissa L. Meyer has noted in the *Oxford Companion to United States History* (2001), by the mid- to late nineteenth century "most Native people east of the Mississippi River had been relocated to 'Indian Territory,' which resembled an ethnic crazy quilt of displaced groups." A series of conflicts and wars led to the decimation of Indian tribes and their cultures—and also to the decision by state and federal governments to determine and provide for Native Americans' "place" in American society as a whole. It was during this period that the U.S. began its policy of placing Indians on "reservations," which were either specially designated lands or lands which "remained" (i.e., were "reserved") after Indian tribes had been forced to cede their homelands for occupancy by whites.

Meyer describes the situation cogently:

> Policy-makers viewed reservations as temporary halfway houses on the road to assimilation. But by the late nineteenth century, they were dismayed that many native people persisted in their customs and beliefs. Easterners hoping to assimilate Indians and westerners hoping to acquire reservation lands coalesced in 1887 to pass the Dawes Severalty Act. Each individual Indian would receive between 40 and 160 acres of land, to be held in trust by the government for twenty-five years while native owners learned how to manage real estate. Homesteaders could buy any land left over. Policy-makers believed that private property would transform Indians' collective values; their cultural traditions would soon follow. The Dawes Act disregarded treaty terms nationwide, except in the arid Southwest. Although some enterprising Indians favored allotment, the vast majority opposed it, but to no avail. In Worcester v. Georgia (1832), the Supreme Court had confirmed the absolute plenary power of the United States over native tribes, and Congress now fully exercised this right.

The reservations created during the nineteenth and twentieth centuries prevented further bloody warfare between whites and Native Americans. But they did not—as federal authorities had hoped—bring about the "assimilation" of Indian peoples into white society: By definition, the "reservations" separated and hence cut off Native Americans from contact with the wider society around them. Today, there are 300 reservations; some are very small, consisting of just a few acres, while others, such as the Navaho Reservation, are very large, in the millions of acres. Nearly all of them have few resources, and their residents suffer from poor education, bad education, and high unemployment. About half of the U.S. Native American population lives on reservations.

The problems that these Native Americans face, as Alexie's poem implies and dramatizes, are severe—unemployment, poverty, disease (tuberculosis and diabetes in particular), alcoholism, crime, suicide. As one scholar has said, "a Native American who wants a middle class job will likely have to leave the reservation."

But for him or her, the immense challenge is how to get away from the reservation, where options and "choices" (Alexie's term) are minimal, even non-existent.

Here is a bit more detail about the conditions of life for Native Americans in one Western state:

> In Arizona, the average age at death for whites is 72, compared with 55 for Native Americans. That's younger than for residents of Bangladesh.
>
> The federal government, which promised in treaties to provide health care for Native Americans, spends less than half as much per tribal member as it does for programs covering other Americans. Private health plans spend more than twice as much per person.
>
> "If this were happening in any other part of America, there would be Senate hearings, commissions," said Sergio Maldonado Sr., an Arapaho who is a program coordinator in the American Indian Studies program at Arizona State University.
>
> "They would be asking, 'Why are these people dying? Is it the water? The air? Anthrax?' But because it's Arapaho, Sioux, the border towns around reservations, no one blinks an eye." *Arizona Central* (April 14, 2002)

Reminder: We include another poem by Alexie, "On the Amtrak," elsewhere in our text.

For a profile of Alexie's life and literary career: Lynn Cline, "About Sherman Alexie," *Ploughshares* 26:4 (Winter 2000/2001), 197–202. See also: John Newton, "Sherman Alexie's Autoethnography," *Contemporary Literature* 42:2 (Summer 2001), 413–28; and Stephen F. Evans, "'Open Containers': Sherman Alexie's Drunken Indians," *The American Indian Quarterly* 25:1 (Winter 2001), 46–72.

JANE FLANDERS
Van Gogh's Bed (p. 556)

Ms. Flanders kindly furnished us with some remarks about her poem. She writes:

> The desire for simplicity [expressed in van Gogh's letters] would seem to be at the heart of the painting. Likewise the poem is "simple," even crude, especially the stubby first line of each stanza with its list of rudimentary adjectives. But what we are given, in both instances, is, of course, the illusion of simplicity. In the painting the room ought to seem restful. Actually it excites the eye with its bright colors, bold strokes, and odd angles. Even the bed itself looks as if it might levitate or drive off like some magical conveyance. A childlike playfulness invites the poet's reverie.

By what wonderful process was it made? What did he dream about when he slept in it? The artist's absence (the empty bed) which may at first seem innocuous or self-evident (he's busy painting the picture, isn't he?) also reminds us that he would have his first mental crisis a few months later and his suicide at the age of thirty-seven was little more than a year away. Likewise, in the poem's final stanza, concrete details give way to something more elusive—light, fragrance, and not happiness itself, but the memory of happiness, with its hint of loss and melancholy.

We hope we are not being presumptuous if we add a few remarks of our own.

1. Using the title as the beginning—the reader more or less has to go back and repeat the title at the start of each stanza—is unusual, interesting, and witty.
2. The bed is orange, "like Cinderella's coach." The coach, of course, was a transformed pumpkin (hence orange), and transforming things is what artists do.
3. The coach-pumpkin-sun image continues into the second stanza, where van Gogh is conceived as being carried "bumpily to the ball." Possibly the idea is that the pumpkin-coach carries him also toward the sun, i.e., he is brought violently toward one of his chief subjects.
4. Although we get some violence in the second stanza ("slept alone, tossing," "bumpily"), in the third stanza we get a glimpse of the "friendly . . . peasant" world that he moved in. If there is violence here ("beat") it is for good domestic purposes ("beat his mattress till it rose like meringue").
5. The last stanza begins a bit desolately ("empty") but immediately is filled with nature ("Morning light pours in"), nature transformed by human beings ("wine"), nature and humanity ("fragrance"), and humanity ("the memory of happiness").

WILLIAM CARLOS WILLIAMS
The Great Figure (p. 559)

The biographical headnote in the text gives Williams's account of the origin of the poem.

When one first encounters the poem, perhaps one takes the title—"The Great Figure"—to be a notable person. Certainly the first two lines, taken in conjunction with the title, allow us to assume that the speaker met someone on a rainy night ("Among the rain / and lights"), but beginning with the third line we adjust this impression and learn that the encounter is not with a notable person but with a notable, even heroic, thing, the number 5, in gold, on a red fire engine. The third line, the line that introduces the fire engine's number, is the longest in the poem (six syllables), suggesting its importance. On the other hand, the very short lines, especially "in gold" and "on a red" are emphatic because of their brevity as well as because of the strong colors.

"Fire truck" appears in the sixth line, just above the middle of the thirteen-line poem. The central line consists of only one word, "moving," and from here on the truck apparently has moved out of sight because the remaining lines about the truck are about its sound ("clangs," "howls"), not its appearance, though the sentence (and the poem) ends with a visual image, but not of the truck; the speaker now sees not the truck but "the dark city."

The poem has been much praised. Dare one say that two lines, each consisting of a single word, are perhaps weak spots? We have in mind "tense / unheeded," words that strike us as weak. The "gong clangs" and the "siren howls" make "tense" unneeded, and we can't quite imagine how anyone, even the most jaded New Yorker, can let a screaming fire engine go by "unheeded." And if New Yorkers *do* let fire engines go by unheeded, well, perhaps it is not for Dr. Williams to announce his superiority to them by saying in effect that *he* is heeding the engine, witness this poem. In fact, "unheeded" seems to shift attention away from the engine, which we take to be the real subject, and to an irrelevant audience.

Now for a brief comment on Demuth's painting. In our headnote we mention that Demuth is sometimes called a Cubist-Realist, a term that more or less fits this atypical painting; more typically Demuth's work is (like the work of Charles Sheeler) characterized as Precisionist, with reference to the almost sterile way in which he delineated architecture. In *I Saw the Figure 5 in Gold* the realism is evident chiefly in the lack of distortion of the number 5; the cubism—of a very tame sort—is a bit more evident, in the diagonals and the planes, and especially in what we take to be the simultaneous treatment of the front (the headlights) and the side (the number 5) of the fire engine.

The three concentric 5s presumably give a violent in-and-out sensation, imitating (with the assistance of the converging diagonals) the onrushing engine. Incidentally, although one often reads, in students' discussions of pictures, that "the eye first sees . . . , and then moves to. . . ." experiments have shown that all such discussions are misguided. The eye does not travel along a path, but rather jumps back and forth all over the place.

A few more words about the figure 5. John Malcolm Brinnin, in *William Carlos Williams* (1963), said that "the possibility that the figure 5, or any other figure, on a fire engine might be 'tense' is absurd" (p. 28). This remark distressed Bram Dijkstra, who, in *The Hieroglyphics of a New Speech: Cubism, Steiglitz, and the Early Poetry of William Carlos Williams* (1969), replied:

> One look at Charles Demuth's visual interpretation of the poem, executed in close association with Williams, should suffice to indicate the appropriateness and accuracy of Williams' use of the word "tense." Demuth's figure 5 strains and pulls, receding and projecting itself again onto the canvas, its original movement in time transformed into visual tensions, caught within the warring pressure lines of darkness and lamplight, a golden object held suspended on the red fires of sound. (p. 78)

You may want to ask students if this is a useful way to talk about the picture—and if it indeed shows that (to go back to Brinnin's point) a digit on a fire engine can be "tense."

The fact that the picture was a sort of portrait of a friend accounts for the inscription of Williams's first name at the top (the letters are partly cut off) and middle name (without the final *s*) in barely discernable letters just below the top of the figure 5. (Conceivably the trimmed names may correspond to the fragmentary glimpses of the moving engine.) The friendly personal connection between Demuth and Williams also accounts for the whimsical "Art Co" at the right, written on what probably is a representation of a storefront. At the bottom left, in small letters, Demuth has written his own initials, and in the bottom center, again in small letters, Williams's initials.

Williams's *Autobiography* (1951), *Selected Essays* (1954), and *Selected Letters,* ed. John C. Thirlwall (1957), are important sources. The *Collected Poems,* 2 vols., ed. A. Walton Litz and Christopher MacGowan (1986–1988), may offer too much for undergraduates, who might do better to start with *Selected Poems,* with an introduction by Randall Jarrell (1969). For an insightful introduction: James E. Breslin, *William Carlos Williams: An American Artist* (1970). See also Kelli A. Larson, *Guide to the Poetry of William Carlos Williams* (1995).

ADRIENNE RICH
Mourning Picture (p. 560)

Edwin Romanzo Elmer's painting has something of the stiffness that one associates with Sunday painters, who until the 1970s were called primitive painters. These painters lacked formal training in art, and as a consequence they were likely to be unskilled in linear perspective and in other ways of suggesting gradual recession in space. They were, however, usually deeply concerned with their own sort of realism, with (for instance) depicting all four legs of a cow because, after all, most cows *do* have four legs—even though in fact in certain positions a leg or two might be invisible. Another characteristic of the work of Sunday painters is that the figures seem posed, as though a photographer using a slow film had arranged his subjects and then told them to be sure not to move.

In fact, Elmer, a native of rural Massachusetts, did receive some formal training in New York at the Academy of Design, but this undated painting probably antedates his stay in New York.

Rich's poem seems to us to have something of the painting's almost unnatural specificity. For instance, the first line is careful to tell us—in a rather flat, unemotional and yet rather solemn tone—that the chair is mahogany and that the rocker is cane: "They have carried the mahogany chair and the cane rocker / out under the lilac bush. . . ." But if the speaker's voice is akin to the world of the painting, matter-of-fact and yet hyper-keen (unblinking, one might say) and otherworldly, these qualities are especially appropriate, since the speaker is the dead girl. That is, the speaker sees things as, in a way, they are but in a way that is not quite natural. For instance, she speaks of "the map of every lilac leaf." When you think of it, leaves do resemble maps because of their veins, but the perception seems unnatural, a sort of perception through a magnifying glass. (By the way, another of Elmer's paintings shows a landscape as seen not simply through a window but through a magnifying glass perched on a vase on a table.)

We don't want to overemphasize the strangeness of the voice, however; the perception of the maplike leaf leads to a more usual perception, "the net of veins on my father's / grief-tranced hand." This chain continues in lines 25–26 with the image of silk thread, which in 27 becomes "a web in the dew." But what exactly do we make of line 25, "the silk-spool will run bare"? These words constitute the end of a sentence about the grieving mother; we might have thought that the silk spool would remain unconsumed, that is, the mother might have put away her domestic work when the child died. But Rich tells us, on the contrary, that the "silk-spool will run bare," possibly suggesting the three fates, who spin, measure, and cut a thread, thereby ending a person's life.

After writing the preceding paragraph, with its conjecture about the silk-spool, we came across an article about Elmer, written by his niece, Maud Valona Elmer (*Massachusetts Review* 6 [1964–1965]: 121–144). She mentions that as a boy Elmer worked in a spool-silk factory (presumably a factory that wound silk thread on spools, or perhaps a factory that prepared silk to be wound on spools). She also mentions that after the death of their daughter, Elmer and his wife left the house shown in the picture and went to live with the wife's mother, in Baptist Corner (cf. line 24). Since other information about Edwin Romanzo Elmer is virtually nonexistent, one can safely say that the article in *Massachusetts Review*—and of course the painting, which the niece sold to the Smith College Museum of Art—inspired Rich to write the poem.

The veins of the leaf become, in line 30, the "skeleton" of the leaf, thereby continuing the death imagery and continuing, too, the somewhat strange quality of the imagery. This strangeness is evident, too, in the "shadowless" house (line 32), shadowless because the time is noonday (line 31), when the sun is directly above us, but also shadowless because death and sadness have not yet come to the house. At the end of the poem the speaker (we think, but we are far from certain) says that if she recreated the world she—having experienced death—could not leave out death from what had seemed an idyllic world, a world of loving parents, placid sheep, and a doll to be cared for.

One other point: we learn from Maud Valona Elmer's article that the lamb in the picture indicates that the child is dead. In old New England cemeteries the tombstones of children are sometimes adorned with a lamb, suggesting that the deceased was "a Lamb of God."

Having said all this, we still remain unsure about the poem, but here are the main lines of our thought:

1. In "Mourning Picture," Effie describes Elmer's picture. In the first stanza she sees that "they" (probably the parents, possibly servants, but it doesn't

matter) have carried out the chair and the rocker, that the parents "darkly sit there," the house "stands fast," the doll lies in her pram. She sees the mourning, but interestingly she does not see herself, with the lamb, the largest figures in the picture. Effie believes that she could remake (like the artist) every particle of that world ("I could remake . . . [I could] draw out") but does not.

2. The second stanza describes Effie's present self, which we are inclined to think means in the hours after death, while she (the shade of the dead) still inhabits the house. What she experiences is that "the dream condenses." (Life here, as at the poem's end, *is* a dream.) It doesn't vanish yet. During this period, while the family mourns, she is "visible and invisible / remembering and remembered."

3. In the last stanza she foresees her parents' future. She imagines making the world "again" (line 29) but will not. Her death ("*this*") is part of her life. She remains "Effie"; "you" (meaning her parents, the painter, the reader?) are *her* dream.

CATHY SONG
Beauty and Sadness (p. 563)

The poem concerns the unhappy artist who creates enduring beauty. In some versions, the artist creates beauty *because* he or she is unhappy, as the oyster creates a pearl out of its discomfort, and this apparently is what Song is suggesting when she says that the "inconsolable" Utamaro—inconsolable presumably because the women were "indifferent" (line 42)—"graced these women with immortality" (line 50). We can go a little further and say that when she speaks of "the dwarfed and bespectacled painter" (line 53) Song implies the Freudian idea of the artist who, suffering from unsatisfied longings, engages in fantasy wish-fulfillment—in this case, making pictures of the beauties he cannot in reality win. Speaking more generally, we can say that Song's poem touches on the venerable theme of *ars longa, vita brevis.*

A few notes: the term *ukiyo* originally was a Buddhist term for "the world of suffering," i.e., the fleeting, transient world of incarnation, but in Japan in the late seventeenth century, by means of a pun, it became "the floating world," i.e., the world of transient pleasure. (The pronunciation is the same, but the initial character is different.) Pictures of the floating world—e.g., of women and of actors—are called *ukiyo-e.* In Song's poem notice "floating world" in line 26 and "fleeting loveliness" in line 13. In line 12, "transfer" probably alludes on the literal level to the thin paper on which the artist drew his design. This paper, placed on the block, provided the carver with a guide for cutting.

Song's books of poetry include *Picture Bride* (1983); *Frameless Windows, Squares of Light* (1988); and *School Figures* (1994). She is eloquent in describing and exploring the relationships between Korean and Chinese cultures and traditions (Song's mother is Chinese, and her father is Korean) and in evoking the history and setting of Hawaii, where she was born.

Mary Jo Salter
The Rebirth of Venus (p. 564)

Botticelli's *The Birth of Venus* (which we will discuss in a moment) is one of the most frequently reproduced paintings in the world. And it does indeed seem to be a favorite of sidewalk artists; we have on several occasions seen the face of Venus done in chalk on the street.

In line 3 Salter mentions chalk, an almost comically inappropriate medium for this goddess who was born in the sea, who is depicted as standing on a floating shell, and who is associated with life-giving fluids. Salter wittily compounds the irony by saying, in her first line, that the artist has "knelt to *fish* her face up from the sidewalk."

In the text we ask students what Salter may mean (lines 6–8) when she refers to "that woman men divined / ages before a painter let them look / into the eyes their eyes had had in mind". We take it that Salter is saying that in this picture of Venus the painter gives form ("an earthly habitation, and a name," to quote Hippolyta, from *A Midsummer Night's Dream*) to what we vaguely intuit or "divine." Perhaps the idea is close to a point that the painter Paul Klee made when he said, "Art does not reproduce the visible; rather, it renders visible."

A query: in lines 5–6, which immediately precede the passage we have just discussed, is Salter getting at the Platonic notion that a work of art is a copy of a copy, i.e., a copy of something on earth, and the something-on-earth is itself only a copy of a heavenly (Platonic) ideal? That is, is Salter saying that the sidewalk artist is copying a reproduction in a book, which itself is a copy of Botticelli's work, and Botticelli's work is the copy of an ideal? (As we will mention in a moment, scholars agree that Botticelli was influenced by Neo-Platonism, and it is likely that Salter knew this.)

In "let there be light" (line 21), we take Salter to be expressing the hope that the afternoon will last long enough for this earnest artist to complete his chalk drawing on the sidewalk, although it is clear that rain is impending and that Venus therefore will soon be returned to her watery element. The tone is genial, even wry ("it's clear enough the rain / will swamp her like a tide") but the poet clearly respects this painstaking artist ("he won't rush") who is constantly "envisioning faces."

A few words about *The Birth of Venus* (c. 1482), by Sandro Botticelli (1445–1510), may be relevant. It is a Renaissance painting, of course, but the nude Venus has little of the obvious voluptuousness—the sense of a ripe, weighty, physical body, we might almost say—that one finds in other Renaissance paintings, especially the Venetian paintings. (Botticelli was a Florentine.) Similarly, there is surprisingly little sense of depth in this picture; aside from the shell, almost everything seems to be at the front. That is,

Botticelli has treated his material in a highly decorative manner (the waves are indicated by little V-shaped squiggles on a flat surface) and has produced a painting of a Venus who has a somewhat etherealized or spiritual quality.

According to a simple, brutal, ancient legend, Saturn (Greek: Cronus) castrated his father, Uranus, and threw the severed genitals into the sea. From the organs, as they gathered foam (*aphros*), was born Venus (Greek: Aphrodite), goddess of love. Botticelli's contemporaries, the Neo-Platonists, in particular Marsilio Ficino, interpreted this myth as an elaborate allegory concerning the birth of beauty in the human soul or mind: when we create or generate some work of beauty, we experience pleasure because we have been fertilized by divinity.

Putting aside allegorical interpretations of the picture—and all scholars agree that Botticelli painted in a Neo-Platonic climate—we can say that the picture shows, at the left, two embracing wind gods (flying Zephyrs) who are blowing Venus (standing on a cockle shell) to her sacred island of Cyprus. At the right a female figure, variously interpreted as representing the Hours or as the nymph Pomona (descended from the ancient goddess of fruit trees), extends to the naked goddess a flower-embroidered cloak.

In the middle of the painting, between these energetic figures and under a shower of roses, stands Venus herself, modestly posed (the posture is called *Venus pudica*, i.e., modest Venus). Although the pose is classic, the rhythmic curve of her body is not, since her weight does not really rest on her feet. As Kenneth Clark puts it, in *The Nude* (1956), "She is not standing, but floating" (p. 102). The figure is also unclassical—that is, it is Gothic (medieval)—in the steeply sloping shoulders and the elongated body. On the other hand, the nudity of course is a sign of classical influence; in the Middle Ages the only nude figures were Adam and Eve, or damned souls. The nudity here, as we have already suggested, is perhaps more ethereal than voluptuous; she looks virginal, and indeed Kenneth Clark has pointed out that Botticelli used the same head for his Madonnas. Clark characterizes her expression as "wistful" (p. 102).

Salter's collections of poetry include *Henry Purcell in Japan* (1985); *Unfinished Painting* (1989); *Sunday Skaters* (1994); and *A Kiss in Space* (1999).

ANNE SEXTON
The Starry Night (p. 567)

We think that one can reasonably call some of the language of this poem surrealistic—particularly the description of a "black-haired tree" that "slips / up like a drowned woman into the hot sky". (A tree presented as having hair, and a woman drowning upward seem to us to qualify; and so does the passage, in the second stanza, about the moon pushing children from its eye.)

Surrealism is characterized by dreamlike, fantastic imagery, often presented in finicky detail and therefore (because the realism seems to be at odds with the subject matter) the more disconcerting. Surrealism is quite different from

Expressionism. Expressionistic painting—and van Gogh is considered to be the father of Expressionism—does not seek to offer the surreal world of dreams and fantasies, nor does it seek to offer the world as perceived by traditional painters, who aimed at reproducing nature. Rather, Expressionist painting, as is evident in many of van Gogh's pictures, seeks to present the artist's emotions or emotional response to the ostensible subject matter. (Sexton, as a "confessional poet," quite naturally found van Gogh's work of special interest.) Thus, as van Gogh's letters indicate, his picture of his bed (see the text and this manual) was supposed to convey the artist's sense of rest. In *The Starry Night* van Gogh gives us not the dark sky with a thousand points of light that all of us can and do see but a blazing heaven that expresses his ecstatic feelings about eternity. (Stars are a traditional symbol of eternity.) Also expressive of his feelings, no doubt, is the writhing cypress. In a letter to his brother, van Gogh says that he sees the sunflower and the cypress as both opposite and equivalent. Bright yellow sunflowers embody the life force, but they go to seed and die; dark cypresses are associated with death, but they energetically rise toward heaven. (See Vojtech Jirst-Wasiutynski on van Gogh's cypresses, in *Art Bulletin* 75 [1993]: 647–670, especially 657–660.) Also expressive is the little town, which is so slight when compared to the grandeur of nature.

But if Sexton's imagery is surrealistic, her poem is nevertheless tightly ordered. (There is no contradiction here. Surrealists such as Dali and Magritte often use conspicuously formal compositions.) The first two stanzas closely resemble each other, most obviously in the number of lines and of course in the identity of the last two lines of each of these stanzas, but in other ways too; for instance, the first line of each of these stanzas is conspicuously shorter than the second line. Doubtless Sexton counted on the reader perceiving the formal connection between the first two stanzas because much of the force of the poem depends on the fact that the last stanza is truncated—five lines instead of six, and only two syllables in the final line, instead of four. That is, "I want to die" (the ending of the first and second stanzas) is diminished to "no cry," a silent ending to an unheroic extinction of the flesh ("no flag," "no belly").

Having said that the poet imagines an unheroic extinction, we are uncomfortably aware that in the first two stanzas she seems to want to go off in a blaze of light ("Oh starry starry night! This is how / I want to die"). Still, our sense is that the third stanza makes a reader see the first two stanzas in a new light.

Two other points: (1) van Gogh's painting, as his letter suggests, is a religious painting, or, rather, an expression of the artist's sense of the divinity of nature, whereas Sexton's poem seems to us to have nothing to do with religion. (2) The poem comes from *All My Pretty Ones* (1962), a book of poems much concerned with death. (The book takes its title from *Macbeth* 4.3.216, where Macduff is speaking of the children whom Macbeth slaughtered. Both of Sexton's parents had died within a few months of each other in 1959, and her father-in-law, of whom she was very fond, had died a few months later.)

For Sexton: *Anne Sexton: A Self-Portrait in Letters,* ed. Linda Gray Sexton (1977); *No Evil Star: Selected Essays, Interviews, and Prose* (1985); and *Selected Poems* (1988). Interviews and essays on Sexton are gathered in *Anne*

Sexton: *The Artist and Her Critics,* ed. J. D. McClatchy (1978). See also *Critical Essays on Anne Sexton* (1989), ed. Linda Wagner-Martin, and Diane Wood Middlebrook, *Anne Sexton: A Biography* (1991).

A note on the assignment in the text: If you use this assignment, which asks students to discuss in what ways the poem does and does not describe the painting, you may want to follow this procedure: Divide the class into two groups. One group, after conferring for 15–20 minutes, would then report on the ways the poem does not reproduce the picture; the other on the ways it does.

W. H. AUDEN
Musée des Beaux Arts (p. 569)

Useful pieces on "Musée" are in *College English* 24 (April 1963): 529–531; *Modern Language Notes* 76 (April 1961): 331–336; *Textual Analysis* (1986), ed. Mary Ann Caws (a relatively difficult essay by Michael Riffaterre); and *Art Journal* 32 (Winter 1972–1973): 157–162—the last useful primarily because it includes reproductions of Brueghel's work and it reprints other poems relating to his pictures. We reproduce Brueghel's picture of Icarus (in the Brussels Museum of Fine Arts, hence Auden's title); for a larger color reproduction see Timothy Foote, *The World of Brueghel* (1968). Auden glances at some of Brueghel's other paintings (the children skating in *The Numbering of Bethlehem* are indifferent to Joseph and Mary, who are almost lost in a crowd; the dogs and the horses in *The Massacre of the Innocents*), and his poem accurately catches Brueghel's sense of nature undisturbed by what rarely happens to the individual.

As Otto Benesch points out (*The Art of the Renaissance in Northern Europe* [1945], p. 99), in *Icarus* Brueghel gives us a sense of cosmic landscape. Plowman, shepherd, and fisherman go about their business, unaware of Icarus, who is represented in the lower right-hand corner simply by his lower legs and feet, the rest of him being submerged in the sea. Daedalus is nowhere represented; the yellow sun sets in the west, and the sea, coasts, and islands are transfigured with a silvery light. It should be noted that in Ovid's account in *Metamorphoses* 8, lines 183–235, the plowman, shepherd, and fisherman beheld Icarus and Daedalus with amazement, taking the two for gods. Given Brueghel's diminution of Icarus—legs and feet, unnoticed by the other figures in the picture—it is fair to say that Brueghel is offering a comment on the pride of scientists. James Snyder, who makes this point in *Northern Renaissance Art* (1985), p. 510, also calls attention to the shiny pate of a recumbent man, a dead man, at the left margin, halfway up and all but invisible even in the original painting. This image, Snyder says, "assuredly is meant to express the old Netherlandish saying, 'No plow stops over the death of any man,' or over Brueghel's Everyman, a clever footnote that reveals, after all, that peasant wisdom can be as profound as that of the ancients."

Students are first inclined to see Auden's poem as an indictment of indifference; our own view is that Auden gives the daily world its due, especially in such phrases as "doggy life" and "innocent behind"; that is, he helps us see that all of creation cannot and need not suffer along with heroes. Auden's poem evoked a pleasant reply by Randall Jarrell, "The Old and the New Masters," *Collected Poems* (1959), pp. 332–333. It begins, "About suffering, about adoration, the old masters / Disagree. . . ."

 Collected Poems (1976) and *The English Auden: Poems, Essays, and Dramatic Writings, 1927–1939* (1977), both edited by Edward Mendelson, are full of interesting work, but they give more than most undergraduates will be able to absorb. We tend to direct students to the selections by Auden that are included in the Norton and Oxford anthologies of English literature and in the *Norton Anthology of Modern Poetry* (1988). *The Dyer's Hand and Other Essays* (1968) and *Forewords and Afterwords* (1973) collect many of Auden's best literary essays and reviews.

 Two useful books for students: John Fuller, *A Reader's Guide to W. H. Auden* (1970), and Monroe K. Spears, *The Poetry of W. H. Auden: The Disenchanted Island* (1963). More advanced students will find value in Anthony Hecht, *The Hidden Law: The Poetry of W. H. Auden* (1993). Biographies have been written by Humphrey Carpenter (1981) and Richard Davenport-Hines (1995). For literary and social contexts: Samuel Hynes, *The Auden Generation: Literature and Politics in England in the 1930s* (1976).

X. J. KENNEDY
Nude Descending a Staircase (p. 571)

Duchamp's picture was exhibited at the famous Armory Show in 1913. This exhibition was chiefly devoted to contemporary American art—quite traditional stuff as we now look at it—but it also included material from the School of Paris. Predictably, the European material provoked indignation, ridicule, and passionate defense. Today the Armory show is regarded as marking the introduction of contemporary European art to America.

 Part of Duchamp's joke in *Nude Descending a Staircase* is that the picture is so *un*sensual, so disappointing to anyone who has expectations of looking at a nude. This is entirely in keeping with Duchamp's interest in the movements of the human body as akin to the movements of a machine. He was influenced by the chronophotographs of Etienne-Jules Marey (1830–1904), who superimposed sequential photographs of a figure in motion. For examples of Marey's work, see Aaron Scharf, *Art and Photography* (1968), and Beaumont Newhall, *The History of Photography* 5th ed. (1999), or, in fact, almost any history of photography. In Duchamp's painting, the curved lines—some made out of dots—derive from Marey, who used such lines to indicate what he called "lines of force." (Duchamp also knew the somewhat comparable photographs of figures in motion made by Eadweard Muybridge.) Photographs of bodies in movement were of considerable interest to scientists.

For instance, Dr. Oliver Wendell Holmes used photographic studies of men walking in his work in designing artificial limbs for soldiers wounded in the Civil War. Photographs, he reported, are

> a new source.... We have selected a number of instantaneous stereoscopic views of the streets and public places of Paris and New York, each of them showing walking figures, among which some may be found in every stage of the complex act we are studying. (qtd. in Newhall, p. 117)

Duchamp's interest in the mechanics of motion continued throughout his life; in his later years, he amused himself by devising complex machines that performed no useful function.

He painted *Nude* not in flesh colors but in the color of wood precisely because he did not want it to be seductive; the picture was to be a sort of scientific study of the machine-like aspects of the body.

> When we consider the motion of form through space in a given time, we enter the world of geometry and mathematics, just as we do when we build a machine for that purpose. Now if I show the ascent of an airplane, I try to show what it does. I do not make a still-life picture of it. When the vision of the *Nude* flashed upon me, I knew that it would break forever the enslaving chains of Naturalism.
> (qtd. in Ian Crofton, *A Dictionary of Art Quotations* [1988], p. 57)

For a longer comment by Duchamp, see *Theories of Modern Art*, ed. Herschel Chipp (1968), pp. 393–395.

What is especially interesting in Kennedy's poem is the engaging sensuous—even sensual—content, evident in such words as "flesh," "A gold of lemon," "She sifts in sunlight," "With nothing on," "We spy," "thigh on thigh," "lips," and "her parts." Surely Kennedy is having a little joke, putting the missing nude back into the picture. In its day, in the Armory show, the picture provoked not only wrath from conventional art critics but also genial humor from those simple souls who wanted a sexy picture of a woman. The most famous quip that came out of all this is that the picture shows not a nude but an explosion in a shingle factory. Where was the nude? *The American Art News* offered a $10 prize. Here is the winning solution:

> You've tried to find her,
> And you've looked in vain
> Up the picture and down again,
> You've tried to fashion her of broken bits,
> And you've worked yourself into seventeen fits.
> The reason you've failed to tell you I can,
> It isn't a lady but only a man.
> (qtd. in Milton W. Brown, *The Story of the Armory Show* (1963), p. 136)

Our point: Kennedy is not simply describing the picture as (dare one say it?) the naked eye sees it. Rather, he is recreating it, turning it into (indeed) a picture of a nude descending a staircase. At the same time, he *does* catch Duchamp's mechanistic view ("the swinging air / That parts to let her parts go by," "Collects her motions into shape") and he does effectively use metaphors to describe what we see ("One-woman waterfall," "she wears / Her slow descent like a long cape").

GREG PAPE
American Flamingo (p. 572)

Greg Pape's poem is a response to "American Flamingo," one of the beautiful hand-colored plates in John James Audubon's *Birds of America,* published in four enormous volumes (each plate is about forty inches tall and thirty inches wide) between 1827 and 1838. Each bird is shown life-size; hence, the flamingo (in order to fit on the page) had to be shown with its head down. Audubon ingeniously shows the bird in other poses in the flamingos in the distance.

The illegitimate son of a French merchant and slave trader and a Creole woman of Saint-Domingue (now Haiti) in the West Indies, and a failure in several business ventures, Audubon had a dream, to which he came to devote his life: He wanted to paint every species of bird in North America. With courage and persistence, Audubon traveled throughout the United States and Canada, seeking always to draw the birds in their natural habitat. The American scientific community failed to recognize the brilliance of his work—his depiction of birds in action, so to speak, as living creatures within a particular environment rather than as inert specimens—and therefore in 1826 he left the United States for England. He found support and collaborators in England, and his work soon went into production and moved forward, even as Audubon himself made return visits to the United States for further research and drawing and painting for the volumes.

Audubon was a passionate writer as well as an artist; with William MacGillivray, he wrote the *Ornithological Biography* (5 vols., 1831–1839) to accompany *Birds of America*. Over the years he has been criticized for sacrificing scientific accuracy for dramatic effect, and there is some truth to this charge. But it is also the case that on occasion Audubon drew birds in strained, near-to-impossible poses because that was, for him, the best means for showing something new and noteworthy—for example, a feature of a bird's coloring that might be hard to glimpse. Remember, he studied the birds in their setting, not in a museum or laboratory.

The force and romantic glamour of Audubon's pioneering personality helps to clarify the quotation from the Southern poet-critic Robert Penn Warren (1905–1989) that Pape gives toward the middle of his poem. It is taken from Warren's long poem *Audubon: A Vision,* published in 1969. (Warren was born in Guthrie, Kentucky, the state where Audubon lived as a young man and tried to make a success of himself in business.) Section I, titled "Was Not the Lost Dauphin," begins with this stanza in part A:

> Was not the lost dauphin, though handsome was only
> Base-born and not even able
> To make a decent living, was only
> Himself, Jean Jacques, and his passion—what
> Is man but his passion?

Referring to Audubon by his baptismal name "Jean Jacques," Warren sets aside the familiar but false story that Audubon was the Dauphin, the son of the dethroned Louis XVI and Marie Antoinette. Interestingly, in the next stanzas, Warren describes Audubon in quest of the Great White Heron, which in *Birds of America* comes just a few plates before the American Flamingo that Pape focuses on. Perhaps the vivid color of the flamingo seized Pape's attention. Or, more simply but importantly, perhaps for this poem of his own, Pape needed to select a different bird from the one that Warren chose: it would hardly do to write about the same one.

Curiously enough—and this point may bear on the solemn, evocative tone of the second half of the poem—the American flamingo is now an infrequent visitor to Florida, and so it would be relatively unusual today to find these birds in Hialeah, the city (and site of the famous race track) in the southeast part of the state to which Pape refers. The birds at the race track are in fact imported captives. According to the Audubon Society's *Encyclopedia of North American Birds* (1995 ed.), the American flamingo "wandered formerly in large numbers to Florida, but now rarely"; to see these brightly hued, long-legged, and long-necked birds in large numbers, one must travel to the West Indies and the Bahamas or to the northern coast of South America.

The *Encyclopedia* also notes that the American flamingo is shy, vigilant, hard to approach, and this may suggest why Pape shows such steady, absorbed interest in the flamingo's watchful eyes. Pape admires and highly values the work that Audubon has done; in line 23, he says that the movements of the flamingos in the background are "stunning"—a tribute to the painter's craftsmanship. And the deliberate pace of Pape's lines itself functions as a more general form of praise, with the passionate care of the poem serving to illuminate Audubon's own passion for detail.

For us, and for students, the challenge of the poem is describing what it all adds up to. Pape's images are striking, especially in the second half, as when he depicts "the satin figures of the jockeys / perched like bright beetles on the backs / of horses. . . ." Here he nicely makes good work of the verb "perched," which we associate for a moment with the posture of a bird only to find that in this instance Pape is attaching it to the beetles on the horses' backs. Still, though they respond to such details, our students have wondered about the broader "point" of the poem, and we find ourselves wondering about the same issue. It could be that this is a mistake on our part—the wrong kind of question to ask. The point of the poem may not be an easily statable theme but, rather, may lie precisely in the exercise of the poet's craft, which, again, is meant richly to compliment the passionate ornithologist Audubon.

But we suspect that there is, after all, a thematic point that Pape seeks to draw in this poem, and it is one that explores the ambiguities of past and present. Many decades ago, Audubon performed his dogged, extraordinary work, and it has eternalized the American flamingo and the other birds upon whom he lavished such care. For Pape, the American flamingo still lives—he saw them. Yet we must be more exact; they live in his memory—he saw them once, in a time now past, and even then part of the reason they awed Pape and the spectators is because they came, it seemed, from "the old world." Seeing them was unforgettable, and Pape records this memory in his poem, as his companion piece to the unforgettable drawing that Audubon has given us.

Note: Students may puzzle a bit over the first lines of the poem: Was this lover of birds a hunter? Audubon was; he hunted all his life and even admitted that when he was a young man he sometimes shot wild animals and birds for the sheer fun of it. Hence Pape may be kinder to him—saying that he shot the birds to study them—than the truth warrants.

The best place to begin the up-to-date study of Audubon's work is *Birds of America: The Watercolors for* The Birds of America, ed. Annette Blaugrund and Theodore E. Stebbins Jr.; catalog entries by Carole Anne Slatkin; with essays by Stebbins and others (1993). For a good short discussion, see Robert Hughes, *American Visions* (1997); also useful is the entry in *The Dictionary of Art* (1996). Somewhat dated, but still useful, is Constance Rourke, *Audubon* (1936). Biographies have been written by Alice Ford (1964) and Alexander B. Adams (1966). For a good selection of Audubon's writings, see the *Audubon Reader,* ed. Scott Russell Sanders (1986).

CARL PHILLIPS
Luncheon on the Grass (p. 574)

We'll begin with a few comments about the painting. According to a contemporary, Manet said, "I'm told that I must do a nude. All right. I will. Back in our studio days, I copied Georgione's women. . . . I'm going to do it over." (The picture that he copied in the Louvre, *The Concert,* is now attributed to Titian.) Manet, regarded as "a painter of modern life" (a term Baudelaire used for slightly earlier realists such as Daumier), chose to do a nude in a modern setting, not in a classical or renaissance setting. Further, it is impossible to give to Manet's naked woman the allegorical implications (ideal beauty, truth, nature, etc.) that customarily were attributed to the nudes of earlier painters. But what is one to make of a nude who cannot be regarded as a part of secular or sacred history (e.g., Bathsheba) or mythology (e.g., Venus) or allegory (e.g., Beauty, or Virtue, or whatever)? A nude of the older sort is acceptable to a bourgeois audience because of its "higher meaning"; on the other hand, a nude who is only a naked woman, a woman stripped in the presence of clothed males, is a problem for the viewer who claims he or she (but it is usually a he) is engaging in a lofty aesthetic experience, looking at art, not at pornography.

We don't want to spend much more space on the painting; pretty much all that needs to be known about it is admirably set forth in Robert L. Herbert's *Impressionism* (1988). The three figures at the left are unquestionably derived from an engraving (where they appear as two nude sea gods and a nude nymph) by Marcantonio Raimondi, based on a lost painting by Raphael of *The Judgment of Paris* (c. 1520). (The engraving, like the Georgione or Titian, is reproduced in Herbert's book.) There is an important point here: artists (and we include poets in this word) like to take earlier works and reinterpret them, partly out of a sense of fun—Manet's painting is almost a parody of his sources—but partly also in order, in Ezra Pound's famous words, to "Make It New." Thus, Shakespeare reworked Plautus in several comedies, and he reworked (and thereby reinterpreted) several earlier English plays, including *King Lear* and a lost *Hamlet*.

To return to Manet: yes, he will do a nude, but he will not disguise the erotic interest in it by claiming that it is a lofty allegory or even history. Rather, he will insist that the viewer recognize the sexual content of the scene. He will "Make It New." The result, of course, was a scandal.

Now for the poem. Phillips begins by recognizing that the picture caused a scandal ("Manet's scandalous / lunch partners"). As a poet, he need not cause a scandal, but his job is to "Make It New," partly by using language in fresh, interesting ways. For a start we can look at a passage in the second and third lines:

> the two men, lost
> in cant and full dress. . . .

Here we get an example of zeugma, since the word "lost" governs two words but in different ways. In "Lost in cant" (incidentally, we might have expected the more flattering "lost in thought"), "lost" suggests some sort of mental failure; in "lost in full dress" the word is used differently, for it now acquires the meaning of being overwhelmed by some sort of physical paraphernalia. Our explanation is clumsy, but the point is evident if you recall some of Alexander Pope's examples of zeugma:

> . . . *stain* her honor, or her new brocade,

and:

> . . . *lose* her heart, or necklace, at a ball.

But of course Phillips does not rely only on zeugma in his effort to make it new. By saying that these pastoral loungers are spreading their legs "subway-style," he makes the picture (1863) new, makes it something of *our* "modern life" rather than only something of Manet's. In fact, this is very much what Ezra Pound was getting at. He did not mean that the poet should turn away from the art of the past but, rather, that the poet should rediscover its vitality and present it in contemporary forms.

And so Phillips says, in his last lines,

> My dear,
> this is not art, we're not anywhere close
> to Arcadia.

This is probably close to what Manet was doing, when he painted his nude in a modern style, i.e., when he painted a scene that (unlike a Renaissance painting) could not possibly be sanitized by being interpreted as an allegory or as an image of a lost pastoral world. Manet in effect said, "Look, *this* is what a nude is—a naked woman, not an allegorical representation of beauty, not a nymph, and if the scene suggests sex, well, why not?"

Phillips sees this in the painting. He imagines his nude as an earthy person, someone who asks, "where's / the *real* party?" Further, he puts himself and a companion into the scene, or, rather, he brings the scene to mind as he contemplates his present condition, nude, with a partner who has removed one boot in order to scratch an itch—and who knows what this will lead to? If Manet's picture is remote from the traditional nude, say, the Renaissance nude by Georgione (or Titian) that he copied, so Phillips's scene is remote from Manet. Manet's picture, in part because the landscape is painted flatly rather than illusionistically, still has something of the artificial world, the "shape of romance" that earlier paintings of nudes had. On the other hand, the details of Phillips's reality—a partner scratching an itchy foot in line 17, a "rusted green dumpster" in line 23, some unwanted chicken salad in line 31, a bottle of beer (not wine) in lines 32–33—take us utterly out of the timeless world of Arcadia. Arcadia endures only in art; in the speaker's world a lover forgets that the speaker dislikes chicken salad, and beer goes flat, and the speaker acts "fitfully." All is not well in this realm:

> My dear,
> this is not art, we're not anywhere close
> to Arcadia.

But of course this *is* art, since it is all set forth in a poem. Phillips is taking the old motif of Arcadia, the old motif of pastoral poetry, and, true to Pound, is making it new.

A publicity release for Phillips's books says that Phillips is a gay African American, so we decided to add this information in one of our questions in the text. In what sense, if any, is this a gay poem? It seemed to us even before we received the publicity release that the partner is male. Why did we have that impression? We aren't sure, but perhaps the reference to boots and athletic socks (lines 16–17) gave us this idea, though women can wear boots and athletic socks. Perhaps we were influenced by the words, "We are two to Manet's main group / of three"; if the first big change is that Manet's female nude is replaced by a male nude, the second, it seems, is that Manet's two clothed males are reduced to one. Or maybe we felt as we did because there is no praise of any aspect of the woman's appearance, whereas heterosexual poems concerned with love usually include such praise.

Phillips is one of the most gifted young poets we have encountered. All three of his collections are excellent, offering subtle and sensitive explorations of the sensual, sexual, and sacred: *In the Blood* (1992), *Cortege* (1995), and *From the Devotions* (1998).

JOHN UPDIKE
Before the Mirror (p. 576)

Updike's poem, we believe, is at least as much about himself as it is about the painting. And many critics today would say that *all* comments about works of art—even allegedly objective accounts—are about the speakers, not the works of art. Works of art say nothing, we often hear; critics are ventriloquists who put words (meanings) into the works that they purportedly describe. We cannot hold such a view—we are pretty sure that *our* comments about works of literature are rooted in the works themselves—but we are uneasily aware, as we read the words of some earlier critics, that *they* certainly made the authors over into their own image.

In an essay called "What MoMA Done Tole Me," written for the magazine *Art and Antiques* and republished in Updike's collection of essays entitled *Just Looking* (1989), Updike anticipated some of the ideas of "Before the Mirror." Of his visits to the museum in 1955–1957, when he lived in New York, he wrote:

> For me the Museum of Modern Art was a temple where I might refresh my own sense of artistic purpose, though my medium had become words. What made this impudent array of color and form Art was the mystery; what made it Modern was obvious, and was the same force that made me modern: time. Indeed, some of the works that arrested me—Picasso's *Girl Before a Mirror,* its ice-creamy colors and fat satisfied black outlines posed in those days at the turning of the main stairs; *Rouault's Christ Mocked by Soldiers,* with its outlines of a coarser sort . . . —dated from 1932 and were thus just my age, which seems to me now very young. (pp. 8–9)

Here is the germ of the poem, the identity of the viewer with the work that is viewed. And so in 1996, when Updike again saw the picture in the great exhibition "Picasso and Portraiture" at the Museum of Modern Art, he returned to the topic, noting with satisfaction that the picture is holding up just fine:

> The blacks,
> the stripy cyanide greens are still uncracked,
> I note with satisfaction; the cherry reds

and lemon yellows full of childish juice.
No sag, no wrinkle. Fresh as paint. *Back then,*
I reflect, *they knew just how to lay it on.*

And yet. . . . One need not be a deconstructionist, committed to the idea that texts are inherently contradictory, to be a bit unnerved by these last lines. The final words, "to lay it on," suggest vigorous action ("lay on, Macduff") but they also undermine the suggestion by implying insincerity (as in, "to lay it on with a trowel"). Or go back to the penultimate line: "Fresh as paint." A chirpy idiom, and witty here, since the speaker is talking about literal paint, but, alas, a cliché; the words (and also others, especially "I note with satisfaction" in line 21) call to mind some oldster cheering himself up.

Updike—do we have to say "the speaker," when the speaker so clearly is the author?—is looking at the picture and seeing himself. He is using the picture as, so to speak, a mirror, most appropriately since the picture itself shows a girl looking into the mirror. But mirrors as symbols have several meanings: The mirror can symbolize truth ("The mirror doesn't lie," "Mirror, mirror, on the wall, / Who is fairest of them all?"); or it can symbolize vanity (again, the wicked stepmother's question, since she believes the mirror will tell her that she is the fairest); or (and Updike, who knows a lot about art, must know this) it can symbolize the passage of time and the coming of death (as in paintings of a young girl looking into a mirror and seeing an ancient crone or a skull). Picasso glances at this last interpretation in *Girl Before a Mirror,* since the girl herself—she is at the left, with her face shown both in profile and frontally—surely is more youthful than the mirror-image (at the right), which seems to reveal a witch-like figure.

The girl's profile has a pale, virginal look; the front view, with lipstick and rouge, suggests a more sexually aware woman; and the face in the mirror suggests advancing years. (The standard comment is that in the frontal view of the girl's face we see the energetic sun, in the mirror-image we see the darkening moon.) Further, the boundary lines of the elongated oval mirror can be seen as suggesting a coffin that contains the image.

If the poem ends with an explicitly cheerful note, this ending only barely conceals intimations of mortality. The painting shows "No sag, no wrinkle," but that is because it is a painting; the viewer, who tells us he is in his sixties, must be showing some sag, some wrinkle. In fact, early in the poem he tells us that he belongs to "a dwindling population." And in lines 9–10 he echoes the line that greets the new arrivals as they enter Hell: "Abandon Hope, ye who enter here." True, Updike's line ("Enter here / and abandon preconception") implies new life, bestowed by a new kind of art, a new way of seeing, but in conjunction with "dwindling population" the line nevertheless casts a shadow over the poem.

Still, he is of a piece with the picture he goes back to a day when "they knew just how to lay it on." Reading this poem about a man looking at a picture of a woman looking in a mirror—a man looking at a picture which, mirror-like, shows him what he takes to be his own image—we perceive a bit of vanity, we sense the approach of death, and perhaps we even think (though this is nowhere explicit in the poem) that Updike's own works are still "uncracked" and full of "juice." Lookers-into-mirrors will go, images in mirrors will go, viewers of pictures will go, but the pictures, the works of art, remain fresh.

What about the girl's gesture toward the mirror? Our guess is that just as the viewer mentally reaches out to the picture, so the girl reaches out to her own image, seeking to make contact with what she knows is an illusion. Perhaps, too, she is (so to speak) saying, "No, this image of decay can't be true," and she reaches out to prove that the image is an illusion. Or perhaps she is moved by sympathy: "There, there, I know how you must feel." Or maybe Picasso simply felt that it was not enough for the two halves of the picture to echo each other, and that they ought to be tied together.

WISLAWA SZYMBORSKA
Brueghel's Two Monkeys (p. 578)

The directness of the first line suggests a matter-of-fact speaker, but of course as soon as one talks about dreams one enters a mysterious world. (Perhaps that is why the sky "flutters" and "the sea is taking its bath.") The speaker gives us no clues about his or her identity, but we may assume that the speaker is a person of some education (perhaps a member of a profession), since dreams about final examinations are said to be fairly common among people with academic credentials. (In such dreams the dreamers are usually baffled and humiliated; the customary analysis suggests that these dreamers believe they are frauds, undeserving of their credentials.)

In the poem, since the examination is History of Mankind, the dreamer can be taken as standing for all of us. We all wonder where we came from (and where we are going), and perhaps most of us are familiar with the experience of talking earnestly about mysterious subjects and then perceiving (or thinking) that our hearer "listens with mocking disdain." In the poem, the second monkey, who "seems to be dreaming away"—i.e., who seems to be a kindred spirit to the dreamer—offers help, but of a terrifying sort: "he prompts me with a gentle / clinking of his chain."

Brueghel's painting shows two chained monkeys, and in the poem the chain is the monkey's, not the dreamer's, but it is easy enough for a reader to think of the dreamer as chained, partly because the dreamer in the poem is unable to escape from the dream and partly because monkeys resemble human beings. Monkeys or apes have been common symbols of humanity, but different artists have put different emphases on the symbolism. In early Christian art the ape symbolizes the devil (a creature who mimics God's concern for humanity but who really is wicked); in later art the ape often symbolizes (usually satirically) the artist, i.e., the maker of imitations. But the ape can also symbolize lechery, pride, folly, and—as perhaps in Brueghel's painting and in Szymborska's poem—baffled humanity. In *Art Bulletin* 63 (1981): 114–126, Margaret A.

Sullivan takes issue with earlier political interpretations of Brueghel's painting and argues that the monkey at the left symbolizes avarice and the monkey at the right (seated among scattered empty nutshells) symbolizes prodigality. Not relevant to the poem, but we thought you might like to know, even if the interpretation is unconvincing.

To return to the poem: What is the significance of the monkey prompting the poet "with a gentle / clinking of his chain"? If there is one thing we can say with some certainty, it is that there is no one right answer to this question. Still, we take the passage to mean (perhaps among other things) something along these lines: the monkey, clinking his chain, "prompts" or reminds the speaker that all of us are fettered, that is, severely restricted in what we can do (and know). This isn't much of an answer, but it is something, and the rhyme at the end of the poem (it is the only rhyme in the poem) provides a note of closure, as if to say, "Well, we know only that we are fettered, but at least we know *something.*"

A good point of departure for further reading of Szymborska's work is *Sounds, Feelings, Thoughts: Seventy Poems,* translated and introduced by Magnus J. Krynski and Robert A. Maguire (1981).

Part III

Standing Back
Arguing Interpretations and Evaluations, and Understanding Critical Strategies

16

Arguing an Interpretation

The entries that we cite in this manual for Chapter 4 are relevant here too. Steven Mailloux's entry on "interpretation" in *Critical Terms for Literary Study,* ed. Frank Lentricchia and Thomas McLaughlin, 2nd ed. (1995), provides a good starting point. You may next want to turn to a short, readable, but highly thoughtful book by Monroe Beardsley, *The Possibility of Criticism* (1970). Also of interest are E. D. Hirsch, *Validity in Interpretation* (1967); Paul B. Armstrong, *Conflicting Readings: Variety and Validity in Interpretation* (1990); and Umberto Eco, with Richard Rorty, Jonathan Culler, and Christine Brooke-Rose, *Interpretation and Overinterpretation* (1992). This last title includes three essays by Eco, with responses by Rorty, Culler, and Brooke-Rose, and a final "Reply" by Eco.

ROBERT FROST
Stopping by Woods on a Snowy Evening (p. 588)

On "Stopping by Woods," see John Lynen, *The Pastoral Art of Robert Frost* (1960), and *Frost: Centennial Essays* (1976), vol. 3, ed. Jac L. Tharpe. We number ourselves among the readers who see in the poem a longing for death ("frozen lake," "darkest evening of the year," "The woods are lovely, dark and deep" seem to support this view), but that is not what the poem is exclusively about. If there is a momentary longing for death in the poem, there is also the reassertion of the will to face the tasks of living. As Frost put it, at the Bread Loaf Writers' Conference in 1960, "People are always trying to find a death wish in that poem. But there's a life wish there—he goes on, doesn't he?"

Frost reads the poem in *Robert Frost Reading His Own Poems* (Record No. 1, EL LCB, 1941), distributed by the National Council of Teachers of English.

Topics for Critical Thinking and Writing

1. As the manuscript indicates, line 5 originally read: "The steaming horses think it queer." Line 7 read: "Between a forest and a lake." Which version do you prefer? Why?

2. The rhyming words in the first stanza can be indicated by *aaba*; the second stanza picks up the *b* rhyme: *bbcb*. Indicate the rhymes for the third stanza. For the fourth. Why is it appropriate that the rhyme scheme differs in the fourth stanza?
3. Hearing that the poem had been interpreted as a "death poem," Frost said, "I never intended that, but I did have the feeling it was loaded with ulteriority." What "ulteriority" is implicit? How is the time of day and year significant? How does the horse's attitude make a contrast with the speaker's?

JOHN MILTON
When I Consider How My Light Is Spent (p. 597)

Argument about the date Milton became blind need not concern us (Miltonists wonder how literally to take "Ere half my days"), but it should be noticed that one critic argues that the sonnet is not about blindness. The common title "On His Blindness" has no authority; it was first used by a printer in 1752. Lysander Kemp held (*Hopkins Review*, 6 [1952]: 80–83) that the sonnet deals with the loss not of vision but of poetic inspiration, but Kemp's view has not been widely accepted. The most sensible view is that the octave assumes that God requires ceaseless labor, and the sestet enlarges the concept of service to include those who though inactive are eagerly prepared for action.

Additional notes: In line 2, "this dark world and wide" suggests not only the dark world of the blind man but is also a religious stock expression for the sinful world; in line 7, "day-labor" suggests not only labor for daily wages but also labor that requires daylight, i.e., the power of vision; in line 14, "wait" perhaps means not only "stay in expectation" but also "attend as a servant, to receive orders."

The library shelves are, of course, teeming with books on Milton's poetry and prose. There is a good book on the sonnets: Anna K. Nardo, *Milton's Sonnets and the Ideal Community* (1979). We have also learned from, and are indebted to, the annotations and commentary in *Milton's Sonnets*, ed. E. A. J. Honigmann (1966). For even more detailed annotation of Milton's poems (including the sonnets), students can be sent to *A Variorum Commentary on the Poems of John Milton* (1970). For a lively, perceptive discussion of this sonnet, we recommend Stanley Fish, "Interpreting the Variorum," included in *Is There a Text in This Class? The Authority of Interpretive Communities* (1980).

ROBERT FROST
Mending Wall (p. 598)

Some critics applaud the neighbor in Frost's "Mending Wall," valuing his respect for barriers. For an extreme version, see Robert Hunting, "Who Needs Mending?" *Western Humanities Review* 17 (Winter 1963): 88–89. The gist of this faction is that the neighbor wisely realizes—as the speaker does not—that individual identity depends on respect for boundaries. Such a view sees the poem as a Browningesque dramatic monologue like "My Last Duchess," in which the self-satisfied speaker unknowingly gives himself away.

Richard Poirier, in *Robert Frost* (1990), makes the interesting point that it is not the neighbor (who believes that "good fences make good neighbors") who initiates the ritual of mending the wall; rather, it is the speaker: "I let my neighbor know beyond the hill." Poirier suggests that "if fences do not 'make good neighbors,' the *making* of fences can," for it makes for talk—even though the neighbor is hopelessly taciturn. For a long, judicious discussion of the poem, see John C. Kemp, *Robert Frost and New England: The Poet as Regionalist* (1979).

Topics for Critical Thinking and Writing

1. Compare and contrast the speaker and the neighbor.
2. Notice that the speaker, not the neighbor, initiates the business of repairing the wall (line 12). Why do you think he does this?
3. Write an essay of 500 words telling of an experience in which you came to conclude that "good fences make good neighbors." Or tell of an experience that led you to conclude that fences (they can be figurative fences, of course) are detrimental.

WILLIAM WORDSWORTH
A Slumber Did My Spirit Seal (p. 599)

This poem has been an object of academic attention for a century, but the early critics were chiefly concerned with the question of whether Lucy was a real person. Then in 1951 Cleanth Brooks used the poem in an essay called "Irony as a Principle of Structure," in *Literary Opinion in America*, ed. Morton D. Zabel. He wrote:

> [Wordsworth] attempts to suggest something of the lover's agonized shock at the loved one's present lack of motion—of his response to her utter and horrible inertness. . . . He chooses to suggest it . . . by imagining her in violent motion. . . . Part of the effect, of course, resides in the fact that a dead lifelessness is suggested more sharply by an object's being whirled about by something else than by an image of an object in repose. But there are other matters which are at work here: the sense of the girl's falling back into the clutter of things, companioned by things chained like a tree to one particular spot, or by things completely inanimate, like rocks and stones. . . .

E. D. Hirsch, in *Validity in Interpretation* (1976), juxtaposed most of this quotation with a very different reading, from F. W. Bateson's *English Poetry: A Critical Introduction* (1950):

The final impression the poem leaves is not of two contrasting moods, but of a single mood mounting to a climax in the pantheistic magnificence of the last two lines. . . . The vague living-Lucy of this poem is opposed to the grander dead-Lucy who has become involved in the sublime processes of nature. We put the poem down satisfied, because its last two lines succeed in effecting a reconciliation between the two philosophies or social attitudes. Lucy is actually more alive now that she is dead, because she is now a part of the life of Nature, and not just a human "thing."

Hirsch decided that these two readings are—if we go no further than the poem—equally acceptable because the poem itself is "indeterminate." (He might have said "ambiguous," but the New Critics had for some decades said that *ambiguity* was a desirable quality in a work of literature.) Hirsch concluded that we must seek the author's intention, which we can find by examining the other writings that Wordsworth produced around 1799. His finding: at that time Wordsworth probably regarded rocks not as "inert objects" but as "deeply alive, as part of the immortal life of nature" (pp. 238–239). In short, Hirsch comes down on Bateson's side and against Brooks.

Putting aside for a moment the question of setting the poem in the context of Wordsworth's thought in 1799, it is our guess that most readers today will read the poem along Brooks's line rather than along Bateson's. Maybe the fault is Wordsworth's. If he had written

> Rolled round in earth's immortal course

or, on the other hand,

> Rolled round in earth's mechanic course

we would know how to take the poem. Still, is the poem "indeterminate" in itself? Need we go, with Hirsch, to the other works of 1799? In *The Possibility of Criticism* (1970), Monroe Beardsley argues that we can stay with the poem itself. In a discussion that we think is the best thing published on the poem thus far, Beardsley says that

> Brooks's reading is (uncharacteristically) distorted. Lucy is not "whirled"; she is "rolled." She does not fall back into a "clutter of things," but is placed among trees, which do not really suggest "dead lifelessness." An orderly "diurnal course" is not "violent motion." (p. 29)

Beardsley goes on to say, speaking of "rocks and stones and trees," that "by putting the word 'trees' at the end, the speaker gives it emphasis; therefore, he is really suggesting that rocks and stones (and *a fortiori* the dead Lucy) are like trees in having an inner life of their own." In short, Beardsley argues that the text itself—not what we may or may not know about Wordsworth's other writings of 1799—refutes Brooks's interpretation.

Now to look at the interpretations offered in our book. We offer our own brief comments, but we realize that other readers may see things very differently.

1. The first is obviously a version of Cleanth Brooks. We think objections along the line of those offered by Beardsley are telling, i.e., "mechanistically hurled into violent motion" is not a fair way of summarizing the condition asserted in the second stanza.
2. The second is a version of Bateson. We think that on the whole it is apt, though, again, we think the poem itself might have made the point more clearly.
3. Again, following Beardsley, we would argue that the poem is not ambiguous, but, yet again, we wish that Wordsworth had used some different language in the second stanza.
4. We do think that *diurnal* adds solemnity, but we think that to see *urn* in it is to see too much.
5. It's our guess that for most of today's readers the poem is about "the brute fact of death." The real questions, then, are these: (a) Should one try to find out what the poem meant to the author? (b) *Can* one find the author's intention? (c) If one should and can find the author's intention, need one then accept it as the only interpretation?
6. We have already touched on these matters in our comments on the earlier assertions.
7. We think there is a good deal of truth in the assertion that the female subject is "not a person," i.e., is not individualized but is valued chiefly in terms of the poet's response. On the other hand, we wonder how many lyric poems—including those by women—are about the nominal subject rather than about the poet's response. That is, we assume that lyric poetry is chiefly the expression of intense feeling.

T. S. ELIOT
The Love Song of J. Alfred Prufrock (p. 601)

Among the useful introductory books are Elizabeth Drew, *T. S. Eliot* (1950); Northrop Frye, *T. S. Eliot* (1968); and Grover Smith, *T. S. Eliot's Poetry and Plays* (1975). On "Prufrock," see also Rosenthal and Smith, *Exploring Poetry* (1955); Hugh Kenner, *The Invisible Poet: T. S. Eliot* (1965), pp. 3–12; and Lyndall Gordon, *Eliot's Early Years* (1977). It is well to alert students to the fact that "Prufrock" is not a Browningesque dramatic monologue with a speaker and a listener, but rather an internal monologue in which "I" (the timid self) addresses his own amorous self as "you." (Not every "you" in this poem, however, refers to Prufrock's amorous self. Sometimes "you" is equivalent to "one.") Possibly, too, the "you" is the reader, or even other people who, like Prufrock, are afraid of action.

Among the chief points usually made are these: The title proves to be ironic, for we scarcely get a love song: "J. Alfred Prufrock" is a name that, like the speaker, seems to be hiding something ("J.") and also seems to be somewhat old-maidish ("Prufrock" suggests "prude" and "frock"); the initial description (especially the "patient etherised") is really less a description of the evening than of Prufrock's state of mind; mock heroic devices abound (people at a cocktail party talking of Michelangelo, Prufrock gaining strength from his collar and stickpin); the sensuous imagery of women's arms leads to the men in shirt-sleeves and to Prufrock's wish to be a pair of ragged claws.

We print the original (1915) version, from *Poetry* magazine, but in line 19 we give *soot* instead of *spot* (an obvious typo in *Poetry*). When the poem later appeared in book form it differed only in punctuation (e.g., square brackets instead of parentheses) and one verbal change—*no doubt* instead of *withal* in line 114.

A "Voices and Visions" videocassette of T. S. Eliot is available from Longman Publishers.

In our study of Eliot's life and literary career, we have also benefitted from the biography by Peter Ackroyd (1984) and from the very interesting volume of Eliot's letters, vol. 1, 1898–1922, expertly edited by Valerie Eliot (1988).

JOHN KEATS
Ode on a Grecian Urn (p. 605)

Let's begin at the end, with the issue of the punctuation of the last two lines. Does the urn speak the two lines, or does it speak only "Beauty is truth, truth beauty"? The matter has been thoroughly discussed by Jack Stillinger, in an appendix to his book called *The Hoodwinking of Madeline* (1971). The problem is this: when the poem was first published, in *Annals of the Fine Arts* (1819), the lines were printed thus:

> Beauty is Truth,—Truth Beauty—That is all
>   Ye know on Earth, and all ye need to know.

When Keats published the ode in his book *Lamia and Other Poems* (1820), the lines were punctuated thus:

> "Beauty is truth, truth beauty,"—that is all
>   Ye know on earth, and all ye need to know.

The two printed versions thus set off "Beauty is truth, truth beauty" as a unit separate from the remaining words. But Keats probably did not supervise the publication in *The Annals,* and because he was ill when *Lamia* was in production he may not have read the proofs or may not have read them attentively. Many scholars therefore do not feel obliged to accept the punctuation of the two printed texts. They point to the four extant manuscript transcripts of the poem (none by Keats, but all by persons close to Keats). Because none of these transcriptions uses quotation marks or a period after "beauty," these scholars argue that the punctuation suggests that the urn speaks all of the last two lines:

> Beauty is Truth,—Truth Beauty,—that is all
>   Ye know on earth, and all ye need to know.

Stillinger points out that none of the six readings (the four transcripts and the two published versions) offers conclusive proof of Keats's intention. He goes on to summarize the interpretations, and we now summarize Stillinger.

1. **Poet to Reader.** The urn speaks the first five words of line 49 ("Beauty is truth, truth beauty"), and the poet, addressing the reader, speaks the rest of the last two lines ("that is all / Ye know on earth, and all ye need to know"). The objection to this view is that earlier in the last stanza the poet and the reader are "us," and the poet says that later woes will belong to a generation other than "ours." Why, then, does the poet shift the address to "ye," where we would expect "we"? Second, the statement is obviously false; we need to know much more than that "Beauty is truth, truth beauty."
2. **Poet to Urn.** The poet speaks the end of line 49, and all of the last line, to the urn. The poet tells the urn that *it* need know no more—but that we need to know a great deal more. The objection, Stillinger points out, is that "ye" is normally a plural pronoun—though in fact Keats did sometimes use it as a singular. A second objection: What can Keats possibly mean by saying to the urn, "that is all / Ye know *on earth* . . ."?
3. **Poet to Figures on Urn.** The poet speaks the end of 49 and all of the last line to the figures on the urn. This fits with "ye" as a plural. The objection is that the figures are not "on earth" and, further, that the poet is no longer thinking of them as alive and capable of hearing. Further, *why* should the figures on the urn know this and only this?
4. **Urn to Reader.** The urn speaks all of the two last lines. The objection is that the statement seems to defy common sense, and more important, it is *not* the way the *Lamia* volume punctuated the line. Some critics have suggested that the quotation marks were meant to set off these five words as a sort of motto within a two-line statement by the urn.

It is our impression that most editors today disregard the *Lamia* punctuation, put the whole of the two lines within quotation marks, and take the lines as spoken by the urn to the reader. In any case, a reader is still left to wonder whether the passage is profound wisdom or nonsense.

Now to begin at the beginning. In the first line "still" probably has several meanings (motionless; as yet; silent); the urn is the "foster-child of silence and slow time" because its real parent is the craftsman who made it, but it has been adopted, so to speak, by silence and the centuries. Although the poet begins by saying that the urn can tell a tale "more sweetly" than a poet can, in fact by the end of the stanza it is clear that the urn cannot tell a tale; it can only (of course) show some isolated moment and let the viewer try to guess what actions came before and will come after. It is worth mentioning, too, that this stanza praises the urns staying-power ("slow time") but is rich in words that imply transience: "Sylvan," "flowery," "leaf-fringed," "haunts" (suggesting the insubstantial or ethereal). The stanza ends with urgent questions conveying agitation and implying that the urn cannot tell a tale satisfactorily.

The second stanza begins on a note of composure; in the space between the stanzas, so to speak, the poet has stilled his questioning spirit and has progressed to a state where he can offer something for meditation ("Heard melodies are sweet, but those unheard / Are sweeter"). As the stanza continues, a slightly painful note is introduced: the pastoral landscape will never die—but the lover will never kiss the woman. The poet urges the lover not to grieve, which means that he in fact introduces into this Arcadian world the idea of potential grief. Although the stanza ends by asserting the youth's eternal love, and the woman's eternal beauty, there is something almost painful in the last words of the next-to-last line of the stanza, "though thou has not thy bliss."

The third stanza begins with a renewed note of joy, again apparently gained in the blank space that precedes the stanza, though perhaps we may also detect a note of hysteria in the repetition of "Ah, happy, happy boughs." This stanza too, despite its early expressions of joy, moves toward distress. We are told that the figures on the urn are "far above" human passion, but the last lines dwell on the pains of human passions: "a heart high-sorrowful and cloyed, / A burning forehead, and a parching tongue."

We cannot quite say that the fourth stanza begins with the by-now expected note of composure because in fact it begins with a question, but it is true to say that in fact this stanza too begins in a quieter mood. The poet is contemplating with interest a new scene on the urn, a scene showing a "mysterious priest" and a "heifer lowing at the skies, / . . . her silken flanks with garlands drest." As the poet describes this highly picturesque scene, again we hear a note foreign to the beginning of the stanza. The poet begins by conveying his interest in what he sees—"the mysterious priest," the "heifer," and the "folk, this pious morn"—but then his mind turns to the "little town" that is "emptied of this folk" and whose "streets for evermore / Will silent be." The last two lines of the stanza are deeply melancholy: "not a soul to tell / Why thou art desolate, can e'er return." Jack Stillinger, in an essay on the odes (reprinted from his *Twentieth Century Views*) in *The Hoodwinking of Madeline* suggests that "'Desolate' in line 40 is the counterpart of 'forlorn' in *Ode to a Nightingale*. It brings the speaker back to his sole self" (p. 106).

The fifth stanza begins with the expected renewed joy, but it is worth noticing that the urn, which in the first stanza was a "Sylvan historian" capable of telling a "flowery tale," now is a "shape" and a "silent form" and a "Cold Pastoral." The poet by now has clearly seen that what he at first took for a world of idealized love is "cold," and its figures are "marble men and maidens." That is, if it is perfect and permanent it is also cold, bloodless, without the passion that (however painful) is what we want from life. Stillinger puts it this way:

> Like the nightingale, [the urn] has offered a tentative idea—momentarily "teas[ing]" the speaker "out of thought"—but has also led the speaker to understand the shortcomings of the ideal. (p. 108)

Stillinger's comment on the last two lines is also worth quoting:

> The final lines present a special problem in interpretation, but it is clear that, while the urn is not entirely rejected at the end, its value lies in its character as a work of art, not in its being a possible substitute for life in the actual world. However punctuated, the urn's "message" amounts to what the speaker has come to realize in his speculations—that the only beauty accessible to mortal man exists "on earth." The urn is "a friend to man" for helping him to arrive at this conclusion through just such ponderings as we have witnessed in the course of the poem. (pp. 108–109)

Bibliographic note: For detailed analyses of the poem, see Earl Wasserman, *The Finer Tone* (1953), and Helen Vendler, *The Odes of John Keats* (1983); for briefer discussions, see the books on Keats by Walter Jackson Bate, *John Keats* (1963), and by Douglas Bush, *John Keats, His Life and Writings* (1966). Also useful is a collection edited by Jack Stillinger, *Twentieth Century Interpretations of Keats's Odes* (1968). Ian Jack, in *Keats and the Mirror of Art* (1967), has an interesting well-illustrated chapter on urns—and pictures of urns—that Keats is likely to have seen, but, unfortunately, no one urn is the model; in fact, "that heifer lowing at the skies" probably came not from an urn but from the Elgin Marbles. Jack's concern is only with identifying motifs; he does not offer an interpretation of the poem.

17

Arguing an Evaluation

MATTHEW ARNOLD
Dover Beach (p. 612)

"Dover Beach" begins with the literal—the scene that hits the eye and ear—and then moves in the second stanza to Sophocles's figurative tragic interpretation, in the third to Arnold's figurative religious interpretation, and finally—the image of the sea now being abandoned—to the simile of the world as a "darkling plain" whose only reality is the speaker and the person addressed. The end thus completes the idea of illusion versus reality that began in the first stanza, where the scene that was "calm" (line 1), "fair" (line 2), and "tranquil" (line 3) actually contained the discords implicit in "grating roar," "fling," and so on. In fact, even the "tonight" of the first line implies some conflict, for the word suggests that on other nights the sea is *not* calm.

For a thought-provoking reading of "Dover Beach," consult A. Dwight Culler, *Imaginative Reason: The Poetry of Matthew Arnold* (1966; rpt. 1976). Culler argues (perhaps too ingeniously) that although some critics complain about a lack of unity in the imagery (no sea in the last section, and no darkling plain in the first), "the naked shingles *are* the darkling plain, and that we have no sea in the last section is the very point of the poem. The sea has retreated from the world. . . ." To this point of Culler's we add that the "pebbles" flung about by the waves (line 10) are an anticipation of "ignorant armies" that are "swept with confused alarms of struggle and flight" (line 36).

Gerald Graff includes a chapter called "How to Save 'Dover Beach'" in his *Beyond the Culture Wars: How Teaching the Conflicts Can Revitalize American Education* (1992). As the title of the essay and the subtitle of the book indicate, Graff believes that works such as "Dover Beach" can best be taught by recognizing that many of today's readers find some of their assumptions unconvincing and even incomprehensible. Graff imagines an older male professor (OMP) who throws up his hands at his students' indifference to the poem and a young female professor (YFP) who says she understands how the students feel. In fact,

Graff's YFP goes on not to express indifference but rather to offer a challenging reading of the poem, or at least of the last lines ("Ah, love. . . ."). She says that this passage adds up to this:

> In other words, protect and console me, my dear—as it's the function of your naturally more spiritual sex to do—from the "struggle and flight" of politics and history that we men have been assigned the regrettable duty of dealing with. It's a good example of how women have been defined by our culture as naturally private and domestic and therefore justly disqualified from sharing male power. (p. 38)

She goes on to say that it is precisely for this reason that we *should* teach the poem—"as the example of phallocentric discourse that it is." OMP objects that such a label "misses the whole point of poetry," and that YFP and her colleagues treat poems "as if they were statements about gender politics" rather than expressions of "universal concerns." YFP replies that literature *is*—among other things—about "gender politics." She goes on:

> What you take to be the universal human experience in Arnold and Shakespeare, Professor OMP, is male experience presented as if it were universal. You don't notice the presence of politics in literature—or in sexual relations, for that matter—because for you patriarchy is simply the normal state of affairs and therefore as invisible as the air you breathe. My reading of "Dover Beach" seems to you to reflect a "special-interest" agenda, but to me yours does, too. You can afford to "transmute" the sexual politics of literature onto a universal plane, but that's a luxury I don't enjoy. (p. 39)

Again, Graff's chief point is that we should face the controversies—should let them enter into our teaching—and not ignore them. "For disagreements about 'Dover Beach' are not peripheral to humanistic culture; they are central to what we mean by humanistic culture" (p. 56). And: "Controversies from which we have been trying to protect 'Dover Beach' can do a lot to save it" (p. 63).

Students will be greatly aided by the detailed annotations in *The Poems of Matthew Arnold*, ed. Kenneth Allott (1965; 2nd ed., ed. Miriam Allott, 1979). *Matthew Arnold: Selections*, ed. Miriam Allott and Robert H. Super (1986), is also well annotated and includes a good selection of Arnold's prose. We also admire the selection of Arnold's poems edited and annotated by Timothy Peltason (1994).

Though now somewhat dated, the range of essays on Arnold's life included in *Matthew Arnold*, ed. Kenneth Allott (1975), is still useful for teachers and students alike. Excellent biographies have been written by Park Honan (1981) and Nicholas Murray (1996). For an insightful brief account: Stefan Collini, *Arnold* (1988). Three books from the 1960s remain valuable: A. Dwight Culler, *Imaginative Reason: The Poetry of Matthew Arnold* (1966; rpt. 1976); G. Robert Stange, *Matthew Arnold: The Poet as Humanist* (1967); and Alan Roper, *Arnold's Poetic Landscapes* (1969). In our view, the most stimulating recent book is David G. Riede, *Matthew Arnold and the Betrayal of Language* (1988).

Topics for Critical Thinking and Writing

1. What are the stated and implied reasons behind Arnold's implication that only love offers comfort?
2. The sea, described in the first stanza, puts the speaker in mind of two metaphors, one in the second stanza and one in the third. Explain each of these metaphors in your own words. In commenting on the first, be sure to include a remark about "turbid" in line 17.
3. Is there a connection between the imagery of the sea in the first three stanzas and the imagery of darkness in the last stanza? If not, is this a fault?

ANTHONY HECHT
The Dover Bitch (p. 613)

Andrews Wanning, to whom the poem is dedicated, is a teacher of literature. Like the title, the subtitle ("A Criticism of Life") is derived from Matthew Arnold, who in "The Study of Poetry," *Essays in Criticism, Second Series* (1880), speaks of poetry as "a criticism of life." Hecht's poem, which at first glance is a parody of Arnold, therefore is also a criticism of poetry (though Arnold's "Dover Beach"—in our text—survives it), and, as we will argue in a minute, also a criticism of life. Hecht's poem must be discussed in connection with Arnold's, but sooner or later the discussion probably ought to get to matters of tone in "The Dover Bitch."

Much of Hecht's poem purports to give the girl's point of view, though we should remember that the speaker is not the girl but a rather coarse fellow who knows her. This speaker sympathizes with her (to "be addressed / As a sort of mournful cosmic last resort / Is really tough on a girl"), but his sensibilities are not of the finest (he tells us that although she is "Running to fat," he gives her "a good time"). If he introduces a note of sexuality that is conspicuously absent from Arnold's poem and that affords some comedy, one's final impression may be that the poem shows us the bleak, meaningless, loveless world that Arnold feared. As Christopher Ricks puts it in *Victorian Studies* 6 (1968), Hecht's "brilliant and poignant poem is by no means flippant. . . . Having subjected Arnold to an unprecedented skepticism, [the poem suddenly reveals] the superiority of Arnold—and of all he epitomized—to that knowing speaker whose worldliness was at first refreshing. The poem, we realize, is in important ways a tribute to Arnold, though hardly a reverential one . . ." (pp. 539–540).

Hecht is also a stimulating critic; his books include *Obbligati: Essays in Criticism* (1986), *The Hidden Law: The Poetry of W. H. Auden* (1993), and *On the Laws of the Poetic Art* (1995).

ROBERT FROST
Design (p. 615)

On Frost's "Design," see Randall Jarrell, *Poetry and the Age* (1953); Richard Poirier, *Robert Frost*; Reuben A. Brower, *The Poetry of Robert Frost* (1963); Richard Ohmann, *College English* 28 (February 1967): 359–367; *Frost: Centennial Essays* (1974); and Reginald Cook, *Robert Frost: A Living Voice* (1974), especially pp. 263–267. Brower is especially good on the shifting tones of voice, for example, from what he calls "the cheerfully observant walker on back country roads" who reports "I found a dimpled. . . "—but then comes the surprising "spider, fat and white"—to the "self-questioning and increasingly serious" sestet. Here, for Brower, "the first question ('What had the flower to do. . . ') sounds like ordinary annoyance at a fact that doesn't fit in." The next question brings in a new note, and irony in "kindred." For Brower, with the last question ironic puzzlement turns into vision: "What but design of darkness to appall?" And then Brower says that in the final line, "The natural theologian pauses—he is only asking, not asserting—and takes a backward step."

The title echoes the "Argument from Design," the argument that the universe is designed (each creature fits perfectly into its environment: the whale is equipped for the sea; the camel for the desert), so there must be a designer, God. Notice that the word—"design"—has two meanings: (1) pattern and (2) intention, plan. Frost certainly means us to have both meanings in mind: there seems to be a pattern and also an intention behind it, but this intention is quite different from the intention discerned by those who in the eighteenth and nineteenth centuries argued for the existence of a benevolent God from the "Argument from Design."

"Design" was published in 1922; below is an early 1912 version of the poem, entitled "In White":

> A dented spider like a snow drop white
> On a white Heal-all, holding up a moth
> Like a white piece of lifeless satin cloth—
> Saw ever curious eye so strange a sight?—
> Portent in little, assorted death and blight
> Like the ingredients of a witches' broth?—
> The beady spider, the flower like a froth,
> And the moth carried like a paper kite.
>
> What had that flower to do with being white?
> The blue prunella every child's delight.
> What brought the kindred spider to that height?
> (Make we no thesis of the miller's plight.)
> What but design of darkness and of night?
> Design, design! Do I use the word aright?

The changes, obvious enough, are discussed by George Monteiro, in *Frost: Centennial Essays* (1974), published by the Committee on the Frost Centennial of the University of Southern Mississippi, pp. 35–38.

By the way, an ingenious student mentioned that the first stanza has eight lines, corresponding to the eight legs of a spider. And the second stanza has six, corresponding to the six legs of a moth. What to do? We tried to talk about the traditional structure of the sonnet, and about relevant and irrelevant conjectures, and about the broad overlapping area. About as good a criterion as any is, does the conjecture make the poem better?

IRA GERSHWIN
The Man That Got Away (p. 616)

We think that the four questions in the text can provide ample material for class discussion, but you may want to get into the first question by asking students to nominate some of their favorite songs. They can then be asked if they think that the lyrics (without the music) stand up as poems. (It doesn't follow, of course, that the song is unworthy if the lyrics do not stand by themselves.) Edgar Allan Poe's comment on the popularity of song as suggesting merit, quoted in our first question, is worth further discussion.

An excellent resource is *The Complete Lyrics of Ira Gershwin*, ed. Robert Kimball (1993).

KATHERINE MANSFIELD
Miss Brill (p. 617)

Few students have any trouble perceiving that Miss Brill is a friendless older woman living in France, seeking out a living by such genteel activities as teaching English and reading the newspaper to an "old invalid gentleman" (who sleeps while she reads). She is "Miss Brill" to us because that is what she is, presumably, to her pupils, to the invalid gentleman, and to anyone else who has any dealings with her. In short, she has no intimate acquaintances. Probably by the end of the first paragraph most readers have a pretty good idea of her emotionally starved life—though to put it this way is perhaps misleading, since Miss Brill herself seems quite content, delighting in the weather and in her shabby fox, as later she will delight in much of what she sees in the park. In the first paragraph most readers probably identify her with the fox—an identification that is insisted on in the final paragraph, when Miss Brill has returned to "the little dark room—her room like a cupboard"—and the fox is returned to its box.

Between the beginning and the end, of course, the unfeeling (or at least careless) boy and girl sitting on the bench jolt Miss Brill out of her comfortable role as delighted spectator at a play, and (in her view of things) as a performer, too.

The third question following the story, asking if Miss Brill is "justly punished for her pride," is the result of several uncomfortable experiences teaching the story. The first time that a student offered this view, we were surprised. It seems evident to us that during most of the story Miss Brill is a sympathetic figure, pitiful, yes, but admirable too, chiefly because she is not given to *self-pity*. She is a bit snobbish about the other regulars who attend the concert ("They were odd, silent, nearly all old, and from the way they stared they looked as though they'd just come from dark little rooms or even—even cupboards!"), but she does no harm to anyone, and she is a person of good will.

Her pride in setting the scene around her is, if anything, pathetic rather than morally offensive. After her rude awakening, we pity her even more. However, students in several classes have argued that Miss Brill seeks to play God, to assign roles, to judge others (as when she says, "The Brute! The Brute!"), and at last she herself is judged by the boy and girl. A slightly less harsh version, also offered in class, goes like this: Miss Brill thinks she plays a significant part in the activities in the park, as a listener, as an appreciator of what is going on, and even as a performer. Stimulated by such thoughts, she seeks to arrange all that goes on, but when the "hero and heroine" (that's the way she sees them) arrive, and Miss Brill is "prepared to listen," reality breaks in, forcing Miss Brill to recognize what she is.

Again, it seems to us to be inappropriate to judge Miss Brill severely, but those students who do judge her severely have not been impressed by arguments to the contrary.

Students are not the only severe judges. In *College English* 23 (1962): 661–663 a university teacher judges her mercilessly. He begins by discussing the action:

> What happens in the story is that with each main event Miss Brill's mind moves higher and higher up the hierarchy of unrealities, until she has reached a point from which she can only fall with a thump back to the hard ground of the real world of her humdrum life. (p. 661)

According to this writer, the first "unreality" is her view of the fox as a "rogue." We realize, he says, "that here is a character who is not averse to wandering in the realms of fancy." He then goes on to assert that "her imaginative coloring of what she sees next is a little more preposterous," for she sees the musicians as (he says) "not a group of hired musicians, but rather a single, responsive and very sensitive creature." This does not seem to us a preposterous way to regard a band of musicians, but the author—very stern with Miss Brill—goes on to assert that she is "ignorant of music." The evidence: she doesn't know whether the "flutey bit" will be repeated, and "the bit to her is 'a little chain of bright drops,' not music." (Teachers who believe that metaphor is not a bad thing, and is indeed a way of conveying fresh perceptions, may be surprised at this condemnation of metaphor.)

The critic continues:

> The episode of the "ermine toque and the gentleman in grey," as it is interpreted by Miss Brill, is considerably more preposterous than her coloring of

her fur and the orchestra. The woman in the ermine hat is obviously a prostitute who is propositioning the gentleman; but to the heroine she is merely a nice lady whose attempt to be friendly is rebuffed by a not-nice man. (p. 661)

There is a great deal more of this sort of thing. Instructors who take up the story in detail in class may want to invite students to express their opinions about the identity of the "ermine toque." (Is she not more plausibly taken as a woman who formerly had a relationship with the gentleman?) More important, of course, is our attitude toward Miss Brill, and our sense of the author's attitude. Although we should always trust the tale, not the teller, following D. H. Lawrence's admirable advice, perhaps it is not utterly illegitimate to keep in mind some words Mansfield wrote in a letter to her husband. She had sent him this story, and in a letter he told her that he shared her enthusiasm for it. In response to his letter she wrote [quoted in Marvin Magalaner, *The Fiction of Katherine Mansfield* (1971), p. 17],

> One writes (*one* reason why is) because one does care so passionately that one *must show* it—one must declare one's love.

Finally, a word about the protagonist's name. we have already mentioned that she is "Miss" because that presumably is the way all of her acquaintances know her, but why "Brill"? James W. Gargano pointed out [*Explicator* 19:2 (November 1960), Item 10] that the brill is a European flatfish, edible though not especially esteemed for its taste. The name certainly does not convey dignity, but whether it conveys ridicule or absurdity is another matter. (The American equivalent would be something like Miss Perch.) In fact, "Brill" is not an exceptionally uncommon name, as a glance at a large telephone directory will reveal. (There are a few dozen in the Boston area.) In any case, students might be invited to discuss the name. Does it fit the person? (Perhaps the important thing is that the name of a character *not* mislead the reader by *in*appropriate connotations, unless these are used for purposes of irony.)

18

Writing about Literature: An Overview of Critical Strategies

Suggestions for Further Reading

For this part of the book, we can only offer the mixed nature of our own experience and invite you to make the decision that feels right to you.

When we teach an introductory course open to all students, we find we usually say little or nothing about critical approaches. We might comment on feminist theory, but we do so within the context of our discussion of a specific literary work. We do not treat the theory in much detail or depth, and about deconstruction and new historicism we are silent. These approaches are too complex for brief comment; the students cannot handle them well and end up feeling mystified or confused. They are, we think, better off focusing on the literary works directly and examining the writer's uses of language in them.

But when we teach an introductory literature or literature and composition course designed for English majors, then we do make an effort to discuss critical approaches. Feminist theory and criticism: this is an approach that students can begin to grasp fairly quickly—they see its relation to the women's movement of the 1960s and 1970s—and can learn to apply themselves. The same holds true for reader-response criticism; students right away can talk about their responses to texts and feel some affinity with the theories that Stanley Fish, Wolfgang Iser, Jonathan Culler, and others have proposed. Deconstruction and new historicism are harder; the first greatly depends on continental philosophy, and the second on a wide and dense range of knowledge about history, society, and culture. But we can make some headway if we are patient enough in our explanations and illustrate how deconstruction, for instance, "works" in the case of a Wordsworth lyric or how a new historicist analysis of the monarchy in Shakespeare's England reveals something new about kingship and the kingdom in *Hamlet*, *Macbeth*, or *King Lear*.

No sooner, however, than we make this distinction between general courses and courses for English majors than we must admit that some of our colleagues hold a different view. Some of them give a good deal of time in all of their literature courses to the subject of critical approaches. Indeed, one or two of our colleagues launch their courses with a discussion of critical approaches. When they use our book, they begin with this chapter, taking it as the point of departure for the rest of the course they are teaching. As one of these instructors said to us, "When the students read and write about a poem, they need to have something to look for, and that's what the critical approaches give them."

To us, this seems an awkward and unpersuasive formulation. Surely there must be "something" in a literary work that can affect us simply because the work is what it is and we are who we are. Must a reader study literary theory before he or she can be moved by a Shakespeare play, a Hawthorne story, or a Dickinson or Frost poem? But we know the point that our colleague is making. He is saying that, in his view at any rate, students need a critical vocabulary, and one that goes beyond such standard terms as plot, character, setting, theme, tone, and the like. Equip the students with the tools, and they will be able to extract meanings from texts. If we don't, so the argument goes, the students will not know what to look for, and they will have little to offer in class and in paper assignments.

In some English departments, this claim has become the principle according to which the curriculum is structured. The introductory courses are theory and criticism courses, and it is only after these are taken that students then move to author, period, and other kinds of literature courses. These teachers maintain that students require a set of terms and interpretive procedures in order to know how to speak and write about the literature they study. The theories, the approaches, it is argued, provide students with the power to read critically and productively.

Perhaps what comes into focus from these examples is a question that teachers and critics have been debating for some years now: How much theory, how much study of critical approaches, do the students in literature courses need? Obviously they need a certain amount of basic work on those familiar and inevitable terms such as character and setting. But after that has been done, how much more is necessary?

A good case can be made that a student planning on graduate school needs a lot more. For better or worse, much of the emphasis in graduate training is placed on theory and criticism; a student starting graduate school without some knowledge of deconstruction, feminist theory and criticism, and other approaches will have some serious catching up to do. For English majors in general, we think the case can be made that they, too, will benefit from courses on critical approaches, but we think that these courses should come in the later stages of the students' undergraduate careers. Why not read many authors and many different kinds of literary works first, and then turn to the project of examining and comparing and contrasting the strengths and limits of critical approaches?

We risk making our point more strongly than we intend. There are many theorists from whom we have learned—Stanley Fish, in his reader-response criticism on Milton's poetry, immediately comes to mind. Others we have learned from and find well worth disagreeing with include Geoffrey H. Hartman and Harold Bloom. But for us what makes the best theorists valuable, stimulating, and provocative is that they are engaged, attentive readers. Even as they work with their theories, they strike us as being responsive to the specific works at hand. This differs from mechanically "applying" this or that theory to a literary work from the outside, with no heed paid to whether the work calls for such a theory or not.

Richard Poirier, Helen Vendler, John Hollander, Frank Kermode—these critics, and others we could name, have an approach but not a theory. They are intensely curious about the ways in which a writer and a literary work can challenge and teach them, explore complex ideas and feelings, spark new insights, expand the borders of consciousness. What matters for them is the writer's relation to the verbal medium—what he or she is doing with words in the literary work—and the reader's engagement with the work that this author has performed. It is this quality of personal commitment and engagement, and the excitement of it, that we do not find often enough in the books of literary theory that we have read. And it is this quality that we believe is the one above all that should be made vivid and rich for students.

We have one or two suggestions to offer you and your colleagues on the vexed matter of critical approaches. We think it is important—though we concede it is not always easy—to make the discussion of and debate about this issue a "public" one for the students. If you are using this book in a multisection course, you and one or two of your colleagues might select a poem by Wordsworth, Blake, or some other poet and each describe how this or that approach illuminates the text. We have often done something like this ourselves, with the help of a colleague or two who visits a class one day, or else we have done a version of it through a panel discussion in the late afternoon that students are encouraged to attend.

There are other topics you could select for one or more panels or faculty presentations:

- The Critics Who Made Us—this would focus on a critic or critics (or a teacher) who played a central role in your own literary education.
- Literary Theory: For and Against—this would center on the question of what is gained, and what is or might be lost, when the study of literary theory and critical approaches takes center stage.
- Close Reading: What It Is and How It is Done—this would explore the question of what it means to "read closely" and what the teacher/critics in your department mean by the term "close reading." What does it mean to be a "close reader" of literature? What makes one close reader better than, or at least different from, another?

We have found that students enjoy these events. It interests them to hear their teachers talking about their own literary experiences and educations. It also helps the students to see connections between the courses they take. Even seeing a difference between one course and another is making a useful connection. And it also clarifies and makes interesting a problem that students often face and wonder about, a problem that may seem quite natural and minor to us but that is very real to them: "My roommate and I are taking the same course, but we're enrolled in different sections. My instructor told our class that . . . but my roommate's instructor said something that sounds completely the opposite. . . ." We should be willing to explain as best we can how and why such situations occur and to explain, furthermore, what would be the consequences for literature and literary study if it turned out instead that instructors and critics were always in agreement.

PART IV
A Thematic Anthology

19

Journeys

JOAN DIDION
On Going Home (p. 644)

In a typical Freshman English class, made up of seventeen- to nineteen-year-olds, some students reading Didion will find her style heady and her topic compelling for their own writing. Others will be irritated, some without knowing why. Still others will be indifferent. Typically, whatever their intellectual range, students at this age vary markedly in emotional maturity. Some, we find, are not ready for the confrontation with their own ambivalence toward their families that a serious engagement with Didion's essay demands. So, although we would assign the essay and discuss it in class, we wouldn't *require* essays written about it. We don't want to read the vague or sentimental essays some would submit; and with so much else to write about, there's no reason to put students on a collision course with failure. For students who can and will use them, the questions following the piece provide some sample essay topics.

Students who admire Didion might be directed to her *Political Fictions* (2001), which includes essays on Newt Gingrich, Bill Clinton, and other political figures and topics, and to *Where I Was From* (2003), which describes her upbringing and experiences in California. The *New York Times* noted of this second book that it is "a reassessment and reappraisal of her thinking about her home state, a love song to the place where her family has lived for generations, but a love song full of questions and doubts." See also *Joan Didion: Essays and Conversations*, ed. Ellen G. Friedman (1984).

MONTESQUIEU (CHARLES DE SECONDAT, BARON DE LA BRÈDE)
Persian Letters (p. 646)

As we say in our headnote, Montesquieu's basic device is the innocent eye, the fairly straightforward reporting of the irrationalities that characterize a society.

Thus, according to him, the King of France is immensely wealthy although he possesses no gold mines. Where does his money come from?

> The vanity of his subjects. . . . He has been known to undertake and wage great wars with no other funds than honorary titles to sell, and by reason of this miracle of human pride, his troops are paid, his fortresses armed, and his navies fitted out.

Some students may not already be familiar with the fact that in Europe titles were sold, but the context makes the practice pretty clear, and few students will be puzzled by anything in the letter. (Most students will be aware that in the United States certain kinds of ambassadorships are given to persons who have donated substantial sums to the party in power.)

Some students will be familiar with *Gulliver's Travels*, a book that often uses Gulliver as an innocent eye but that also uses other characters similarly. Thus, Swift's Lilliputians comment on Gulliver's pocket watch—a device unfamiliar to them—in order to satirize our enslavement to time:

> [Gulliver] put this engine to our ears, which made an incessant noise like that of a watermill. And we conjecture it is either some unknown animal, or the god that he worships: but we are more inclined to the latter opinion, because he assured us (if we understood him right, for he expressed himself very imperfectly), that he seldom did any thing without consulting it. He called it his oracle, and said it pointed out the time for every action of his life.

Yes, there is some satire here of the self-satisfied Lilliputians who are convinced that Gulliver "expressed himself very imperfectly," but chiefly the satire is directed against Europeans, persons who let their timepieces run their lives.

We include Montesquieu chiefly in order to give students an idea of how they might write their own Persian Letter. They may want to talk about such national matters as war, political campaigns and elections, the death penalty, gay marriage, abortion, and public safety, or they may want to talk about more local matters such as applying to college, college courses and requirements, and family customs. The satire may be directed against any of these (e.g., it may call attention to the irrationality of what we normally accept), or on the other hand the letter may satirize the letter-writer, who sees and who speaks reasonably but who utterly fails to understand what he or she sees.

TONI CADE BAMBARA
The Lesson (p. 648)

It would be hard to find a less strident or more delightful story preaching revolution. At its heart, "The Lesson" calls attention to the enormous inequity in the distribution of wealth in America, and it suggests that black people ought to start thinking about "what kind of society it is in which some people can spend on a toy what it would cost to feed a family of six or seven" for a year. That the young narrator does not quite get the point of Miss Moore's lesson—and indeed steals Miss Moore's money—is no sure sign that the lesson has failed. (Presumably, Miss Moore doesn't much care about the loss of her money; the money is well lost if it helps the narrator, who plans to spend it, to see the power of money.) In any case, the narrator has been made sufficiently uneasy ("I sure want to punch somebody in the mouth") so that we sense she will later get the point: "I'm goin . . . to think this day through." The last line of the story seems to refer to her race to a bakery, but it has larger implications: "Ain't nobody gonna beat me at nuthin."

The difference between Sylvia's response and Sugar's response to Miss Moore's lesson is worth discussing in class. As Malcolm Clark, of Solano Community College, puts it in a letter to us, "The obvious question of the story is, 'What is the lesson?' . . . It's clear that Miss Moore is trying to teach these children a lesson in economic inequity. . . . Sugar learns this lesson, as her comments to Miss Moore indicate. However, Sylvia has also learned this lesson, though she does not reveal her understanding to Miss Moore." As Clark goes on to point out, Miss Moore's lesson is not simply that some people are rich and others are not. She wants to bring the children to a state where they will demand their share of the pie. And it is in learning this part of the lesson that Sylvia and Sugar part company. Despite Sugar's obvious understanding of the lesson and her momentary flash of anger—strong enough to make her push Sylvia away—her condition is only temporary.

"At the end of the story she is unchanged from the little girl she was at the beginning. It is she who wants to go to Hascomb's bakery and spend the money on food, essentially the same thing they intended to do with the money before the lesson began. . . . Sylvia, however, is greatly changed. She does not intend to spend the money with Sugar; instead, she plans to go over to the river and reflect upon the lesson further."

For students who would like to read more of Bambara's work, the best place to begin is with her two collections of stories: *Gorilla, My Love* (1972) and *The Sea Birds Are Still Alive* (1977). A posthumous book, *Deep Sightings and Rescue Missions: Fiction, Essays, and Conversations* (1996), is also well worth reading. For secondary sources: Keith Byerman, *Fingering the Jagged Grain: Tradition and Form in Recent Black Fiction* (1986), and Elliott Butler-Evans, *Race, Gender, and Desire: Narrative Strategies in the Fiction of Toni Cade Bambara, Toni Morrison, and Alice Walker* (1989). See also the entry in the *Dictionary of Literary Biography,* vol. 38 (1985), pp. 12–22. There is a section on Bambara in *Black Women Writers (1950–1980): A Critical Evaluation,* ed. Mari Evans (1984), pp. 41–71.

Topics for Critical Thinking and Writing

1. Let's suppose Bambara had decided to tell the story through the eyes of Miss Moore. Write the first 250 words of such a story.

2. Miss Moore says, "Imagine for a minute what kind of society it is in which some people can spend on a toy what it would cost to feed a family of six or seven. What do you think?" In an essay of 500 words, tell a reader what you think about this issue.

BOBBIE ANN MASON
Shiloh (p. 653)

Writers in all periods have occasionally used the historical present in telling stories (Katherine Anne Porter, for example, used it for "Flowering Judas"), but in America in our century—until the early 1970s—few storytellers used it, except for melodramatic historians eager to convey a sense of immediacy: "The German armies march into Paris...." At first glance it seems that Updike uses the present in "A & P," a story whose opening line is this: "In walks these three girls in nothing but bathing suits." But Updike uses a first-person narrator, who occasionally talks in a sort of "So he says to me... and I says to him" manner.

Exactly why so many writers in the 1970s and 1980s used the present tense (Mason wrote her story in 1982) is not clear, but some explanations attribute its widespread use to television, film, the new journalism, and drugs. But what sort of useful generalization can one make about the effect of this device? Usually it is said that the present adds realism and immediacy, but such an assertion is dubious.

Still, it seems true that contemporary writers who narrate in the present usually write in what can be called a plain style, i.e., they use (for instance) little subordination, few words with strong connotations, and few figures of speech. (In fact, in "Shiloh" Mason uses more figures than are commonly found in fiction of its type.) Such writing often seems "flat," lacking in energy, free from value judgments, uninvolved. Sample:

> When Leroy gets home from the shopping center, Norma Jean's mother, Mabel Beasley, is there. Until this year, Leroy has not realized how much time she spends with Norma Jean. When she visits, she inspects the closets and then the plants, informing Norma Jean when a plant is droopy or yellow. Mabel calls the plants "flowers," although there are never any blooms. She always notices if Norma Jean's laundry is piling up.

The narrator is just reporting on what passes before his or her eyes, not responding or evaluating. In "Shiloh," after the first surprising sentence ("Norma Jean is working on her pectorals"), almost no sentence seems to have been written to give the reader a special little thrill. But this is only to say that Mason writes the story in an appropriate style, since the story is about confused, almost numbed people, people whose lives (like their child) seem to have died, people who can't make out who they are, what they are, or even where they are:

Now that Leroy has come home to stay, he notices how much the town has changed. Subdivisions are spreading across western Kentucky like an oil slick. The sign at the edge of town says "Pop: 11,500"—only seven hundred more than it said twenty years before. Leroy can't figure out who is living in all the new houses. The farmers who used to gather around the courthouse square on Saturday afternoons to play checkers and spit tobacco juice have gone. It has been years since Leroy has thought about the farmers, and they have disappeared without his noticing.

Perhaps when storytellers customarily used the past tense they were (to some degree) implying that something had happened, was over and done with, and they were reporting on it because they thought they had made something out of it; further, they thought that what had happened and what they had made out of it were worth reporting. Perhaps when writers use the present tense they are (to some degree) implying that "such-and-such is passing in front of my eyes, I'm telling you about it, but I am not able to interpret it any more than the participants themselves are able to." In any case, "Shiloh" is obviously a story about a man and wife who don't know what to make of each other or of themselves. Leroy has his kits and his hope of building a real log cabin, and Norma Jean has her weights, her music, her cooking, and her English composition course, but none of these things provides a center. There was once a marriage, and there was once a baby, but the baby died and the marriage has fallen apart. This is not at all the world that existed when Leroy and Norma Jean got married; it's a new world, a world in which women engage in weight-lifting, men engage in needlepoint, and a doctor's son pushes dope. It's all very confusing, especially to Leroy.

Mabel, Norma Jean's mother, thinks things can be as they were in the past (Norma Jean should be a dutiful daughter and not smoke, Leroy and Norma Jean should go on a second honeymoon—to Shiloh, where Mabel went on her honeymoon), but of course there is no going back to the way things were. The trip to Shiloh proves to be a disaster. Norma Jean walks away from Leroy, leaving him to realize that he doesn't understand his wife, himself, or their marriage. He remembers some events, but

> he knows he is leaving out a lot. He is leaving out the insides of history. History was always just names and dates to him. It occurs to him that building a house out of logs is similarly empty—too simple.

Early in the story, when we first hear about Leroy's interest in kits, we are told that "Leroy has grown to appreciate how things are put together" (that's the way he sees it, of course), but at the end of the story we see that he has no idea of how the pieces of his life can be put together.

A few words about the names "Leroy" and "Norma Jean." Some readers suggest that Leroy (French for "the king") puts us in mind of Elvis Presley. Further, they say, the name evokes an image of a romantic knight errant, now reduced to a maimed man who does needlepoint of a scene from *Star Trek* while his truck rusts. Norma Jean, of course, evokes Marilyn Monroe.

For Mabel, Shiloh has the pleasant associations of a honeymoon, and she thinks that the happiness she experienced at Shiloh can now be transferred to Leroy and Norma Jean. But Shiloh, though now a site for picnics, was a scene of vast destruction, and it is at Shiloh that Leroy sees that his marriage has come apart.

(The Battle of Shiloh took its name from Shiloh Church, a meeting house at the site. The church was named for the ancient Hebrew sanctuary about ten miles north of Bethel. It is thought that the word means "tranquility," so the name adds irony to the story.)

We admire Mason's novels, *In Country* (1985) and *Spence and Lila* (1988), but value her short stories, in *Shiloh and Other Stories* (1982) and *Love Life: Stories* (1989), even more. For studies of "Shiloh": Leslie White, "The Function of Popular Culture in Bobbie Ann Mason's *Shiloh and Other Stories* and *In Country*," *Southern Quarterly* 26 (Summer 1988): 69–79; and Barbara Henning, "Minimalism and the American Dream: 'Shiloh' by Bobbie Ann Mason and 'Preservation' by Raymond Carver," *Modern Fiction Studies* 35 (Winter 1989): 689–698.

ANONYMOUS JAPANESE FOLK TALE
The Mountain-Climber (p. 663)

Our text includes Katherine Min's "Courting a Monk," an extremely engaging story that raises some Buddhist issues, and in our discussion of that story (this manual, p. 418), we offer a relatively extended commentary on some chief Buddhist ideas. If the present folk tale interests you, please look at the discussion of Min's story for some further comment about Buddhism.

Here we will talk about Buddhism much more briefly. For Buddhists, this visible world of transience, of suffering, of death, is *samsara*, a Sanskrit word translated as "journeying" or "wandering." (This is why we place the story in a chapter called "Journeys.") The idea is this: Caught in a seemingly endless cycle of birth, death, and rebirth, we wander through a changing world, looking for a permanent home. There is much argument about *what* is reborn, since most Buddhist thinking denies that we have a soul, something independent of the body. If there is no soul, and no "self," what is reborn? The usual explanation offers an analogy to the flame of a candle that lights another candle, the idea being that the flame on the second candle is and is not the first flame. (For a good, short discussion of this issue see Rupert Gethin, *The Foundations of Buddhism* [1998], in the comment on "no self," pages 136–44.)

Many of your students will be familiar with the term *karma*, the doctrine that one's condition of rebirth depends on the good or evil deeds that one has done in a previous existence. Thus, a wicked person may be reborn as an animal, or as a human in hell, a place of punishment (but in Buddhist thinking hell is *not* a place of eternal punishment, so therefore it is more like the Christian Purgatory than it is like hell). An especially good person may be reborn in a

Pure Land, a sort of heaven but again not a place of eternal joy, simply a place in which further merit can be achieved, so that ultimately one can entirely cease to crave, and can thus be liberated from *trishna*, "attachment," a quality that binds us to the cycle of birth, death, and rebirth. In short, Buddhist enlightenment consists in learning not to crave. (Again, we go into this in our discussion of Min's story in this manual, pages 418–422.)

"The Mountain-Climber" represents the struggle to achieve *nirvana* (i.e. freedom from attachment, enlightenment) as an exhausting climb up a mountain, aided by a bodhisattva, a being who himself has achieved freedom from desire but who paradoxically desires to help others to achieve this condition of freedom from desire. Let's begin by thinking a moment about the symbolism of a mountain. Mountains, reaching into the sky, are widely associated with deities, and the ascent of the mountain often implies an ascent toward divine knowledge. Moses received the Ten Commandments on Mount Sinai (Exodus 20.1–17), and Jesus preached a Sermon on the Mount (Matthew 5–7). Christ's Transfiguration (when Moses and Elija appeared to him, and a voice spoke from the heavens) occurred on "a high mountain" (Mark 9.2) and his Ascension into heaven took place on the Mount of Olives (Luke 24.50; Acts 1.2–11). Taoist immortals are associated with mountain tops, and the Buddha preached from the Vulture Peak. It is not at all surprising, then, that in the Japanese tale the quest for spiritual knowledge is symbolized by the attempt to ascend a mountain.

The tale interestingly represents our world of *samsara*, ordinarily envisioned as filled with attractions (good food, good sex, lovely nature, etc.) as a barren mountain, with the implication that this is a good metaphor for what *samsara* really is. (One thinks of those European folk tales about a young knight who embraces a beautiful woman and then wakes from his dream and finds that he holds nothing but bones and ashes.) In the Japanese story we are not told until fairly late that the mountain is made up of skulls. At first we hear only of "tumbled fragments that rolled or turned beneath the foot" and of "trodden [material that] would burst like an empty shell." Then the priest touches something and sees that it is not a stone but a skull. Still, we are not told until the final paragraph that the mountain of skulls consists entirely of skulls of the priest's former lives.

The story does not tell us whether the priest achieves nirvana, only that he is instructed in the nature of the mountain, but we can perhaps assume that he profits from the instruction. Some students find the story unpleasantly macabre, and others find it excessively negative since it suggests that what we normally think of as life is better thought of as death. But the New Testament is not lacking in passages that connect with this motif, passages suggesting that we must free ourselves from attachment to this world. One example is Jesus' assertion,

> Whosoever looketh on a woman to lust after her hath committed adultery with her already in his heart.
> And if thy right eye offend thee, pluck it out, and cast it from thee: for it is profitable for thee that one of thy members should perish, and not that thy whole body should be cast into hell.

And if thy right hand offend thee, cut it off, and cast it from thee: for it is profitable for thee that one of thy members should perish, and not that thy whole body should be cast into hell. (Matthew 5. 28–30)

(We give additional texts in our discussion of Min's "Courting a Monk.")

In our "Topic for Critical Thinking and Writing," through Tennyson's metaphor of "stepping-stones / Of [our] dead selves" and Augustine's metaphor of mounting upward by climbing on a ladder of vices that we trample underfoot, we try to help students to see that the idea that some experiences are to be triumphed over, and are a kind of sickness or death, is not exclusively a Buddhist idea.

JOHN KEATS
On First Looking into Chapman's Homer (p. 665)

In "On First Looking into Chapman's Homer," Keats uses figures to communicate to the reader the poet's state of mind. Figures of traveling (appropriate to a poem about the author of *The Iliad* and *The Odyssey*, and also, via "realms of gold" or El Dorado, to the Elizabethans) give way in the sestet to figures of more breathtaking exploration and discovery. (By the way, it is not quite right to say that at line 9 we pass from the octave's images of land to the sestet's images of discovery. An important shift occurs in line 7, with "Yet" no less important than line 9's "Then." "Breathe" in line 7 is probably transitional, linked to the octave's idea of foreign travel and also to the sestet's early reference to the skies.)

It is probably fair to say that the octave (or at least its first six lines as compared with the sestet) has a somewhat mechanical, academic quality. "Realms of gold," "goodly states," "bards in fealty to Apollo," "demesne," etc., all suggest something less than passionate utterance, a tone reinforced by the rather mechanical four pairs of lines, each pair ending with a substantial pause. But in the sestet the language is more concrete, the lines more fluid (it can be argued that only line 10 concludes with a pause), and the meter less regular, giving a sense of new excitement that of course corresponds to the meaning of the poem.

Almost all critics agree that Keats erred in giving Cortez for Balboa, but C. V. Wicker argues in *College English* 17 (April 1956): 383–87 that Keats meant Cortez, for the point is not the first discovery of something previously unknown, but an individual's discovery for himself of what others have earlier discovered for themselves. Still, it seems evident that Keats slipped, and instructors may want to spend some class time discussing the problem of whether such a factual error weakens the poem.

In line with much contemporary criticism that sees poetry as being reflective discourse concerned with itself, Lawrence Lipking, in *The Life of the Poet* (1981), sees this poem as being about Keats's discovery of Keats. Well, yes, in a way, but surely the poem is also about the discovery of the world's literature, a world other than the self. See also P. McNally, in *JEGP* 79 (1980): 530–40.

Percy Bysshe Shelley
Ozymandias (p. 666)

James Reeves, in *The Critical Sense,* does a hatchet job on Shelley's "Ozymandias." (Ozymandias, incidentally, was the Greek version of the name User-ma-Ra, better known as Ramses II, the name the Greeks used for the thirteenth century B.C. pharaoh who, like other pharaohs, built monuments to celebrate his own greatness. One such monument was a colossus sixty feet tall, carved in stone by Memnon. Diodorus, a Sicilian Greek historian of the first century, saw the statue and wrote that it was inscribed, "I am Ozymandias, King of kings; if any would know how great I am, and where I lie, let him excel me in any of my works." At some later date, the statue tumbled, leaving only fragments.) Reeves's objections include: "vast" (2) means "of great extent," but the legs would be tall rather than vast; "on the sand" (3) is hardly necessary after "in the desert"; if the visage is "shattered" (which Reeves takes to mean "broken to pieces"), it would be difficult to recognize the facial expression; the speaker says that the sculptor "well . . . read" the subject's passions, but we cannot know if this is true, since we have no other information about the subject; if it is argued that the inscription is evidence of cold-hearted tyranny, the sestet should begin "For," not "And"; to speak of "the decay" of a "wreck" is tautological; in lines 13–14 "boundless" makes unnecessary "stretch far away," and "bare" makes "lone" unnecessary. Some of Reeves's objections are telling, some are niggling; in any case, the power of the poem is chiefly in the essential irony and the almost surrealistic scene of legs arising in the desert, the face on the ground nearby, and no trunk anywhere.

A small point: Lines 4–8 are unclear, for it is not certain if "the hand . . . and the heart" belong to the sculptor, in which case the idea is that the sculptor "mocked" ("mimicked," "imitated in stone") the passions and "fed" them by creating them in stone, or if the hand and the heart belong to Ozymandias, whose hand mocked the passions of his foes and whose heart fed his own passions.

Shelley's friend, Horace Smith, a banker with a taste for literature, wrote a sonnet on Ozymandias at the same time that Shelley did. You may want to ask students to compare the two poems:

On a Stupendous Leg of Granite, Discovered Standing by Itself in the Desert of Egypt

In Egypt's sandy silence, all alone,
Stands a gigantic Leg, which far off throws
The only shadow that the desert knows.
"I am great Ozymandias," said the stone,

"The King of kings; this mighty city shows
The wonders of my hand." The city's gone!
Naught but the leg remaining to disclose
The sight of that forgotten Babylon.

We wonder, and some hunter may express
Wonder like ours, when through the wilderness
Where London stood, holding the wolf in chase.
He meets some fragment huge, and stops to guess
What wonderful, but unrecorded, race
Once dwelt in that annihilated place.

For additional background material on Shelley's poem, see H. M. Richmond, "Ozymandias and the Travellers," *Keats-Shelley Journal* 11 (1962): 65–71. For a discussion of Shelley's poem and Smith's, see K. M. Bequette, "Shelley and Smith: Two Sonnets of Ozymandias," in *Keats-Shelley Journal* 26 (1977): 29–31.

There are excellent biographies by Richard Holmes (1974) and Kenneth Neill Cameron (2 vols., 1950, 1974), and many critical studies, including those by Carlos Baker (1948), Harold Bloom (1959), Earl Wasserman (1971), and William Keach (1984). The scholarship on Shelley, because of its engagement with the poet's dense ideas and passionate, but often obscure, social and philosophical views, can prove daunting to undergraduates. It might be preferable to recommend instead two books that combine primary texts with extensive annotations and contextual materials: *The Lyrics of Shelley*, ed. Judith Chernaik (1972), and *Shelley's Poetry and Prose,* ed. Donald H. Reiman and Sharon B. Powers (1977).

ALFRED, LORD TENNYSON
Ulysses (p. 667)

Robert Langbaum, in *The Poetry of Experience* (1957), and Christopher Ricks, in *Tennyson* (2nd ed. 1989), offer some good remarks; Paul Baum, in *Tennyson Sixty Years After* (1948), assaults the poem. Henry Kozicki, in *Tennyson and Clio* (1979; a book on Tennyson's philosophy of history), argues that "Ulysses" reveals Tennyson's optimism about historical progress and his despair about the role of a hero. For a review of much that should not have been written, see L. K. Hughes in *Victorian Poetry* 17 (Autumn 1979): 192–203. By the way, it is worth mentioning to students that Homer's hero wanted to get home, Sophocles's (in *Philoctetes*) is a shifty politician (as is Shakespeare's), and Dante's Ulysses (*Inferno* XXVI) is an inspiring but deceitful talker whose ardent search is for *forbidden* things.

The first five lines emphasize, mostly with monosyllables, the dull world Ulysses is leaving. With line 6 ("I cannot rest from travel") we see a rather romantic hero, questing for experience, and indeed "experience" is mentioned in line 19, but it must be added that something is done in the poem to give "experience" a social context: Ulysses has fought for Troy (17), he wishes to be of "use" (23), and he wishes to do "some work of notable note" (52). Lines 22–23 apparently say the same thing four times over, but readers are not likely to wish that Tennyson had deleted the superbly appropriate metaphor of the rusting sword. "Gray spirit" (30) and "sinking star" (31) help (along with the heavy pauses and monosyllables in 55–56) to define the poem as a piece about dying, though students on first reading are likely to see only the affirmations. Even the strong affirmations in 57 ff. are undercut by "sunset" (60), "western" (61), etc. But the last line, with its regular accents on the meaningful words, affords a strong ending; perhaps the line is so strong and regular that it is a bit too easy. In line 45 Ulysses directly addresses the mariners, yet we hardly sense an audience as we do in Browning's dramatic monologues. If he is addressing the mariners, who are aboard, where is he when he refers to "this still hearth" (2) and when he says, "This is my son" (33)? (Some critics claim that lines 1–32 are a soliloquy: Ulysses supposedly would not speak publicly of Ithaca as stagnant and savage, or of his wife as "aged." Lines 33–43 are his farewell to the Ithacans, and the remainder is an address to his mariners.)

Probably the reader ought to see the poem not as a muddled attempt at a Browningesque dramatic monologue but as a somewhat different type of poem—a poem in which the poet uses a fairly transparent mask in order to express his state of mind and to persuade his readers to share that state of mind. The poem thus is closer to, say, "Prufrock" than it is to "My Last Duchess."

CARL SANDBURG
Limited (p. 669)

Carl Sandburg was the brawny, big-hearted poet of immigrants and laborers, of common men and women, an enemy of exploitation and injustice, a celebratory singer of the working people of America, its industries and factories, and its grand panoramas of mountains, rivers, and landscapes. "The great mid-West," observed the poet, critic, and anthologist Louis Untermeyer, "that vast region of steel mills and slaughterhouses, of cornfields and prairies, of crowded cities and empty skies, spoke through Carl Sandburg."

Sandburg was a very popular poet (he said he wrote "simple poems for simple people"), but during the 1920s he launched a biographical project on Abraham Lincoln—it required six volumes to complete (1926–39)—and today perhaps even more people are aware of him for the Lincoln biography than for his verse.

Sandburg also wrote books of children's tales, including *Rootabaga Stories* (1922) and *Rootabaga Pigeons* (1923). In addition, he made important contributions to the study of American song, folklore, and oral tradition through his compilations *The American Songbag* (1927) and *The New American Songbag*

(1950). Often he toured the country, reading his own poems and reading the poems and singing the ballads (accompanying himself on the banjo or the guitar) included in these books.

"Limited," from *Chicago Poems* (1916) is a more complicated and suggestive work than it might seem at first encounter. The title refers to a "limited train," which is a train "having a limited number of cars and making a limited number of stops in order to provide fast through service." The most famous of such trains probably was the Twentieth Century Limited, inaugurated as early as 1902. Between 1910 and 1912 the wooden cars were replaced by all-steel cars, and in Sandburg's day the train made the run from New York to Chicago in a bit under twenty hours, an astounding time—comparable in its day to something like the now-discontinued Concorde flights from New York to London and Paris. The Twentieth Century Limited, at that time the fastest train in the world, was an emblem not only of speed but also of luxury: Passengers could eat in a special dining car, could get a haircut and shave, and could have their clothes pressed. After World War II railroad service went downhill, and the limited trains—once the world's symbols of American know-how and can-do—lost out to the airlines. Even the famed Twentieth Century Limited was discontinued in 1967.

Back to Sandburg's poem. The body of the poem implies that Sandburg is using "limited" not just with reference to the kind of train but also in the sense of "confined within limits, restricted in extent, number, or duration." Lives, and material possessions, are limited, as line three reminds us. The emphasis on the "hurtling" movement of the train indeed intimates the "limited" control that we exercise over our lives. We are at the mercy of the machines we have made, and, more broadly, at the mercy of mighty forces that greatly exceed our own all-too-human, all-too-limited powers. "Limited" is perhaps, too, a sly joke about the final word "Omaha": this is a very limited, one-word answer to the speaker's question.

It's intriguing to wonder why Sandburg picked Omaha. It is the largest city in Nebraska (population in 2000: 390,007), and today, and even more in Sandburg's time, it was a "major transportation center" and the site of "one of the largest livestock markets in the world and a market for agricultural products." Much business, crucial to the nation, was (and is) conducted there, in the nation's heartland. (See *The Columbia Gazetteer of North America*, 2000 ed.)

The name of the city may be, for Sandburg, less significant than the man's tone when he replies "Omaha." The man knows where he is going; he is blunt, definite, decisive. In another sense, however, the man does not at all know where he is going. Or, rather, to state the point directly: he thinks he is going to Omaha but he is really headed toward death and oblivion.

Possibly there's a bit of ironic play in the connection between the image of the "ashes" and the presence of the man in a "smoker." A few students may be familiar with the phrase "ashes to ashes, dust to dust," which sounds Biblical but which does not appear in the Bible. It comes from the Burial section of the first *English Book of Common Prayer* (published in the mid-sixteenth century): "Earth to earth, ashes to ashes, dust to dust."

When you teach "Limited," you might ask students to examine large and small details in the text. Why, for example, does Sandburg use the present tense ("I am riding...")? Why, too, does he specify "fifteen" coaches and one "thousand" people? (Our view is that he offers these numbers because they are amazing: The train is as vast as a city.) Does it matter that the speaker directs his question to a man who is in "the smoker," as opposed, say, to being in the dining car or in a non-smoking passenger car? There's a chance, by the way, that some students will need to be told that "smoker" refers to a car on a train where smoking is permitted.

Another detail, connected to the poem's structure: Ask the students why Sandburg includes the third line, and why he places it in a parenthesis. What would be our response if this line were omitted? And what would be our response if the line were retained but without the parenthesis?

For further study: Joseph Haas and Gene Lovitz, *Carl Sandburg: A Pictorial Biography* (1967); Penelope Niven, *Carl Sandburg: A Biography* (1991); North Callahan, *Carl Sandburg: His Life and Works* (1987); and Philip R. Yannella, *The Other Carl Sandburg* (1996).

COUNTEE CULLEN
Incident (p. 670)

The poem seems to be of the utmost simplicity: twelve lines without any figures of speech and without any obscure words. But it has its complexities, beginning with the title.

Our first question in the text asks students to think about the word "incident." It's our impression that an "incident" is usually a minor affair—something detached from what comes before and after, and of little consequence. For instance: "During the banquet a waiter dropped a tray full of dishes, but apart from this incident the affair was a great success." There are of course plenty of exceptions, such as the famous "Incident at Harpers Ferry," but we think that on the whole an incident is (1) minor and (2) a distinct occurrence.

Cullen's title therefore is ironic; the episode might seem to be minor, but in fact it has left an indelible mark on the speaker's mind (and on the minds of countless readers). And since it continues to have its effect, it is not something separate and done with. The apparent simplicity, then, of the title and of the entire poem, is deceptive, since this seemingly trivial and unconnected episode stands for, or embodies, an enormous force in American life.

It's a good idea to ask a student to read the poem aloud in class (true for all poems, of course), so that students can hear the rhythms. On the whole, "Incident" sounds like a happy jingle, but of course that is part of the irony. Two details that strike us as especially effective are the enjambments in lines 7 and 11.

Of the other ten lines, nine end with some mark of punctuation, and the other one ("I saw the whole of Baltimore") could be complete in itself. But in the seventh line we are propelled into the horrible event of the eighth line ("And so I smiled, but he poked out / His tongue, and called me 'Nigger'"); and in the eleventh line we are propelled into the final line, the line that tells us that this whole "incident" was by no means trivial ("Of all the things that happened there / That's all that I remember").

Studies of Countee Cullen include Helen J. Dinger, *A Study of Countee Cullen* (1953); Stephen H. Brontz, *Roots of Negro Racial Consciousness—The 1920s: Three Harlem Renaissance Authors* (1954); Blanche E. Ferguson, *Countee Cullen and the Negro Renaissance* (1966); and Margaret Perry, *A Bio-Bibliography of Countee P. Cullen* (1971).

Instructors will find these secondary sources to be helpful, but none of them offers help on one issue that will be in the air when Cullen's poem is discussed. "Nigger," in line 8, is an ugly, offensive word—which is central to Cullen's point in the poem, but which is nonetheless a hard word for the teacher and for students to say aloud and to analyze.

We know some instructors who press hard on the word "Nigger" in class; they want the students to feel very vividly the crude bigotry and shock of the term. This approach, we confess, does not work for us, and so we follow a different path. Often, after we have read the poem and begun to examine it with students, we have paused to say outright that it's hard to use and talk about offensive racial and ethnic slurs and epithets. Yes, one of them is in Cullen's poem, and thus it has to be considered as essential to its meaning. But, still, we tell and teach ourselves that such words are wrong—that they should not be used, ever, because they are offensive—and thus it cuts against our principles and (we hope) our practice to hear ourselves voicing them.

This may or may not be the best approach, but at the least it acknowledges for students that *something* is awry and uncomfortable in the room when the instructor and students start using the word "nigger" or other words like it. Keep in mind what the students are or might be thinking and feeling. Be aware of, and talk about it. The tone of the class will be better, we believe, if you are sensitive to this issue and seek as best you can to address it carefully. The mistake would be to assume that, in a classroom context, ugly, offensive words will be heard by students neutrally, dispassionately.

WILLIAM STAFFORD
Traveling Through the Dark (p. 671)

The speaker is matter-of-fact, but by the end of the poem we realize that he is not only thoughtful in the sense of considerate of others (unlike the motorist who killed the deer, he pushes the deer off the road so that others won't have an accident) but also thoughtful in the sense of meditative. Although he realizes that he cannot possibly save the unborn fawn, he cannot dispose of the doe casually, knowing that he will also be killing its fawn.

We take it, then, that when he says "I thought hard for us all" (line 17) he means not only "our group" (line 10), but everything including the fawn. He briefly hesitates—his "only swerving"—but he does what he has to do, lest a motorist "swerve [and] . . . make more dead" (line 4).

In teaching this poem we usually try to reserve comment on the title until late in the discussion. If the poem has been talked about for a while, students can usually see that the title implies something about the human condition. All of us are "traveling through the dark," moving through a difficult, demanding world, sometimes swerving a bit, but by and large guided by principles. The resonance of Stafford's title will become especially clear if you ask students how it compares with some invented title, such as "The Dead Deer," or "On the Edge of the Wilson River."

A postscript. Is it absurd to compare the poem to Frost's "Stopping by Woods on a Snowy Evening"? We have in mind especially Frost's contrast between the speaker and the little horse that, being only a horse, can't share the speaker's values. In Stafford's poem, the automobile serves somewhat as the horse; its parking lights are on, and its engine purrs steadily. No swerving here, no decisions to make. But unlike machines, human beings have to make hard decisions in a world of danger (the tail-light turns the exhaust red).

For biographical background and context: William Stafford, *Down in My Heart* (1998); and Kim Stafford, *Early Morning: Remembering My Father, William Stafford* (2002). For an introduction: Jonathan Holden, *The Mark to Turn: A Reading of William Stafford's Poetry* (1976). See also: *On William Stafford: The Worth of Local Things,* ed. Tom Andrews (1993); and Judith Kitchen, *Writing The World: Understanding William Stafford* (1999).

ROBERT FROST
The Pasture (p. 671)

Frost wrote "The Pasture" in 1913, and beginning in 1930 he used it as the first poem—a sort of prologue—to all editions of his *Collected Poems*.

There isn't a word here that is unusual, not a word that any of us might not say, except perhaps the word "shan't," but even this word doesn't cause a reader any difficulty.

In many ways this short poem is typical of Frost: First of all, the language—the diction that he uses—is drawn from ordinary life. Second, the poem is a kind of miniature drama, a little play in which there is not only a speaker but also another character, here an unidentified "you," someone who is obviously dear to the speaker. Third, and this may be a bit less obvious to students in an introductory course in literature, the poem is about more than it seems to be.

There is always the danger, of course, that students will hunt too avidly for symbols, especially if they have to write a paper about it. In one lecture, for instance, he warned students, "You just don't chew a poem, take it all to pieces." On the other hand, Frost at least as often assured his audiences that poems have multiple meanings, are symbolic, and he on several occasions used the somewhat odd word "ulteriority" to talk about a quality in poems. For instance, in an essay in the *Atlantic Monthly* in 1946 ("The Constant Symbol," much reprinted) he says:

> There are many . . . things I have found myself saying about poetry, but the chiefest of these is that it is metaphor, saying one thing and meaning another, saying one thing in terms of another, the pleasure of ulteriority.

Still, before getting into Frost's "ulteriority," we suggest that you first help students to enjoy the miniature drama enacted in the "The Pasture."

This little dramatic monologue consists of two stanzas, and these divisions alert us to something; they are, so to speak, part of the meaning. After all, Frost didn't have to put that break between the fourth line and the fifth. He wants to tell us that there are two phases to this drama. This sounds strange, since the last line of the poem merely repeats the last line of the first stanza, but students will easily see that there is a development in the poem. Ask them if they agree that if the second stanza came first, the poem would be *less* effective, *less* interesting; almost all students will see that there is a development, a point we will get into in a moment.

The first line, "I'm going out to clean the pasture spring," is a simple enough assertion, yet the idea of "clearing" something, of cleaning up or *clarifying* something, can obviously have big implications, especially if we are talking about "the pasture spring." A spring is a source of life, a vitalizing power. Frost can be hinting at being witness to a new beginning. Next we get,

> I'll only stop to rake the leaves away
> (And wait to watch the water clear, I may):

That "wait to watch the water clear, I may" comes as a bit of a surprise. We thought he was just going out to complete a chore, and now we find that he is going to enjoy the job, he is going to loaf a bit, and enjoy the spectacle. There are additional little surprises, and it is worth reminding students that almost all poetry—almost all writing of any sort that is interesting, including each essay that students will write in your courses—should offer the reader small pleasant surprises as it progresses. That is, each line takes us to a place that we had not quite anticipated, but once we are there, we mentally say, "of course, that's exactly right."

Students will probably agree that we find this speaker an engaging fellow; he begins by announcing, in simple terms, that he is setting out to do what sounds like a routine job, but then he confesses—though he doesn't come out and say it directly—that this is a job that has its pleasures, it will afford him the opportunity to see the water clear up, a visual experience that for whatever reason is fascinating—we like to see the darkness yield to clarity, and, as we have already suggested, there is a hint here—since we are talking about a spring in a pasture—of a new beginning, a renewal, a freshening of life.

The first stanza ends, "I shan't be gone long.—You come too." That's a surprise, a big one—the speaker wants the listener to join him. So, even though the speaker is saying that he is *leaving* the person whom he is addressing, by this stage of the poem—just the fourth line—he indicates that, no, he doesn't really want to go and watch the water clear just by himself; he wants his companion to share the experience. He doesn't come out and say so, in so many words—we might say that his natural modesty prevents him from doing that—but it is evident that he values companionship, human society, just as much as he values enjoying the sight of watching the water clear. He wants to share the enjoyment, he wants his companion to experience it also.

Everything we are saying, we hasten to add, is something that students will easily see for themselves, if you just get them thinking and talking about the lines.

Now for the second stanza. We see the lines set off as a stanza on the page, so there is no surprise in its mere presence. And the rhyme scheme is the same, no surprise there.

> I'm going out to fetch the little calf
> That's standing by the mother.

We don't want to press this tiny poem too hard, but we think that with the introduction of the cow and the calf, Frost provides the reader with another surprise, the introduction of *relationships,* of *family.* Certainly there is nothing unnatural about finding a cow and a calf in a pasture, but the reader hadn't quite expected them. Frost is complicating the poem, giving us an additional pleasure and an additional view of life.

> It's so young,
> It totters when she licks it with her tongue.

And of course the calf itself is *new* life, a sort of parallel or analog to the pasture spring, the spring that, after raking, will be clear, a sort of new spring.

> I shan't be gone long.—You come too.

So the division of the poem into two stanzas marks the division between watching the spring clear, and watching the mother cow care for its offspring. And you can help students to find other dualities in the poem: the *speaker* and the *listener*; *solitude*—which is what the speaker first talks about—and *society* ("You come too"); *work* (raking the pasture spring) and *pleasure* or *meditation* ("wait to watch the water clear, I may"). The poem, despite its evident simplicity and its lucidity, is interestingly complex.

We don't want to say—by any means—that the spring is "a symbol of new life," or that the cow and the calf are "symbols of society"—but we do want to say that this spring, this pasture, this cow and calf—are loaded with what Frost called "ulteriority."

We want to mention again that Frost put this little poem at the beginning of every edition of his *Collected Poems.* The poem itself does not contain a single metaphor, and yet the entire poem can reasonably be called a metaphor, or a symbol. Surely Frost was addressing the reader, not just an imagined partner on the farm. Surely he was inviting the reader into his pasture, his world of poems; and surely he was saying to the reader, "here, in these poems, are the clear springs, the clarifications, that I have produced by raking away the muck—the usual incoherent thoughts that are in my mind or anyone's mind. The water is clear now. I took pleasure in writing these poems, and now, well, they are out there, in the pages ahead. Join me in the world that I see: 'You come too.'"

WENDELL BERRY
Stay Home (p. 672)

We included this poem largely because we took it to be an entertaining response to Frost's "The Pasture." For Frost's "You come too," Berry substitutes "You stay home too."

Having included it, well, now we are not so sure we should have done so. We like poems that connect with other poems—notably parodies—and we admire Wendell Berry, but we wonder how well "Stay Home" stands up to the poem that prompted it. "The Pasture" seems to us to be an unqualified success, a wonderful piece, largely because of the varying tones, from the matter of fact opening, "I'm going out to clean the pasture spring" to the qualification in the second line when he says he will "only stop to rake the leaves away," and then the further qualification in the third line when he says he "may" wait "to watch the water clear," and so on, to the engaging "You come too." Irresistible. But beyond the varying tones is the human being who speaks the lines, someone who wants a fellow-human being to share a quiet but a rich experience.

Against this is Berry's speaker, who wants to preserve his solitude. Yes, there are times when we all want to be alone—nothing wrong with that—but is this speaker a bit too insistent on his special aptitude for experiencing nature and history? Does he have to tell us that he is "at home" (line 6) with "the labor of the fields / longer than a man's life"? Does he have to tell us that he is "at home" (line 13) with "the stillness of the trees"? Would it not have been enough if he had told us that he wants to "wait here in the fields" and stand "in the woods / where the old trees / move only with the wind / and then with gravity"?

Perhaps we take the piece too seriously, and don't see that it should be read as a jest, a good-natured reply to Frost's "The Pasture."

A good introduction to Wendell Berry's work are the twenty-one essays, spanning two decades, included in *The Art of the Commonplace: The Agrarian Essays of Wendell Berry*, ed. Norman Wirzba (2002). We also recommend *That Distant Land: The Collected Stories* (2004).

ADRIENNE RICH
Diving into the Wreck (p. 673)

Most responses identify the wreck as either (1) the speaker's life (persons familiar with Rich's biography may identify it specifically as her unhappy marriage to a man who committed suicide in 1970, about three years before the poem was published), or (2) more broadly, our male-dominated society. Another way of putting it is to say that the poem is about sexual politics. The poem is discussed by Wendy Martin and by Erica Jong in *Adrienne Rich's Poetry* (1975), ed. Barbara C. Gelpi and Albert Gelpi. Part of the following comment is indebted to their discussions.

Armed with a book of myths (an understanding of the lies society has created?) and a camera and a knife (an instrument of vision and an instrument of power?) she goes, alone, in contrast to Cousteau assisted by a team, to explore the wreck. (This sort of exploration can be done only by the individual. One might add, by the way, that it is a new sort of exploration, an exploration for which Rich had no maps. Before the second half of the twentieth century, there was virtually no poetry about what it was like to be a wife or a woman living in a male-dominated society. The earlier poetry written by women was chiefly about children, love, and God.) More exactly, she is there, exploring the wreck ("I came to explore the wreck" implies that she is speaking from the site itself). She has immersed herself in the primal, life-giving element and has now arrived in order "to see the damage that was done / and the treasures that prevail," that is, to see not only what is ruined but also what is salvageable. Her object is to find truth, not myth (62–63).

Lines 72–73, in which she is both mermaid and merman, and line 77, in which "I am she; I am he," suggest that she has achieved an androgynous nature and thus has become the sort of new woman who will tell the truth. According to lines 92–94, the names of such true persons, or androgynes, persons who may rescue civilization, do not appear in the book of myths.

DEREK WALCOTT
A Far Cry from Africa (p. 675)

Many students—partly because they think that puns are always comic and that literature is always serious—will not see the double meaning in the title: (1) the poem is a lament from Africa, violated by colonialism and also by Africans themselves, and (2) the poet—a West Indian who lives part of the year in the West Indies and part in the United States—is a very considerable distance away from Africa.

Walcott, a black, sees not only the wickedness of British colonial rule but also the wickedness that Africans visit upon other Africans. Further, Walcott's tongue is English; he utters his cry (to use a word from the title of the poem) in English, not in an African language. In short, the two meanings of the title embody the themes of the poem—the pain that Africa is experiencing (inflicted not only by colonialists but also by Africans), and the dilemma of the English-speaking poet, who is black but who lives thousands of miles from Africa and who feels a loyalty to (and a love for) "the English tongue."

The place to begin is with Walcott's *Collected Poems, 1948–1984* (1986), but your more advanced students might enjoy exploring his epic poem, *Omeros* (1990). See also *The Art of Derek Walcott*, ed. Stewart Brown (1991); Rei Terada, *Derek Walcott's Poetry: American Mimicry* (1992); and *Critical Perspectives on Derek Walcott*, ed. Robert D. Hamner (1993).

SHERMAN ALEXIE
On the Amtrak from Boston to New York City (p. 677)

This piece takes the Anglo reader deep into the heart of "the Other." On the surface, the speaker is an affable guy—in a conversation with a stranger he nods his head acquiescently, he does not embarrass the woman by telling her she is talking foolishly, and he even brings her an orange juice from the food car. But we feel his rage at her superficiality and at Don Henley's show of concern for Walden. We also intensely feel his impotence as he makes plans (34–37), which of course he will not act on, for the next occurrence of the same situation. The last line makes it explicit that whites are his enemy, but the reader knows that the whites who meet him on the train will never know it.

The woman's idea that "history" has been made only by whites is presented here in such a way that it is obviously absurd. But it is an idea that almost all whites have held until very recently. For instance, Robert Frost in "The Gift Outright" speaks, without any irony, of the pre-white world as "unstoried, artless, unenhanced."

Alexie is a poet, novelist, short story writer (we include one of his stories in the text here), and screenplay writer. Our favorite among his books is *Reservation Blues* (1996), which *The Reader's Catalog* summarizes as "a mythic tale of an all-Indian rock band traveling from reservation bars to Seattle and on to Manhattan." According to one review, *Reservation Blues* "does for the American Indian what Richard Wright's *Native Son* did for the Black American in 1940." An issue of the journal *Studies in American Indian Literatures*, 9:4 (Winter 1997), is devoted to Alexie. See especially John Purdy, "Crossroads: A Conversation with Sherman Alexie," 1–18.

Lynn Cline presents an illuminating profile of Alexie's life and literary career in "About Sherman Alexie," *Ploughshares* 26:4 (Winter 2000/2001): 197–202. Also helpful is Stephen F. Evans, "'Open Containers': Sherman Alexie's Drunken Indians," *The American Indian Quarterly* 25:1 (Winter 2001): 46–72, which treats Alexie's techniques as a satirist and social critic, in particular his exploration of ethnic stereotypes. See also John Newton, "Sherman Alexie's Autoethnography," *Contemporary Literature* 42:2 (Summer 2001): 413–28, included in a special issue on the topic "American Poetry." "Sherman Alexie: The Official Site" can be found at http://www.fallsapart.com/.

Christina Rossetti
Uphill (p. 678)

How can one be sure that the poem is metaphorical? This is part of what we are getting at in our first question, in which we ask the student to respond to a reader who assumes the speaker is making inquiries preparatory to a bit of touring.

The question is not meant to be frivolous. Instructors know that this is a poem about larger matters, but that's because instructors are used to reading poems and are therefore used to figurative language. Most students are unfamiliar with the way poems work—which is why they sometimes read too literally and why, on other occasions, they read too freely, ignoring some passages and imposing highly personal readings on others.

Our second question asks, Who is the questioner? The poem is not a Browningesque dramatic monologue, and we think it is enough to say that the questioner is the poet, or the poet as a universal spokesperson. By the way, we don't know exactly what to make of the suggestion of a student that the answerer in "Uphill" is a ghost, that is, someone who has made the journey and who therefore answers authoritatively.

As for our final question in the text, we do find the answers (with their dry understatement, as in "You cannot miss that inn," i.e., "Don't worry, you will certainly die") chilling as well as comforting, but we are unconvinced that a reader is supposed to imagine a dialogue between the poet and a revenant. Rather, we believe (guided by Jerome J. McGann's essay on Christina Rossetti in his *The Beauty of Inflections*) that the poet is speaking with what McGann calls "her divine interlocutor" (242). McGann points out that the ending of "Uphill" is easily misinterpreted. Rossetti is not saying that the pilgrimage of the Christian soul ends with an eternal sleep. Rather, she is alluding to the Anabaptist doctrine known as "Soul Sleep" (technically, psychopannychism), which holds that at death the soul is put into a condition of sleep until the millennium. On the Last Day the soul awakens and goes to its final reward. McGann fully discusses the point in his essay.

From time to time, we have taught students who have become very interested in Rossetti's verse. For specialized work, we can recommend *The Complete Poems of Christina Rossetti,* ed. R.W. Crump, 3 vols. (1979–90). But students might profit even more from reading Rossetti in the midst of other Victorian women poets; see *Victorian Women Poets: An Anthology,* ed. Angela Leighton and Margaret Reynolds (1995). See also Dolores Rosenblum, *Christina Rossetti: The Poetry of Endurance* (1986); Antony H. Harrison, *Christina Rossetti in Context* (1988); and Angela Leighton, *Victorian Women Poets* (1992), 118–63.

Emily Dickinson
Because I could not stop for Death (p. 679)

In Dickinson's "Because I could not stop for Death," the fact that a grave is suggested in lines 17–20 eludes many students; the reference to the grave contributes to toughening the poem. This stanza, by the way, is a good example of the closeness of some metaphors to riddles, a point worth discussing in class. Allen Tate, in a famous essay, praised the poem because "we are not told what to think." J. J. McGann, rightly taking issue with Tate, points out that "the message about the benevolence of Death is plain enough." McGann also takes issue with the widespread idea that in this poem death is a "gentlemanly suitor." He argues, on the contrary, that since the penultimate line speaks of "horses," Dickinson is talking not about a suitor—who would drive only one horse—but about an undertaker, who is driving a hearse. (McGann's essay originally appeared in *New Literary History*, 12 [1981], and is reprinted in *Literary Theories in Praxis* [1987], ed. Shirley F. Staton.) Selections from a number of commentaries (including, among others, Allen Tate, *Reactionary Essays* (1936), Yvor Winters, *In Defense of Reason* (1947), and Richard Chase, *Emily Dickinson* (1951) are collected in *Fourteen by Emily Dickinson* (1964), ed. Thomas M. Davis. See also Clark Griffith, *The Long Shadow* (1964), pp. 128–134, and Charles R. Anderson, *Emily Dickinson's Poetry* (1960), pp. 241–246.

Topics for Critical Thinking and Writing

1. Characterize death as it appears in lines 1–8.
2. What is the significance of the details and their arrangement in the third stanza? Why "strove" rather than "played" (line 9)? What meaning does "Ring" (line 10) have? Is "Gazing Grain" better than "Golden Grain??
3. The "House" in the fifth stanza is a sort of riddle. What is the answer? Does this stanza introduce an aspect of death not present—or present only very faintly—in the rest of the poem? Explain.
4. Evaluate this statement about the poem (from Yvor Winters's *In Defense of Reason* [1947]): "In so far as it concentrates on the life that is being left behind, it is wholly successful; in so far as it attempts to experience the death to come, it is fraudulent, however exquisitely."

20

Love and Hate

SEI SHŌNAGON
A Lover's Departure (p. 683)

Our first question in the text, concerning a reader's initial response and a subsequent response, derives from our experience in teaching this selection. On first reading it, most students don't see much here—they are too intent on looking for an important message. When they reread it, however, they usually enjoy the visual picture of the lover's departure, and, more important, they enjoy the strong irritation that Sei Shonagon displays at the end.

We are reminded of two remarks (in letters) by John Keats: "The excellence of every Art is its intensity, capable of making all disagreeables evaporate," and

> the poetical character [i.e., the artist] . . . enjoys light and shade; it lives in gusto, be it foul or fair, high or low, rich or poor, mean or elevated—It has as much delight in conceiving an Iago as an Imogen.

So, too, readers delight in villains as well as heroes, or, in this case, we delight both in the lover's conceit and also in Sei Shonagon's detestation of him. (She was, of course, no Keats, no practitioner of "negative capability." Rather, she was what Keats called "the egotistical sublime," but this quality is part of what delights the reader.)

The second question in the text asks students to speculate about Sei Shonagon's personality. Almost nothing is known about her other than what she reveals in her book, but the book amply testifies to the one significant external comment about her, a remark in a diary by the other great prose writer of the early eleventh century, Lady Murasaki (author of *The Tale of Genji*): "Sei Shonagon: The very picture of conceit and arrogance." Murasaki goes on to say that Shonagon is "pretentious," "inane," and "notorious for her triviality." Anyone who reads Shonagon's *Pillow-Book* (in Arthur Waley's translation, or, even better, in Ivan Morris's) will agree—but will probably also add, "yes, and isn't she marvelous!"

Our third question suggests that students emulate Sei Shonagon and write some observations about hateful things. Among Shonagon's entries are comments on an unwelcome visitor who chatters, elderly people who have the gall to warm themselves near a brazier in a most unceremonious way ("I have seen some dreary old creatures actually resting their feet on the brazier and rubbing them against the edge while they speak"), crying babies, and people who tell a story that she was about to tell. Her writings reveal her keen perceptions and her self-centeredness—and one doesn't know which to enjoy more. She apparently was the Erica Kane of her day.

JUDITH ORTIZ COFER
I Fell in Love, or My Hormones Awakened (p. 684)

Our first question in the text asks about the humor in the essay. Almost every paragraph provides examples. For instance, in the first paragraph there is (in the first sentence) the comic drop from "I fell in love" to "my hormones awakened"; later in the paragraph we hear that she fell in love with "an older man"—a senior, when she was a first-year student. But the humor does not consist entirely in defeating the reader's expectations; much of it is in the author's genial presentation of her silly, romantic—and very human—self, for instance in the second paragraph the revelation that she drank milk, which she hated, so that she would have an excuse to go to the store to see the boy who worked there.

Nothing in the essay will cause readers any difficulty, we think, and it lends itself very well to writing assignments, some of which we suggest in the text.

We recommend Cofer's *The Latin Deli: Prose and Poetry* (1995), which includes poetry, personal essays, and short stories about the lives of Puerto Ricans in a New Jersey barrio.

ERNEST HEMINGWAY
Cat in the Rain (p. 688)

The best published discussion is David Lodge's "Analysis and Interpretation of the Realist Text," *Poetics Today* 1 (1980): 5–19, conveniently reprinted in Lodge's *Working with Structuralism* (1981). Lodge begins by summarizing Carlos Baker's discussion, in which Baker (in *Ernest Hemingway: The Writer as Artist* [1952]) assumed that the cat at the end is the cat at the beginning. As Lodge puts it, in this reading

> [T]he appearance of the maid with a cat is the main reversal in Aristotelian terms in the narrative. If it is indeed the cat she went to look for, then the reversal is a happy one for her, and confirms her sense that the hotel keeper appreciated her as a woman more than her husband.

238 Chapter 20: *Love and Hate*

On the other hand, Lodge points out, if the cat is not the same cat,

> We might infer that the padrone, trying to humour a client, sends up the first cat he can lay hands on, which is in fact quite inappropriate to the wife's needs. This would make the reversal an ironic one at the wife's expense, emphasizing the social and cultural abyss that separates her from the padrone, and revealing her quasi-erotic response to his professional attentiveness as a delusion.

Lodge goes on to discuss a very different interpretation by John Hagopian, published in *College English* 24 (Dec 1962): 220–222, in which Hagopian argued that the story is about "a crisis in the marriage . . . involving the lack of fertility, which is symbolically foreshadowed by the public garden (fertility) dominated by the war monument (death)." For Hagopian, the rubber cape worn by the man in the rain "is a protection from rain, and rain is a fundamental necessity for fertility and fertility is precisely what is lacking in the American wife's marriage." Put bluntly, Hagopian sees the rubber cape as a condom. Lodge correctly points out that although rain often stands for fertility, in this story the rainy weather is contrasted with "good weather." What the rubber cape does is emphasize the bad weather, and thus it emphasizes the padrone's thoughtfulness (and the husband's indifference).

Lodge's careful and profound article can't be adequately summarized, but we'll give a few more of his points. Near the end of the story, when we read that "George shifted his position in the bed," a reader may feel that George will put down the book and make love to his wife, but this possibility disappears when George says, "Oh, shut up and get something to read."

Taking Seymour Chatman's distinction between stories of *resolution* (we get the answer to "What happened next?") and stories of *revelation* (events are not resolved, but a state of affairs is revealed), Lodge suggests that this story seems to share characteristics of both: it is, one might say, a plot of revelation (the relationship between husband and wife) disguised as a plot of resolution (the quest for the cat). The ambiguity of the ending is therefore crucial. By refusing to resolve the issue of whether the wife gets the cat she wants, the implied author indicates that this is not the point of the story.

On point of view, Lodge demonstrates that Hemingway's story is written from the point of view of the American couple, and from the wife's point of view rather than the husband's. (Of course, he doesn't mean that the entire story is seen from her point of view. He means only that we get into her mind to a greater degree—e.g., "The cat would be round to the right. Perhaps she could go along under the eaves"—than into the minds of any of the other characters.) Lodge's argument is this: at the end, when the maid appears, "the narration adopts the husband's perspective at this crucial point," and so that's why we are told that the maid held *a* cat rather than *the* cat. After all, the man had not seen the cat in the rain, so he can't know if the maid's cat is the same cat.

Finally, another discussion of interest is Warren Bennett, "The Poor Kitty . . . in 'Cat in the Rain,' " *Hemingway Review* 8 (Fall 1988): 26–36. Bennett reviews Lodge's discussion of Baker and Hagopian and insists that the wife is not pregnant (Lodge had suggested, in arguing against Hagopian, that the wife *may* be pregnant). Bennett says that

> [T]he girl's feelings as she thinks of the padrone pass through three stages, tight inside, important, and of momentary supreme importance, and these stages reflect a correspondence to the sensations of desire, intercourse, and orgasm.

Not all readers will agree, though probably we can all agree with Bennett when he says that "The wife's recognition of the padrone's extraordinary character suggests that her husband, George, lacks the qualities which the wife finds so attractive in the padrone. George has neither dignity, nor will, nor commitment."

In any case, Bennett suggests that when the wife returns to the room "her sexual feelings are transferred to George. She goes over to George and tries to express her desire for closeness by sitting down 'on the bed.'"

Bennett's article makes too many points to be summarized here, but one other point should be mentioned. He says that female tortoise-shell cats do not reproduce tortoise-shells and that males are sterile. Since he identifies the woman with the cat, he says that the woman's "destiny is that of a barren wandering soul with no place and no purpose in the futility of the wasteland *In Our Time.*"

Bennett's article is reprinted in the excellent collection, *New Critical Approaches to the Short Stories of Ernest Hemingway*, ed. Jackson J. Benson (1990). There have been a number of noteworthy biographies of Hemingway published recently, including Kenneth S. Lynn, *Hemingway* (1987), and James R. Mellow, *Hemingway: A Life without Consequences* (1992).

WILLIAM FAULKNER
A Rose for Emily (p. 702)

The chronology of the story—not very clear on first reading—has been worked out by several writers. Five chronologies are given in M. Thomas Inge, *William Faulkner: "A Rose for Emily"* (1970); a sixth is given in Cleanth Brooks, *William Faulkner: Toward Yoknapatawpha and Beyond* (1978) (pp. 382–384). Brooks conjectures that Miss Emily is born in 1852, her father dies around 1884, Homer Barron appears in 1884 or 1885, dies in 1885 or 1886, the delegation calls on Miss Emily about the smell in 1885/86. In 1901 or 1904 or 1905, Miss Emily gives up the lessons in china-painting. Colonel Sartoris dies in 1906 or 1907, the delegation calls on her about the taxes in 1916, and Miss Emily dies in 1926.

The plot, of course, is gothic fiction: a decaying mansion, a mysteriously silent servant, a corpse, necrophilia. And one doesn't want to discard the plot in a search for what it symbolizes, but it is also clear that the story is not only "about" Emily Grierson but also about the South's pride in its past (including its Emily-like effort to hold on to what is dead) and the guilt as well as the grandeur of the past. Inevitably much classroom discussion centers on Miss Emily's character, but a proper discussion of her character entails a discussion of the narrator.

(This next paragraph summarizes an essay on this topic by John Daremo, originally printed in early editions of S. Barnet, *A Short Guide to Writing about Literature*.) The unnamed narrator is never precisely identified. Sometimes he seems to be an innocent eye, a recorder of a story whose implications escape him. Sometimes he seems to be coarse: he mentions "old lady Wyatt, the crazy woman," he talks easily of "niggers," and he confesses that because he and other townspeople felt that Miss Emily's family "held themselves a little too high for what they really were," the townspeople "were not pleased exactly, but vindicated" when at thirty she was still unmarried. But if his feelings are those of common humanity (e.g., racist and smug), he at least knows what these feelings are and thus helps us to know ourselves. We therefore pay him respectful attention, and we notice that on the whole he is compassionate (note especially his sympathetic understanding of Miss Emily's insistence for three days that her father is not dead). True, Miss Emily earns our respect by her aloofness and her strength of purpose (e.g., when she publicly appears in the buggy with Homer Barron, and when she cows the druggist and the alderman), but if we speak of her aloofness and strength of purpose rather than her arrogance and madness, it is because the narrator's imaginative sympathy guides us. And the narrator is the key to the apparently curious title: presumably the telling of this tale is itself the rose, the community's tribute (for the narrator insistently speaks of himself as "we") to the intelligible humanity in a woman whose unhappy life might seem monstrous to less sympathetic observers. Another meaning, however, may be offered (very tentatively) for the title. In the story Faulkner emphasizes Miss Emily's attempts to hold on to the past: her insistence, for example, that her father is not dead, and that she has no taxes to pay. Is it possible that Homer Barron's corpse serves as a sort of pressed or preserved will, a reminder of a past experience of love? If so, the title refers to him.

For a feminist reading, see Judith Fetterley, in *The Resisting Reader: A Feminist Approach to American Fiction* (1978), reprinted in *Literary Theories in Praxis*, edited by Shirley F. Staton (1987). Fetterley sees the story as revealing the "sexual conflict" within patriarchy (whether of the South or the North, the old order or the new). Emily's confinement by her father represents the confinement of women by patriarchy, and the remission of her taxes reveals the dependence of women on men. Emily has been turned into a "Miss," a lady, by a chivalric attitude that is "simply a subtler and more dishonest version of her father's horsewhip." The narrator represents a subtle form of this patriarchy. According to Fetterley, the narrator sees her as "'dear, inescapable, impervious, tranquil, and perverse'; indeed, anything and everything but human."

Fetterley—the "resisting reader" of her title, that is, the reader who refuses to accept that text—argues that the story exposes "the violence done to a woman by making her a lady; it also explains the particular form of power the victim gains from this position and can use on those who enact their violence. . . . Like Ellison's invisible man, nobody sees *Emily*. And because nobody sees *her*, she can literally get away with murder."

We have enjoyed and learned from the biographies of Faulkner by David Minter (1980), Joseph Blotner (the one-volume abridgment, 1984, of his three-volume work), Joel Williamson (1993), and Richard J. Gray (1994). We have also roamed around in the meticulously detailed biography written by Frederick R. Karl (1989), but we confess that, at 1,200 pages, it feels long to us. There are far too many critical studies to mention here. But we will say that two older books still strike us as good introductions for undergraduate readers: Michael Millgate, *The Achievement of William Faulkner* (1966), and Irving Howe, *William Faulkner: A Critical Study*, 3rd ed., rev. and expanded (1975).

Topics for Critical Thinking and Writing

1. How valid is the view that the story is an indictment of the decadent values of the aristocratic Old South? Or a defense of these values (embodied in Emily) against the callousness (embodied in Homer Barron) of the North?
2. Suppose Faulkner had decided to tell the story from Miss Emily's point of view. Write the first 200 or 300 words of such a version.
3. Characterize the narrator.

ZORA NEALE HURSTON
Sweat (p. 713)

Zora Neale Hurston was not simply a black writer or a woman writer; she was a black woman writer, and much of her fiction comes from this perspective. (bell hooks, in *Ain't I a Woman,* interestingly discusses black women and feminism.)

The contrast between the two chief characters is boldly drawn—clearly Delia is good and Sykes is bad—but it is not without complexity. After all, Delia does allow Sykes to die, and Sykes, though a brute, obviously suffers (despite his boasting and his bullying) from a sense of inferiority which apparently is heightened by the sight of his wife engaged in a menial task for white people: "Ah done tole you time and again to keep them white folks' clothes outa dis house." Though Hurston does not explicitly make the point that black men had a harder time than black women in finding employment, a reader presumably is aware of the fact that an oppressive white society made black men feel unmanly and that they sometimes compensated by brutal expressions of what they took to be manliness. When Sykes deliberately steps on the white clothes, we understand that he is expressing not only a cruel contempt for his wife but also hostility toward white society.

Still, that Sykes is a brute cannot be doubted; the other black men in the story testify to this effect. This is the intent of question 2, below. Notice especially the longish speech to the effect that some men abuse women simply because the men are bad:

> Taint no law on earth dat kin make a man be decent if it aint in 'im. . . . Dey knows whut dey is doin' while dey is at it, an' hates theirselvs fuh it but they keeps on hangin' after huh tell she's empty. Den dey hates huh fuh bein' a cane-chew an' in de way.

Further, even before Sykes came to hate his wife, he never loved her but only lusted after her.

> She had brought love to the union and he had brought a longing for the flesh.

In this respect, however, he apparently is not much different from the other men in the story, who seem to regard an attractive woman only as a commodity, not as a person with ideas and feelings. Thus one of them, commenting on Delia's good looks in her earlier days, says, "Ah'd uh mah'ied huh mahself if he hadn'ter beat me to it." It does not occur to him that she might have had a say in the choice of her husband.

Classroom discussion will probably focus on Delia, especially on the question of whether a woman as devout as Delia would stand by and allow even the worst of husbands to die. (Question 3 approaches this point.) But "stand by" is misleading, since Hurston takes pains to emphasize not only the suffering that Delia has undergone at Sykes's hands but also the helplessness she experiences when the snake bites him. She becomes "ill," and we are told that "Delia could not move—her legs were gone flabby." Seeing him in agony, she experiences "a surge of pity," but "Orlando with its doctors was too far." All of these statements extenuate—indeed, eliminate—any blame that otherwise a reader might conceivably attach to Delia.

Further, Sykes is responsible for his own death since he malevolently introduces the snake into the house, and it is presumably Sykes who has transferred the snake from the box to the laundry basket, in an effort to murder Delia. He is thus justly punished, undone by his own hand. Interestingly, a passage in Ecclesiastes (10:8–9) uses the image of a snake:

> He that diggith a pit shall fall into it; and whoso breaketh an hedge, a serpent shall bite him.
> Whoso removeth stones shall be hurt therewith; and he that cleaveth wood shall be endangered thereby.

We are thus in a world of tragedy, where a person aiming at good (doubtless in his brutal mind Sykes thinks that it will be good—for him—to eliminate Delia) destroys himself. With the passage from Ecclesiastes in mind, one can almost speak of the physics of the world: for every action, there is an equal and opposite reaction. Delia, one notices, tells Sykes that she now hates him as much as she used to love him, and he counters that his hatred for her equals her hatred for him. At the start of the story he torments Delia by terrifying her with what seems to be a snake, and at the end of the story he is terrified by a snake. He puts the snake in her laundry basket, but the snake crawls into his bed—where Sykes is bitten. A final comment on the reciprocal structure or geometry of the story: "Sweat" begins late at night and ends with "the red dawn," which gradually changes into full light, as "the sun crept on up." The image of daylight implies a new day, a new life for Delia, though of course nothing can bring back her youth or her love.

For an extensive discussion of the economics of the sexist and racist society depicted in "Sweat," see Kathryn Lee Seidel, "The Artist in the Kitchen: The Economics of Creativity in Hurston's 'Sweat,'" in *Zora in Florida* (1991), ed. Steve Glassman and Kathryn Lee Seidel.

Hurston is best known for her novel *Their Eyes Were Watching God* (1937)—which, according to recent surveys, is the most widely taught book in U.S. colleges and universities. But Hurston is also the author of an interesting autobiography, first published in 1942; see *Dust Tracks on a Road: An Autobiography*, edited and with an introduction by Robert Hemenway (1970; 2nd ed., 1984). Her writings have been collected in a two-volume set in the Library of America series (1995).

Robert Hemenway's biography (1977) is excellent. For students, two reference works are helpful: Adele S. Newson, *Zora Neale Hurston: A Reference Guide* (1987), and Rose Parkman Davis, *Zora Neale Hurston: An Annotated Bibliography and Reference Guide* (1997). There are a number of books, as well as chapters in books, that focus on Hurston. Students might do best to start with a good, brief survey of the life and writings: Lillie P. Howard, *Zora Neale Hurston* (1980). Then they can sample the critical approaches included in *Zora Neale Hurston,* ed. Harold Bloom (1986), and *Zora Neale Hurston: Critical Perspectives Past and Present*, ed. Henry Louis Gates Jr. and K. A. Appiah (1993).

Topics for Critical Thinking and Writing

1. Summarize the relationship of Delia and Sykes before the time of the story.
2. What function, if any, do the men on Joe Clark's porch serve?
3. Do you think Delia's action at the end of the story is immoral? Why, or why not?

BEL KAUFMAN
Sunday in the Park (p. 721)

This short, easy story can be used effectively in the first days of class if you want to teach something about character, conflict, or irony—or almost anything else about the conventional well-made story. Or if the story is taught in conjunction with Chapter 4 (Analysis) or 9 (Fiction), it's worth spending a little time on the ways in which Kaufman characterizes Morton and the other man: Morton reads *The New York Times Magazine*, the other man reads the comics; Morton speaks standard English, the other man says "this here" and "yeah" and uses blasphemy ("take your kid the hell out of here").

The title probably conjures up images of children romping in the park, young people playing or flirting, and old people decorously sunning themselves and vicariously enjoying the pleasures of the young. (A few students may even have encountered that great representation of Sunday leisure, Georges Seurat's *Sunday Afternoon on the Island of La Grande Jatte*, now hanging in the Art Institute, Chicago.) And of course the first paragraph—until near its end—encourages us to think along these lines:

> It was still warm in the late-afternoon sun. . . . Morton was reading the *Times Magazine* section, one arm flung around her shoulder; their three-year-old son, Larry, was playing in the sandbox; a faint breeze fanned her hair softly against her cheek. . . . *How good this is,* she thought. . . .

The point of view is third person, but we gain entrance only into the mind of the woman. Perhaps the idea is that we see Morton and Larry as she sees them—persons she thinks about by name—whereas we see her as she sees herself, unnamed. (Instructors might ask students why, in their opinion, Kaufman does not name the woman.)

The first hint of something wrong is not, perhaps, when the little boy throws sand at Larry; maybe it is, in retrospect, given even earlier in the paragraph, when we hear of the woman's apparently affectionate but nevertheless somewhat condescending view of Morton:

> They must go out in the sun more often; Morton was so city-pale, cooped up all week inside the gray factorylike university.

When we have finished the story we probably believe that despite all of her affection for Morton—and there is little doubt that the affection is genuine—she harbors a certain contempt for him because of his physical weakness and his awareness that in any physical contest he is sure to be bested.

Some students may argue that the woman rebukes her husband not because he is weak but because he is bullying her and the child ("'If you can't discipline this child, I will,' Morton snapped"), but such an argument ignores the fact that the woman experiences a strange sensation *before* the husband bullies her:

> Her first feeling was one of relief that a fight had been avoided, that no one was hurt. Yet beneath it there was a layer of something else, something heavy and inescapable. She sensed that it was more than just an unpleasant incident, more than defeat of reason by force. She felt dimly it had something to do with her and Morton, something acutely personal, familiar, and important.

(Students might be invited to speculate about what "it" is.) A few sentences later—but still before Morton threatens the child—we hear of something "glued like heavy plaster on her heart." (In some ways the story resembles Kate Chopin's "The Story of an Hour," in Chapter 2, with its female protagonist who struggles against an unwelcome sensation.)

Presumably the woman unconciously has been disappointed with her husband; the episode with the aggressive man triggers a release, and she sees that her husband is unambiguously weak. Nevertheless it would be wrong to say that her earlier expression of joy and affection is insincere. It may be closer to the truth to say that, although the belated conscious recognition of her husband's weakness is true in itself, it is false to her usual or essential loving nature. Notice Kaufman's wording at the end:

"Indeed?" she heard herself say. "You and who else?"

"She heard herself say." The words indicate that there are two "hers," the her that speaks these cruel words, and the usual her, the her that hears them. The idea that sometimes we are not ourselves is by no means unfamiliar; we often excuse ourselves with the expression "Forgive me, I'm not myself." Similarly, when we say, "I was beside myself with anger," we are suggesting that the *real me* was somewhere else and is not to be confused with the "me" of this momentary performance.

On the other hand, in the real world we can hardly excuse all of our nasty words by saying that they don't represent "the real me." We must recognize that we are responsible for our words. "The spoken word," Horace says, "can never be recalled"; Menander's version is, "It is as easy to recall a stone thrown violently from the hand as a word which has left your tongue." What, then, is the reader's attitude toward the woman at the end of the story? (This question is addressed in the text, in question 3.) Is she deliberately cruel to her husband, needling him about something (his physical weakness) that he can't change? Or do the words come not out of her mouth but (so to speak) out of the mouth of another self, a worse self that is not unlike the worse self that we harbor inside us but that we usually manage to keep gagged and locked up? There will be no shortage of class discussion on this issue.

RAYMOND CARVER
Mine, Little Things (p. 724)

The usual characteristics of Minimalism are alleged to be:

- lower-middle-class characters, who are relatively inarticulate and out of touch with others and with themselves
- little if any setting
- little action of any apparent importance

- little if any authorial comment, i.e., little interpretation of motive
- a drab style—fairly simple sentences, with little or no use of figurative language or allusions

Almost no story perfectly exemplifies this textbook paradigm. In fact, "Mine" is an excellent way of seeing the *in*adequacy of such a view of minimalism.

Let's look at this very short story—certainly minimal in terms of length—from beginning to end, though for the moment we'll skip the title. Here is the first paragraph:

> Early that day the weather turned and the snow was melting into dirty water. Streaks of it ran down from the little shoulder-high window that faced the back yard. Cars slushed by on the street outside, where it was getting dark. But it was getting dark on the inside too.

If you read the paragraph aloud in class, students will easily see that Carver very briefly establishes an unpleasant setting ("dirty water," "streaks," "cars slushed by"), giving us not only a sense of what we see but also the time of day ("dark"). But of course Carver is *not* giving us mere landscape and chronology. When we read "But it was getting dark on the inside too," we anticipate dark passions. A reader can't be sure that such passions will materialize or how the story will turn out; the darkness may dissipate, but at this stage a reader is prepared for a story that fits the rotten weather. (Another way of putting it is to say that Carver is preparing the reader, i.e., is seeking to control our responses.) Perhaps, then, it is incorrect to say that minimalists do not use figurative language; surely the dark weather is figurative. And on rereading the story a reader may feel that the metamorphosis of snow into dirty water is an emblem of the history of this marriage.

Ask students to compare the opening paragraph with an earlier version. Perhaps the chief differences are the elimination of the sun from the revised version—there is no sunshine in this world—and the emphasis, in the last sentence of the revised paragraph, on the internal darkness. In the earlier version, "It was getting dark, outside and inside;" in the later version, the inside darkness gets a sentence to itself: "But it was getting dark on the inside too." The real point of asking students to look at the revisions "to account for the changes" is to help them to look closely at what Carver has written, so that they will give his words a chance to shape their responses.

As we read the story, we never get inside the heads of the characters. The author tells us nothing about them, other than what they say and what they do. We don't know why they behave as they do. We know very little about them, not even their names, since Carver calls them only "he" and "she." The first line of dialogue is angry, and all of the remaining dialogue reveals the terrific hostility that exists between the two speakers. As the author presents them to us, the alienation of these characters does seem to fit the textbook description of minimalist writing.

The quarrel about the picture of the baby leads (because Carver is an artist, not a mere recorder) to the quarrel about the baby. (These people may hate each other, but apparently they both love the baby, although of course it is possible that each wants to possess the picture and the baby simply in order to hurt the other. Again, the author gives no clues.) The adults' angry passions contaminate the baby, so to speak, for the baby begins to cry and soon is "red-faced and screaming."

Even a little detail like the flowerpot is relevant. In the fight, the adults could have knocked over some other object, for example, a kitchen chair. But it is a flowerpot—a little touch of life and presumably a small attempt at beautifying the house—that is upset. Norman German and Jack Bedell, *Critique* 29 (1988): 257–260, make the interesting point that no plant is mentioned, only a pot. "The empty pot," they suggest, "is like the house, a lifeless hull." Carver isn't just recording; he is choosing what he wishes to record because he wants to evoke certain responses.

We can't tell what ultimately happened to the baby, but there is every reason to believe that he is physically harmed, possibly even killed, and this point gets back to the title. Why did Carver change the title from "Mine" to "Popular Mechanics" and then to "Little Things"? The second title summons to mind the magazine of that name, but the magazine is never mentioned. What, then, is the relevance of the title? First, it probably calls to mind the male blue-collar world, the chief readership of *Popular Mechanics*. Second, by the time one finishes the story and thinks about the title, one sees a sort of pun in "popular," one of whose meanings is "Of or carried on by the common people" (*Webster's New World Dictionary*). And in "mechanics" we see the forces at work—the physical forces operating on the baby as the two adults each pull him. We wish Carver had retained this title.

The last sentence surely is worth discussing in class: "In this manner, the issue was decided." The language seems flat, unadorned, merely informative. But "decided" is monstrously inappropriate. The word suggests thought rather than sheer violence; even if, say, we decide an issue by tossing a coin, the decision to toss a coin is arrived at by thinking and by common consent. Perhaps the word "issue," too, is significant; German and Bedell find in it a pun (*offspring* as well as *argument*). To find a parallel for Carver's last sentence we probably have to turn to the world of Swiftian irony.

Invite students to compare the last line with Carver's earlier version, "In this manner they decided the issue." In the revision, by means of the passive, Carver makes the sentence even flatter; the narrator seems even more effaced. But he is therefore, to the responsive reader, even more present. As Tobias Wolff puts it, in the introduction to *Matters of Life and Death* (1983), "Irony offers us a way of talking about the unspeakable. In the voices of Swift and Nabokov and Jane Austen we sometimes hear what would have been a scream if irony had not subdued it to eloquence."

The circumstances and the word "decided" may remind the reader of another decision concerning a disputed child, the decision Solomon made (1 Kings 3:16–27) when confronted with two prostitutes who disputed over which was the true mother of the child. One woman, you'll recall, was even willing to murder the child in order to settle the dispute.

In short, Carver's language is not so drab as it sometimes appears to be, which disputes the contention that his stories—especially the early ones—are "thin." He developed as a writer, but in some ways the body of his work is consistent. Late in his life, in the preface to *The Best American Short Stories 1986*, he described his taste:

> I'm drawn toward the traditional (some would call it old-fashioned) methods of story-telling: one layer of reality unfolding and giving way to another, perhaps richer layer; the gradual accretion of meaningful detail; dialogue that not only reveals something about character but advances the story.

In interviews shortly before his death he freely admitted that his view of life had changed; he was in love, and things didn't seem as bleak as they had seemed earlier. But this does not mean that his early stories are less skillfully constructed than are his later, more tender stories.

Carver's plain, pointed realism has proven very influential; many writers of short stories (e.g., Ann Beattie, Bobbie Ann Mason) learned from him and have said they were inspired by his example. Students can be directed to the following collections: *Will You Please Be Quiet, Please?: The Stories of Raymond Carver* (1976); *What We Talk about When We Talk about Love* (1981); *Cathedral* (1983); and *Where I'm Calling From* (1988). We should also mention *All of Us: The Collected Poems* (1998).

There are three good studies of Carver, and all of them are fairly accessible to undergraduates: Arthur M. Saltzman, *Understanding Raymond Carver* (1988); Randolph Runyon, *Reading Raymond Carver* (1992); and Kirk Nesset, *The Stories of Raymond Carver* (1995). Another resource is Sam Halpert, *Raymond Carver: An Oral Biography* (1995).

Topics for Critical Thinking and Writing

1. Some readers object to "minimalist" writings on the grounds that the stories (1) lack ideas, (2) do not describe characters in depth, and (3) are written in a drab style. Does Carver's story seem to you to suffer from these alleged weaknesses?
2. When Carver first published the story, the opening paragraph was slightly different. Here is the earlier version:

   > During the day the sun had come out and the snow melted into dirty water. Streaks of water ran down from the little, shoulder-high window that faced the back yard. Cars slushed by on the street outside. It was getting dark, outside and inside.

   Which version do you prefer? Why?
3. The last line—"In this manner, the issue was decided"—in the original version ran thus: "In this manner they decided the issue." Do you consider the small change an improvement? Why, or why not?

4. The original title was "Mine." Again, what do you think of the change, and why?

RAYMOND CARVER
What We Talk about When We Talk about Love (p. 726)

This story is Carver's dark version of Plato's *Symposium*, even though there are no direct echoes beyond the situation (people talking and drinking) and the subject (love). Carver's story begins in daylight and moves into darkness, with the talk seeming (at least on the surface) to clarify nothing, whereas Plato's dialogue moves from late afternoon or evening through the night and into the daylight. True, at the end of *The Symposium* we are told that some of the participants have fallen asleep and others are drowsy and unable to follow the argument that Socrates is presenting, but presumably the reader has been persuaded by Socrates's words (Socrates modestly attributes them to the priestess Diotima) concerning the nature of love.

In ordinary talk, love means many things, ranging from (say) a passion for the movies or for shopping to more serious things, such as love of one's country, love of God, love of humanity, love of parents for children, and erotic love of human beings. Even if we confine our attention to erotic love—the only kind of love discussed in Carver's story—we probably can hardly come up with a narrow definition; rather, when we think about what love is, we think of three things. First, we think of our own experiences; second, we think of the lovers around us, whose secrets we don't know but whose relationships we can guess to be widely (and wildly) varied; and third—or perhaps really first—we think of famous stories of love, for it probably is these (e.g., Romeo and Juliet, Othello and Desdemona, Beatrice and Benedict, Petruchio and Kate, Tristan and Isolde, perhaps even Edward VIII and Wallie Simpson) that give us our clearest and most memorable ideas about what love is. These fictions help to create life. (Someone—maybe La Rochefoucauld—said that people would not fall in love if they had not read about it in a book.) In *The Symposium*, too, there is a range of kinds of love, though it is clear that for Plato the highest is love of wisdom.

Carver's story resembles Plato's *Symposium* not only in the setting and in the topic of discussion but also in form. We say that "What We Talk About" is a short story, but perhaps we ought to call it (following Northrop Frye) an anatomy, a prose fiction characterized by debates or dialogues. Frye used the word to distinguish such long prose fictions as *Gulliver's Travels* and *Point Counterpoint* from the novel; he pointed out that it was not very useful to discuss all long prose fictions as though they are novels, with realistic characters and plots that moved to resolutions. Similarly, we can say that not all short works of fiction need be short stories, if by "short story" we mean, again, a work with realistic characters participating in a plot that is resolved. Frye himself saw some short prose fictions as *tales* (narratives with the emphasis on the improbable), and perhaps we can see others—those that explore ideas and that do not come to a resolution—as anatomies.

In any case, it is evident that we can distinguish between literature of *resolution* and literature of *revelation,* that is, between (1) literature that stimulates us to ask, "And what happened next?" and that finally leaves us with a settled state of affairs, and (2) literature that causes us to say, "Ah, I understand what they mean." But we should add that in Carver, and, for that matter, in *The Symposium* too, the more the characters talk, the more mysterious the topic becomes. Doubtless one reason Socrates attributed to the priestess Diotima his vision of the love of the ideal was to make it unearthly, mysterious, overpowering—in short, to make it emotionally appealing.

In the case of "What We Talk about When We Talk about Love," we can—by "consistency-building," to use a term from reader-response criticism—try to make some sense of the characters. There is, for instance, Mel, the cardiologist who had been a seminarian and who "would like to come back again in a different life, a different time and all, . . . as a knight." Yet this knight—if we have stock ideas we think of chivalry—fantasizes killing his wife by releasing a swarm of bees in her home. We can put together all that we see and hear of each character and can try to make sense of the bundle, but the characters remain elusive. Terri, for instance, insists that the man who beat her up and who tried to kill her *did* love her, and though Mel can say, "I just wouldn't call Ed's behavior love," *we* are hardly in a position to pass judgment. The reader can only say what the narrator says: "I'm the wrong person to ask. . . . I didn't even know the man. . . . I wouldn't know. You'd have to know the particulars." Terri *did* know the particulars, and she says that Ed—a suicide—died for love (paragraph 37), to which Mel replies, "If that's love, you can have it."

That is, the characters are insulated from each other just as we are insulated from the characters. The extreme example is the old couple in the hospital, swathed in bandages with only "little eye-holes and mouth-holes. . . . The man's heart was breaking because he couldn't turn his goddam head and *see* his goddam wife." These two characters are probably pretty clear to the reader, and they are clear to Mel, too, but (given his experience with his former wife) he can hardly believe what he knows is true. In any case, the image of the elderly swathed lovers, unable to communicate, is connected with the image of knights in heavy armor—protective but also suffocating—and with the image of the beekeeper wearing "a helmet with the plate that comes down over your face, the big gloves, and the padded coat." A moment after he gives us this description, Mel decides not to telephone his children (by his first marriage), again emphasizing the gaps between people. Immediately after Mel makes this decision, the narrator speaks of heading "out into the sunset," to which the narrator's wife asks, "What does that mean, honey?" "It just means what I said," the narrator curtly replies, "That's all it means." This communication that does not communicate is immediately paralleled by words that do not lead to actions or, more precisely, by words that are not accompanied by the appropriate action: Terri offers to get some cheese and crackers but in fact she makes no move to do so, and the characters remain sitting in the dark room, their heartbeats audible.

We can, of course, chart some patterns. There is the bandaged couple (old, devoted lovers); Mel and Terri (lovers for a considerable time, but not old); the narrator and Laura ("going on a year and a half"); but these characters are not set within a traditional plot, and nothing in the way of obvious action happens. Nothing is resolved, but (paradoxically) something is revealed in the darkness; readers may feel that Carver has drawn them more deeply into the mystery of love—perhaps even given them one more picture of lovers to add to the literary gallery that helps to give us an idea of what love is.

Topics for Critical Thinking and Writing

1. Terri believes Ed's dealings with her (as well as his suicide) show that he loved her. How else might his actions be interpreted? And in your opinion, why does she interpret his actions the way that she does?
2. Mel says that if he could come back in a different life, he would come back as a knight. What does this tell us about Mel?
3. What *kinds* of love get discussed? Sexual attraction, of course, but what other kinds of love?
4. We usually expect something to *happen* in a story, an action to reach some sort of completion. What, if anything, happens in this story? For instance, can we say that such-and-such a character changes?
5. Mel asks his companions, "What do any of us really know about love?" What is *your* response? What do *you* know about love?
6. Probably the conventional—maybe literary or maybe movie—ideas of love are these, some of which contradict others:
   a. Love is usually a matter of love-at-first-sight.
   b. Love may be acted on in defiance of convention.
   c. Love is not mere physical attraction but depends on other things, for example, shared interests.
   d. Love is an ennobling passion (the lover finds his or her better self and engages in virtuous actions that might not be undertaken had the person not fallen in love).
   e. Lovers ought to be true, faithful to the beloved.
   f. Love can cause the lover to violate social obligations.

When *you* talk about love, do you talk about any of these things? If so, what do you say? If you talk about other aspects of love, what are they, and what are your views?

RAYMOND CARVER
Cathedral (p. 734)

You might begin by asking students to indicate what sort of impression the narrator makes on them in the first paragraphs. (You may want to assign a short writing requirement of this sort along with the story. If students come to class with a paragraph or two on the topic, the discussion is usually good.)

Probably no single word adequately describes the narrator at this stage, but among the words that students have suggested in their paragraphs are "mean," "cynical," "bitter," "sullen," (this seems especially apt), "unfeeling," "cold," and "cruel"; all of these words are relevant. He is also (though fewer students see this at first) jealous, jealous both of the blind man and of the officer who was his wife's first husband. His jealousy of the officer emerges in his wry reference to "this man who'd first enjoyed her favors." (Later in the story his hostility to the officer is more open, for instance, in this passage: "Her officer—why should he have a name? he was the childhood sweetheart, and what more does he want?—came home from somewhere, found her, and called the ambulance.")

With the blind man, too, the narrator's characteristic form of aggression is the ironic or mocking comment, as when he tells his wife that he will take the blind man bowling. His jealousy of the affectionate relationship between his wife and Robert is understandable if unattractive, and equally unattractive is the way in which he at last reveals that he does not fear this intruder into his house, when he flips open her robe, thus "exposing a juicy thigh." Still, this action is a step toward his accepting Robert and ultimately responding to Robert's influence. One other characteristically aggressive response also should be mentioned: only rarely does he call Robert by his name. In speaking about him, as early as the first sentence of the story but pretty much throughout the story, he usually calls him "the blind man," a way of keeping him at a distance. (Not surprisingly, we soon learn that the narrator has no friends.) Late in the story, when Robert asks the narrator if he is "in any way religious," the narrator replies, "I guess I don't believe in it. In anything." This reply is not surprising; all of his behavior has shown that he doesn't believe "in anything."

The narrator seems to us, until near the end, to be a thoroughly unattractive figure. His irony is scarcely witty enough to make us deeply interested in him, so why do we continue reading the story after we have read the first few paragraphs? Mark A. R. Facknitz interestingly suggests in *Studies in Short Fiction* (Summer 1986) that "perhaps what pushes one into the story is a fear of the harm [the narrator] may do to his wife and her blind friend" (p. 293).

Despite the narrator's evident aggressiveness, fairly early in the story he does profess some sympathy for Robert and especially for Robert's late wife, who died without her husband

> having ever seen what the goddamned woman looked like. It was beyond my understanding. Hearing this, I felt sorry for the blind man for a little bit. And then I found myself thinking what a pitiful life this woman must have led. A woman whose husband could never read the expression on her face, be it misery or something better. Someone who could wear makeup or not—what difference to him? . . . And then to slip off into death, the blind man's hand on her hand, his blind eyes streaming tears—I'm imagining now—her last thought maybe this: that he never even knew what she looked like, and she on the express to the grave. Robert was left with a small insurance policy and half of a twenty-peso Mexican coin. The other half of the coin went into the box with her. Pathetic.

But to say that the narrator displays "sympathy" here is, obviously, to use the word too loosely. What is displayed, again, is his bitterness, cynicism, and (despite his "imagining") his utter inability to understand the feelings of others. (Later, when the blind man's hand rests on the narrator's as the narrator draws a box—like his house—that turns into a cathedral, he will presumably come close to the experience that here he so ineptly imagines.)

Almost by chance the blind man enters into the narrator's life and thaws the ice frozen around his heart, or better, the blind man enables the narrator to see. As Facknitz puts it,

> Carver redeems the narrator by releasing him from the figurative blindness that results in a lack of insight into his own condition and which leads him to trivialize human feelings and needs. Indeed, so complete is his misperception that the blind man gives him a faculty of sight that he is not even aware that he lacks. (p. 293)

The narrator so dominates the story that there is a danger in class that no other matters will get considered, but it's worth asking students to characterize the wife and also Robert. Carver has taken care not to make Robert too saintly a fellow, full of wisdom and goodness and all that. True, Robert does have an uncanny sense of the difference between a black-and-white television set and a color set, but Carver nicely does not dwell on this; he just sort of lets it drop. Further, Robert's use of "bub" is maddening, and his confidence that he has "a lot of friends" in "Guam, in the Philippines, in Alaska, and even in Tahiti" suggests that he takes quite a bit for granted. It is easy, in fact, to imagine that one wouldn't much like Robert. The man who brings the narrator to a new consciousness is not sentimentalized or etherealized.

The story also invites comparison with Flannery O'Connor's "Revelation," which is about unearned grace, although the word "grace" should be used metaphorically when talking about Carver, whereas O'Connor was literally concerned with the working of the Holy Spirit. Talking of several of Carver's stories (including "Cathedral"), Facknitz puts the matter thus:

> Grace, Carver says, is bestowed upon us by other mortals, and it comes suddenly, arising in circumstances as mundane as a visit to the barber shop, and in the midst of feelings as ignoble or quotidian as jealousy, anger, loneliness, and grief. It can be represented in incidental physical contact, and the deliverer is not necessarily aware of his role. Not Grace in the Christian sense at all, it is what grace becomes in a godless world—a deep and creative connection between humans that reveals to Carver's alienated and diminished creatures that there can be contact in a world they supposed was empty of sense or love. Calm is given in a touch, a small, good thing is the food we get from others, and in the cathedrals we draw together, we create large spaces for the spirit. (pp. 295–296)

One last point: obviously a cathedral is a more appropriate and richer symbol for what Carver is getting at than is, say, a gas station or shopping mall. Notice, too, that in the television program about cathedrals there is an episode in which devils attack monks; that is, an assault is made on the soul. Presumably the narrator is unaware of morality plays, but some readers will understand that this scene introduces the possibility of a sort of spiritual change. A little later the inner change is further prepared for by the narrator's comments about a change in physical sensation. When he goes upstairs to get a pen so that he can draw a cathedral, he says, "My legs felt like they didn't have any strength in them. They felt like they did after I'd done some running."

Topics for Critical Thinking and Writing

1. What was your impression of the narrator after reading the first five paragraphs?
2. Why does the narrator feel threatened by the blind man? Has he any reason to feel threatened?
3. What attitude does the narrator reveal in the following passage:

   > She'd turned so that her robe slipped away from her legs, exposing a juicy thigh. I reached to draw her robe back over her and it was then that I glanced at the blind man. What the hell! I flipped the robe open again.

4. Why does the narrator not open his eyes at the end of the story?
5. The television program happens to be about cathedrals, but if the point is to get the narrator to draw something while the blind man's hand rests on the narrator's, the program could have been about some other topic, for example, about skyscrapers or about the Statue of Liberty. Do you think that a cathedral is a better choice, for Carver's purposes, than these other subjects? Why?
6. In what ways does Carver prepare us for the narrator's final state of mind?

MICHAEL GERBER AND JONATHAN SCHWARZ
What We Talk about When We Talk about Doughnuts (p. 746)

When you assign this selection, you may want to remind students that in Chapter 5 in *Literature for Composition* we talk a bit about parody. Then, when you discuss the piece in class, you can ask them how they might improve the discussion in Chapter 5. But chiefly you probably will want them to discuss the parody in terms of its object, Carver's writing, especially "What We Talk about When We Talk about Love."

As we see it, the parody—which we take to be affectionate, not scathing or corrosive—picks up the following qualities in Carver's writing.

1. The narrator is working class. His language is ordinary and indeed sometimes ungrammatical ("there was Jim and me"). He tends to report things

by saying "He said . . . She said" and he rarely interprets what he reports, but he does appreciate excellence (of his friend Jim, the fish-measurer, he says, "I mean, there was a man who could measure a fish!").
2. Given the narrator, the setting is usually working class. In Carver we do not find stories set in doctors' offices, or cruise ships, or the faculty lounge.
3. Nothing seems to happen. "There was a bowl of peanuts sitting on the table, but nobody ate many of them, because we were drinking and smoking." If we were asked, "Well, what *does* happen in a Carver story?" we would probably say, maybe a bit desperately, "People engage seriously with each other. In 'What We Talk about When We Talk about Love' Mel asks, 'What do any of us really know about love?' and the answer may be that they don't know much, and they certainly don't come to any answers that we can take away with us, but they do share serious moments that at least briefly seem to unite them, to give them memorable experiences." "What We Talk About" ends, you will recall, thus: "I could hear my heart beating. I could hear everyone's heart. I could hear the human noise we sat there making, not one of us moving, not even when the room went dark."
4. There is a strong undercurrent of conflict, especially between the sexes, and especially concerning issues that seem trivial. When Jim says that he likes doughnuts at breakfast and sometimes also at lunch, his wife, Elizabeth (also called Lisa and sometimes called Frank), says, "Now, hon, you know that's not true," and an angry exchange follows.
5. The dialogue has a slightly dislocated or screwy tone, partly because the narrator doesn't make connections clear (why is a woman whose name is Elizabeth, and who is called Lisa, sometimes called Frank?), but also partly because the narrator's experiences and values are not quite the reader's. So in this parody we hear, from Lisa, that her ex-boyfriend would sometimes put doughnuts on the floor, get up on the coffee table, "and then jump off directly on top of them." "'It was scary,' she said." In our view, the parody is least successful when it moves to the fanciful: Jim's wife is his forty-fifth, and she "inhaled too much helium and just floated away."

But we don't want to end on a negative note. We think the parody is delightful, it does catch Carver's tone and subject matter, and it in no way lessens our regard for Carver.

ANONYMOUS
Western Wind (p. 748)

"Western Wind" has been much discussed. Probably most readers will find acceptable R. P. Warren's suggestion (*Kenyon Review*, 1943, p. 5) that the grieving lover seeks relief for the absence of his beloved in "the sympathetic manifestation of nature." But how do you feel about Patric M. Sweeney's view (*Explicator*, October 1955) that the speaker asserts that "he will come to life only when the dead woman returns, and her love, like rain, renews him"? In

256   Chapter 20: Love and Hate

short, in this view the speaker "cries out to the one person who conquered death, who knows that the dead, returning to life, give life to those who loved them." We find this reading of the poem hard to take, but (like many readings) it is virtually impossible to *dis*prove.

One other point: some readers have asked why other readers assume that the speaker is a male. A hard question to answer.

CHRISTOPHER MARLOWE
Come Live with Me and Be My Love (p. 748)

SIR WALTER RALEIGH
The Nymph's Reply to the Shepherd (p. 749)

JOHN DONNE
The Bait (p. 750)

Marlowe's poem will probably cause no problems. We hope, however, that students do not reject it because it depicts an idealized, idyllic, pastoral world. It gives us, of course, not the real world but a world that we might sometimes dream of.

Raleigh's bitter (but engaging) response does not quite say that Marlowe's world is utterly fanciful. Raleigh seems to grant the truth of Marlowe's springtime world, but he points out that there is a further truth—the truth of change. Spring becomes fall and winter. (Topic 2 in the text asks about line 12. We hear puns in *spring* [the season, and also the watery source] and *fall* [the season, and a downfall].)

We find the last stanza of Raleigh's poem especially interesting. The poem does not cynically glory in debunking Marlowe's poem; rather, the final stanza expresses a poignant wish that Marlowe's vision were true.

Donne's "The Bait" begins with Marlowe's words, and the shift to "golden sands, and crystal brooks" hardly seems to change the landscape, though of course it does in fact get us into the world of fisherfolk. The idealized motif is continued in the second stanza, though "betray" in line 8 introduces a dark note. Still, the next stanza (lines 9–12) seems chiefly to continue the motif of a golden world, but in lines 13–16 we get two additional words that cause unease, "loath" and "darknest." The next two stanzas vigorously introduce the real world of hardships; fishing is no longer a delightful sport, but something that requires people to "freeze," and it will "cut" their legs. Further, we now hear of "poor fish," and the fisherfolk behave "treacherously." This is a bit odd, since at the start the speaker invited the beloved to fish in a world of "golden sands" and "crystal brooks," with "silken lines" and "silver hooks." That is, as the poem continues, the act of fishing is seen as less pleasant (to those who fish and to the fish themselves). In fact, where the speaker was a fisherman in the first stanza, in the last stanza he is a victimized fish, taken by the bait (attractiveness?) of the beloved. The beloved, therefore, is (at the start) a fellow-fisher or a companion at the start and (at the end) is also a deceiver who snares the speaker. On the other hand, although the speaker seems to lament his lot, he also evidently enjoys it. The idea that lovers enjoy suffering, enjoy thralldom, is of course commonplace.

When we teach sixteenth- and seventeenth-century poetry, we try always to find time to mention two books that we greatly valued when we were beginning our own efforts to become literary critics: William Empson, *Seven Types of Ambiguity* (1930; 3rd ed., rev. 1953), and F. R. Leavis, *Revaluation: Tradition & Development in English Poetry* (1936; rpt. 1975). For us, the virtue of both Empson and Leavis lies in their keen attentiveness to the poet's uses of language; Empson is adroit in showing the rich and mind-testing complexities of specific words, images, and lines, while Leavis excels in evoking the tone and movement of the poet's voice and in making forthright judgments about when a poem is effective and when it is not.

Not all readers share our esteem for Empson and Leavis. But our point here has less to do with the particular critics we grew up on than it does with the lesson or example that you can communicate to the students. Take a few moments to tell them about the critics who have been important to you. Who were the critics who have taught you in illuminating and inspiring ways, and who have enabled you to understand what it means to study and teach literature?

To most students, there you stand at the front of the room, speaking in an informed and confident (well, at least much of the time!) voice about a wide range of poems, plays, and stories. It is something of a mystery, and you can help to solve it for them: How did you become the critic and teacher that you are? Who were the critics who made you?

Don't underestimate the power of your own example. Your best students—those with a real love for the subject—will be looking to you for guidance about how to become a serious reader of literature. If you name the critics and books that you found crucial to your own literary education, you can be certain that some of your students will seize the tips you give them. Not all of them will, of course. But we need to offer something from time to time for the best students in the room, the students who want *more*. They are eager for a push, a challenge, a new path to follow. Keep them in mind.

WILLIAM SHAKESPEARE

Sonnet 29 ("When, in disgrace with Fortune and men's eyes") (p. 752)

Shakespeare's 154 sonnets were published in 1609, although it is thought that most of them were composed in the middle 1590s, around the time *Romeo and Juliet* and *A Midsummer Night's Dream* were written. Francis

Meres spoke of Shakespeare's "sugared sonnets" in 1598, and two were published in an anthology in 1599. The order of the sonnets is probably not Shakespeare's, but there are two large divisions (with some inconsistent interruptions). Sonnets 1–126 seem to be addressed to, or concerned with, a handsome, aristocratic young man who is urged to marry and thus to propagate his beauty and become immortal. Sonnets 127–152 are chiefly concerned with a promiscuous dark woman who seduces a friend, at least for a while.

Both you and your students will find all the commentary you need in three insightful, meticulously written books: *Shakespeare's Sonnets*, edited with analytic commentary by Stephen Booth (1977); *Shakespeare's Sonnets*, ed. Katherine Duncan-Jones (1997); and Helen Vendler, *The Art of Shakespeare's Sonnets* (1997).

The rhyme scheme of Sonnet 29 is that of the usual Shakespearean sonnet, but the thought is organized more or less into an octave and a sextet, the transition being emphasized by the trochee at the beginning of line 9. The sense of energy is also communicated by the trochee that begins line 10 and yet another that introduces line 11, this last being especially important because by consonance and alliteration it communicates its own energy to the new image of joy ("Like to the lark"). As in most of Shakespeare's sonnets, the couplet is more or less a summary of what has preceded, but not in the same order: line 13 summarizes the third quatrain; line 14 looks back to (but now rejects) the earlier quatrains.

The first line surely glances at Shakespeare's unimpressive social position, and line 8 presumably refers to his work. Possibly the idea is that he most enjoyed his work before it became the source of his present discomfort. Edward Hubler, in *The Sense of Shakespeare's Sonnets* (1952), notes that "the release from depression is expressed through the image of the lark, a remembrance of earlier days when the cares of his London career were unknown."

To this it can be added that although the poem employs numerous figures of speech from the start (e.g., personification with "Fortune," synecdoche with "eyes" in line 1, metonymy with "heaven" in line 3), line 11, with the image of the lark, introduces the poem's first readily evident figure of speech, and it is also the most emphatic run-on line in the poem. Moreover, though heaven was "deaf" in line 3, in line 12 it presumably hears the lark singing "hymns at heaven's gate." "Sullen" in line 12 perhaps deserves some special comment too: (1) The earth is still somber in color, though the sky is bright, and (2) applied to human beings, it suggests the moody people who inhabit earth.

Topic for Critical Thinking and Writing

Disregarding for the moment the last two lines (or couplet), where does the sharpest turn or shift occur? In a sentence, summarize the speaker's state of mind before this turn and, in another sentence, the state of mind after it.

WILLIAM SHAKESPEARE
Sonnet 116 ("Let me not to the marriage of true minds") (p. 753)

Although the poem is almost certainly addressed to a man, because it is a celebration of the permanence of love it can apply equally well to a woman or, in fact, to a parent or child.

The first words, "Let me not," are almost a vow, and "admit impediments" in the second line faintly hints at the marriage service in the Book of Common Prayer, which says, "If any of you know just cause or impediment. . . ." In line 2 "admit" can mean both "acknowledge, grant the existence of" and "allow to enter."

The first quatrain is a negative definition of love ("love is not . . ."), but the second quatrain is an affirmative definition ("O no, it is . . ."). The third begins as another negative definition, recognizing that "rosy lips and cheeks" will indeed decay, but denying that they are the essence of love; this quatrain then ends affirmatively, making a contrast to transience: "bears it out even to the edge of doom." Then, having clinched his case, the speaker adopts a genial and personal tone in the couplet, where for the first time he introduces the word "I."

Speaking of couplets, we can't resist quoting Robert Frost on the topic. Once, in conversation with Frost, the boxer Gene Tunney said something about the price of a poem. Frost replied: "One thousand dollars a line. Four thousand for a quatrain, but for a sonnet, $12,000. The last two lines of a sonnet don't mean anything anyway." Students might be invited to test the sonnets against this playful remark.

JOHN DONNE
A Valediction: Forbidding Mourning (p. 754)

Instructors may be so familiar with this poem that they may not recognize the difficulties it presents to students. The title itself leads many students to think (quite plausibly) that it is about death, an idea reinforced by the first simile. But this simile is introduced to make the point that *just as* virtuous men can die quietly because they are confident of a happy future, *so* the two lovers can part quietly—that is, the speaker can go on a journey—because they are confident of each other.

The hysterics that accompany the separation of less confident lovers are ridiculed ("sigh-tempests," "tear-floods"); such agitation would be a "profanation" of the relationship of the speaker and his beloved and would betray them to the "laity."

Thus the speaker and the beloved are implicitly priests of spiritual love.

The poem goes on to contrast the harmful movement of the earth (an earthquake) with the harmless ("innocent") movement of heavenly bodies, thereby again associating the speaker and the beloved with heavenly matters. (The cosmology, of course, is the geocentric Ptolemaic system.) The fourth stanza continues the contrast: other lovers are "sublunary," changeable, and subject to the changing moon. Such earthbound lovers depend on the physical things that "elemented" their love ("eyes, lips, and hands"), but the love of the speaker and his partner is "refined" and does not depend on such stuff. Moreover, if their love is like something physical, it is "like gold to airy thinness beat."

The three last stanzas introduce the image of a draftsman's (not an explorer's) compass, and they also introduce the circle as a symbol of perfection.

See Theodore Redpath's edition of *The Songs and Sonnets of John Donne* (1983), and see especially Clay Hunt, *Donne's Poetry* (1969), and Patricia Spacks, *College English* 29 (1968): 594–595. Louis Martz, *The Wit of Love* (1969), p. 48, says of line 20: "'Care less,' but is it so? The very rigor and intricacy of the famous image of the compass at the end may be taken to suggest rather desperate dialectical effort to control by logic and reason a situation almost beyond control."

For students, there is plenty to learn from and profitably argue with in these two books: Wilbur Sanders, *John Donne's Poetry* (1971), and John Carey, *John Donne: Life, Mind, and Art* (1980).

Andrew Marvell
To His Coy Mistress (p. 755)

Marvell's "To His Coy Mistress" is well discussed by J. V. Cunningham, *Modern Philology* 51 (August 1953): 33–41; by Francis Berry, *Poets' Grammar*; by Joan Hartwig, *College English* 25 (May 1964): 572–575; by Bruce King, *Southern Review* 5 (1969): 689–703; and by Richard Crider, *College Literature* 12 (Spring 1985): 113–121. Incidentally, "dew" in line 35 is an editor's emendation for "glew" in the first edition (1681). Grierson suggests "glew" means a shining gum found on some trees. Other editors conjecture "lew"—that is, warmth.

Naturally none of the early discussions of the poem consider whether it is outrageously sexist—and, if it is, whether it should be taught. Such a discussion is probably inevitable in the classroom today, and no reader of this manual can be in need of our opinion on this topic. We will therefore comment only on some formal matters.

The poem consists of three parts, developing an argument along these lines: "If . . . But . . . Therefore." The first of these three parts is playful, the second wry or even scornful or bitter, and the third passionate. Or, to put it in slightly different terms, the poem is an argument, spoken (as the title indicates) by a male suitor to a reluctant woman. It begins with a hypothetical situation ("Had we but world enough and time") in which the speaker playfully caricatures Petrarchan conventions (fantastic promises, incredible patience). Then (lines 21–32), with "But at my back," he offers a very different version of life, a wry, almost scornful speech describing a world in which beauty is fleeting. Finally (lines 33–46) he offers a passionate conclusion ("Now therefore").

The conclusion, and especially the final couplet, perhaps require further comment. The "amorous birds of prey" of line 38 replace the doves of Venus found in more traditional love poetry. The destructiveness suggested by the birds is continued in the image of a "ball," which is chiefly a cannonball hurtling "through the iron gates of life" but is also the united lovers—that is, the ball is made up of their "strength" (chiefly his?) and "sweetness" (chiefly hers?). Some commentators find in "Tear" a suggestion of a hymen destroyed by "rough strife." The violence and the suggestions of warfare are somewhat diminished in the final couplet, but they are not absent, for the sun, though advancing, is partly imagined as an enemy that is being routed ("yet we will make him run").

We have some small uncertainties about the metrics of lines 21–22, "But at my back I always hear / Time's winged chariot hurrying near." Are "chariot" and "hurrying" disyllabic or trisyllabic? If they are trisyllabic the line contains two extra syllables, forcing the reader to hurry through the line. But of course different readers will read almost any line differently. For instance, in the first of these lines some readers will put relatively heavy stresses on the first four syllables ("But at my back"); others may rush through the first three words and put an especially heavy stress on "back," compensating for the lack of an earlier stress. In any case, these two lines surely are spoken differently from the earlier lines. Similarly, the third section, beginning with line 33, starts by sounding different. In this case almost everyone would agree that "Now therefore" gets two consecutive stresses.

Good selections of Marvell's poetry have been edited by Frank Kermode (1967), George de F. Lord (1968), and Elizabeth Story Donno (1972). Students might enjoy John Dixon Hunt, *Andrew Marvell: His Life and Writings* (1978), which includes well-chosen illustrations. Our favorite book on Marvell is still Rosalie Colie, *"My Echoing Song": Andrew Marvell's Poetry of Criticism* (1970).

WILLIAM BLAKE
The Garden of Love (p. 757)

Instead of the freedom and innocence of the echoing green (a poem we print later in the text) we now have the restraint of the priest-ridden garden, where desires are constrained by repressive authority.

The chapel is closed (a sign of repressiveness), priests are dressed in black, the garden has become a cemetery, and "Thou shalt not" is the prevailing spirit. To our ear, the tone is jingly, which might suggest merriment but (given the context) perhaps is meant to indicate a mechanical, lifeless place. All of the lines except the last two have three stresses each; in each of the last two lines there are four stresses, and there are also internal rhymes, which, in the context, serve to "bind" the poem, i.e., to emphasize the oppressiveness of the place.

In the illustration, children stare into a grave, and the window in the church is dark.

WILLIAM BLAKE
A Poison Tree (p. 757)

The first three lines of the last stanza are primarily trochaic, each beginning with a heavily stressed hammer-stroke emphasizing the speaker's deliberation. The last line, however, is iambic, and the shift probably contributes to our sense of the speaker's relief in contemplating the result of his perverse activity.

Fruitful images ("I watered," "I sunned," "it grew," "it bore") are used here to describe a death-giving repressive activity, the speaker delighting in his sick productivity. E. D. Hirsch Jr., in *Innocence and Experience* (1964), calls attention to the fact that the poem is not simply an attack on hypocrisy but is also a description of "the causes and characteristics of human fallenness."

What is the reader's attitude toward the speaker? Do we listen with horror—or are we engaged, and even delighted? After all, a reader's response to a work of literature is not at all the same as a viewer's response to a real-life happening. The problem has been discussed at least since the days of Aristotle, who in the course of his remarks on tragedy sought to explain why we take delight in literary versions of actions that in real life would distress us. But even in real life some morally repulsive actions may give us pleasure. One thinks of Keats's famous remark, in a letter of March 19, 1819: "Though a quarrel in the streets is a thing to be hated, the energies displayed in it are fine." Is the energy displayed in this poem "fine"?

One can, of course, disagree with Keats's general comment—or even if one agrees with Keats one can say that Keats does not speak for Blake. Does Blake give us any guidance? If we turn to *The Marriage of Heaven and Hell* (1790–1793), we find many statements suggesting that Blake, like Keats, delighted in energy, and (we are going a bit further) that Blake might approve of the speaker of "A Poison Tree." Here, from *The Marriage,* are some of the "Proverbs of Hell":

> Drive your cart and your plow over the bones of the dead.
> The road of excess leads to the palace of wisdom.
> If the fool would persist in his folly, he would become wise.

On the other hand, also among the "Proverbs of Hell" is this:

> He who desires but acts not, breeds pestilence.

And from elsewhere in *The Marriage of Heaven and Hell*:

> Expect poison from standing water.
> The weak in courage is strong in cunning.
> Sooner murder an infant in its cradle than nurse unacted desires.

If we were to choose a single line that seems best to represent Blake—that is, our understanding of Blake—it would be (also from *The Marriage of Heaven and Hell*) this:

> Energy is Eternal Delight

The question, then, is whether the speaker of the poem is indeed showing admirable energy, and whether we (in line with Keats's view) inevitably delight in his delight however wicked its sources, or, on the other hand, whether the speaker is one of those who are "weak in courage," a person equivalent to "standing water," someone who "desires but acts not," i.e., who acts only in piddling ways (watering, sunning, smiling) and therefore is someone who "breeds pestilence."

Perhaps, too, the whole issue is complicated by the fact that the speaker's foe is disreputable, since he steals into the garden at night. (Surely we *can* believe the speaker on this matter.)

If in class you raise the issue of to what degree, if any, we can approve of the speaker, you might wish to compare the poem with Browning's "Soliloquy of the Spanish Cloister."

WALT WHITMAN
When I Heard at the Close of the Day (p. 762)

First, a few words about Whitman's sexual orientation. As the biographical note indicates, Whitman's heterosexual poems (partly remarkable because of their passages about female eroticism) aroused more indignation than what we take to be his homosexual ones, which were passed off as celebrating some sort of pure "manly love." For instance, in the first biography of Whitman, *Walt Whitman* (1883), written by Dr. Richard Maurice Bucke in collaboration with the poet, one reads that "Calamus" presents "an exalted friendship, a love into which sex does not enter as an element" (p. 166). Some admirers saw the poems differently, but in a letter (written in response to an inquiry by John Addington Symonds, famous for his interest in "Greek love") Whitman wrote, "Though unmarried, I have had six children." Symonds apparently accepted this at face value, and in his *Walt Whitman* (1893) he said that what Whitman calls "the 'adhesiveness' of comradeship is meant to have no interblending with the 'amativeness' of sensual love" (p. 93). But Symonds also wrote:

> Those unenviable mortals who are the inheritors of sexual anomalies, will recognize their own emotions in Whitman's "superb friendship . . . latent in all men." (p. 93)

In the text, in our discussion of gay criticism, we mention some recent work on Whitman.

Now for a few words about "When I Heard." David Cavitch, in *My Soul and I: The Inner Life of Walt Whitman* (1985), places the poem in the context of Whitman's development:

> "When I Heard at the Close of the Day" reveals Whitman's dissatisfaction with his long-standing discipline of ambition and solitary creativity. His achievements, his acclaim, and his cronies no longer delight him, he says;

he is happy only when he withdraws from it all to be with his lover at a rendezvous. But Whitman is not just on vacation: He dismisses the rewards of national fame and high accomplishments, and he emphasizes his perfect gratification in actual, private intimacy. (p. 132)

We may add two points to this comment: (1) the "plaudits in the capital" were in fact muted; Whitman seems to be alluding to a single cautious newspaper review; (2) nature—the sound of the water and the sand—seems to "congratulate" him, offering an approval beyond what the public can offer.

Some commentators speak of this poem as a sort of free verse sonnet. We discuss this idea in our comment on the next poem.

WALT WHITMAN
I Saw in Louisiana a Live-Oak Growing (p. 762)

Whitman spent two months in New Orleans, in the spring of 1848.

As Whitman sees it, the tree is like him in that it is "rude, unbending, lusty" (this is the Whitman who from the first version of *Leaves of Grass* onward celebrated himself as "one of the roughs, a kosmos, / Disorderly, fleshly and sensual. . . eating drinking and breeding"), but the tree is *un*like him in that it grows in solitude.

In line 3 "uttering" ("uttering joyous leaves") strikes us as especially interesting, since it attributes to the tree a voice, or, rather, sees its organic growth as akin to human speech. Whitman conceived himself as one who by nature writes poetry, as a tree by nature produces leaves.

On at least one occasion Whitman suggested that the poems in "Calamus" could be thought of as something like a group of sonnets, and some readers have felt that this poem has the feel of a sonnet with an octave and a sestet, even though it is not rhymed, is not in iambic pentameter, and has thirteen rather than fourteen lines.

The first four lines can be thought of as a quatrain (or, in terms of the structure of the whole, as roughly equivalent to the octave in an Italian sonnet) in which the poet presents the image—the tree—and relates it to himself. Then, at the beginning of line 5, comes a turn (the *volta* in an Italian sonnet), strongly marked by "But," and we get a sort of comment on the first unit, rather as a sestet in an Italian sonnet may comment on the octave. (Here the second unit runs to nine lines rather than to six.) The gist is this: the poet dwells on his difference from the tree—even as he talks about the souvenir twig that he has brought back with him. One can of course divide this second unit variously, for instance, one can distinguish between the first five lines (5–9)—a group about the twig—and the remaining four lines (10–13)—a group in which the poet's thought returns to the original tree that is not only like him ("joyous") but is also unlike him ("without a friend a lover near").

Edna St. Vincent Millay
Love Is Not All: It Is Not Meat nor Drink (p. 763)

Late in the poem a phrase in line 12 ("the memory of this night") identifies the speaker (a lover), the audience (the beloved), and the time (a night of love), but the poem begins drily, even rather pedantically. A somewhat professorial voice delivers a lecture on love, beginning authoritatively with four almost equally stressed monosyllables ("Love is not all"). Then, warming to the subject, the speaker becomes more expansive, with "It is not . . . nor . . . Nor . . . nor . . . And . . . and . . . and . . . and . . . can not . . . Nor . . . nor," all in the octave. Of course, in saying that love cannot do this and that we sense, paradoxically, a praise of love; if we have read a fair amount of love poetry, perhaps we expect the octave to yield to a sestet that will say what love *can* do. But this sestet too begins with apparent objectivity, as if making a concession ("It well may be"). Then, like the octave, the sestet introduces a romantic note while nominally proclaiming realism, although its images are somewhat less exotic (there is nothing like the "floating spar" of line 3, for instance) than the images of the octave. On the other hand, insofar as it introduces a more personal or a more intense note ("the memory of this night") and reveals that the poem is addressed to the beloved, it is *more* romantic. In any case the sestet comes down to earth and at the same time reaches a romantic height, in its last line, which consists of two sentences: "It may well be. I do not think I would." The brevity of these two sentences, and the lack of imagery, presumably convey a dry humor that the octave lacks, and at the same time they make an extremely romantic claim. (Surely "I do not think I would" is an understatement; in effect, it is a passionate declaration.) Put it this way: although the octave asserts, for example, that love is not meat and drink and cannot heal the sick, and the first part of the sestet asserts that the speaker "might" give up the beloved's love in certain extreme circumstances, the understated passion of the conclusion serves to dismiss these assertions as unlikely—indeed, a reader feels, as untrue. Although to the rational mind "love is not all," to the lover it is "all," and a lover here is doing the talking.

Robert Frost
The Silken Tent (p. 764)

The idea of comparing a woman to a silken tent in the summer breeze seems fresh enough to us (probably swaying silken tents have been compared to young women, but did anyone before Frost see it the other way around?), and given this idea, one would expect passages about gentle swaying. If one knew the piece were going to be an allegory worked out in some detail, one might expect the tent pole to be the soul. But who could have expected the brilliant connection between the cords and "ties of love and thought," and the brilliant suggestion that only rarely are we made aware—by "capriciousness"—of our "bondage"? The paradoxical idea that we are (so to speak) kept upright—are what we are—by things that would seem to pull us down is new to most students, who think that one "must be oneself." With a little discussion they come to see that what a person is depends largely on relationships. We are parents, or students, or teachers, or—something; our complex relationships give us our identity. Sometimes, in trying to make clear this idea that our relationships contribute to (rather than diminish) our identities, we mention the scene in Ibsen's *Peer Gynt* where, in an effort to get at his essential self, Peer peels an onion, each removed layer being a relationship that he has stripped himself of. He ends with nothing, of course.

In short, we think this poem embodies a profound idea, and we spend a fair amount of our class time talking about that idea. But we also try to look at the poem closely. Students might be invited to discuss what sort of woman "she" is. What, for instance, do "midday" and "summer" in line 2 contribute? Frost could, after all, have written "In morning when a sunny April breeze" but he probably wanted to suggest—we don't say a mature woman—someone who is no longer girlish, someone who is of sufficient age to have established responsibilities and to have experienced, on occasion, a sense of slight bondage. Among the traits that we think can be reasonably inferred from the comparison are these: beauty, poise, delicacy (in lines 1–4), and sweetness and firmness of soul (in lines 5–7).

ADRIENNE RICH
Novella (p. 766)

The third-person point of view (for what the reader almost surely takes as an episode from the author's life), the flat tone, and the title serve to distance the work, serve, we might say, to make it prosaic, since poems usually express passion. But of course these devices, like other devices such as understatement, mask deep feeling.

Despite the man's return to the house and the somewhat absurd situation where he finds that because he has forgotten his key he must ring the bell of his own house in order to enter, we take it that the quarrel is not resolved. That is, he *does* return, and "The lights go on in the house"—this might seem to be a sign of reunion, the dispelling of the darkness of anger, etc.—but the last two lines ("Outside, separate as minds, / the stars too come alight") seem to us to indicate that the man and the woman remain "separate." Some of our students have disagreed with us.

Topics for Critical Thinking and Writing

1. Rewrite the poem along these lines:

   My husband and I are in a room, speaking harshly.
   He gets up, goes out to walk.

I go out into the next room
and wash the dishes, cracking one.
It gets dark outside.

Has the poem been improved, or weakened, or simply changed? Explain.

2. What, if anything, do the last two lines contribute to the poem?
3. A *novella* is a long short story or a short novel (usually about 50–100 pages). Why do you suppose Rich called this short poem "Novella"?
4. In one typed page, write your own "Novella." You may be a character in the plot, but keep your voice third person.

ADRIENNE RICH
XI. (from *Twenty-One Love Poems*) (p. 766)

Nothing in this poem specifies the sex of the speaker, but since the author is a woman perhaps most readers assume that the speaker is a woman. Such an assumption is usually fairly safe but certainly not always. In this case, however, it is true; the surrounding poems make it clear that the speaker is a woman.

Topic for Critical Thinking and Writing

We know from the context—the poem is one of a group of twenty-one poems—that it is about two women in love. But can the poem—at least out of context—be read equally well as a poem about heterosexual lovers?

ROBERT PACK
The Frog Prince (p. 767)

The tale recorded by the Grimm Brothers is not quite as we remembered it. In our memory—and we think that perhaps most people share this view—a handsome young prince has been turned into a frog by a witch, and he cannot regain his human shape until a beautiful woman kisses him, i.e., loves him, or at least pities him. It all works out all right, and the implicit moral is (as in the story of "Beauty and the Beast") that love is so powerful that it can transform the beloved, or that those who pity the unfortunate will themselves be rewarded, or something along those lines.

In fact, the Grimm story is rather different. The trouble is, even the earliest English translation of Grimm, *German Popular Tales* (1823), changed the story considerably. (The version given in this first English translation is reprinted in Iona and Peter Opie, *The Classic Fairy Tales* [1974].) The Grimm version is, however, readily available in *The Juniper Tree* (1973), trans. Lore

Segal. In the original story (i.e., the German version printed by the Grimm Brothers), the girl does not love the frog; she promises him that she will let him live with her if he retrieves a golden ball. She makes the promise lightly, assuming that the frog cannot get out of the well. Her father, however, insists that she keep the promise. In a fit of anger, she throws the frog against a wall, and it becomes the human being that it earlier was. Folklorists believe that the Grimm Brothers probably added the bit about the father insisting that the girl keep her promise, in order to make the story suitably instructive for children, but even with this added bit of moralizing the story as a whole remains morally chaotic. As Maria Tatar says, in *Off with Their Heads! Fairy Tales and the Culture of Childhood* (1992),

> Although the princess of "The Frog King" is selfish, greedy, ungrateful, and cruel, in the end she does as well for herself as all the modest, obedient, magnanimous, and compassionate Beauties of "The Search for the Lost Husband." Much as the Grimms tried to rewrite the tale with paternal prompts about the importance of keeping promises and showing gratitude, they could not succeed in camouflaging the way in which the tale rewards indignant rage. (p. 154)

This is not really surprising. Nineteenth-century versions of fairy tales *don't* usually have nice morals; on the contrary, they are often nightmarish things, especially nightmarish because their arbitrariness seems meaningless. We should mention, however, that in Freudian thought the meaning is evident: the slimy frog who seeks to get into the princess's bed is a scarcely veiled phallic symbol; the penis attains completeness only when accepted by a partner.

It may be useful to ask students if they have encountered the story of the prince who, transformed into a frog, can regain his human shape only when accepted by a beautiful woman. Probably some will report a saying popular among young women, "You have to kiss a lot of frogs before you find a prince."

We don't know what version of the story Robert Pack started from, but since he does not mention the startling episode of the princess hurling the frog against the wall, we suspect that he may have drawn on a moralized version of the sort we mentioned at the outset, where the princess out of love or tenderness or sympathy accepts the frog. Pack's first quatrain deals chiefly with the princess's surprise at the change in the frog; in the second quatrain and in the first part of the third quatrain her thoughts turn from the frog to herself—first, to the thought that *she* has transformed him, and then to the thought that in turn *she has been transformed* by the sexual act. The second half of the third quatrain and the final two lines of the poem (we can't quite call them a couplet since they don't rhyme with each other, and in fact the fourteenth line rhymes with the twelfth) bring us down to earth when the mother sees the girl with the prince: "What was it that her mother said?" Obviously Pack is making a little joke: he takes a myth (a puzzling one, if he is working from the original version, or a pretty one, if he is working from the moralized version) and he subjects it to a common-sense mentality. But the joke is also serious; the poem forces the reader to think of the gap between the mother and the transformed girl. In line 6 the word "wonder"—in the sense of "marvelous thing"—explicitly refers to the transformation of the frog, but we can apply it also to the transformation of the girl. Of course the mother once was similarly transformed, but in the poem the contrast is between the girl, who has suddenly entered into a marvelous new world, made by love, and the mother, whose remarks, though not given, can easily be imagined.

Pack is not only an accomplished poet—see *Waking to My Name: New and Selected Poems* (1980)—but he is also a stimulating critic and essayist, as the work in *Affirming Limits: Essays on Mortality, Choice, and Poetic Form* (1985) and *The Long View: Essays on the Discipline of Hope and Poetic Craft* (1991) attests.

JOSEPH BRODSKY
Love Song (p. 768)

For this poem, we think the best way to proceed is to examine closely each of the poet's two-line units. Consider, for example, the first two lines:

> If you were drowning, I'd come to the rescue,
>   wrap you in my blanket and pour hot tea.

This sounds noble enough. The speaker presents himself as an intrepid rescuer of his drowning beloved, and he wittily shows the follow-up to his effort: he will even wrap her in *his* blanket and pour the tea for her. But in the next two lines, the emphasis changes:

> If I were a sheriff, I'd arrest you
>   and keep you in the cell under lock and key.

Is this more wit? Yes, to an extent. But the image is a little disquieting too: is the beloved a lawbreaker of some kind? No, she is not, but the "sheriff" speaker would pretend that she is, and would keep her "under lock and key." No freedom for her: she is under the authority of her sheriff-jailer.

We have taught this poem twice, and at this point in the discussion, the students tend to say that they enjoyed the poem and found it funny, but also sensed an ironic and even unpleasant edge to it. One student said she thought the poem is "coercive," because in it the speaker keeps imagining how *he* will portray the relationship—which, our student said, suggests that the speaker insists on being the person always in control.

The poem is very carefully put together, for all of its seemingly free and easy manner. "Wrap you in the blanket" is innocent—a good thing to do for a person who needs warming up. But "wrap you in a blanket" may sound more disconcerting when we return to it after reading the next two lines. "Keep you in the cell" is just a more extreme version of the idea of enclosure and containment that "wrap you in a blanket" intimates.

We had good luck on one occasion when we asked students, as a writing assignment, to compose a poem of their own that used the if/then pattern that Brodsky follows here. For your women students, you might suggest that they write the poem from the point of view of the beloved, as she responds to Brodsky's speaker. Our students had fun with this assignment. We gave them as much leeway as they wanted to make the stanzas entertaining, funny, outlandish, macabre. All we required—a good touch, we think—is that the students preserve the rhyme scheme.

Though we admire Brodsky as a poet, the book by him we have enjoyed the most is one that he coauthored with Seamus Heaney and Derek Walcott: *Homage to Robert Frost* (1996). Brodsky's commentary on Frost's "Home Burial" is very penetrating and sensitive, and it is well worth recommending to students as an example of a powerful critical mind in action.

NIKKI GIOVANNI
Love in Place (p. 769)

Although (we think) the title of the poem—see question 5—is not immediately self-evident, by the end of the poem the title is clear. "In place" has the sense of "in the same place," "unchanging," as in "The soldiers marched in place," meaning that they did not move forward. Here, then, the speaker finds that although the years have passed, she is (because she sees herself through the eyes of her lover) "still young and slim and very much committed to the / love we still have." Her love is still "in place," fixed where it was. There is thus something of a pun on "still"—"continually," and "without moving."

Our sixth question invites students to talk about the idea of "falling in love." They might discuss it in the context of another familiar phrase, "Love is blind" (an idea that goes back to Theocritus and is found later in Plautus, Chaucer, and Shakespeare).

Students might begin with Giovanni's *Selected Poems* (1996) and then turn to Virginia C. Fowler, *Nikki Giovanni* (1992), a good overview of the writer's life and literary career. Also recommended: Giovanni, *Gemini: An Extended Autobiographical Statement on My First Twenty-Five Years of Being a Black Poet* (1971); and *Conversations with Nikki Giovanni*, ed. Virginia C. Fowler (1992).

CAROL MUSKE
Chivalry (p. 770)

We begin by asking students about the meanings of the word "chivalry." Students usually know that the term refers to the medieval system, principles, and customs of knighthood—bravery, honor, loyalty. They are not always aware that it also connotes gallantry toward women.

The central claim that Muske makes, in stanza 3, then becomes the focus of our discussion. The speaker says that she has seen few acts that are like this one—an act of "true chivalry." But the act itself is one that may make many American readers, accustomed to different burial practices, uneasy and uncomfortable. Not all of our students, but a fair number of them, have found this poem disturbing: How could a man who loved his wife burn her body?

Yet this is the point of the poem, or, rather, the burden of meaning that Muske has taken on, as she declares and seeks to convince us that this is a noble, loving act. She uses the word "reverence," which connotes profound love, awe, deep respect. Muske wants to claim about this scene what we might at first find hard to accept—that it is a beautiful gesture that shows the "bereavement" (the desolate loneliness) that the old man feels.

Muske sets this moment against the broader span of the "familiar carnage of love." We ask students why they think Muske ended the poem with this line: Does it fittingly conclude Muske's reflections on the scene, or, instead, does it somewhat jar against the solemn mood she has created? Is there anger in this final line? Bitterness? "Carnage" is a strong word—massive slaughter, as in war, a massacre; corpses, especially of those killed in battle. Such "carnage" is "familiar," Muske observes: we have witnessed it all too often.

But we push this point further: What kinds of experiences is Muske alluding to through this phrase? Do members of the class agree with this claim, which is after all a grand and shocking one? Should Muske have done more to establish for us what "the familiar carnage of love" (at least it still *is* love) entails and how it stands in contrast to the kind of chivalric gesture she has depicted here?

In *An Octave Above Thunder: New and Selected Poems* (1977), Muske presents twenty years of work in verse. For interested students, this book pairs nicely with another that she has written in prose, a collection of essays titled *Women and Poetry: Truth, Autobiography, and the Shape of the Self* (1977).

KITTY TSUI
A Chinese Banquet (p. 771)

We don't think students will have any difficulty with this poem, or, rather, we don't think there are any lines or images in the poem that students will find difficult to understand except the reference to the dragon, in line 50—more about that in a moment—though some students may find it difficult to talk about the subject matter, a lesbian relationship.

The title suggests fun, "A Chinese Banquet," but the dedication *"for the one who was not invited,"* immediately undermines any such suggestion. The language of the opening stanza (and of the entire poem) is conversational, the language one uses in speaking with friends and family, but the report immediately sets the speaker apart:

> it was not a very formal affair but
> all the women over twelve
> wore long gowns and a corsage,
> except for me.

Ask your students why she was not wearing a corsage. They will explain that presumably all the other women had been given corsages by their husbands or boyfriends. Ask them, too, why the second stanza begins with the same words as the first stanza, "it was not a very formal affair." Here there may be less unanimity. Our own reading is that the repetition suggests that the speaker is hurt and is going over and over the event in her mind, returning so to speak to the scene of the crime, wishing it could have been different. As the poem proceeds, she recalls the typical talk, buying a house, traveling, but she is "dreaming" of her partner, who has not been invited. Instead of the banquet being a pleasant social occasion for the speaker, it is a trial, with her mother speaking sarcastically, nagging her. The banquet is "very much a family affair" but so far as the mother is concerned, the daughter has no partner and indeed the partner has not been invited. Isolated from the family by her sexual orientation, she cannot (or at least she thinks she cannot) join in the conversation even about food and cars, or tell her family that her "back is healing," i.e., she thinks she cannot talk about what matters to her, her health and her partner.

A few words about line 50, "i dream of dragons and water." In Western thinking, the dragon is a symbol of Satan and of evil in general, but in East Asia the dragon is beneficent, the male principle associated with rain (hence it is associated with the air, and in the poem with "the wide open sky"), bringer of nourishment and good harvest. The complement of the dragon is the tiger, the female principle. We don't want to press the poem for autobiographical significance, but if the speaker is the author, Kitty Tsui, and if she conceives of herself (somewhat playfully) as a tiger—Kitty?—then it is not surprising that she dreams of "dragons and water," i.e., of her partner, her complement.

One other point: Why does the speaker not use any capital letters? We don't know. If she did not use a capital for the first person singular pronoun but used capitals at the beginnings of sentences, we probably would suggest that the lack of capitalization in the pronoun suggested her sense of littleness, apartness, unconventionality. But the lack of capitalization at the beginning of sentences suggests there must be a different reason. Perhaps—and this would be a perfectly good reason—it is just to set the work apart from prose, i.e., to indicate that this utterance is distinctive.

Additional Topic for Discussion

Is the poem rooted in specific ethnic behavior, or might this family equally have been, say, of Russian Jewish background, or Italian Catholics, or WASPs?

TERRENCE MCNALLY
Andre's Mother (p. 773)

Andre's Mother says nothing, so it is difficult for us (or any reader or spectator) to offer evidence in support of any characterization that we might propose. Still, the fact that she says nothing says something. Her refusal to join in the conversation—her insistence on isolating herself from the three other characters—tells us she is deeply hurt, but it does not tell us *what* she is hurt by. By her son's immorality (as she sees it)? By Cal, who may, in her view, have corrupted her son and then killed him (again, in her view)?

We learn that Andre had two reasons for not telling his mother that he had AIDS: He was "afraid of hurting [her] and [he was afraid] of [her] disapproval." The mother's continued silence, even near the end of the play, causes Cal to say, "I'm beginning to feel your disapproval and it's making me ill," and a moment later he leaves the stage, without a comforting word from the mother. She presumably cannot accept her son's homosexuality—or if she can accept it, she probably blames it and his death on Cal, although Cal tells her that he himself "tested negative."

We know nothing of Andre's Mother other than that she probably lived in a rural society (Cal says that Andre was "a country boy"), but even this information is a bit soft: A New Yorker such as Cal might jokingly say that someone from, oh, maybe Kansas City, is a country boy. Probably it is enough for us to say that the mother is hostile toward homosexuality and quite understandably is grieved by the death of her son and that she in some degree blames the boy's partner.

What do we make of the ending, when the mother finally let go of the balloon? Cal gives a rather constricted interpretation of the balloons:

> They represent the soul. When you let go, it means you're letting his soul ascend to Heaven. That you're willing to let go. Breaking the last earthly ties.

Surely other people, even at this very graveside, might offer a different interpretation. One might reasonably say that one is not and should not be willing to "let go," i.e., one will treasure the memory and perhaps will daily or at least often engage in actions that are motivated by the enduring connection with the dead partner, but one lets the balloon sail into the air as a sort of emblem of the deceased's new kind of existence.

In any case, the final stage direction tells us several things about Andre's Mother:

> *Her lips tremble. She looks on the verge of breaking down. She is about to let go of the balloon when she pulls it down to her. She looks at it awhile before she gently kisses it. She lets go of the balloon. She follows it with her*

eyes as it rises and rises. The lights are beginning to fade. Andre's Mother's eyes are still on the balloon. The lights fade.

It would be absurd for us to speak dogmatically about the thoughts of Andre's Mother. For one thing, she is a fictional character—she has no existence other than the words that her author puts into her mouth. But even if she were a historical figure, in which case we might more reasonably speak of her personality, we would have to be cautious lest we project our own views onto the subject.

Still, perhaps we can say something of use. First of all, we can assume that Cal's view of the symbolism may have had some effect on her. That is, her reluctance to let go of the balloon may suggest her reluctance to let go of her ideas about her son—that he *couldn't* have been gay, or if he was gay, that he was somehow seduced from his natural heterosexuality by Cal and that Cal is responsible for Andre's death. Perhaps when she lets go of the balloon she is letting go of some or all of these mistaken, destructive ideas.

McNally tells us in the stage direction that Andre's Mother "follows [the balloon] with her eyes" and that when the lights fade, at the very end, "Andre's Mother's eyes are still on the balloon." This does not sound to us as though she is "willing to let go," and indeed we—the writers of this page—don't think she should "let go" her love for and memory of her son. On the other hand, yes, she should "let go" whatever false ideas she had about him, and she should "let go" whatever anger she feels toward his lover.

She *does* let go—literally—of the balloon, so in a way she lets go of this symbol of her son, or, rather, this symbol of her son's soul. We take the white balloon to be a fairly obvious symbol of the soul. The sphere, a sort of three-dimensional circle, is a common emblem of endlessness and perfection. White is a common symbol of purity and of rebirth, even (we are told) in Black Africa, where young men after circumcision may cover their faces with white chalk, indicating that they are now "reborn" as responsible adults. In Japan the white lotus is associated with the Buddha's perfect knowledge. For all of these reasons, then, and because the helium-filled balloon rises into the heavens, the white balloon seems to us to be a pretty clear symbol of the soul released from the body.

One final point about the play, and then we will say something about McNally's video version of his play. As far as readers and an audience are concerned, the play ends with Andre's Mother releasing the balloon *after* Penny and Arthur and (a bit later) Cal have left. Nothing indicates that these others know her final action. Cal's last words to her are, as we said a moment ago, "I'm beginning to feel your disapproval and it's making me ill. . . . Goodbye, Andre's Mother." If at the very end the Mother undergoes some change, however small, viewers must find it painful—can we say tragic?—that Cal does not know of the change. Although it is commonplace to say that in a tragedy the tragic hero experiences an *anagnorisis*, a recognition, a final illumination, in fact tragic heroes often do *not* know the whole truth, do *not* fundamentally change. For example, in *Oedipus the King*, the self-confident protagonist is, at the end of the play, still being bossy: In the next-to-last speech of the play (except for the final words of the Chorus), Oedipus tries to hold on to his children, and in the last speech (again, except for the Chorus) Creon quite reasonably tells Oedipus that he is no longer in a position to give orders. In *King Lear*, almost surely Lear dies with the mistaken belief that Cordelia is alive. Romeo unquestionably dies thinking Juliet is dead. Many other instances might be given. Our point simply is that tragedy usually deals with mistakes, with mistakes that contain an element of irony—Lear banishes the daughter who loves him most—and sometimes the mistakes, the ironies, persist even unto death. In *Andre's Mother* surely our sympathy is chiefly with Cal but probably it finally extends to Andre's Mother, and perhaps we feel a twinge that Cal, a bit too self-satisfied at the end, does not see that she is not beyond redemption.

McNally's video, *Andre's Mother* (starring Richard Thomas and Sada Thompson), done for American Playhouse, runs 58 minutes, obviously far longer than the original play takes. The opening shot shows Andre's Mother, then her son, then we hear the narrator's voice, and then the mother says, "You took my son from me." We next gets shots of a street, a vendor with white balloons, a released balloon, the interior of a church, the funeral service complete with white lilies and a singer rendering Mozart's *Shepherd King* ("I love him, I will be constant"), shots of people in pews, another shot of Andre's Mother in a pew, a scene at an airport in which Cal meets Andre's Mother and explains that Andre has just left for Hartford to try out for a role. Andre's Mother and Cal go to Cal's apartment and we learn that Cal is writing a book about a gay composer, Samuel Barber. On the wall of the apartment is a poster of Hamlet: Remember, Andre is an actor, and in the printed version Cal pays tribute to Andre by reciting a line that Horatio addresses to the dead Hamlet, "Good night, sweet prince, and flights of angels sing thee to rest."

The Mother—we are still talking about the television version—says "Maybe there's some things I'd just as soon not know," and then there is a cut back to the church which is the site of the funeral service. There is a scene in a museum with Andre's Mother and her own garrulous mother, then a scene in a restaurant with Cal, the two women, and an evidently gay waiter. In the cemetery, Cal denounces Andre's Mother but embraces her, and he lets his balloon slip away. Cut to a scene of a young mother with a small boy on the beach—this is presumably Andre and his mother in happier days—and then we go back to Andre's Mother in the cemetery, where we see her release the balloon. You get the idea; the play is "opened up," with lots of scenes that are not in the original. This is not a bad thing, and indeed we think the video is quite effective—but it is different from (much more explicit than) the original text.

For biography and context, see interviews in: *A Search for a Postmodern Theater: Interviews with Contemporary Playwrights*, ed. John L. DiGaetani (1991), 219–28; *The Playwright's Art: Conversations with Contemporary American Dramatists*, ed. Jackson R. Bryer (1995), 182–204; and *Speaking on Stage: Interviews with Contemporary American Playwrights*, ed. Philip C. Kolin and Colby H. Kullman (1996), 332–45.

21

Making Men and Women

STEVEN DOLOFF
The Opposite Sex (p. 778)

Although this essay is more than two decades old, we find that it still works well in the classroom.

Before you begin, you might give students some help with a few references. Most of them will not know the film *Tootsie* (1982), starring Dustin Hoffman, which depicts an obnoxious, unemployed actor in New York City who becomes a better person after he disguises himself as a woman to land a job. *Gentleman's Quarterly*, with the motto "Look Sharp/Live Smart," is a magazine of style, advice, and commentary for men; as one of its promotions says, it offers "fashion, sports, women, journalism, fitness, and more for the modern man. It's about fashion. It's about style. It's about journalism. It's about guy stuff." "Mr. Hyde" is one of the characters in Robert Louis Stevenson's mystery novel, *The Strange Case of Dr. Jekyll and Mr. Hyde* (1886); the physician Jekyll is transformed into the evil figure Hyde. The Ford Foundation is a major international grant-making and funding agency, dedicated to a four-fold mission: "Strengthen democratic values, reduce poverty and injustice, promote international cooperation and advance human achievement."

This is one of those occasions when the blackboard comes in handy. We make two columns and ask students to list the activities that the women-as-men performed, and then the activities that the men-as-women performed, according to Doloff's article. Once we have the lists, we then ask the class to comment on how accurate these seem: Do the students find that this account rings true to their own experiences and speculations?

The next step we take is obvious enough: We invite the students to comment on whether such a list would be different today. Have things changed a lot, a little, or not at all since 1983?

Before we leave "The Opposite Sex," we make sure to prompt students to think about it—its strengths, its limitations—as a piece of writing. In particular we press the class to identify what, in their view, is its purpose. It is jaunty, engaging, fun to read and debate. But what, if anything, does it offer beyond that? Is the article itself a little like the results that Doloff describes—"both entertaining and annoying in its predictability?" This draws us, in turn, to remind the students that "The Opposite Sex" was published in a newspaper, as a kind of "opinion" piece.

Here are some questions for the class: Why would *The Washington Post* select for publication "The Opposite Sex" from the many submissions it receives each week? Would you have accepted it if you were in charge of the op-ed page? If it were submitted today just as it is (maybe with one or two of the references updated) would you accept it, or not? Would you conclude that it needed revision, or that it could go straight into print exactly as it stands?

GRETEL EHRLICH

About Men (p. 779)

This essay will cause readers no difficulty, but it may provoke some lively discussion, especially in states where students may know something (perhaps firsthand maybe even secondhand, or perhaps merely from movies and advertisements) about the life of a cowboy. Does Ehrlich go too far in debunking the stereotype? Does she replace the familiar strong-but-silent macho guy (from the Mexican-Spanish *macho*, "showing a strong sense of masculinity, given to aggressiveness") with a tenderhearted androgyne? (She says he is "androgynous" in her fourth paragraph. This is almost the only word in the essay that may puzzle some students, but you may also want to talk about "*macho*," which appears in her first paragraph. You might ask students how they define it. Dictionaries vary slightly, but among the traits listed are, usually, "courage, aggressiveness, and domination of women.")

Ehrlich offers plenty of generalizations; you may want to ask students (a) *if* she supports them adequately, and then, pressing a bit further, (b) *how* she supports them. They will see, when they look again at the essay, that many of her generalizations are supported, presumably, by her close observation of what is going on around her—she tells us how many hours a cowboy works, what the wage is, what a cowboy has to do when a calf is stuck in a boghole, etc.—but she also offers quotations (e.g., "one old-timer told me" in paragraph 1, "My friend Ted Hoagland wrote," in paragraph 8). In effect, then, she sometimes cites authorities—not necessarily erudite sources but people who have lived the life of a cowboy and who therefore are presumed to be trustworthy authorities on this subject.

In her fifth paragraph Ehrlich says, "So many of the men who came to the West were Southerners . . . that chivalrousness and strict codes of honor were soon thought of as western traits." In our discussion, in this manual (p. 365) of Bierce's "A Horseman in the Sky," we offer a conjecture about why a code of chivalry developed in the South.

CHARLOTTE PERKINS GILMAN
The Yellow Wallpaper (p. 782)

In this story the wife apparently is suffering from postpartum depression, and her physician-husband prescribes as a cure the things that apparently have caused her depression: isolation and inactivity. Victorian medical theory held that women—more emotional, more nervous, more fanciful than men—needed special protection if they were to combat lunacy. As Gilman tells us in her autobiography, *The Living of Charlotte Perkins Gilman* (1935), the story (published in 1892) is rooted in the author's experience: after the birth of her child, Gilman became depressed and consulted Dr. S. Weir Mitchell (physician and novelist, named in the story), who prescribed a rest cure: "Live as domestic a life as possible. Have your child with you all the time. Lie down an hour after each meal. Have but two hours intellectual life a day. And never touch pen, brush or pencil as long as you live." Gilman in fact tried this routine for a month, then took a trip to California, where she began writing and recovered nicely. Thinking about Mitchell's plan later, Gilman concluded that such a way of life would have driven her crazy.

Although the prescribed treatment in the story is not exactly Mitchell's, it does seem clear enough that the smug husband's well-intended treatment is responsible for the wife's hallucinations of a woman struggling behind the wallpaper. The narrator is mad (to this degree the story resembles some of Poe's), but she is remarkably sane compared to her well-meaning husband and the others who care for her. Elaine R. Hedges, in the afterword to the edition of *The Yellow Wallpaper* published by the Feminist Press (1973), comments on the narrator:

> At the end of the story the narrator both does and does not identify with the creeping women who surround her in her hallucinations. The women creep through the arbors and lanes along the roads outside the house. Women must creep. The narrator knows this. She has fought as best she could against creeping. In her perceptivity and in her resistance lie her heroism (or heroineism). But at the end of the story, on her last day in the house, as she peels off yards and yards of wallpaper and creeps around the floor, she has been defeated. She is totally mad. But in her mad sane way she has seen the situation of women for what it is. (p. 53)

Judith Fetterley offers a thoughtful interpretation of Gilman's story in "Reading about Reading" in *Gender and Reading: Essays on Readers, Texts, and Contexts*, edited by Elizabeth A. Flynn and Patrocinio P. Schwieckart (1986), pp. 147–164. Here (in direct quotation) are some of Fetterley's points, but the entire essay should be consulted:

> Forced to read men's texts [i.e., to interpret experience in the way men do], women are forced to become characters in those texts. And since the stories men tell assert as fact what women know to be fiction, not only do women

lose the power that comes from authoring: more significantly, they are forced to deny their own reality and to commit in effect a kind of psychic suicide. (p. 159)

The nameless narrator of Gilman's story has two choices. She can accept her husband's definition of reality [that his version is sane and that her version is mad] . . . or she can refuse to read his text, refuse to become a character in it, and insist on writing her own, behavior for which John will define and treat her as mad. (p. 160)

Despite the narrator's final claim that she has, like the women in the paper, "got out," she does not in fact escape the patriarchal text. Her choice of literal madness may be as good as or better than the "sanity" prescribed for her by John, but in going mad she fulfills his script and becomes a character in his text. Still, going mad gives the narrator temporary sanity. It enables her to articulate her perception of reality and, in particular, to cut through the fiction of John's love. (p. 163)

The narrator's solution finally validates John's fiction. In his text, female madness results from work that engages the mind and will; from the recognition and expression of feelings, and particularly of anger; in a word, from the existence of a subjectivity capable of generating a different version of reality from his own. (pp. 164–165)

More insidious still, through her madness the narrator does not simply become the character John already imagines her to be as part of his definition of feminine nature; she becomes a version of John himself. Mad, the narrator is manipulative, secretive, dishonest; she learns to lie, obscure, and distort. (p. 164)

This desire to duplicate John's text but with the roles reversed determines the narrator's choice of an ending. Wishing to drive John mad, she selects a denouement that will reduce him to a woman seized by a hysterical fainting fit. Temporary success, however, exacts an enormous price, for when John recovers from his faint he will put her in a prison from which there will be no escape. (p. 164)

Of the many feminist readings of the story, perhaps the most widely known is that of Sandra M. Gilbert and Susan Gubar, *The Madwoman in the Attic* (1979). For Gubar and Gilbert, the wallpaper represents "the oppressive structures of the society in which [the narrator] finds herself" (p. 90). The figure behind the wallpaper is the narrator's double, trying to break through. But Jeanette King and Pam Morris, in "On Not Reading Between the Lines: Models of Reading in 'The Yellow Wallpaper,'" *Studies in Short Fiction* 26 (1989): 23–32, raise questions about this interpretation. Their essay, influenced by Lacan, is not easy reading (one finds such terms as "decentered subject," "signified and signifier," "a polysemic potential"), but they present some impressive evidence against the widespread view that the woman behind the paper is "the essential inner psyche which has been trapped by repressive social structures" (p. 25). First, they argue that if the woman indeed is the essential inner psyche, "the breaking free, even if only in the hallucination of madness, ought surely to indicate a more positive movement than the chilling conclusion of the tale suggests" (p. 25). They point out that the wallpaper is not described in terms of "a controlling order"; rather, the narrator says it has "sprawling flamboyant patterns," and it resembles "great slanting waves" that "plunge off at outrageous angles . . . in unheard-of contradictions." For King and Morris, the wallpaper's "energy and fertility are anarchic and lawless, at times aggressive. It displays, that is, an assertive creativity and originality that have no place in the wifely ideal constructed by patriarchal ideology" (p. 29). They therefore interpret it not as a metaphor of a repressive society but as a metaphor of the "forbidden self" (p. 29), "the repressed other" (p. 30). The narrator, seeking to comply with the male ideals, is thus threatened by the wallpaper, and her "attempts to tear down this obdurate wallpaper are not intended . . . to free her from male repression . . . but to eliminate the rebellious self which is preventing her from achieving ego-ideal" (p. 30). That is, she wishes to remove the paper (the image of her secret self, which she strives to repress) in order to gain John's approval. "When the woman behind the paper 'gets out,' therefore, this is an image not of liberation but of the victory of the social idea." We get a "grotesque, shameful caricature of female helplessness and submissiveness—a creeping woman." Nevertheless, King and Morris argue, the narrator does indeed have "a desperate triumph . . . : she crawls over her husband" (p. 31).

King and Morris assume that "Jane" (mentioned only near the end of the story) is the narrator, but, like most earlier critics, they do not greatly concern themselves with arguing this point. William Veeder, in "Who Is Jane?," *Arizona Quarterly* 44 (1988): 41–79, does argue the point at length. He writes, "By defining a context beyond Poesque horror and clinical case-study, Kolodny, Hedges, and others have convincingly described the heroine's confrontation with patriarchy. What remains to be examined is another source of the heroine's victimization. Herself" (p. 41). Veeder discusses Gilman's difficult childhood (an absent father and a "strict and anxious mother") and, drawing on Freud and Melanie Klein, argues that the story is not only about a repressive marriage but also about "the traumas wrought by inadequate nurturing in childhood" (p. 71). To escape bondage to men, "Jane moves not forward to the egalitarian utopia of *Herland* but back into the repressive serenity of the maternal womb" (p. 67).

We've had good luck recently with a paper assignment keyed to the final paragraphs of Gilman's story. It takes as its point of departure an observation by Edith Wharton, a contemporary of Gilman's and the author of *The House of Mirth* (1905) and *The Age of Innocence* (1920), who said that in structuring her novels she sought to "make my last page latent in my first."

Wharton wanted her readers, after they had completed the final page, to be able to return to the first chapter and see the sources for the conclusion there: the novel would have a logic that would be developed throughout the story, which would give the whole work its effectiveness and coherence. Ask the class to apply Wharton's statement to the conclusion of "The Yellow Wallpaper" where the narrator "creeps" over her husband. Is Gilman's last page "latent in her first?"

Topic for Critical Thinking and Writing

In the next-to-last paragraph the narrator says, "I've got out at last." What does she mean, and in what way (if any) does it make sense?

RICHARD WRIGHT
The Man Who Was Almost a Man (p. 793)

There is no shortage of initiation stories, especially those about young males, but Wright's story is especially interesting because the ending is relatively ambiguous. Is the ambiguity, one wonders, rooted in the idea that in a world dominated by whites an African American cannot (or could not, in Wright's day) achieve the sort of full development that a white can achieve? (Conceivably the title implies that in white America a black man is kept from fully achieving manhood.)

In the early part of the story Dave is very much a boy, not a man: his pay goes to his mother, and he feels, rightly, that everyone treats him "as though he were a little boy." In order to establish himself as an adult, he thinks, he needs a gun. (The limited omniscient point of view helps us to share his feelings, but it also lets us have a larger view than Dave himself has.) The connection between adulthood and a gun is made explicit by Joe, the merchant, who says, "You ain't nothing but a boy. You don't need a gun."

His parents, unsurprisingly, treat Dave like a child, and of course he *is* immature. Just before he fires the pistol, he speaks to the mule, telling her not to "acka fool now," but it is Dave who acts the fool, firing the gun, not recognizing what has happened to the mule, chasing the mule, trying to plug the bullet hole with handfuls of earth, and inventing a preposterous story to account for the mule's death. When his fabrication is exposed, the entire crowd laughs, a point that Wright stresses by adding that at night Dave "remembered how they had laughed." Firing the gun successfully thus becomes an urgent matter. He retrieves the gun, fires it until it is empty, and then, seeing Jim Hawkins' "big white house," he wishes he had just one more bullet:

> Lawd, ef Ah had just one mo bullet, Ah'd taka shot at tha house. Ah'd like t scare ol man Hawkins jusa little. . . . Jusa enough t let im know Dave Saunders is a man.

This bit of dialogue is especially interesting for two more or less contradictory reasons. First, although we sympathize with Dave when we hear him swagger, we also smile at a boy who is talking big; it's all very well for him to say that if he had one bullet left he would "scare old man Hawkins," but he is safe in saying this because he knows that he does not have one bullet left. If in fact he had more ammunition, he might say no such thing. Second, not until this point do we learn Dave's full name: "Jusa enough t let im know Dave Saunders is a man."' In short, this *is* the point when Dave achieves an adult identity; he is not just "Dave" the boy, but "Dave Saunders," a young man with a last name as well as a first name.

The end of the story is similarly ambiguous. Viewed one way, Dave is fleeing from society, even from his own family; viewed another way, Dave is heading for a new beginning, "somewhere where he could be a man. . . ." In fact, irony is at the heart of the story: Dave thinks that a gun will make him a man, and in a way it does, but not in the way that he anticipates. It causes him to incur a man-sized debt, and it causes him to make a break with his home.

John E. Loftis, in *Studies in Short Fiction* 23 (1986): 437–442, sees the story as "Richard Wright's parody of the hunt tradition," i.e., a parody of stories of white youths who achieve maturity through the hunt. Loftis argues that "In American literature . . . the hunt is a European and thus white tradition, and its heroic and mythic dimensions hardly seem available to black American writers. . . ." In Wright's hands, however, "the hunt can embody the hero's maturation at the same time that its parodic implications dramatize the disparity between black and white possibilities of growth and development in American society" (p. 437).

Toward the end of his essay Loftis makes another point that you may want to discuss in class. He says,

> Jenny is short for Jennifer which derives from Guinevere which in turn derives from the Welsch "gwen," white. Dave's society is one dominated by whites who refuse to allow any black male to truly mature, and Dave must symbolically kill this domination before he is free to grow up. . . . Through this parody [of stories of white youths who achieve maturity via a hunt] Wright shapes a convincing and moving account of the black experience of growing up in the rural South in the second quarter of the twentieth century. (p. 442)

How much weight ought a reader to put on the mule's name? After being educated by Loftis, do we feel that the name Jenny is a subtle touch, a sign of Wright's concern for details, or do we feel that Loftis is pressing too hard? Before we can find the name significant must we first be assured that Wright knew about the Welsh meaning? Or do we agree with Robert Frost, who once said that the author is entitled to the credit for anything good that the reader finds in the work?

Wright's reputation has fallen in recent years, in part because of the rise to prominence of Toni Morrison, Alice Walker, and other important African-American women writers. In the view of feminist critics, Wright portrays women in a hostile, demeaning, and cruel fashion, and hence he is less relevant for contemporary readers than are Morrison and other women authors. Furthermore, Wright, it is claimed, fails to value properly the rich resources of the African-American folk and oral traditions that his contemporary Zora Neale Hurston and her modern-day successors draw upon so richly.

There is some truth to this charge. But we still think that Wright is a tremendously powerful writer, in his novels and stories and in his autobiographies as well. *Native Son* (1940) remains one of the landmarks of modern American and African-American literature, and students, we find, are quickly caught up in its searing portrait of Wright's angry, confused, murderous protagonist Bigger Thomas. The stories in *Uncle Tom's Children* (1938) are also gripping, as is the first volume of Wright's autobiography, *Black Boy* (1945).

There is a very good biography by Michel Fabre (1973) and a first-rate collection of commentaries: *Critical Essays on Richard Wright,* ed. Yoshinobu Hakutani (1982). Students might also find stimulating the discussions of Wright's legacy in James Baldwin, *Notes of a Native Son* (1955); Irving Howe, *A World More Attractive* (1963); and Ralph Ellison, in both *Shadow and Act* (1964) and *Going to the Territory* (1986).

GLORIA NAYLOR
The Two (p. 802)

Although instructors will be interested in matters of technique—especially the metaphors of the quilt and of the smell, and the shift in point of view from (at the start) the outside view of the two women to (midway) the inside view of Lorraine and Theresa—discussion in class is likely to center on the characterization of "the two" (we don't learn even their names until we have read about one-third of the story), their relationship to each other, and society's relationship to them.

The differences between the two women are clear enough—Lorraine is shy, soft, and in need of the approval of the community; Theresa is tougher (but "the strain of fighting alone was beginning to show")—but both are at first lumped together as "nice girls," and this point is worth discussing in class. Why, at first, does the community find them acceptable? Because they don't play loud music, they don't have drunken friends, and—the next most important point—they do not encourage other women's husbands to hang around, that is, they are not a threat to the married women. But it is precisely this "friendly indifference to the men on the street" that (when its source is detected) becomes "an insult to the [neighborhood] women."

By the way, we have fairly often encountered in the popular press articles with such titles as "Why Are Gay Men Feared?" (the usual answer is that men insecure about their own heterosexuality feel threatened by gay men, who, the theory goes, in effect tell the supposed straight men that maybe they aren't really so straight), but we don't recall ever encountering an article on the response of heterosexual women to lesbians. Perhaps some students will want to confirm or dispute

Naylor's view of why the straight community resents "the two." As we understand the story, Naylor is suggesting that heterosexual women welcome other women who are not threats to their relationships with men but then reject lesbians (who fit this category) because lesbians, by virtue of their indifference to or independence from males, seem to be a criticism of heterosexuality. (Can we go so far as to say that lesbians, in this view, upset straight women because lesbians make other women aware of their need for men?)

There are two stories in this story, the story of the relationship between the community and "the two," and the story of the relationship between Lorraine and Theresa. This second story, we take it, is about two women who (like the members of most straight couples) differ considerably in personality and who have their problems but who are tied to each other by deep affection. The last we hear in the story is a bit of good-natured bickering that reveals Lorraine is doing her best to please Theresa. Lorraine, who had tried to talk Theresa into avoiding fattening foods, is preparing a (fattening) gravy for the chicken, and Theresa is pretending to disapprove.

"The Two" is included in Naylor's first and, we think, her best book, *The Women of Brewster Place* (1982). But students might be directed to her later novels: *Linden Hills* (1985); *Mama Day* (1988), which blends African-American folklore with stories derived from Shakespeare's *The Tempest;* and *Bailey's Cafe* (1992).

For background and context: Gloria Naylor and Toni Morrison, "A Conversation," *Southern Review* 21 (July 1985): 567–593; Gloria Naylor, "Love and Sex in the Afro-American Novel," *Yale Review* 78 (Autumn 1988): 19–31; and Barbara Christian, "Gloria Naylor's Geography: Community, Class, and Patriarchy in *The Women of Brewster Place* and *Linden Hills*," in *Reading Black, Reading Feminist*, ed. Henry Louis Gates Jr. (1990), pp. 348–373.

ALICE MUNRO
Boys and Girls (p. 808)

A good way to begin the discussion of this story is to have a student read the first paragraph aloud, and then ask if the sentences about the calendar have any relevance to the rest of the story. Of course this passage would be justified if it did no more than give a glimpse of the sort of decorations that might be found on a Canadian fox farm, and one doesn't want to press too hard for a deep meaning, but surely the picture of "plumed adventurers" (male, naturally) who use "savages" as pack animals introduces, however faintly, a political note that can be connected with the treatment of distinctions between the sexes.

This is not to say that the story suggests that women are comparable to the Indians who bend their backs in service to the whites. The wife works hard, but so does the husband. And the early part of the story indicates that the female narrator, when a child, eagerly engaged in what the mother must have thought was "man's work." Certainly the girl, feeling quite superior to her little brother, had no sense that she was oppressed. She came to learn, however, that she must "become" a girl. If we hear a note of protest in this statement that society expects us to assume certain roles, the story nevertheless seems also to suggest that females are, by nature rather than by nurture, mentally or emotionally different from males. Despite the narrator's early enthusiasm for her father's work, and despite her sense of superiority to her brother (she can handle the wheelbarrow used for watering the foxes, whereas Laird, carrying a "little cream and green gardening can," can only play at watering), she is more shaken by the killing of Mack than she will admit. "My legs were a little shaky," she says, and later she adds that she "felt a little ashamed," but for the most part she deals with her response by talking about another episode, the time when she endangered Laird's life, and afterwards felt "the sadness of unexorcised guilt." Of course, we may think that anyone—male or female—might feel shaky and guilty upon first witnessing the death of a harmless animal, but in fact Laird does not seem even mildly disturbed. Rather, after witnessing the shooting of Mack, Laird is "remote, concentrating."

The guilt engendered by watching Mack die prompts the narrator to let Flora escape. (A question: If the first horse killed had been a female, would the narrator have let the second horse, a male, escape? One answer: The story is right as it is. Don't monkey with it. If the horses were reversed, the story would be less coherent.) The narrator is irretrievably female. (Notice too the passage recounted after the episode with Flora, about the narrator's attempt to prettify her part of the bedroom and, in the same paragraph, the discussion of her new fantasies, in which she no longer performs heroic rescues but is now the person rescued and is wondering about her hairstyle and her dress.) Having let Flora escape, she of course has no desire to join in the chase, but Laird does, and when he returns, daubed in blood (this passage, however realistic, seems almost a parody of Hemingway and Faulkner on rituals of initiation), he is quite casual about what happened: "'We shot old Flora,' he said, 'and cut her up in fifty pieces.'" Laird, no longer his sister's partner but now firmly aligned with the men, soon betrays the narrator, reducing her to tears. Her father means well in absolving her ("She's only a girl"), but, as the narrator says, the words not only absolve but also "dismiss" her. On the other hand, the narrator recognizes that the father's words may be "true."

In teaching this story, one might get around to making the point that a work of literature doesn't "prove" anything. *Hamlet* doesn't prove that ghosts exist, or that one should not delay, or that revenge is morally acceptable. Similarly, Munro's story doesn't prove that girls are by nature more sensitive to the killing of a horse than boys are. We won't attempt here (or anywhere) to say what a work of fiction does do, but the point is worth discussing—probably early in the course and again near the end, after students have read a fair amount of literature.

Among Munro's books, we remain partial to her first two collections of stories: *Dance of the Happy Shades* (1968) and *Lives of Girls and Women* (1971). But the best point of departure for students is her volume *Selected Stories* (1996). For a concise survey: E. D. Blodgett, *Alice Munro* (1988).

Anonymous Nursery Rhyme
What Are Little Boys Made Of (p. 818)

Fairy tales have come in for a good deal of criticism, on various grounds: they often show women as passive and men as active (Sleeping Beauty is awakened by the kiss of Prince Charming); they depict old women as ugly and evil (witches); they contain terrifying elements (people fall into boiling cauldrons). To the best of our knowledge, nursery rhymes have not come in for comparable criticism—perhaps because the implications about gender are less evident (there is a good deal of rhyming nonsense in nursery rhymes), perhaps because nursery rhymes are regarded as less important than fairy tales, or (more or less the opposite of the last conjecture) perhaps because nursery rhymes are treasured and few if any of us want to debunk the material that we loved in our earliest years.

"*What Are Little Boys Made Of?*" We give the version that we have known since childhood, but when we decided to print the verses we checked Iona and Peter Opie, *The Oxford Dictionary of Nursery Rhymes* (1997), and we were surprised to find in line 3 not "Snips and snails" but "Frogs and snails." The Opies report, however, that our version is at least as old as 1820.

The additional stanzas that we give in our second topic for discussion were reported in 1844, but to the best of our knowledge they are not widely known. Why? Is it that whereas the better known lines are purely imaginative—boys are *not* made of "snips and snails / And puppy dogs' tails" and girls are *not* made of "sugar and spice"—the less well known lines do have (or can have) a literal truth; young men can sigh and leer, and young women can wear ribbons and laces and can have pretty faces. Is it possible that these lines about young men and young women are less well known because they are less metaphoric?

Anonymous
Higamus, Hogamus (p. 818)

We don't want to make a big deal of these four lines (or they are sometimes printed as two lines), but we do find them amusing. Nonsense often is charming (here "hogamus higamus / higamus hogamus"), a charm increased if the hearer recognizes a parody of Latin conjugations ("amo, amas, amat, amamus, amatis, amant") and declensions ("hic, haec, hoc"). Schoolchildren who laboriously learn Latin grammar are delighted to parody it—perhaps as a childish way of mocking the teachers who impose such tasks. Further, polysyllabic rhymes often are comic—especially when, as here, one of a pair of rhyming words is nonsense. But under all the fun is an assertion that one has to seriously. Of course it is not invariably true, but it probably strikes many people as largely true. (See not only the following poem by Dorothy Parker but especially the comment by a sociologist that we quote in the second question following Parker's verse.)

In our first question in the text we ask whether it makes any difference if the couplets are reversed. We think there is a slight difference, or, rather, two slight differences. First of all, anyone who had a year of Latin is familiar with the declension that runs "hic, haec, hoc," which is better echoed (parodied) in "higamus hogamus" than in "hogamus higamus." But perhaps more important, we think the joke—sad though it may be, if it is true—is sharper in the movement from monogamy to polygamy than the other way around. That is, the jingle ends with a bit of locker-room humor: women are monogamous, but men (nudge, nudge, wink, wink) are polygamous.

So far as the second question in the text goes, we strongly prefer the following version: "Men are from Mars, women from Venus." The second and third versions that we give seem needlessly wordy—the second "are" slows the thing down. But suppose we compare "Men are from Mars, women from Venus" with "Women are from Venus, men from Mars." One might argue that this version has the advantage of ending emphatically: the second clause uses alliteration, and it uses shorter words. And yet, to our ears this version is less effective than "Men are from Mars, women from Venus," which might be thought to end weakly, with an unstressed syllable. Why? Perhaps after the initial onslaught of the original ("Men are from Mars"), a reader welcomes the more bouncy or tripping "women from Venus."

DOROTHY PARKER
General Review of the Sex Situation (p. 819)

The title suggests an academic treatise, so that's the first joke. The second joke perhaps is that the poem is so short; the "general review" of an immense topic is reduced to eight end-stopped lines, i.e., the topic is treated in a tiny space, in a no-nonsense manner, and with the implication that there is no more to be said. Further, this authoritative characterization of the presumably inevitable differences between the two sexes—no talk about "the construction of gender" here—concludes with the suggestion that *of course* things are a mess, but what can we expect?

On Parker: Arthur F. Kinney, *Dorothy Parker* (1978). See also *The Collected Dorothy Parker* (1973) and *The Portable Dorothy Parker,* ed. Brendan Gill (rev. ed., 1973).

RITA DOVE
Daystar (p. 820)

The poem comes from Dove's Pulitzer-Prize book *Thomas and Beulah* (1986), which contains sequences of poems about African Americans who migrated from the South to the North.

In thinking about a poem, one can hardly go wrong in paying attention to the title. Here, why "Daystar"? "Daystar" can refer either to a planet—especially Venus—visible in the eastern sky before sunrise, or to the sun. Both meanings are probably relevant here. The speaker's brief period of escape from (at one extreme) the children's diapers and dolls and (at the other) Thomas's sexual demands are perhaps like the brief (and marvelous) appearance of a planet at a time when one scarcely expects to see a heavenly body; and this moment of escape—a moment of wonderful independence—is perhaps also like the sun, which stands in splendid isolation, self-illuminating. Sometimes, as she sits "behind the garage," she is closely connected to the visible world around her (the cricket, the maple leaf), but sometimes, with her eyes closed, she perceives only her self. (The mention, in the last line of the poem, of "the middle of the day" perhaps indicates that the chief meaning of "daystar" here is the sun, but we see no reason to rule out the suggestion of the other meaning.)

ROBERT HAYDEN
Those Winter Sundays (p. 821)

Students can learn something about writing by thinking about the length of the four sentences that constitute this poem. The first stanza consists of a fairly long sentence (four and a half lines) and a short one (half a line, completing the fifth line of the poem). The brevity of that second sentence reinforces the content—that no one thought about the father—and the brevity also, of course, adds emphasis by virtue of its contrast with the leisurely material that precedes it. Similarly, the fourth sentence, much shorter than the third, adds emphasis, an emphasis made more emphatic by the repetition of "What did I know?"

Next a confession: we thought about glossing "offices" in the last line, for students will almost surely misinterpret the word, thinking that it refers to places where white-collar workers do their tasks. But we couldn't come up with a concise gloss that would convey the sense of ceremonious and loving performance of benefits. And it may be just as well to spend some class time on this important word, because the thing as well as the word may be unfamiliar to many students. After the word has been discussed, the poem may be read as a splendid illustration of an "office." Like the father in the poem, who drives out the cold and brings warmth (by means of love, of course, as well as coal) to an unknowing child, an "austere and lonely" writer performs an office, shaping experience for another person's use.

One may want to raise the question in class of whether the knowledge that the author was black affects the poem's meaning.

The most important books for the study of Hayden are *Collected Poems*, ed. Frederick Glaysher (1985), and *Collected Prose*, foreword by William Meredith, ed. Frederick Glaysher (1984). Students can begin with this cogent introduction: Fred M. Fetrow, *Robert Hayden* (1984). And, for more depth and detail, they can next consult John Hatcher, *From the Auroral Darkness: The Life and Poetry of Robert Hayden* (1984).

THEODORE ROETHKE
My Papa's Waltz (p. 822)

Writing of Roethke's "My Papa's Waltz" in *How Does a Poem Mean* (1975), John Ciardi says that the poem seems to lack a "fulcrum" (Ciardi's word for a "point of balance" or point at which there is a twist in the thought), but that the fulcrum "occurs after the last line." In his terminology, "The fulcrum exists outside the poem, between the enacted experience and the silence that follows it" (p. 253).

See *The Collected Poems of Theodore Roethke* (1966); *On the Poet and His Craft: Selected Prose of Theodore Roethke*, ed. Ralph J. Mills Jr. (1965); and *Straw for the Fire: From the Notebooks of Theodore Roethke, 1948–63*, ed. David Wagoner (1972). Critical studies include Karl Malkoff, *Theodore Roethke: An Introduction to the Poetry* (1966), and Rosemary Sullivan, *Theodore Roethke: The Garden Master* (1975).

SHARON OLDS
Rites of Passage (p. 823)

One of our students wrote a good paper about this poem, calling it a "poem about perspective." We liked the way he noted the difference in size between the speaker and her son and the other "short men" attending the party, and his movement from this observation to verbal details that illuminate the speaker's point of view. This student said that the speaker in fact takes two points of view—two perspectives—on the boys, seeing them as children and as small adults (i.e., the persons they will grow up to be). We think it's helpful to ask students to consider how the speaker perceives the boys, how they view themselves ("they eye each other"), and—a broader issue—how Olds means for readers to understand the lesson of the poem. What exactly is its tone? What is our own perspective on its descriptions supposed to be?

Here one can focus on Olds's title. What is a "rite of passage" and in what respect is this birthday party an example of one? Turn next to specific moments in the poem's language, as when the speaker quotes the boys' warnings: "I could beat you up" and "We could easily kill a two-year-old." Students, we have found, react very differently to these phrases. Some judge them to be comic—it's funny and familiar to hear little boys making large threats—whereas others maintain that Olds wants us to hear these words as ominous, as a sign of the hard masculine world that these "short men" will inhabit (and promote) when they get older.

The discussion of "Rites of Passage" is always lively and becomes more so as it proceeds. A student in one of our classes wondered if this is a political poem. Is Olds using this scene to assail patriarchy, a system in which boys "naturally" assume manly poses and, while still small, are already looking and sounding like "bankers" and "Generals"? It is intriguing, too, to invite students to imagine other perspectives on this same subject. Would the boy's father (note that no mention is made of him) interpret the scene differently from the mother? Is there a similar kind of typical scene at a girl's birthday party against which this one could be compared?

Responses to these questions can be keyed to the poem's final phrase: "celebrating my son's life." The word "celebrate" can be connected to the word "rites"—it has a sacred and solemn meaning, as in celebrating a marriage or a mass. More commonly, "celebrate" suggests showing joy at an event; being part of a festive, happy occasion; rejoicing in an opportunity to honor someone (i.e., celebrating a person's achievements). Does Olds want her readers to hear her final line as ironic, or, as students have sometimes told us, does she instead mean it more straightforwardly, as if she were saying, "I've made my amused, satiric points, but it's really a happy day after all, and I do love my son"? Don't neglect the word "my," however. It's one of those small words that students tend to pass by, but it's an important one. It indicates the speaker's connection to the child (he is *her* child), renewed at the end of the poem. Yet while the speaker takes responsibility for him in one sense, this is balanced against the detachment, the separation, evident in the speaker's perception that her small boy is a man in miniature, not her child as much as an adult in the making. The words in this last line are finely placed, reaching a complicated, disquieting balance.

Students might be encouraged to start with *The Matter of This World: New and Selected Poems* (1987). For critical analysis: Suzanne Matson, "Talking to Our Father: The Political and Mythical Appropriations of Adrienne Rich and Sharon Olds," *American Poetry Review* 18 (1989): 35–41, and Calvin Bedient, "Sentencing Eros," *Salmagundi* 97 (1993): 169–181.

Frank O'Hara
Homosexuality (p. 824)

We have enjoyed teaching this poem, and it has gone over well in the classroom. But we are not confident that we really understand it. It is shocking, and it is entertaining; the word play is both unnerving and wonderful to behold. But the movement of the poem is hard to figure out: Does O'Hara's poem grow into a unified whole, or does his array of details come to seem confusing, signs of inconsistency, as if the poet had examined his rich theme only partially, without the further effort to gauge and order what everything he sees and feels amounts to?

Our text is taken from O'Hara's *Collected Poems,* published in 1971, and this is an editorial point that we mention to the class because for many students nowadays "homosexuality" has a different charge of meaning than it did three decades ago. So we start our analysis of "Homosexuality" by talking about the title.

Some of our students, it must be said, believe that homosexuality is sinful; and on their course evaluations, some students have objected to studying poems like this one that they say "go against" their religious faith. For our part, we think that these literary works should be taught; if they are not, the students will fail to learn about a range of human feeling and love that, in our view, they should know about. If a student's religious faith is strong, it will not be undermined through an exposure to a poem or story about homosexuality.

Our gay and lesbian students value the opportunity to read, study, and write about these poems and stories. But for them, "homosexuality" is a dated term—indeed, it is a term that most of them associate with people who are anti-gay and anti-lesbian. These students define themselves not as homosexual but as gay or lesbian or (a term which for them has a sharper, more militant edge) "queer." (Cf. the slogan of an activist group: "We're here, we're queer, get used to it.")

When we last taught the poem, we asked the students to describe their responses to the title. The responses were interesting, ranging from "I found the title made me uncomfortable" to "I really liked the bold and direct use of the word"—which, this student said, must have seemed even more forthrightly so when the poem was first published. But looking back on the discussion, we suspect we have may erred a bit in how we set it up. The question "How do you respond?" is a good point of departure, for this and with most other poems. But we should have linked this question to another: "In the poem itself, as it unfolds, how is O'Hara using or not using the responses we have—that he knows we will likely have—to his title?"

It is important to take this step, moving from the responses of the reader to the poet, to the work that the poet has done in *making* the poem. The risk of relying too much on the responses of the students is that they may conclude, "Well, it is all subjective. When I read a poem, what matters is how I feel about it." While this is an important part of the story, it is not the entire story. You have to turn the discussion back toward the poet—what he or she does with language (the poet's medium), what he or she has created, constructed, put together. The poem is something we respond to, but it is also something that a writer has *made,* a work of art.

When you pitch the discussion in this form, you can help the students to see the value of literary analysis—there is an object that we can analyze. This does not mean that all of us will interpret this or that detail the same way, or even that we will agree on large matters. But we do have something that we can look at together, discuss, debate—organizations of language that we can inquire into, tones of voice that we can listen to carefully.

This point takes us to the first stanza, which seems to mark a point in the middle of a conversation already underway. "So we are talking . . .": the implication is that something has been said that precedes the words of the poem at hand. Imagine the situation in these terms: you and I are having a talk; we agree about some important matter; and I then say to you, as if coming from both of us: "So we have decided then. . . ."

At first this speaker's words seem confident, even defiant: "So we are taking off our masks." But this tone shifts with the phrase "are we," which turns the apparent assertion into a question. "Keeping" is a little tricky—O'Hara puts us off-balance with it. On one level it is a strong word, as in the phrase "I am keeping this for myself." But following the tentative "are we," "keeping" may have for us the echo of "keeping on," which doubles back on the phrase "taking off."

This, we suspect, is the association that O'Hara is working with, even as he sharply starts the second line with "our mouths shut." Not "keeping on," but "keeping shut." The poem, one might suggest, is moving backwards from the heady claim (or so it seemed) of its first few words. We are taking off our mask. But are we? Are we keeping our mouths shut?

What appeared at first to be a poem through which a speaker proclaims his acceptance of his and others' homosexuality—no more masks, this is who we are—now seems more cautious, hesitant. Maybe there is even some frustration, or a touch of self-directed impatience and anger: so that is what we are doing after all, just "keeping / our mouths shut"?

"As if we'd been pierced by a glance"—an intriguing phrase. One wonders whether O'Hara might have in mind here a moment in the Passion story:

> But when they came to Jesus, and saw that he was dead already, they brake not his legs. But one of the soldiers with a spear pierced his side. . . . (John 19:33–34)

Perhaps instead, or in addition, O'Hara is seeking to evoke the apprehension that T. S. Eliot's speaker expresses in "The Love Song of J. Alfred Prufrock" (1917):

> And I have known the eyes already, known them all—
> The eyes that fix you in a formulated phrase,
> And when I am formulated, sprawling on a pin,
> When I am pinned and wriggling on the wall,
> Then how should I begin
> To spit out all the butt-ends of my days and ways?
> And how should I presume? (lines 55–61)

This passage reminds us of another, perhaps more pertinent poem, Eliot's "The Love Song of St. Sebastian," which Eliot included in a notebook manuscript of poems that in 1968, three years after the poet's death, was shown as part of the Berg Collection of the New York Public Library. The manuscript has now been published, included in *T. S. Eliot: Inventions of the March Hare: Poems 1909–1917*, meticulously edited by Christopher Ricks (New York, 1996).

Sebastian was a Roman officer who served in Diocletian's Praetorian Guard; when he refused to worship idols and identified himself as a

Christian, he was shot with arrows. He did not die from these wounds—he was left for dead but was nursed back to health, again testified to his faith, and was then clubbed to death—but pictures of his martyrdom show him as a beautiful nearly nude young man bound to a tree or column and pierced with arrows. His martyrdom was a popular subject for late medieval and Renaissance artists, including Piero della Francesca, Bellini, and Mantegna. At the turn of the century, Sebastian also was a favorite saint for homosexuals. Oscar Wilde, for instance, after his release from prison in 1897, took the name Sebastian Melmoth—Sebastian for the martyr, and Melmoth from C. R. Maturin's Gothic novel *Melmoth the Wanderer* (1820). Ricks quotes from the scholar Ian Fletcher: "Homosexuals had a particular cult of Saint Sebastian. The combination of nudity and the phallic arrows was irresistible." So much was this the case that Eliot, in a letter that Ricks cites, felt obliged to say about his own aims in his poem: "There's nothing homosexual about this."

Perhaps we may seem to have gone far afield. Obviously one can bypass this possible line of literary and cultural context and can simply dwell on the word "pierced" in its own right. Pierce: to cut or pass through with or as if with a sharp instrument; stab or penetrate. But we thought the discussion grew richer to the students when we introduced this material. There was disagreement about how much of this is "in" the poem, but this phase of the conversation in class was itself stimulating, and we think it was valuable for the students.

The kind of close attention we have described here for the first stanza shows the way we proceed in our work on "Homosexuality." The class can perform some rigorous analysis on this poem, and they can also have some fun with it. Moving to the second stanza: Ask the students, "What does 'the song of an old cow' sound like?" How can such a song be "full of judgment?" "Judgment" of what kind? But not *more* judgment than. . . . The "vapors which escape one's soul when one is sick": this evocative phrase has at least two intimations of meaning. The vapors come from a soul who is sick; at the same time, the vapors "escape," suggesting that there is a release or liberation associated with them. Though we must then add: if the vapors gain release, they seem to stand in judgment, as if to pronounce a person diseased, unhealthy. Maybe O'Hara's self-lacerating point is: there are moments when we homosexuals feel weighed down by self-judgments from which we otherwise seek, and succeed, in staying free.

One can see how quick and sly and fast this poem is. We said that you can have some fun with it, noting the fine phrase "the song of an old cow," but no sooner did we make this suggestion than our commentary became darker, more disquieting. This in miniature gets at the power and the perplexity of the poem. We take delight in the keen, witty images and turns of phrase in it, and their vivid interaction, even as we strain to describe the meaning or meanings of the poem as a whole.

When you reach the end of the poem, you might ask the class, "What kind of statement is O'Hara making about homosexuality?" In a way this is not a good question; we do not usually want our students to be understanding poems as "statements." But we think that this is the right question for O'Hara's poem, and that is because the students will soon show through their differing observations that if "Homosexuality" is a statement, it is not a clear or simple one. They will see that "statement" is less helpful than other words, such as "expression" or "exploration." We know that a statement can be provocative, but so can an exploration, through the range of feelings and sensations that it can lead us to experience. Homosexuality cannot be reduced to *this* or *that* alone. If you can enable the students to perceive homosexuality as involving everything and more that the complicated range of "Homosexuality" connotes, you will perform for them an important literary and cultural service.

Frank O'Hara was not only a prolific poet, but he also was actively involved in the New York art scene, with the painters Jackson Pollock, Franz Kline, and others. He worked on the staff of the Museum of Modern Art and was a member of the editorial group for the periodical *Art News*. For a detailed account of O'Hara's tragically short life (he died in an accident on Fire Island in 1966, at the age of forty) and literary career, see Brad Gooch, *City Poet: The Life and Times of Frank O'Hara* (1993). Another useful book, which delves into O'Hara's interest in modern art, is Marjorie Perloff, *Frank O'Hara: Poet Among Painters* (1977).

TESS GALLAGHER
I Stop Writing the Poem (p. 825)

Here is how we get acquainted with a poem: we take in the title, pause for a breath, and then turn to the opening line where, we assume, the poem itself will begin. Tess Gallagher knows this, and here she chooses to work against our usual practice. We read her title, pause (one hears a period after "Poem"), and then discover that the first four words of line 1 are a continuation of the title: "I stop writing the poem to fold the clothes." The title refers to a decisive action—"I stop"—only to undo our own act of stopping as the first line opens up a sentence that seemed closed.

What kind of poem is this? For a time it may strike us as a protest poem: this woman writer cannot focus on her literary work because she is obliged to take care of domestic chores, including the folding of her husband's (or lover's) shirts. But is this really a protest poem? Line 5 might have led to a line like this:

Line 5:   Nothing can stop

Line 6:   My hurt, pain, anger, etc.

But line 5 leads instead to "our tenderness," which is puzzling. One is unsure how to hear these words. Could Gallagher mean them ironically, bitterly? Or maybe the point is that the woman speaker is trying to convince herself that since she and her husband love one another, she should not (and does not) object to taking care of his shirts and momentarily losing contact with her poetry-writing. Perhaps. But we ourselves hear "our tenderness," in its plain, direct statement, as an authentic witness to the woman's feelings and to her perception of her husband's feelings about her. Gallagher places the period after "tenderness," in the middle of the line, so that we must linger over the word, absorbing it before we can move on. "Tender": delicate or gentle, as in the tender touch of a hand; easily moved to sympathy or compassion; kind, as in a tender heart; affectionate.

At this point we ask the students: What would be the meaning of the poem if it ended at lines 6–7 ("I'll get back / to the poem.")? How would the speaker thus have characterized herself and her relationships to the man in her life and to her poetry and domestic work? We then ask the same question about our response if the poem had ended with lines 7–8 ("I'll get back to being / a woman.").

Through these questions, you can help the students to understand how Gallagher extends, and deepens, the psychological portrait that she draws of her woman-speaker. You can then ask a version of the same question about the larger unit from the middle of line 8 to line 12, with which the poem concludes. There are only two adjectives in this poem, so consider both of them—and their interconnection—carefully. The speaker refers to the shirt but then immediately states more precisely that it is a "giant" shirt. It is extraordinary, superhuman, of great size and importance—and hence it stands in stark contrast to the smallness of the girl whom we hear about in line 10.

Encourage the students to tell you as clearly as they can how they "hear" the tone of this poem. As we said a moment ago, it seems that it could, or should, be angry and resentful, or at least troubled and pained. But are these feelings in the tone? Possibly Gallagher's aim is in fact *not* to write such a poem, of which there have been many since the surge of feminist poetry in the 1960s; she may indeed be working against our expectation that this will, or should, be such a poem—that the elements of a situation like this one inevitably mean that the woman will feel indignant at being separated from the creative labor (writing poems) that she most cares about. But where is the indignation in this case? It does not appear to be here, unless—ask the students—it is intimated just beneath the surface of the closely controlled phrasing.

Is Gallagher dramatizing a point of view on the situation she describes, or, instead, is she concerning herself with the bare bones of the situation itself—and thus leaving it to us to articulate our own point of view, our sense of what this incident means? It is an incident that happens in the present (e.g., "I bring"), but that looks to the future (e.g., "I'll get back"), and yet that closes with a backward glance toward the small girl and her mother. Perhaps to us it is regrettable that the speaker must stop writing the poem—folding clothes interferes with this literary work. But we should then take note that Gallagher's speaker has nonetheless composed a poem: she has written—she has completed—a poem about the writing of a poem she was not able to complete. She copes well with the problem she faces.

Gallagher is an interesting if uneven poet; her best volume is *Amplitude: New and Selected Poems* (1987). She is also the author of *Concert of Tenses:*

Essays on Poetry (1986) and *The Lover of Horses and Other Stories* (1992). Gallagher was married to the poet and short-story writer Raymond Carver; a number of poems to and about him are included in *Willingly* (1984).

JULIA ALVAREZ
Woman's Work (p. 826)

When we read line 1 for the first time, we thought "Woman's Work" would be a protest poem in which Alvarez argued that the domestic work that many women have performed (and still perform) is, in truth, a form of art, and "high art" at that. But when we moved to line 2, we realized that line 1 comes not from the poet herself but from another woman, who is, we later learn, the speaker's mother. The mother's question is really a challenge to her daughter, and it is a challenge that the mother backs up through her own physical work—the first detail we hear about her is her scrubbing of the bathroom tiles. Not wash, but *scrub,* which means to remove dirt or grime by rubbing *hard* with a brush or cloth. A detail like this tells us something about the mother—who she is, what she's like, how she affects others.

Line 3 is a bit of a puzzle. It seems to be part of the challenge that the mother issues. But these are not words we can easily imagine that this mother would speak. They strike us instead as the poet's words, as she expresses in her own terms the injunction that the mother gives. But what exactly does the line mean? Part of its interest, and elusiveness, is the result of the sudden shift from inner to outer. At one moment the emphasis falls on the scrubbing of the tile, keeping house; and at the next the emphasis is on the heart. Alvarez, it seems, is suggesting that caring for the house is as important—at least in the mother's view—as caring for one's deepest thoughts and feelings.

Like many of us when we were young, the speaker feels dismayed by her chores: she must clean the house with her mother while her friends have fun outside. The touch of humor here is her observation that if keeping house is a high art, it is also a difficult art—difficult to practice when pleasures beckon.

For students, one of the sources of interest in the poem is the nature of the speaker's relationship to her mother. You can focus this issue by asking them to comment on line 9: "She kept me prisoner in her housebound heart." Does this line affect us as a piece of resigned wit?—the speaker, stuck indoors, feels like a prisoner. Or is this line a sharper complaint?—the speaker judges that her life is rigidly confined by the rules that the mother has laid down. These readings are both possible, though we also notice that it is the mother's heart that is "housebound": her feelings too have become restricted by the round of domestic duties she undertakes.

The heart/house imagery becomes even more forcefully present in the next-to-last stanza. Ask the students if they hear bitterness in the speaker's reference to herself as her mother's "masterpiece." We think that bitterness, anger, regret are there, but perhaps also some humor, even self-mockery. That is quite a series of verbs in line 14; the poet Alvarez must have enjoyed bringing these verbs together, and thus one wonders whether "masterpiece" has the edge we might have thought for a flash that it possessed.

When you work with students on this or any other poem, you can gain a great deal, and do them a very useful service, if you spur them repeatedly to consider and explore the meanings of words. This point is displayed well in the final stanza, which begins with the speaker's outcry: "I did not want to be her counterpart!" "Counterpart" means:

1. a person or thing closely resembling another, esp. in function
2. a copy or duplicate, as of a legal document
3. one of two parts that fit, complete, or complement one another

The speaker did not want to be a copy or duplicate of her mother: she had in view a different kind of life for herself. But the discovery she makes is that she can be a counterpart in a different sense—not a copy of her mother, but a complement to her mother. Her mother performed one type of work—and for her it was an art. The poet-speaker in turn, taking her mother's words to heart, is an artist as well, tending to the poems she writes with the same vigor and dedication that her mother had demonstrated in her actions.

MARGE PIERCY
Barbie Doll (p. 827)

The title alerts us to the world of childhood, so we are not surprised in the first line by "This girlchild" (like "This little pig") or by "pee-pee" in the second line. The stanza ends with the voice of a jeering child. The second stanza drops the kid-talk, adopting in its place the language of social science. We have not, then, made much progress; the "girlchild" who in the first stanza is treated like a Barbie doll is in the second treated like a healthy specimen, a statistic. The third stanza sounds more intimate, but she is still an object, not a person, and by the end of this stanza, there is a painful explosion. The two preceding stanzas each ended with a voice different from the voice that spoke the earlier lines of the stanza (in line 6, "You have a great big nose and fat legs," we hear a jeering child, and in line 11, "Everyone saw a fat nose on thick legs," we hear an adolescent imagining how others see her), but the third stanza ends with something of the flatly stated violence of a fairy tale: "So she cut off her nose and her legs / and offered them up." In the fourth and final stanza she is again (or better, still) a doll, lifeless and pretty.

In recent years, in addition to white Barbies there have been African-American, Hispanic and Asian Barbies, but until the fall of 1990 the TV and print ads showed only the fair-skinned, blue-eyed version. For additional information about Barbie, see Sydney Ladensohn Stern and Ted Schoenhaus, *Toyland: The High-Stakes Game of the Toy Industry* (1990), and M. G. Lord,

Forever Barbie (1994). Barbie's wardrobe has changed from flight attendant to astronaut, and from garden-party outfits to workout attire. She has a dress-for-success outfit and a briefcase—but they are pink.

We think that Piercy's best books of poetry are *Circles on the Water: Selected Poems* (1982) and *Available Light* (1988). She explores some of the same feminist and political themes in her utopian novel *Woman on the Edge of Time* (1976).

HENRIK IBSEN
A Doll's House (p. 828)

First, it should be mentioned that the title of the play does *not* mean that Nora is the only doll, for the toy house is not merely Nora's; Torvald, as well as Nora, inhabits this unreal world, for Torvald—so concerned with appearing proper in the eyes of the world—can hardly be said to have achieved a mature personality.

A Doll's House (1879) today seems more "relevant" than it has seemed in decades, and yet one can put too much emphasis on its importance as a critique of male chauvinism. Although the old view that Ibsen's best-known plays are "problem plays" about remediable social problems rather than about more universal matters is still occasionally heard, Ibsen himself spoke against it. In 1898, for example, he said, "I must disclaim the honor of having consciously worked for women's rights. I am not even quite sure what women's rights really are. To me it has been a question of human rights" (quoted in Michael Meyer, *Ibsen* [1967], 2:297). By now it seems pretty clear that *A Doll's House*, in Robert Martin Adams's words in *Hudson Review* 10 (Autumn 1957), "represents a woman imbued with the idea of becoming a person, but it proposes nothing categorical about women becoming people; in fact, its real theme has nothing to do with the sexes. It is the irrepressible conflict of two different personalities which have founded themselves on two radically different estimates of realty." Or, as Eric Bentley puts it in *In Search of Theater* (p. 350 in the 1953 Vintage edition), "Ibsen pushes his investigation toward a further and even deeper subject [than that of a woman's place in a man's world], the tyranny of one human being over another, in this respect the play would be just as valid were Torvald the wife and Nora the husband."

Michael Meyer's biography, *Ibsen,* is good on the background (Ibsen knew a woman who forged a note to get money to aid her husband, who denounced and abandoned her when he learned of the deed), but surprisingly little has been written on the dramaturgy of the play. Notable exceptions are John Northam, "Ibsen's Dramatic Method," an essay by Northam printed in *Ibsen* (1965), ed. Rolf Fjelde (in the Twentieth Century Views series), and Elizabeth Hardwick's chapter on the play in her *Seduction and Betrayal* (2001). Northam calls attention to the symbolic use of properties (e.g., the Christmas tree in Act I, a symbol of a secure, happy family, is in the center of the room, but in Act II, when Nora's world has begun to crumble, it is in a corner, bedraggled, and with burnt-out candles), costume (e.g., Nora's Italian costume is suggestive of pretense and is removed near the end of the play; the black shawl, symbolic of death, becomes—when worn at the end with ordinary clothes—an indication of her melancholy, lonely life), and gestures (e.g., blowing out the candles, suggesting defeat; the wild dance; the final slamming of the door).

For a collection of useful essays on the play, see *Approaches to Teaching Ibsen's "A Doll's House* (1985)," ed. Yvonne Shafer. Also of interest is Austin E. Quigley's discussion in *Modern Drama* 27 (1984): 584–605, reprinted with small changes in his *The Modern Stage and Other Worlds* (1985). Dorothea Krook, in *Elements of Tragedy* (1969), treats the play as a tragedy. She sets forth what she takes to be the four universal elements of the genre (the act of shame or horror, consequent intense suffering, then an increase in knowledge, and finally a reaffirmation of the value of life) and suggests that these appear in *A Doll's House*—the shameful condition being "the marriage relationship which creates Nora's doll's house's situation." Krook calls attention, too, to the "tragic irony" of Torvald's comments on Krogstad's immorality (he claims it poisons a household) and to Nora's terror, which, Krook says, "evokes the authentic Aristotelian pity."

One can even go a little further than Krook goes and make some connection between *A Doll's House* and *Oedipus the King*. Nora, during her years as a housewife, like Oedipus during his kingship, *thought* that she was happy but finds out that she really wasn't, and at the end of the play she goes out (self-banished), leaving her children, to face an uncertain but surely difficult future. Still, although the play can be discussed as a tragedy and cannot be reduced to a "problem play," like many of Ibsen's other plays it stimulates a discussion of the questions, "What ought to be done?" and "What happened next?" Hermann J. Weigand, in *The Modern Ibsen* (1925), offered conjectures about Nora's future actions, saying,

> But personally I am convinced that after putting Torvald through a sufficiently protracted ordeal of suspense, Nora will yield to his entreaties and return home—on her own terms. She will not bear the separation from her children very long, and her love for Torvald, which is not as dead as she thinks, will reassert itself. For a time the tables will be reversed: a meek and chastened husband will eat out of the hand of his squirrel; and Nora, hoping to make up by a sudden spurt of zeal for twenty-eight years of lost time, will be trying desperately hard to grow up. I doubt, however, whether her volatile enthusiasm will even carry her beyond the stage of resolutions. The charm of novelty worn off, she will tire of the new game very rapidly and revert, imperceptibly, to her role of songbird and charmer, as affording an unlimited range to the exercise of her inborn talents of coquetry and playacting.

Students may be invited to offer their own conjectures on the unwritten fourth act.

Another topic for class discussion or for an essay, especially relevant to question 4 in the text: Elizabeth Hardwick suggests (*Seduction and Betrayal*, p. 46) that Ibsen failed to place enough emphasis on Nora's abandonment of the children. In putting "the leaving of her children on the same moral and emotional level as the leaving of her husband Ibsen has been too much a man in the end. He has taken the man's practice, if not his stated belief, that where self-realization is concerned children shall not be an impediment." But in a feminist reading of the play, Elaine Hoffman Baruch, in *Yale Review* 69 (Spring 1980), takes issue with Hardwick, arguing that "it is less a desire for freedom than a great sense of inferiority and the desire to find out more about the male world outside the home that drives Nora away from her children" (p. 37).

Finally, one can discuss with students the comic aspects of the play—the ending (which, in a way, is happy, though Nora's future is left in doubt), and especially Torvald's fatuousness. The fatuousness perhaps reaches its comic height early in Act III, when, after lecturing Mrs. Linde on the importance of an impressive exit (he is telling her how, for effect, he made his "capricious little Capri girl" leave the room after her dance), he demonstrates the elegance of the motion of the hands while embroidering and the ugliness of the motions when knitting. Also comic are his ensuing fantasies, when he tells the exhausted Nora that he fantasizes that she is his "secret" love, though the comedy turns ugly when after she rejects his amorous advances ("I have desired you all evening"), he turns into a bully: "I'm your husband, aren't I?" The knock on the front door (Rank) reintroduces comedy, for it reduces the importunate husband to conventional affability ("Well! How good of you not to pass by the door"), but it also saves Nora from what might have been an ugly assault.

Students will enjoy Frederick J. Marker and Lise-Lone Marker, *Ibsen's Lively Art: A Performance Study of the Major Plays* (1989), which examines the main characters in a number of Ibsen's works through a review of important performances. For a good short introduction: David Thomas, *Henrik Ibsen* (1983). Students eager for more can turn to the massive biography by Michael Meyer (1971).

Topics for Critical Thinking and Writing

1. To what extent is Nora a victim, and to what extent is she herself at fault for her way of life?
2. Is the play valuable only as an image of an aspect of life in the later nineteenth century, or is it still an image of an aspect of life?
3. In the earlier part of the play Nora tells Helmer, Mrs. Linde, and herself that she is happy. Is she? Explain. Why might she be happy? Why not? Can a case be made that Mrs. Linde, who must work to support herself, is happier than Nora?
4. Write a dialogue—approximately two double-spaced pages—setting forth a chance encounter when Torvald and Nora meet five years after the end of Ibsen's play.
5. Write a persuasive essay, arguing that Nora was right—or wrong—to leave her husband and children. In your essay recognize the strengths of the opposing view and try to respond to them.

22

Innocence and Experience

Maya Angelou
Graduation (p. 879)

Many students do not perceive that the elevated or heroic diction of the first part (e.g., "glorious release," "nobility," "like travelers with exotic destinations," all in paragraph 1) is an essential prelude to the descent in the middle ("It was awful to be Negro"). Neither do these students see the comedy, mixed of course with pathos, in such a passage as "My academic work was among the best of the year. I could say the preamble to the Constitution even faster than Bailey." Nor, often, do they see the comedy in the paragraph beginning with "The school band": "We stood," "we sat," "we rose again," "we remained standing for a brief minute before the choir director and the principal signaled to us, rather desperately I thought, to take our seats." Nor do they always realize, even after finishing the essay, that this confusion about sitting and standing resulted from the deletion of the Negro national anthem, presumably out of deference to the white speaker. The difficult thing about teaching this essay, then, is showing some students that they missed a good part of an essay that they read with ease and believed they fully understood. Probably they miss some of the comedy because they can scarcely believe that an essay on graduation can be even partly amusing—unless it is an out-and-out spoof.

We try, then, in teaching this chapter from *I Know Why the Caged Bird Sings*, to help students see the difference between the youthful (and, from an adult's point of view, touching yet amusing) excitement and confidence of the beginning and the mature, partly understated knowledge of the final three paragraphs. In this narration of the movement from innocence to experience, the last paragraph is especially tight-lipped and tough-minded, with its "If we were a people much given to revealing secrets," "slavery cured us of that weakness," and "it may be enough, however. . . ."

In addition to *I Know Why the Caged Bird Sings*, we recommend *The Complete Collected Poems of Maya Angelou* (1994) and *Conversations with Maya Angelou*, ed. Jeffrey M. Elliot (1989). For introductions to Angelou's life and work: Lynn Z. Bloom, "Maya Angelou," in the *Dictionary of Literary*

Biography, vol. 38 (1985), pp. 3–12, and Grace E. Collins, "Maya Angelou," in *Notable Black American Women*, ed. Jessie Carney Smith (1992), pp. 23–27.

Topics for Critical Thinking and Writing

1. Question 2 following the essay can be used as an assignment for writing one paragraph; question 3 for a brief essay of two to four paragraphs.
2. In 500 to 750 words describe your own graduation from grade school or high school. (Before setting out on your first draft, think about your experience and jot down some words that summarize your chief impression—"exciting," "boring," "hot," "nervous," "disappointing," "fun," or whatever. Think about these, and pick out one or two that on reflection seem truest to the experience. You may even choose two that are contradictory. Then, with this as a thesis, jot down supporting details, and finally begin to draft your essay.)
3. Narrate an experience that disclosed a lesson of some value to you. (Students should be cautioned not to look exclusively at momentous events in their lives or to expect to make startling discoveries. Most of us can, on reflection, recall experiences from which we learned—however dimly we perceived the lesson at the time—something that was and continues to be of value to us.)
4. Write an essay whose title might be: "From Innocence to Experience—A Comparison of Maya Angelou's 'Graduation' and Toni Cade Bambara's 'The Lesson'" (Toni Cade Bambara's "The Lesson," text p. 858).

NATHANIEL HAWTHORNE
Young Goodman Brown (p. 888)

Lea. B. V. Newman's *A Reader's Guide to the Short Stories of Nathaniel Hawthorne* (1979) provides a valuable survey of the immense body of criticism that "Young Goodman Brown" has engendered. (By 1979 it had been discussed in print at least five hundred times.) We can begin by quoting Newman's remark that the three chief questions are these: "Why does Brown go into the forest? What happens to him there? Why does he emerge a permanently embittered man?"

Newman grants that there is a good deal of "ambivalence" in the story, but she finds most convincing the view that Brown is a victim, a man who "is deluded into accepting spectral evidence as conclusive proof of his neighbors' depravity." Newman also finds convincing another version of the "victim" theory, this one offered by psychologists who hold that "Brown is a sick man with a diseased mind who cannot help what he sees in the forest or his reaction to it." But her survey of course also includes references (pp. 342–344) to critics who see Brown "as an evil man who is solely responsible for all that happens to him."

Various critics—it almost goes without saying—press various details very hard. For instance, one critic says that Faith's pink ribbons symbolize Brown's "insubstantial, pastel-like faith." (Instructors expect to encounter this sort of reductive reading in essays by first-year students, but it is disappointing to find it in print.) How detailed, one might ask, is the allegory? Probably most readers will agree on some aspects: the village—a world of daylight and community—stands (or seems to stand) for good, whereas the forest—a dark, threatening place—stands (or seems to stand) for evil. The old man—"he of the serpent"—is the devil. But, again, as Newman's survey of criticism shows, even these interpretations have been debated.

The journey into the forest at night (away from the town and away from the daylight) suggests, of course, a journey into the dark regions of the self. The many ambiguities have engendered much comment in learned journals, some of which has been reprinted in a casebook of the story, *Nathaniel Hawthorne: Young Goodman Brown*, ed. Thomas E. Connolly. Is the story—as David Levin argues in *American Literature* 34 (1962): 344–352—one about a man who is tricked by the devil, who conjures up specters who look like Brown's neighbors in order to win him a damnable melancholy? Does Faith resist the tempter? Does Goodman (i.e., Mister) Brown make a journey or does he only dream that he makes a journey? Is the story about awareness of evil, or is it about the crushing weight of needlessly assumed guilt? That is, is the story about a loss of faith (Austin Warren, in his *Rage for Order,* says it is about "the devastating effect of moral skepticism"), or is it about a religious faith that kills one's joy in life? And, of course, the story may be about loss of faith not in Christ but in human beings; young Goodman Brown perceives his own corruption and loses faith in mankind.

With a little warning the student can be helped to see that the characters and experiences cannot be neatly pigeonholed. For example, it is not certain whether or not Faith yields to "the wicked one"; indeed, it is not certain that Brown actually journeyed into the woods. Richard H. Fogle points out in *Hawthorne's Fiction* (1964) that "ambiguity is the very essence of Hawthorne's tale." Among other interesting critical pieces on the story are Marius Bewley, *The Complex Fate* (1967); Thomas Connolly, "Hawthorne's 'Young Goodman Brown': An Attack on Puritanic Calvinism," American Literature 28 (November 1956): 370–375; and Frederick C. Crews, *The Sins of the Fathers: Hawthorne's Psychological Themes* (1989). Connolly argues that Brown does not lose his faith, but rather that his faith is purified by his loss of belief that he is of the elect. Before the journey into the woods, he believes that man is depraved, but that he himself is of the elect and will be saved. In the forest he sees "a black mass of cloud" hide "the brightening stars," and (according to Connolly) his faith is purified, for he comes to see that he is not different from the rest of the congregation.

On the other hand, one can point out (as J. L. Capps does, in *Explicator,* Spring 1982), that only once in the story does Hawthorne use the word "hope" ("'But where is Faith?' thought Goodman Brown; and as hope came into his heart, he trembled"), and the word "charity" never appears, indicating that Brown lacks the quality that would have enabled him to survive despair.

Speaking a bit broadly, we can say that critics fall into two camps: those who believe that Goodman Brown falls into delusion (i.e., misled by the devil, he destroys himself morally by falling into misanthropy), and those who believe that he is initiated into reality. Thus, for readers who hold the first view, Brown's guide into the forest is the devil, who calls up "figures" or "forms" of Brown's acquaintances, and it is Brown (not the narrator) who mistakenly takes the figures for real people. Even what Brown takes to be Faith's pink ribbon is for the narrator merely *"something* [that] fluttered lightly down through the air, and caught on the branch of a tree." In this view, (1) the fact that Faith later wears the ribbon is proof that Brown has yielded to a delusion, and (2) we are to judge Brown by recalling the narrator's objective perceptions. For instance, Brown's guide says that "evil is the nature of mankind," and Brown believes him, but the narrator (who is to be trusted) speaks of "the good old minister" and of "that excellent Christian," Goody Cloyse. There is much to be said for this view (indeed much has been said in journals), but against it one can recall some words by Frederick Crews: "The richness of Hawthorne's irony is such that, when Brown turns to a Gulliver-like misanthropy and spends the rest of his days shrinking from wife and neighbors, we cannot quite dismiss his attitude as unfounded" (*The Sins of the Fathers,* p. 106).

Topics for Critical Thinking and Writing

1. What ambiguities do you find in "Young Goodman Brown"?
2. What are the strengths and weaknesses of the view that Brown is tricked by the devil, who stages a show of specters impersonating Brown's neighbors, in order to destroy Brown's religious faith?
3. Brown's guide says, "Evil is the nature of mankind," but does the *story* say it?
4. Is the story sexist, showing Brown more horrified by his wife's sexuality than his own?
5. Retell the story using a modern setting. Make whatever changes you wish, but retain the motif of the temptation of a man and a woman by evil.

JAMES JOYCE
Araby (p. 896)

Probably the best discussion of "Araby" remains one of the earliest, that of Cleanth Brooks and Robert Penn Warren in *Understanding Fiction* (1943). Among more recent discussions, L. J. Morrissey, "Joyce's Narrative Strategies in 'Araby'" *Modern Fiction Studies* 28 (1982): 45–52, is especially good.

Students have difficulty with the story largely because they do not read it carefully enough. They scan it for what happens (who goes where) and do not pay enough attention to passages in which (they think) "nothing is happening." But when students read passages aloud in class, for instance the first three paragraphs, they *do* see what is going on (that is, they come to understand the boy's mind) and enjoy the story very much. To help them hear the romantic boy who lives in what is (from an adult point of view) an unromantic society, it is especially useful to have students read aloud passages written in different styles. Compare, for instance, "At night in my bedroom and by day in the classroom her image came between me and the page I strove to read" with "I asked for leave to go to the bazaar on Saturday night. My aunt was surprised and hoped it was not some Freemason affair."

That the narrator is no longer a boy is indicated by such passages as the following:

her name was like a summons to all my foolish blood.

Her name sprang to my lips at moments in strange prayers and praise which I myself did not understand. My eyes were often full of tears (I could not tell why).

What innumerable follies laid waste my waking and sleeping thoughts. . . .

Morrissey points out that in addition to distancing himself from his past actions by such words as "foolish" and "follies" (and, at the end of the story, "vanity"), the narrator distances himself from the boy he was by the words "imagined" and "seemed," words indicating that his present view differs from his earlier view.

The narrator recounts a story of disillusionment. The first two paragraphs clearly establish the complacent middle-class world into which he is born—the houses "conscious of decent lives within them" gaze with "imperturbable faces." This idea of decency is made concrete by the comment in the second paragraph that the priest's charity is evident in his will: he left all of his money to institutions and his furniture to his sister. (Probably even the sister was so decent that she too thought this was the right thing to do.) Morrissey, interpreting the passage about the priest's will differently, takes the line to be the boy's innocent report of "what must have been an ironic comment by adults."

As a boy he lived in a sterile atmosphere, a sort of fallen world:

- The house is in a "blind" or dead-end street.
- The rooms are musty.
- The priest had died (religion is no longer vital?).
- A bicycle pump, once a useful device, now lies rusty and unused under a bush in the garden.
- An apple tree stands in the center of the garden in this fallen world.
- Nearby are the odors of stable and garbage dumps.

Nevertheless the boy is quickened by various things, for instance by the yellow pages of an old book, but especially by Mangan's sister (who remains unnamed, perhaps to suggest that the boy's love is spiritual). He promises to visit "Araby" (a bazaar) and to return with a gift for her.

The boy for a while moves through a romantic, religious world:

- He sees her "image."
- He imagines that he carries a "chalice."
- He hears the "litanies" and "chanting" of vendors. He utters "strange prayers."

Delayed by his uncle, whose inebriation is indicated by the uncle's "talking to himself" and by "the hall-stand rocking" (his parents seem not to be living; notice the emphasis on the boy's isolation throughout the story, e.g., his ride alone in the car of the train), he hears the clerks counting the day's receipts—moneychangers in the temple.

"The light was out. The upper part of the hall was now completely dark." The darkness and the preceding trivial conversations of a girl and two young men reveal—Joyce might have said epiphanize—the emptiness of the world. The boy has journeyed to a rich, exotic (religious?) world created by his imagination and has found it cold and trivial, as dead as the neighborhood he lives in.

The boy's entry through the shilling entrance rather than through the sixpenny (children's) entrance presumably signals his coming of age.

This brief discussion of "Araby" of course seems reasonable to its writer, even the remarks that the rusty bicycle pump suggests a diminished world and that the entry through the shilling entrance rather than the sixpenny entrance suggests, implies, or even—though one hesitates to use the word—symbolizes (along with many other details) his initiation into an adult view. But how far can (or should) one press the details? An article in *James Joyce Quarterly* 4 (1967): 85–86 suggests that the pump under the bushes stands for the serpent in the garden. Is there a difference between saying that the rusty pump—in the context of the story—puts a reader in mind of a diminished (deflated) world and saying that it stands for the serpent? Is one interpretation relevant and the other not? Students might be invited to offer their own views on how far to look for "meaning" or "symbols" in this story, or in any other story. They might also be advised to read—but not necessarily to swallow—the brief discussions of symbolism in the text and in the glossary.

There is an immense body of biographical and critical work on Joyce. For undergraduates at an introductory level, we suggest keeping things simple. Probably you should make mention of Richard Ellmann's biography (new and rev. ed., 1982), a classic of the biographer's art. But from there, keep the focus on the story itself. We were disappointed by the poor response to "Araby" that we received the first two or three times we taught it. Eventually we realized that in the case of Joyce, the teacher may need to do more work than usual in the classroom. We now spend a fair amount of time lecturing on Joyce's life and on the Irish background. This is not an approach we favor, especially in a course on literature and composition, where so much should depend on the questions and comments from students. But we discovered that Joyce's characters and settings seemed far away in time and place to many students, even those from an Irish background themselves. To get the benefit we want from Joyce's stories, we need to make him and his era vivid for the students.

Fortunately, we have a good array of sources to help us. These include *Dubliners: Text, Criticism, and Notes,* ed. Robert Scholes and A. Walton Litz (1969); *James Joyce's Dubliners: An Illustrated Edition with Annotations,* ed. John Wyse Jackson and Bernard McGinley (1993); Don Gifford, *Joyce Annotated: Notes for Dubliners and A Portrait of the Artist as a Young Man* (2nd ed., 1982); Bruce Bidwell and Linda Heffer, *The Joycean Way: A Topographic Guide to Dubliners & A Portrait of the Artist as a Young Man* (1981); and Donald T. Torchiana, *Backgrounds for Joyce's Dubliners* (1986).

Topics for Critical Thinking and Writing

1. What do the first two paragraphs tell us about the boy's environment? What does the second paragraph tell us about his nature?
2. Of course none of us can speak authoritatively about what life was *really* like in Dublin around 1900, but would you say that Joyce gives—insofar as space allows—a realistic picture of Dublin? If so, was his chief aim to give the reader a slice of Dublin life? What do you think Joyce wants us to believe that life in Dublin was like?
3. The boy says that when his uncle returned he heard his uncle talking to himself, and he heard the hallstand (coatrack) rocking. Then he says, "I could interpret these signs." What do "these signs" mean? How is the uncle's behavior here consistent with other details of life in Dublin?

LANGSTON HUGHES
One Friday Morning (p. 901)

This story produces a vigorous reaction in the classroom, but not always a positive one: "One Friday Morning" is not a story that students like very much, not at first at any rate. To them everything seems painfully obvious: Nancy Lee is earnest, accomplished, hard-working, admirable; she deserves the scholarship that then is cruelly taken away from her on purely racist grounds. We begin by conceding this point: yes, the story line and characterization do seem obvious. But we know that Langston Hughes is a thoughtful, skillful writer, in both prose and poetry: What if we assume that he knew what he was doing, and that he wrote the story as he did for a specific purpose? What will be the interpretive result if we proceed on this basis?

In our view, the obviousness of the story line is meant to prepare for an unobvious ending. Most of us expect that Nancy Lee will be outraged by the unfair treatment she receives. We expect her—in fact, we likely want her—to lash out against the racism embedded in America that denies deserving people their rewards simply on the basis of skin color. But Hughes's character does not do that. The ending of the story is self-affirming and highly patriotic. Nancy Lee is not embittered; she is not defeated. She takes Miss O'Shay's words to heart and renews her allegiance to the United States as a nation where the ideals of liberty and justice will one day be secured for all people. Nancy Lee will continue her struggle, and she is confident that friends like Miss O'Shay will support her.

Some students, we find, are quick to judge this ending "sentimental." Sometimes they use even stronger terms—unrealistic, phony, sappy. But challenge these judgments; ask the students directly how *they* would have written the ending? Nancy Lee should have.... Well, what should she have done? Denounced American racism and given up her aspirations? Concluded that all white people are racists? For Hughes it was important that Nancy Lee experience racism in all of its gross unfairness but not give up on herself, on white people, or on American ideals. From one point of view, this may seem a conveniently optimistic, too-comforting ending. But from another, it is a hard ending: it is difficult to continue to think and feel as Nancy Lee does; if anything, it would be far easier not to.

We suggest that when you teach this story, you probe and test the students' habitual ways of thinking and feeling. Your students probably will be inclined to conclude, "Nancy Lee is so naive, such a dreamer." But you then can press the students to imagine the possibility that Nancy Lee is not naive, but is, instead, strong and courageous, a person who will not surrender the dreams she holds for herself, for her fellow African Americans, and for the nation.

There is an excellent two-volume biography of Hughes by Arnold Rampersad (vol. 1, 1986; vol. 2, 1988); another good resource is Thomas A. Mikolyzk, *Langston Hughes: A Bio-Bibliography* (1990). The short stories have been edited by Akiba Sullivan Harper (1996). But most of the scholarly books focus on the poetry, rather than on the fiction. The best points of departure for studying Hughes are two recent collections: *Langston Hughes: Critical Perspectives Past and Present* (1993), ed. Henry Louis Gates Jr. and K. A. Appiah, and *Langston Hughes: The Man, the Art, and His Continuing Influence* (1995), ed. C. J. Trotman.

Isaac Bashevis Singer
The Son from America (p. 907)

The first question in the text invites students to formulate their attitudes toward Berl and Berlcha. Responses will of course vary, from respect to condescension and perhaps even contempt, but many students probably will offer a response along this line: they are good but rather stupid people. If something like this is said, you may want to begin by asking students to distinguish between stupidity and ignorance. That the peasants are ignorant is beyond doubt, but that they are stupid is less certain. They share the values of the village (although they don't go for newfangled kerosene lamps), and by the end of the story the reader sees that these values—rooted in piety—bring contentment and are life-sustaining. Yes, if Berl and Berlcha were a bit more adventurous they would at least have bought eyeglasses so that they could see better—although, when one thinks about it, except for being unable to make much out of the photographs that Samuel sends, they can see as much as they have to.

Singer makes clear the ignorance of his peasants, for instance, in the business about the people in America walking with "their heads down and their feet up," and "since the teacher said so it must be true." Further, we smile at the characters when, by taking us inside their minds, Singer delicately reveals their uncomprehending views. For instance, we know that Samuel is embracing his mother, but Singer gives us Berl's view thus:

> At that moment Berl came in from the woodshed, his arms piled with logs. The goat followed him. When he saw a nobleman kissing his wife, Berl dropped the wood and exclaimed, "What's this?"

It is useful to discuss the point of view in the story. In "When [Berl] saw a nobleman," Singer conveys the sight from Berl's naive point of view. Much of the story, however, is told from a relatively objective point of view, though surely even in the first paragraph a reader perceives the narrator's affection for this fairy-tale-like place:

> The village of Lentshin was tiny—a sandy marketplace where the peasants of the area met once a week. It was surrounded by little huts with thatched roofs or shingles green with moss. The chimneys looked like pots.

For the most part the narrator is content to report in what passes for an objective manner, but in the final paragraph, after the dialogue has convincingly done its work, the narrator offers a judgment:

> But this village in the hinterland needed nothing.

Few American readers in the late twentieth century will envy the life of the villagers, but these readers may nevertheless see that the villagers do not need what Samuel can give. Which is not to say that Samuel has become corrupted. From all that we can see, he is a dutiful son and a generous man. He is, moreover, a man who has kept the faith. But (as the last paragraph makes clear), some of the things that give him his identity—"his passport, his checkbook, his letters of credit"—are not needed in Lentshin.

The Collected Stories of Isaac Bashevis Singer (1982) is a source of much wisdom and delight.

WILLIAM BLAKE
Infant Joy (p. 912)

In addition to the infant there is a second speaker, an adult—presumably the mother, but nothing in the text rules out the possibility that the adult speaker is the father.

The infant speaks the first two lines, the adult (asking what to call the infant) speaks the third. The infant replies, "I happy am, / Joy is my name," and the adult is then moved to say, "Sweet joy befall thee." Is it too subtle to detect a difference between the infant, who knows only that it is happy, and the adult, who, in saying "Sweet joy befall thee" is introducing (to the edges of our mind or, rather, to the depths of our mind) the possibility that—life being what it is—joy may *not* befall the infant? That is, even here, in the *Songs of Innocence*, we may detect an awareness of a fallen world, a world where in fact people do not always encounter "Sweet joy."

The second stanza apparently is spoken entirely by the adult, but the language of the first two lines ("Pretty joy! / Sweet joy but two days old") is close to the language of the infant—not to the language of a real infant, of course, but to the language of Blake's infant, who began the poem by saying "I have no name, I am but two days old." Still, there is a difference between the speakers. The mother sings (a lullaby?), partly out of her own joy, and partly, perhaps, to reassure the infant (at least that is more or less the function of lullabies in real life).

What of Blake's illustration for the poem? The best discussion of the picture is Andrew Lincoln's, in his edition of Blake's *Songs of Innocence and Experience* (1991), which is volume 2 in the series called *Blake's Illuminated Books*, gen. ed. David Bindman. We quote Lincoln's chief points:

> The figures within the opened petals enact an Adoration scene. A mother in a blue dress nurses a baby in her lap, while a winged girl-angel stands with arms reaching out towards the infant.
>
> The petals of the flower seem protective, although those that curl over from the left may suggest containment, hinting perhaps at the potential constraints that face the newborn child.
>
> There are other images of constraint here. In the design, the drooping bud at the right may recall the temporal process in which flowers unfold and decay, while in the song joy is at once a present state of being and a hope for an uncertain future.

WILLIAM BLAKE
Infant Sorrow (p. 912)

In "Infant Joy" we saw not only the child's view but also the parent's. Here we see only the child's view, which regards the adult embrace not as an act of love but as a threatening constraint. It's not a question of which view—"Infant Joy" or "Infant Sorrow"—is truer. Both are true. In "Infant Sorrow" Blake lets us see life from the point of view of the infant, a creature who is helpless, distrustful of the parents, presciently aware that it has entered a "dangerous world" and that its cries sound like those of a "fiend" to all who cannot understand its distress.

The first stanza emphasizes physical actions—of the mother in labor, of the sympathetic father, and of the babe itself ("piping loud"). There is action in the second stanza too, but there is also something more; there is thought, really strategy. Confined by the father at the beginning of the second stanza, the infant decides it is best to turn to the mother ("I thought best / To sulk upon my mother's breast"), but in any case the infant is still trapped.

Andrew Lincoln points out that the illustration seems to represent a rather "comfortable and secure interior." He goes on to say that "In the light of the poem, the protection that surrounds the child here must itself seem threatening, potentially stifling."

WILLIAM BLAKE
The Echoing Green (p. 914)

E. M. W. Tillyard discusses this poem in *Poetry Direct and Oblique* (1977). Among his points are these:

- Blake "finds in the traditional village sports and pieties a type of his world of innocence".
- The poem moves from dawn in the first stanza, to midday in the second (presumably Old John sits under an oak to protect himself from the noonday sun), to evening in the third stanza, and thus "the form is a stylized day-cycle".
- Beginning and end are balanced (echoing green, darkening green; waking birds, birds in their nest).
- "The old unfreeze and join their mirth to make up a full chorus with children."

According to Tillyard, all of this is an indirect way of expressing "desire satisfied" and "fruition." He goes on: "At the end of the 'echoing green' is 'the darkening green' because its function is fulfilled." All of this seems reasonable to us, if fulfillment is recognized as including weariness and the coming of darkness.

Some other points: Who is the speaker? Apparently a young person, if one leans on lines 9 ("our sports"), 15 ("our play"), and 24 ("our sports"), but not a child; the vision is that of a mature person, at least someone mature enough to know that "our sports have an end."

In the first stanza, one action almost automatically generates the next: the sun rises, making the skies happy; the merry bells ring, stimulating the birds, who "Sing louder around / To the bells' cheerful sound."

Why "echoing green"? Because it resounds with the noise of children playing, of course, but also because the children are a renewed version of the old people, or, to put it the other way around, the old people are the distant echoes of the children. There are other echoes, too, in the repeated words: the title is repeated in the last lines of the first and second stanzas, and it is varied ("the darkening green") at the end of the third stanza. Other repeated words are "sun" (1, 23), "bells" (3, 6), "birds" (6, 27), "seen" (9, 19, 29), "sports" (9, 24, 29), "laugh" (12, 15), and "such" (in 17 we get "Such, such").

Allen Ginsberg sings "The Echoing Green" on *Songs of Innocence and Experience by William Blake, Tuned by Allen Ginsberg.*

GERARD MANLEY HOPKINS
Spring and Fall: To a Young Child (p. 916)

In our experience, students will have considerable difficulty if they simply read the poem silently to themselves, but if they read (and reread) it aloud, it becomes clear—and more important, it becomes something they value.

We begin, then, as we usually do with poems, by having a student read the poem aloud, and then we invite comments about the title and its connection with the two people in the poem. Students usually see that the poem presents youth and age, that Margaret is associated with spring and the speaker with the fall, and this leads to discussion of the Fall in Christian thought. Many students, however, do not know that in Christian thought the disobedience of Adam and Eve brought consequences that extended to nature and that the perennial spring of Eden therefore yielded to autumn and winter; that is, "Goldengrove" inherited death. ("Goldengrove," incidentally, might seem to suggest preciousness and eternity, but here the golden leaves are a sign of transience and death.)

In the original version of "Spring and Fall" (1880), line 8 ran, "Though forests low and leafmeal lie." When he revised the poem in 1884, Hopkins changed "Though forests low and" to "Though worlds of wanwood," thus introducing the pallor of "wanwood" and also wonderfully extending the vista from "forests" to "worlds." Margaret's sorrow for the trees stripped of their golden foliage is finally sorrow for the Fall, whose consequences are everywhere. Her mouth cannot formulate any of this, but her spirit has intuited it ("ghost guessed").

On "Spring and Fall," see Paul L. Mariani, *A Commentary on the Complete Poems of Gerard Manley Hopkins* (1970); Marylou Motto, *"Mined with a Motion": The Poetry of Gerard Manley Hopkins* (1984); and Peter Milward's essay in Milward and R. V. Schoder, *Landscape and Inscape* (1975). George Starbuck has a modern version ("Translations from the English") in his book of poems, *White Paper* (1966).

There is an excellent biography by Robert B. Martin: *Gerard Manley Hopkins: A Very Private Life* (1991). For students, a helpful beginning is Norman H. MacKenzie, *A Reader's Guide to Gerard Manley Hopkins* (1981). For a selection of criticism: *Gerard Manley Hopkins*, ed. Harold Bloom (1985). See also the suggestive commentary in Helen Vendler, *The Breaking of Style: Hopkins, Heaney, Graham* (1995).

A. E. HOUSMAN
When I Was One-and-Twenty (p. 917)

The "wise man" seems to offer two pieces of wisdom, but they are closely related. One is, in effect, "Don't give your heart away," that is, don't fall in love; the second is, "If you do give your heart away, you will suffer." The speaker ignored the advice, and now, at twenty-two, has learned its truth. The last line of the poem, with its repetition, suggests that the speaker takes his youthful sorrow very seriously ("And oh 'tis true, 'tis true"), but surely the line strikes readers (and is intended to strike them) as a trifle maudlin. And since the poem jingles nicely and almost suggests a nursery rhyme, we can hardly take the grief too seriously. We listen with sympathetic amusement to this tale of disillusionment.

Norman Page has written a good biography (1983), and there is a valuable, if dated, selection of criticism in *A. E. Housman: A Collection of Critical Essays,* ed. Christopher Ricks (1968). For students, we recommend B. J. Leggett, *The Poetic Art of A. E. Housman: Theory and Practice* (1978). But John Bayley, *Housman's Poems* (1992), is worth consulting as well.

E. E. CUMMINGS
in Just- (p. 918)

Of course a reader's response to any sort of print on a page is partly conditioned by the appearance of the page. Nice margins and creamy paper can make a so-so story seem pretty good, and double columns and thin paper that allows for show-through can make reading even an absorbing work difficult. And probably any poet would be distressed to find the first twelve lines of his or her sonnet printed on a right-hand page, and the final couplet—invisible to the reader of the three quatrains—on the next page.

Our point, again, is that the physical appearance of any work counts, but with Cummings's work it counts a great deal more, in a variety of ways. For instance, "eddieandbill" catches the child's way of speaking, and also conveys a sense of an inseparable pair, just as "bettyandisabel" does. (When the youngsters grow up, they will be Eddie and Betty, and Bill and Isabel, but Cummings is giving us children in the stage when boys play with boys and girls with girls.) As for the variations in which the words "far and wee" appear, we can say only that the spaces (in line 5, "far and wee"; in line 13, "far   and   wee"; in lines 22–24, "far / and / wee") convey the variations in the balloonman's whistle, and the last of these perhaps suggests that he is moving away.

The allusion to Pan (via the goatfoot and the whistle) seems clear to us. Pan is the woodland god of Arcadia, a land usually depicted as a world of perpetual spring. Of course Pan is especially associated with the pursuit of nymphs, but Cummings here gives us a rather sexless world, though we can hardly repress the thought that this world of childhood (with its inseparable boys and its inseparable girls) and of springtime play (marbles, dancing) will in time become something else.

One other point: most students, in the course of class discussion, will see that the repeated "wee" (lines 5, 13, 14) works several ways. The balloon man is "little" (line 3); his whistle makes the sound of "wee"; "wee" is a child's exclamation of delight; and "we" children go running to buy balloons.

Louise Glück
The School Children (p. 919)

On the surface, the poem seems loaded with pictures of cute children on their way to school, bringing the traditional apples for the teachers: "with their little satchels," "apples, red and gold," "their overcoats of blue or yellow wool." Even "how orderly they are" (said of the nails on which the children hang their coats) can be taken as a benign comment on this happy scene.

But by the time we finish the second stanza we realize that this is not a Norman Rockwell scene. The children must cross to "the other shore" where they are confronted by people "who wait behind great desks." Further, these people are not presented warmly. Rather, they are presented (we never see them) as godlike figures who wait "to receive these offerings."

The third stanza is perhaps even more menacing, with that orderly row of nails, waiting to accept the pretty coats. The text speaks—horribly—of "the nails / on which the children hang. . . ." As we continue to read the sentence the meaning changes radically, of course, and we see that it is not the children but "their overcoats" that hang on the nails, but the thought lingers; the mind retains a vision of the children hanging from nails.

The last stanza reintroduces us to the teachers, who "shall instruct them in silence," a menacing expression that we take to mean (1) shall teach them silently (a terrifying way of teaching), and (2) shall teach them to be silent (a terrifying condition). The stanza does not end, however, with the teachers or with the children. Rather, it ends with the mothers, who "scour the orchards for a way out," i.e., who seek to equip their children with the "offerings" (line 7) that the gods require. That is, the mothers seek (by propitiating the gods) to protect their children from the severe socialization that awaits them, but it is already too late, because "the gray limbs of the fruit trees" (it is now autumn) bear "so little ammunition."

In the last stanza, why "The teachers *shall* instruct them," and "the mothers *shall* scour the orchards," rather than "will instruct" and "will scour"? Although older handbooks say that *shall* expresses simple futurity in the first person (and *will* expresses determination in the first person), it is our impression that *shall* has almost disappeared. Indeed, part of what made Douglas MacArthur's "I shall return" so memorable was that he used an unusual construction. To our ear, the use of *shall* in the last stanza of Glück's poem has a voice-of-doom quality; the teachers must act as they will, and the mothers must act as they will—and the children will be the victims.

Students might continue their study of Glück by reading *The First Four Books of Poems* (1995), which brings together separate volumes of her work published from 1969 to 1985. Another important book is Glück's *Proofs and Theories* (1994), a collection of essays on the art of poetry that includes commentary on the autobiographical sources for a number of her poems. The best critical commentaries on Glück can be found in Helen Vendler, *The Music of What Happens* (1988) and *Soul Says* (1995).

Louise Glück
Gretel in Darkness (p. 919)

In *New Voices in American Poetry,* ed. David Allan Evans (1973), p. 106, Ms. Glück comments on her poem:

> To Hansel the escape from the forest was a means to an end: a future. To Gretel the escape is an end in itself. No moment in the ordinary existence she made possible by killing the witch and rescuing her brother can touch for her the moment of the escape. That moment was her triumph: it provided Gretel with an opportunity to experience herself as powerful. The whole episode, the drama in the forest, remains for her charged and present. It is in that episode that she wishes to imbed herself. Unfortunately, she is alone in this desire. Their adventure grows increasingly remote to Hansel, presumably because the new life answers his needs. The Gretel of the poem perceives, and passionately wishes to alter, the discrepancy between her investment in the forest and Hansel's.

William Shakespeare
Hamlet (p. 932)

This long discussion will consist of:
- some general introductory remarks
- a note on staging scenes in the classroom
- a note on writing a review
- a fairly detailed scene-by-scene commentary on the entire play

Probably the best short study of *Hamlet* is Maynard Mack's "The World of Hamlet," *Yale Review* 41 (1952): 502–523, reprinted in the Signet paperback edition of *Hamlet*, in *Tragic Themes,* ed. Cleanth Brooks (1955), and elsewhere. Maurice Charney's *Style in Hamlet* (1969) is excellent, and so too is Harley Granville-Barker's book-length essay in *Prefaces to Shakespeare*

(1984). For an essay that draws on the tenets of reader-response criticism, see Stephen Booth, "On the Value of *Hamlet*," in *Reinterpretations of Elizabethan Drama* (1969), 137–176. See also *Approaches to Teaching Hamlet* (2001), ed. Bernice W. Kliman.

We will give some additional bibliography in the course of the following comment, but here we want to mention two very different works, both of great value. For a highly intelligent scene-by-scene commentary, we know of nothing better than Alfred Harbage's *William Shakespeare: A Reader's Guide* (1963), a book that is very wise but utterly unpretentious. (Nevertheless, in this manual we offer our own scene-by-scene commentary.) For persons concerned with textual issues, the three earliest texts of *Hamlet* are assembled in *The Three-Text "Hamlet": Parallel Texts of the First and Second Quartos and First Folio*, ed. Paul Bertram and Bernice W. Kliman (1991).

The nature of the Ghost has produced a good deal of commentary, most of it summarized in Eleanor Prosser's *Hamlet and Revenge* (1971). She says that for the Elizabethans a ghost can be only one of three things: the soul of a pagan (impossible in this play, for the context is Christian); a soul from Roman Catholic purgatory (impossible in this play, because it seeks revenge); or a devil (which is what Prosser says this Ghost is). Prosser argues that the Ghost is evil because it counsels revenge, it disappears at the invocation of heaven, and it disappears when the cock crows. But perhaps it can be replied that although the Ghost indeed acts suspiciously, its role is to build suspense and to contribute to the play's meaning, which involves uncertainty and the difficulty of sure action. Prosser sees Hamlet as a rebellious youth who deliberately mistreats Ophelia and descends deep into evil (e.g., he spares Claudius at his prayers only in order to damn him), but when he returns from England he is no longer the "barbaric young revenger . . . but a mature man of poise and serenity" (p. 217). He is generous to the gravediggers and Laertes, "delightful" with Osric. In short, the young rebel has been chastened by experience and by the vision of death, and so he is saved. He "has fought his way out of Hell" (p. 237). Prosser offers a useful corrective to the romantic idea of the delicate prince, as well as a great deal of information about the attitude toward ghosts, but one need not accept her conclusion that the Ghost is a devil; her evidence about ghosts is incontrovertible on its own grounds, but one may feel that, finally, the play simply doesn't square with Elizabethan popular thought about ghosts.

A Note on Staging Scenes in the Classroom

In the course of teaching *Hamlet* we usually have students stage four or five parts of scenes, each about two or three pages long. (We devote five or six meetings to the play, so we usually have one performance for each meeting after the first meeting.) For the first production, we ask for volunteers because it has been our experience that the students who immediately volunteer are those who have had some experience on the stage, and thus the first production is likely to be pretty good. For later productions we usually simply assign parts rather than accept volunteers.

We set the thing up about a week in advance of each performance, and we ask one student to serve as director, and two or three or four students—however many are necessary for the scene—to play the parts. They are told that they must get together at least once for a rehearsal, i.e., on the day that parts are assigned they must, immediately after class, agree on a time when they will rehearse. (Unfortunately this requirement will eliminate some students, who simply cannot be present for a rehearsal.) We give the performers and the director photocopies of the relevant pages, with marginal annotations offering a few suggestions about how this or that speech might be delivered, e.g., about what gestures might be appropriate, etc. but we emphasize that what they do in class is up to them. They are not expected to memorize the parts—they read from the pages while they act—but they do gesticulate and move about, sit, etc. as seems appropriate.

Among the passages from the first two acts that we have used in class (we believe with some success) are the first 62 lines of the play (up through Horatio's remarks following the departure of the Ghost); 1.3 (Laertes, Ophelia, Polonius); 2.2.1–57 (Claudius, Gertrude, Rosencrantz, Guildenstern, Polonius); 2.2 169–324 (Hamlet, Polonius, Rosencrantz, Guildenstern). But there is no need for us to specify additional passages; if you like the idea, you know which passages you want to assign.

This business of staging scenes has several good effects. For one thing, we have been impressed with how competent most students are, even the shy ones. The rehearsal gives them some confidence, and they almost always do quite well. (We should add that the casting is gender-blind, or almost so. Because there are far more male than female parts, we regularly ask women to play some male roles, though we confess that we have never cast a man in a female role.) Second, when students prepare to act a part, they begin to see the complexities, the multiplicity of ways that a speech or line or word may be delivered. Further, they begin to see how important tones of voice, pauses, and gestures can be.

Take, for instance, 3.4, the "closet" (private chamber) scene, in which Hamlet kills Polonius and then sternly—ferociously? almost insanely?—lectures the Queen. When he urges Gertrude to "Look here upon this picture, and on this" (3.4.54), exactly what *are* the pictures? From Marvin Rosenberg's admirable *The Masks of Hamlet*—a massive account of the stage business that has developed over the centuries—we learn that there are three chief ways of staging this passage. There may be large portraits on the wall (students who choose this route will simply draw two large frames on the blackboard before the production begins), or two framed portraits on a table; or—the second of the three ways—the performers may use two miniature pictures (for instance, Hamlet may wear, hanging from a chain around his neck, a miniature of Hamlet Senior, and Gertrude may wear a miniature of Claudius, either around her neck or on a bracelet). The third approach is to use no pictures other than the word-pictures that Hamlet evokes in his speeches.

If miniatures are used, and one miniature hangs on Hamlet's chest and the other is in Gertrude's bosom, the scene may be charged with sexual overtones as Hamlet closely grasps his mother and lifts the picture from her bosom. (In our notes to the students, we simply alert them to the several ways of playing the scene—the three methods that we have mentioned, and we also tell them that they may use a combination, e.g., there may be a large picture of Claudius on the wall, which Hamlet may contrast with a miniature of his father that he wears.)

Although it takes time to have students perform several passages, we believe that your students—the actors and the spectators—will enjoy the performances and will learn a good deal.

A Note on Writing a Review

Students enjoy writing reviews of a film. Most of them see lots of films, and thus they feel in this area at least they possess some real expertise and experience. The reviews that they write in our courses are lively and entertaining; the students are more honest and open about stating what they really think than they are in their assignments on literary works, where, unfortunately, they are inclined to worry too much about "what the professor thinks and wants to hear."

The most common flaw in these reviews is that students tend to say what they think without explaining what led them to this or that response, judgment, conclusion. In one sense they are right to see a review of a film or novel or new book of non-fiction as an opportunity to express their own opinion: "This is my opinion." Nothing wrong with that. But students need to realize that simply giving an opinion does not amount to much. A reviewer needs to do *that* but, at the same time, should explain what it is in the story, characterization, setting, etc., that led to this opinion: What is it based upon? If all that counted were the act of stating an opinion, there would be little need to write about it: you could simply tell yourself what you think. Writing means not only clarifying an opinion, a response, a judgment for yourself but also for the reader, the person to whom you are speaking, to whom you are seeking to make a connection.

Explicitly or implicitly, when we write a review, we are attempting both to state what we think and to convince our readers to think the same way that we do. You might say that this places us under an obligation: we must give the evidence in the film or the book that impelled us toward our opinion. A review would not be effective otherwise; it would be an opinion with nothing underneath supporting it.

If, for example, we decide that Derek Jacobi excelled in his performance of Claudius in Branagh's film version of *Hamlet,* we want to highlight how he spoke his lines at an important moment, how he looked, how he acknowledged or ignored the others around him, how he responded to Gertrude, how he addressed and engaged Hamlet, etc. When writing a review, we usually have only a limited amount of space: we have to be economical and concise. But we can be selective and yet still be specific. Remind your students that they need to be pointing to this, to that, example or set of examples in order to *share* their opinion with the reader. Whether we are analyzing a poem or writing a review, we must bring forward the evidence, the examples from the text or film itself that shape and support our conclusions.

Bibliographic note: For film and television versions, see Bernice Kliman, *Hamlet: Film, Television, and Audio Performance* (1988); H. R. Coursen, *Shakespearean Performance as an Interpretation* (1992); and H. R. Coursen, *Watching Shakespeare on Television* (1993). The Olivier and Branagh film versions have been published.

Scene-by-Scene Commentary

In a moment we will offer a scene-by-scene commentary on the play, but we want to mention again that another commentary of this sort—and a very good one—is available in Alfred Harbage's *A Reader's Guide to Shakespeare* (1963). For a commentary of more than 900 pages, emphasizing theatrical productions, consult Marvin Rosenberg, *The Masks of Hamlet* (1992). We make no claims for the originality of any of the following remarks. They are derived from decades of reading commentaries, seeing productions, teaching the play, and conversing with colleagues.

When we teach *Hamlet* in an introductory course, we usually allot five days to it, doing roughly an act per day. We spend part of at least two meetings having students perform a short scene or part of a scene. Our practice is to use volunteers for the first of these scenes, but we then usually assign students for any other scenes that we may want to stage, simply because we have found that some students who hesitate to volunteer will nevertheless gladly participate if asked. We give each actor a photocopy of the pages of the scene, on which we have jotted some minimal bits of direction, and we assign another student to serve as the director. Sometimes we recommend that the director read the relevant pages in Rosenberg's book, so that he or she may try out some approaches. It is the responsibility of the students to meet twice for rehearsal. In order to make certain that they can indeed all meet, during the class meeting when we choose the performers, we set a time when they can meet to rehearse, e.g., Monday and Thursday, 4:00–6:00 P.M. The students are not expected to memorize the parts; while performing they read from the text, but they do engage in a certain amount of movement, e.g., sitting, embracing, gesticulating.

1.1 The play begins with soldiers and ends with a soldier's funeral. Although the idea that Hamlet is a romantic, melancholy figure who cannot make up his mind still has currency, we tend to emphasize Hamlet's energy, resourcefulness, courage, and even military skill. He is involved in a battle to the death, and we do not think it incongruous to conceive of Hamlet as a soldier. Fortinbras (literally "strong-in-arm"), you will recall, at the end of the play says that had Hamlet become king, he would in all likelihood have "proved most royal." (How Fortinbras could know this is, admittedly, unclear, but we assume that Shakespeare wanted his audience to take the comment seriously, and so we tend to interpret the play in a way that fits with this final evaluation.)

This opening scene is chiefly in blank verse, but most of the first twenty-five lines, chiefly short, often iambic, could pass as prose. These lines, though simple and direct, introduce the note of mystery. Further, as is apparent when one sees this scene on the stage, the element of unstabilizing doubt is strong:

Francisco is the soldier on duty, so he ought to challenge the apparent interloper, but it is Bernardo (coming to relieve Francisco) who utters the first words, the challenging "Who's there?" Later in the scene we will learn that Bernardo and Marcellus have seen the Ghost on two previous nights, so it is not surprising that Bernardo is jumpy and (hearing or seeing something) calls out "Who's there?" Francisco's response ("Nay, answer me. Stand and unfold") is not an answer to the question, and it thus further indicates to us the state of uncertainty and confusion. Our point: Hamlet is not the only character in the play who is puzzled by his encounters and who is unsure of what is what and who is who.

In this commentary we will try to confine ourselves to the text, but here we want to mention that although we admire Kenneth Branagh's film (1996), we are not wild about its opening, with its shots of Elsinor in snow, an immense statue of Hamlet Senior, a rasping noise, and (here we quote from the printed version of the screenplay) "CRASH! A body, from right of frame, bundles [Francisco] forcibly to the ground. On the frozen ground they struggle, dangerous flashing blades in the gloom." All of this before the second line of dialogue is spoken. We think that if you simply read the first twenty lines aloud or have students perform them, students will see that none of Branagh's embroidery is necessary.

Because the play was originally staged in daylight, Shakespeare has to inform his audience that the scene takes place at midnight, and this he does by having Bernardo say, "'Tis now struck twelve," a good dramatic hour. Francisco goes on to set the psychological scene: "'Tis bitter cold, / And I am sick at heart." The uncertainty is emphasized by additional questions ("Who is there?" "Who hath relieved you?" "What, is Horatio there?"), all within the first twenty lines. We in the audience are kept in the dark. Marcellus says, "What, has this thing appeared again tonight?" He goes on to speak of "this dreaded sight," and Horatio says, "Tush, tush, 'twill not appear," but the spectator or reader still does not know what "this . . . sight" or "this apparition" or this "it" is.

Bernardo begins to narrate the events of "last night," setting a cosmic stage ("When yond same star that's westward from the pole / Had made his course t'ilume that part of heaven / Where now it burns"), and in the very act of narration the Ghost appears, almost as though he has been waiting for his cue. How the Ghost entered in Shakespeare's theater we do not know. Perhaps he merely walked on, perhaps he rose through a trapdoor. Whose ghost is it? It is said to *look* like the king, but perhaps it is an imposter. Horatio asks, "What art thou . . . ?" (again, the element of uncertainty), and when "by heaven" he charges it to speak, it stalks away. Marcellus says the Ghost is "offended," but why? Because it is an evil spirit, disguised as the king, who cannot respond when charged "by heaven"? Or because it indeed is the king and is offended by Horatio's charge that it "usurps" the night and the "fair and warlike form" of the dead king of Denmark? The audience thus far has been put into suspense and then partly gratified: we at last see the "thing" or "apparition," but we still do not know whether it is the ghost of the king or a usurper, presumably an evil spirit in the form of the king. And all this within fifty lines.

Horatio informs us that "This bodes some strange eruption to our state," and (whether the Ghost is or is not the dead king) we are ready to believe him. Marcellus tells the men to "sit down," and presumably they do so, somewhat relaxing the tension—but only somewhat, since the narrative that Horatio proceeds to set forth, concerning King Hamlet and the Norwegians, is filled with anticipation of a future struggle. Bernardo conjectures that the Ghost is associated with the war with Norway; Horatio (evoking Julius Caesar) gives it a cosmic dimension. Probably we are so absorbed with the narrative that we are taken by surprise when the Ghost reappears.

Usually we linger a bit over Horatio's speech, in order to make sure that the students pick up the important political background that it provides about the former kings of Denmark and Norway, the men whose sons bear the same name as their fathers—Hamlet and Fortinbras. The elder Hamlet, "our last king," Horatio explains, fought a deadly duel with King Fortinbras of Norway. He states that old Fortinbras was incited by pride and that Hamlet's father was obliged to accept the challenge.

It is not surprising that Horatio seeks to cast the king of his own country in a favorable light (though some scholars have wondered whether Horatio, who has come from Wittenberg University, is a Dane or not), but Shakespeare has crafted the line so that it is somewhat ambiguous. "Thereto pricked on by a most emulate pride" is meant by Horatio to refer to Fortinbras, but when we hear the line it seems for a moment also to refer to Hamlet. The annotation in our text states, "refers to old Fortinbras, not the Danish king," which bears witness to the ambiguity of the line: our editor feels that there is something in the line he needs to straighten out. He is right, but part of the meaning is in our response to the line *before* it is straightened out.

Our editor glosses "emulate" as "ambitious," but in addition to this older meaning, we think that "emulate" also suggests "to strive to equal or excel, especially through imitation; to compete with successfully; to approach or attain equality with." Shakespeare is prompting us to consider how these two kings are both different and the same, both of them moved by pride and honor, both of them setting an example that their sons in their different ways—Hamlet with much more complexity and difficulty—will respond to powerfully.

Horatio says that Hamlet's success in the dual enabled him to gain Fortinbras's lands. But now, in violation of the pledge which the old kings made before the duel (the winner gets the other's lands), young Fortinbras is on the march for revenge. Horatio then reports that young Fortinbras has "sharked up a list of lawless resolutes" and is planning to regain what his father lost.

The shark is a predator of the sea—fierce, dangerous, deadly; here the word connotes something of the angry, indiscriminate way that the shark feeds on other fish—which looks forward to the imagery of food and eating in the next lines. The word can also refer to a ruthless, greedy, dishonest person (e.g., a loan shark)—which gives all the more charge to the word "lawless"—or to a person unusually skilled in a particular activity (e.g., a card shark). As a verb, "shark" means "to obtain by deceitful means; to practice or live by fraud and trickery." It's a wonderfully chosen word that reveals a central feature of both Fortinbras's character and the kind of men he has enlisted in his army of mercenaries, against whom Denmark is now hastily making preparations to defend itself.

"Lawless resolutes": such is Fortinbras's force as Horatio apprehensively describes it here. When we actually see the army in 4.4, it seems well-organized and disciplined, a fine fighting force, capably led by a "hot" (Horatio's word) but decisive and efficient Fortinbras. His narrow intensity is impressive, and to an extent it dramatizes a limitation in young Hamlet, as he observes himself. But while Fortinbras is more focused, not deterred by brooding doubts, he is for that very reason less interesting than the self-examining Hamlet, who has so many more elements in his character.

Why in fact is the Ghost walking? To warn the Danes against a Norwegian threat? Or to warn against some other "feared events," perhaps of a cosmic nature? Later we will learn that it walks because its death is unavenged, but of course none of the figures on the stage knows that the king was murdered, so they have no reason to offer this explanation. The closest anyone comes to touching on this point is Horatio's suggestion that perhaps the Ghost appears because one of the living may do something to "ease" it, but this hypothesis appears along with several others, thereby emphasizing the uncertainty.

The cock crows, the Ghost mysteriously appears in various parts of the stage ("'Tis here" "'Tis here"), and then it vanishes. Just as no one knows how the Ghost appeared in the Elizabethan stage, no one knows how it vanished. Conceivably it excited through one door just as another identically costumed actor appeared briefly at a second door; or perhaps it disappeared through one trapdoor and rose through another. The ambiguous nature of the Ghost is sustained by the contrast between Marcellus's assertion that it is "majestical" and Horatio's assertion that "it started, like a guilty thing / Upon a fearful summons" and that it cannot appear in the daylight. Marcellus goes on to suggest that it may be an evil spirit, something that cannot appear at Christmas time.

Is the Ghost "an honest ghost" or is it, as Eleanor Prosser learnedly argues in *Hamlet and Revenge* (1967), a demon impersonating Hamlet's father, with the aim of enticing Hamlet to damnation? Prosser assembles massive evidence that Elizabethans did not regard a son as obligated to avenge the death of a murdered father and massive evidence to the effect that most Elizabethan revenge plays condemn revenge. Looking specifically at *Hamlet*, she argues that the Ghost is hellish (i.e., a demon, not the spirit of Hamlet's father) because it urges revenge, it leaves when heaven is invoked and again when the cock crows, and it darts about suspiciously. Nevertheless, against all of her evidence, the writers of these pages believe that the Ghost is what it claims to be, the spirit of Hamlet's dead father. We take the play *not* to be about what Prosser in effect suggests it is chiefly about (Hamlet's escape from the devil's plot to ensnare his soul) but, rather, to be about a man's heroic fulfillment, at the expense of his life and the lives of others, to bring a murder to justice.

You may want to suggest to your students that they keep an eye out for passages concerned with Christianity. How Christian is the play? Probably the most explicitly Christian passages are Marcellus's speech here, the Ghost's later reference to purgatory, the scene in which Claudius prays, the burial of Ophelia, and

Hamlet's comments on providence and on the Christian prohibition against suicide. On the other hand, all of these passages exist in a play in which revenge is never condemned. And it is scarcely an exaggeration to say that one of the moments when Christian doctrine is most in evidence is the passage when Hamlet decides not to kill the praying king (he believes that to kill the praying king would send Claudius to heaven rather than to hell), and it is precisely this bit of theological reasoning that has most deeply offended many viewers and readers.

Although 1.1 is filled with doubt, with surprise, and with dire talk, it ends lyrically, with the coming of dawn, described (not shown, of course, on the Elizabethan stage) by Horatio. We have moved from midnight to dawn and from armed figures and an armed Ghost to a description of the dawn walking in homespun clothing, i.e., we have moved into a more comfortable world—but only for a brief while.

1.2 This scene is a bit long to do in class with student actors, but we have sometimes done the first part, up through Hamlet's first line ("A little more than kin, and less than kind"), or even up through the end of Hamlet's first soliloquy.

In contrast to the "dark" and sparsely populated opening scene, 1.2 begins with a fanfare of trumpets ("Flourish") and lots of colorfully dressed figures. Handsomely dressed members of the court crowd the stage, but Hamlet is set apart from these colorful figures, probably physically and certainly by black garments ("nighted color," "inky cloak"). This contrast is evident whether the costumes are Elizabethan (doublet and hose) or modern, or something in between, as in Branagh's film, which was set in the late nineteenth century, with the women in ball gowns and the men in colorful military attire—except for Hamlet, in black. One of the characteristics of any tragic hero is his isolation—his sensibilities set him apart—here made visible by Hamlet's costume and probably by his position on the stage. Branagh's published text tells us that Hamlet stands at the other end of the hall, "a black silhouette." Even when the tragic hero has a confidant such as Horatio he is, finally, alone, as we will see. Claudius engagingly—or is it unctuously?—summarizes the recent history of Denmark. He assures his hearers that although the dead king still is very much remembered, the time has come to go about new business. Claudius has married the queen, with the full knowledge and presumably the advice and consent of the court, and he thanks them for their help. He then turns to the present difficulty, young Fortinbras.

The speech, again, seems highly competent, even masterful, but perhaps its very polish, its abundant and perhaps too-adept use of antitheses, makes a hearer uneasy, makes a hearer sense that Claudius is trying to make the hasty marriage acceptable by tying it to the funeral. Consider the following passage:

> Therefore our sometime sister, now our Queen,
> Have we, as 'twere, with a defeated joy,
> With an auspicious and a dropping eye,
> With mirth in funeral, and with dirge in marriage,
> In equal scale weighing delight and dole,
> Taken to wife.

That image of one eye joyful and the other downcast (or perhaps dropping tears), as well as the mixture of "mirth in funeral" and "dirge in marriage" and "delight and dole," is enough (a) to reveal Claudius's skill as a shrewd politician and (b) to make us a bit queasy. The audience does not yet know that Claudius is a villainous hypocrite, but the lines certainly allow us to suspect hypocrisy.

A word about the marriage between Claudius and Gertrude. Hamlet will later call it incestuous, but if the Elizabethans regarded the marriage of a man to his sister-in-law as incestuous, why does Claudius go out of his way to speak of Gertrude as "our sometime sister, now our Queen"? Theoretically such a marriage was incestuous, but Elizabeth's father, Henry VIII, had married Catherine of Aragon, his sister-in-law, after the death of her husband, Henry's brother, Prince Arthur. Before making this marriage he had sought advice and was assured it was acceptable. Later, after he became infatuated with Anne Boleyn (and anxious for a male heir), he had moral doubts and was assured that the marriage was not acceptable. In short, the Elizabethans were of two minds about whether such a marriage was incestuous; it seems that Claudius's view was acceptable, and so was Hamlet's.

The rest of this long speech by Claudius shows him efficiently going about his business as king, explaining to the court the state of affairs with Norway, and dispatching Cornelius and Voltemand to the king of Norway. We notice that whereas Hamlet Senior conquered Fortinbras Senior in battle, King Claudius—apparently not a heroic figure—prefers diplomacy; he instructs the messengers to tell old Norway to restrain young Fortinbras.

Claudius's next speech is one of our favorites for revealing Shakespeare's skill in suggesting character:

> And now Laertes, what's the news with you?
> You told us of some suit. What is't, Laertes?
> You cannot speak of reason to the Dane
> And lose your voice. What wouldst thou beg, Laertes,
> That shall not be my offer, not thy asking?
> The head is not more native to the heart,
> The hand more instrumental to the mouth,
> Than is the throne of Denmark to thy father.
> What wouldst thou have, Laertes?

If we ask students to perform this scene, in the annotated pages that we give them we call attention to Claudius's repetition of "Laertes"—an obvious attempt (presumably successful) to ingratiate himself. A master of what Dale Carnegie later formalized as *How to Win Friends and Influence People*, Claudius names Laertes four times in nine lines, thus verbally caressing him. In our notes to student performers of the scene we suggest that perhaps Claudius put both hands on Laertes's shoulders at the beginning of the last of these lines. Or perhaps he puts an arm around Laertes's shoulders, or even around his waist.

Students will immediately see the effect of the repetition of "Laertes"; they are less likely, however, to notice another method Claudius uses in order to ingratiate himself with Laertes, his shift from the royal first person plural ("You told *us* of some suit") to the first person singular ("*my* offer"), and in addressing Laertes the shift from "you" to the more intimate "thou."

Laertes makes his brief speech (he came to witness Claudius's coronation; Horatio will explain that *he* came for the funeral of Hamlet's father), and Claudius—apparently deferring to Polonius in yet another ingratiating touch—grants Laertes's wish, such is the power of a king. Claudius then turns to Hamlet, again putting aside the royal form: "my cousin" and "my son" (not "our cousin" and "our son"). His response is a one-line speech with a bitter pun, probably uttered as an aside, and when Claudius speaks another line and is greeted with another bitter one-line answer, Gertrude intervenes, telling Hamlet not to "forever" mourn his father. Hamlet, still bitter, picks up Gertrude's word "seems" and insists that his feelings are genuine. This is one of the passages that have caused some interpreters to say that Hamlet is a nasty self-centered figure, always whining, morally quite inferior to King Claudius, who is doing his best to govern a kingdom that has recently lost its leader and that is threatened by Norway. (This interpretation never ceases to amaze us.) Claudius—a man who has murdered his brother—in the next speech has the chutzpah to tell Hamlet that his grief is "unmanly" and even "impious," that "It shows a will most incorrect to heaven." Claudius's moralizing lecture continues:

> Fie, 'tis a fault to heaven,
> A fault against the dead, a fault to nature,
> To reason most absurd, whom common theme
> Is death of fathers, and who still hath cried.
> From the first corse till he that died today,
> "This must be so."

The speech takes one's breath away, especially when one recalls that "the first corse" was that of Abel, killed by his brother, Cain—a parallel to the murder that Claudius has committed.

Having delivered this stern rebuke, Claudius again seeks to ingratiate himself with Hamlet, in effect announcing that Hamlet is his heir ("let the world take note / You are the most immediate to our throne"). At the same time he makes it clear that he wants to keep Hamlet under surveillance: "For your intent / In going back to school in Wittenberg, / It is most retrograde to our desire." The "our"—the royal plural—makes it clear that Claudius is issuing a command. Gertrude adds two lines, and Hamlet (in effect snubbing Claudius) says, "I shall in all my best obey you, madam." Claudius politely ignores the slight, seizes the favorable aspect of Hamlet's response, and puts the best gloss on it: "Why, 'tis a loving and a fair reply." Announcing that he is pleased by this response, he informs the court that when he drinks, the cannon will join the celebration, "Respeaking earthly thunder." Readers and viewers may remember this passage (and the later sounds of the cannon when the king drinks) at the end of the play, when Fortinbras orders the soldiers to fire cannon as a tribute to the dead Hamlet.

Hamlet's first soliloquy: Our text gives "sullied," in the famous passage ("O, that this too, too sullied flesh would melt"); the quartos read "sallied" (probably an alternative form of "sullied") but the Folio reads "solid." Students need not be bothered with a textual problem; "sallied" or "sullied" makes sense, but in our view "solid" goes better with "melt."

In this soliloquy Hamlet calls attention to the Judeo-Christian prohibition against suicide, and in the final scene of the play (5.2) he will make explicit reference to "Providence," but, interestingly, nowhere in the play does Shakespeare raise the issue of the relation of revenge to Christian morality. The point is important because one sometimes hears that Hamlet's delay is due to a conflict in his mind between the Ghost's command that Hamlet avenge his death and the Biblical injunction, "To me belongeth vengeance" (Deuteronomy 32:35; Hebrews 10:30). To repeat: the issue of the morality of revenge is never raised in the play.

The soliloquy clearly reveals Hamlet's sense of despair, despair engendered not only by the death of his father but by the hasty (as it seems to him) remarriage of his mother. Indeed, his mother's action seems to be the greater cause of pain. We pause here to mention that this tragedy is unusual in that the hero's tragic situation is *not* of his own making. For the most part, tragic heroes (e.g., Macbeth, Othello, Lear) take some action that brings about their suffering, but Hamlet has done nothing. He suffers, but not because of any action he has taken. And at this moment he gets, again without initiating the action, news of the Ghost, news that will somewhat lift his spirits. With Horatio, Marcellus, and Bernardo, Hamlet is among friends, though, as we will see, even Horatio cannot fully share his feelings. The scene ends (we are skipping a lot) with Hamlet significantly rejecting the formal farewell of the friends ("Our *duty* to your honor") and substituting for it the much more intimate "Your *loves,* as mine to you." The very last lines of the scene, like the last lines of the first scene, end with a note of hope.

With so much to cover in each scene and act and in the play as a whole, we always feel hard-pressed to decide what to include in (and what, reluctantly, to exclude from) class discussion. But we do try to give special attention to one or more of Hamlet's soliloquies, both for their dramatic importance and for the immediate connection they have for the students, who are familiar with many of the famous lines. In this soliloquy, as we have noted, Hamlet is in despair, especially from the pain of his mother's remarriage. "That it should come to this!" Hamlet cries out:

> But two months dead—nay, not so much, not two.

Hamlet corrects himself sharply in the middle of the line, with three negatives. He is wounded by the hard fact of how recently it was that his mother remarried and insists on getting the period of time right, perhaps because to do otherwise would almost amount to excusing his mother's deed: no, she could not claim it was as long as two months; it was less than that.

> So excellent a king, that was to this
> Hyperion to a satyr, so loving to my mother
> That he might not beteem the winds of heaven

Visit her face too roughly. Heaven and earth,
Must I remember?

"Excellent": this is Hamlet's word to describe his father's quality as king. His father, as king, was outstanding, superior, but more than that. In his *Dictionary* (1755), Samuel Johnson defines *excellent* as meaning "of great virtue; of great worth; of great dignity; eminent in any good quality." Virtue; dignity; worth; eminence. The word evokes a great deal about Hamlet's sense of his father's distinction and the specialness of his reign.

Hamlet's father was Hyperion to the satyr that is Claudius. Hyperion, in Greek mythology, is one of the Titans, the father of Helios, god of the sun; Selene, goddess of the moon; and Eos, goddess of the dawn. The satyr, on the other hand, is one of the deities of the mountains and the woods, with horns, tail, and, sometimes, the legs of a goat. The satyrs are portrayed in Greek mythology as the companions of Dionysus; they drink, dance, play music, and pursue nymphs. And in these activities, the satyr, for Hamlet, makes a fitting figure for the dissolute and lecherous Claudius.

Hamlet is angry, grievously hurt, and his intense language shows how much he has suffered—and how punished he is each time he remembers and recapitulates to himself what his mother and uncle have done. Hamlet, at this point, is overwhelmed by the profligate sexuality his mother has displayed in remarrying so quickly; he does not yet know about his father's murder—this will not come until the Ghost's appearance in 1.5. What comes painfully to mind for Hamlet now are images of his father's graciousness and sensitivity; he loved his wife so much that he wished that the winds might not blow too harshly on her face. The delicacy of this image—though the reference to the "heavens" also conveys its grandeur—is in striking contrast to the next one:

Why, she would hang on him
As if increase of appetite had grown
By what it fed on.

Hamlet represents his father as a man of power, of prominence, yet one who is lovingly attentive to his wife. She, however, crudely hangs on him, her sexual appetite increasing each time it is satisfied. The image Hamlet uses for her suggests a person somewhat desperate, out of control, who cannot keep in check her erotic desires. The implication is that she could not handle being without a husband—a husband who is depicted here as a victim, a man oppressed by his wife's sexual demands. Hamlet, too, may feel victimized by his mother's sexuality, which saturates his consciousness and which in this speech hits home for him with sickening force. His mother might say in her own defense that she was deeply in love with her husband, but Hamlet's vision of this love is coarse, burdensome—she "hang[s] on him," consuming (as the image shifts) one meal after another.

The line concludes:

And yet within a month.

The two months have been reduced to less than two and, now, to less than a single month. And the impact of these adjustments in time reinforces Hamlet's indignation. To Hamlet, it feels if anything less than a month; the new marriage seemed almost instantaneous. We realize we are stretching a point, but to us Hamlet suggests that his mother was unfaithful to her husband's memory, *and* unfaithful to this memory with such disturbing speed that she may have been unfaithful to him even when he was alive. How much longer could Hamlet's father have succeeded in satisfying her ever-growing sexual appetite? It was only a matter of time before she would betray him, if she had not already done so. The Ghost's characterization of Claudius as "adulterate" (1.5.42) suggests that Gertrude had been unfaithful while married to Hamlet Senior.

This soliloquy also offers a fine opportunity to work with videos of the play. Nearly always, we focus on the text first, reading the lines aloud, exploring the meanings and implications of words and images, getting a feel for the tone, the movement, the organization. Then we turn to one or two video clips to reflect on how much or how little the actor has come close to our own interpretation and sense of how Shakespeare is characterizing Hamlet—or maybe we should say, how Hamlet is characterizing himself—through this speech.

Laurence Olivier, in his film version, begins this soliloquy in voiceover; we hear Hamlet's words as we watch him move silently, thinking to himself and walking slowly in the shadowy hall that Claudius, Gertrude, and the others have just left. But we see and hear Olivier himself uttering the bitter words, "Nay, not so much, not two," as though this point is one he cannot keep held within. He does the same thing later, with "and yet within a month," emphasizing once more the unmistakable speed of his mother's remarriage: he cannot think of this in silence.

While Olivier's tone is haunted, soft, painfully internalized, Kenneth Branagh's in his film is fiercer, angrier, more aggressively agonized. Through his tone of voice he makes his contempt for Claudius very vivid in the "Hyperion to a satyr" contrast, and as he declares "Heaven and earth / Must I remember," he holds his hands against his head, wishing he could protect himself from the memories and images that cut into his consciousness.

This might be a good occasion for you to explain to students that there is a long, rich, complicated tradition of "playing Hamlet," and that indeed each new Hamlet is more or less obliged somehow to make *his* Hamlet different. When Branagh performed the part on the stage (and later on film) he was keenly aware of how the great Olivier had done the part. One way of understanding Branagh's performance in his film is in fact to perceive it as a response to Olivier's, every detail of which Branagh knows and is acting (or, rather, reacting) against.

This movement from the text to the film helps to remind students that *Hamlet* is a work to be read—enjoyed and explicated—and a work to be acted, brought to life anew in each production. Often, we have found that watching a film clip—say, of one of the soliloquies—enables students to understand a word or line or image that they could not quite grasp while they were reading the text on their own. Sometimes, too, it works in the other direction; the students will conclude that an actor is misinterpreting a line, misrepresenting the tone of the speech as (according to the students) Shakespeare wants it to be heard and experienced.

1.3 This rather domestic scene with Laertes, Ophelia, and Polonius comes between Hamlet's plan to meet the Ghost and the meeting itself. It is sometimes said to relieve the tension, but it might also be said to increase the tension: we listen with some interest to these lightweight people—but perhaps we also have, at least at the edges of our minds, thoughts about how Hamlet and the Ghost will meet.

Laertes has inherited something of his father's windiness, and in his dispensing of worldly knowledge he also resembles his father. Ophelia, significantly, has little to say in the scene; her longest speech occupies six lines, but most of her speeches consist of one line or half a line, such as "Do you doubt that?" and "No more but so?" Some recent Ophelias, with heightened feminist consciousness, have delivered these lines forcefully, or playfully, rather than meekly. And during Laertes's long speech some Ophelias have glared, smiled contemptuously or condescendingly, or in other ways indicated their independence. After this sort of thing, it is not surprising to hear her say to her father, "I do not know, my lord, what I should think" and "I shall obey, my lord." On the other hand, she is certainly not without spirit. After enduring Laertes's thirty-four-line lecture, she amusingly urges him to follow his own advice.

"Enter Polonius" the text says, but how does he enter? Given his propensity to eavesdrop, in some productions he enters silently at the rear, unseen by Ophelia and Laertes, and he observes them for a while before he makes his presence known. What to make of Polonius's advice? It can be delivered mechanically or absent-mindedly, making Polonius seem a fool. But certainly much of the advice is sound, and at least half a dozen lines (probably more) have found their way into common speech with no ironic implications, e.g., "Neither a borrower nor a lender be," "The apparel oft proclaims the man," and "This above all, to thine own self be true." Putting aside this last bit for the moment, one can say that Polonius's advice consists of worldly wisdom, much of it venerable, with sources in Isocrates, Cato, and other ancients. Is it good advice? In William Blake's words (though we can't recall the source), "Good advice for Satan's kingdom." Consider "Give thy thoughts no tongue." We can all agree that there are times when it is right to hold one's tongue (not just shrewd and self-serving, but morally correct), but Polonius's words easily include advice to be hypocritical. "Neither a borrower nor a lender be," but surely there are times when we should be generous, willing to lend money even though it may not be returned. "Beware / Of entrance to a quarrel; but being in, / Bear't that th' opposed may beware of thee." Perhaps Laertes heeds this advice too well; once he enters into the quarrel, he will stop at nothing, not even at the use of a poisoned foil. The bit of advice that is perhaps most memorable is

> This above all, to thine own self be true,
> And it must follow, as the night the day,
> Thou canst not then be false to any man.

Exactly what "self" does Polonius have that he can be "true" to it? If he is essentially a somewhat fatuous dispenser of platitudes, and one who fawns on the king, is this the self he should be true to? As for Laertes, he talks about honor, and in 5.2 he is so concerned with his honor that he accepts Hamlet's apology only tentatively, explaining that before he fully accepts it he wishes to consult "some elder masters of known honor"—but while he is saying this very line he holds in his hand a weapon he knows has been tipped with poison. If anyone in the play strives to be true to himself, it is Hamlet. For what it's worth, when the writer of this paragraph discusses in class the idea of being true to oneself, he customarily mentions the scene in Ibsen's *Peer Gynt* when Peer, an individualist whose motto has been "Peer, to thyself be enough," finds that by living this sort of life he has lost himself. He strips off layer upon layer of an onion, each layer representing a human relationship that he has cast off, and of course he finds there is no core, no self, because, Ibsen suggests, the nature of the self is social. Another way of getting at this idea is to look at Frost's "The Silken Tent" (in our text), where Frost makes the point that the tent stands up because it is tied down by guy lines, "countless silken ties of love and thought / To everything on earth the compass round." A discussion of this sort does, admittedly, get pretty far from the play, from talk about Shakespeare's art, about Hamlet's problem, about revenge, about tragedy, but we think it is worth it. It's our guess that students will never again speak of "being true to themselves" without thinking hard about what they mean.

To get back to the play, and to 1.3, we like to tell students that although Shakespeare's genius is evident in the famous lines, some of which we have just quoted, it is evident too in Polonius's "Affection, pooh," his contemptuous (and contemptible?) but marvelously revealing response to Ophelia's comment that Hamlet "has made many tenders of his affection." Polonius, full of worldly wisdom, cannot imagine that Prince Hamlet may indeed love Ophelia and will not seek to seduce her. We mentioned that the tragic hero is isolated from others; certainly Hamlet's world is not Polonius's. And, not surprisingly, in his last speech in this scene, Polonius forbids Ophelia from maintaining any contact with Hamlet, which, of course, serves to isolate Hamlet still further, depriving him of a connection with a loving, decent woman.

1.4 The setting is the cold guard-platform on the battlements, but the flourish of trumpets and the firing of cannon ("two pieces go off") remind us that Claudius and his court are comfortably reveling. Hamlet's comments on this habit of firing cannon when the king drinks are worth discussing in class. First, we notice that although Hamlet is "native" and "to the manner born" (i.e., he is familiar with the custom from birth), he dislikes the custom; he is isolated, separated from his fellows. Second, commentators who see Hamlet as prone to delay because he thinks too much see in the long speech he makes just before the Ghost appears a tendency to philosophize, to generalize. The argument goes thus: Hamlet begins with a specific situation (cannon being fired when the king drinks), and from this he moves, first, to commenting that Danes drink too much and then that because they are known for their heavy drinking they have a bad reputation that overshadows their good qualities. From this he goes on to reflect about "some vicious mole of nature" or "the stamp of one defect" that destroys a person. He gives several possibilities: the mole (blemish) may be (1) "in their birth—wherein they are not guilty," or (2) it may be "some complexion" (i.e., a dominant trait of temperament), or (3) it may be "some habit." When he goes on to say that it may be "nature's livery, or fortune's star," we may be justified in thinking that we are not quite clear about the categories, but in any case we do understand his point that whatever the virtues of the Danes, in the view of other people they "take corruption / From that particular fault."

The gist of the entire passage is clear enough, but the details are obscure, especially the end of the speech: "The dram of evil / Doth all the noble substance often dout, / To his own scandal." (The passage appears only in Q2, and what in our text appears as "evil" in Q2 is "eale," usually taken to be an error for "evil" but perhaps a word whose meaning we have lost. And where our text gives "often dout," Q2 gives "of a doubt.") In any case, some critics, as we have said, see in this episode a tendency for Hamlet to move from the particular to the general, or (to put it severely) to lose sight of the immediate issue. For them, this is Hamlet's tragic flaw. (We disagree.)

This speech about the "vicious mole of nature" is sometimes regarded as Shakespeare's discussion of Aristotle's concept of *hamartia,* a term that used to be translated as "tragic flaw" but now is more usually translated as "tragic error."

Despite the common image of Hamlet as melancholy, romantic, and indecisive, in the latter part of this scene he acts swiftly and bravely. He vigorously rejects the entirely reasonable warnings of Marcellus and Horatio, and he bravely approaches the Ghost. In fact, when he defies his comrades, he probably draws his sword when he says, "I'll make a Ghost of him that lets me" ("lets" of course means "hinders," as in a let ball in tennis, not "allows"). A Hamlet who draws his sword here may then hold it in front of him, using the hilt as a cross that offers protection. Hamlet exits, following the Ghost; he will receive the information that will change his life and all of Denmark.

1.5 The Ghost says Hamlet is bound to "revenge" the father's death, and this issue has given rise to an immense amount of comment. We have already referred to Eleanor Prosser, who in her book argues that Hamlet does *not* have a duty to avenge his father. A good deal of comment along these lines argues that Shakespeare regularly recommends forgiveness, for instance, Cordelia forgives Lear. On the other hand, Macduff vows vengeance on Macbeth for killing his family, and no critics object.

The Ghost imposes restrictions: "Taint not thy mind, nor let thy soul contrive / Against thy mother aught. Leave her to heaven." Hamlet now has acquired devastating knowledge (his uncle has murdered his father, and his beloved mother not only has married promptly but married the murderer), and he has also acquired the duty to avenge his father. This is not all; he must, again, not contrive against his mother, and he must not taint his mind, i.e., he must not become so consumed with hatred that he himself becomes villainous. If readers or viewers ever thought that he should heed the platitudinous remarks of his uncle and his mother in 1.2, to the effect that his grief was excessive and that he should reconcile himself to his father's death, surely they now realize that, given the new information and the new charges laid upon him, his grief can only deepen.

In the ensuing soliloquy he is not mad but he is somewhat hysterical (consider his odd injunction to himself to record his observation that a villain can smile), as well he might be, given his experience. His mother is a "most pernicious woman," his uncle a "villain, villain, smiling damned villain." When Horatio and Marcellus return, Hamlet goes on to speak what Horatio accurately calls "wild and whirling words," but, again, one must consider the revelations that have been made to him.

When the Ghost speaks from below, telling the mortals to swear, it is unclear what they say or do. The stage direction ("They swear") is an editorial addition—there is no such authentic direction and there is no dialogue. Possibly they simply place their hands on the cross-like hilt of the sword, or they may kiss the sword.

Why does Hamlet caution his friends that he may put on an "antic disposition"? In the source, it was known who killed the king, and Hamlet was guarded lest he attack the killer. He therefore feigned idiocy in order to deceive the guards into thinking he was harmless. But in Shakespeare's play Claudius has no reason to think that Hamlet knows of the murder, and therefore Claudius has no reason to fear Hamlet. By feigning madness Hamlet can only attract attention to himself and cause Claudius to be suspicious. The commonest explanation for Hamlet's announcement that he may feign madness is that (given the burden placed upon him by the Ghost's revelations and commands) perhaps he knows that he will not always be able to control himself and he therefore is cautioning his fellows about his possible odd behavior. Later in the play he insists he is not mad (e.g., in 3.4, when he says to Gertrude, "I essentially am not in madness, / But mad in craft"), but in 5.2, when he apologizes to Laertes, he twice alludes to his madness and his "sore distraction."

The scene ends not with a couplet (a fairly common way of ending a scene) but with an unrhymed line following the couplet, which, so to speak, weakens what might otherwise be a strong ending. That is, the vigor of a pair of rhymed lines ("The time is out of joint. O cursèd spite / That ever I was born to set it right") is diminished by "Nay, come, let's go together." Possibly Horatio and Marcellus have stepped back, maybe even bowing, to allow their social superior to go out first, but Hamlet insists on their leaving with him, partly out of courtesy, partly out of a need for human closeness.

2.1 This scene, like the next (the act consists of only two scenes), is largely concerned with spying, in this instance a father spying (through his agent, Reynaldo) on his son. Hamlet's father was, from all that we are told about him, a heroic figure; the father whom we see in this scene is a very different sort of person. Reynaldo protests that the false charges Polonius suggests be spoken of Laertes would "dishonor" Laertes (line 27), but in fact they dishonor Polonius. Polonius in this scene is despicable, but he is also something of a comic figure, which is to say that the first part of the scene offers some comic relief.

Ophelia's report of Hamlet's visit to her closet (private chamber) has been variously interpreted. Our own view is—this seems perfectly obvious to us—

that Hamlet, having been cut off by Ophelia, as Polonius had ordered ("I did repel his letters and denied / His access to me"), has now lost not only his father and (for all purposes) his mother but also the woman whom he loves, and this final loss has very nearly driven him mad. Ophelia says he looked at her "As if he had been loosèd out of hell / To speak of horrors," and indeed he can speak of horrors, the report of the Ghost, who has been loosed out of purgatory. Polonius interprets Hamlet's behavior as a sign that Hamlet is "mad for thy love," which is almost right, but, more exactly, we take it that Hamlet is maddened not by love (Polonius's view) but by Ophelia's rejection of his love. His mother (by her marriage) shut the door on him, and the woman whom he loves has now shut him out of her life. Ophelia's report is of his anguished farewell to his beloved.

There are, of course, other interpretations. Bradley sees in Hamlet's visit a stratagem: Hamlet is putting on the antic disposition he mentioned earlier (he knows Ophelia will report his behavior to Polonius, who will report it to the king). Why? In order to disarm Claudius, i.e., in order to seem a harmless lunatic, mad for love. In our view, the description is too convincing, too moving, for us to take Hamlet's behavior as feigned. The most astounding interpretation we have encountered, however, is that of Harold Goddard, who in *Yale Review* (March 1946) argues that the episode reported by Ophelia never really took place. The whole thing, Goddard says, is Ophelia's hallucination; nothing in the play, he argues, confirms it, i.e., Hamlet never mentions the episode and no other character claims to have witnessed it. To the extent that there is no scrap of evidence in the play that specifically supports the view that the episode actually occurred, Goddard is right, but it seems to us so clear that Ophelia is speaking the truth that no confirmation is needed.

Polonius, we believe, is right in thinking that Hamlet's behavior shows "the very ecstasy [i.e., madness] of love," but wrong in not seeing that the "ecstasy" is caused by the anguish Hamlet experiences when rejected by Ophelia. A few more words about Polonius: the stage direction in Q2, "Old Polonius," easily lets us think of him as slightly doddering. Notice line 6, "Marry, well said, very well said. Look you, sir," with its repetition and its insistence on being heeded (note also "Mark you" in line 42), and especially lines 50–51, when he loses his train of thought, lapses into prose, and then asks, "Where did I leave?"

2.2 This scene, the longest of the play, affords several passages that students can effectively perform in class. Consider the possibility of asking students to do the first thirty-nine lines, in which the king and queen talk with Rosencrantz and Guildenstern. This unit begins with Claudius preparing to make use of the two young men—the scene will end, many lines later, with Hamlet preparing to make use of the Players—and with a little coaching the student actor who plays Claudius can convey the cunning that lies beneath the apparent geniality. Although Claudius seems to be solicitous for Hamlet's sake, his real concern is his own well-being, and when in lines 14–17 he asks Rosencrantz and Guildenstern to "gather" and to "glean" information from Hamlet, he is in effect urging them to spy.

The queen immediately adds a bit of flattery ("Good gentlemen, he hath much talked of you"), and she ends her short speech with a thinly disguised offer of bribe: "Your visitation shall receive such thanks / As fits a king's remembrance." Then comes this dialogue:

> *Rosencrantz.* Both your Majesties
> Might, by the sovereign power you have of us
> Put your dread pleasures more into command
> Than to entreaty.
> *Guildenstern.* But we both obey
> And here give up ourselves in the full bent
> To lay our service freely at your feet,
> To be commanded.
>
> *King.* Thanks, Rosencrantz and gentle Guildenstern.
>
> *Queen.* Thanks, Guildenstern and gentle Rosencrantz.

The repetition of the word "both" (in the first line of Rosencrantz's speech and the first line of Guildenstern's) probably goes unnoticed, but no one can miss the almost comic repetition in the lines of the king and queen, where the names of the friends are reversed. The passage hints at the interchangeability of these two friends, two ciphers, we might say, which leads us to quote Goethe's shrewd remark in *Wilhelm Meister*:

> What these two persons are and do [Wilhelm says] it is impossible to represent by one.... These soft approaches, this smirking and bowing, this assenting, wheedling, flattering, this whisking agility, this wagging of the tail, this allness and emptiness, this legal knavery, this ineptitude and insipidity, ... how can they be expressed by a single man? There ought to be at least a dozen of these people ... for it is only in society that they are anything. They are society itself, and Shakespeare showed no little wisdom and discernment in bringing in a pair of them. Besides, I need them as a couple that may be contrasted with the simple, noble, excellent Horatio.

(When we coach students for the scene, we usually read this passage to them and briefly discuss it.)

Another scene that acts well in class and helps students to see something of the ways in which Shakespeare characterizes his figures is the episode in which Polonius diagnoses Hamlet and reads Hamlet's letter while the king and queen, barely able to contain themselves, listen to him. Polonius is so full of himself, so confident of his perceptiveness, that he probably doesn't realize he is lying when he tells Claudius and Gertrude that he had perceived Ophelia's love for Hamlet "Before [his] daughter told [him]."

Soon after Polonius proposes using Ophelia as bait ("I'll loose my daughter to him") so that Claudius can verify Polonius's diagnosis, a stage direction reads, *"Enter Hamlet reading a book."* Some directors, following a suggestion first made by John Dover Wilson, have Hamlet enter a dozen lines earlier, unseen; he hears the plot, retreats, and then enters more audibly. The idea behind this staging is to communicate to the audience that in the next scene, 3.1, when Hamlet speaks to Ophelia, he is really speaking for the benefit of the hidden Claudius and Polonius. You may want to raise the issue now and discuss it when you talk about 3.1.

Hamlet's conversations with Rosencrantz and Guildenstern, after Polonius leaves, also work well in the classroom. The passage begins with conventional phrases from Rosencrantz and Guildenstern ("My honored lord," "My most dear lord"), phrases that contrast with the earnestness or almost boyish enthusiasm of Hamlet's "My excellent, good friends! How dost thou, Guildenstern? Ah, Rosencrantz! Good lads, how do you both?" But Hamlet's remarks soon turn bitter. Of course in the first dozen or so lines he does not yet know that they are in effect spies, but presumably he senses (and we know) that they are not people with whom he can speak with ease, and very soon he sees through them, saying directly, "Were you not sent for?" They are no match for Hamlet, and a dozen or so lines later the two collapse and Guildenstern confesses, "My lord, we were sent for."

You may want to comment on Shakespeare's use of prose, or, rather, his uses of prose. We saw Polonius slip into prose when he lost his train of thought in 2.1.50; later in the play, when Ophelia becomes mad, she speaks in prose, a form that, in a play that is predominantly in blank verse, can indicate a loss of command of language. We have already seen prose used for Hamlet's letter, in 2.2, where Shakespeare wants to set off a form of discourse from the normal language of the play. (In blank verse plays, letters and proclamations normally are in prose.) In short, Shakespeare uses prose for a variety of purposes, and his prose is as shapely, as artful, as his poetry. Although prose is commonly regarded as the language of normal speech, we should remember that despite M. Jourdain's joke in *The Bourgeois Gentleman,* prose is *not* what most of us speak. Normally we utter repetitive, shapeless, and often ungrammatical torrents; prose is something very different—a sort of literary imitation of speech at its most coherent.

Shakespeare often uses prose for small talk, such as Hamlet's conversations with Rosencrantz and Guildenstern, but he uses it also for princely reflections on "What a piece of work is a man" in the present scene. Perhaps he uses prose here because in the very act of speaking about man's nobility he wishes to undercut the assertions—the "goodly frame" is for Hamlet a "sterile promontory," and the creature who is "like an angel" is for him the "quintessence of dust." In any case Shakespeare conducts his prose as carefully as his verse. One might, in fact, contrast this speech, with its deeply moving contrasts, with Polonius's rather dotty verse speech describing Hamlet, which also abounds in contrasts, but entertainingly pointless ones: "My liege and madam, to expostulate / What majesty should be, what duty is, / Why day is day, night night, And time is time, / Were nothing but to waste night, day, and time."

In the Player's speech, as in a letter or a proclamation in a play, Shakespeare uses a distinctive style—as he will again in the play-within-the-play—to separate it from its context. True, in the Player's speech he uses blank verse rather than, say, octosyllabic couplets, but it sounds different from the rest of the blank verse in *Hamlet*. Conveying this difference to students is not easy, however, because to inexperienced readers most of Shakespeare's verse sounds pretty strange, pretty extravagant. That's one reason why when we teach *Hamlet* we call attention to the apparent naturalness of the verse in the very first scene, for instance, in such a speech as "Horatio says 'tis but our fantasy, / And will not let belief take hold of him / Touching this dreaded sight twice seen of us," or even in the heightened language at the end of 1.1: "But look, the morn in russet mantle clad / Walks o'er the dew on yon high eastward hill." This language, they can see (with a little help), differs from the Player's bombastic speech: "The rugged Pyrrhus, like th' Hyrcanian beast," or "The rugged Pyrrhus, he whose sable arms, / Black as his purpose, did the night resemble / When he lay couchèd in th' ominous horse. . . ." Students may at first not quite hear the difference, but as you go on with the speech they probably will perceive its difference, its strangeness, at least in some lines.

But of course you won't talk only about the style of the speech, or even about the nice bit of imitation where "Did nothing" is emphasized (some would say "enacted") by the nothingness that makes up the rest of the line:

So as a painted tyrant Pyrrhus stood,
And like a neutral to his will and matter
Did nothing.

A question: Is the "hellish Pyrrhus" an image of Claudius, or is he an image of the avenging Hamlet? Or both? Certainly he resembles Hamlet in his quest for revenge and in (temporary) paralysis, and one can also argue that Pyrrhus, "horribly tricked / With blood of fathers, mothers, daughters, sons," anticipates Hamlet, who is at least partly responsible for the deaths not only of Polonius, Rosencrantz, Guildenstern, and Claudius but also of Ophelia and Laertes (and perhaps we can add Gertrude). Our own view is that in the picture of Pyrrhus we see a bloodthirsty avenger who is an image of what Hamlet might be if he went cold-bloodedly or hot-bloodedly about his task; that is, ultimately the spectator (on reflection) contrasts Hamlet with Pyrrhus, to Hamlet's credit.

The scene ends with a long soliloquy in which Hamlet reproves himself, a soliloquy that provides some of the evidence for the view that Hamlet delays, that Hamlet is a man who cannot make up his mind, that Hamlet knows what he should do but invents excuses for not doing it. And yet, would one want him to go about his work as Pyrrhus does? Best not to be dogmatic here. Many intelligent readers and spectators have felt that Hamlet's plan to confirm the honesty of the Ghost ("the spirit that I have seen / May be a devil") is mere stalling; others have felt that it is entirely reasonable and, further, quite in character for a man who is thoughtful, unlike (for instance) the impetuous Laertes, who is easily manipulated by Claudius.

3.1 "To be, or not to be" is among the most famous lines in Shakespeare, and the soliloquy in which it occurs is probably the most extensively discussed passage in Shakespeare. In reading some of the scholarship, one inevitably recalls James Joyce's comment (well, OK, it's a comment that Joyce puts into the mouth of Buck Mulligan), "Shakespeare is the happy hunting ground of all minds that have lost their balance." Rather than seek to review the arguments about the precise meanings of certain words and about the degree to which the speech is about human existence as opposed to being about Hamlet's particular problems, we refer you to Harold Jenkins's Arden edition (1982) of *Hamlet,* pp. 484–490.

Spectators last saw Hamlet when he was energized by his plot to trap Claudius; now, in the soliloquy, he meditates. His problem is not merely to find a way to kill Claudius but to find some meaning in life, in a world of injustice and infidelity. Here again we call attention to the tragic hero as someone isolated from others, isolated by his heightened consciousness. True, Hamlet casts a wide net in his meditations; he has not (for instance) personally suffered "the law's delay." We can say, however, that his reflections are significantly rooted in his experience. If he has not in any very obvious way experienced "the insolence of office," he has nevertheless experienced Claudius's power to prevent him from returning to Wittenberg, and with Ophelia's rejection he has experienced "the pangs of disprized [i.e., unvalued] love."

Incidentally, "disprized" is the Folio reading; Q2 has "despiz'd." A small difference, but there are so many small differences that no two modern eclectic editions of *Hamlet* are the same. And while we are touching on small textual matters, we want to mention that when, after this soliloquy, Ophelia first addresses Hamlet and asks "How does our honor for this many a day?" he replies, in F (the text chiefly used in our book), "I humbly thank you; well, well, well." In Q2 there is only one "well," and many editors take F's repetition to be an unauthorized actor's addition—and indeed it may well be. No one doubts that this is the sort of thing that actors do, and F affords several examples. Still, and here is our point, the larger issue is this: Is the text of a play the play that the author drafts, or the play that the actors perform, with revisions made in the course of rehearsals and perhaps with the permission (or reluctant permission) of the dramatist? Since Shakespeare was a member of the company that performed his plays, we can be sure that he was aware of actors' interpolations. What he thought of them is something we cannot be sure of. Once a director has settled on a text, there is still the problem of how to deliver the lines. It's too simple to say, "Just speak the lines, don't 'interpret' them, don't 'give a reading' of them." One *must* interpret them, one *must* give a reading. In the present instance, does Hamlet speak "Well, well, well" bitterly? Absent-mindedly? Cautiously?

The verbal assault on Ophelia is shocking and distressing, especially since we have no doubt that Hamlet in the main is a noble figure. An occasional critic has argued that Hamlet thinks Gertrude is eavesdropping and that his words are really directed at her. We find this view unconvincing, but we do believe that the attack on women is prompted chiefly by Hamlet's thoughts of Gertrude, though the words fall on Ophelia's ears. In any case, surely the words are provoked by the unendurable distress he has experienced, caused by (a) the death of his father; (b) the murderer's apparent success (the unsuspected Claudius rules Denmark); (c) Gertrude's swift marriage to the murderer; and (d) Ophelia's rejection of Hamlet's love. We might also add (e) Hamlet's awareness that his friends Rosencrantz and Guildenstern are spying on him, but in the context of these other agonizing experiences, their treachery is almost beneath attention. And we might also add (f) Dover Wilson's theory that Hamlet has heard Polonius tell the king that he and the king should eavesdrop on Hamlet's conversation with Ophelia—but we do not believe this to be the case.

In any case, Hamlet's comments on the discrepancy between appearances and reality (e.g., "I have heard of your paintings, too, well enough. God hath given you one face, and you make yourselves another") have already been anticipated by several passages in the play. The most notable anticipation is Claudius's own reflection about cosmetics earlier in this scene, in the speech immediately preceding "To be, or not to be," when in an aside Claudius comments on Polonius's assertion that often with "pious action we do sugar o'er / the devil himself." Claudius's words are:

> O, 'tis too true!
> How smart a lash that speech doth give my conscience!
> The harlot's cheek, beautied with plastering art,
> Is not more ugly to the thing that helps it
> Than is my deed to my most painted word.

Claudius's words are very important because they seem to confirm that he is as guilty as the Ghost claimed. His words indicate that his conscience torments him: he recognizes that his pious actions conceal the work of a man who (in the word that Polonius used) is the devil himself. But it is not clear what Claudius is, or might be, guilty of: Is he referring here to the murder of his brother, or to the over-hasty marriage to Gertrude, or to both?

Whatever its exact source, Claudius's guilt cuts him like the lash of a whip—he feels its searing pain. "Smart" is a keenly chosen word, wonderfully fitting in this context. It means, first, "with a stinging sensation." But, second, it implies mental alertness, shrewdness, intelligence, as if to suggest that the lash itself knows the depth and degree of Claudius's guilty conscience. Claudius is looking inward, with self-contempt, and he sounds in his awareness of his inauthenticity a little like Hamlet in some of his brooding soliloquies.

In the next lines, Claudius compares himself to a "harlot." This word originally referred to a vagabond, beggar, rogue, rascal, villain, low fellow, knave, and (by the 16C–17C) a man of loose life, a fornicator; later, it came to refer to an unchaste woman, a prostitute, a strumpet, though it could apply to men as well. Claudius is suggesting that he is as false as a whore, who commits sexual sin while making herself look pretty—attractive on the outside, ugly within. To put the point more exactly: Claudius is saying that the harlot's cheek is to his deed as the harlot's makeup is to the fine-sounding (but false and falsifying) words he uses. Perhaps the cheek is pockmarked, scarred from smallpox, implying that this woman can only make her way in life by trying to cover up what she looks like and selling her body. The sexual reverberations of these lines may intimate that what is really on

Claudius's mind is not the murder but the remarriage or, more likely still, the connection of the murder to the marriage. Possibly he wanted Gertrude as much as or more than he wanted the crown, and it was for this reason that he killed his brother.

In some productions, these lines are cut, perhaps because the director does not want Claudius to expose himself to the audience before the dumbshow and the Players' spoken play in 3.2. Apparently some directors conclude that if the lines are retained, 3.2 loses its suspense. On the other hand, one could argue that the suspense would still be there, just in a different form. The audience would come to 3.2 in possession of this revelation in 3.1 spoken by Claudius himself. The question, How will the King react?, will be vivid and suspenseful in either case.

When Hamlet suddenly asks Ophelia, "Where's your father?" he may be manifesting his antic disposition (the question seems to come out of nowhere), or he may have seen the arras stir (in some productions, Polonius sticks his head out in order to see or to hear better, and Hamlet catches a glimpse of him), or he may see a foot protruding beneath the arras. In Branagh's film, responding to what Branagh's stage direction calls "a tiny noise," Ophelia "glances across the room. And then it dawns." Best, in our view, Hamlet may just suddenly—mysteriously, instinctively—sense that something is wrong, that he is being spied on.

The scene ends with Claudius correctly perceiving that Hamlet's condition is not due merely to love of Ophelia. In his next-to-last speech in the play, Claudius astutely speaks of Hamlet's "brains still [i.e., continually] beating" on a "something-settled [i.e., lodged] matter in his heart," and here he puts his finger on Hamlet's distinctive quality, a mind that cannot dismiss what he has experienced.

3.2 Hamlet's speech about acting and about the nature of drama may well tell us something about Shakespeare's own ideas, but we may also connect it with Hamlet's own character, particularly with his intense concern to get things right—again, that continually beating brain. The comment that drama holds the mirror up to nature, showing "virtue her own feature, scorn her own image," is ancient. Donatus attributed it to Cicero, and it was a Renaissance commonplace. In particular, the idea was especially relevant to satiric comedy. The theory basically holds that a spectator watches the play, sees how foolish certain behavior is (e.g., miserliness, or jealousy, or love-sickness), and, not wanting to be like the absurd person on the stage, reforms his or her own behavior. Whether anyone today believes this idea about the social function of comedy is perhaps questionable, but it is worth thinking about Bernard Shaw's formulation of it in the Preface to his *Complete Plays* (1931):

> If I make you laugh at yourself, remember that my business as a classic writer of comedies is "to chasten morals with ridicule"; and if I sometimes make you feel like a fool, I have by the same action cured your folly, just as the dentist cures your toothache by pulling out your tooth. And I never do it without giving you plenty of laughing gas.

After the Players leave the stage, Horatio enters, the true friend, in contrast with Rosencrantz and Guildenstern, whom Hamlet now dismisses from the scene. Hamlet tells Horatio that he has selected him as his special friend because Horatio is a stoic. Horatio is:

> As one, in suffering all, that suffers nothing,
> A man that Fortune's buffets and rewards
> Hast ta'en with equal thanks. . . .

(There is a pun in "suffering": undergoing; experiencing pain.) Hamlet continues in this vein, praising the stoical man, the man who is "not a pipe for Fortune's finger," the man who "is not passion's slave." Such a man, he says, is Horatio, and therefore Hamlet has taken him to his bosom. We must believe that Hamlet's characterization of Horatio is apt, and we can see why Hamlet admires him, but it is also appropriate to point out that the very qualities that Hamlet praises in Horatio are qualities that make him *less* than Hamlet, *less* than a tragic hero. Hamlet's intense feeling or obsessiveness (remarked on by Claudius at the end of 3.1, when Claudius speaks of Hamlet's "brains still beating" on a "something-settled matter in his heart") is part of the essence of a tragic hero, whose response to experience is not stoical acceptance but rather a passionate and an everlasting "no." The stoic is an unimpassioned bystander, not a heroic doer, not one who feels an obligation to set the time right.

The dumbshow has caused a good deal of odd comment: Why, critics ask, does Claudius tolerate the sight of the crime in the dumbshow, since he finds the sight intolerable when the Players follow it up in a spoken performance? Answers vary. The chief answers are: (1) Claudius doesn't see the dumbshow because he has been chatting with Gertrude; (2) the printed text mistakenly conflates two versions, i.e., in one version there was a dumbshow, to which the king responded, and in another version there was a spoken text, to which the king responded; (3) the king can put up with the dumbshow because he is not convinced that it proves Hamlet is aware of his crime, but when the crime is enacted a second time, he realizes that Hamlet indeed is sending him a message; (4) the dumbshow is necessary for *us* (not for Claudius) because the spoken performance will be interrupted, i.e., Shakespeare considerately shows us the whole thing and then shows us what happens when Claudius responds in the middle of the spoken version. In our view, the last explanation is the most satisfactory. In fact, we see no problem.

The style of the play-within-the-play, especially its beginning, is notably old-fashioned (couplets in an elaborated style):

> Full thirty times hath Phoebus' cart gone round
> Neptune's salt wash and Tellus' orbèd ground,
> And thirty dozen moons with borrowed sheen
> About the world have times twelve thirties been. . . .

The reason for this distinctive style is of course to set it off from the "normal" verse language of the play. Invite students to think of comparable examples in film and television, where a flashback or a fantasy is presented. (Color may yield to black and white, or normal speed to slow motion.)

In talking about the Player King's speeches we almost always call attention to two passages that are relevant to thematic concerns:

> What to ourselves in passion we propose,
> The passion ending, doth the purpose lose.
> The violence of either grief or joy
> Their own enactures with themselves destroy.

(Late in 4.7, Claudius will say something quite similar to Laertes: "That we would do / We should do when we would, for this 'would' changes, / And hath abatements and delays".) The second passage that we sometimes dwell on is this:

> Our wills and fates do so contrary run
> That our devices still are overthrown;
> Our thoughts are ours, their ends none of our own.

Examples of ironic happenings abound in the play, for instance, Claudius prepares poison for Hamlet, but Hamlet forces Claudius to drink it, and Laertes's poisoned foil similarly is used against Laertes himself.

When the king rises, thereby interrupting the performance, he provides proof that he is the murderer. But exactly *why* does he rise? Is it because (1) he is shocked to learn that Hamlet knows that Claudius is the murderer, or because (2) he is struck with guilt? This second interpretation gains some confirmation from several passages in the play. Earlier, Claudius has indicated that indeed he has a conscience, when in an aside he says (3.1) of Polonius's speech about hypocrisy, "How smart a lash that speech doth give my conscience." Later, in the scene when he is praying (3.3), he does not spare himself: "O, my offense is rank." It is not foolish to say that Claudius may be guilt-struck when he sees the crime enacted in the play-within-the-play.

The delightful passage in which Hamlet plays upon Rosencrantz and Guildenstern, while accusing them of trying to play upon him, can go over very well in class. Again, we like to impress upon students that Shakespeare is not all fancy language and high sentiments; he can write wonderful colloquial prose. A line such as "It is as easy as lying" (often said to be proverbial, but we have never seen an earlier citation) is just as Shakespearean, and just as good, as "To be or not to be." And it is noteworthy that after Hamlet has finished playing upon his former friends, he turns to Polonius and plays a bit on him, with the business about the shape of the cloud.

In the final speech in 3.2, for instance, when he says, "Now could I drink hot blood," Hamlet is rather like the poisoner Lucianus ("Thoughts black, hands apt, drugs fit"), and in the next scene, when he contemplates killing the king but holds off because he wants to be sure to send the king's soul to hell, he perhaps sounds like a Machiavellian villain such as Iago, but for the most part

Hamlet retains our sympathy. Even the speech about drinking hot blood modulates into this:

> Soft, now to my mother
> O heart, lose not thy nature! Let not ever
> The soul of Nero enter this firm bosom.
> Let me be cruel, not unnatural;
> I will speak daggers to her, but use none.

Still as becomes evident in a moment, his hope that in dealing with his mother he will not become "unnatural" (e.g., unfilial) does not prevent him from formulating an almost diabolic design against Claudius.

3.3 Claudius's first speech lets us know that he knows Hamlet is at war with him; Claudius is obviously getting Hamlet out of the way, but only later will we learn of Claudius's plot to have Hamlet killed. Guildenstern's first speech here is typical in its obsequiousness and its windiness ("Most holy and religious," "many many," "live and feed"). Rosencrantz's speech is no less obsequious, but it also sets forth the traditional view that the fall of a king is essentially different from the fall of a lesser person: "The cess of majesty / Dies not alone, but like a gulf doth draw / What's near it with it." Like Guildenstern in the preceding speech, Rosencrantz goes on to (in effect) repeat himself: "or it is. . . ." However true the speech is, it is (a) windy, and (b) unconsciously ironic, since these words consciously refer to Claudius but can be applied to Hamlet Senior, whose death in fact was brought about by Claudius. That is, this apparent praise of Claudius is utterly misplaced, since it was Claudius's act of murder that has brought suffering to Denmark.

In discussing the episode of the king at prayer, students may need some help in understanding the difference between remorse and repentance. Claudius himself is clear about the difference. He knows that he feels a gnawing distress or mental anguish for his action (remorse, from the Latin *re + mordere,* to bite), but he also knows that if he were repentant (from *re + pentir,* to be sorry) he would resolve to change. The obvious sign of a change would be that he would give up the fruits of his action (the crown and the queen), but he cannot bring himself to this second stage:

> But O, what form of prayer
> Can serve my turn? "Forgive me my foul murder"?
> That cannot be, since I am still possessed
> Of those effects for which I did the murder:
> My crown, mine own ambition, and my Queen
> May one be pardoned and retain th' offense?

He knows the answer. Still, he tries to pray. As it turns out, he knows that his prayer is not heartfelt; again, he is remorseful but not repentant—but Hamlet, observing Claudius at prayer but not knowing Claudius's state of mind, does not realize that Claudius is in effect unconfessed.

What are we to make of Hamlet as he contemplates killing the praying king? Almost all commentators agree that Hamlet's sentiments are dreadful. For those with an Aristotelian bent, Hamlet here commits *hybris,* trying to kill not only Claudius's body but also his soul. We may as well toss in the term *hamartia*; the word is commonly translated as "tragic flaw" or (better) "tragic error," but etymologically it is a matter of "missing the mark," and Hamlet indeed misses, not only in the sense of passing up an opportunity but also in the sense of misinterpreting what is happening, since the king in fact is not contrite. We hasten to add that we do not encourage the application of these Greek terms, at least not in this episode, but some students are familiar with them (or at least with "tragic flaw") and may bring them up. For most critics, Hamlet here is at his worst. For some critics, however, the words are so dreadful that he cannot really mean them. In this view, Hamlet is looking for an excuse not to kill Claudius, and so he falls upon this ingenious way of not acting. Such was Coleridge's view, and it survives in Bradley: "That this again is an unconscious excuse for delay is now pretty generally agreed."

Let's look at the situation a bit differently: How does an audience respond at this point? Our hunch is that most people (a) do not want Hamlet to kill Claudius while the king is praying and has his back to Hamlet, and (b) they do not want Hamlet to kill while he is in this somewhat demoniacal mood. Most of us probably feel immense relief when, a moment before he might strike, he interrupts his own action.

A few words about the staging: Claudius often kisses a cross before praying and after his unsatisfactory prayer brushes the cross aside, or he may remove a crucifix that he has been wearing. Some Hamlets leave a token that the king (to his great distress) finds when he stops praying. Among the things that Hamlet has left in stage productions are a coxcomb that the antic Hamlet has worn, a gown that he has worn, or a weapon. In some productions Claudius puts down his own sword before kneeling to pray; Hamlet, unseen, removes the sword, and Claudius discovers the loss when he has finished praying.

3.4 This is the famous "closet" scene, almost always staged as a bedroom scene, but a closet is merely a private room (as opposed, for instance, to an audience chamber) and it therefore need not contain a bed. The Freudian reading (Hamlet, endowed with an Oedipus complex, desires to kill his father and sleep with his mother, and therefore he cannot bring himself to kill the man—Claudius—who in fact has done what Hamlet himself wanted to do) is widely popular and doubtless has contributed to the strongly sexual staging that the scene often gets today. But we do not need Freud or Ernest Jones to tell us that in this scene Hamlet is intensely concerned with his mother's sexuality, and as Rosenberg points out in *The Masks of Hamlet,* pre-Freudian productions often made use of a bed in this scene.

When Hamlet compares the picture of his father with the picture of Claudius, in the twentieth century he has usually pulled from his bosom a miniature of his father and from Gertrude's bosom a miniature of Claudius (lots of room for sexuality here), but sometimes the pictures are framed canvases hanging on a wall, and sometimes they are two coins that Hamlet pulls out of his pocket. Occasionally they are not a pair; the picture of Claudius may be a framed picture on a table, and the picture of Hamlet Senior may be a miniature that Hamlet wears on a chain around his neck.

We have not discussed the question of why Hamlet delays, or (as some critics put it) *whether* he delays. The implication in this last view is that although he reproaches himself for delay (in the present scene he speaks of himself as "tardy" [line 110] and the Ghost speaks of Hamlet's "almost blunted purpose" [line 115]), Hamlet in fact acts quite vigorously, i.e., he quite reasonably and systematically must first verify the Ghost. When he has established Claudius's guilt, he promptly stabs him, or thinks he does, only to find that he has killed Polonius rather than Claudius. In this view, although Hamlet reproaches himself for delay, and the Ghost also does, both of these figures are (understandably) impatient and they do not accurately represent the facts. Then there is the Freudian view, already mentioned, that Hamlet delays because he cannot kill the man who has done what he himself wishes to do. And there is a very old no-nonsense view, attributed to Thomas Hanmer: if Hamlet acted promptly the play would end too soon, so the playwright had to find excuses for delaying the killing. Our own experience, most recently confirmed when we saw Branagh's film, is that despite the occasional reference to delay, a spectator does not (so to speak) *feel* that Hamlet delays.

Two other points about the scene, or, perhaps, one point drawing on two passages. When we merely read the play, we hear Hamlet lecture his mother at some length but we may forget that his moralizing is delivered in the presence of a bloody corpse. When we *witness* the play, the corpse can be relatively inconspicuous, e.g., behind the bed, but usually it is very conspicuous, and presumably its presence strongly colors our response to Hamlet in this scene. It can be unnerving to hear Hamlet lecture in the presence of a bloody body. The second passage that we have in mind is his final speech in the scene, where, thinking about Rosencrantz and Guildenstern ("adders fanged") he seems to take a bit too much relish in the thought of destroying them:

> For 'tis the sport to have the enginer
> Hoist with his own petard, and 't shall go hard
> But I will delve one yard below their mines
> And blow them at the moon. O, 'tis most sweet
> When in one line two crafts directly meet.

One doesn't want to press the point too hard, but isn't it reasonable to say that this is not the mood the viewer wants Hamlet to be in when he finally brings Claudius to justice?

This entire speech, in fact, presents Hamlet in a disturbing light. Not only does he show a zesty glee about the fate he will contrive for Rosencrantz and Guildenstern—he will "blow them at the moon"—but he also speaks demeaningly, coarsely, about Polonius, whose "guts" Hamlet hauls away. Perhaps Hamlet is correct to term Polonius a "foolish prating knave," but one need not conclude that Polonius therefore deserved to be killed. Hamlet acted hastily when he thrust the sword through the arras, and, one could say, he excuses himself for his dreadful error by putting the blame on his victim. Polonius, we should remember, is not only the overbusy counselor to the King but also the father of Ophelia, and she (and Laertes too) suffer grievous pain because of Hamlet's bloody deed.

In some productions we have seen, Hamlet speaks the lines of this speech hysterically. He is very worked up, frenzied, distracted. There's something to be said for this approach. It removes some of the coarseness from Hamlet's words about Polonius and some of the formality of his goodbye to his mother ("good night," he says twice—sincerely? mockingly? sorrowfully?). From this point of view, Hamlet is not in full possession of his faculties as the tremendously charged scene with his mother concludes; and so we should not pin him too literally to the words that he uses. The words matter less than the complex feelings behind the words.

Hamlet's words have also been spoken in a soft, quiet, even contrite tone, the tone thereby taking some of the harshness out of the words. In more than one production we attended, the phrase "lug the guts" was omitted.

One more point, which you may wish to mention to the class: lines 209–217 ("There's letters sealed . . ." to ". . . two crafts directly meet") are not in F and may pose a bit of a problem. They do not seem to jibe with what Hamlet later (5.2.4ff.) reports to Horatio, where he tells of discovering the murder order in Rosencrantz and Guildenstern's papers. How, one wonders, has he found the "letters sealed," to which he refers?

The play is filled with intriguing puzzles of this kind. Some of them are hard (if not impossible) to resolve; others, it seems, can be resolved with interpretive effort and ingenuity. We try to find moments during class to bring up examples of the play's textual cruxes and perplexities—we mention a number of them in this commentary. It is important to explain to students what a Shakespeare play is—that an edition of the play that we read is the result of a demanding editorial process that involves the study of texts and manuscripts often filled with mysteries and contradictions. But we need to remind ourselves that *Hamlet* is a big challenge for students, and it may be risky to linger too much over this or that textual problem or issue. When we teach the play, we find that the students do best when they keep their attention on the main lines of character development and organizing themes.

4.1 It is impossible to know if Gertrude really believes Hamlet is "mad as the sea and wind" (line 7) or if she is covering for Hamlet. Similarly, her assertion that Hamlet "weeps for what is done" (line 27) cannot be verified. But what is especially interesting about this short, urgent scene is the growing separation between Claudius and his queen. In line 28 he says, "O Gertrude, come away!"; in line 38, "Come Gertrude"; in line 44, "O, come away!" Throughout this speech she remains silent, presumably moved by what Hamlet has told her during the closet scene. In stage productions, if Claudius seeks to put his arm around her waist or shoulder, she usually draws away from him. Note, too, that in his last line in the scene ("My soul is full of discord and dismay") he reveals that the battle with Hamlet (and with his own conscience?) is indeed unnerving him. And why shouldn't he be unnerved? If in the prayer scene Hamlet has left with Claudius a token, for instance, a coxcomb, Claudius may now be holding it nervously.

4.2 A reader may take this scene to be chiefly one in which Hamlet verbally displays his antic disposition, but in fact the scene is filled with physical action. There are the offstage shouts, then the bustling entrance of Rosencrantz and Guildenstern who in effect have been pursuing Hamlet. Branagh's stage direction in the script for his film gives an idea of the physical business: "They circle each other in the large room. Wary of a quick move." In the film, as in many productions, courtiers and soldiers enter, and attempts are made to lay hands on Hamlet. In Branagh's film, "Hamlet grabs Rosencrantz around the neck, taking him hostage against the growing crowd," and ultimately "Hamlet throws Rosencrantz back to the crowd." Incidentally, the last sentence in the scene, Hamlet's "Hide fox, and all after" (doubtless a line from a game of hide-and-seek) appears only in F, and it is commonly regarded, probably rightly, as an actor's addition. So again we can raise the question: What is the text of a play by Shakespeare—the play that he wrote or the play that was produced?

4.3 In line 14 we learn that Hamlet now is "guarded," and when he appears on the stage his hands may be bound, or he may be surrounded by armed guards. In Daniel Day-Lewis's production he was confined in a straitjacket. The wit-battle concerning the trip to England makes it clear that Hamlet and Claudius are at war. Here is how Branagh presents this passage in his film-script. (We do not preserve Branagh's typography, punctuation, or spelling, only his words.)

> *Claudius:* . . . Therefore prepare thyself.
>   The bark is ready, and the wind at help,
>   Th' associates tend, and everything is bent
>   For England.
> *Hamlet:* For England!
> *Claudius:* Ay, Hamlet.
> *Hamlet:* Good.
> *(Claudius will not give in to Mr. Smart-arse.)*
> *Claudius:* So it is, if thou knew'st our purposes.
> *Hamlet:* I see a cherub that sees them. But come, for England! Farewell, dear mother.
> *Claudius:* Thy loving father, Hamlet.
> *Hamlet (brightly):* My mother. Father and mother is man and wife, man and wife is one flesh, and so my mother. *(This last with real hatred.)*

This is warfare, and we are not surprised to hear, a few moments later, the king confess in a soliloquy that he has ordered "the present [i.e., instant] death of Hamlet." In our view (here we tip our hand) it is entirely appropriate at the end of the play for Fortinbras to order the soldiers to treat Hamlet as a soldier who died doing his duty: "Let four captains, / Bear Hamlet, like a soldier, to the stage. . . ."

4.4 This scene (along with Fortinbras's other scenes) is often deleted in productions, but it is an important scene, not only because it shows a contrast between Fortinbras in command and Hamlet in custody but also, of course, because of the great soliloquy in which Hamlet meditates on the distinction between man and beast, characterized by the human being's possession of (a) rationality and (b) a sense of honor. These two qualities may be in conflict: rationality may cause us to think carefully (we may find ourselves "thinking too precisely on th' event"), whereas our sense of honor may cause us to act impetuously, even rashly. Hamlet praises Fortinbras as a man of action, but notice how some of the diction in his speech quietly undermines the praise. Expressions such as "divine ambition puffed," "eggshell," "straw," "fantasy and trick of fame" make the hearer doubt the worth of the quarrel motivated by honor. True, the speech ends strongly: "O, from this time forth / My thoughts be bloody or be nothing worth!" yet even here, in "bloody," we may have mixed feelings about what Hamlet apparently is praising.

4.5 The scene begins with the queen, obviously agitated ("I will not speak with her"), seeking to put off an encounter with Ophelia, partly of course to avoid a stressful situation, but partly because the queen herself is almost distraught (in line 17 she speaks of her "sick soul"). Perhaps the Gentleman's speech describing the mad Ophelia is meant to prepare the viewers, lest they laugh when they next see her. What has driven Ophelia mad? Among the possible causes: (1) the death of her father, at the hands of the man she loved; (2) Hamlet's rejection of her; (3) guilt at the thought that, on her father's order, she betrayed Hamlet.

In 1.4.90 Marcellus had said, "Something is rotten in the state of Denmark," and the truth of his remark is everywhere in evidence here—in Ophelia's madness, in Gertrude's soul-sickness, in Claudius's uneasiness in this scene ("Where is my Switzers? Let them guard the door" he calls out when he hears "a noise outside"). In fact, when Claudius speaks to Gertrude and enumerates the causes of Ophelia's madness, saying "When sorrows come, they come not single spies, / But in battalions," we can rightly take his words to apply to his own distress, we might say his dis-ease. And notice, too, in this speech, how Claudius is becoming isolated from his wife. Twice he addresses her, once near the beginning of the speech and once near the end ("O Gertrude, Gertrude," "O my dear Gertrude") but he gets no response from her. (A bit later, however, Gertrude seizes Laertes in order to protect Claudius.)

We need comment only briefly on Laertes here. It is obvious that his angry words about the death of his father can be compared and contrasted with Hamlet's:

> How came he dead? I'll not be juggled with.
> To hell, allegiance! Vows to the profoundest devil!
> Conscience and grace, to the profoundest pit!
> I dare damnation. To this point I stand.
> That both the worlds I give to negligence,
> Let come what comes, only I'll be revenged
> Most thoroughly for my father.

Having seen Claudius work his charms upon Laertes in 1.2, we are not surprised to see that Claudius can easily disarm this angry young man, indeed partly by the same device of unctuously repeating Laertes's name:

> What is thy cause, Laertes,
> That thy rebellion looks so giantlike?
> Let him go, Gertrude. Do not fear our person.
> There's such divinity doth hedge a king
> That treason can but peep to what it would,
> Acts little of his will. Tell me, Laertes,
> Why thou are thus incensed. Let him go, Gertrude.
> Speak, man.

Claudius calms Laertes, assures him that the crown is innocent, and that justice will be done. Claudius's last words in the scene are, "And where th' offense is, let the great ax fall." At the end of the play we will see that the ax falls on Claudius as well as on the others, innocent and guilty.

4.6 Hamlet's letter (in prose, as usual) reveals a confident tone, and it reports energetic action—in effect it refutes the idea that Hamlet is someone who cannot act decisively. Also noteworthy is the fact that Hamlet tells Horatio to give the letter (his word is "letters," but the plural form regularly has a singular sense) to the king, i.e., Hamlet does not contrive to make an unexpected appearance. As we will see in subsequent passages, his mood now differs from his earlier moods; he now is beyond contriving. Incidentally, in the next scene Claudius assures Laertes that Laertes can use an unbated foil without Hamlet noticing it because Hamlet is "Most generous, and free from all contriving."

4.7 The dialogue between Laertes and Claudius, or especially the portion beginning after Hamlet's letter and continuing up to the entrance of the queen, is a bit long, but students can perform it effectively in class. Laertes is not exactly dumb, but he is no match for the Machiavellian Claudius, and one almost feels sorry for him when Claudius says, "Can you devise me?" and Laertes replies, "I am lost in it, my lord." A moment later, when Claudius says, "Will you be ruled by me?" Laertes replies, "Ay, my lord, / So you will not o'errule me to a peace," and of course peace is the last thing that Claudius has in mind for Laertes. Claudius flatters Laertes ("You have been talked of since your travel much, / And that in Hamlet's hearing"), telling him that Lamord's report of Laertes "Did Hamlet so envenom with his envy / That he could nothing do but wish and beg / Your sudden coming o'er to play with you. / Now, out of this—" and Laertes, who has not quite followed what Claudius is getting at, rather simply asks, "What out of this, my lord?" Notice that Claudius does not directly answer the question, but instead keeps Laertes in suspense and whets his appetite by asking, "Laertes, was your father dear to you?" One cannot help admiring Claudius, so skilled is he in manipulating the impetuous young man. Claudius continues, bringing up again the motif of action that may dissolve into nothing ("Time qualifies the spark"). Laertes assures Claudius that he would "cut [Hamlet's] throat in' the church," a sentiment seconded by the murderer

Claudius, who piously observes that "No place, indeed, should murder sanctuarize." And then on to a passage we mentioned a moment ago, when Claudius rightly says that Hamlet, being "generous, and free from all contriving, / Will not peruse the foils." True, earlier Hamlet had been engaged in contriving, but when he returns from the sea journey he is changed for the better, willing to act at the right moment ("the readiness is all") but not plotting to establish the conditions of the moment.

If one wants to talk about *hamartia*, one can say that Hamlet is guilty of a "tragic error" (he does not peruse the foils), but certainly this error or mistake proceeds not from a flaw in character but from a virtue. In contrast to Hamlet's virtue is Laertes's dishonorable behavior; Claudius has suggested using an unbated foil, and Laertes not only consents to using it but adds that he will also poison the tip. Claudius then suggests that as a backup he will prepare a poisoned chalice. Surely it makes no sense to see Hamlet as flawed when one sees villainy such as this.

Laertes is (from the spectators' view) at a low point, but the report of Ophelia's death does get some sympathy for him. The audience's response, however, is probably complex. We sympathize, and perhaps are even touched by his grief, but we also know that the reason why he does *not* utter the "speech of fire" that blazes within him is that he is confident he will kill Hamlet in the duel.

5.1 The dialogue between the clowns is amusing even when it is acted by amateurs, and even when it is delivered to people not familiar with the footnotes. But why does Shakespeare include in this dialogue passages insisting on Hamlet's age? Doubtless he wanted to convey the irony inherent in the fact that Hamlet was born on the very day that the gravedigger began his trade—it is almost as though the gravedigger has all this time been digging in anticipation of Hamlet's death—and Shakespeare also wanted to connect Hamlet's birth with the triumph of Hamlet's father over Fortinbras. Still, why did Shakespeare insist on Hamlet's age? Perhaps he wanted to emphasize Hamlet's maturity, lest the audience think too much about Hamlet as the moody student of 1.1.

We want to talk a bit about Hamlet's famous leap into the grave—a leap that maybe he does not make. Certainly Laertes leaps into the grave first. Laertes's dialogue clearly calls for his leap, and stage directions in Q1 and F confirm it. He says, "Hold off the earth awhile, / Till I have caught her once more in mine arms" and then, after leaping into the grave, he says, "Now pile your dust upon the quick and dead." Hamlet's leap is far less clearly established; in fact, it depends entirely on a stage direction a bit later in Q1, a so-called "Bad Quarto": "Hamlet leaps in after Laertes." This direction, not in Q2 or F, may well merely reflect a provincial production. It is attractive in some ways, since the leap into the grave can be taken as a sort of symbolic entrance into death, and the leap out as a sort of renewal of life. On the other hand, it serves to make Hamlet the aggressor, and many students of the play wish to see in the Hamlet who has returned from the sea journey a new, mature Hamlet, a Hamlet who proclaims his kingly identity with "This is I, / Hamlet the Dane." (Cf. Claudius's earlier use of "the Dane" to mean the king, when he says to Laertes, in 1.2, "You cannot speak of reason to the Dane, / and lose your voice."

Further, the dialogue pretty clearly indicates that Laertes is the aggressor. Hamlet says, "I prithee, take thy fingers from my throat," and "Hold off thy hand," perhaps indicating that Hamlet's mere announcement that he is "the Dane" has caused Laertes to climb out of the grave and to seize him. Such is the way the episode is staged in Branagh's film. Somewhat strangely, Laertes has no lines in this scene after he and Hamlet are separated, even though Hamlet directly addresses him, for instance, with "Hear you, sir, / What is the reason that you use me thus?" (By the way, one may wonder how Hamlet can be unaware of why Laertes is enraged.) In some performances, Hamlet offers a hand or arm to Laertes is enraged.) In some performances, Hamlet offers a hand or arm to Laertes, who angrily (and silently) rejects the offer. In other performances, Laertes is still being restrained by those who separated him a moment ago during the fight. You may want to invite students to talk about how they would stage the fight and the remainder of the scene.

5.2 We spend a lot of time discussing this scene in class, much of it on the question of whether Hamlet's change of mood after the sea journey is (to put the matter crudely) a Good Thing or a Bad Thing. Our own view is that he has brought himself into the proper frame of mind, proper in that it ultimately is satisfactory to the spectator. That is, he pretty much ceases to be the bloodthirsty avenger, the man scheming and at the same time upbraiding himself for not accomplishing his purposes. He becomes, in our view (speaking a bit broadly), the man who rightly understands that he has a task to fulfill and that he *will* fulfill it, but in a way not yet known to him. The Ghost had enjoined him, "Taint not thy mind" (1.5.86) but we have seen that Hamlet in his bloodthirsty moments, and especially in his desire to catch the king's soul, comes close to violating this command. Even the passage at the end of 3.4, when he contemplates with pleasure outwitting and destroying Rosencrantz and Guildenstern, has a disturbing edge to it:

> For 'tis the sport to have the enginer
> Hoist with his own petard, and 't shall go hard
> But I will delve one yard below their mines
> And blow them at the moon.

Now, however, in the final act his mood is different. In his second speech in 5.2 he tells Horatio that he acted rashly:

> Rashly
> And praised be rashness for it—let us know
> Our indiscretion sometimes serves us well
> When our deep plots do pall, and that should learn us
> There's a divinity that shapes our ends,
> Rough-hew them how we will. . . .

Telling Horatio about the letter ordering his death, he rightly says:

> Being thus benetted round with villains,
> Or I could make a prologue to my brains,
> They had begun the play.

Thus, in a situation *not of his own making* (just as his initial situation—the death of his father and the remarriage of his mother—was not of his making), he responds more or less spontaneously, i.e., without the calculated villainy that characterizes a Machiavellian. His response, a forged letter that sends Rosencrantz and Guildenstern to death, has distressed some commentators, but we confess that our own uneasiness is *very* slight. In the traditional legend, Hamlet contrives a successful revenge, and obviously in Shakespeare's play there are traces of Hamlet as an intriguer. But in Shakespeare's play, interestingly, most of Hamlet's intriguing comes to nothing. The obvious exception is the execution of Rosencrantz and Guildenstern, but whatever uneasiness a spectator or reader might have about their end is diminished: (a) The deaths are reported, not seen; (b) we have little sympathy for the two victims; (c) Hamlet is acting under great pressure, with his own life at stake; (d) asked by Horatio how Hamlet "sealed" the letter, Hamlet replies, "Why, even in that was heaven ordinant," and we are inclined to believe him (more about this in a moment); and (e) no one in the play expresses grief over the deaths of Rosencrantz and Guildenstern. Horatio's dry comment probably expresses much the audience's sentiment: "So Guildenstern and Rosencrantz go to 't."

What about this business of heaven being "ordinant"? The play (unlike *Lear*) is set in a Christian world, with a ghost from purgatory, talk of "our Savior's birth," and so on. When we experience this play, do we strongly feel a divine providence? *Hamlet* is not a medieval biblical play with a heaven-sent avenging angel. On the whole, things seem to work out on a purely naturalistic level. And yet: The Ghost gives Hamlet information that is otherwise unknown; the traveling players appear from nowhere, so to speak, allowing Hamlet to confirm the Ghost's message; during the sea voyage Hamlet, unable to sleep, is mysteriously prompted to examine the commission from Claudius; he forges a different commission and providentially (he says) is able to seal it with the king's signet; a pirate ship comes out of nowhere, and Hamlet alone boards it; Laertes and Claudius, *not* Hamlet, prepare the unbated poisoned foil that will enable Hamlet to fulfill his revenge; and this fulfillment is accomplished publicly, in circumstances arranged not by Hamlet but by Claudius. (Whether Hamlet holds the poisoned rapier by chance or not is something we will look at in a moment.) We do *not* want to say anything to the effect that the play shows God is always at work in the world in mysterious ways, but we do want to say that in some mysterious way things work out, and that Hamlet fulfills his revenge without becoming a villainous avenger.

We have not yet looked at several speeches in 5.2, after Osric's departure, in which Hamlet seems to some commentators to have achieved an inner peace (in contrast, for instance, to the end of the soliloquy in 4.4, when he says "O, from this time forth / My thoughts be bloody or be nothing worth!"). To other commentators, however, these speeches indicate that he has lapsed into further inaction, inaction that he masks as resignation to heaven's will. The two most explicit passages are:

> (1) I am constant to my purposes; they follow the King's pleasure. If his fitness speaks, mine is ready; now or whensoever, provided I be so able as now.

> (2) Not a white, we defy augury. There is special providence in the fall of a sparrow. If it be now, 'tis not to come, it will be now; if it be not now, yet it will come. The readiness is all.

In the second speech, the line about the "special providence in the fall of a sparrow" echoes Matthew 10:29: "Not a sparrow shall fall on the ground without your Father's knowledge." Writing about this passage, A. C. Bradley in *Shakespearean Tragedy* (1904) said that he did *not* find "any material change in [Hamlet's] general condition or the formation of any effective resolution to fulfill the appointed duty. On the contrary [the speech and some other speeches] seem to express that kind of religious resignation which, however beautiful in one aspect, really deserves the name of fatalism rather than of faith in Providence." H. B. Charlton, essentially a Bradleyite, in his own *Shakespearean Tragedy* (1949) says pretty much the same thing:

> Worst of all, recognition of the will's impotence is accepted as . . . the calm attainment of a higher benignity, whereas it is nothing more than a fatalist's surrender of personal responsibility. That is the nadir of Hamlet's fall. (p. 103)

We see the point, but we differ. We don't know how either of the two contrasting views (Hamlet as lapsing in fatalism vs. Hamlet as achieving a heightened state of awareness) can ever be proved to the satisfaction of those who begin by holding the other view, but it seems to us that Hamlet's move from bloodthirsty plotting to an awareness that he must make himself ready to act when the right moment comes represents progress. Further, his apology to Laertes indicates a healthier state of mind than he has sometimes earlier displayed. And what of his comment, shortly before the duel, that the culprit was not Hamlet but "Hamlet's madness"? We are uneasy here. Is he lying? If so, his behavior is reprehensible. We prefer to think he now understands that indeed some of his earlier behavior (his cruel rejection of Ophelia comes to our minds) was the result of an emotional stress that caused him to behave in ways that would be shameful for a rational person. Remember, too, that we in the audience know, but Hamlet does not know, that the man to whom he is apologizing is prepared to murder Hamlet. Surely the spectator's response during this speech when Hamlet shifts some of the blame for his actions to his madness is not condemnation of Hamlet for evading responsibility but wonder about what Laertes's response will be. And what is Laertes's response? This man who is planning to use a poisoned foil insists in a fatuous and finicky way that he can accept Hamlet's apology only provisionally, and that before he can be certain that Hamlet's apology leaves Laertes's honor unbesmirched, he will consult "some elder masters of known honor." An audience that responds intelligently to Laertes's twisted sense of honor can hardly judge Hamlet adversely.

The duel between Hamlet and Laertes perhaps brings to mind thoughts of the conflict between Hamlet Senior and Fortinbras, an honorable battle, in the heroic manner, that contrasts strongly with the treachery that underlies the present encounter. Exactly what happens in this final duel is a bit uncertain. Does Hamlet, wounded by Laertes's unbated foil, suddenly realize that Laertes is out to kill him, and does he therefore wrest the weapon from Laertes's hand? Q1 (the "Bad Quarto") says, *"They catch one anothers Rapiers, and both are wounded, Laertes falles downe, the Queene falles downe and dies."* The Folio says, *"In scuffling they change Rapiers."* Q2, a good quarto, has no stage direction here. The problem, then, is this: Do they exchange rapiers because Hamlet knows that Laertes holds an unbated rapier? Or does the exchange result from chance, from a scuffle in which the weapons are accidentally exchanged? Is this fatal exchange one of "accidental judgments, casual slaughters" ("casual" from the Latin *casus,* "chance") that Horatio will mention when he tells Fortinbras what has just occurred?

Olivier in his film has Laertes thrust at Hamlet and draw blood. Hamlet, realizing that Laertes's foil is unbated, in the next round knocks the foil out of Laertes's hand, retrieves it for his own use, and gives Laertes the blunt-tipped foil. Branagh in his film has Laertes rush at Hamlet, nick Hamlet's shoulder, then run past him, stop, and face him. After a few seconds of slow circling, *"suddenly it's a free-for-all, and now Hamlet chases Laertes round the hall, in amongst the crowd. . . . A great leap from Hamlet trips Laertes up. His sword skids away. Hamlet rushes for it. He looks at the tip—enraged. He throws his own sword to Laertes and retains the poisoned one."*

Laertes confesses his treachery ("The foul practice / Hath turned itself on me"), blames the king and says Claudius "is justly served," thus publicly vindicating Hamlet. "Exchange forgiveness with me, noble Hamlet," Laertes says, and we take seriously the word "noble." As we have earlier said at some length, Hamlet fulfills the Ghost's command, and—remarkably—he does so in a way that does not taint him with murder.

Horatio summarizes the "woe and wonder" (standard characteristics of heroic tragedy) that Denmark has witnessed:

> So shall you hear
> Of carnal, bloody, and unnatural acts,
> Of accidental judgments, casual slaughters,
> Of deaths put on by cunning and forced cause,
> And, in this upshot, purposes mistook
> Fall'n on th' inventors' heads.

"Purposes mistook" are evident: Laertes prepares a foil to poison Hamlet, but he himself dies by that foil; the king prepares a poisoned drink for Hamlet, but

Gertrude drinks it, and ultimately Hamlet forces the king to drink it. The "carnal" and "unnatural acts" may include Gertrude's incest; the "casual slaughters" may include the murder of Polonius and the drowning of Ophelia. But we need not try to identify each of Horatio's words with a particular happening in the play. It is enough, we think, to see that Hamlet, thrust into a tragic situation that is *not* of his own making, has at last performed the arduous task that he was ordered to do. T. S. Eliot, in "Shakespeare and the Stoicism of Seneca," a bit snidely says that Hamlet, having made a mess, "dies fairly well pleased with himself." In our view, Eliot misunderstands the play, partly because he does not see that Hamlet has indeed been successful (though at a terrible cost), and partly because he does not realize that it is appropriate for the tragic figure to make a dying speech in which he sums up his essence. (Othello has been similarly criticized for, in Eliot's words, "cheering himself up.") Many of your students will know *Macbeth,* so you may want to remind them that we get a report of the final speech made by the traitor Cawdor, just before he was executed: "Very frankly he confessed his treasons, / Implored your Highness' pardon and set forth / A deep repentance: nothing in his life / Became him like the leaving it."

The play ends with Fortinbras ("strong arm," the man of action) awarding Hamlet a salute from the cannon ("*a peal of ordnance is shot off*"), a military tribute to a heroic figure, a tribute to a man who, though he apparently preferred the meditative life associated with the university, nevertheless fulfilled a tremendously demanding task. When we hear the sounds of the cannon at the end of the play, we may recall that earlier in the play the cannon were set off when the base king drank. Now at the end, it is evident that Denmark has been purged of a criminal king, by a man who "was most likely, had he been put on, / To have proved most royal."

23

Studying America in Crisis: Responding to Literature of the Civil War, the Great Depression, the Vietnam War, and September 11, 2001

JEFFERSON DAVIS
Inaugural Address (p. 1057)

Jefferson Davis resigned his seat in the U.S. Senate in 1861 when his home state of Mississippi seceded from the Union. A graduate of West Point and an experienced soldier and officer who had served in the Mexican War, Davis expected that he would be placed in command of the Confederate armies, but instead he was named President of the Confederate States of America.

During the war, and in the decades after the South's defeat, President Davis was criticized, as one biographer has commented, "for intervening in the military's policies and for assuming near-dictatorial executive powers." The Texas senator and governor Sam Houston said of Davis at the time that he was as "ambitious as Lucifer and cold as a lizard." This judgment was pointedly echoed by Winfield Scott, a Virginian serving as a lieutenant general in the U.S. Army, who observed: "I am amazed that any man of judgment should hope for the success of any cause in which Jefferson Davis is a leader. There is contamination in his touch." Then and later on, Davis was assailed too for his inability to weld the slave states into a true "nation," united in common political and military purpose.

On the other hand, more sympathetic biographers and scholars have noted that Davis was in a near-impossible position: How could anyone lead a "nation" that in fact was based on a staunch and strident, indeed extreme, "states' rights" theory? The entire point of secession, after all, was that it was undertaken as an act of principled opposition to a coercive national government. Perhaps something of Davis's strengths and limitations is summed up by the historian David M. Potter: He was "a man who thought in terms of principles rather than of possibilities and who cared more about proving he was right than about gaining success."

The most obvious thing about the style of Davis's Inaugural Address is that it uses, appropriately enough, what will seem to students to be a highly elevated style, though in fact it is not far removed from presidential addresses even in the twentieth and twenty-first centuries. Typically such speeches use periodic sentences, that is, sentences whose meaning is not syntactically complete until the end or near the end. This means the sentences often begin with a series of dependent clauses and often use parallels until—after many words—they at last reach the independent clause that makes the meaning clear. The formula can be illustrated simply by this much abbreviated invented example: "Of X, of Y, of Z, I say nothing." Davis's first sentence is not wholly typical, since the main verb and its subject ("I approach") appear after a mere twenty words, but it can be used to illustrate something of the style: Davis begins with "Called to the . . . station. . . , I approach. . . ."

The first sentence of the third paragraph is a more typical example. It begins, "Looking forward," and it goes on for another forty-two words before we get the main verb, "I enter." Also characteristic of the speech are doublets, triplets, and parallels: "difficult and responsible situation," "guide and aid," "virtue and patriotism," "courage and patriotism," "honor and security," "no aggression . . . no domestic convulsion," "to success, to peace, and to prosperity." As we can see from the last example, with its "peace" and "prosperity," we also find alliteration. Other examples of alliteration are "discharge of the duties" and "policy is peace."

Although Davis's Address is far removed from ordinary speech—probably far removed even from the ordinary speech of highly educated Southern gentlemen of the mid-nineteenth century—it causes readers no difficulty. The diction is simple and the syntax does not befuddle. It is, in short, good political rhetoric, not far removed from the usual State of the Union address. You might ask students to chart the gist of the presentation. As we see it, it goes somewhat along the lines of what is outlined on the next page—but first we should mention that it was delivered from the top step of the Capitol in Montgomery, Alabama (at that time the capital of the Confederacy, though the capital was later moved to Richmond, Virginia). The building at Montgomery drew on Greek and Roman architecture and Jeffersonian classicism, which is to say that it was white, simple, and dignified rather than exuberant, fronted by a columned portico and topped with a dome; in short, it was big and blocky (Roman *firmitas*), and it proclaimed to viewers that ancient Roman traditions such as civic duty, the rule of law, and the institution of slavery were alive and well in the New World. Students should be reminded that the *setting* of a speech (for instance, the area in front of the Lincoln Memorial, for Martin Luther King Jr.'s "I Have a Dream") is an important part of the speech. That is, the setting *says* something, is part of the speech.

Paragraph 2: Presentation of the self: "humble" but confident because of "the wisdom" of those who will "guide and aid" him. (The speaker is establishing what rhetoricians call *ethos*, or "ethical appeal," i.e., his honorable character.)

Paragraph 3: Optimistic; reasserts "the right of the people to alter or abolish governments whenever they become destructive of the ends for which they were established."(Here we are getting *logos*, "logical appeal," reasons.)

Paragraph 4: The Confederacy represents the original principles of the nation.

Paragraph 5: The high-minded principles that motivated the formation of the nation in the eighteenth century and that now motivate the formation of the Confederacy justify our position. Further, we hope that if war is forced upon us, posterity will know who is the aggressor.

Paragraph 6: We are an agricultural people, and "our true policy is peace and the freest trade." Reason says there should be no conflict between us and the North, but if "passion or the lust of dominion should cloud the judgment or inflame the ambition" of the North, we must fight. (Lots of *logos* and *ethos* here.)

Paragraph 7: We must provide certain departments and services.

Paragraph 8: "For the purposes of defense" we will need an army and a navy.

Paragraph 9: Given the fact that our constitution is true to the original constitution, some states may seek to join us, and we welcome them—but we will not return to the society from which we have seceded.

Paragraph 10: We are motivated only by "the desire to preserve our own rights and promote our own welfare"; we have offered no "aggression" and we have caused no "domestic convulsion." It is the North that has not been guided by "reason."

Paragraph 11: My experience in lesser offices has taught me to expect "toil, and disappointment" but I will work hard in an effort to merit your confidence (the usual expressions of humility that political candidates offer).

Paragraph 12: Our constitution is true to the original Constitution (reaffirmation of American principles).

Paragraph 13: Reaffirmation of the justice of the cause and of the speaker's dedication to it and to those who have chosen him.

Paragraph 14: The concluding paragraph, so it appropriately begins affirmatively ("It is joyous"), yet reaffirms the danger of the moment ("perilous times"), compliments the audience ("a people united in heart"), speaks of "sacrifices," and brings God into the argument ("sanctified," "reverently," "God of our fathers," "his blessing"). This paragraph also makes obvious use of the parallels and triplets and alliteration that we noted earlier ("perpetuate the principles," "vindicate, establish, and transmit," "to success, to peace, and to prosperity").

If you ask students to make a paragraph outline something like this, in which they indicate the gist of what each paragraph *says* and (equally important) what each paragraph *does*, they will learn a good deal about the rhetoric of political speeches.

MARY BOYKIN MILLER CHESNUT
November 28, 1861 (p. 1061)

Chesnut's diary was private, not intended for publication, and the author makes no effort to reconcile passages that seem to us to be contradictory. Thus, she can say—and we take her to be speaking truthfully—that she hates slavery, but she can also say in effect that blacks are fit only to be slaves, and that whites have a duty to guide blacks, a duty that in effect means to keep them in a condition of slavery. In short, her view is paternalistic: Slaves owe their masters labor, and masters owe their slaves—childlike creatures—housing and guidance. Her paternalism is in the tradition of a famous passage by Thomas Jefferson, who wrote,

> We should endeavor, with those whom fortune has thrown on our hands, to feed and clothe them well, protect them from ill usage, require such reasonable labor only as is performed voluntarily by freemen, and be led by no repugnancies to abdicate them, and our duties to them.

Students are likely to say that Chesnut is hypocritical, but hypocrisy involves professing beliefs that one does not in fact hold, and Chesnut very clearly *does* hold the beliefs she professes. (Again, her writing was not intended for publication; she is not trying to deceive anyone, though we may argue that she is self-deceived.) Notice, too, that Chesnut does not quite accuse Mrs. Stowe and other Yankees of hypocrisy. She says, as we read her, that they are naive idealists, living in libraries, and—unaware of the actual conditions in the South—dangerously shooting their mouths off. She is contemptuous of them, but she stops short of accusing them of hypocrisy.

A word about slavery in the South, and especially about the plantation system: We gather, from a bit of reading, that between 1800 and 1850 the number of slaves in the South more than doubled, in response to the increased cultivation of cotton. By the middle of the century, Southern economy depended almost entirely on cotton. True, other crops (hemp, rice, tobacco, sugarcane) were grown, but cotton was king, especially from southern Virginia into Alabama, Mississippi, Louisiana, Arkansas, and central Texas. And although most white Southerners did not own slaves, and of the slave-owners most owned fewer than five slaves, there nevertheless also were vast plantations with hundreds of slaves on them, and these were the moneymakers in the world of King Cotton. In our limited reading we have encountered books that argue that slavery was inefficient and would soon have been abandoned, and books that argue to the contrary; clearly we are in no position to offer an opinion, but we believe that Chesnut was speaking sincerely (though possibly she was mistaken) when she says that her husband's plantation "is running him in debt."

It is hard to like Mary Boykin Miller Chesnut, and it is hard to sympathize with most of her complaints. (In several famous passages that we do not reproduce, she complains about white men who sleep with black women, but her lament is chiefly based on the wrong these men do to their wives, not on the wrong they do to the blacks, and indeed she is inclined to think that black women are the seducers.) Still, she sets forth her thoughts in vigorous sentences, and her writing has the great virtue of letting us know exactly how one white woman of high social status in the South viewed African Americans and their Abolitionist champions. It is impossible for anyone today to share her views, but it is important to know that people *did* hold such views. We are reminded of a favorite quotation, L. P. Hartley's remark in the Prologue to his *The Go-Between* (1953): "The past is a foreign country; they do things differently there."

ABRAHAM LINCOLN
Address at the Dedication of the Gettysburg National Cemetery (p. 1062)

Lincoln delivered this "Address" on November 19, 1863, at the site where four months earlier 179,000 Americans had fought. There were 51,000 casualties in the battle.

One reason that the "Address" is brief is that, as Richard A. Lanham points out in *Revising Prose* (1979), the brevity is expressive. "Lincoln took for his subject the inevitable gap between words and deeds. At Gettysburg, this gap was enormous, and the shortness of Lincoln's speech symbolizes just this gap. . . . Lincoln's brevity did not remove the emotion of the occasion but intensified it" (p. 108).

An instructor can profitably go through the address, sentence by sentence, helping students to see that although it seeks by praise to arouse the audience's respect for the dead, it also seeks to move the audience to action. It begins by speaking of an action even earlier than the battle (the bringing to birth of a new nation); it then turns to the present ("now we are engaged"), and it ends by calling upon the hearers to resolve that the dead did not die in vain, that is, it calls upon the hearers to act so that the nation "shall have a new birth of freedom." The structure is thus past, present, future. The "Address" is at least as much about future deeds of "us the living" as it is about the past deeds of "these honored dead." The praiseworthy deeds of our forefathers and of our dead contemporaries are to be a stimulus to our own future deeds. This emphasis on the future is, of course, related to the praise of the past through the imagery of birth: "conceived in Liberty," "a new birth of freedom."

Garry Wills, in his "Prologue" to *Inventing America* (1978), pushes the imagery rather far: "The suggested image is . . . a marriage of male heaven ('our fathers') and female earth ('this continent'). And it is a miraculous conception, a virgin birth. The nation is conceived by a mental act, in the spirit of liberty, and dedicated (as Jesus was in the temple) to a proposition." Maybe. A bit more conservatively one can suggest that the biblical echo of "Four score and seven" (cf. "the days of our years are three score and ten") is picked up in "our fathers" (cf. the beginning of the Lord's Prayer) and perhaps in "brought forth" (cf. "and she brought forth a babe").

Another way of putting the matter is to say that Lincoln delicately enlarges his hearers' understanding of the event. His second paragraph tells them why they are at Gettysburg, and it concludes by affirming that "it is altogether fitting and proper" that they gather for their avowed purpose. The next paragraph, however, courteously diminishes this purpose ("But, in a larger sense, we cannot dedicate . . ."), and it substitutes a grander purpose or obligation.

Philip B. Kunhardt, Jr., in an appendix to his *A New Birth of Freedom* (1983), prints the seven early texts of the speech. Two are drafts that Lincoln wrote before he gave the address, two are contemporary reports, and three are versions that Lincoln wrote in the months following his delivery of the speech. Thus, the two drafts say, "We are come to dedicate a portion of it"; and the three later autographs say, "We have come to dedicate a portion of this field." All of the variations are slight, and the wording in modern texts represents a consensus. It is not known exactly what Lincoln actually said at Gettysburg.

In short (as we say in Barnet et al., *A Short Guide to College Writing*) we think an analysis of Lincoln's speech will probably make some or all of the following points below.

An *analysis* of the Gettysburg Address—an attempt to show *how* it works, *how* it achieves its special effects—will not simply restate (paraphrase) the text. Rather, it will make such points as these:

- "Four score and seven years" evokes the Bible, which in Psalm 90 speaks of human life as "three score years and ten"; Lincoln thus begins the speech by solemnly introducing a holy context.
- "Four score and seven" is not the only evocation of the Bible; Lincoln also uses "dedicate" (in the Bible the word commonly means "set aside for a divine purpose"), "consecrate," "hallow" (to make holy), "devotion" (this word contains the word "vow"), "under God"—words appropriate to the creation of a cemetery, and words suggesting that the dead soldiers were sacrifices to a divine purpose.
- The address moves from the past (the first sentence refers to the Revolution in 1776) to the present (for instance, "Now we are engaged," "We are met," "we cannot") and then to the future ("shall have a new birth," "shall not perish").
- A metaphor of birth begins the speech ("conceived" in the first sentence), and another ends the speech ("new birth" in the last sentence); somewhat fainter images of birth are also present in "brought forth" and "created."
- Alliteration helps to bind words together ("*f*our score . . . *f*athers. . . *f*orth; *n*ew *n*ation"), and moves the language from ordinary prose toward the more highly textured language of poetry; in fact, speaking of poetry, the first two words ("four score") rhyme.
- Triads also elevate the language beyond ordinary prose ("we cannot dedicate—we cannot consecrate—we cannot hallow," "of the people, by the people, for the people").

For a richly detailed, illuminating study of "The Gettysburg Address," we recommend Garry Wills's *Lincoln At Gettysburg: The Words That Remade America* (1992). Wills's central insights and argument are also available, in a condensed form, in an essay of the same title published in *The Atlantic Monthly* (June 1992).

Martha Liggan
Dear Madam (p. 1063)

As our headnote explains, Martha Liggan treated and comforted a Confederate soldier, O. H. Middleton, who had been mortally wounded in a battle in Virginia in May 1864. After his death, Liggan sent this letter to his mother.

When we teach the selection, we seek first to remind students of the human reality that it dramatizes. It's not just a selection in a book for study and analysis. It's a wrenching letter from one mother to another, a letter that a flesh-and-blood woman produced with much care for the benefit of a woman whose son had been killed. What could cause more anguish than the death of a child? Is there a task more difficult than telling a parent that his or her child has died?

Our point is to make students *feel* the presence of the persons involved in this intense situation: These are real people who faced and somehow had to absorb a grievous loss. Liggan does not know Mrs. Middleton, yet, as the letter bears witness, she feels an intimate connection to her, one that she is impelled to express in written form.

After the formal (i. e., respectful) salutation, "Dear Madam," Liggan sets out her purpose in a focused single-sentence first paragraph. "I now seat myself," implies the serious dutifulness of her action—"this is something I must do now"; and it implies also the *hardness* of this act of writing—"this letter takes resolve to write, and it will take even greater courage and strength for you, Mrs. Middleton, to read it."

Notice, too, the precision of the phrase "the death of your noble son." No sooner does Liggan state the fact of the death than she stresses that this son was "noble." He was a decent, dignified young man. No doubt this is how Mrs. Middleton always thought of him—and that is why Liggan reinforces this image now, as if to say, "In death your son was the same fine and beautiful person he was in life." Later, Liggan uses the word "noble" again, linking this death to the deaths that mothers all across the South have endured. This is one mother's loss and, emblematically, the same loss that many have known in the South and, of course, in the North as well—and as the war continues, this loss will be felt again and again.

One of the most moving features of Liggan's letter is that while it has awkward usages and phrases, it is written with a special kind of craft. The brief opening leads to a long, detailed second paragraph that describes the scene. The details are few, but perhaps for this very reason all the more evocative—one thinks of Hemingway's practice of restraint and his economical use of detail.

Liggan explains that after she bathed and washed this wounded soldier-son (one hears in the background Christ's injunctions to minister to the sick and dying), she observes that he "would raise his head from the pillow" and that he would then "speak very distinctly" (note the emphatic "very").

Here, you might ask the class why Liggan clarifies her intent in asking young Middleton who he was and where he lived. Perhaps she feels that her and the others' questions might seem to the Middleton family more than a little forward and intrusive. It's striking that she was aware, and says so to Mrs. Middleton, that even as they cared for this soldier, they realized he "would die." We feel that the son knew this himself—that he was on his deathbed.

Several of our students said they were uneasy about the reference to young Middleton's "delirium." To them, it would have been better if Liggan had omitted this aspect of the death-scene: Why make Mrs. Middleton suffer *this* picture? But we believe that Liggan wanted to tell the whole truth, however painful, and even as she does so in this paragraph, she concludes by emphasizing the soldier-son's patience and fortitude, as if to say: His final moments were agonizing, but he was brave and strong to the bitter end, and you would have been (and should be now) proud of him.

Students also have expressed discomfort about the boy's burial; they wonder why Liggan refers to the possible "decay" of the body if, as she indicates, there is no proper burial in a coffin. But, again, this is part of Liggan's honest account of the scene and situation: The honesty is a compliment, indeed a tribute, to Mrs. Middleton, as though Liggan were implying, "I know you would want to know everything." Remember, too, that the letter is composed in a time of horrifically bloody civil war; by May 1864, hundreds of thousands of men, North and South, had been killed, and many more had been wounded and mutilated. Liggan is dealing here with terrible, tragic, and all-too-familiar realities.

And remember as well that one of Liggan's aims, in this act of consolation, is to say that young Middleton became transformed for her from a stranger to a member of her family. He was buried in the Liggans' own "burying ground," and Liggan has cried over his body and his grave. Indeed, one senses that she may have visited the grave more than once already.

One other point about students' responses: You may find, as we have, that students judge the final paragraph to mark an abrupt break in tone. Perhaps it does. But to us it brings piercingly home the human dimension of this incident. Liggan cannot, *as she writes*, restrain herself any longer: She is angry, bitter, vengeful. This is what she feels, and she may sense that Mrs. Middleton has similar feelings: My boy is gone; the "enemy" took my boy away from me.

For further background and context on the Northern and Southern home fronts, see: *The War Was You and Me: Civilians in the American Civil War*, ed. Joan E. Cashin (2002); and *Southern Families at War: Loyalty and Conflict in the Civil War South*, ed. Catherine Clinton (2000).

For background about the soldiers of the Civil War, two books by Bell Irvin Wiley remain valuable: *The Life of Billy Yank, The Common Soldier of the Union* (1952) and *The Life of Johnny Reb, The Common Soldier of the Confederacy* (1943). For a more recent study, see James M. McPherson, *What*

They Fought For, 1861–1865 (1994), which draws upon the letters and diaries of 1,000 Union and Confederate soldiers. For a selection of letters that span U.S. history, we recommend *War Letters: Extraordinary Correspondence from American Wars*, ed. Andrew Carroll (2001).

W. E. B. DU BOIS
The Lesson for Americans (p. 1065)

Most of your students will know that slavery was widespread in North America and in the Caribbean region before, during, and after the era of the American Revolution. They may be aware, too, of the specific "compromises" made by delegates to the Constitutional Convention in 1787—compromises to which W. E. B. Du Bois refers in this selection. These include the infamous clause in Article I, section 2, counting each slave as "three-fifths of all other persons"— the words *slave* and *slavery* never appear in the Constitution—in determining a state's number of seats in the U.S. Congress. The greater the number of slaves, the greater was the South's power at the federal level, enabling the slave states to protect and expand their institution of human bondage.

But perhaps we can offer you here some additional background and detail for our selection, which is taken from Du Bois's first book, *The Suppression of the African Slave-Trade to the United States of America, 1638–1870* (1896). This may aid you in bringing home to students the deep reality of the general points about slavery they already may be familiar with.

America's leading statesmen of the Revolutionary era did indeed live in the midst of slavery. When the Declaration of Independence was issued in 1776, one in every six Americans was a slave; and the members of the Constitutional Convention in 1787 included seventeen slaveholders (e. g., George Washington and James Madison) who held a total of 1,400 slaves. And, as Du Bois emphasizes, the U.S. Constitution allowed slavery to remain intact.

It seemed to many in the North, however, and to others in the South, that the American Revolution would make a moral and, eventually, a political and economic difference and that slavery would, somehow, fade away. This occurred in the North, where black and white resistance and state abolition-societies, inspired by the ideals of the Revolution, dealt slavery a fatal blow, as anti-slavery argument and activism dovetailed with the system's ebbing profitability. In 1787, the Northwest Ordinance prohibited slavery in the Ohio Valley; and slavery was abolished by the constitutions of Vermont (1777), Ohio (1802), Illinois (1818), and Indiana (1816); by judicial decision and by the state bill of rights in Massachusetts (1783); by gradual abolition acts in Pennsylvania (1780), Rhode Island (1784), Connecticut (1784, 1797), New York (1799, 1817), and New Jersey (1804, 1820); and by constitutional interpretation in New Hampshire (1792).

There were encouraging trends on the national scene as well. In 1794, U.S. law prohibited "American ships or foreign ships clearing American ports from carrying on the slave trade between foreign ports"; and in 1808, the Atlantic slave trade (the importation of slaves) was abolished as a provision in the Constitution (Article I, section 9) had allowed. Both of these changes were met with opposition. The slave trade in Rhode Island had reached its height *after* the Revolution and the merchants there "did everything they could to save it," fighting abolition, agitating Congress, and breaking laws, as the scholar Jay Coughtry has demonstrated. As early as 1785, in "The Slave Trade and Slavery," the anti-slavery Congregational minister Samuel Hopkins observed that "trade in human species has been the first wheel of commerce in Newport [Rhode Island], on which every movement in business has chiefly depended."

While ending the slave trade was significant, this was, as the historian James H. Broussard has indicated, "the aspect of slavery most easily dispensed with, for it did not touch the heart of the system at all, and there were strong economic arguments against a large influx of new slaves." Many might detest the overseas slave trade yet not agree that slavery should cease where it was central to the economy. Maintaining fewer slaves if anything kept their value high, and eliminating the overseas trade induced the development of a well-paying trade—"Negro speculation"—within and between states. As the writer and reformer Lydia Maria Child said in 1833, "the breeding of Negro cattle for the foreign markets (of Louisiana, Georgia, Alabama, Arkansas, and Missouri) is a very lucrative branch of business."

The first U.S. Census in 1790 counted nearly 700,000 slaves. Two decades later, and even with the foreign slave trade having been banned for two years, the census count of slaves had jumped to 1.2 million.

During the period from 1780 to 1810, almost as many Africans were shipped to the United States as in the 160 years from 1620 to 1780. The slave population expanded by thirty-three percent between 1800 and 1810 and by another twenty-nine percent between 1810 and 1820. Despite the Atlantic slave trade's termination in 1808, the slave population in the United States soared, its number boosted by illegal trading (approximately 1,000 per year brought in illegally) and slave breeding and interstate slave trading. Between 1808 and 1860, the slave population tripled; and the profit from investment in slaves averaged an impressive ten percent during the 1840s and 1850s. In Virginia alone, 300,000 slaves were sold out-of-state between 1830 and 1860.

As Toni Morrison, author of a powerful novel about slavery, *Beloved* (1987), reflected in an interview (*Time* magazine, May 22, 1989), trading and selling slaves, evil yet addictive, "was like cocaine is now . . . Imagine getting $1,000 for a human being. That's a lot of money. There are fortunes in this country that were made that way."

Du Bois is sharply making this point when he condemns the "cupidity and carelessness" of the Founding Fathers. They had the opportunity—no, he insists, the moral obligation—to end slavery when the new nation was begun. They chose not to, and the tragic and terrible consequence was the Civil War. The day of reckoning was postponed, and thus the price was far higher than it would have been if action had been taken in the 1770s and 1780s.

During the Civil War, 1861–1865, between 700,000 and 800,000 men served in the Confederate armies, and about 2.3 million in the Union armies.

The number of casualties was 1 million, in a country whose population was 31 million. The death toll was 618,000: 360,000 North, 258,000 South. This exceeds the number of deaths in all of America's other wars combined.

For an excellent overview of Du Bois's life and career, see Arnold Rampersad, *The Art and Imagination of W. E. B. Du Bois* (1976). A good, brief biography: Manning Marable, *W. E. B. Du Bois: Black Radical Democrat* (1986). A major two-volume study: David Levering Lewis, *W. E. B. Du Bois— Biography of a Race, 1868–1919* (1993); and Lewis, *W. E. B. Du Bois: The Fight for Equality and the American Century, 1919–1963* (2000). See also: *Critical Essays on W. E. B. Du Bois*, ed. William L. Andrews (1985); Shamoon Zamir, *Dark Voices: W. E. B. Du Bois and American Thought, 1888–1903* (1995); and Raymond Wolters, *Du Bois and His Rivals* (2002).

AMBROSE BIERCE
A Horseman in the Sky (p. 1067)

We take it that the narrator (see our first question in the text) is matter-of-factly stating the rules of war, and is not to be regarded by the reader as a nut case. But the severe rules that govern an army are not the only rules in this story; there is also the stern code of chivalry that governs the behavior of the Virginians. The son tells his father that he is going to fight on the opposing side, and the father does not protest. Rather, he says only,

> Well, go, sir, and whatever may occur do what you conceive to be your duty. Virginia, to which you are a traitor, must get on without you. Should we both live to the end of the war, we will speak further of the matter.

We take it that Bierce wants us to admire these gentlemen, each of whom has a firm sense of what is right, though the story will tell us that this inflexible code, this sense of duty, results in one man destroying the other.

Speaking of duty, we can't resist mentioning that in *The Devil's Dictionary* Bierce offers this definition:

> DUTY: That which sternly impels us in the direction of profit, along the line of desire.

This definition is all too typical of many of the cynical and insufficiently amusing entries in *The Devil's Dictionary*, and though we quote it here, we do *not* think it is relevant to Bierce's story. We take the story to be a straightforward telling of a horrifying incident in a horrifying war, and we assume that Bierce sees something heroic—though also appalling—in Druse's performance of duty.

At the risk of talking about things we are far from expert in, we want to say a bit more about the principled, high-minded—can we say "courtly" and in a way "chivalric"?—code of honor that Bierce attributes to the father and son.

Most people probably would agree that there was and perhaps still is a difference in behavior between Northerners and the Southerners. (John F. Kennedy wittily glanced at it when he said that Washington D.C. was a city of Southern efficiency and Northern charm.) The writer of this page, a Northerner, recalls his surprise when, as an eighteen-year-old in the South, he occasionally heard himself addressed as "Sir," and apparently this word was regularly used not only when college students addressed their male professors but also when professors addressed their male students. The usual explanation for the South's code is that it is largely if not entirely (like so much else in the South) the product of a slave society. (Alexis de Tocqueville in 1831 wrote, "I could easily prove that almost all the differences which may be noticed between the character of the Americans in the Southern and Northern states have originated in slavery." This makes sense to us.) The South, having in the late eighteenth and early nineteenth centuries become a society that depended heavily on slave labor, needed to dehumanize slaves (blacks had to be seen as naturally inferior to whites), and therefore whites had to see themselves as some sort of higher order, people whose moral code was far above that of the allegedly shiftless, lying, sexually promiscuous persons whom they had enslaved. The South, or at least some of it, convinced itself that by enslaving Africans it was in effect civilizing them and (by converting them to Christianity) saving their souls. Thus, the argument goes, the South developed paternalistic, patriarchal, chivalric concepts.

Whatever the truth of this theory—and it has been widely embraced—we think all readers, Southern and Northern, will agree that (a) the behavior seems possible for Virginians and (b) impossible for Yankees.

Surely the sergeant's ejaculation at the end of the story, "Good God," reflects the reader's response. Presumably we feel that *we* could not have done such a thing as Druse did, but we also know that we do not live by the code of honor that Druse and his father lived by. There is something here of the world of tragedy, not simply a world in which bad things happen, but a world in which figures do deeds of horror that are almost beyond our comprehension—Oedipus kills his father and sleeps with his mother and ultimately blinds himself, Othello strangles Desdemona, Lear curses his daughters, Hamlet directly kills five people and indirectly some others—but they also somehow are larger than life and in a way are admirable. The spectacles they produce evoke (to quote Horatio) not only "woe" but also "wonder." In Bierce's story, the sergeant's "Good God"—a comment that any of us might make when we see a tragic hero do a deed of horror—forces us to contrast the normal human response (amazement) with the high tragic codes that have been briefly instilled in us in the early part of the story, when we hear about the crime of falling asleep and when we witness the brief scene of the two Virginians, each doing his duty.

Finally, we think (here we touch on the fourth question in the text) that the emphasis on the aesthetic response to the horseman is a way of distancing or elevating the story, a way of, so to speak, putting the story within a proscenium. Notice that in addition to telling us that Druse sees the horseman as an equestrian statue, Bierce uses a fair number of words that suggest art: In paragraph 8 we get "costume," "harmonized," "foreshortened," "profile," and "outline." Our point, again, is that Bierce is doing two things: He is telling us a story about the horrors of war, but he is also elevating these horrors into a tragic world that is somehow greater than our own. We are certainly not saying that Bierce's achievements are anywhere near to Shakespeare's, but we are saying that readers of the story might well feel that they have been taken into a world of woe and wonder, a world that in some ways is greater than the daily world we move in.

Mordant, misanthropic, and wickedly entertaining, Bierce is a limited but compelling writer. His most accomplished work is *Tales of Soldiers and Civilians* (1892), though his best known is *The Cynic's Word Book* (1906), later republished under its more familiar title, *The Devil's Dictionary* (1912). It includes such entries as the following:

HAPPINESS, n.: An agreeable sensation arising from contemplating the misery of another.

PHILOSOPHY, n.: A route of many roads leading from nowhere to nothing.

Bierce believed that life was futile and compromised, doomed, with no exceptions, to a bad ending. "Bierce would bury his best friend with a sigh of relief," concluded the novelist Jack London, "and express satisfaction that he was done with him."

For an overview: M. E. Grenander, *Ambrose Bierce* (1971). Critical discussion can be found in: *Critical Essays on Ambrose Bierce*, ed. Cathy N. Davidson (1982); and Cathy N. Davidson, *The Experimental Fictions of Ambrose Bierce: Structuring the Ineffable* (1984). See also: Lawrence I. Berkove, *A Prescription for Adversity: The Moral Art of Ambrose Bierce* (2002). Another good resource: Robert L. Gale, *An Ambrose Bierce Companion* (2001).

STEPHEN CRANE
An Episode of War (p. 1072)

Long before it became fashionable to talk about "indeterminacy" in literature, we were uncertain about the thrust of this story. That is, we did not (and still do not) feel confident about how we were to understand the last line of the story, when the lieutenant, accompanied by his sobbing relatives, says, "I don't suppose it matters so much as all that."

Are we to take this remark as revealing a depth of perception that has been gained at the cost of great suffering? Or is the remark meant chiefly to comfort the relatives? Or does the remark show that the lieutenant is unaware of his own situation: He is a marked man, a man whom others will always regard with awe, but he doesn't know it. Although this last view seems to us the least convincing, it does gain considerable support from the comment in paragraph 7 that "A wound gives a strange dignity to him who bears it. Well men shy from this new and terrible majesty."

We need not comment further about the ending, other than to say that we believe several interpretations are equally plausible. The one other point we want to make about the story—well, maybe we want to make two points—is this: To the men at the front, the war is unheroic, a matter of getting hit while in the routine business of dividing coffee beans. (Crane makes a little joke in the second paragraph when he characterizes the lieutenant's action of allotting portions as "a great triumph in mathematics.") Here, at the front, activities—even those that result in the loss of an arm—are mere episodes, to quote the title. Probably the lieutenant is *un*named in order to diminish him, i.e., to make him not a heroic individual but an anonymous figure who participates not in a grand battle but in an "episode." Behind the front lines, however, things look different, and the war indeed seems romantic and heroic. Thus, in paragraph 10 the lieutenant sees a general mounted on a horse, an aide saluting and presenting a paper—all of which is "a wonder, precisely like a historical painting." Two paragraphs later we are told that the deployment of the battery "stirred the heart," and that the "aggregation of wheels, levers, motors had a beautiful unity." We take Crane to be saying that the man in the front lines has all he can do to get routine tasks done, and has no thoughts about the heroism or beauty of war. Such thoughts are for observers behind the lines.

This last comment of ours provokes us to make one additional related point: In paragraph 17 the lieutenant sees a gray-faced man "serenely smoking a corncob pipe." And then Crane writes, "The lieutenant wished to rush forward and inform him that he was dying." We take it that Crane is making the point that the gray-faced man—the man who has really experienced the war—is unaware of the experience; he is dying but he doesn't know it. But—and here we are very unsure—is the reader to apply this vignette to the lieutenant's remark at the end, i.e., is the lieutenant like the gray-faced man, unaware of his plight? Or, to return to our opening comment, are we to understand that the lieutenant has achieved some sort of deep insight into the littleness of the suffering of any human being?

In his critical study *Stephen Crane* (1962), John Berryman observes that the lieutenant's wound "is described with such deliberation and force as to make one feel that no wounded man has ever been correctly described before" (256). We've found that this claim makes a good point of departure in the classroom for a close study of Crane's language: What makes Crane's description so distinctive? Where in the text are the signs of his "deliberation and force" as a craftsman?

Crane is also a master of irony. As R. W. Stallman notes in an essay in *The Houses That James Built and Other Literary Studies* (1961) Crane possesses the great writer's "gift of ironic outlook, that grace of irony which is so central to his art. Irony is Crane's chief technical instrument" (105). This too is a good means through which to examine Crane's organizations of language—the scale and kind of ironies that he deploys from sentence to sentence.

For a brief biography: James B. Colvert, *Stephen Crane* (1984). For fuller accounts, see: Christopher Benfey, *The Double Life of Stephen Crane* (1992);

and Linda H. Davis, *Badge of Courage: The Life of Stephen Crane* (1998). Also valuable: *The Crane Log: A Documentary Life of Stephen Crane, 1871–1900*, ed. Stanley Wertheim and Paul M. Sorrentino (1994). For commentary on the stories: Chester L. Wolford, *Stephen Crane: A Study of the Short Fiction* (1989); and Michael W. Schaefer, *A Reader's Guide to the Short Stories of Stephen Crane* (1996).

DANIEL DECATUR EMMETT
Dixie's Land (p. 1075)

In our headnote in the text we give what we take to be the essential background, but a few details can be added here. Emmett sold the publication rights for the song to a New York publisher, for a flat $500, but with the outbreak of the Civil War the South felt free to use the song without paying royalties to the owner, so neither the author nor the composer ever made much profit from "Dixie."

One other point: The day after Lee surrendered, a brass band led some three thousand celebrants to the White House, where they hoped to hear Lincoln speak. Lincoln asked the band to play "Dixie," saying something to the effect that the rebels claimed the tune for themselves, but it was one of his own favorites and he was now taking it back. The crowd went wild with approval, and the band played "Dixie" and then "Yankee Doodle." Our point in recounting these two bits of information is that although the song is indisputably associated with the South, it has had Northern admirers from the very beginning.

We think that our "Topics for Critical Thinking and Writing" raise important issues, but we will comment only briefly on some of them. Are renditions in dialect offensive? Our own response is that in many cases they *ought* not to be—they were not intended to ridicule, but on the contrary were intended to convey that these speakers are distinctive and ought to be valued as such—but we do understand that today such writings may seem condescending. At their worst, dialect writings may in effect say, "See and hear these quaint folks, aren't they delightfully naive, utterly charming! Let's not corrupt them with education or money; let's keep them ignorant and poor, so they can retain their charm and they can continue to amuse us." In fact, we have never heard a singer of "Dixie" who preserved the pronunciations indicated by the spelling—we have heard only "land of cotton," never "land ob cotton."

Doubtless for many Southerners—white and black—the line "I'll take my stand to live and die in Dixie" has a resonance that it cannot have for Northerners, though many Northerners, like Lincoln, cherish the song. For persons not from the South, perhaps the song has the appeal that most good lyric poems have: They convincingly tell us how certain persons feel, i.e., how it feels to be a particular person in a particular situation (e.g., Frost's "Stopping by Woods on a Snowy Evening"), and we readers are glad that for a moment we can enter this mind, can have this sensation, can, so to speak, for a moment intensely *feel* a state of mind.

Julia Ward Howe
Battle Hymn of the Republic (p. 1077)

Although in the last few decades women in considerable numbers have written poetry on political and social issues, in earlier periods their chief topics were love, children, death, and God, for the most part treated personally, intimately, rather than publicly. But religion allowed, in hymns, for personal expression on a public topic, and the Abolitionist movement especially provided a subject about which women could exhort society to action.

Lines 1–4 of "Battle Hymn of the Republic" are indebted to Revelations 19.11 ("And I saw heaven opened, and behold a white horse; and he that sat upon him was called Faithful and True, and in righteousness he doth judge and make war"), 14 ("And the armies which were in heaven followed him upon the white horses"), and 15 ("And out of his mouth goeth a sharp sword, that with it he should smite the nations: and he shall rule them with a rod of iron: and he treadeth the winepress of the fierceness and wrath of Almighty God"). Isaiah 63.3–6 ("I have trodden the winepress . . . ; I will tread down the people in mine anger"), describing God's punishment of His enemies, also exerted an influence. Line 15 is indebted to Genesis 3.15 (God tells the serpent that woman's seed shall bruise the serpent's head), and in line 18 "sift" is related to Isaiah 30.28 (God will "sift the nations"). The "fiery gospel" of the third stanza perhaps comes from Deuteronomy 33.2 ("from his right hand went a fiery law"). The lilies of line 21 probably come from the Song of Songs and the Sermon on the Mount; the connection between holiness and freedom (23) is common in Paul, though of course in "Battle Hymn" (published in 1862) the allusion to freedom in line 23 is to freeing the black slaves.

In *Redeemer Nation*, Ernest Tuveson briefly discusses the poem in the context of American apocalyptic writing. He points out that although many who have sung the hymn have thought that the biblical images are merely "fitting metaphors for a war between right and wrong," the images in fact convey "a message about the precise place and point of the war in the pattern of salvation." (The idea was that the Civil War is the fruit of the accumulated evils of the reign of Satan; the day of the Antichrist is ending.)

The hymn has recently been the subject of some controversy. In July 1986 a committee of the United Methodist Church (a denomination formed in 1968 when the Methodist Church and the Evangelical United Brethren merged) narrowly voted to eliminate "Battle Hymn of the Republic" (along with "Onward, Christian Soldiers") from the hymnal. The committee received thousands of letters of protest and reversed its decision in July 1987. Students might well be invited to discuss the appropriateness (or inappropriateness) of the military metaphor and the reasons for the appeal of the hymn.

Two other issues: "Glory, Glory, Hallelujah" (a shout of triumph at the fall of Babylon) was not in the "Hymn" when it was first published. The final stanza, with its two lines about Christ, may seem incongruous or inept, but it introduces the Incarnation and Atonement, which made possible the last triumphs over evil on earth. Hermes Nye sings "Battle Hymn" on a record entitled *Ballads of the Civil War*, Vol. 1 (Folkways FA 2187 [FP 48/7]).

HERMAN MELVILLE
The March into Virginia (p. 1078)

It is hard for anyone today to think of war as romantic—if nothing else, televised images of the dead and wounded have pushed romance out of the picture—though of course individual acts may be heroic, and possibly (a topic much debated by philosophers) some wars may be "just." But on the whole the war poems that have found their way into today's anthologies are not celebrations of military exploits. Poems such as Browning's "Incident of the French Camp," Longfellow's "Paul Revere's Ride," and Kipling's "Gunga Din"—standard stuff in schoolbooks of the 1930s—have all but vanished. In their place are such deeply ironic favorites as Hardy's "The Man He Killed" and Wilfred Owen's "Dulce et Decorum Est."

As we read it, Melville's "The March into Virginia" is somewhere in between these two extremes. Certainly there is abundant irony—the boyish "champions and enthusiasts" (lines 6–7), "Chatting left and laughing right" (30) will move from their innocence to experience:

> But some who this blithe mood present,
>   As on in lightsome files they fare,
> Shall die experienced ere three days are spent
>   Perish, enlightened by the vollied glare. . . .

The "lightsome files" are soon "enlightened by the vollied glare," i.e., their superficial joy is turned into first-hand knowledge of what war—accompanied by death—is really like. (The irony is heightened by the fact that gunfire literally produces light.) On the other hand, some of the men will survive, and will become "like to adamant" (35), battle-hardened veterans who will continue the fight. That these survivors, Melville tells us, will go on to a second defeat ("the throe of Second Manassas share") does not minimize their achievement; ultimately the Union forces won the war and preserved the United States. Although we hear in the poem a voice pitying the innocence of the inexperienced warriors, and we hear a judgment on war ("All wars are boyish, and are fought by boys"), we do not hear a denunciation of this war, or of war in general.

As we read the poem, Melville is saying that wars would not be fought if the warriors knew more, for instance that war offers more than "glory" (26)—but they don't know this, and so they go into battle and (often) die. He does *not* say that the battle cannot be for a noble cause, and there is ample evidence that Melville was a strong Unionist. We would go so far as to say that this poem might stand, in a textbook, next to "The Gettysburg Address" and there would be no argument, no ironic contrast between the two works, although the thrust of each work differs greatly. In fact, although *Battle-Pieces* (the book from which the poem comes) is dedicated "to the memory of the three hundred thousand who in the war for the maintenance of the Union fell devotedly under the flag of their fathers," the book has much of the tone of Lincoln's Second Inaugural Address, which concluded by exhorting the nation to proceed "with malice toward none, with charity for all." *Battle-Pieces* includes two poems praising a Southern general, Stonewall Jackson—the subject of Lanier's poem later in this chapter.

In a "Supplement" at the end of *Battle-Pieces* Melville talks at some length about heroic ideals, both on the side of the North and the South. He sees the Southern cause as seriously tainted, but he also sees noble ideals. Here is a small sample from the "Supplement":

> It was in subserviency to the slave-interest that Secession was plotted; but it was under the plea, plausibly urged, that certain inestimable rights guaranteed by the Constitution were directly menaced that the people of the South were cajoled into revolution. Through the arts of the conspirators and the perversity of fortune, the most sensitive love of liberty was entrapped into the support of a war whose implied end was the erecting in our advanced century of an Anglo-American empire based upon the systematic degradation of man.
>
> Spite this clinging reproach, however, signal military virtues and achievements have conferred upon the Confederate arms historic fame, and upon certain commanders a renown extending beyond the sea—a renown which we of the North could not suppress, even if we would. . . . Dishonorable would it be in the South were she willing to abandon to shame the memory of brave men who with signal personal disinterestedness warred in her behalf. . . .
>
> Barbarities also there were [in the South], . . . but surely other qualities—exalted ones—courage and fortitude matchless, were likewise displayed, and largely. . . .

Melville takes a deeply tragic view of the Civil War, seeing it as something that may have conferred on the nation—at a tremendous cost—a wisdom that perhaps can be born only of tremendous suffering. The final paragraph of the "Supplement" begins thus: "Let us pray that the terrible historic of our time may not have been enacted without instructing our whole beloved country through terror and pity. . . ." Here the words "pity" and "terror" make it perfectly clear that Melville has in mind an Aristotelian concept of tragedy, and it is evident that he held the view (common in the nineteenth century and most famously formulated in the early twentieth century by A. C. Bradley in his book on Shakespeare's tragedies) that these emotions, properly evoked, bring forth a kind of wisdom otherwise unattainable.

Melville's language is sometimes condensed, but we think the only passage that may cause students any difficulty is this one, at the end of the first stanza:

> Turbid ardors and vain joys
> > Not barrenly abate—
> Stimulants to the power mature,
> > Preparatives of fate.

As we understand the words, the gist is this: The turbid ardors (tumultuous passions?) of the young do not end in nothing ("not barrenly abate"); rather, they are stimulants for the powerful actions of mature men, and it is these that produce the future ("Preparatives of fate").

One other point: After writing the preceding paragraphs we happened to come across Robert Penn Warren's *Selected Poems of Herman Melville* (1970). Warren suggests that in "berrying party" (line 18) there is "really a secret, and grim pun: *burying party*," i.e., a glimpse of soldiers burying the dead after the battle. We had read the poem dozens of times without this thought having occurred to us, and we are now inclined to think that the pun is accidental—but of course we cannot talk fruitfully about Melville's intention in this matter. In any case, our own feeling is that even if Melville did not intend the pun, now that Warren has pointed it out a reader cannot *not* think of it. It is here to stay. You may want to ask your class (1) whether they noticed it, (2) if they didn't, do they imagine that it was intended, and (3) does the author's intention—at least in this issue—matter?

In his Introduction to Melville's *Selected Poems*, F. O. Matthiessen points out that while this great writer's verse is sometimes "stiff and clumsy," it reflects the strain and difficulty of the ideas and feelings that Melville seeks in time of war to express. Throughout the Civil War poems, says Matthiessen, the reader senses Melville's "continuing concern with the unending struggle, with the tensions between good and evil: within the mind and in the state, political, social, and religious" (8).

For biography: Laurie Robertson-Lorant, *Melville: A Biography* (1996); and Hershel Parker, *Herman Melville: A Biography* (2 vols., 1996, 2002). Older but still valuable studies include: Newton Arvin, *Herman Melville* (1950); Lawrance Thompson, *Melville's Quarrel with God* (1952); and Warner Berthoff, *The Example of Melville* (1962). A helpful resource is: *A Companion to Melville Studies*, ed. John Bryant (1986). On Melville's poetry, see Stanton Garner, *The Civil War World of Herman Melville* (1993), and, especially, William C. Spengemann "Melville the Poet," *American Literary History* 11:4 (1999): 571–609.

HERMAN MELVILLE
DuPont's Round Fight (p. 1080)

Melville opposed slavery and he unambiguously supported the North, but he saw the Civil War as something more (or deeper) than right versus wrong. He seems to have regarded it as the product of tragic human error and unthwartable historic forces, and he thought that out of the bloodshed would come some sort of purification. Here we can repeat his comment (quoted in our discussion of "The March into Virginia") from his "Supplement": "Let us pray that the terrible historic of our time may not have been enacted without instructing our whole beloved country through terror and pity. . . ."

In "DuPont's Round Fight," however, he does clearly indicate that one side is "Right" (line 5), and the other side is unambiguously characterized as "The rebel." This explicit partisanship is, as we say, somewhat unusual in Melville's poems, but even in this poem one feels that Melville is less concerned with celebrating the North than he is with celebrating order, or "time and measure" (line 1), geometry (line 7), and law (12).

For a fairly obvious reason, Melville's reference to "stars" (3) and "LAW" (12) brought to our mind George Meredith's "Lucifer in Starlight," which we quote here, on the off chance that an instructor may happen to want to quote it if the discussion in class turns to the idea that the stars are a type (i.e., prototype) of law, law that binds poems and everything else.

> **Lucifer in Starlight**
>
> On a starred night Prince Lucifer uprose.
> Tired of his dark dominion swung the fiend
> Above the rolling ball in cloud part screened,
> Where sinners hugged their spectre of repose.
> Poor prey to his hot fit of pride were those.
> And now upon his western wing lie leaned,
> Now his huge bulk o'er Afric's sands careened,
> Now the black planet shadowed Arctic snows.
> Soaring through wider zones that pricked his scars
> With memory of the old revolt from Awe,
> He reached a middle height, and at the stars,
> Which are the brain of heaven, he looked, and sank.
> Around the ancient track marched, rank on rank,
> The army of unalterable law.
>
> [1883]

For Melville, no less than for Meredith, the stars represent heavenly law and order, and therefore rebellion—whether that of Lucifer or of the South—is bound to fail.

For bibliographic suggestions, see the preceding entry.

HERMAN MELVILLE
Shiloh (p. 1080)

The subtitle, "A Requiem," perhaps does not prepare us for the opening lines ("Skimming lightly, wheeling still, / The swallows fly low") though even as we read these lines we can guess that Melville will go on to contrast the pleasant natural scene with the terrible human things that happened at this site. Incidentally, the Shiloh of the Hebrew Bible, a sanctuary and the seat of the priesthood, was itself not exempt from tragedy: The Philistines destroyed it after the Battle of Ebenezer (about 1050 BC).

The Civil War has sometimes been called the Brothers War, alluding to the fact that in some instances brothers joined opposing armies (in the story by Bierce that we reprint, it is father and son who are on opposing sides), and in "Shiloh" Melville emphasizes the fact that at Shiloh "dying foemen mingled," brought together by death. Further, it is worth pointing out (as we mentioned in our discussion of "DuPont's Round Fight") that although Melville opposed slavery and unambiguously supported the North, in most of his poems he is not partisan. A line such as "What like a bullet can undeceive" (line 16) applies equally to the Blue and the Gray.

The poem ends as it began, with the swallows skimming over the field. One can take the line to suggest that nature is indifferent, or that nature pays tribute. Discuss.

For related discussion and bibliography, consult the entry for Melville's "The March into Virginia."

SIDNEY LANIER
The Dying Words of Jackson (p. 1082)

As we mentioned in the comments on Melville's "The March into Virginia," Melville's *Battle-Pieces* includes two poems on Jackson. In the first of these, Melville clearly states that Jackson "devoutly stood for Wrong," but he finds he must praise him nevertheless:

> Earnest in error, as we feel;
> True to the thing he deemed was due,
> True as John Brown or steel.

Melville's second poem on Jackson, subtitled "Ascribed to a Virginian," offers undiluted praise (or praise diluted only in so far as the subtitle implies a modification). Given the fact that Sidney Lanier's poem makes such considerable use of star imagery, it is interesting to notice Melville's comment that "Stonewall followed his star" (in fact he uses these words five times, with minor variations, and he also speaks of "Stonewall's star"). One can hardly escape the idea that Melville is suggesting a comparison with the Magi, who followed a star, i.e., who were divinely guided in their activity. True, Melville's invented speaker is a Virginian, but surely Melville would not have written the poem if he had not been immensely impressed by Jackson's deeds.

Lanier's poem begins with Jackson's dying words, in which Jackson showed himself to be, to the last, a soldier devoted to duty. Students may have trouble with the first stanza, which we interpret thus: The stars take up the work of the sun ("the glittering Day") and "rain his glory down with sweeter grace / Upon the dark World's grand, enchanted face / All loth to turn away," i.e., the world still seeks (needs?) Jackson's illuminating spirit. In the second stanza, the dying Day turns its commission over to the stars, "To stand for burning fare-thee-wells of light," i.e., in traditional elegiac form, nature itself mourns the death of the hero. Further, the heavenly imagery suggests that the dead hero is not really dead but has achieved immortality.

The third stanza explicitly compares Jackson to the sun (life-giving), and his words to the stars (i.e., heavenly, illuminating), and sets him above "the gloomy wars" in which he gave his life, i.e., the man is even greater than his deeds. The fourth stanza brings us into the delirious mind of the general (as the epigraph has already done) and sees in his dying words his solicitude for his soldiers. In the fifth stanza, Jackson, having done all that a man can do, is now ready to die, and to let God decide the battle. The final stanza continues the imagery of the sun and stars: The sun is gone (i.e., it is nighttime, and Jackson-the-sun has departed), but "thy stars remain" (i.e., Jackson's words remain, words "that miniature his deeds"). The poem thus ends where it began, with Jackson's words, and with the stars replacing the sun. But the final stanza also introduces a new note; whereas the earlier parts of the poem have emphasized Jackson's loving care, the final stanza tells him that he himself is "Thrice-Beloved," and therefore he can draw solace.

What Lanier is doing in most of the poem is what most writers of elegies do, i.e., Lanier is giving new life to the deceased. That is, he is apotheosizing Jackson, making him into a heavenly body. This is in accord with Greek and Roman thought (influenced by Persian and Babylonian thought), which worshipped stars and planets as deities, but the idea is not only pagan; Christ speaks of himself as the "bright star of dawn" in Revelation 22:16. In the next-to-last line, where Lanier says that Jackson's "great heart bleeds," he comes pretty close to evoking an image of the crucified Christ. We don't mean to say that Lanier is equating Jackson with Christ, but he does suggest that Jackson's deeds and words continue to sustain those who knew him.

In our fourth question we ask students to name some military figures who, like Stonewall Jackson (a name given to Jackson because he and his brigade at Bull Run stood "like a stone wall") were given metaphoric nicknames. The following come immediately to our minds: In the American Revolution, the Swamp Fox (Francis Marion, known for his habit of evading the British by disappearing into the swamps); in the Civil War, Fighting Joe Hooker; in World War I, Black Jack Pershing—so called because in 1895 he willingly commanded African-American troops (against the Plains Indians) at a time when few military leaders accepted blacks in combat units; in World War II, Admiral Bull Halsey, Vinegar Joe Stilwell, Blood and Guts Patton, the Desert Fox (the German commander, Erwin Rommel). Of these, perhaps the only inappropriate nickname is "Fighting Joe" Hooker; at Chancellorsville—in our text we include Hudgins's poem "At Chancellorsville"—Hooker, head of the Army of the Potomac, outnumbered Lee's forces by 2 to

1, yet Hooker unaccountably retreated to Chancellorsville. His later explanation: "To tell the truth, I just lost confidence in Joe Hooker." The point of our question is to get students talking and thinking about metaphor, in life as well as in literature.

ANONYMOUS
Women at the Grave of Stonewall Jackson
(photograph, p. 1083)

Grief knows no gender, but in wartime traditionally men are supposed to embody the manly virtues, which means heroic action, and women are supposed to embody the womanly virtues, which means grief. At the sight of the death of a hero, for instance, men are (or were) supposed to remain stoic, and women are (or were) supposed to collapse, overcome by emotion. The women here have not collapsed, but presumably Jackson had died some time ago, and they are now paying tribute by their presence.

Students might be invited to discuss the usual demeanor of men versus women on occasions of mourning. They might also discuss the various forms that mourning takes in different cultures. And they might well relate this picture and Lanier's poem to Auden's elegy, "Funeral Blues," in Chapter 15.

The historian Roy R. Stephenson has pointed out, in a discussion of "death and mourning" in the Confederacy, that the extremely high casualty rate "made Southerners acutely aware of mortality." Of a "potential military population of about a million," he explains, "750,000 soldiers served in the Confederate armies, and approximately 250,000 died during the war—about one in four Southern white men of military age in contrast to the Northern rate of one in ten." See *Encyclopedia of the Confederacy* (4 vols., 1993), 2:459–61.

As Stephenson and others have shown, Southern women during the first years of the war mourned their own dead loved ones in "public" ways, transforming their personal grief into a ritual that honored and heightened their sense of the rightness of the Confederate cause. As the war dragged on, however, as the casualties mounted, and as the eventual collapse of the Confederacy became clear, Southern women turned increasingly to the personal cost of the war: Above all they grieved over their lost husbands, sons, and brothers, not ever the death of the Confederate nation. Yet after the war, the elements of public ritual again became prominent, with memories of the dead tied repeatedly to the nobility of the "Lost Cause."

Students interested in this rich topic might consult: Anne Firor Scott, *The Southern Lady: From Pedestal to Politics* (1970); Rollin G. Osterweis, *The Myth of the Lost Cause: 1865–1900* (1973); George Rable, *Civil Wars: Women and the Crisis of Southern Nationalism* (1989); and Drew Gilpin Faust, "Altars of Sacrifice: Confederate Women and the Narratives of War," *Journal of American History* 76 (1990): 1200–28.

WALT WHITMAN
Reconciliation (p. 1084)

In "Reconciliation" Whitman celebrates not simply the end of the war—though that in itself was a cause of celebration—but a loving union, or reunion, daringly symbolized by a kiss bestowed upon the dead enemy. The poem begins by announcing (1) that the very word *reconciliation* has an affinity with heaven ("beautiful as the sky"), and (2) that the fact of reconciliation will "in time" obliterate the terrible carnage of the clash of cultures. Whitman goes on to call Death and Night sisters; that is, he constructs a mythology—at least we are not aware of any system of mythology in which they are sisters. (In Greek mythology, Night is the mother of Death.) Whitman's two allegorical figures "incessantly softly wash again, and ever again, this soil'd world." Once he has given us this image, it seems obvious enough, but, again, it is new to us. Far from being portrayed as a cleansing force, Death customarily is portrayed as destructive (think of the classical image of the inverted torch, or the late medieval and Renaissance image of a skeleton carrying a scythe), or at best as offering an anodyne, a release from an unbearably painful world. Night, in traditional mythology, is not quite so grim, and is even beneficent to the extent that she brings her son, Sleep, but she is nevertheless destructive since, like Day, she leads to decay and death. In contrast, Whitman imagines Death and Night as washing (purifying) "this soil'd world"; in this specific context of this poem, which speaks of a corpse in a coffin, the allegorical figures surely are meant to be associated with persons washing (symbolically purifying) a corpse.

The purification effected by Death and Night is a purification of the speaker and of his enemy; now that the "carnage" has been washed away, the former enemies are (in the word of the title) reconciled, and the new relationship is symbolized (daringly) by a kiss. But we should notice that, almost as daring as the gesture of the kiss, Whitman daringly ends this poem with the dead man still dead; the last word in the poem is *coffin*. Unlike (say) Lanier's Stonewall Jackson, Whitman's dead soldier does not become enshrined in the heavens, nor does he, through noble words, live eternally in the minds of survivors. The closest a reader gets to heaven is in the first line, where (as we have seen) the word *reconciliation* is said to be "beautiful as the sky." Still, at least in our reading of the poem, the gesture of the kiss is so daring, so original, that it overcomes the horror of the carnage and the continuing death of the former enemy.

WALT WHITMAN
Vigil Strange I Kept on the Field One Night (p. 1085)

When we begin work in the classroom on this poem, we try to dramatize for students the literary and cultural richness of Whitman's experience of, and response to, the Civil War. In his essay "Walt Whitman, Mark Twain, and the

Civil War," *The Sewanee Review* 69 (April–June 1961), 185–204, James M. Cox states the central point:

> Whitman's role in the Civil War stands as one of the triumphs of our culture. That this figure should have emerged from an almost illiterate background to become a national poet, that he should have at the age of forty-two gone down into the wilderness of Virginia to walk across the bloody battlefields ministering to the sick and wounded, that he should have paced through the hospitals and kept a vigil over the mutilated victims on both sides, that he should have created the war in prose and poetry of an extraordinarily high order—that he should have done these deeds shows how truly he had cast himself in the heroic mould.

What works well, we find, is to move from this big statement to the organization and details of specific poems, so that the students can perceive the vivid forms through which Whitman explores wartime scenes and relationships. But here the issue becomes complicated: Did the scene depicted in "Vigil Strange" actually take place? How do we know the answer to this, one way or the other? What difference, if any, does the answer make?

These are questions that we put to the students. We want them to feel the power of the biographical and historical dimensions of the poem, even as we prompt them to recall that this is a poem, a product of the creative imagination, not a piece of biography or history.

Usually we then take a breath and ask the class (sometimes in the form of a brief in-class writing assignment) to summarize in a paragraph or two the "story" that "Vigil Strange" tells. This, too, helps to sharpen the class's perception of this poem *as* a poem. Next, we proceed, line by line, to examine what Whitman's language "does" to this story. What, for example, is a "vigil"? And what are the meanings of the key word "strange," both as we encounter it the first time through the text, and then again as we return to it once we have completed our reading?

Notice, too, the terms that Whitman's speaker uses for the fallen soldier, including "son," "comrade," "boy." These terms, and others, with their choice of adjectives, establish and evoke the range of the speaker's feeling for the soldier—and for the multiple nature of the soldier's identity as the speaker portrays it.

The rhythm of Whitman's language is a curious blend of the active and the passive. This leads us to ask a series of similar, but importantly different, questions: How is the language representing the dead soldier? What is the language doing *for* him? What is it doing *to* him?

In response to this question when we taught the poem recently, one student protested, in a nicely provocative way, that in her view Whitman is "objectifying" the dead comrade—that the speaker cares less about the soldier himself than about the soldier as a focal point for "feelings" that the speaker wishes to release. Some good discussion followed from this, and you might look for a way to imply or raise this critical point yourself.

In our own case, we sought to counter it by highlighting the "delicacy" of Whitman's language. "Delicacy" is a term that we came across some years ago in an essay by James A. Wright, "The Delicacy of Walt Whitman," in *The Presence of Walt Whitman: Selected Papers from the English Institute*, ed. R. W. B. Lewis (1962). Wright refers to Whitman's "powers of restraint, clarity, and wholeness, all of which taken together embody that deep spiritual inwardness, that fertile strength, which I take to be the most beautiful power of Whitman's poetry" (165).

"Beautiful power" is a suggestive phrase. It has impelled us to ask students, Do you find this poem "beautiful"? What makes it so?

We think it's important to consider the poem, at some point in the discussion, in relation to the sizable body of work that has been done on gay and homoerotic themes in Whitman's poetry and prose. Much of this scholarship is stimulating, and it makes Whitman all the more complicated and absorbing as a writer and cultural icon. It also calls attention, in fresh ways, to details in the texts that might otherwise be overlooked or under-interpreted. In *Masculine Landscapes: Walt Whitman and the Homoerotic Text* (1992), for example, Byrne R. S. Fone observes:

> When [Whitman] speaks in "Vigil Strange I Kept on the Field One Night" about a "boy of responding kisses," implicit therein is the presumption that most boys do not respond to the kisses of men and that boys who do are "men like me," who, like those in *Calamus* 4, love "as I am capable of loving." The qualifications of his texts are significant, not the presumed subjects or actions. Here *responding*, *like*, and *as*—not kisses or loving or men—are the key signs that show the nature of the discourse. (15)

Whitman is, however, a gay poet and more than that, or much in addition to that. You could say that there is a gay aspect or element to "Vigil Strange," and you would be right. But you could also say that the poem is operating to show strong currents of emotional and physical affection between men that might be, yet that do not *have* to be, gay, homosexual, or homoerotic. Sexuality in Whitman is capacious and multifaceted. Everyone can find his or her place in it.

For biography: Justin Kaplan, *Walt Whitman: A Life* (1980); Philip Callow, *From Noon to Starry Night: A Life of Walt Whitman* (1992); Jerome Loving, *Walt Whitman: The Song of Himself* (1999); and Roy Morris, Jr., *The Better Angel: Walt Whitman in the Civil War* (2000). See also: David S. Reynolds, *Walt Whitman's America* (1995); *Breaking Bounds: Whitman and American Cultural Studies*, ed. Betsy Erkkila and Jay Grossman (1996); and Vivian R. Pollak, *The Erotic Whitman* (2000).

ANDREW HUDGINS
At Chancellorsville (p. 1086)

Chancellorsville, in Virginia, was the site of a major battle between the Confederate and Union armies, fought May 1–4, 1863. It was a stunning victory for the South, whose main army was led by Robert E. Lee, but it proved a costly one as well, for one of the Confederate losses was the charismatic general Thomas "Stonewall" Jackson, who was killed by friendly fire.

There's something puzzling about the next line (or is it intended as a subtitle?), "The Battle of the Wilderness," and its bearing on the title. The Battle of the Wilderness was waged exactly one year later in the thick woods of northern Virginia, a few miles to the west of Chancellorsville. This time, Lee engaged in a bloody stand-off with a formidable Union force under the command of Ulysses S. Grant. It's not clear what the connection is, for Hudgins, between the two military engagements.

That issue aside, the key point you might make to the students is that both sides in the Civil War suffered horrific losses. At Chancellorsville, Union casualties were 17,000, and Confederate casualties were 14,000. For the Battle of the Wilderness, the Union figure was 18,000, and the Confederate was 12,000.

By the war's end in April 1865, this was the cost in human lives:

Union: Battle deaths: 110,070; disease, etc.: 250,152. Total: 360,222.
Confederacy: Battle deaths: 94,000; disease, etc.: 164,000. Total: 258,000.

Note: In 1860, the white population of the entire country was 26.7 million. The slave population was 3.95 million.

Once the historical context is set, we read the poem aloud and then ask a few questions about structure. Why does Hudgins begin with the description given in lines 1–4? These lines surprise us a bit. Or, rather, we should say that line 5 surprises us, with its first word "my," which makes an account that seemed to be rendered in the third person turn out to be one given in the first person. It's interesting to consider the different movement of the poem, and in our response, if lines 1–4 were located between the current lines 9 and 10.

On a related matter, you might ask the students to ponder why Hudgins includes two Confederate soldiers rather than just one, and, furthermore, why he makes them brothers. Notice also that it's only Clifford whose actual words of dialogue are quoted. Sid emphasizes the ferocity of his curses, but the specifics of his cursing are not presented. Why does Hudgins make this choice?

Another source of interest is the slight but suggestive shifting back and forth between Sid's narration and Hudgins's signs of his presence as poet. Such phrases as "their line broke / in animal disarray" and "the other-person stink" evoke Hudgins's own presence. Compare to: "I cursed Clifford from his eyeballs to / his feet," a phrase that gives us a form of language that Sid himself likely would use. At some moments, then, Hudgins's poem dramatizes the speaking voice of Sid, while at others it intimates the poet behind this first-person speaker.

When you reach line 20, invite the class to explain the insight or lesson that Sid calls attention to. Why does he say he "had compromised my soul?" The poem could have ended here, at lines 20–22. But it keeps going: three more sentences remain, and it's not until the sentence that occupies lines 25–26 that Hudgins brings the poem to its conclusion. This final sentence takes the action some months beyond the scene of the dead Indiana corporal whom Sid has described. The point is that later these Confederate soldiers overcame any unease about, and objection to, wearing the uniform of the other side. What does this detail in the last lines indicate about the two sides in the conflict?

Some important general points about war emerge from the study of "At Chancellorsville." For example: the two sides kill each other even as they resemble one another (symbolized by the shared uniforms), and cruel and callous deeds, rejected early on, later grow acceptable and widespread. That's the bitter, wrenching course that war takes.

True enough, but after you make such general points, shift the discussion back to the more particular: "But isn't this poem, in crucial respects, a Southerner's poem about the war?" Here's an opportunity to prompt students to think about the idea of a "Southern" American literature, a Southern literary point of view on the Civil War and its aftermath.

Among Hudgins's books, we especially value *Babylon in a Jar: New Poems* (1998). We also recommend *The Glass Anvil* (1997), in which Hudgins explores a range of topics, including language, autobiography, religion, racism, and Southern literature. For Civil War background: Stephen W. Sears, *Chancellorsville* (1996), and Ernest B. Furgurson, *Chancellorsville, 1863: The Souls of the Brave* (1992).

STUDS TERKEL
Interviews (p. 1090)

As our headnote in the text indicates, Terkel has compiled a fair number of books of interviews, so it is possible that some of your students have encountered one or another of his books, perhaps on their own, perhaps in a course in sociology or economics. In these books he presents what seem to be raw interviews, with only the briefest of introductions, though doubtless he edited the material that he collected. A related genre is the essay based on an interview, where the writer describes the setting, includes some of the questions that prompted the responses, and perhaps concludes with some remarks of his or her own. Many students have had experience writing this sort of paper in courses in Women's Studies, Education, and Sociology, and they report that they enjoy working on these assignments, so if you have never made such an assignment, you may want to consider asking students to interview someone, for example, a great grandparent or an elderly neighbor who remembers the Great Depression, and then write an essay about the person's memories. If you do ask your students to conduct an interview and to write an essay based on it, you may want to equip them with the following suggestions (abridged from our material in *The Little, Brown Reader*).

A Note on Conducting an Interview

In preparing to write about some of the thematic topics in *Literature for Composition*, you may want to interview faculty members or students, or persons not on the campus. For instance, if you are writing about the Great Depression you may want to talk to instructors who teach economics or American history or sociology. If you are writing about September 11, 2001, you may simply want to collect the views of people who have no special knowledge but who may offer thoughtful responses. Obviously topics such as love, American identity, and law addressed in this book are matters that you might profitably discuss with someone whose experience is notably different from your own.

A college campus is an ideal place to practice interviewing. Faculties are composed of experts in a variety of fields and distinguished visitors are a regular part of extracurricular life. In the next few pages, we'll offer some advice on conducting interviews and writing essays based on them. If you take our advice, you'll acquire a skill you may well put to further, more specialized use in social science courses; at the same time you'll be developing skills in asking questions and shaping materials relevant to all research and writing.

Guidelines for Conducting an Interview and Writing an Essay

You can conduct interviews over the telephone or online using electronic mail, but in the following pages we assume that you are conducting the interview face-to-face.

1. Finding a subject for an interview. If you are looking for an expert, in the college catalog, scan the relevant department and begin to ask questions of students who have some familiarity with the department. Then, with a name or two in mind, you may want to see if these faculty members have written anything on the topic. Department secretaries are good sources of information, not only about the special interests of the faculty, but also about guest speakers scheduled by the department in the near future.

2. Preliminary homework. Find out as much as you can about your potential interviewee's work. If the subject of your interview is a faculty member, ask the department secretary if you may see a copy of that person's vita (Latin for "life," and pronounced vee-ta). Many departments have these brief biographical sketches on file for publicity purposes. The vita will list, among other things, publications and current research interests.

3. Requesting the interview. In making your request, don't hesitate to mention that you are fulfilling an assignment, but also make evident your own interest in the person's work or area of expertise. (Showing that you already know something about the work, that you've done some preliminary homework, is persuasive evidence of your interest.) Request the interview, preferably in writing, at least a week in advance, and ask for ample time (probably an hour to an hour and a half) for a thorough interview.

4. Preparing thoroughly. If your subject has written on the topic, read and take notes on the publications that most interest you. As you read, write out the questions that occur to you. As you work on them, try to phrase your questions so that they require more than a yes or no answer. A "why," or "how" question is likely to be productive, but don't be afraid of a general question such as "Tell me something about. . . ."

Revise your questions and put them in a reasonable order. Work on an opening question that you think your subject will find both easy and interesting to answer. "How did you get interested in . . ." is often a good start. Type your questions or write them boldly, so that you will find them easy to refer to.

Think about how you will record the interview. Although a tape recorder may seem like a good idea, there are good reasons not to rely on one. First of all, your subject may be made uneasy by its presence and freeze up. Second, the recorder (or the operator) may malfunction, leaving you with a partial record, or nothing at all. Third, even if all goes well, when you prepare to write you will face a mass of material, some of it inaudible, and all of it daunting to transcribe.

If, despite these warnings, you decide (with your subject's permission) to tape, expect to take notes anyway. It's the only way you can be sure you will have a record of what was important to you out of all that was said. Think beforehand, then, of how you will take notes, and if you can manage to, practice by interviewing a friend. You'll probably find, that you'll want to devise some system of shorthand, perhaps no more than using initials for names that frequently recur, dropping the vowels in words that you transcribe—whatever assists you to write quickly but legibly. But don't think you must transcribe every word. Be prepared to do a lot more listening than writing.

5. Presenting yourself for the interview. Dress appropriately, bring your prepared questions and a notebook or pad for your notes, and appear on time.

6. Conducting the interview. At the start of the interview, try to engage briefly in conversation, without taking notes, to put your subject at ease. Even important people can be shy. Remembering that will help keep you at ease, too. If you want to use a tape recorder, ask your subject's permission, and if it is granted, ask where the microphone may be conveniently placed.

A good interview develops like a conversation. Keep in mind that your prepared questions, however essential, are not sacred. At the same time don't hesitate to steer your subject, courteously, from apparent irrelevancies (what one reporter calls "sawdust") to something that interests you more—"I'd like to hear a little more about . . ." you can say. Or, "Would you mind telling me about how you . . ." It's also perfectly acceptable to ask your subject to repeat a remark so that you can record it accurately, and if you don't understand something, don't be afraid to admit it. Experts are accustomed to knowing more than others do and are particularly happy to explain even the most elementary parts of their lore to an interested listener.

7. Concluding the interview. Near the end of the time you have agreed upon, ask your subject if he or she wishes to add any material, or to clarify something said earlier. Express your thanks and, at the appointed time, leave promptly.

8. Preparing to write. As soon as possible after the interview, review your notes, amplify them with details you wish to remember but might have failed to record, and type them up. You might have discovered during the interview, or you might see now, that there is something more that you want to read by or about your subject. Track it down and take further notes.

9. Writing the essay. In writing your first draft, think about your audience. Unless a better idea occurs to you, consider your college newspaper or magazine, or a local newspaper, as the place you hope to publish your interview. Write with the readers of that publication in mind. Thinking of your readers will help you to be clear—for instance, to identify names that have come up in the interview but which may be unfamiliar to your readers.

As with other writing, begin your draft with any idea that strikes you, and write at a fast clip until you have exhausted your material (or yourself). When you revise, remember to keep your audience in mind; your material should, as it unfolds, tell a coherent and interesting story. Interviews, like conversations, tend to be delightfully circular or disorderly. But it is legitimate to edit the interview in order to give it some shape.

If you've done a thorough job of interviewing you may find that you have more notes than you can reasonably incorporate without disrupting the flow of your story. Don't be tempted to plug them in anyway. If they're really interesting, save them, perhaps by copying them into your journal; if not, chuck them out.

In introducing direct quotations from your source, choose those that are particularly characteristic, or vivid, or memorable. Paraphrase or summarize the rest of what is usable. Although the focus of your essay is almost surely the person you interviewed, it is your story, and much of it should be in your own words. Even though you must keep yourself in the background, your writing will gain in interest if your reader hears your voice as well as your subject's.

You might want to use a particularly good quotation for your conclusion. Now make sure that you have an attractive opening paragraph. Identifying the subject of your interview and describing the setting is one way to begin. Give your essay an attractive title. Before you prepare your final draft, read your essay aloud. You're almost certain to catch phrases you can improve, and places where a transition will help your reader to follow you without effort. Check your quotations for accuracy; check with your subject any quotations or other details you're in doubt about. Type your final draft, then edit and proofread carefully.

10. Going public. Make three copies of your finished essay, one for the person you interviewed, one for your instructor—hand it in on time—and one for yourself.

Topic for Writing

Write an essay based on an interview. Among possible interviewees are: Someone who remembers the Great Depression; a recent immigrant; the adolescent child of a recent immigrant; a veteran of the Vietnam War; a veteran of the war in Iraq. If you can manage to do so, include a few photographs of your subject, with appropriate captions.

TILLIE OLSEN
I Stand Here Ironing (p. 1095)

The story ends ("she is more than this dress on an ironing board") with an echo of its beginning ("I stand here ironing"). In a sense, there are two stories in between: the story of the mother, whose monologue we hear, and the story of her nineteen-year-old daughter as told by the mother. The two, of course, are connected. The mother was nineteen when she bore the daughter; the mother and daughter have had a difficult life in the "prerelief, pre-WPA world of the depression"; they both resist the conventions of the conformist society as embodied by the guidance counselor or psychiatrist who has told the mother that her daughter "needs help." As the mother tries to understand the forces that have shaped her daughter, she is also trying to understand the mysterious, irresistible forces that surround us all. Life for mother and daughter has been a struggle—for the mother to work and to make a success of her second marriage and her family, for the daughter to survive nurseries, schools, clinics, and a convalescent home.

Both *have* survived, though not in the view of the counselor who seeks a meeting with the mother to discuss the child's "problems." The child, though damaged, is strong, demanding, and entertaining (she "does not smile easily," but she can compel to laughter a "roaring, stamping audience, unwilling to let this rare and precious laughter out of their lives"). "Let her be" is the mother's strong view. True, "all that is in her will not bloom," she thinks, "but in how many does it? There is still enough to live by." And so we come to the end of this story: whatever the counselor may think, the task is not to manipulate the young woman but "only [to] help her to know . . . that she is more than this dress on the ironing board, helpless before the iron."

Students are often angry with the mother for sending the girl to a sanitarium, or for now not wanting to talk to the counselor. But the mother—who, like the daughter, resists being flattened like an ironed dress—is distressed by her daughter's suffering. Sometimes she seems to engage in self-justification, blaming the depression and the war, but on the whole we see compassion and (perhaps more important) an intelligent belief that Emily will "find her way," or at least an awareness that even a mother does not have all the answers.

Note: Students may need help in seeing that despite the "you" (mentioned in the first line and persistently throughout), the piece is a soliloquy, a reflective monologue. For the most part, the "you" is, as we have mentioned, some sort of conscientious, but insensitive counselor. In the paragraph beginning "Afterwards," however, the "you" is the mother being addressed by the remembered counselor, and we are almost surprised to learn that the counselor has a sense of humor after all, as well as an awareness of talent that enables him (or her) to recognize the child's special gift. But the very next paragraph, beginning "She is coming," indicates that the counselor does not call to commend the child, or to talk about successes and happy days, but to report trouble.

As the entry on Tillie Olsen in *The Columbia Companion to the Twentieth-Century American Short Story* (2000) notes, "I Stand Here Ironing" introduced "a voice rarely heard in fiction until this time, the voice of a poor single mother. . . . It depicts all the anguish and guilt of a mother who, in order to work to support her children, has been forced to leave them in inadequate care." In keeping with Olsen's work in general, this story acknowledges "the harm done by poverty and powerlessness," but also insists on "the presence of creativity among those in whom it is least nurtured socially" (435).

For further background and discussion, see Elaine Neil Orr, *Tillie Olsen and a Feminist Spiritual Vision* (1987); *The Critical Response to Tillie Olsen*, ed. Kay Hoyle Nelson and Nancy Huse (1994); and Joanne S. Frye, *Tillie Olsen: A Study of the Short Fiction* (1995).

E. Y. HARBURG
Brother, Can You Spare a Dime? (p. 1101)

With lyrics by E. Y. Harburg, and music by Jay Gorney, "Brother, Can You Spare a Dime?" was featured in *Americana*, a musical revue that opened at the Shubert Theatre in New York City, on October 5, 1932. The song—sometimes termed "the anthem of the Great Depression"—is a painful, bitter one, and we think it will give students a keen insight into the hurt and anger that Americans during this period experienced.

When we have taught this selection, students always comment on how "little" a dime is: "Things must have been really rough if people were begging for just a dime." But in the Depression decade, a dime both was and was not a significant amount of money. It's just a dime, ten cents. But wages and costs were of course much lower then.

Consider, for example, the cost in the early 1930s of some items of women's and men's clothes:

WOMEN'S CLOTHES
Winter Coat	$28.00
Leather or Suede Bag	$2.25
Bathrobe	$1.00
Sweater	$1.00

MEN'S CLOTHES
Broadcloth Shirt	$1.00
Wool Sweater	$1.00
Bathrobe	$4.90
Overcoat	$18.50

And here are examples of weekly wages, comparing then and now:

WEEKLY WAGES	THEN	NOW
Manufacturing—Production Worker	$16.89	$500
Cook	$15.00	$236
Doctor	$61.11	$1800
Accountant	$45.00	$700

(Note: Our source is the Michigan Historical Center.)

The following figures, which compare 1927 (two years before the Depression hit) and 1999 prices, are also revealing:

- In 1927, baked ham cost thirty cents per 8- to 12-pound slabs, averaging each pound at about three cents. Now a baked ham costs about $3.59 per pound.
- Milk in 1927 was twenty-five cents for three tall cans, averaging eight cents per can. Today a gallon of milk costs $2.49.
- Eggs in 1927 cost twenty-four cents per dozen. Today a dozen large eggs costs eighty-nine cents.
- A 24-ounce loaf of wrapped split bread sold for nine cents in 1927. Today a single 16-ounce loaf costs sixty-nine cents.

As one scholar has noted:

In 1927, a dollar sounded more exciting and valuable than it does today. Today when you walk down the street and see a nickel or dime, it seems easier just to walk on by than take the effort to pick it up. In 1927 though, a nickel or dime was enough to buy a whole pound of baked ham or a tall can of milk. If you found a couple nickels or dimes, you could have bought dinner for the whole family.

(Note: For these figures and the comment, we are indebted to the *News-Sun* newspapers of northeastern Indiana.)

For a more personal kind of testimony, here's a recollection by the eminent film-critic Pauline Kael (1919–2001), who was enrolled at the University of California, Berkeley, during the Depression:

When I attended Berkeley in 1936, so many of the kids had actually lost their fathers. They had wandered off in disgrace because they couldn't support their families. Other fathers had killed themselves so the family could have the insurance. Families had totally broken down. Each father took it as his personal failure. These middle class men apparently had no social sense of what was going on, so they killed themselves. . . . There were kids who didn't have a place to sleep, huddling under bridges on the campus, I had a scholarship, but there were times when I didn't have food. . . .

(Included in Studs Terkel, *Hard Times: An Oral History of the Great Depression*, published in 1970.)

The keynote sounded in the first lines of Harburg and Gorney's song is betrayal. An unspecified "they" told the speaker that he and the others were fulfilling the American dream as they worked hard on the land or took up arms to serve in the military. The speaker was always "right there," ready and willing. The implication is that he was lied to, and, furthermore, that he and others like him perhaps were foolish to be taken in by false promises. This second meaning may be suggested too by the word "mob." Those in a mob follow the crowd, unthinkingly, in a frenzy. It is a demeaning term, and yet it is one that at the very outset of this song the speaker applies to himself and to others who acted as he did.

Now, the speaker has been reduced to standing (i. e., he is not working, he is not doing anything), waiting for a handout, and for no more than bread. Compare *this*, he says, to the big job of building a railroad, with all of its speed and power. That's done: his labor is no longer needed, and he has been cast off. He then makes his appeal to the hearer (or reader): "Brother, can you spare a dime?," addressing someone better off than he is, whom he views as a "brother"—or else, whom he is addressing as a "brother" in the hope that such a pitch will gain him the desperately needed dime.

The word "tower" in the second stanza is intriguing. It may imply the large structures that the speaker has helped to erect. More precisely, it may invoke the skyscrapers and tall office-buildings of America's major cities. The Empire State Building, on Fifth Avenue in New York City, for instance, had been completed in 1931 and officially opened by President Hoover on May 1st of that year—just a year and a half before the revue *Americana* opened at the Shubert Theatre. This building, 102 stories high, took just eighteen months to construct. It is the kind of extraordinary feat that the speaker is referring to, in order to dramatize the terrible fall into inactivity and poverty he has suffered.

In the final stanza, the speaker recalls with pride his Army uniform, and the sound and spirit of the rousing patriotic song "Yankee Doodle Dandy," which was very popular at the time of America's entry into World War I. But the last lines are troubled, even pathetic. No one seems to remember who the speaker is. Will the hearer be his "Buddy" and give him a dime? No, not "give," but (as in the earlier use of the same phrase) "spare": "spare a dime." The listener has enough; the speaker has nothing.

You might ask your students to explore some additional details. Why the reference to the speaker as "the kid with the drum?" Well, it's noteworthy that he was no more than a "kid"—young, hopeful, and (it now appears to him) naïve, deceived by others and self-deceived. The drummer of any band is special; attention focuses on him, for even when the wind instruments are silent he is hammering out the beat. And why "Al?" One reason is that "Al" rhymes with "Pal": Harburg may have wanted "Pal" and thus chose "Al" as the obvious name to use in the preceding line for the rhyme to work. But to us "Al" also has a clear, simple, even casual sound to it as a name. It's a nickname, short for Albert, Alfred, and Aloysius, and it's the name that Ring Lardner chose for the title of his well-known baseball book, *You Know Me Al*, published in 1916.

A final point: Note that the song uses "Brother" midway through, but then shifts to "Buddy" at the end. What might be the reason for this?

We tend to think of "brother" as having a strong, political, spiritual, or universalist connotation—all of us, in this or that united cause, or because we all are human beings, are brothers (and sisters). And it has been used in this way very often. The emblem of Great Britain's Society for the Abolition of Slavery, for example, depicted a kneeling, enchained African slave and the appeal coming from him, "Am I Not a Man and a Brother?" And in "Black English," "brother" refers to a black man in general, but even more, to a soul brother, a comrade.

Slang dictionaries, however, frequently make a different point about the term, noting that "brother" was used (perhaps it still is) when addressing a man whose name was not known. "Used in addressing strangers," is how one such dictionary defines "brother."

"Buddy" carries these same senses, but it also implies the meaning "to be friendly or associate," "to pair up to provide mutual help or support." "Brother" may sound more intimate, but in the 1930s, there may have been a slightly more formal, distanced resonance to the word. "Buddy" may have dramatized greater closeness—and hence, for the speaker of this song, a need that is all the more piercing.

ANONYMOUS
My God, How the Money Rolls In (p. 1102)

In our Topics in the text we give one alternate version. Here is another:

> My sister she works in a laundry,
> My father he fiddles for gin,
> My mother she takes in washing,
> My God, how the money rolls in.

Students may be familiar with yet other versions. Of the ones that we know, we prefer the version that we give in the text, partly because it seems to us to be the bitterest: "My sister makes love for a living" takes the singer into a realm darker than work in a laundry or even bootlegging gin. And the alliteration in "love for a living" seems to us to make the line the most memorable in the song, bringing together two words that in one sense belong together (love and life properly seem inseparable) but here "living" means mere sustenance, not the rich experience of being alive.

Why has the song endured (our second question in the text)? Well, doubtless the tune ("My Bonnie Lies Over the Ocean") has something to do with its popularity, but we do think the words themselves are powerful, especially the line that we have just talked about. Sung today by kids who are comfortably off, the song is not much more than a pleasant joke, a bit of recreation; sung during the Depression, it must have been a way of expressing bitterness and an attempt to master the hard facts by giving them a memorable form. The words are bitter, but the song also expresses a kind of stoicism, a certain resilience, a sense of "We'll get by, somehow."

A final point: Interesting, isn't it, that the speaker talks about the money his mother, father, and sister bring in, but never mentions any contribution of his own. He seems to be one of those amiable rogues who is quite happy to live off the labors of others. Is it possible that this fact accounts for a large part of the appeal? As one sings the song, one is living in a sort of Cloud-cuckoo-land, a Big Rock Candy Mountain, a place where work is something other people do.

ALFRED HAYES
Joe Hill (p. 1103)

We include this poem partly because it is a significant part of twentieth-century American history, and partly because it allows the class to think about the differences between a *traditional ballad* (or *popular ballad*), such as "Sir Patrick Spence" and "The *Titanic*" (some students may know these), and what in effect is a *broadside ballad*. Broadside ballads (so called because they were printed, double-column, on a large sheet of paper and were hawked in the streets like newspapers) were typically on recent accidents or miraculous events, but they included the last repentant speeches of criminals from the gallows—or at least the songs were alleged to report the last repentant words; "Joe Hill" is a variant on this type, but whereas the usual dying speech is full of repentance, Joe Hill urges his followers to continue the struggle. In terms of form, the poem clearly is by a single author; it has none of the sharp contrasts or breaks in narrative that are typical of a poem that has been passed down through the centuries (or even through a couple of generations).

"Joe Hill" is also unlike traditional ballads—and like broadside ballads reporting last words—in its didacticism. This song by Alfred Hayes and Earl Robinson is in accordance with the ideas of their friend Charles Seeger, musicologist and composer and father of the folk singer Pete Seeger: Music, Charles Seeger (and many other left-wing musicians of the Depression) believed, should be traditional in form and revolutionary in content. Pete Seeger sings it in *Carry It On: Songs of American Working People* (Flying Fish, 1989) and also in *If I Had a Hammer: Songs of Hope and Struggle* (Smithsonian Folkways, 1998). Other versions: Paul Robeson's 1958 rendition, on *Paul Robeson in Live Performance* (Columbia Records, 1971); Joan Baez, *Rare, Live, and Classic* (boxed set, Vanguard, 1993).

Although in our headnote we give a bit of information about the Industrial Workers of the World (IWW), you may want to ask students to do a little research about them. The IWW goal was to overthrow capitalism and to introduce socialism by uniting all workers, unskilled and skilled; its greatest strength, however, was with unskilled migrant workers, miners, loggers, and dockhands. It scorned political activity, favoring instead the strike and the boycott. For background: Gibbs M. Smith, *Joe Hill* (1969).

Probably from the day of his death Joe Hill became a mythic figure, standing for the IWW ideal of a world of united workers, but he was especially in the public mind during the Great Depression of the 1930s, even though by this date the IWW itself had become ineffectual, partly because its opposition to the World War allowed its opponents to call the Wobblies draft dodgers.

LANGSTON HUGHES
Out of Work (p. 1105)

When we teach "Out of Work" we make sure to give the students some background about the Great Depression. Most of them know in a general way what this period of American history involved, but they have little concrete knowledge about it. For some reason, the Depression and New Deal do not seem to be studied in much detail or depth in high schools. And the challenge is, for us, all the more difficult because in our courses we teach many students from abroad, who possess limited knowledge of American history. Many of them have not encountered the term "the Great Depression."

So we review some basic facts, beginning with the stock-market crash of October 1929 and the sudden, shocking loss of 40 percent of the value of commonly held stocks. Many Americans lost everything, as the market continued to plummet. By 1933, the value of stock had fallen by 80 percent. Unemployment was 25 percent, perhaps higher; farm income had declined by 60 percent; manufacturing output had fallen by 50 percent, and in the manufacturing sector 40 percent of the workforce had lost their jobs.

For the study of Hughes's poem, you'll want to add that for African Americans the situation was even worse. By 1932, 50 percent of African Americans were unemployed, and in both the North and the South many white Americans demanded that black workers should be fired so that these jobs could be made available to white workers. The lynching of African Americans during this painful period also increased; in both 1932 and 1933 at least twenty were lynched, compared to only four in 1929.

White Americans, then, suffered greatly during the Depression years, but black Americans suffered even more. One historian has noted, as a typical example, that the unemployment rate in Pittsburgh was 31 percent for whites, and 48 percent for African Americans.

President Roosevelt's New Deal programs and policies made a difference to the nation as a whole, but these did not provide equal treatment for all. The National Recovery Administration allowed for the payment of lower wages for black workers than for white workers performing the same jobs. And there was much segregation and discrimination in employment and housing of the Civilian Conservation Corps and the Tennessee Valley Authority. African Americans also voiced complaints about the Works Progress Administration (WPA), which, again, far more favored whites than blacks.

To be sure, African Americans did receive some significant benefits from these programs, and for this reason the vast majority of them supported President Roosevelt even as they rallied and agitated for more, and for fairer treatment. And Langston Hughes was among the fervent and determined authors calling for better conditions for African Americans. He was very much on the political left, having visited the Soviet Union and published widely in liberal, left, and Communist Party-sponsored newspapers and magazines.

"Out of Work," April 1940, appeared not in a left-wing publication, however. Hughes placed it instead in *Poetry* magazine, one of the nation's premier literary journals, founded in 1912—which suggests both Hughes's literary stature and the pervasive presence of political themes and topics in literary and cultural venues and periodicals during these hard years.

"Out of Work" is structured as a blues song, on an A-A-B pattern, with the first set of two lines echoed by the next two and the third responding to them. The poem is written in dialect, the first-person voice bringing home Hughes's affinity for the common man and woman, and testifying to his commitment to their plight and cause, which he is seeking to dramatize to the audience of *Poetry*.

Notice that by 1940, life remains rough for African Americans, and the New Deal's programs are not working effectively for them. You might mention to the class that World War II had begun in September 1939 with Hitler's invasion and conquest of Poland. This may be in the background, with all of its fear and uncertainty for the nation, still struggling to cope with the Great Depression's impact.

We stress the poem's grim humor—the speaker says he could starve for a year, but "that extra day" would be too much for him to bear. Even more, we highlight the final stanza, and ask the class to describe Hughes's tone in it. The implication here is that African Americans are worse off than others. Maybe times are tough for everybody, but the audience of *Poetry* at least is saved from the predicament of living on *nothing*, "on two-bits minus two." The tone, we think, suggests an appeal for sympathy, but it's also confrontational, perhaps hostile. It's bitter, and the use of the word "folks" may mark less of a plain-spoken bond than a put-down: "You are really no better than me, so show more attention to and concern about what I and others like me are experiencing."

For biography: Arnold Rampersad, *The Life of Langston Hughes*, 2 vols. (1986, 1988; 2nd ed., 2002). Critical studies include: Onwuchekwa Jemie, *Langston Hughes: An Introduction to the Poetry* (1976); R. Baxter Miller, *The Art and Imagination of Langston Hughes* (1989); and *Langston Hughes: Critical Perspectives Past and Present*, ed. Henry Louis Gates, Jr. and K. A. Appiah. See also Hans Ostrom, *A Langston Hughes Encyclopedia* (2002).

DAVID WAGONER
Hooverville (p. 1107)

Hooverville was the semi-jocular semi-bitter name given to the hobo encampments—shantytowns—on the outskirts of the cities in the 1930s. Still, those who lived in Hoovervilles at least had a roof over their heads, and thus were somewhat better off than those who slept on the streets, under newspapers

(Hoover blankets). David Wagoner, born in 1926, is old enough to remember the Great Depression firsthand.

The speaker (our second question in the text) clearly is from a middle-class family: He lives in a proper house (line 13), and his family has enough money to give food to beggars. His respectable parents have instructed him not to get too close to the bums (line 1), and presumably he has obeyed them because the worst he has done is to sneak out of bed at night in order to observe Hooverville's distant fires. (These fires, we hasten to add because some students may misinterpret the line, are not houses going up in conflagrations, but small outdoor fires where hobos cook their food. The dwellings in Hooverville have no kitchens, they are not much more than improvised walls and a roof that give minimal shelter.) Like many youngsters, the speaker is enchanted by the seeming romance of the life of the hobos, who sing and dance in the firelight (19–20). He contrasts their life favorably (in this respect at least) with his own: "Nobody danced in our yard" (20), and in the final stanza (our fourth question in the text) he contrasts the middle-class "short front lawns" that end "in cindery ditches" with the land beyond the crossties, "Where tumbleweeds, on the loose, were ready to roll," i.e., where the very vegetation seems to partake of the life of the wanderer.

The hobos of the 1930s (our third question in the text) were for the most part unemployed men, people who did not work simply because they could not find employment. In this sense, they were—admittedly we are speaking broadly—different from many of the homeless in the last two decades, who often are mentally ill, or are drug addicts, or are welfare mothers who have dependent children but no one to help support them. Today's bag lady was almost unknown, or so it seems, in the Great Depression. Unemployment today is also a problem, but it is nothing in comparison with the unemployment of the Great Depression, when one-third of the labor force was unemployed. Take, merely as an example, these figures: In 1932, U.S. Steel, formerly the nation's largest producer of steel, operated at only 12 percent, and the American Locomotive Company, which in the 1920s produced about six hundred locomotives a year, in 1932 produced exactly one locomotive (James L. Roark et al, *The American Promise*, 2nd ed., pages 843–44).

For further study: Sanford Pinsker, *Three Pacific Northwest Poets: William Stafford, Richard Hugo, and David Wagoner* (1987), and Ronald E. McFarland, *The World of David Wagoner* (1997).

MOLLY IVINS

A Short Story about the Vietnam War Memorial (p. 1110)

Ivins is primarily an essayist, and this piece could easily be published as an essay, but the title tells us that it is a short story. You may well want to involve the class in a discussion of this issue: Can we always make a distinction between a story and an essay? Some essays clearly have no narrative content—no characters, no plot—and are frankly presented only as the meditations of the writer, but others, such as Orwell's "A Hanging" (elsewhere in our book) report a narrative. Indeed, some biographers of Orwell have investigated the background of "A Hanging" and also of Orwell's "Shooting an Elephant" and have been distressed to find there is no evidence that the events actually took place. Was Orwell inventing the episodes, and if he was inventing, was he really writing short stories and passing them off to a gullible public as essays?

It is perfectly possible that Ivins is reporting episodes from her own life, but if so, she chooses to put them (by means of the title) into the form of a short story. Incidentally, the title is not unprecedented: Hemingway has a story entitled "A Very Short Story," and we seem vaguely to recall a few other stories with comparable titles that we can't name the authors. As we see it, an author who uses this sort of title is, paradoxically, announcing that the work is fiction but is at the same time adopting a sort of "I-am-telling-it-as-it-was" attitude, saying something like "No fancy titles here, just read this."

In our view, the final paragraph, with its simple sentences and a compound sentence ("She thinks.... He would.... He did not.... There just were... and...."), reflects the unheroic—and numbing and literally deadening—experience that is reported. In effect it says: No eloquence here; just the facts.

Molly Ivins's lively columns and witty, barbed critiques of Republicans and conservatives have been published in *The Nation, The Progressive, Mother Jones,* and other liberal and left-leaning magazines and journals. Her books include *Molly Ivins Can't Say That, Can She?* (1991) and *You Got to Dance with Them What Brung You: Politics in the Clinton Years* (1998).

TIM O'BRIEN
The Things They Carried (p. 1112)

A few words should be said about the movement away from the highly anecdotal story of, say, the Middle Ages and even of the late nineteenth century (e.g., Maupassant)—a movement toward what has been called the lyric style of, say, Chekhov and Joyce.

Most stories, even those of the twentieth century, retain something of the anecdotal plot, a fairly strong element of conflict and reversal. Howard Nemerov offers a satirical summary in *Poetry and Fiction* (1963):

> Short stories amount for the most part to parlor tricks, party favors with built-in snappers, gadgets for inducing recognitions and reversals; a small pump serves to build up the pressure, a tiny trigger releases it, there follows a puff and a flash as freedom and necessity combine; finally a celluloid doll drops from the muzzle and descends by parachute to the floor. These things happen, but they happen to no one in particular.

Some writers, however, have all but eliminated plot, and it's not unusual for twentieth-century writers of stories to disparage narrative (especially the novel) and to claim some affinity with poets. Frank O'Connor, in an interview in *Paris Review* (reprinted in *Writers at Work* [1958], edited by Malcolm Cowley), said that the short story was his favorite form

> because it's the nearest thing I know to lyric poetry—I wrote lyric poetry for a long time, then discovered that God had not intended me to be a lyric poet, and the nearest thing to that is the short story. A novel actually requires far more logic and far more knowledge of circumstances, whereas a short story can have the sort of detachment from circumstances that lyric poetry has.

In his book on the short story, *The Lonely Voice* (1963), O'Connor amplifies this point.

Faulkner makes pretty much the same point in another *Paris Review* interview that is reprinted in the same collection. Faulkner says:

> I'm a failed poet. Maybe every novelist wants to write poetry first, finds he can't, and then tries the short story, which is the most demanding form after poetry. And failing at that, only then does he take up novel writing.

Doubtless, Faulkner is being at least somewhat facetious, but we can't quite dismiss his implication that the short story is allied to the poem—by which he must mean the lyric.

If the course is being taught chronologically, students probably have already encountered Chekhov, Joyce, and Hemingway; if, for instance, they have read "Araby" they have read a story in which (many of them think) "nothing happens." In the "lyric story" (if there is such a species) the emphasis is not on telling about a change of fortune, marked by a decisive ending, but rather is on conveying (and perhaps inducing in the reader) an emotion—perhaps the emotion of the narrator. There is very little emphasis on plot, that is, on "What happened next?" (Chekhov said, "I think that when one has finished writing a short story one should delete the beginning and the end"), though of course there is a good deal of interest in the subtle changes or modulations of the emotion.

Certainly in "The Things They Carried"—a story set in a combat zone—there is none of the suspense and catastrophic action that one would expect in a war story of the nineteenth century, say a story by Ambrose Bierce or Stephen Crane. In "The Things They Carried" we learn fairly early that Ted Lavender got killed; because no one else gets killed, an inexperienced reader may conclude that nothing much happens in the story.

Of course, as far as plot is concerned, what "happens" is that Lieutenant Cross, feeling that his thoughts of Martha have led him to relax discipline with the result that one of his men has been killed, determines to pay attention to his job as a military leader, and he therefore burns Martha's letters and photographs. But this narrative could scarcely sustain a story of this length; or, to put it another way, if that's what the story is about, much of the story seems irrelevant.

Even inexperienced readers usually see that "The Things They Carried" is not to be judged on its plot, any more than is (say) "Born in the U.S.A." If some passages are read aloud in class, even the least-experienced readers—who may miss almost all of the subtleties when they read the story by themselves—will see and hear that O'Brien interestingly varies "the things they carried," from physical objects (chewing gum and the latest gear for killing) to thoughts and emotions. In short, he uses verbal repetition (which creates rhythm) and metaphor to a degree rarely if ever found in the novel.

Not least of "the things they carried" are themselves and their minds. "For the most part they carried themselves with poise, a kind of dignity." "For the most part" is important. O'Brien doesn't sentimentalize the soldiers; they can be afraid and they can be wantonly destructive. He tells us, fairly late in the story, that "They shot chickens and dogs, they trashed the village well." He tells us, too, that "They carried the soldier's greatest fear, which was a fear of blushing." "They carried all the emotional baggage of men who might die." "They carried shameful memories." This insistent repetition, rather like the incremental repetition in the old popular ballads (e.g., "Edward," "Lord Randall," "Barbara Allen"), serves less to record a sequence of events than to deepen our understanding of a state of mind.

Still, there is, as has already been said, something of the traditional narrative here: Lieutenant Cross at last does something overt (burns Martha's letters and photographs). He thus "carries" less, literally, since the first line of the story is "First Lieutenant Jimmy Cross carried letters from a girl named Martha." Whether by burning the letters and photos he will in fact lighten his load—his guilt—is something about which readers may have different opinions. He may indeed impose stricter discipline, but it's hard to imagine that he will think less of Ted Lavender. Cross himself seems skeptical. "Lavender was dead. You couldn't burn the blame." One may lighten one's load by shooting off fingers and toes, and thus gain release from combat, and one can dream of flying away ("the weights fell off; there was nothing to bear"), but a reader may doubt that when Cross lightens his physical load he will find that the weights will fall off, and that he will have nothing, or only a little, to bear. He will still be a participant in a war where "men killed and died, because they were embarrassed not to." One may wonder, too, if Cross will be able to forget about Martha, or, so to speak, to keep her in her place. He thinks he will be able to do so, but the matter is left unresolved:

> Henceforth, when he thought about Martha, it would be only to think that she belonged elsewhere. He would shut down the daydreams. This was not Mount Sebastian, it was another world, where there were no pretty poems or midterm exams, a place where men died because of carelessness and gross stupidity. Kiowa was right. Boom-down, and you were dead, never partly dead.

This quotation, however, raises yet another question, and perhaps a central question if one takes the story to be about Cross rather than about the soldiers as a group. Cross here seems to assume that death comes only to those who are careless or stupid. He thinks, presumably, that it is his job as an officer to prevent the carelessness and the stupidity of his men from getting them killed. But of course we know that in war even the careful and the bright may get killed.

Further, nothing in the story tells us that Lavender was careless or stupid. He was killed while urinating, but even the careful and the bright must urinate. We are told that he was shot in the head, and perhaps we are to understand that, contrary to standard operating procedure, he was not wearing his helmet, but the point is not emphasized. When we first hear of Lavender's death we are told that Cross "felt the pain" and that "he blamed himself," although the reader does not know exactly why the lieutenant is blameworthy. Later perhaps a reader concludes (though again, this is not made explicit) that it was Cross's job to insist that the men wear their helmets. In any case, the reader is probably much easier on Cross than Cross is on himself.

To the extent that the story is about Cross's isolation—and, as Kiowa knows, Cross is isolated—it fits Frank O'Connor's remark (in *The Lonely Voice*) that a short story is "by its very nature remote from the community—romantic, individualistic, and intransigent." But, to repeat, it's probably fair to say that O'Brien is as much concerned with celebrating the state of mind of all the "legs or grunts" as he is with recording the sequence of actions that constitutes Lieutenant Cross's attempts to deal with his sense of guilt.

This story has been reprinted in a book called *The Things They Carried,* where it is one of twenty-two related but discontinuous pieces ranging from two to twenty pages. The book is dedicated to "the men of Alpha Company," and the names in the dedication correspond to the names in the stories. Further, in the book the narrator identifies himself as Tim O'Brien. A question thus arises: Is *The Things They Carried* a collection of stories, or is it biography, history, or whatever? Perhaps one's first thought, given the dedication and the name of the narrator, is that the book reports what O'Brien experienced—and yet in an interview in *Publisher's Weekly* O'Brien said, "My own experience has virtually nothing to do with the content of the book." He claims he used his own name for that of the narrator merely because he thought it would be "neat." (In another interview, he said the use of his own name was "just one more literary device.") If we believe what he told the interviewer, the book is fiction. But perhaps O'Brien is toying with the interviewer. Or perhaps he is behaving in accordance with a point made in the book: "In war you lose your sense of the definite, hence your sense of truth itself, and therefore it's safe to say that in a true war story nothing is ever absolutely true." Has O'Brien been infected by the "fact-or-fiction?" game of much recent writing? If so, should someone tell him that what we value in his writing is his ability to bring the Vietnam War home to us, rather than his philosophizing?

YUSEF KOMUNYAKAA
Facing It (p. 1124)

The title is both literal (he is facing the wall) and figurative (he is confronting the terrible memories of past experiences).

Soldiers in other wars, too, underwent traumatic experiences, and the experience of a combatant is almost bound to include episodes that seem unreal or surreal. But the fact that the Vietnam War had so little popular support—was not convincingly bolstered by the idea that it was being fought for a good cause—was particularly disconcerting and demoralizing. Much of Komunyakaa's poem catches a sense of unreality and a sense of the loss of self. Thus, a black man looking at his reflection in the black wall finds his reflection literally disappearing; at the same time, if the wall has caused his reflection to disappear, it has nevertheless caught the man himself, drawn him back into the horrible experiences that the wall in effect memorializes. (Strictly speaking, the wall memorializes those who died, not the war itself. That is, the memorial does not say that the war was either good or bad, only that certain people died in the war.)

From the title on, the speaker is "facing it"—facing the painful memories aroused by standing in front of the wall and confronting or reliving the war experiences. He sees a vision of the booby trap that killed a comrade, Andrew Johnson, and, as reflected in the wall, the loss of the arm of a veteran, who therefore is standing near the poet. At the end of the poem the violence is transformed by the return to the world outside of the wall. In the wall the poet sees a woman "trying to erase names," that is, apparently engaged in a futile action, though one hopes that the memories of the war can be diminished if not erased. But then he corrects himself and realizes that the wall is in fact mirroring an act of affection: "No, she's brushing a boy's hair."

Some of your students may have visited the wall. If so, you may want to ask them to report their experiences.

For a good selection of Komunyakaa's verse, we recommend *Neon Vernacular: New and Selected Poems* (1993). Students might also enjoy *The Jazz Poetry Anthology,* ed. Sascha Feinstein and Yusef Komunyakaa (1991), and *The Second Set: The Jazz Poetry Anthology,* vol. 2, ed. Feinstein and Komunyakaa (1996). Komunyakaa has discussed his life and work in two interviews: Vicente F. Gotera, "'Lines of Tempered Steel': An Interview with Yusef Komunyakaa," *Callaloo: A Journal of African American and African Arts and Letters* 13:2 (Spring 1990), 215–229, and Muna Asali, "An Interview with Yusef Komunyakaa," *New England Review* 16:1 (Winter 1994), 141–147. For critical commentary on *Dien Cai Dau* (1988), Komunyakaa's poems about the Vietnam War, see Vicente F. Gotera, "'Depending on the Light': Yusef Komunyakaa's *Dien Cai Dau*," in *America Rediscovered: Critical Essays on Literature and Film of the Vietnam War,* ed. Owen W. Gilman Jr. and Lorrie Smith (1990), pp. 282–300, and Kevin Stein, "Vietnam and the 'Voice Within': Public and Private History in Yusef Komunyakaa's *Dien Cai Dau*," *Massachusetts Review* 36:4 (Winter 1995–1996), 541–561.

MAYA LIN
Vietnam Veterans Memorial (photograph, p. 1125)

The monument was commissioned by the Vietnam Veterans Memorial Fund, which held a design competition. Any U.S. citizen over the age of eighteen could enter a design. The criteria were as follows: The monument had to (1) be reflective and contemplative in character; (2) be harmonious with its surroundings; (3) include the names of the nearly 58,000 persons who died or who remain missing in action; (4) make no political or military statement about the war; (5) occupy no more than two acres of land. The competition was won by Maya Ying Lin, an undergraduate at Yale University. Her design consists of two 250-foot walls of polished black granite, meeting at a 136-degree angle. The walls are ten feet tall where they meet but taper off into the sloping ground. The names of the dead are inscribed chronologically in order of death. The names begin not at the left end of the monument but at the intersection of the two walls, at the top of the right-hand wall. The names continue along the wall, and when space on the right-hand wall is exhausted (where the tip of the wall points to the Washington Monument) they continue at the western end of the left-hand wall (whose tip points to the Lincoln Memorial). Thus, the names of the first who died in the war (on the left-hand side of the right-hand wall) are adjacent to the names of the last to die (on the right-hand side of the left-hand wall).

When the winning design was announced—there were 1,421 entries—it was met with much opposition. It did not convey heroism, it was not made of white marble (the traditional material of memorials), and it was not representational. Despite the controversy, the memorial was built—though as a compromise, a flagpole and a realistic sculpture of three soldiers (two white, one black) were erected nearby. Today the monument is universally recognized as a masterpiece, though it is very difficult to explain why visitors find it so deeply moving. Something has to do with the site (pointing, as we have said, to the Washington Monument and the Lincoln Memorial), something has to do with the sequence in which the names are inscribed, but much has to do with the reflective black granite sinking into the sloping grass. The criteria, you will recall, included the monument be reflective—and it *is* reflective, in a literal way that the committee doubtless had not envisioned. Visitors looking for the names of friends and loved ones see themselves in the monument. It is not too much to say that the living and the dead meet here, set in an area rich in historical associations. Perhaps we can also say that although the Vietnam Veterans Memorial is indeed a memorial, it is not gloomy, chiefly because it is animated by images of the living, but also because of the site, a grassy slope in an area flanked by memorials to Washington and Lincoln.

One wonders, too, to what extent viewers are moved by the knowledge that the memorial was created by a young woman—an undergraduate!—of Asian ancestry. It is appropriate at this point to quote Maya Lin's own comment on her work. We find it interesting but far from definitive:

> I thought about what death is, what a loss is . . . a sharp pain that lessens with time, but can never quite heal over. A scar. The idea occurred to me there on the site. Take a knife and cut open the earth, and with time the grass would heal it. As if you cut open the rock and polished it.
> —*American Institute of Architects Journal* 72 (May 1983):151

Useful discussions of the memorial can be found in Jan C. Scruggs and Joel L. Swerdlow, *To Heal a Nation: The Vietnam Veterans Memorial* (1992), and in an article by Charles L. Griswold in *Critical Inquiry* 12 (1986): 688–719. (Griswold's article is reprinted in *Critical Issues in Public Art*, ed. Harriet F. Senie and Sally Webster, rev. ed., 1998.) Somehow, no discussion does much to account for the experience of visiting the memorial.

JOHN UPDIKE
Talk of the Town: September 11, 2001 (p. 1127)

This is an interesting though disquieting essay to teach and to ask students to write about, not only because of its horrifying subject but also because of Updike's approach to and point of view toward it.

You might, for example, help students to see the indirectness and impersonality of moments in Updike's language, as they alternate with the vivid phrase-making and image-creating that is Updike's stock in trade as a writer. As the piece begins, "Suddenly summoned to witness something great and horrendous . . . ," we are not told who is doing the summoning, nor whom, for that matter, is being summoned; the "we," as the sentence continues, is not identified.

The second sentence is dramatically more specific, though shaded by the suggestion of the random, the accidental: "From the viewpoint of a tenth-floor apartment in Brooklyn Heights, where I happened to be visiting some kin, the destruction of the World Trade Center twin towers. . . ." The sentence takes a disconcerting turn: ". . . had the false intimacy of television, on a day of perfect reception." Updike does not describe what he sees but what it felt like or, rather, what it resembled but in truth did not feel like—"the false intimacy."

The next sentence focuses attention on the scene itself: "A four-year-old girl and her babysitter called from the library, and pointed out through the window the smoking top of the north tower, not a mile away. . . ." Again the language is indirect, deliberately imprecise: Who is this girl? What is her relation to Updike? "Kin" of some kind, we know that much. But why not be more explicit? Why does Updike keep back a detail that he could easily reveal?

Because Updike's essay is short, it's possible to work one's way through it sentence by sentence, keying in on tone, point of view, the nature of the language. But as you do so, you might lead students into thinking about more general questions as well:

What, in broad terms, is Updike's point of view?

How would you characterize his response? What is he trying to express for himself and to convey to his reader?

A topic for discussion: Given that Updike wrote this essay in the immediate aftermath of the World Trade Center attack, how would you assess it? Might a reader have responded to it one way the week after the attack and differently (very differently?) now?

A related topic: Does Updike offer you a description of the scene, or a description of his response, or both?

A student to whom we showed this essay objected to it, saying that for her "Updike's language gets in the way"—that is, the language is intrusive, distracting. This is a version of a criticism sometimes made about his novels and stories as well—that it flaunts its own inventiveness, that it is more style than substance. We don't agree with this criticism: we greatly admire Updike as a writer, in part for his sheer brilliance as a stylist, but also because we find him a very keen, incisive observer, critic, and explorer of contemporary art, culture, and American life. But, we confess, this particular essay does not quite work for us. And yet we cannot quite articulate our reasons for feeling this way, since the essay has the marks of Updike's intelligence and imagination, is serious and striking. It is not that we expect Updike to make us comfortable or even to comfort us. But the tone of the essay overall seems slightly awry, as is perhaps evident—you might ask your students about this—in the final paragraph:

> The next morning, I went back to the open vantage from which we had watched the tower so dreadfully slip from sight. The fresh sun shone on the eastward façades, a few boats tentatively moved in the river, the ruins were still sending out smoke, but New York looked glorious.

Maybe the city did look "glorious" from a very faraway perspective, but did it really, up close? And in a sense everyone in the country felt very up close to New York City during those days. Could one truly register that, the glory, the morning after this nightmarish event? If the glory was there, it had been so shattered, menaced, violated. Isn't that what we were intensely conscious of?

Suggested Topic for Writing

In the immediate aftermath of the September 11th tragedy, many people expressed the view that American life "would be forever changed." In your experience, has this prediction proven true?

MICHAEL KINSLEY
How to Live a Rational Life (p. 1130)

The preceding essay in our text, Updike's "Talk of the Town: September 11, 2001," was published a few days after the attack. We end our discussion of it in this manual with a suggested writing assignment, in which students would assess the assertion that the attack would change American life "forever."

Kinsley, writing on the first anniversary of the attack, offers a view that may then have struck many readers as radical, but now, a few years after the attack, he seems to us to be right on the mark. He begins:

> For most of us, airports are the only places where life has really changed since 9/11.

Kinsley was writing before the invasion of Iraq, and of course anyone who has served in Iraq or—worse—lost a beloved person in Iraq—is bound to feel differently, but Kinsley's assertion nevertheless continues to strike us as true: "For most of us, airports are the only places where life has really changed since 9/11." The nation has not drafted young men and women to serve in the armed forces, has not rationed food or gasoline, has not imposed curfews, has not raised taxes to pay for "the war against terror." Aside from the minor inconveniences that Kinsley specifies in his opening paragraph (long lines in airports, persons asking us to remove our shoes or to put cell phones into bags), life—real life, not political oratory—is pretty much what it used to be.

Kinsley is arguing the surprising thesis that we should do *less* about terrorism, rather than more. The thesis is arguable in the two usual senses, i.e., it is plausible enough so that it can be advanced with rational arguments, and it is uncertain enough so that it can be contested. In the text, we invite students to develop the best counter-argument that they can, whatever their own position. It is our hunch that most students initially will find Kinsley's thesis astounding, so in effect this assignment asks them to set forth their stock response and *then to examine it, to find reasons to support their view*. If the assignment helps them to examine their own views, whatever these views are, it will have fulfilled an important function.

We think the essay is admirably written, and we plan to teach it in our role as composition teachers, not in any grand role of Political Indoctrinator. In discussing it in class, we intend to go through it paragraph by paragraph, pointing out such things as these:

The Title: "How to Live a Rational Life" is not the greatest title in the world, but it is sufficiently catchy. Most of us do want to live a rational life, so we are willing to devote the necessary three minutes to this article in order to find a key to the rational life, a key to the happy life.

Paragraph 1: The boldly assertive opening paragraph begins with a sentence (quoted above) that probably surprises most readers, although by the end of the paragraph these readers may well agree with Kinsley's assertion. Certainly the concrete details that he immediately offers (long lines, inspections of shoes, cell phones in suitcases, federal employees saying "Now I'm going to run my hands around your waist") are pretty compelling. So also is his report of the PA system that tells passengers that they should "report any suspicious activity." Is there anything in this paragraph that any first-year student couldn't write? No; there are no quotations from learned sources, no details known only to lawyers or civil rights activists, nothing at all but what any of us can see and hear at any airport. The lesson for students: Provide your reader with details that support you generalizations.

Paragraph 2: Kinsley offers an engaging statistic in support of his thesis. Statistics are usually impressive, or at least attention-getting; and, again, this is the sort of thing that almost any writer can provide. Quite possibly Kinsley saw this figure in a newspaper. Our only quibble is that he doesn't cite a print source, but *Time*, where this piece appeared, doesn't give citations.

Paragraph 3: This short paragraph—it contains only two sentences—offers no details. Rather, it briefly summarizes the gist of the preceding paragraphs (actions have been trivial or excessive), adds one qualifying generalization ("not counting the military effort"), and then (by asking a question) gives a strong hint of what the rest of the essay will be devoted to: "Is there a middle ground?" Readers at this point know, even if they don't verbalize the point, that Kinsley will devote the rest of his essay to what he promises in the title: "How to Live a Rational Life."

Ask students to think about the construction of this brief paragraph, and with little or no prompting they will see that much of its effect depends on the fact that the first sentence is relatively long and the second ("Is there a middle ground?") is relatively brief. The second sentence gains weight precisely because it is brief, its five words being equivalent, so to speak, to the twenty-eight words of the preceding sentence. Kinsley has put aside the kidding around (e.g., the joshing in the first paragraph, about old ladies in tennis shoes and about putting cell phones into bags or taking them out) and puts the question on the table.

Paragraph 4: If you ask student to talk about aspects of Kinsley's style here, they will see that he does not scorn such a simple but immensely useful device as explicitly indicating that he will be going on to make a number of points. Having said that dealing with terrorists is difficult "for several reasons," he does not hesitate to say "First," so we know that here or in later paragraphs he will give us additional points. That is, he sets up expectations, and he will then go on to fulfill them. We recall that last year a student in one of our courses wrote an argumentative essay that we found hard to get through—we were not sure where one supporting argument ended and the next began—and we suggested that this essay would have been clearer if he had said, early in the paper, something to the effect that he would be offering three arguments, and then if as he was making his points he had simply said, "First . . . , Second . . . , Finally. . . ." He expressed amazement, and said that his high school teacher had warned him that such writing was "too obvious." It turned out that other students had been given similar advice in high school, advice that we consider as foolish as "Never begin a sentence with 'But.'"

In looking at this paragraph we also plan to call attention to Kinsley's use of repetition and of parallels: "Our legal culture, our political culture and our media . . . ; Lawyers will sue, politicians will hold hearings, newspapers and newsmagazines will publish. . . ." Perfectly simple, anyone can do it, but lucid and effective, something students may well emulate.

Paragraph 5: Kinsley makes his second point, and he is not afraid to label it "Second." His concern for his readers is further seen when he clarifies the distinction between "risk" and "uncertainty" by defining the words. In short, like all good writers, he is keeps his audience in mind, anticipates uncertainties that they may have, and resolves the uncertainties.

Paragraphs 6 and 7: Kinsley makes his third and fourth points, again numbering them. Readers will not, we hope, think that Kinsley is writing down; rather, they will be pleased that they can move easily through the essay.

Paragraph 8: Kinsley begins his summary: "What all this adds up to is . . . ."

Paragraph 9: Kinsley offers some general advice, and he drives his point home with a statistic (more people die annually from accidental drowning than died in the attack of September 11), again the sort of figure one might find in a newspaper or *Time* magazine. That is, he is not and he does not present himself as a statistician or an expert, but he knows that a statistic can contribute to good writing. And this sort of good writing is within almost everyone's reach. Perhaps the one sentence that most of us could not have thought of is his final sentence, where he amusingly reverses a familiar saying: "We need the courage and good sense to bury our heads in the sand a bit."

We don't want to minimize the horror of September 11, 2001, but in teaching Kinsley's essay we would concentrate on his rhetoric, and we would tell our students that in their own writing they should try to achieve clarity and interest by some of the methods he employs.

CATHARINE R. STIMPSON
Staffing (p. 1133)

"Staffing" works very well for teaching students about "tone." This is a common term in literary analysis, but sometimes we forget that it is a bit mystifying to many students. We tell them in a writing assignment, for example, to examine a passage and describe its "tone," and this seems clear enough to us. But it may not be clear to the students: They are unsure about what "tone" means and what it involves. They see words on the page and wonder: "How am I supposed to figure out the tone of this? What does *that* oblige me to do?"

For this reason, when we focus on "tone," we remind students that they are more familiar with the term than they realize. We begin with a few phrases from the definition in the dictionary: Vocal or musical sound; accent or inflection of the voice as adapted to the emotion or passion expressed; style or manner of approach in speaking or writing; general or prevailing character, quality, or trend of moral or social behavior; frame of mind; mood; temper.

What we stress to the class, is that when we explore and discuss "tone," we are asking, "What does this speaker or narrator *sound like*, and how does the tone, or tones, of voice, create for us an image, a portrait, of this speaker or narrator?" Tone, then, is a matter of specific words, phrases, rhythms, but, more broadly, it is a technique for identifying or rendering character, as when we say, "I really liked the tone of his remarks at the conference," or, "She set just the right tone when we met to work out the deal."

After you say this, your students may still be somewhat perplexed, but you can next remind them that they are themselves keenly aware of, and sensitive to, *tone* in their person-to-person interactions with professors, coaches, parents, friends, and everyone else. And they are as much, or more, alert to questions of tone when they send or receive letters or e-mails. We are, and often in vivid and complex ways, "getting a feeling" for the other person, and for his or her attitude toward us, as we listen to the tone he or she uses in a meeting or in an e-mail message to us.

The first time we taught "Staffing," we started class by asking, "What kind of person is this speaker?" The discussion went pretty well. But next time, we began with the details of the text itself, listening to and commenting on the tone as it develops and moves, and from *there* we progressed to more general questions about the speaker's life, work, and relationships. This produced even better results because it obliged the students to respond to particulars: They had to be more precise in showing and clarifying how they reached the conclusions they did, and the general points they were led to make.

It is tempting always to proceed in this fashion, moving from the particular to the general. But we will mention in passing that both approaches have merit: Students need to feel equipped to answer a local, specific question, "What is the tone of this sentence?" and also a more general one, "How would you characterize the tone of voice in this story?"

By highlighting "tone," you will develop your students' skills as critical readers, but you will also be giving them good lessons for becoming more effective writers. So much of writing well is a matter of handling tone: "How do I sound in this sentence? If I say and sound like *this* in my first paragraph, what impression of myself will I be conveying to my reader? And is *that* the effect I want, or not?"

What's nice about "Staffing," is that it's not Stimpson who is speaking, but, rather, a character, a voice that Stimpson has created and designed. You can ask good questions about Stimpson's choices: Why does she begin the story this way? How does she want her narrator to sound here? Is the narrator at any point conscious herself of how she sounds?—and how does Stimpson achieve this effect?

Please take a look for a moment at the opening sentences of "Staffing." The narrator comes across to the reader as a friendly, personable woman—we know she is a woman by the reference to the "bozos" who make sexual advances toward her. Of course, she does not use the phrase sexual advances; if she did say that, instead of "hits on me," she would be a different kind of character, one whose tone is different.

She is a churchgoer, and is earnest, nice, though (as one of our young daughters would say) maybe not the brightest bulb on the planet. She explains that she sees the bishops' staffs, which she then calls "sticks," and which she then clarifies further as having "a crook at the end." Well, maybe we should feel a touch impatient at the implication that we would not know what a bishop's staff is. But would this be a right hearing of the narrator's tone? She is more than a little absorbed in her own doings, but aren't we all? And she is trying to make sure we understand what she is referring to. She is not someone who "puts on an air," as the saying goes; she attends church, but seems not to be especially devout. No effort on her part to cover this up: she is a dutiful member of the flock, but (this is part of the narrator's appeal) she is outside as well as inside her churchgoing experiences.

"But my position is Administrative Staff, Grade 13. . . ." It isn't quite clear how the narrator gets to *this* from the previous sentences. For Stimpson, the transition proceeds from the pun on "staff," which the bishops carry, to member of the "Staff," which is the narrator's job. But it's something of an open question as to whether the narrator herself really hears the staff/Staff wordplay. That's a key dimension of tone, after all—not only how we sound, but how much or how little we hear how we sound.

The first two sentences of the paragraph are roughly the same length; they establish a rhythm that Stimpson plays against, with the long sprawl of a sentence with which the paragraph concludes.

We had a nice back and forth with the class when we asked about the tone of this third sentence. A few students heard in it something random, or freely associative in the speaker's words, as she moves (or is it "jumps"?) from phrase to phrase. But others in the class, while understanding this response, proposed instead that in her own way this narrator is pretty careful and exact: *If* she protects anybody, it is her boss, and she does *that* because he is nice to her, and she is all the more inclined to protect him because his wife is nice (or, at least, "pretty nice") to her too, and because he does not cheat on his wife, and because, furthermore, he does not "hit" on her sexually—which is something that many others in her workplace do (they are "bozos," so much for them: she is no doubt right). Even more: her boss "takes care" of her when she does suffer being "hit on," which, it seems, has happened more than once. A well-made sentence that Stimpson has crafted—casual-sounding yet rigorously clear in its own genuine way.

These comments indicate why we admire and value "Staffing." It functions very well for the teaching of "tone" in interpretation and in writing. And as you make your way through it, and get more deeply into the "September 11" subject, you'll find that the class will build to a powerful and moving conclusion.

BILLY COLLINS
The Names (p. 1135)

When we typed "Billy Collins" into Google, among the things that came up was a short piece he wrote in 2002, "Poetry and Tragedy," in which Collins, then the nation's poet laureate, offered a two-paragraph comment about poetry and the aftermath of September 11, 2001. Here is the second half of the second paragraph:

> It's not that poets should feel a responsibility to write about this calamity. All poetry stands in opposition to it. Pick a poem, any poem, from an anthology and you will see that it is speaking for life and therefore against the taking of it. A poem about mushrooms or about a walk with a dog is a more eloquent response to Sept. 11 than a poem that announces that wholesale murder is a bad thing.

That's worth discussing in class. Sooner or later one wants to talk in some detail about this particular poem, "The Names," and one way of getting into it is by asking students to think of names or naming in association with disaster or tragedy. Some of them will mention Maya Lin's *Vietnam Veterans Memorial,* where the names of the Americans who died are inscribed not in alphabetic order (Collins's principle) but in the order of the dates of their deaths.

Discussion may include comment on names on tombstones, inscribed in an effort to give the deceased a continuing life in the mind of the viewer. And in a discussion of names it is conceivable that if you are blessed with exceptionally well-prepared students someone may mention Yeats's "Easter 1916," which concludes thus:

> I write it out in a verse—
> MacDonagh and MacBride
> And Connolly and Pearse
> Now and in time to be,
> Wherever green is worn,
> Are changed, changed utterly:
> A terrible beauty is born.

Yeats here is working in the tradition of the epic catalog, naming the heroes. (Epic catalogs are not limited to heroes: They include names of beautiful people, ships, places, even—in *Paradise Lost*—fallen angels.) The inventory is normally presented in order to honor its subject, to give new life to it, to remind hearers that these people or things or traits must never be forgotten. The catalog, often presented in ritualistic or incantatory manner, summons up things that have vanished and thus gives them new life. Some students may be familiar with genealogical passages in the Bible, for instance the descendants of Noah in Genesis 5.1–30, or the descendants of Adam down to the descendants of Saul (I Chronicles 1.1–9), where, again, the act of naming affirms the importance of persons and gives them new life in the minds of the hearers. (The New Testament also includes genealogies, naming the ancestors of Jesus [Matthew 1.1–17; Luke 3.23–38], but here the primarily purpose is to establish Jesus as the prophesied Messiah.)

Collins, working in the epic tradition, celebrates the individuals. The poem begins with the sleepless poet, "unhelped by any breeze" (no quickening breeze animates his mind, apparently there is no *inspiration* in the literal sense of "breathing into"), yet the "soft rain" stimulates thought of the names, and perhaps it is not fanciful to see a connection between the "soft rain" and new life. Collins begins with five names, in alphabetic order, then comments a bit (lines 7–14), mentioning "Twenty-six willows," at which point we can guess that the twenty-six willows will stand for the letters of the alphabet. Why willows? Because the willow, especially the weeping willow, is an emblem of mourning: During the Babylonian exile the Jews wept for Zion and they hung their harps on willows (Psalms 137. 1–2); rejected by her husband, Desdemona sings a song about a rejected woman ("The poor soul sat sighing by a sycamore tree, / Sing all a green willow," *Othello* 4.3); a somewhat comic version of the suicidal lover appears in *The Mikado* ("On a tree by a willow a little tomtit / Sang 'Willow, titwillow, titwillow'"). The willow is a common motif on nineteenth-century tombstones. But from this motif of nature, Collins then moves to walking "barefoot / Among thousands of flowers" (11–12), and it is easy enough to see the flowers as emblems of rebirth.

He then moves to the next five letters of the alphabet, F, G, H, I, and J, cleverly connecting this list with his previous reference to flowers by calling up a victim named Fiori, Italian for "flower." After this second group of five names, he again comments (lines 17–23), sometimes speaking figuratively ("Names written in the air") and sometimes literally ("A name under a photograph taped to a mailbox"). Then come what at first might seem to be five more names, K, L, M, N, and O, but after a very brief comment we get six additional names, beginning with P, Q, R, S, T, and U, providing some variety, assuring us that the poem is not proceeding mechanically by fives. And then another comment, again part metaphoric ("Names written in the pale sky") and part literal ("Names silent in stone / Or cried out behind a door").

The final group of five names includes X, but probably there was no victim whose name began with X, so Collins effectively solves the problem by saying "let X stand, if it can, for the ones unfound." The poem ends by at first taking us out into green nature—a world of fields and birds—but that might seem too glib an ending so Collins takes us from nature to

> the dim warehouse of memory.
> So many names, there is barely room on the walls of the heart.

That is, Collins returns us to the victims themselves ("so many names") and to ourselves, the living, who in "the walls of the heart" give the victims whatever life they retain.

In our fourth question we invite students to think about defining "sentimentality," and to discuss Collins's poem in the context of their definition. We suggest that when you assign the poem, you might ask students to come to class prepared to discuss question 4.

You might dare to ask the students, is "The Names" truly a moving and effective poem, or does it possess power primarily because of its connection to a terrible and tragic event?

In an interview published in the *New York Times*, December 19, 1999, Collins emphasizes his keen attention, as he constructs his poems, to the responses of the reader. "As I'm writing," he says "I'm always reader conscious. . . . I have one reader in mind, someone who is in the room with me, and who I'm talking to, and I want to make sure I don't talk too fast, or too glibly. Usually I try to create a hospitable tone at the beginning of a poem. Stepping from the title to the first lines is like stepping into a canoe. A lot of things can go wrong." This implies one of Collins's strengths, but perhaps also one of his limitations. Sometimes he seems less to be expressing and exploring—really exploring—an issue or theme than presenting it in a form that will surprise, disconcert, or ruffle the reader a little but not a lot. Collins is clever and sincere, and that does not always lead to complex poems.

The poet-critic Jeredith Merrin, in "Art Over Easy," *The Southern Review* 38:1 (Winter 2002), 202–214, has sharply criticized Collins as superficial and unchallenging. She concludes he "is not without some rhetorical skills, charm, and wit. . . . But what he finally offers is disappointingly monotonous and slight."

DEBORAH GARRISON
September Poem (p. 1137)

For this poem, you need only to read it aloud and await the immediate responses—usually, objections—to begin. Not all, but many, students find the focus of "September Poem" to be offensive, outrageous, self-indulgent. They say either that Garrison should not feel that the September 11 attack make her desire to become pregnant or, if she did feel this, that she should have kept it to herself.

We give students a chance to vent their opinions, but we do some shaping of these, and some connecting of them to larger issues about poets' choice of subject. *Why* does Garrison want to become pregnant? What is *in* the nature of the terrorist attack that triggers this impulse? If this is indeed what she felt, should she have kept it to herself? Is *that* a lesson that a poet, a writer, must learn—that some subjects, attitudes, and feelings should be kept to oneself? Is this an exercise of good taste and judgment, or is it self-censorship? After all, we claim that writers should be honest, and that they should be courageous, willing to go against the grain of conventional feeling and point of view. What is the basis, then, for any objection to Garrison's poem? Perhaps, at bottom, there is none.

One or two or more of your students may make this argument for you, and that's good: it's always better if the case for the defense comes from the class, rather than from you. But there's a risk that the discussion will then peter out somewhat: the students may agree all too readily that, yes, writers should say what they think and feel, and thus what Garrison has done is troubling but legitimate (if daring) for her to articulate. This, roughly, is our own position, but we would not want the students to occupy it too quickly or comfortably. Ask the students: But should such a poem be *published*?—which is different from saying, Should it be written? Shouldn't Garrison have considered whether her poem would prove hurtful to those who suffered grievous losses from the attacks?

We hold in reserve a question about "September Poem" we like to end on: Why does Garrison use this particular structure? What is the relationship between the form and the content? This takes us directly to the text itself, and to the places in it where Garrison queries the feelings and points of view she voices. Readers may be inclined to criticize Garrison, but there are signs of self-criticism, self-scrutiny, and self-awareness in the movement of the poem: she knows what she is saying, as the form and turns of phrase reveal.

24

Identity in America

THOMAS JEFFERSON
The Declaration of Independence (p. 1142)

This document was addressed not to the King of Great Britain or to the English people but to the world ("mankind," in the first sentence), to the community of nations ("the powers of the earth"), and especially to France and Spain, from which the colonists expected help. That is, the Declaration does not appeal (as earlier revolutionaries in Britain did appeal) to the historical right of Englishmen. Rather, appealing to a universal standard of human rights, it assures the world that the revolution is not an irresponsible upheaval but a principled action.

But of course the Declaration was also in a sense especially addressed to the British people, since the King—not the entire British government or the people—is made the villain. And the Declaration was also directed to the states themselves, for it is a pact between "these free and independent states."

The speakers are "the representatives of the United States," who "hold these truths to be self-evident." That is, the speakers are reasonable and God-fearing men (they trust in Providence) who offer a thoughtful argument. They set forth principles at the start, then offer a catalog of facts, and then arrive at conclusions. Instructors who are teaching the techniques of persuasion will find the Declaration admirably suited to their purpose.

Herbert Aptheker, in *The American Revolution* (1985) (Part II of his *History of the American People*), usefully points out that the enunciation of the colonists' cause has three basic parts: (1) human beings (essentially equal in attributes and needs) possess rights to life, liberty, and the pursuit of happiness; (2) to obtain these rights, they create government; (3) governments destructive to these rights are tyrannical and should be altered or abolished by the people, who then have the right and duty to create a government which (in the words of the Declaration) "to them shall seem most likely to effect their safety and happiness."

One can put the argument this way:

Major premise: Governments denying that men are created equal and are endowed with inalienable rights may be altered or abolished by the people, from whose consent the governments derive their just powers.
Minor premise: The King has repeatedly acted tyrannically over the American states.
Conclusion: The states may renounce allegiance to the King.

As for the revisions in the first part of the second paragraph (the second question in the text), we offer a comment from Carl Becker's *The Declaration of Independence* (1966):

> When Jefferson submitted the draft to Adams the only correction which he made was to write "self-evident" in place of "sacred & undeniable." It is interesting to guess why, on a later reading, the other changes were made. I suspect that he erased "& independent" because, having introduced "self-evident," he did not like the sound of the two phrases both closing with "dent." The phrase "they are endowed by their creator" is obviously much better than "from that equal creation"; but this correction, as he first wrote it, left an awkward wording: "that they are endowed by their creator with equal rights some of which are inherent & inalienable among which are." Too many "which ares": and besides, why suppose that some rights given by the creator were inherent and some not? Thus we get the form, which is so much stronger, as well as more agreeable to the ear: "that they are endowed by their creator with inherent & inalienable rights." Finally, why say "the preservation of life"? If one has a right to life, the right to preserve life is manifestly included.

This passage from Becker's book, along with an extract from Aptheker's book as well as extracts from many other valuable sources, is given in *A Casebook on the Declaration of Independence*, edited by Robert Ginsberg. One other important source (published after Ginsberg's book) must be mentioned: Gary Wills, *Inventing America* (1979).

Additional Topic for Writing

Write a persuasive Declaration of Independence for some imagined group. Examples: adolescents who declare that their parents have no right to govern them; young adolescents who declare that they should not be compelled to attend school; parents who declare that the state has no right to regulate the education of their children; college students who declare that they should not be required to take certain courses.

ANNA LISA RAYA
It's Hard Enough Being Me (p. 1146)

Most students are concerned with being themselves (more specifically, with being true to themselves), with being individuals, with establishing their identity, and only a curmudgeon would point out that some students who are confident that they are highly individualized in fact wear the clothing of the tribe. They may think they would wear "any old thing," but they wouldn't be seen dead in the wrong kind of jeans; they cut their hair after the current fashion, and so on.

In talking about identity—for instance, in speaking about Raya's conclusion, in which she determines that she will be true to herself—we have found, over the years, that we sometimes talk about Frost's "The Silken Tent" (Chapter 20), where the suggestion is that our "self" in large measure is established by the "countless silken ties of love" that connect us to others, let's say to our parents, our siblings, our friends, our—well, the list is endless. Or we sometimes mention the episode in Ibsen's *Peer Gynt* in which Peer, seeking to find his essential self, peels an onion—each layer represents a relationship or tie that he has freed himself from (business partner, lover, etc). He finds that there is no essential self, no core to the onion. (In teaching *Hamlet* we mention that Polonius's intelligent-sounding and obvious advice to Laertes—"to thine own self be true"—is not at all obvious and perhaps is not very intelligent, since we are likely to have several selves. Hamlet, we notice, must work very hard before he is able to be true to himself, and the effort costs him his life.)

As Raya observes, when she was in Los Angeles, with her family and close friends, she was Mexican, but when she visited her maternal grandmother she was Puerto Rican. Now, at Columbia, she finds that she is, or must consider herself, Latina. What she is saying, of course, is that peer pressure is forcing an identity on her that is new to her and that she does not want to accept. (In the text, we touch on this point in our second question, and in our third question we ask students to think about terms—whether *Hispanic* or *Latino*—that assemble Spanish-speaking people—including those like Lisa, who says she doesn't speak Spanish well—into a single group.)

It seems evident to us that politically Raya is to the right of the center. For instance, she expresses skepticism about multiculturalism, and she speaks disparagingly of bilingual education. Her political stance will please some students and displease others, and they may well be more concerned with her politics than with the quality of her essay as a piece of argumentative writing. We include the essay, however, because we think it shows students that they themselves can write interestingly and effectively. In our view, most students who are native speakers can write an essay about as good as Raya's, if they will take the trouble to draft it well in advance of the due date, revise it, perhaps submit it to peer review, and revise it yet again.

Raya's conclusion (in her two final paragraphs) is that she is going to be herself, not someone manufactured by others. As we indicate at the beginning of this comment, we think this conclusion needs further thinking, but we also think the essay is clear, intelligent, and interesting.

ANDREW LAM
Who Will Light Incense When Mother's Gone? (p. 1149)

This piece is recent (March 2003), and we have taught it only once. The class was a successful one, but not in the manner we had expected.

We admired Lam's essay when we came across it, and we promptly assigned it for class discussion. To us, it seemed to describe poignantly the separation of feelings between a Vietnamese mother and her son. Writing from the son's perspective, Lam sensitively treats a familiar dimension of immigrant experience: the older generation clings to beliefs, customs, and practices from which the younger generation feels distant. Alice Walker, Amy Tan, Julia Alvarez, and many others have in their own ways explored these divisions, fears, and resentments between generations—and also the possibilities and prospects for acceptance and reconciliation. In multiethnic, multicultural fiction, non-fiction, poetry, and drama, this is an important storyline and recurring theme.

This helps to explain why we responded with interest and pleasure to the essay and put it on the syllabus. We were sure that students would respond well to it, and quickly. But what happened instead, is that the class proved slow at first to say much at all. One student said she liked the detail of the incense; another said she was amused by the meaning attached to the word "cowboy"; and a couple of others spoke approvingly (though not with much enthusiasm) about the narrator-son as he portrays himself, afflicted by doubts and concerns. That was about it.

Finally, one student said, "I've read lots of things like this before." Others in the class then chimed in, saying the same. With something of a start, we realized that the familiarity of Lam's account implied a problem with it for students. In grammar school and high school, and now again in college, students today read many works about multicultural and multiethnic America, and the topic of immigration, with its rewards and sorrows and splits between generations, is treated with great frequency. Our students respected the situation that Lam presents, but the nature of the situation, the cultural and emotional predicament, was not new to them.

For once we had our wits about us, and we asked: "Does an essay have to say something new in order to be good?" Some in the class spoke cogently about the importance for any piece of writing from a new angle, a fresh point of view; one student said, "a writer has to make you pay attention." But others maintained that if a work is well-written, it does not have to say something new—that there's a value in the telling and hearing of the same or similar stories. One of the students said something like this: "Maybe if it's the same story you'll realize you're not alone, that your experience is shared."

We next asked, "Well, if it's the case that nearly all of you find this article to be the same as other articles you've read, how would you make it different?" One student jumped right in. She said she was tired of reading about mothers and fathers and grandparents who are attached to the old ways; this student wanted to read a story or an essay in which the members of the older generation insist that the children reject the old ways, even as the children for their part are determined to embrace and perpetuate them. The class liked that idea: never underestimate the yearning for novelty. But this also gave us an opening: "That sounds good, but is that really true to life? Is that what typically happens in an immigrant family?"

The students' response to Lam's essay made us wonder whether we had overvalued it. Maybe there's not enough that's new in it. But the fact remains that the class we devoted to this essay was a very good one, and we think you'll benefit from using it. Perhaps there's something to be learned about our work as teachers from this experience. It's true that sometimes we want to resist the students if we think they are missing a point in a stubborn way, or dismissing this or that literary work because it fails immediately to engage them. But it's also true that we can gain something by letting the students have their say, and then working with that. Agree with them, and then kindle their curiosity about why they have the response they do. Give them a chance to do some teaching and learning.

AMY TAN
Two Kinds (p. 1151)

It's not a bad idea to ask a student to read the first two paragraphs aloud and then to invite the class to comment. What, you might ask them, do they hear besides some information about the mother's beliefs? Probably they will hear at least two other things: (1) the voice of a narrator who does not quite share her mother's opinion, and (2) a comic tone. You may, then, want to spend some time in class examining *what the writer has done* that lets a reader draw these inferences. On the first point, it may be enough to begin by noticing that when someone says, "My mother believed," we are almost sure to feel some difference between the speaker and the reported belief. Here the belief is further distanced by the fivefold repetition of "You could." The comedy—perhaps better characterized as mild humor—is evident in the naivete or simplicity of ambitions: open a restaurant, work for the government, retire, buy a house with almost no money down, become famous. Many readers may feel superior (as the daughter herself does) to this mother, who apparently thinks that in America money and fame and even genius are readily available to all who apply themselves—but many readers may also wish that their mother was as enthusiastic.

The second paragraph adds a sort of comic topper. After all, when the mother says, in the first paragraph, "you could be anything you wanted to be in America," the ambitions that she specifies are not impossible, but when in the second paragraph she says, "you can be prodigy too," and "you can be best anything," we realize that we are listening to an obsessed parent, a woman ferociously possessive of her daughter. (In another story in Tan's *Joy Luck Club* a mother says of her daughter, "How can she be her own person? When did I give her up?") Obsessions, of course, can be the stuff of tragedy—some students will be quick to talk about Macbeth's ambition, Brutus's self-confidence, and so forth—but obsessions are also the stuff of comedy; witness the lover who writes sonnets to his mistress's eyebrow, Harpo Marx in pursuit of a blonde, the pedant, and all sorts of other monomaniacs whose monomania (at least as it is represented in the work of art) is not dangerous to others.

The third paragraph, with its references to the terrible losses in China, darkens the tone, but the fourth restores the comedy, with its vision of "a Chinese Shirley Temple." The fifth paragraph is perhaps the most obviously funny so far: when Shirley Temple cries, the narrator's mother says to her daughter: "You already know how. Don't need talent for crying."

There's no need here to belabor the obvious, but students—accustomed to thinking that everything in a textbook is deadly serious—easily miss the humor. They will definitely grasp the absurdity of the thought that "Nairobi" might be one way of pronouncing Helsinki, but they may miss the delightful comedy of Auntie Lindo pretending that Waverly's abundant chess trophies are a nuisance ("all day I have no time to do nothing but dust off her winnings"), and even a deaf piano teacher may not strike them as comic. (Of course, in "real life" we probably would find pathos rather than comedy in a deaf piano teacher—and that's a point worth discussing in class.) So the point to make, probably, is that the story is comic (for example, in the mother's single-mindedness, and in the daughter's absurd hope that the recital may be going all right, even though she is hitting all the wrong notes) but is also serious (the conflict between the mother and the daughter, the mother's passionate love, the daughter's rebelliousness, and the daughter's later recognition that her mother loved her deeply). It is serious, too, in the way it shows us (especially in the passage about the "old Chinese silk dresses") the narrator's deepening perception of her Chinese heritage.

As a child, she at first shares her mother's desire that she be a "prodigy," but she soon becomes determined to be herself. In the mirror she sees herself as "ordinary" but also as "angry, powerful"; she is an independent creature, not an imitation of Shirley Temple. The question is, Can a young person achieve independence without shattering a fiercely possessive parent? Or, for that matter, without shattering herself? We can understand the narrator's need to defy her mother ("I now felt stronger, as if my true self had finally emerged"), but the devastating effect when she speaks of her mother's dead babies seems almost too great a price to pay. Surely the reader will be pleased to learn that the narrator and her mother became more or less reconciled, even though the mother continued to feel that the narrator just didn't try hard enough to be a genius. It's worth reading aloud the passage about the mother's offer of the piano:

> And after that, every time I saw it in my parents' living room, standing in front of the bay window, it made me feel proud, as if it were a shiny trophy that I had won back.

As a mature woman, the narrator comes to see that "Pleading Child" (which might almost be the title of her early history) is complemented by

"Perfectly Contented." Of course, just as we have to interpret "Pleading Child" a bit freely—let's say as "Agitated Child"—so "Perfectly Contented" must be interpreted freely as, say, "Maturity Achieved." We get (to quote the title of the story) "two kinds" of experience and "two kinds" of daughter in one.

See Marina Heung, "Daughter-Text/Mother-Text: Matrilineage in Amy Tan's *Joy Luck Club*," *Feminist Studies* 19 (Fall 1993): 597–616.

ALICE WALKER
Everyday Use (p. 1159)

The title of this story, like most other titles, is significant, though the significance appears only gradually. Its importance, of course, is not limited to the fact that Dee believes that Maggie will use the quilts for "everyday use"; on reflection we see the love, in daily use, between the narrator and Maggie, and we contrast it with Dee's visit—a special occurrence—as well as with Dee's idea that the quilts should not be put to everyday use. The real black achievement, then, is not the creation of works of art that are kept apart from daily life; rather, it is the everyday craftsmanship and the everyday love shared by people who cherish and sustain each other. That Dee stands apart from this achievement is clear (at least on rereading) from the first paragraph, and her pretensions are suggested as early as the fourth paragraph, where we are told that she thinks "orchids are tacky flowers." (Notice that in the fifth paragraph, when the narrator is imagining herself as Dee would like her to be on a television show, she has glistening hair—presumably because the hair has been straightened—and she appears thinner and lighter-skinned than in fact she is.) Her lack of any real connection with her heritage is made explicit (even before the nonsense about using the churn top as a centerpiece) as early as the paragraph in which she asks if Uncle Buddy whittled the dasher, and Maggie quietly says that Henry whittled it. Still, Dee is confident that she can "think of something artistic to do with the dasher." Soon we learn that she sees the quilts not as useful objects but only as decorative works; Maggie, on the other hand, will use the quilts, and she even knows how to make them. Dee talks about black "heritage," but Maggie and the narrator embody this heritage and they experience a degree of contentment that eludes Dee.

Many white students today are scarcely aware of the Black Muslim movement, which was especially important in the 1960s, and they therefore pass over the Muslim names taken by Dee and her companion, the reference to pork (not to be eaten by Muslims), and so on. That is, they miss the fact that Walker is suggesting that the valuable heritage of American blacks is not to be dropped in favor of an attempt to adopt an essentially remote heritage. It is worth asking students to do a little work in the library and to report on the Black Muslim movement.

Houston A. Baker Jr. and Charlotte Pierce-Baker discuss the story in *Southern Review* (new series 21 [Summer 1985]), in an issue that was later published as a book with the title *Afro-American Writing Today*, ed. James Olney (1989). Their essay is worth reading, but it is rather overheated. Sample:

418   *Chapter 24: Identity in America*

> Maggie is the arisen goddess of Walker's story; she is the sacred figure who bears the scarifications of experience and knows how to convert patches into robustly patterned and beautifully quilted wholes. As an earth-rooted and quotidian goddess, she stands in dramatic contrast to the stylishly fiery and other-oriented Wangero. (p. 131)

The essay is especially valuable, however, because it reproduces several photographs (in black and white only, unfortunately) of quilts and their makers. Lots of books on American folk art have better reproductions of quilts, but few show the works with the artists who made them. It's worth bringing to class some pictures of quilts, whether from the essay by the Bakers or from another source. Even better, of course, is (if possible) to bring some quilts to class.

Many students have read Walker's novel *The Color Purple* (1982)—it is one of the most widely taught novels in U.S. colleges and universities—and seen the film adaptation directed by Steven Spielberg (1985). In our judgment this is Walker's best book, though we also value an earlier novel, *Meridian* (1976), and two collections from the 1980s: *In Search of Our Mothers' Gardens: Womanist Prose* (1983) and *Living by the Word: Selected Writings, 1973–1987* (1988). For a selection of critical essays on the story we have chosen, see *Everyday Use*, ed. Barbara T. Christian (1994). Also helpful: *Alice Walker: Critical Perspectives Past and Present*, ed. Henry Louis Gates Jr. and K. A. Appiah (1993).

Topics for Critical Thinking and Writing

1. "Everyday Use" is by a black woman. Would your response to the story be the same if you knew it were written by a white woman? Or by a man? Explain.
2. How does the narrator's dream about her appearance on the television program foreshadow the later conflict?
3. Compare "Everyday Use" with Bambara's "The Lesson." Consider the following suggestions: Characterize the narrator of each story and compare them. Compare the settings and how they function in each story. What is Miss Moore trying to teach the children in "The Lesson?" Why does Sylvia resist learning it? In "Everyday Use," what does Dee try to teach her mother and sister? Why do they resist her lesson? How are objects (such as quilts, toys) used in each story? How in each story does the first-person narration enlist and direct our sympathies?

KATHERINE MIN
Courting a Monk (p. 1166)

Readers of this story need to know nothing, or almost nothing, about Buddhism, and we decided to limit our annotations to a single note, on *dukkha* in paragraph 67, a Pali word literally meaning "unpleasant," "dis-ease," but usually translated as "suffering"—not merely physical suffering but also the suffering that results from desire. "Desire" (or "craving" or "thirst for life" or "attachment to the world") in Buddhist thought is not merely the desire of the flesh—the sort of desire that St. Augustine saw all around him in Carthage, and, for that matter, that he himself felt when he prayed, "Give me chastity and continence, but not just now." Nor is it merely desire for worldly goods; rather, it is any sort of attachment, even to things and ideas that the West considers noble. We will speak further (very briefly) about Buddhism, but first we want to make a few obvious comments about the structure of the story.

Broadly speaking, Min's structure employs *chiasmus*, an X-like arrangement, "a placing crosswise." (The classical example of the ABBA structure that constitutes chiasmus is Shakespeare's "Remember March, the Ides of March remember," in *Julius Caesar* 4.3.18.) What we have in mind is this: the story begins with Micah as a chaste monk and Gina (the narrator) as a woman consumed by desire. At the end, although Gina tells us that Micah sometimes appears to be removed from the world, he is a high school teacher of biology, the father of two children, and a man who "makes it sound as though he were crazy to ever consider being a monk." Gina, by contrast, has "taken to reading books about Buddhism," and in the penultimate paragraph she briefly recounts the story of how Siddhartha (the Historical Buddha) gained enlightenment (Sanskrit *bodhi*, in the United States, best known by the Japanese word *satori*, which some specialists prefer to translate as "awakening"). Obviously chiasmus can be a highly effective way of concluding, as the very brief example from *Julius Caesar* indicates. When we go beyond a sentence or two and get into a plot, this structure can provide not only a sense of finality but also a rich sense of irony. In "Courting a Monk" the irony is evident but the finality is diminished; although Micah has put aside his early ambitions and views, he is still (at least according to Gina) given to moments of meditation, and although Gina is studying Buddhism, she has by no means achieved enlightenment ("Awakening"). Gina is still attached to the world, but she is pondering a *koan* of her own invention, "What is the sound of a life not lived?" (We will talk about *koans* later.)

Within the story there is another sort of X that deserves a bit of comment. The narrator's father opposes his daughter's marriage to a Caucasian, yet during the dinner, despite his insistence on his daughter's Korean blood, he says to her, "This boy more Korean than you." Interestingly, what apparently appeals to the father is Micah's fondness for Korean food (cabbage kimchi), which Gina does not care for. Micah's interest in Buddhism does engage the father's attention, but chiefly as something to react against; the father is no longer a Buddhist, and Buddhism does not provide a bond. Food is another thing; we do find kinship with the people who share our tastes in food. One can almost say that shared tastes for food are in the blood (we have in mind the father's insistence that blood makes for identity), something deeper than shared intellectual interests. It is our impression that for many Americans, their deepest connection with their European or Asian or African backgrounds is not in their religion but in the foods they ate as children and (despite assimilation in other matters) continue to cherish.

We said at the outset that readers need no knowledge of Buddhism, but we nevertheless want to offer a few comments about it since the subject may come up in class, especially if you have some Asian or Asian-American students or indeed native-born Caucasian students who have converted to Buddhism. (*Caution:* Do not assume that your Asian students are Buddhists. Most of the Korean and Korean-American students whom we have met in our classes have been Christians.)

The subject of desire (Sanskrit: *trishna*), or attachment, is emphasized in the story. In paragraph 35 Micah tells Gina that "Buddhism is all about the renunciation of desire," and the topic is discussed in the ensuing paragraphs. In paragraph 44 Gina offers an extremely interesting definition: "I understood what desire was then, the disturbance of a perfect moment in anticipation of another." The discussion of desire reappears in paragraph 70, when Gina says that Buddhists "believe in physical desire. . . . They have sex," but Micah parries with "Buddha believes in physical desire. . . . It's impermanent, that's all. Something to get beyond." All of this talk may lead to some classroom discussion of Buddhism, so we will offer a brief comment.

Buddhism of course is immensely complicated. It has a long history, and it has developed many schools, and there is much argument about terms such as "self" (see paragraphs 95–96), but we can probably say that the heart of Buddhism is the belief that suffering *(dukkha)* is omnipresent. The Four Noble Truths (paragraph 67) are these:

1. All existence is characterized by suffering; the human condition (though it includes temporary pleasures) is one of dis-ease.
2. Suffering is caused by desire (or "craving," or "attachment"), by a thirst for selfish pleasure, by orientation to the transient.
3. Suffering can be eliminated, but only by ceasing to crave.
4. One can cease to crave only by leading a disciplined, moral life, and this is set forth in the Eightfold Path, which takes one from the realm of suffering to Nirvana.

Before we go on to list the constituents of the Eightfold Path we want to say, in all seriousness, that the image of the father trying to hard-boil an egg by running hot water over it strikes us as a wonderful metaphor for the life of craving. Doubtless the father had been frustrated in earlier endeavors, and later he would be frustrated by others, most notably by his desire to have a daughter whose behavior shows filial piety. Indeed, in the final paragraph of the story Gina specifically connects the father's futile effort to cook the egg with his futile effort to shape his daughter. But, again, we think this image of the father trying to boil an egg by putting it in a sock and holding it under hot water wittily (and in a very Zen-like way) conveys the Buddhist idea of the suffering inherent in desire, or, to put it only a bit less grandly, the image embodies the frustration that the unenlightened mind experiences.

With some hesitation—this is getting complicated—we give one version of the Eightfold Path, which the Buddha taught in his first sermon. These are not eight successive stages but eight practices that are engaged in simultaneously. We are aware that each of the following points needs considerable amplification, and it may be that you will want some students to give reports on some aspects of Buddhism.

1. Right understanding, or right views (understanding reality, which means understanding the Four Noble Truths)
2. Right thinking (resolution to renounce desire, ill will, and cruelty)
3. Right speech (avoidance of lying, angry words, gossip)
4. Right action (avoidance of stealing, rape, pederasty, etc.)
5. Right livelihood (avoidance of harmful ways of making a living, e.g., hunting, fishing, palmistry, astrology)
6. Right effort (cultivation of what is wholesome)
7. Right mindfulness (good thoughts, contemplation, including—as a corrective to vanity—contemplation of corpses)
8. Right concentration (a stage in meditation in which mental activity ceases and the mind is united with the object of meditation)

By these practices, it is said, one extinguishes the passions (which produce ignorant actions) and arrives at enlightenment. Attempts to eliminate passion, to detach oneself from the things of this world, are not, of course, limited to Buddhism. One can easily find Christian texts that urge renunciation.

> But I say unto you, That whosoever looketh on a woman to lust after her hath committed adultery with her already in his heart. / And if thy right eye offend thee, pluck it out, and cast it from thee: for it is profitable for thee that one of thy members should perish, and not that the whole body should be cast into hell.
>
> Matthew 5:28–29

> He that loveth father or mother more than me is not worthy of me: and he that loveth son or daughter more than me is not worthy of me.
>
> Matthew 10:37

> And everyone that hath forsaken houses, or brethren, or sisters, or father, or mother, or wife, or children, or lands, for my name's sake, shall receive an hundredfold, and shall inherit everlasting life.
>
> Matthew 19:29

We are not saying that in the matter of renunciation Christianity and Buddhism are the same. We daily try (especially when we ask students to write a comparison) to keep in mind a profound remark by Bishop Joseph Butler: "Everything is what it is, and not another thing." Still, if some students find the Buddhist ideal of renunciation odd, we think it is worth citing some Christian texts.

One other aspect of Buddhism that is given some emphasis in the story is the *koan*, which Micah introduces in paragraph 48. In 52 he explains that "It's a question that has no answer, sort of like a riddle. You know, like 'What is the sound of one hand clapping?' Or, 'What was your face before you were born?'" (By the way, although "What is the sound of one hand clapping?" is probably the best-known *koan* in the United States, in fact the correct translation of this *koan* invented by the Japanese monk Hakuin is "What is the sound of one hand?" (For a painting by Hakuin, showing him with one hand raised, and inscribed at the top, "Young people, no matter what you say, everything is nonsense unless you hear the sound of one hand," see Sylvan Barnet and William Burto, *Zen Ink Paintings* [1982], p. 54, or Penelope Mason, *History of Japanese Art* [1993], p. 285.) Buddhist teachers (especially Zen Buddhists of the Rinzai sect) use *koans*, which are often paradoxical and which in any case cannot be solved by logic, as a device to force the student to make an intuitive leap into a world beyond logical contradiction. Here are two of the responses that are said to have satisfied some Zen masters: (1) the pupil said, "Whether it's from the front or the back, you can hear it as you please"; (2) the pupil thrust one hand forward. (These are given in *The Sound of One Hand,* trans. Yoel Hoffman [1975], pp. 47–49.)

Gina in one of her least likeable moments trivializes the whole procedure by asking (paragraph 57), "What's the sound of one cheek farting?" Even as late as paragraph 130 she is clowning around when, in the ice cream parlor, she asks, "What is the sound of Swiss chocolate almond melting?" By the way, the *koan* about the sound of a hand is so well known that journalists take it for granted. On the very day that we drafted this page (August 6, 1999) *The New York Times* had an article (C5) about Abercrombie and Fitch's advertising campaign that featured "lubricious images of toothsome campus types." The article ended, "It's not unlike the riddle asking about the sound of one hand clapping. What does a college student tugging off his boxers sound like?"

The coarseness of the newspaper account is more or less of a piece with Gina's coarseness during most of the story, but, again, at the end she is a different person. Not enlightened, but seriously meditating: "What is the sound of a life not lived?"

Suggested reference: The literature, even in English, on Buddhism is enormous, but in our view the best introduction is a collection of Buddhist texts with admirable short introductions: W. M. Theodore De Bary, ed., *The Buddhist Tradition in India, China, and Japan* (1969). We have also profited from Rupert Gethin, *The Foundations of Buddhism* (1998).

EMMA LAZARUS
The New Colossus (p. 1176)

The poem (which should be compared with the next poem, by Aldrich), is almost inseparable from its history. It was written in support of a campaign to raise funds for a pedestal for the *Statue of Liberty*—the manuscript was auctioned and the proceeds given to the fund. In 1886 the poem was read at the dedication of the statue, and in 1903 (the twentieth anniversary of the writing of the poem) a bronze tablet with the poem was placed on an interior wall of the pedestal. In 1945 the bronze tablet was moved from the second-story landing inside the pedestal to the main entrance of the statue. The poem is inevitably joined to a cherished national image, and probably millions of schoolchildren (among them the writer of this note) took pride in memorizing the lines.

When we came to prepare this section of our book, there was never any doubt that we would include the poem—the last four and a half lines alone demand inclusion. But in rereading the poem we did feel a tad uneasy about the highfalutin' opening lines, with their classical allusion and their overall "poetic" tone. Lazarus is writing in the genteel tradition—the tradition that derived from classically educated English poets such as Tennyson—rather than, obviously, in the tradition of Whitman. No "barbaric yawp" would come from the mouth of this New Yorker who was descended from a prosperous Sephardic family that had lived in the United States since the eighteenth century. Her lines praise America in a rather academic way, by comparing it favorably to the classical world.

It is not surprising, therefore, that the colossus is periphrastically evoked as "the brazen giant of Greek fame," or that electricity in the torch is "the imprisoned lightning," or that ancient lands are places of "storied pomp." It is all very declamatory, possibly right for a bronze plaque—but (at least to our ear today) a trifle inflated or stiff. Having said this, we want to add that we are still moved by the final words, spoken by the statue. The words spoken by this colossal symbol of a lofty ideal seem to us less inflated than the earlier lines, spoken by the poet or by the reader. (Here we are expressing the idea that when readers read lyric poems, as opposed to dramatic monologues such as "My Last Duchess," the readers themselves are the speakers, the poems are *their* utterances).

A few additional points:

1. Lazarus calls the statue "Mother of Exiles," thereby anticipating the great final passage, in which the statue welcomes "the wretched refuse" of countries across the sea, i.e., low-status persons scorned by the powerful. In France the statue was officially called *Liberté Eclairant le Monde* ("Liberty Enlightening the World"), though in the United States it is popularly known as the *Statue of Liberty*. (The French title emphasizes the torch, symbolizing illumination, i.e., knowledge, and, by extension, freedom since knowledge is supposed to free us from the bonds of ignorance. The French did not intend to symbolize America as a haven for the oppressed, but as an example of a republican government. But the great increase in immigration in the following years, and Lazarus's poem, have given the statue a meaning it did not originally have.)
2. In line 8, "air-bridged" and "twin cities" deserve a bit more comment than we give them in our headnote in the text. New York (which was confined to the island of Manhattan) and Brooklyn were separate cities when Lazarus wrote the poem; not until 1898 did the two cities, and some other communities, combine into "Greater New York." The Brooklyn Bridge was the world's first great suspension bridge, i.e., the roadway is supported not on arches or pillars but rather is suspended from vertical cables that are attached to main cables; the main cables are hung on two towers, and their ends are anchored in bedrock. This method of construction requires far

fewer intermediate supports beneath the bridge, thus giving it a sense of airiness (hence "air-bridged" in line 8).

3. The words "wretched refuse" in line 12 have disturbed some people, and we raise this point below, in our first question. Our own feeling is that there is nothing bothersome here. The poet is not saying that these people are unworthy or without value; rather, she is saying that they are distressed or afflicted ("wretched") and they are rejected ("refuse") by those in power in their own lands.
4. The poem ends with the words, "the golden door." Naive immigrants supposedly thought that the streets were paved with gold—the idea goes back at least to the conquistadors who searched for El Dorado, the legendary kingdom rich in precious metals—but surely "the golden door" is a metaphor for opportunity, for a chance not only to make money but also to live a new kind of life, a life of freedom.

Lazarus wrote the poem in 1883; obviously in discussing the poem in a course in literature it is not essential to talk about the pros and cons of today's immigration policies. Still, an instructor may well be interested in relating the poem to the life around us, so here is a brief history of our immigration policy. The Open Door policy of nineteenth- and early twentieth-century America was changed, in 1924, to a nationalorigins quota system which favored Northern and Western Europe and severely restricted immigration from everywhere else. This system was replaced in 1965 by a law (with amendments) that said there were three reasons to award visas to immigrants:

1. An immigrant might possess certain job skills, especially skills that this country needs. (Relatively few visas were awarded on this basis.)
2. An immigrant might be a refugee from war or from political persecution, and we would offer "political asylum."
3. An immigrant might be related to an American citizen or to a legal alien (the "family reunification policy").

In 1965, when this policy was formulated, there was little immigration from Latin America, the Caribbean, and Asia. Today, 90% of all immigration to the United States comes from those areas. Upwards of 80% are people of color. Whatever our policy is, is it *not* racist? What about numbers, rather than percentages? The peak decade for immigration was 1901–1910, when about 8.7 million immigrants arrived, chiefly from Southern and Eastern Europe. Probably 1981–1990 matched this, if illegal immigrants are included, but in any case in 1901–1910 the total United States population was less than one-third of what it is today. After 1910, immigration declined sharply; in all of the 1930s, only about 500,000 immigrants came to the United States, and in all of the 1940s there were only about 1,000,000, including refugees from Hitler. The figure now is about 1.5 million annually, plus an unknown number of illegal immigrants (the usual guess is half a million annually). In 1970 Latino immigration was 4.5%; in 1990 it was 9%.

Topics for Critical Thinking and Writing

1. At the International Arrivals Building of John F. Kennedy Airport a plaque, with large gold letters, quotes some of the most famous words in the poem—the speech in the last five lines—but it omits the third line from the end, "The wretched refuse of your teeming shore." Apparently those who installed the plaque thought that Lazarus regarded the immigrants as trash, "wretched refuse." Is this the way you read the line? Or do you think Lazarus is giving not her view but the view of the European ruling classes? Or what?
2. A question about the first lines: Why does Lazarus begin with a negative, saying what the Statue of Liberty is *not?* Does this form for the opening of the poem strengthen or weaken it?
3. In the first two lines of the poem, Lazarus mistakenly says that the colossus of Rhodes symbolized tyranny, when in fact it symbolized resistance to tyranny. In your opinion, how damaging to the poem is this factual error?

TSENG KWONG CHI
Statue of Liberty, New York City (photograph, p. 1177)

Before we offer a very brief comment on the photograph, we want to give a little additional background about the statue, supplementing our headnote to Emma Lazarus's poem.

Strictly speaking, Auguste Bartholdi's sculpture is entitled *Liberty Enlightening [i.e. illuminating] the World*. Paid for by public subscription, it was the gift of the French people (not the government), presented in memory of French assistance during the War of Independence. The statue was built in sections in France, shipped to the United States, and unveiled and inaugurated in October 1886.

The statue, 150 feet tall, is made of thin sheets of beaten copper affixed to an iron and steel framework designed by Gustave Eiffel, who later built the Eiffel Tower. A classically draped woman, her left foot advanced and stepping on the broken shackles of tyranny, she holds a torch in her raised right hand and a tablet in her left hand. Her face is traditionally said to be that of Bartholdi's mother, but even if this pleasant story is true, the face is highly stylized in a severe classic manner.

Liberty was an ancient Roman goddess—but she was the goddess of personal freedom (i.e., of the condition opposite to slavery), not the goddess of a political idea. From the late eighteenth century, however, the goddess was interpreted in terms of political freedom and democracy. The symbolism of Bartholdi's statue is very clear:

1. The tablet, which doubtless is meant to call to mind the tablets held by Moses, is inscribed "JULY IV MDCCLXXVI." Thus, Liberty is associated

both with God and with American history; the idea is that liberty, divinely ordained, flourished in America in 1776 and will spread throughout the world.
2. The torch represents the dispelling of darkness, i.e., the dispelling of political ideals which enslave. Probably, too, there is an association here with Christ, who in John 8:12 calls himself "the light of the world".
3. The radiant or sunburst crown is a sort of halo, making the figure a secular saint. The seven rays suggest the seven planets, the seven seas, the seven continents, etc.
4. The base stands on a star fortress (Fort Wood, on what used to be called Bedloe's Island but is now Liberty Island), suggesting that liberty is indomitable.

For a readable account, see Marvin Trachtenberg, *The Statue of Liberty* (rev. ed. 1986). Also useful is June Hargrove et al., *Liberty: The French-American Statue in Art and History* (1986).

There are plenty of pictures of the *Statue of Liberty* shot, like this one, against a heavenly background, i.e., shot from below in order to emphasize the heroic, godlike quality of the figure, but this photo by Tseng Kwon Chi is unusual, not least because it contains a comparable image of him as well as of the statue. There he stands, self-assured, taking his own picture along with Liberty (notice the cable release in his hand). The fact that the picture is in black and white helps to unify the photographer with the image and its pedestal, and for that matter, with the background.

Also unusual, of course, is the fact that the man is an Asian. Until fairly recently, most Asians entered the United States through Angel Island, the largest island in San Francisco Bay, not through Ellis Island (a few hundred yards from the small island on which the statue stands), and probably few Asian tourists bothered to photograph themselves with the Statue of Liberty. Viewers are used to seeing pictures of immigrants from Europe approaching the Statue of Liberty, but they are probably surprised by a picture of an Asian with the statue. It is a vigorous reminder that the old patterns of immigration and also of tourism, in which immigrants and tourists came chiefly from Europe, have been markedly changed.

THOMAS BAILEY ALDRICH
The Unguarded Gates (p. 1177)

One can hardly neglect the opportunity to compare this narrow-minded poem with the poem that precedes it in the text, Emma Lazarus's "The New Colossus." Lazarus—imaginatively looking from the European immigrant's point of view—sees New York Harbor as enriched and purified by "sea-washed, sunset gates," where a beacon "Glows world-wide welcome." Aldrich—looking from his Boston nest—sees the "Wide open and unguarded . . . gates" and the "sacred portals" (lines 1 and 16) as the entries through which we foolishly admit destructive hordes. Are all immigrants potential threats? No, lines 12–17 specify the people whom we must care for, "sorrow's children" and so forth. How can we recognize them, or, rather, how can we recognize the others, people who threaten our civilization? Easily, by their place of origin and (in most cases) color or religion:

> Men from the Volga and the Tartar steppes,
> Featureless figures of the Hoang-Ho,
> Malayan, Scythian, Teuton, Kelt, and Slav,
> Flying the Old World's poverty and scorn;
> These bringing with them unknown gods and rites,
> Those tiger passions, here to stretch their claws.

From 1865 onward Aldrich lived chiefly in Boston, so one is not entirely surprised to find the hostile reference to the "Kelt"—Protestant Bostonians were known for their hostility to the recent Irish immigrants—but the reference to the Teuton is a bit puzzling, since persons like Aldrich identified themselves as Anglo-Saxons and therefore as related to German stock. It's our guess that Aldrich had in mind Catholic German peasants. In any case, Aldrich's terrific hostility to what is now called the Other is evident. For him, the people who constitute the Other are "a wild, motley throng," without recognizably human faces ("featureless figures"), and they bring not only "unknown gods and rites" but also their "tiger passions."

The hostile references to people from Asia (given the context, the Kelts and the Teutons are sort of dishonorary Asians) allow us to say that Aldrich was openly racist—though we should add that, by today's standards, almost everyone else was racist too, and indeed racism was respectably founded in what was thought to be the most advanced science of the day. Doubtless when he speaks of Liberty as a "white goddess" he has in mind a classical structure of white marble, but surely he would say that the material aptly symbolizes the superior—most highly evolved—people that he has in mind.

Putting aside what we can call the basic ideas of the poem, what can we say about it as poetry? We can say something rather similar to what we said about Emma Lazarus's poem—that is, Aldrich is writing poetry in the manner of a proper Victorian, i.e., in accordance with the classical tradition. Like Lazarus, he cannot think of sounding a Whitmanian "barbaric yawp." Predictably, he sees the United States as another Rome (line 20) and the new immigrants as barbarian invaders. But what sort of United States does he see? It is white, it is entered through "sacred portals" (line 16), and it is a place of "freedom" (line 17). Evidently it is not the America that Emerson, in "The Poet" (1841), said awaited its poets:

> Our log-rolling, our stumps and their politics, our fisheries, our Negroes and Indians, our boasts and our repudiations [i.e., refusals to acknowledge debts], the wrath of rogues, and the pusillanimity of honest men, the north-

ern trade, the southern planting, the western clearing, Oregon and Texas, are yet unsung. Yet America is a poem in our eyes; its ampler geography dazzles the imagination, and it will not wait long for metres.

Aldrich is a singer of a very limited America.

ANONYMOUS
The Registry Room, Ellis Island, ca. 1912 (photograph, p. 1178)

The room was modified in various ways—for instance, a decade or so earlier it had a great staircase descending in the middle of the floor—but essentially this is the room through which millions of immigrants passed, or hoped to pass, into America. We say "hoped to pass" because a small percentage was not allowed entry, chiefly for reasons of health.

It is easy to talk about this image. The immigrants, crowded into lanes, hope to pass through the narrow gate in the center, beneath the flag. (Gates of course customarily mark restricted areas, keeping out the uninitiated.) Above the flag, the light of heaven! How fragile the barrier-gate seems, and yet how impenetrable to those who suffered from a communicable disease, or who were mentally retarded, or who somehow gave the wrong answers to the questions put to them by the immigration officials.

For some additional details about Ellis Island, see our comment on Joseph Bruchac's poem above.

JOSEPH BRUCHAC III
Ellis Island (p. 1179)

Ellis Island, in Upper New York Bay, southwest of Manhattan Island, from 1892 until 1943 was the chief immigration station of the United States. In its first year, it saw 450,000 immigrants arrive, and in its peak years in the first decade of the twentieth century the annual number exceeded a million; the total number of Ellis Island graduates was over seventeen million. When the island closed, immigration was at a low point, and for some years the buildings fell into ruin. They have now been renovated and form a museum of immigration. In 1965 Ellis Island became part of the Statue of Liberty National Monument (the statue—on its own island, separated from Ellis Island by a few hundred yards of water—had been declared a national monument in 1924).

In our discussion of Emma Lazarus's "The New Colossus" we mention that in the first decade of the twentieth century about 8.7 million immigrants entered the country, most of them via Ellis Island. This means, of course, that the great-grandparents or even the grandparents or parents of an enormous number of today's Americans are alumni of the island, and it has a hold on their affections.

Bruchac begins by calling up an image of two of his grandparents who had endured the long journey and "the long days of quarantine." He implicitly contrasts their journey and their anxiety—about 10% of the visitors were denied admission for reasons of health—with "a Circle Line ship," a ship that makes a daily pleasure cruise of a few hours around the islands, chiefly patronized by tourists. He goes on to evoke "the tall woman, green / as dreams of forests and meadows," i.e., the green patina of the *Statue of Liberty* connects it with nature.

In the second stanza he says that like millions of others he has come to the island, but of course there is a distinction between the millions who, pursuing a dream (lines 10 and 17) came as immigrants and the millions who now come as tourists, perhaps in homage to their ancestors and to the nation that accepted them.

There is, then, a contrast between the first and second stanzas, but the two harmonize. The third stanza, however, introduces a serious complication: if the immigrants were pursuing a dream, they nevertheless also were invading the "native lands" (lines 20–22) of others. (Bruchac himself, as we mention in the headnote, is part Native American and part Slovak.) The Native Americans are characterized as people "who followed / the changing Moon," people who have or who had "knowledge of the seasons / in their veins," so they too, like the green statue, are associated with nature. Is the reader to think that these people are gone—or, on the contrary, that their heritage lives on, for example, in the "veins" of the poet? To our mind, the fact that Bruchac *ends* the poem with a reference to a knowledge that is in the "veins" suggests that he sees the heritage as still living—and the violence wrought by later immigrants as also still living.

Bruchac is a prolific author who has written poetry, fiction, and many books for children and young adults. We especially value the work he has done as an editor; his edited collections include *Breaking Silence: An Anthology of Contemporary Asian American Poets* (1983); *Songs from This Earth on Turtle's Back: Contemporary American Indian Poetry* (1983); and *Survival This Way: Interviews with American Indian Poets* (1987).

ANONYMOUS

Slavic Women Arrive at Ellis Island in the Winter of 1910 (photograph, p. 1179)

We chose this image partly because it relates closely to Joseph Bruchac's poem (he mentions his Slavic heritage) but also because it gives a somewhat unusual image of Ellis Island, which is rarely associated with snow, or, for that matter, with an allfemale group. Probably the husbands of these women had come earlier, found work, and then had sent for their wives. And probably, too, what the women carry on their backs and over their arms is all that they have brought with them.

We have sometimes used this photograph and others in this section as an occasion for recommending novels and stories about immigrant life. See, for example, Abraham Cahan, *Yekl, a Tale of the New York Ghetto* (1896) and *The Rise of David Levinsky* (1917), and Anzia Yezierska, *Bread Givers*

(1925). For an evocative account of the East European Jews, see Irving Howe, *The World of Our Fathers* (1976).

EDWIN ARLINGTON ROBINSON
Richard Cory (p. 1180)

The point is not that money doesn't bring happiness; even a thoroughly civilized spirit (grace, taste, courtesy) does not bring happiness. The protagonist's name is significant. "Richard" suggests "Rich," and probably his entire name faintly suggests Richard Cœur de Lion (and *cœur* = heart and core, and also suggests *cour* = court). These suggestions, along with "crown," "favored," "imperially," "arrayed," "glittered," and "king," emphasize his superiority. Other words emphasize his dignity, courtesy, and humanity: "gentleman," "clean favored," "quietly," "human," "schooled," "grace." Everything combines to depict him as a man of self-sufficiency, dignity, and restraint—yet he kills himself. Still, even his final act has some dignity: it is stated briefly, and it takes place on "one calm summer night." Students might be asked if anything is lost by substituting (what might on first thought seem more appropriate) "one dark winter night." If this rewriting is not bad enough, listen to Paul Simon's version of the poem. He sings it, with Art Garfunkel, on *Sounds of Silence*, Columbia CS 9269.

There is a *Collected Poems* (1937) but this huge volume (1,500 pages) is not the place where students should begin. Direct them instead to *Selected Poems*, ed. M. D. Zabel (1965). They will profit from these secondary sources: Emory Neff, *Edwin Arlington Robinson* (1948); Ellsworth Barnard, *Edwin Arlington Robinson: A Critical Study* (1952); and Wallace Anderson, *Edwin Arlington Robinson: A Critical Introduction* (1967). See also Nancy Carol Joyner, *E. A. Robinson: A Reference Guide* (1978).

AURORA LEVINS MORALES
Child of the Americas (p. 1181)

The author, born in Puerto Rico of a Puerto Rican mother and of a father whose origins went back to the ghetto in New York and beyond that to Europe, came to the United States when she was thirteen and has lived in Chicago, New Hampshire, and now in the San Francisco Bay Area. Her heritage and her experience thus are considerably different from those of most Puerto Ricans who are now in the United States.

Whereas other Latinas in this book emphasize the difficulties of their divided heritage (see Pat Mora's "Immigrants"), Morales celebrates her diversity and apparently is at ease as a Latina in the United States: she is "a light-skinned mestiza of the Caribbean, / a child of many diaspora," she was born "at a crossroads," she is "a U.S. Puerto Rican Jew, / a product of the ghettos of New

York," "Spanish is in [her] flesh," but in the next-to-last stanza she insists that she is "not african," "not taína," "not european." Most significantly, she insists that she is not fragmented but is, on the contrary, "whole."

In short, Morales holds to the old idea of the United States as a melting pot, an idea not heard so often today. The conception of the melting pot has largely given way to the conception of America as a "gorgeous mosaic," a "salad bowl," a kaleidoscope, i.e., a place where there is great variety but where each ingredient maintains its identity.

You can recommend to students two books by Morales. The first, coauthored with her mother, Rosario Morales, *Getting Home Alive* (1986), includes short essays, stories, and poems about their lives, languages, cultures, and religions. Rosario was born in Puerto Rico, the daughter of Russian Jewish immigrants who moved to New York when she was a child; Aurora was born in New York and, when she was a child, moved with her parents to Puerto Rico. In *Medicine Stories: History, Culture and the Politics of Integrity* (1998), Morales presents essays on social identity, ecology, children's liberation, and other topics.

GLORIA ANZALDÚA
To Live in the Borderlands Means You (p. 1182)

As we say in our headnote in the text, obviously the "borderlands" are not merely physical locales. Among other things, they are the multicultural heritage *within* a single individual, as expressed, for example, in Joseph Bruchac's poem, "Ellis Island," where he finds his cherished Slovak heritage doing violence to his Native American heritage.

The poem is macaronic, that is, the writer uses one language chiefly but includes foreign words. The origin of the term *macaronic* is uncertain but is commonly said to be due either to the fact that *maccarone* is a mixture (a dumpling made of flour, butter, and cheese) or that macaroni is heaped on a plate and sauce is dribbled over it. Earlier macaronic poetry was chiefly comic ("Mademoiselle got the croix de guerre / For washing soldiers' underwear, / Hinky, dinky, parlez-vous"), but some was serious, and in modern times it usually is serious. Consider, for instance, Eliot's use of foreign terms in *The Waste Land*. Today it is especially common in serious poems by Chicanos or by persons from Puerto Rico; obviously it indicates, among other things, that the writers value Spanish as well as English.

The entire poem is of great interest, but the second stanza especially strikes us, with its assertion that the *india* had been betrayed for 500 years, and that

> denying the Anglo inside you
> is as bad as having denied the Indian or Black. . . .

The first point, about the *india,* strikes us as especially contemporary because until almost yesterday all Spanish-speaking people of South America were called "Hispanic," even though many of them were evidently of Indian origin. It's our impression that only recently, perhaps along with a heightened awareness of ethnic values in the United States, are persons of Indian origin insisting on this heritage, rather than gliding over it and characterizing themselves as Hispanic—a Eurocentric term that implies a European heritage.

If in your classes you have students from Central or South America, you may want to ask them how they identify themselves—as Hispanics, Latinos/Latinas, Chicanos? It is our impression that most people from Central or South America define themselves in terms of the country of their origin, rather than with any of these all-embracing terms. But insofar as one of the broader terms is used, it probably is Latino/Latina, rather than Hispanic; both are Eurocentric, but the former is not English and therefore seems to be preferred by people who wish to distinguish themselves from Anglo culture.

Anzaldúa's work includes *Borderlands: The New Mestiza=La frontera* (1987), a book of essays and poems, written in English and Spanish, in which she explores her identity as a lesbian and a Chicana writer.

JIMMY SANTIAGO BACA
So Mexicans Are Taking Jobs from Americans (p. 1184)

The title, the first line, and indeed the whole poem have the flavor of ordinary but forceful speech, and we think this closeness to pugnacious speech, on both sides of the fence, accounts for much of the work's power. That is, it is not enough for a poem to set forth admirable sentiments, let's say, sympathy for the disenfranchised. We want it to be a poem, not just the expression of ideas we approve of.

Here we find art in the contrast between the title, which evokes the ordinary world, and the first line and a half, which give us a preposterous world of mounted bandits, and then the third line, which gives us, even more preposterously, a bandit asking us to hand over not money but our job: "Ese gringo, gimmee your job."

To our ears, the most successful lines in the poem are of this sort—lines that show an ear for common speech and a sense of the absurd—and the least successful are the straight, earnest lines of the advocate, such as "I see the poor marching for a little work, / I see small white farmers selling out / to clean-suited farmers living in New York." But we realize that what we have been saying, which in some measure separates literature from political activity, may be unconvincing to others.

In fact, *are* Mexicans taking jobs from Americans? Well, first of all, many of these "Mexicans" are themselves Americans of Mexican origin. Second, although the subject is much disputed, some reputable authorities insist that much of the work that Chicanos do—as migrant laborers, domestic workers, gardeners, and so forth—is in fact so low-paying that Anglos and African Americans will not do it. That is, the jobs wouldn't exist except for the fact that "Mexicans" are willing to do them.

Of Baca's books, we especially value *Immigrants in Our Own Land and Selected Early Poems* (1990 ed.) and *Working in the Dark: Reflections of a Poet of the Barrio* (1992).

LANGSTON HUGHES
Theme for English B (p. 1185)

We have found this poem to be very provocative for getting students to think about what constitutes the *identity* of a poet. The question has always been an important one, but perhaps in the highly multicultural 1990s it has become especially vexed and contentious. "Will my page be colored that I write?" Hughes's speaker asks. Does a poem inevitably reflect the race, ethnicity, gender, and/or class of its author? Can members of a different group *really* read and understand such a poem, or is a poem a circuit of communication that passes only from the author to the members of the group whose identity he or she shares?

For Hughes, persons cannot be separated off into groups, however much they might wish they could be. "That's American," he says. If there is an essential America, it lies in the fact that in America no one is truly separate from anyone else. Everyone is "part" of one another and has much to learn: no one can claim to be beyond the need of knowing about what others have to teach them. We like at this point both to commend Hughes's faith and to query students whether they can accept it for themselves.

PAT PARKER
For the white person who wants to know how to be my friend (p. 1187)

We begin with a quotation from Shirley Chisholm, an African American who served in the U.S. House of Representatives (elected 1968) and who was an unsuccessful candidate for the Democratic presidential nomination (1972). The line comes from her book, *Unbought and Unbossed* (1970):

> Racism keeps people who are being managed from finding out the truth through contact with each other.

Now a second quotation, this one by Abraham Joshua Herschel, from *The Insecurity of Freedom: Essays on Human Existence* (1967):

> We appreciate *what* we *share*, we do not appreciate *what* we *receive*. Friendship, affection is not acquired by giving presents. Friendship, affection comes about by two people sharing a significant moment, an experience in common.

To take Chisholm's comment first: Chisholm sees a better society emerging if blacks and whites can make contact. But blacks and whites report that making contact is not easy. Many of our white students report that black students do not welcome their friendship (they cite the fact that blacks often sit in groups in the dining halls and cafeterias), and many of our black students report offers of friendship from white students bear marks of condescension and inauthenticity (they cite their particular experiences with whites who apparently have bolstered their self-esteem by reaching out toward blacks).

Now for Herschel's comment: we assume it contains a good deal of truth, but the question is, How much "experience in common" do blacks and whites have? No one can doubt that most neighborhoods are segregated—not *de jure*, of course, but *de facto*. It is our impression that many of our students, black and white, have not had much opportunity to share experiences until they come to college.

We offer the preceding comments as background to the poem, but in fact, attempts to discuss Parker's poem almost always quickly move from the poem to the background, that is, from art to life. In a way, this is a tribute to the power of the poem—it certainly touches a nerve—but we want students to *enjoy the poem* as well as to talk about their experiences. We want them to take pleasure in the title (we begin by asking them what effect Parker gains by not capitalizing the first letter in each word of the title), we want them to be stimulated by the paradox in the first two lines, we want them to hear the increasing irritation in tone by the time the reader gets to the second part of line 6 ("They made us take music appreciation too"). And so on, to the end of the poem ("I'm lazy. Remember"), where Parker ironically evokes a stereotype of African-American behavior. (In the text, in our third question, we call attention to the stereotypes.)

Perhaps by talking about this poem—not just by talking about their experiences outside of the classroom—black and white students can share an experience.

MITSUYE YAMADA
To the Lady (p. 1188)

First, some background. In 1942 the entire Japanese and Japanese-American population on America's Pacific coast—about 112,000 people—was incarcerated and relocated. More than two-thirds of the people moved were native-born citizens of the United States. (The 158,000 Japanese residents of the Territory of Hawaii were not affected.)

Immediately after the Japanese attack on Pearl Harbor, many journalists, the general public, Secretary of the Army Henry Stimson, and congressional delegations from California, Oregon, and Washington called for the internment. Although Attorney General Francis Biddle opposed it, on February 19, 1942, President Franklin D. Roosevelt signed Executive Order 9066, allowing military authorities "to prescribe military areas . . . from which any or all persons may be excluded." In practice, no persons of German or Italian heritage were disturbed, but Japanese and Japanese Americans on the Pacific coast were rounded up (they were allowed to take with them "only that which can be carried") and relocated in camps. Congress, without a dissenting vote, passed legislation supporting the evacuation. A few Japanese Americans challenged the constitutionality of the proceeding, but with no immediate success.

Many students today may find it difficult to comprehend the intensity of anti-Japanese sentiment that pervaded the 1940s. Here are two samples, provided by David Mura, whose poem about the internment camps appears in Appendix C of the text. Lt. General John DeWitt, the man in charge of the relocation plan, said:

> The Japanese race is an enemy race and while many second and third generation Japanese born on United States soil, possessed of United States citizenship, have become "Americanized," the racial strains are undiluted. To conclude otherwise is to expect that children born of white parents on Japanese soil sever all racial affinity and become loyal Japanese subjects. . . . Along the vital Pacific Coast over 112,000 enemies, of Japanese extraction, are at large today. There are indications that these are organized and ready for concerted action at a favorable opportunity. The very fact that no sabotage has taken place to date is a disturbing and confirming indication that such action will be taken.

One rubs one's eyes in disbelief at the crazy logic that holds that *because* "no sabotage has taken place," such action "will be taken." The second quotation Mura has called to our attention is a remark made in 1942 by Senator Tom Steward of Tennessee:

> They [the Japanese] are cowardly and immoral. They are different from Americans in every conceivable way, and no Japanese . . . should have the right to claim American citizenship. . . . A Jap is a Jap anywhere you find him. They do not believe in God and have no respect for an oath of allegiance.

By the way, not a single Japanese American was found guilty of subversive activity. For two good short accounts, with suggestions for further readings, see the articles entitled "Japanese Americans, wartime relocation of," in *Kodansha Encyclopedia of Japan* (1983), 4:17–18, and "War Relocation Authority," in 8:228.

It may be interesting to read Yamada's poem aloud in class, *without* having assigned it for prior reading, and to ask students for their responses at various stages—after line 4, line 21, and line 36. Line 14 poses a question that perhaps many of us (young and old, and whether of Japanese descent or not) have asked, at least to ourselves. The question, implying a criticism of the victims, shows an insufficient awareness of Japanese or Japanese-American culture of the period. It also shows an insufficient awareness of American racism; by implying that protest by the victims *could* have been effective, it reveals ignorance of the terrific hostility of whites toward persons of Japanese descent.

The first part of the response shows one aspect of the absurdity of the lady's question. Japanese and Japanese Americans were brought up not to stand out in any way (certainly not to make a fuss), and to place the harmony of the group (whether the family or society as a whole) above individual expression. Further, there was nothing that these people could effectively do, even if they had shouted as loudly as Kitty Genovese did. For the most part they were poor, they had no political clout, and they were hated and despised as Asians. The absurdity of the view that they could have resisted effectively is comically stated in "should've pulled myself up from my / bra straps" (echoing the red-blooded American ideal of pulling oneself up by one's bootstraps), but of course the comedy is bitter.

Then the speaker turns to "YOU," nominally the "lady" of the title but in effect also the reader, and by ironically saying what we would have done points out what in fact we did not do. (The references to a march on Washington and letters to Congress are clear enough, but most students will not be aware of the tradition that the King of Denmark said that he would wear a Star of David [line 27] if Danish Jews were compelled by Nazis to wear the star.)

Thus far the speaker has put the blame entirely on the white community, especially since lines 5–21 strongly suggest that the Japanese Americans *couldn't* do anything but submit. Yet the poem ends with a confession that because Japanese Americans docilely subscribed to "law and order"—especially the outrageous Executive Order 9066—they were in fact partly responsible for the outrage committed against them. The last line of the poem, "All are punished," is exactly what Prince Escalus says at the end of *Romeo and Juliet*. Possibly the echo is accidental, though possibly the reader is meant to be reminded of a play, widely regarded as "a tragedy of fate," in which the innocent are victims of prejudice.

From this poem, students might proceed to two other books by Yamada: *Desert Run: Poems and Stories* (1988) and *Camp Notes and Other Poems* (2nd ed., 1992).

Dorothea Lange

Grandfather and Grandchildren Awaiting Evacuation Bus (photograph, p. 1189)

Lange, working for the War Relocation Authority, photographed the proceedings as part of a program documenting the relocation. What can we say about the picture that we reproduce? Lange probably asked the family to pose, and she may have created the composition (the grandfather seated, the smaller boy in front of the taller boy) but she didn't create the tags, she didn't create the little packages wrapped in newspaper, and she didn't create the expressions on the faces. Most interesting is the grandfather's grim and dignified manner, chiefly created by his face, but also by his erect posture and his cane. Also interesting is the echo of the grandfather in the smaller boy's expression and the angle of his head.

Studies of Lange include Milton Meltzer, *Dorothea Lange: A Photographer's Life* (1978); Karin Ohrn, *Dorothea Lange and the Documentary Tradition* (1980); and *Dorothea Lange: A Visual Life,* ed. Elizabeth Partridge (1994).

LUIS VALDEZ
Los Vendidos (p. 1191)

Students who have been told that stereotyping people is wicked and that characters (whether in fiction or in drama) should be well motivated, believable, and so on may find it difficult to see anything of value in a work that uses one-dimensional stock characters. Perhaps one way to help them enjoy such a work is to talk briefly about stereotypes in films they have enjoyed and admired. The roles performed by Chaplin, the Marx Brothers, Bogart—or even some roles in soap operas—may help them to see that stereotyped characters can be powerful.

Los Vendidos is comic in the sense of having some laughs in it, and also (at least to a degree) in the more literary sense of being a play with a happy ending. If one stands at a distance, so to speak, and looks at the overall plot, one sees the good guys outwitting the bad guys (Ms. Jimenez). In the talk about going to a party, there is even a hint of the traditional *komos* or revel.

It is of course entirely appropriate that the play includes amusing passages. Valdez has said that he wanted to lift the morale of his audience (chiefly striking workers), and he wrote and staged comedies—in the sense of plays with happy endings—because he wanted to help change society. He did not want, obviously, to show the tragic nature of the human condition. He makes his aims clear in his short essay, "The Actos." One might ask students to think especially about whether in this play he does anything to "show or hint at a solution" to the "social problem." In some *actos* the message is clear, for instance, "Join the union."

It's our view that *Los Vendidos* does not at all suffer by failing to give a "solution." (Of course it's implied that Anglos should not think of Mexican Americans as stupid and lazy, should not expect them to be subservient, and should value them as people, but Valdez does not offer a solution for Anglo prejudice.) Much of the strength of the play seems to us to lie in the wit with which the stereotypes are presented, and also in the ingenuity of the plot, when the robots come alive and thus reverse the stereotype: the Mexican Americans are shown to be shrewd and enterprising, and Honest Sancho is shown to be lifeless.

For further study, students might begin with Jaime Herrera, "Luis Miguel Valdez," in *Updating the Literary West,* ed. Max Westbrook and Dan Flores (1997), pp. 379–385. See also Harry J. Elam Jr., *Taking It to the Streets: The Social Protest Theater of Luis Valdez and Amiri Baraka* (1997).

Topic for Critical Thinking and Writing

At the end of the play the Mexican Americans are shown as shrewd and enterprising. Has Valdez fallen into the trap of suggesting that Mexican-American culture is not distinctive but is just about the same as the Anglo imperialistic (capitalistic) culture that he satirized earlier in the play?

CASE STUDY: WRITING ABOUT AMERICAN INDIAN IDENTITY

"Indian" or "Native American"?

In the text, at the beginning of the case study, we mention that although the term "Native American" is now sometimes used, especially by people of European origin, "Indian" remains the preferred word by the descendants of the people whom the Europeans encountered after 1492. Here are a few examples: the Navaho Indian Nation, the American Indian Movement, the National Indian Youth Council, the National Congress of American Indians, and the editors and readers of *American Indian Culture and Research Journal* and *American Indian Quarterly*. In short, the word "Indian" is the preferred word among the people most concerned, and we therefore use this word rather than "Native American."

A Few Generalizations

If we think for a moment about the deep differences that separate some Catholics in Ireland from some Protestants in Ireland, and then think further about the differences between, say, a Swiss businessman and a Serbian farmer, or a Norwegian fisherman and an Italian filmmaker, we realize how odd it is to lump all of these (and countless others) together as "Europeans." What, one wonders, unites these people? What can possibly be usefully said about all of them? But this is what we do, or have done, when we speak of "Indians," as though (for instance) the Iroquois and the Navaho—who did not share a language—are or were pretty much alike. (Anthropologists distinguish at least six distinct Indian cultures, excluding that of the Arctic: Northwest Coast, Plains, Plateau, Eastern Woodlands, Northern, and Southwestern.) In today's language, because these are all seen as "Other" they are reduced to a common identity. To take a simple instance, in the common view, Indians wore feathers in their hair—especially backward-leaning feathered bonnets with trains—and practiced scalping. In fact, the feathered bonnet with a train was worn only by some members of some Indian nations, and scalping was practiced only by some nations.

Perhaps we can say that whites defined Indians chiefly by negative qualities:

They didn't look like whites.
They weren't Christians.
They didn't have certain kinds of technology (notably, guns).

By the way, the English settlers did *not* regard the Indians as racially different; in the seventeenth century Indians were never called "Red" but were regarded merely as darker people, tanned. (For that matter, the English did not call themselves "white" until around 1700, when they used the word to distinguish themselves from slaves brought from Africa, whom they called "Negroes," the Spanish and Portuguese word for black.) The essential thing for the English was that Indians were uncivilized—if the commonest name was "Indians," the next most common was "savages."

A small digression or bit of pedantry: in William Strachey's *The True Repertory of the Wrack* (1610), a report of a shipwreck off Bermuda and almost surely a document that Shakespeare drew on when he wrote *The Tempest*, Strachey comments on the "barbarous disposition" of the natives. His editor, Samuel Purchas, in the 1625 edition of Strachey's papers, adds a humbling note, suggesting that the British themselves had been savages—like the natives of Virginia—until the Roman conquerors used swords to civilize the British: "Can a savage remaining savage be civil? Were not we ourselves made and not born civil in our progenitors' days? And were not Caesar's Britons as brutish as Virginians? The Roman swords were best teachers of civility to this and other countries near us."

Let's return to the main issue, of "us" versus "the Other." Some of us have imposed an identity on populations that certainly did not think of themselves as sharing an identity. Nor do Indians today think of themselves as sharing an identity—since money and privileges may be involved, many tribes are quite insistent about who does or does not qualify as a member of the tribe—although for some purposes Indians unite in seeking certain kinds of legislation. The question of identity is further complicated by the fact that Indian nations, like others, have not been static. They have a *history,* that is, they have changed over the decades and centuries. Thus, nineteenth-century treaties moved tribes, united them with others on reservations, and produced new societies. For instance, the Creeks are (we have heard) an eighteenth-century group formed when several distinct groups merged in what is now Alabama and Georgia, and today's Seminoles (again, we have heard) were Creeks who in the nineteenth century were moved from Alabama and Georgia and established in Florida after wars and disease had decimated the earlier Seminole population. In any case, with the passing of years the cultures inevitably changed. The old idea, however, was that Indians—just "Indians," as a whole—were "a Vanishing Race," a single group doomed to extinction because they could not adapt to new ways. (It was less commonly said that they were vanishing because of physical assaults on them and because of diseases introduced by whites. On the motif of the Vanishing Race, or the Vanishing Red, see the poem by Robert Frost and the picture by Edward S. Curtis, included in the text, and our discussions in this manual, especially our comment on Curtis.)

The chief degree of complexity in the white view of the Indian was that the Indian was a "noble savage," i.e., a person close to nature and thus unspoiled by luxury (that's the "noble" part) and yet a warlike, uncivilized, un-Christian person (that's the "savage" part). Some representations emphasized the savagery (scenes of massacres or even scenes of hunting), but it can also be argued that even those images that call attention to nobility (a handsome muscular chief standing tall in a landscape) in fact also imply savagery in the unsmiling face, in the feathered bonnets, in the necklaces of bear claws.

Visual Images of American Indians

Bush, Alfred L., and Lee Clark Mitchell, *The Photograph and the American Indian* (1994)

Capps, Benjamin, *The Great Chiefs* (1975)

Fleming, Paula Richardson, and Judith Lynn Luskey, *The North American Indians in Early Photographs* (1986)

Fleming, Paula Richardson, and Judith Lynn Luskey, *Grand Endeavors of American Indian Photography* (1993)

Goetzmann, William, *The First Americans: Photographs from the Library of Congress* (1991)

Johnson, Tim, ed., *Spirit Capture: Photographs from the National Museum of the American Indian* (1998)

Lubbers, Klaus, *Born for the Shade: Stereotypes of the Native American in United States Literature and the Visual Arts, 1776–1894* (1994)

Troettner, William, ed., *The West as America* (1991)

ANONYMOUS ARAPAHO

My Children, When at First I Liked the Whites and *Father, Have Pity on Me (Two Ghost-Dance Songs)* (p. 1200)

These songs (with others) were first printed by James Mooney, in "The Ghost Dance Religion and the Sioux Outbreak of 1890," in *Fourteenth Annual Report of the Bureau of American Ethnology* (1896). A selection can be found in John Hollander, ed., *American Poetry: The Nineteenth Century* (1993) 2:727–735.

Of the first of our two songs, "My Children, I Gave Them Fruits," Mooney writes that the song was composed by a Southern Arapaho chief named Nawat (Left Hand). Mooney goes on to say:

> In his trance vision of the other world, the father showed him extensive orchards, telling him that in the beginning all these things had been given to the whites, but that hereafter they would be given to his children, the Indians.

Of the second song, "Father, have pity on me," Mooney says:

> This is the most pathetic of the Ghost-dance songs. It is sung to a plaintive tune, sometimes with tears rolling down the cheeks of the dancers as

the words would bring up thoughts of their present miserable and dependent condition. It may be considered the Indian paraphrase of the Lord's prayer.

As students of English and American literature, we formally studied some important works of oral literature (e.g., *Beowulf,* popular ballads, African-American spirituals); in recent years we have tried to learn something about American Indian literature, partly by reading anthologies of the primary material and partly by reading recommended secondary material. The secondary material reveals a vigorous conflict between scholars who insist on the Otherness of the material and scholars who insist that non-Indians can indeed experience this material in some significant way. At one extreme, then, are those who adopt highly technical methods of transcribing the material, making it unreadable to the lay reader; at the other extreme are those who present "versions," "adaptations," and so on. One other concept should be mentioned: in reading about theories of translation, and in reading translations, fairly often one finds two people collaborating, a scholar who is a specialist in the culture and a poet. Presumably the scholar provides some sort of fairly literal text, with explanatory notes, and the poet then turns this stuff into poetry. The result is a work that seeks to be both artistic and also faithful. Not surprisingly, scholars usually find this practice objectionable, and poets too may object, saying that this is not the way readable poems—even translations of poems—get produced. On this issue, you may want to look at Brian Swann's "A Note on Translation and Remarks on Collaboration," in *Recovering the Word,* eds. Brian Swann and Arnold Krupat (1987), pp. 247–254.

Oral literature of non-whites was not taken very seriously by most whites until fairly recently. For early explorers in the New World, or in Africa, the indigenous people spoke gibberish, and they had no literature at all (true only if we insist that *literature* implies *written* material); their stories and songs were childish if not wicked. In the early nineteenth century the Romantic Movement did much to widen the concept of literature (think, for instance, of the interest in folk material and of Wordsworth's emphasis on the language of ordinary people), but it is probably true to say that there was only a severely limited interest in American Indian oral material until the last two or three decades of the nineteenth century. At that time, however, with the concept of "the Vanishing Red," anthropologists began to engage in salvage operations, recording what they believed were the remnants of dying cultures. Inevitably, however, the anthropologists could not escape their own nineteenth-century culture, with the result that, in the view of most of today's specialists, the published translations of American Indian literature are more Victorian than Indian. [See Dennis Tedlock's "On the Translation of Style in Oral Narrative," in *Journal of American Folklore* 84 (1971), rpt. in *Smoothing the Ground,* ed. Brian Swann (1982).]

For one thing, as we remark in our headnote in the text, the early printed versions simply provided words, without indications of pitch, tone, and pace; that is, they were offered as literature (where words supposedly are everything) rather than as *event-oriented performances*. The trouble with much of the work of today's anthropologists, however, is that it is offered in so forbidding a form, with such foreign-looking symbols, that the lay reader is turned off. The specialist is likely to say, in effect, "I won't falsify this material just to make it easy for you. It is Other, and you must recognize it as such." The result is that material presented in this fashion does not get into the dominant culture. What to do? The chief alternative, many specialists warn, is to offer readable stuff that falsifies the original and that gives us a deceptive belief that we have entered into another culture.

JAMES MOONEY
Ghost Dance (photograph, p. 1201)

Probably most people would agree that photographs of all but the most contemporary subjects evoke pathos. We look at a picture and we inevitably say to ourselves, "These people [or these buildings, or these open spaces, or these forests, or whatever] are gone." Of course paintings, too, sometimes show "real" things, but the painting nevertheless is taken as something that is made up, constructed, fabricated by an artist. The painting—whatever its subject—is meant to be valued in itself, a work that is independent. The photograph may be regarded as a work of art, but we know that it once was regarded chiefly as a way of saying to the viewer, "Look, here is something in the world around us that you may have overlooked, or that perhaps is in a place so far from you that you don't even know that things like this exist. This is *real*, not something invented by an artist. These people are alive, and they are leaving their traces on this paper that you are now looking at."

Walter Benjamin was saying something like this, in "The Work of Art in the Age of Mechanical Reproduction," when he wrote, "The camera introduces us to unconscious optics as does psychoanalysis to unconscious impulses." Although Benjamin was talking about motion pictures, still photographs too help us to see what, unphotographed, is invisible. Today everyone knows that a running horse never assumes the rocking horse position (front legs thrust forward, rear legs thrust backward), but we know it not because we have observed horses closely but because we have seen photographs, in particular Eadweard Muybridge's classic photographs of animals and humans in motion. For centuries artists had painted the rocking horse pose, not because they saw horses in that pose but because they had been taught that the pose conveyed the idea of a running horse.

Photographs give us a keen sense of reality partly by (this is paradoxical) conveying to us the strangeness of reality. The camera, accidentally catching overlapping forms or accidentally cropping the subject, helps us to see things freshly. Thus, in the picture in the text, we see and are convinced of the reality of a lost world—a world in which warriors were adorned with ritual paint that they thought would give them immortality, and then danced, with upraised hands, in an effort to communicate with the dead. (The term "ghost dance" was applied by whites because the ritual centered on making contact with the dead.) Here, in this one picture we see the two stages—in the center a dancer with uplifted hands, and in the foreground a dancer who has fallen into a trance. How strange, how interesting, we reflect, is this composition. We see all this, and we know it was real. What we don't see, but what we know, is that the beliefs of the men in the picture (probably 1889), along with the men themselves or men like them, were destroyed in December 1890 in South Dakota, at the Battle of Wounded Knee. Wounded Knee in fact was less a battle than a massacre; when a group of Sioux warriors refused to surrender their weapons to the U.S. Seventh Calvary, the soldiers attacked, killing nearly 150 Sioux men, women, and children. This was the last military engagement to take place between federal troops and Native Americans.

LYDIA HOWARD HUNTLEY SIGOURNEY
The Indian's Welcome to the Pilgrim Fathers (p. 1201)

A good entry into Sigourney's poem is through its descriptive language—about, for example, the ominous landscape that the Pilgrims confronted, and even more, the figure of the Indian chief who appears to them. Notice that the chief at first seems fearsome and threatening, but Sigourney's point is precisely to show that however fierce he seemed, he came to speak welcome and bring words of peace. Indeed, Sigourney emphasizes that the Indians' "welcome" was the word that marked their downfall. She does not say so explicitly, but Sigourney leaves the implication that perhaps the Indians would have done better *not* to welcome these first settlers, who at the beginning were vulnerable, exposed intruders—"a weak, invading band."

The word choices in this poem are suggestive and pointed. Sigourney writes that the Indians and their children were "swept" from the land that belonged to them. On one level, this may seem untrue, for the Indians did resist; they did not give up as easily as the ease and absoluteness of "swept" indicates. But Sigourney wants to accent the point that, ultimately, the Indians had no chance once they welcomed the settlers and thus allowed the "weak, invading band" to remain. "Swept" is a word that captures much of the callousness of the white settlers and the helplessness of the Indians to defend their rights against a power that would soon overwhelm them.

Students who wish to explore the historical context might consult Harold E. Driver, *Indians of North America* (1961); Alvin M. Josephy Jr., *The Indian Heritage of America* (1968); Francis P. Prucha, *The Great Father: The United States Government and the American Indian*, 2 vol., (1984); and Russell Thornton, *American Indian Holocaust and Survival* (1987).

ROBERT FROST
The Vanishing Red (p. 1202)

This must be one of Frost's most terrifying poems because, in our reading of it, Frost implies that in the human heart there is a sort of maniacal hatred of what now is called the Other. He is not saying we all would kill those who are different from us, but he is saying that if we were the Miller's contemporaries, we might not judge him as we now do:

> It's too long a story to go into now.
> You'd have to have been there and lived it.
> Then you wouldn't have looked on it as just a matter
> Of who began it between the two races.

That is, for the modern reader, it seems to be a matter of who first did what to whom. Did the white people injure the Indians, so that any counterattacks by Indians are more or less excusable, or did the Indians savagely (!) attack the new immigrants? (We might remember that although we now speak of "Native Americans," these people in fact were not native to the continent; they migrated to this hemisphere, but a good deal earlier than the whites did. And while we are remembering things, we might also remember that until recently it was regularly said that when Indians killed whites it was a "massacre," but when whites killed Indians it was a "battle.")

Well, why isn't it a matter "Of who began it"? Or, to put the question a bit differently, why did the Miller kill the Red Man? In lines 14–18 Frost gives us as much of an answer as he will give:

> Some guttural exclamation of surprise
> The Red Man gave in poking about the mill
> Over the great big thumping shuffling mill-stone
> Disgusted the Miller physically as coming
> From one who had no right to be heard from.

"Some guttural exclamation of surprise." About what? About the Miller's prices? About the Miller's behavior? About the way the mill worked? Frost doesn't tell us—because it doesn't matter. What matters is that the Red Man expressed something and he was a person "who had no right to be heard from," in the Miller's opinion. The Red Man was, we might say, a non-person, and here he was, like a person, acting uppity. By the way, when the poem was originally published in *The Craftsman* (October 1916), what is now line 18 ("From one who had no right to be heard from") was not one line but two:

> From a person who the less he attracted
> Attention to himself you would have thought the better.

The early version is interesting, but it does not convey the intensity and the craziness of the revised version, where Frost does what he can to tell us of the Miller's reason for his act: the Indian had "no right" to open his mouth.

And so the Miller decides to show John the wheel pit. (By the way, the Indian is named, but not the Miller, almost as though the Miller is not meant to be a single person.) The Miller shows John "The water in desperate straits"—in a moment John himself will be in desperate straits—then closes the trap door, whose jangling ring serves as a sort of funeral knell. Obviously self-satisfied, the Miller "said something to a man with a meal-sack / That the man with the meal-sack didn't catch—then." Frost doesn't tell us what the Miller said, but we can go back to lines 6–8, where Frost does tell us what the Miller's face seemed to say. And we can easily imagine that the last line of the poem ("Oh, yes, he showed John the wheel pit all right") is what he may have said to the man with the meal-sack. Frost tells us that whatever it was he said, it was something that the man "didn't catch—then." The "then," preceded by a dash, implies that later the man *did* get the words. Presumably at some point the Red Man was missed, perhaps the man with the meal-sack said he had seen him at the mill—and then, suddenly, the significance of the words became clear.

But we are offering mere conjectures about the narrative, about what the Miller's motive was, about what he said, about what made the man with the meal-sack later "catch" the meaning of the words. What is *not* conjecture, however, is the irony of the title. "The Vanishing Red" sounds as though the Red Man did some sort of magic trick and made himself disappear into thin air. The term (or a variant such as "The Vanishing Indian" or "The Vanishing Race") was of course a euphemism; white society liked to believe that the Indians simply faded away, not that they were killed or that they died of diseases brought by whites. Why, according to the old mythology, did Indians "vanish"? They "vanished" because whether they were imagined as noble savages (persons living close to nature, filled with natural goodness) or imagined as diabolical figures (persons lacking the virtues of civilization), they lived in an unchanging world, a world that did not participate in progress (technology). When technology came to dominate the land—when their world was superseded—they simply vanished. Such was the comforting view held by many whites. Frost gives us quite another view of the vanishing act. (We will return to this issue in a moment.)

The poem is unusual among Frost's work not only in its subject matter but also in its form. We are not thinking so much of the fact that the lines do not rhyme—Frost wrote a fair amount of blank verse—but of the fact that the pentameter is only loosely iambic. One other point: in a conversation, Frost once mentioned that he never read this poem publicly. He put it in a class with "Out, Out" (the poem about the boy who loses his hand while operating a buzz-saw), something too terrifying to inflict on a captive audience.

A few more words about the title, and about the representation of American Indians. First, a word about the word "Indian." It is Eurocentric, of course, and in recent years it has been somewhat displaced by "Native

American," but many American Indians still prefer to call themselves Indians; in fact, it is our impression that whites are more likely than Indians to use "Native American." Second, whatever term is used, it probably erodes important ethnic and individual differences. One hears generalizations about Native Americans (or Indians) that would be inconceivable in speaking of "Europeans." For instance, in *The West as America* (1991), ed. William H. Truettner—a book that accompanied a highly controversial exhibition of art—the authors are very careful to indicate their views that the Indians were far superior to the whites who maltreated them, but we get such sweeping, unsupported comments as this: "Individuality, material status, and vanity . . . [are] all notions less highly regarded in Indian culture [than in white culture]" (p. 149). It might come as a surprise to, say, the Sioux, the Navaho, the Pawnee, and the Seneca, that they have much in common. Still, *The West as America* is an invaluable resource for images of Indians.

Another resource is Edward S. Curtis's massive collection of photographs, *The North American Indian*. The first picture in the first volume (1907—only nine years before Frost's poem) is called *The Vanishing Race*. It shows a line of Indians riding from the foreground into a dark background—vanishing. We reproduce it with Frost's poem.

EDWARD S. CURTIS
The Vanishing Race (photograph, p. 1203)

Curtis (1868–1952), who dedicated most of his life to recording (with the camera) what he thought was a vanishing way of life, has come in for strong criticism in recent years. Born in Wisconsin, he moved to Seattle in 1887, where he made his first photographs of Indians. In 1899 he went to Alaska with the E. H. Harriman expedition as an official photographer. For the next thirty years—the first seven of them at his own expense—he worked on a monumental project, traveling at least 9,000 miles, visiting at least 80 tribes from Canada to Mexico, and taking more than 40,000 photographs of Indians. Of those, 1,500 appeared in his twenty-volume work, *The North American Indian* (1907–1930), a publication supplemented by 20 larger folios of 722 unbound plates. About half of the cost was paid by J. P. Morgan at the request of President Theodore Roosevelt.

The chief criticisms of Curtis are two: (1) his desire to show Indians in a pre-contact (or pre-conquest) condition caused him to pose his subjects so that no evidence of white civilization appeared (e.g., the white man's cooking gear), and he sometimes clothed his subjects in costumes that he carried with him; (2) he believed (as the title of our photograph indicates) that the Indians he photographed were members of a vanishing race, the last survivors of a way of life that was doomed to disappear. That is, he did not conceive of Indians as persons who might—like other persons—adapt to new conditions, persons who might wear jeans and yet preserve important values of their own. He is thus regarded by some critics as, finally, condescending toward (if not contemptuous of) the people whose life he recorded.

We think we do understand the objections to Curtis's view, and it is indeed clear that he did not anticipate the sort of survival shown in a relatively recent photograph that we reprint, *Three American Indian Students at Princeton*. On the other hand, given what he saw, his belief that the Indians were a vanishing race is not surprising, and his response was entirely sympathetic. He knew that many Indian languages had become extinct—for instance, all that we know of Virginia Algonquian (one of the many languages now extinct) is what John Smith wrote down in the seventeenth century—and he knew that some Indians were being converted to Christianity and were being educated in the white man's schools. And of course he saw the devastating effects of the forcible removals that had taken place in the mid-nineteenth century.

It has been estimated that when Columbus arrived there were some 2.5 million Indians, but by 1890 only about 250,000. Everyone knew that they had been killed by disease and by federal soldiers. (In 1864 Col. John M. Chivington became a local hero in Denver when he attacked a camp of unarmed Cheyenne and Arapaho at Sand Creek—they had given up their weapons thinking that peace had been agreed on—killing 105 women and children along with 28 men.) Enforced relocations, under the eyes of federal troops, were devastating: about a quarter of the Cherokee who in 1838 were compelled to march twelve hundred miles from Georgia to what is now Oklahoma died en route. In 1887 Congress passed the General Allotment Act (popularly called the Dawes Act), which sold to whites some of the land that had been set aside as Indian reservations. Between 1887 and 1930 Indian lands were reduced to a little more than one-third of what they had been. In 1890, when Curtis was twenty-two, five hundred soldiers at Wounded Knee surrounded three hundred and forty Indians and killed or wounded two-thirds of them. Why would not a viewer think of the Indians as a vanishing race? Throughout the nineteenth century one hears and sees the motif: early in the century William Cullen Bryant, writing about Indians, ended "The Disinterred Warrior" with the words, "A noble race! But they are gone"; around the middle of the century Tompkins H. Matteson painted *The Last of the Race* (1847), showing an Indian family on a cliff, at the water's edge, the sky filled with dark clouds; at the end of the century James Earle Fraser produced a bronze sculpture, *End of the Trail* (c. 1894, enlarged to heroic size for the Panama-Pacific Exposition of 1915 in San Francisco), showing an exhausted Indian, head down, slumped on an exhausted horse. (Matteson's painting and Fraser's sculpture are reproduced in *The West as America*, ed. William Truettner [1991], pp. 168 and 174. And while we are citing material, we want to call attention to Christopher Lyman, *The Vanishing Race and Other Illusions: The Photographs of Edward S. Curtis* [1982].) Nominally the choice seemed to be maintenance on a reservation or (for a few) assimilation, but a reasonable observer might conclude that the end would be extinction.

Now, at the beginning of the twenty-first century, we can see that many aspects of Indian cultures have survived, and the Indian population (according to the 1990 census) has risen to 1.9 million. Partly because of the activities of fairly recent Indian groups such as the National Indian Youth Council (established in 1961) and AIM (American Indian Movement, 1968), Indians are more visible, on and off the reservation. (Although some whites who advocated putting Indians on reservations doubtless had the Indian's best interests in mind, for the most part the idea was to get the Indians out of the way, to keep them helpless, and to let them dwindle into nothingness.) Indians recently have regained some of their old rights, and they have regained some money—for instance, the government has paid the Sioux $100 million for lands that were taken when gold was discovered on them in the nineteenth century. Increasing numbers are enrolled in colleges and universities, courses are given in Indian culture, and, all in all, there is a new awareness of Red Power. But Curtis, essentially a man of 1900, can hardly be expected to have anticipated the 1990s. The worst that can be said of him, we think, is that he did not call attention to the abuses the Indians had suffered. His desire to exhibit their dignity prevented him from showing them in degraded circumstances, circumstances that ought to have aroused the viewer's indignation.

But let Curtis speak for himself. Here is what he said in 1911 to a reporter for the *New York Times,* as quoted in William Goetzmann, *The First Americans* (1991), p. 20:

> [The Indians] have grasped the idea that this is to be a permanent memorial of their race, and it appeals to their imagination. Word passes from tribe to tribe. . . . A tribe that I have visited and studied lets another tribe know that after the present generation has passed away, men will want to know from this record what they were like, and what they did, and the second tribe doesn't want to be left out.

He thought of himself as what today we would call a documentary photographer, but it is now evident that he was a pictorialist—a photographer who wanted to elevate photography to the ranks of serious art and who therefore composed his subjects carefully. Curtis's *The Vanishing Race* (c. 1904) shows Indians riding off, single file, into obscurity. The title guides us into what we take the picture to show. But a title cannot force us to interpret a picture a certain way. If the picture showed Indians riding at us, three abreast, we could hardly agree that it shows "the vanishing race." Curtis may or may not have asked these Indians to ride in a certain direction, but of course the picture is, as we now say, "constructed," even if only by the angle from which Curtis chose to shoot it. Everyone now understands that virtually all pictures are constructed, beginning with the family photo ("Say cheese—and John, make the dog sit"). As the photographer Minor White memorably said, "I don't take pictures, I make them." Part of "making" a picture is the choice of focus. Curtis, like other pictorialists of his day, often used a soft focus, getting a slightly blurred or dreamy effect.

Topic for Critical Thinking and Writing

1. What would your response to the picture be if it were entitled, "Hunters Returning Home Laden with Game"?

WENDY ROSE
Three Thousand Dollar Death Song (p. 1204)

First, a bit of background. Until 1960 or so, the white world's awareness of Indians was probably formed chiefly by stereotypical images in films, advertisements, and toys. A relatively small number of whites was of course aware of serious anthropological studies—and that's where we get into trouble, since these studies included unearthing the bones of the deceased. Perhaps from about 1960 Indian voices of protest were heard, but not until 1990—ten years after Rose published her poem—did the Native American Graves Protection and Repatriation Act require federally funded museums and institutions to compile inventories of their collections and to work with Indian nations for the return of their human remains. (The Act also was concerned with the return of sacred ritual objects and items of cultural patrimony, but these are not central in Wendy Rose's poem.)

Surely the gist of the poem is clear—that whites buy and sell Indian bones is a sign of the white violation of Indian culture—but we find that we differ in one respect from most other readers of the poem. Our students and colleagues assume that the "museum invoice" of the epigraph indicates that the museum bought the nineteen skeletons for $3,000. But an invoice is a list of goods shipped or services rendered, so if the word is used in the strict sense, the museum sold the bones. (Another possibility, of course, is that the "museum invoice" is an invoice not prepared by the museum but something in the files of the museum, in which case it could indeed indicate that the museum purchased the bones.) The point is not crucial—in either case the whites are dealing in sacred Indian material—but we do think that the skeletons probably were sold rather than bought by the museum. Line 24, "we explode under white students' hands," would thus mean that the bones were sold to a medical school or to some other educational institution that would use the bones for anatomical study. (If the museum bought the bones, then perhaps the line alludes to student anthropologists who study the bones in the museum.)

The poem begins by pretending to be businesslike ("in cold hard cash? . . . Or in bills? . . . Or / checks"), but the businesslike tone is obviously a transparent satiric mask for the speaker's indignation. The indignation becomes explicit with the reference in line 6 to "paper promises."

The second half of the poem moves from the assault on the bones to the larger issue of how the white world not only turned the Indian "dead into specimens" (line 34) but also stole everything from the Indians—"turquoise / and copper, blood and oil, coal / and uranium," of course, and even (and this is a surprising note in such a list) "children" (line 50). But the speaker warns (possibly drawing on Ezekiel 37:1), "watch our bones rise" (line 43).

The central point is the white despoilment of Indian culture, and we don't want to trivialize this issue by turning to what may seem to be a minor matter, but we do want to say that one way of approaching the poem is to ask students if they have ever seen any Indian artifacts in a museum. If so, how were the objects treated? Were they treated as the Other, something odd, primitive, crude, uncivilized or even barbaric, less than (for example) the beautiful art objects of white culture? Museum administrators face a real problem here; if they treat the material in a more or less ethnographic way, the museum is open to the charge of condescending to the culture ("See how curious the customs of these people were!"). If, on the other hand, they treat the material as important works of art, objects of rare beauty, the museum is open to the charge of taking objects out of their indispensable cultural context and seeing them as "mere" esthetic objects rather than as, say, part of the religious life of a people.

Students might be asked why a museum would possess skeletons. We take lines 18–19 to suggest that the bones might be used in a display of Indian burial practices, some stretched out, some assembled in a fetal position. Why is it—what does it say about us—students might be asked, that a museum of natural history might display the bones of Indians but would not conceivably display the bones of whites? Does such an exhibition become something of a freak show? And why is the display of bones offensive to some—perhaps most—people? In particular, is the display of Indian bones especially offensive because some Indians (like some other people) believe that the dead cannot rest until their bones are buried?

Students have told us they enjoyed Rose's collection *Bone Dance: New and Selected Poems, 1965–1993* (1994).

NILA NORTHSUN
Moving Camp Too Far (p. 1206)

The first stanza evokes the world of the Indian, though the very first words ("i can't") make it clear that this world is lost, at least to the speaker. We are in the world not of the Vanishing Red (cf. Frost's poem with this title) but of the Vanished Red.

The second stanza begins by evoking a contrast (that's what second stanzas often do)—but a moment later the contrast proves to be illusory, since the affirmative words ("i can see an eagle") become negative ("almost extinct"). The second stanza, then, does not really contrast with the first; rather, it intensifies the first (again, that's what second stanzas often do). Further, the second stanza builds to a climax of degradation; the affirmative "i can dance to indian music" descends into "rock-n-roll hey-a-hey-o," and then to the further, and final—and surprising, but in retrospect almost inevitable—collapse of "& unfortunately / i do." The degradation is evident, and what perhaps is most painful is that the speaker implicitly accepts at least some of the responsibility.

For background information, consult Klaus Lubber, *Born for the Shade: Stereotypes of the Native American in United States Literature and the Visual Arts, 1776–1894* (1994).

JAMES LUNA
The Artifact Piece (photograph, p. 1206)

Not every student will know that an artifact (or artefact) is an object produced or shaped by humans, especially a tool, weapon, or ornament. Ethnographic museums commonly have rooms with names like "Artifacts of the American Indian" or "Hall of the Congo," in which bows and arrows, knives, bracelets, baskets, and so forth are displayed, in an effort to help the viewer understand what kinds of lives the people lived. Exhibitions may also include life-size sculptures of persons making or using the artifacts, let's say of a waxwork figure of an Indian weaving a blanket or making a basket. Labels in the cases or nearby on the wall explain that over here is a hank of wool that is not yet dyed, and over there is a hank of wool that has been dyed and is drying, and here is a knife used to cut the wool. Inevitably, especially if the exhibition includes images of human beings, the effect is to suggest a mummified culture. How can it be other, with those unmoving figures, preserved behind glass?

James Luna, born in 1950 on the La Jolla Indian Reservation in California, was educated at the University of California, Irvine (B.F.A.) and at San Diego State University (M.F.A.). He studied painting but then found that he could better express himself as a performance artist. In *The Artifact Piece* (performed in 1987 and 1990), Luna, clad in a loincloth, lies in a museum exhibition case on a bed of sand. Here, in effect, he is saying, "You want to know about Indians? You think you can understand us by looking at statues of basket-makers and baskets? Here is something for you to look at." Labels in the case call attention to wounds gained in drunken brawls. Additional display cases contain family photographs, his college diplomas, and divorce papers. It is hard for us to imagine a more educational—a more thought-provoking—exhibition concerned with Indian life. As Lisa Roberts says, in her entry on Luna in the *St. James Guide to Native North American Artists* (1998),

> The presence of a real, or undead Indian displayed as artifact questioned the underlying premise of museums' authoritative role in defining perceptions of cultural authenticity and identity. (p. 343)

Topic for Critical Thinking and Writing

Describe Luna's artifact, and explain its effect on you. In your answer, take account of the following:
- What is an artifact?
- If you have ever been in an ethnographic museum or a museum of natural history, report what artifacts are commonly displayed in such museums.

25

Law and Disorder

HENRY DAVID THOREAU
From *"Civil Disobedience"* (p. 1212)

Your students may already know that Thoreau's essay was an important influence on, and inspiration for, Mohandas K. Gandhi and Martin Luther King, Jr., in their reform campaigns. But we think it is valuable for students to see Thoreau's essay in its biographical and historical contexts, which we describe in our headnote. It's a timeless essay, a classic, but like all timeless works, it is nonetheless the result of—it is a response to—a specific moment in the writer's life and history.

We also remind students that Thoreau's act of civil disobedience, while courageous, was unusual for him. He was a staunch individualist, not really a social reformer; he believed that social life would inevitably become better as persons reformed themselves, and thus that the project of transforming individual hearts and minds should be the main focus. In this one instance, Thoreau took a moral stand against an unjust war, and he paid a price for it—though, to be honest, it was not much of a price, only a single night in the hometown jail. He never did anything as sustained, as difficult and demanding, as the work that Gandhi and King performed, work that took enormous effort and resolve over a span of many years.

If Thoreau was an activist, he was above all an activist through and in his writing. Thoreau loved the sheer act of writing, and he wrote constantly. Indeed, living at Walden Pond in the 1840s was for him less an immersion in nature than an opportunity for sustained literary labor, away from the busy family home with its boarders and pencil business. As soon as Thoreau arrived, he started composing two lectures about what he was doing and why. He was hard at work all the time on essays and books, including a book about his stay at Walden (which hadn't yet ended), and he was generating page after page of journal entries and revising and reorganizing them. In *Walden* Thoreau chooses not to divulge how much time he spent at his writing desk, but in truth he was at Walden an indefatigable writer who was almost always writing. It's a wonder he had the time now and then to take a walk in the woods.

Thoreau lived only to age forty-four, yet he managed to write two major books (*A Week on the Concord and Merrimack Rivers* and *Walden*), many lectures and essays, thousands of pages of manuscript for other essays and books (a number of which were published after his death), thousands of more pages of notebooks, hundreds of poems, many letters, and millions of words in his journal. He lived to put pen to paper, and he made everyone and everything else secondary to that. Even nature, however dear it was to him, was in essence raw material for literary activity. Thoreau was possessed and driven by a will to write that few American authors have equaled.

We emphasize this fact about Thoreau in order to lead to a question we ask the students: Does "Civil Disobedience" stand on its own, or should we weigh and appraise it alongside the realities of the writer's most urgent commitment?—which, in Thoreau's case, was his writing. Yes, Thoreau took a stand, but do the arguments of "Civil Disobedience" suggest that he should have taken such stands more often than, in truth, he did? We then press the students (and ourselves) a bit: But is this question about, or, rather, criticism of, Thoreau really a fair one? Should we expect—can we expect—a person to be in his or her life completely faithful to the principles that Thoreau outlines? How do we know when we must resist an unjust law or practice, as opposed to a law or practice with which we disagree but which we judge to be tolerable?

Our best classes on "Civil Disobedience" have been a little messy and disorderly, with lots of questions raised and with issues debated and (usually) left unresolved. One problem with the essay, we have found, is that it is too easy for students to admire it. We think that they ought to admire it but also that they should test and inquire into the grounds for their admiration and return to the text for a fresh look. For this reason, we always give the paper assignment on "Civil Disobedience" after the class has discussed it. This makes the essay harder for the students to write, but of course the advantage is that it requires them to think more analytically, to be more reflective about Thoreau's arguments and their own and others' responses to them.

The best recent discussion of Thoreau's essay is Lawrence A. Rosenwald's "The Theory, Practice, and Influence of Thoreau's Civil Disobedience," in *A Historical Guide to Henry David Thoreau*, ed. William E. Cain (2000), pp. 153–179. Rosenwald concludes:

> Thoreau undogmatically sorted through all of the traditions available to him, rejecting what he could not use and holding fast what was good. The non-resistance of Garrison, Ballous, and Alcott, the revolutionary action of 1775, the Transcendentalist emphasis on conscience, the large historical events and small personal accidents of Thoreau's own time, his mechanical expertise, and his masculine insecurity are all sifted for use in the essay. What has made the essay capable of exerting so great an influence is not only the severity of its idea but also its concreteness and unsystematic pragmatism. (p. 173)

Note: By "mechanical expertise," Rosenwald is referring to Thoreau's expert knowledge as a surveyor and as a scientist, including one who was involved in his family's pencil-making business; as Thoreau states in "Civil Disobedience," "Let your life be a counter friction to stop the machine."

For a stimulating essay on changing interpretations of "Civil Disobedience," see Evan Carton, "The Price of Privilege: 'Civil Disobedience' at 150," *The American Scholar* 67:4 (Autumn 1998): 105–112. "Civil Disobedience," Carton contends,

> exposes and undoes the psychological training that in one way or another we have all internalized. It dissolves the buffer between us and the host of distant sins that, in Thoreau's stunningly precise formulation, "from immoral have become, as it were, unmoral, and not quite unnecessary to that life which we have made." When we "just do it" in our Nikes, my students hear Thoreau whispering: Are you in fact doing it on the shoulders of the Indonesian (or now, because of a recent rise in the price of Indonesian labor, Vietnamese) sweatshop workers who make those Nikes for pennies an hour?

For a keen, accessible overview, we recommend Leo Marx, "The Struggle over Thoreau," *The New York Review of Books*, June 24, 1999. Biographies include Walter Harding, *The Days of Henry Thoreau* (1965; rev. ed., 1992), and Robert D. Richardson Jr., *Henry Thoreau: A Life of the Mind* (1986). For other teaching tips: Laraine Fergensen, "'Civil Disobedience' (or Is It 'Resistance to Civil Government'?) in a Composition Course," in *Approaches to Teaching Thoreau's Walden and Other Works*, ed. Richard J. Schneider (1996).

If time permits, you might bring to class some passages from Thoreau's later political essays, "Slavery in Massachusetts" (1854) and "A Plea for John Brown" (1859, 1860). Both of these essays are more violent in their rhetoric and more sympathetic toward violence as a form of social and political protest than is "Civil Disobedience." The best collections of Thoreau's writings are the two volumes in the Library of America Series, published in 1985 and 2001; the second contains the essays.

For cogent discussions of nonviolent and violent forms of civil disobedience: Michael Martin, "Ecosabotage and Civil Disobedience," *Environmental Ethics* 12 (Winter 1990): 291–310; and Gerald D. Coleman, "Civil Disobedience: A Moral Critique," *Theological Studies* 46 (March 1985): 21–37.

Some of your students might enjoy examining the impact of Thoreau on Gandhi and King. See, for example, Manfred Steger, "Mahatma Gandhi and the Anarchist Legacy of Henry David Thoreau," *Southern Humanities Review*, 27:3 (Summer 1993); and Anita Haya Goldman, "American Philosophy as Praxis: From Emerson and Thoreau to Martin Luther King," *Salmagundi* 108 (Fall 1995).

GEORGE ORWELL
A Hanging (p. 1215)

The business at the end of Orwell's essay, with the superintendent offering a drink after the hanging ("You'd better all come out and have a drink") reminded us of a passage at the end of Kipling's "Danny Deever," another work about a hanging. When we decided to add a unit called "Law and Disorder" to *Literature for Composition*, we immediately thought of Orwell's essay, and when we turned our minds to poems about law, we thought of Housman's "The Carpenter's Son" and his "Eight O'Clock" (both are in our book) and also of "Danny Deever." Three poems on hanging, however, seemed a bit too much, so we dropped "Danny Deever." Still, because we encountered "Danny Deever" when we were young and it has lasted with us for decades, we think that perhaps young people may still respond to it, i.e., you may want to give your students a chance to be taken by the powerful rhythms and, indeed, the powerful situation it presents. So here it is.

Danny Deever

"What are the bugles blowin' for?" said Files-on-Parade.
"To turn you out, to turn you out," the Color-Sergeant said.
"What makes you look so white, so white?" said Files-on-Parade.
"I'm dreadin' what I've got to watch," the Color-Sergeant said.
    For they're hangin' Danny Deever, you can bear the Dead March play, 5
    The regiment's in 'ollow square—they're hanging' him today;
    They've taken of his buttons off an' cut his stripes away,

An they're hangin' Danny Deever in the mornin'.
"What makes the rear rank breathe so hard?" said Files-on-Parade.
"It's bitter cold, it's bitter cold," the Color-Sergeant said. 10
"What makes that front-rank man fall down?" said Files-on-Parade.
"A touch o' sun, a touch o' sun," the Color-Sergeant said,
    They are hangin' Danny Deever, they are marchin' of 'im round,
    They 'ave 'alted Danny Deever by 'is coffin on the ground;
    An' 'e'll swing in 'arf a minute for a sneakin' shootin' hound— 15
    They're hangin' Danny Deever in the mornin'!

" 'is cot was right-'and cot to mine," said Files-on-Parade.
"'E's sleepin' out an' far tonight," the Color-Sergeant said.
"I've drunk 'is beer a score o' times," said Files-on-Parade.
"'E's drinkin bitter beer alone," the Color-Sergeant said. 20
    They are hangin' Danny Deever, you must mark 'im to 'is place,
    For 'e shot a comrade sleepin'—you must look 'im in the face;
    Nine 'undred of 'is county an' the Regiment's disgrace,
    While they're hangin' Danny Deever in the mornin'.

"What's that so black agin the sun?" said Files-on-Parade. 25
"It's Danny fightin' 'ard for life," the Color-Sergeant said.
"What's that that whimpers over'ead?" said Files-on-Parade.
"It's Danny's soul that's passin' now," the Color-Sergeant said.
    For they're done with Danny Deever, you can 'ear the quickstep play,

The regiment's in column, an' they're marchin' us away;   30
Ho! the young recruits are shakin', an' they'll want their beer today,
After hangin' Danny Deever in the mornin'.

[1890]

In case you do teach this poem, a few notes may be useful. Lines 1–2: *Files-on-Parade . . . Color-Sergeant,* army private . . . noncommissioned officer; 6: *'ollow square,* the troops line the four sides of a square (the prisoner will be marched into the center); 7: *buttons . . . stripes,* the buttons on the condemned man's uniform, bearing royal insignia, are cut off, as are the chevrons (stripes denoting his rank). Incidentally, in the United States armed forces, when a man was given a dishonorable discharge and condemned to prison for some crime, a similar ritual prevailed, at least up through the first World War. The writer of these lines remembers his father (who had served in the U.S. Navy in World War I) telling him about witnessing such an event. The ship's entire crew was assembled, the guilty man was brought forth by several sailors armed with rifles equipped with bayonets (bayonets appear, too, in Orwell's essay), and the buttons—because "U.S." was stamped on them—were cut off so that they would not suffer the ignominy of being worn by a man who was about to be imprisoned.

Back to Orwell's "A Hanging." We'll offer our own responses to the questions that we give in the text.

1. *The two delays.* In our view, both delays—that provided by the dog and that provided by the prisoner's prayer or cry for help—are designed to cause the reader to experience increasingly uneasy feelings concerning the monstrosity of the hanging. The narrator seems to offer a camera's eye view, without comment, and this apparently objective presentation in itself moves the reader to protest—at the very least we very much want to know, What did this man do? Why is he being hanged? The interruption of the dog, which licks the man and frolics, shows us a little burst of life, life that in a moment will be taken from the condemned man. It gives the man an extra minute or two, and perhaps we find ourselves hoping for a last-minute reprieve. In any case, this energetic and affectionate dog reminds us of the joy of living, and we are forced to wonder why this man, of whom we have heard no ill, should have his life taken away. The second delay, when "the prisoner began crying out to his god" (paragraph 12) is caused by the superintendent, who "was slowly poking the ground with his stick; perhaps he was counting the cries, allowing the prisoner a fixed number—fifty, perhaps, or a hundred." Orwell doesn't tell us why the superintendent poked at the ground, just as the author of the narrative of "The Woman Taken in Adultery" (in our text) doesn't tell why "Jesus stooped down, and with his finger wrote on the ground." In both cases, we are eager to know, but we will never know, and the narrated action generates in us a tension, an uneasiness, that is unresolved but that is perhaps a sort of tiny analog to the uneasiness experienced by the silent figures (Jesus, the superintendent) whose actions are described but not explained.

2. *The paragraphs after the hanging.* Presumably the nervousness and the joking—and the joking seems to be a sign of the nervousness—help the reader to

reflect on the inhumanity of the hanging. Nothing in these paragraphs reassures the reader that justice has been done. The closest that we come to hearing someone express feelings about the execution is the superintendent's "Well, that's all for this morning, thank God" (paragraph 16) and the narrator's comment on the "enormous relief" (paragraph 17) that came over the group. But surely we feel that they are "chattering gaily" not because they are cruel or callous but because they are desperately trying to put the hanging out of their minds.

3. *The prisoner stepping aside to avoid a puddle.* We think there are at least two reasons why Orwell reports this detail (paragraph 9). First, it shows that the man still is attached to life, still is careful about his behavior. When you think about it, it is absurd that a man who in a minute or two will be killed is worrying about stepping in a puddle, but in his small action we see a concern for proper behavior, for decency. Later (paragraph 18) we will learn that "when he heard his appeal had been dismissed, he pissed on the floor of his cell. From fright." This reflexive action is countered by the—shall we call it "civilized"?—detail about the care with which the man steps around the puddle. We know almost nothing about the victim, but we treasure this concern for propriety. Or put it this way: this detail reveals, in a surprising, even shocking context, the condemned man's connection to us, his connection to the reader's world. He is doing something that we imagine we ourselves would do, and thus we are brought disquietingly close to him—he has our habits, our preoccupations, our foibles. Perish the thought, but if we faced execution, we would likely behave as he did. In light of this fact, how do we feel about his execution now?

4. *The last two sentences.* Orwell's version is right, and our revisions are disasters. In his version, but not in ours, the final sentence is devoted exclusively to the dead man. A short, simple sentence, it contrasts starkly with the the preceding sentence, in which Asians and Europeans find something to laugh about.

ZORA NEALE HURSTON
A Conflict of Interest (p. 1219)

As we mention in our headnote, in the late 1950s and the 1960s, Hurston's reputation went into a decline; in a period of enormous gains in civil rights she seemed both naive, and reactionary, a sort of Aunt Jemima. Even then it was hard—for African Americans as well as whites—to understand the mind-set of this African American woman of the 1940s, and perhaps today we still cannot understand how any black person could have behaved the way Hurston did in the episode (undated, but probably in the 1920s) that she reports. Can we possibly agree with her that "self-interest rides over all sorts of lines"?

Well, although most of us doubtless hope that *we* would act altruistically, probably most of us are, at our best, guided by what Burke called "enlightened self-interest." Kahlil Gibran maybe was uncomfortably close to the truth when he said, "We are all practical in our own interest and idealists when it concerns others." We can agree that a truly enlightened self-interest would have led

Hurston and her colleagues to see that it was in the interest of *everyone* that the stranger be given a haircut, that Jim Crow be abandoned, but it is easy to say this at our comfortable distance. As Hurston indicates, she and her fellows felt that their livelihoods were threatened; not until she had gained a bit of distance—a few hours—could she see things differently:

> It was only that night in bed that I analyzed the whole thing and realized that I was giving sanction to Jim Crow, which theoretically, I was supposed to resist. But here were ten Negro barbers, three porters and two manicurists all stirred up at the threat of our living through loss of patronage. Nobody thought it out at the moment. It was an instinctive thing. (Paragraph 17)

In our second question in the text we ask students to evaluate the view that Hurston's piece is comic as well as tragic. We will tip our hand here: We think Hurston presents the episode partly in comic terms. Imagine if it were filmed: We would watch the barber Updyke whirling his chair around so that the intruder could not sit in it, and saying, almost farcically, "Don't you touch *my* chair," and we would watch "barbers, customers all lathered and hair half cut, and porters," rushing around to "throw the Negro out." Where have we seen "customers all lathered up and hair half cut" leaping out of barber chairs? Only in silent film comedies, or in the early talkies. It is simply impossible to see a guy lathered up, wrapped in a sheet, leaping out of a chair and not see him as funny.

Hurston goes on to say,

> Perhaps it would have been a beautiful thing if Banks had turned to the shop crowded with customers and announced that this man was going to be served like everybody else even at the risk of losing their patronage, with all of the other employees lined up in the center of the floor shouting, "So say we all!" It would have been a stirring gesture, and made the headlines for a day. Then we could all have gone home to our unpaid rents and bills and things like that.

We know that a few decades later, heroic figures did indeed engage in actions that not only made headlines for a day but that also changed America forever. (Rosa Parks, who in 1955 dared to sit in the "whites only" section of a bus comes to mind.) But this gets us into issues of the man versus the moment: Was Rosa Parks possible, or rather, was the success of Rosa Parks possible before World War II?

In any case, we find Hurston's narrative gripping, partly because she honestly presents herself in an unflattering light, partly because she forces us to think about what our own reactions might have been in this situation, and partly because, by presenting some aspects in comic terms, she helps us to see that maybe, just maybe, we ourselves might *not* see the episode as we think we would see it if it happened today.

For further reading, see *Dust Tracks on a Road: An Autobiography*, ed. Robert E. Hemenway (2nd ed., 1984); and *Zora Neale Hurston: A Life in Letters*, ed. Carla Kaplan (2002). Also recommended: Robert E. Hemenway, *Zora Neale Hurston: A Literary Biography* (1977); Lillie P. Howard, *Zora Neale Hurston* (1980); *Zora Neale Hurston: Critical Perspectives Past and Present*, ed. Henry Louis Gates, Jr. and K. A. Appiah (1993); and Susan Edwards Meisenhelder, *Hitting a Straight Lick with a Crooked Stick: Race and Gender in the Work of Zora Neale Hurston* (1999).

Martin Luther King Jr.
Letter from Birmingham Jail (p. 1222)

King's letter was prompted by a letter (printed in the text) by eight Birmingham clergymen. His letter is unusually long ("Never before have I written so long a letter") because he was jailed at the time and thus was unable to speak to audiences face to face.

King goes to some length to show that his work is thoroughly in the American (and Judeo-Christian) tradition. That is, although he rebuts the letter of the eight clergymen, he represents himself not as a radical, nor in any way un-American (and of course not as an opponent of the Judeo-Christian tradition), but as one who shares the culture of his audience. Thus, although he rejects the clergymen's view that he is impatient, he begins by acknowledging their decency. They are, he says, "men of genuine goodwill"—and in saying this King thereby implies that he too is a man of goodwill. Moreover, King's real audience is not only the eight clergymen but all readers of his letter, who are assumed to be decent folk. Notice, too, in his insistence that he is speaking on an issue that involves all Americans, his statement (paragraph 4) that "injustice anywhere is a threat to justice everywhere." But his chief strategy early in the letter is to identify himself with Paul (paragraph 3), and thus to guide his mainly Christian audience to see him as carrying on a tradition that they cherish. Notice also the references to Niebuhr, Buber (a Jew), and Jesus.

It is usual, and correct, to say that King is a master of the appeal to emotion. This essay reveals such mastery, as in paragraph 14, when he quotes a five-year-old boy: "Daddy, why do white people treat colored people so mean?" And because King is really addressing not so much the eight clergymen as a sympathetic audience that probably needs encouragement to persist rather than reasons to change their beliefs, an emotional (inspirational) appeal is appropriate. But the essay is also rich in lucid exposition and careful analysis, as in paragraph 6 (on the four steps of a nonviolent campaign) and paragraphs 15–16 (comparing just and unjust laws).

Topics for Critical Thinking and Writing

1. Think of some injustice that you know something about, and jot down the facts as objectively as possible. Arrange them so that they form an outline.

Then, using these facts as a framework, write an essay (possibly in the form of a letter to a specific audience) of about 500 words, presenting your case in a manner somewhat analogous to King's. For example, don't hesitate to make comparisons with biblical, literary, or recent historical material, or to use personal experiences, or to use any other persuasive devices you wish, including appeals to the emotions. Hand in the objective list along with the essay.
2. If some example of nonviolent direct action has recently been in the news, such as actions by persons opposed to nuclear power plants, write an essay evaluating the tactics and their effectiveness in dealing with the issue.

AESOP
A Lion and Other Animals Go Hunting (p. 1236)
A Note on Fables, Parables, and Other Moral Stories

Because the didactic story in effect offers a statement about reality, it thereby seeks to alter the reader's attitude toward reality—and perhaps even the reader's behavior. Such a story clearly differs from one chiefly concerned with making the reader understand or experience the consciousness of a character engaged in certain actions. The emphasis in the moral story is not on the ideas of a character but on an idea about life. Even when such a story (e.g., the Aesopian fable of the ant and the grasshopper) does not question a traditional value but merely reaffirms it, the story seeks to make us feel its truth with new force. The mere fact that the story is told is itself an assertion that the traditional value is held only weakly, only nominally subscribed to but not lived by; the story implicitly urges the reader to move from lip service to action.

Early in *Literature for Composition* we give the Parable of the Prodigal Son, a classic of its kind. If you discuss this parable, or the short narratives in the present unit, you may want to invite students to consider this comment from H. W. Garrod's The *Profession of Poetry* (p. 264):

> Literature does not please by moralizing us; it moralizes us because it pleases.

The question to be asked is this: Why do works such as Aesop's fables, Jesus's parables, and the story of the Woman Taken in Adultery—not a parable but presumably history—please us? One answer may be that the moral is itself pleasing, but other answers involve matters of plot and characterization—in short, matters of artistry.

Now, for Aesop's "A Lion and Other Animals Go Hunting."

A few students will know this fable, but it is not nearly so familiar as some others, for instance, "The Grasshopper and the Ant" (whose moral strikes us as typically cruel in its delightful way) or "The Tortoise and the Hare," or "The Boy Who Cried Wolf."

In our second question we ask students to comment on the explicitly stated morals. In our view, the difference between a moral story and its moral is considerable, not because the moral can't be stated but because the moral, however true it may seem to us, is usually obvious, boring, forgettable, whereas the story gives us vivid, memorable characters. Something along these lines can be said of all literature. More than one great love poem, for instance, can be reduced to "I love her not only because she is beautiful but, more important, because she is also virtuous." Not something that makes the pulse beat faster or that (in Housman's formula) makes the hairs bristle. We can quote Emily Dickinson: "If I feel physically as if the top of my head were taken off, I know that is poetry." Philosophic abstractions, however lofty, however noble, do not have this sort of effect on anyone except perhaps the philosophers who formulate them. Most of us need concrete images, sensory material, and this is what literature gives us.

Consider the difference between enduring proverbs and the moral formulations that many students are familiar with. In the text (Chapter 3) we talk at some length about a proverb that many students are familiar with, "A rolling stone gathers no moss." At that point in the text we are chiefly concerned with the effectiveness of the statement (e.g., "stone" vs "moss", with the contrast of hard and soft, inorganic and organic), and we compare it with a paraphrase, "If a stone is always moving around, vegetation won't have a chance to grow on it." But we might also have contrasted it with an abstract formulation, something like "Constantly varying activity inhibits substantial accomplishment."

Or take, to get back to Aesop, one we sometimes hear today, "Boy, out there it's a jungle." This metaphor evokes the view that "life is fraught with dangers and difficulties" with a vitality that the abstract statement lacks. Indeed, the figure of the jungle is surprisingly close to Aesop's view of the world, as is shown by the fable that we reprint in the text, and the fact that these fables have been read for more than two centuries says something.

JOHN (?)
The Woman Taken in Adultery (p. 1237)

As we say in our headnote, most scholars agree that this story, which is not found in the earliest Greek manuscripts, is not really part of the Gospel According to St. John but is an account that somehow got inserted into late manuscripts. On grounds of diction it is said to resemble Luke far more than John.

The Mosaic law required that an adulterer be put to death (Lev. 20:10, Deut. 22:22), but it scarcely required the scribes and Pharisees to be so callous toward the woman or so eager to trip Jesus. They hoped to force Jesus to reject the Mosaic law; or, alternatively, possibly they sought to make him vulnerable to a charge (by Roman authorities) that he incited people to murder the woman. Note how they use the woman for their own purposes:

> And the scribes and Pharisees brought unto him a woman taken in adultery; and when they had set her in the midst, they say unto him, "Master, this woman was taken in adultery, in the very act. Moses in the law commanded us that such should be stoned: but what sayest thou?

That business of setting her in the midst and of specifying "in the very act" has an ugly sound.

The scribes and Pharisees "continued asking him," pressing for an answer that would damage him. Jesus's unexplained gesture of writing on the ground can never be decisively explained, but perhaps it indicates his distress (which he seeks to relieve by a physical distraction) at seeing and hearing this malicious spectacle. A second interpretation, not incompatible with what we have just said, is that the episode keenly involves the readers, making us wonder what Jesus's words might have been. But in time he answers. His response does not mean that he dismisses the sin of adultery as trivial; it does mean, however, that he refuses to condemn the woman and that he sees in the scribes and Pharisees behavior at least as sinful, which ought to teach them to temper justice with mercy. His words strike home: the judges "are convicted by their own conscience." Note that Jesus bids the woman to give up her sinful life. He does not always speak so gently to sinners, and so we must assume that here he perceived she was not fixed in evil but was contrite.

The exact lesson can be much debated, but we think *The Jerome Biblical Commentary* (1968) gives a summary (p. 441 in the portion of the book devoted to the New Testament) to which many readers can subscribe. It says,

> The lesson of the story is, of course, not that sin is of no importance, nor that God does not punish sin, but that God extends mercy to the sinner that he may turn from his sin. The picture of the sinner and the Sinless standing face to face exemplifies the call to repentance. Thus, though Jesus himself does not judge (8.15), it is nevertheless for judgment that he has come into the world (9.39).

One final point, relevant to the important issue of Christian and non-Christian responses. This episode is the only place recorded in the New Testament where Jesus confronts the issue of legal execution. Does the episode suggest that devout Christians must oppose the death penalty?

ANONYMOUS
Three Hasidic Tales (p. 1238)

1. *Keeping the Law*. The story begins with a question that seems insoluble: How could Abraham have kept all the law if all the laws had not yet been specified? The answer turns out to be simple: "All that is needful is to love God." The idea of course is that all the laws—those that Abraham knew and those not yet given to him—are part of one overarching law, "Love God."

Probably all religions are in danger of developing such complex codes that devotees fear they may inadvertently neglect some law or other, and probably all religions have stories somewhat like "Keeping the Law." In Judaism, for instance, the Scripture is divided into three parts, The Law (the Torah, the first five books), the Prophets, and the Writings, and one finds not only the Ten Commandments (Exodus 20:1–17, Deuteronomy 5:6–21) but also innumerable laws concerning such matters as the preparation of food, taxation, the distribution of booty, and recompense for death caused by animals. But Judaism also prizes a famous comment by Rabbi Hillel (fl. 30 BC–AD 10). Asked to summarize the Scriptures very briefly, he replied: "What is hateful to you, do not do to your fellow creature. This is the whole of the Law."

Hillel's comment of course reminds us of what has come to be called the Golden Rule (the term seems to be no older than the eighteenth century), Jesus's teaching, "Do unto others as you would have them do unto you" (Luke 6:31; Matthew 7:12). Most scholarly interpretations of Jesus's comment see it as more than a mere ethical commonplace; in its context, it grows out of the commandment to love God and one's neighbor. In 22:40 Matthew reports that when Jesus said we should love God and should love our neighbor as ourself, he added, "On these two commandments hang all the law and the prophets."

2. *Noting Down.* One way to teach this story is to ask students why a congregation might expect each new leader to write down a new regulation. The text does not tell us, but presumably the implication is that a new leader has some insight, some way of furthering his congregation to behave virtuously, and he ought to put this insight into writing. Such a principle sounds plausible enough—at least it is plausible enough for the reader to keep reading—and then we get the complication in this simple plot: Rabbi Shmelke "put it off from day to day." What, we wonder, is the matter with the rabbi, why is he stalling? The teller of the tale devotes two additional sentences to a report that the rabbi did not comply, thus building the suspense (the reader shares the emotion of Gwendolyn in *The Importance of Being Earnest:* "The suspense is terrible. I hope it will last"), and then comes the eminently satisfying resolution, when the rabbi writes the Ten Commandments. The rabbi has done what Ezra Pound (if we may mention an anti-Semite in this context) says all good writers do: "Make it new." That is, Rabbi Shmelke revivified the old truths, made his congregation see them freshly.

3. *The Recipient.* We believe that our question in the text is niggling, but we ask it in an effort to help students to think hard about the story. True, Zusya is mistaken when he tells the rich man that he gave without thinking about to whom he was giving. Of course the rich man had thought about the object of his charity—he had chosen Zusya because Zusya was desperately poor and was devout. But in the context of the story we are to feel that the rich man was originally motivated not by a spirit of calculation but by a generous impulse. And in a world governed by a loving God, such action is rewarded. The loving action of man, we might say, provokes a loving reaction from God. The story ends with a sort of a joke: when the rich man began "to seek out especially noble and distinguished recipients, God did exactly the same." Of course we are not to

believe that in fact God became as calculating (and selfish) as the rich man. But we can believe that this rich man, despite his wealth, was no longer "noble and distinguished," i.e., no longer acting morally, and so God turned to others.

FRANZ KAFKA
Before the Law (p. 1240)

"Before the Law" is short enough for you and your students to make your way through it line-by-line. Kafka's writing often strikes many students as all too ominously (and obscurely) allegorical, and they may have some trouble figuring out what are the probable and possible meanings of this story. We are not sure about these ourselves! But we have found that if we move patiently through the text, we can convey to the students the interest and effectiveness of Kafka's work as a writer, however much his point (to use a simplifying term we should avoid) may prove elusive.

"The Law" may refer to the laws of the land, or the Mosaic law (that is, the ancient law of the Hebrews, attributed to Moses and contained in the Pentateuch), or perhaps to an authority or power or fate mightier still. What does "admittance to the Law" mean? Well, we thought as we began our first reading that the answer is, the "man from the country" simply wants to become a lawyer. But the story suggests more than that. "Admittance" means: (1) the act of admitting or entering; (2) permission to enter. To gain "admittance to the law" is, we think, to be granted access to an inner understanding of it—not only what the Law is but also what makes the Law what it is and who, ultimately, defines and administers it. Passing through the doorway thus may imply passing evermore deeply and profoundly into the formidable mystery of the Law until, perhaps, its truth is reached and apprehended.

There are touches in the story that give to it a grim humor—the scary gatekeeper, for instance, whose appearance prompts the man from the country to take a seat (on a stool, not a chair) and remain there. He has a Tartar beard. (A Tartar is a member of any of the Turkish and Mongolian peoples of central Asia who invaded Western Asia and Eastern Europe in the Middle Ages, or, more generally, a person regarded as ferocious or violent.) The poor persistent "man from the country" suffers one disappointment after another, concluding, finally, that only a bribe may do the trick. But the bribe fails: the doorkeeper has an answer to that, one that drives home to the man from the country his own insufficiency: he must think of everything, but nothing he will think of will win him the "admittance" he seeks.

This is all puzzling enough, yet clearly presented in its own strange way. The truly challenging part comes when the aged man from the country senses a "radiance" (the emission of heat or light, glowing or beaming) from the "gateway of the Law." There is something wondrous (though the source is at a distance) that bears witness to the rightness, one might propose, of the man's intense, prolonged wish to enter through the door.

The man, it should be noted, while powerless, has a measure of dignity. He is importunate (troublesomely urgent or persistent in requesting; pressingly entreating); he does not give up and return home; and he wins from the gatekeeper the acknowledgment, "you are insatiable" (impossible to satiate or satisfy). And the final lines are unnerving but also a compliment, however harsh in tone: this gate was made only for the man from the country, for no one else. He will never enter, but it is not stated that anyone else will either, assuming (a big assumption, perhaps) that there is a special and separate gate for each of them, too. It is, on the one hand, terrifying to be singled out, yet, on the other hand, there is something grimly comforting in knowing that one has indeed been singled out.

Edy Sagarra and Peter Skrine, in *A Companion to German Literature: 1500 to the Present* (1999), speak of Kafka's penetration "behind the surface of everyday reality" and his ability to "lay bare its deeper paradoxes and implications" (p. 199). Working with this observation, you might ask students what is "on the surface" of Kafka's story and what, in turn, might lie behind or beneath it. On a related note, the Kafka entry in *The Oxford Companion to German Literature* (3rd ed., 1997) refers to "Kafka's highly symbolical and oblique style of writing which makes his work subject to widely divergent interpretations" (p. 440). Here again, you might invite the students to consider whether a discussion of the story leads us to an interpretation we more or less agree on or, instead, to very different interpretations that may not fit together.

The books and essays on Kafka that we have read could prove a little difficult, even intimidating, for most students. We have found helpful Frederick C. DeCoste, "Kafka, Legal Theorizing and Redemption," *Mosaic: A Journal for the Interdisciplinary Study of Literature* 27:4 (December 1994): 161–178. About Kafka and the law, he concludes:

> Kafkian jurisprudence is a jurisprudence of despair. There are no alternatives in history, and there is no alternative but history. Furthermore, because history is dystopic, there is no possibility of a coherent future, and no opportunity to reshape our moral and communal lives and commitments. We are, instead, forever condemned to the estranging and alienating now.

This is certainly bleak, and it accurately reflects the main force of "Before the Law." But, in our view, there are line-to-line perplexities, bits of tough humor, and details of characterization (which need not be there, but which Kafka wants there) that play against or complicate the argument that DeCoste advances.

We have also benefited from Robert Alter, "Franz Kafka: Wrenching Scripture," *New England Review* 21:3 (Summer 2000): 7–19. He does not examine "Before the Law," but his commentary on Kafka's novel *Amerika* brings out cogently this writer's relation to the Bible. *Amerika,* says Alter,

> invokes an elaborate network of conflated allusions to Genesis and Exodus, which are thematically imperative, for all their transmogrification in a fantasized American setting. This use of biblical materials in a modern setting, at

once playful and thematically serious, reflects both the after-life of authority and the altered standing of the Bible in modernist writing.

"Before the Law" has the quality of a parable, or of a Biblical episode, maybe a little like the Book of Job (e.g., "he curses his bad luck"). Possibly, in line with Alter's essay, one could see Kafka to be writing modernist scripture, Biblical stories without God in them.

For good overviews, see George Steiner, "Man of Letters," *The New Yorker*, May 28, 1990; Gabriel Josipovici, "The Dream Fulfilled: Kafka's Search for His True Voice," *Times Literary Supplement*, October 8, 1993; David Foster Wallace, "Laughing with Kafka," *Harper's Magazine*, July 1998; and Cynthia Ozick, "The Impossibility of Being Kafka," *The New Yorker*, January 11, 1999. For biography: Frederick R. Karl, *Franz Kafka, Representative Man* (1991).

Elizabeth Bishop
The Hanging of the Mouse (p. 1242)

Most students will be familiar with animal fables, especially perhaps those of Aesop (we give one of Aesop's fables earlier in this chapter), the semi-legendary Greek slave of the sixth century BC. They may never have read any of the fables, but they will have heard of such memorable characters as the ant and the grasshopper, the tortoise and the hare, and the dog in the manger. They will know, too, that such fables are characterized by (1) animals who have human traits, especially human weaknesses, and by (2) a moral, usually explicitly set forth at the end.

Bishop's little animal story is somewhat different. True, the animals reveal human foibles, but there is no explicit authorial moral statement at the end. The narrator apparently merely reports an episode and lets it go at that. In fact, when we read Bishop's story we probably make a pretty clear mental distinction between the narrator who tells the story and the author who wrote it. The narrator earnestly reports what he or she (let's say "he," for the sake of simplicity) sees. Thus, "a vague feeling of celebration"—there will be a public hanging!—fills the air on the night preceding the event. The animals decide "several times" (i.e., they are an irresolute, irrational bunch, unaware of their motives and purposes) to "wander about the town," and then, since it is late, this mindless crew decides it is "only sensible" (we always assure ourselves that our actions are "sensible") to arrive at the square in time for the hanging.

In short, despite some sophisticated vocabulary such as "lassitude" in the first paragraph, the narrator is of the type customarily called an *innocent eye*, or a *naive narrator*, or an *unrealiable narrator*. This narrator is impressed, for instance, by the brisk military behavior of the "two enormous brown beetles in the traditional picturesque armor of an earlier day," and because he is impressed by their precision he is faintly annoyed by the mouse, whose inept behavior somewhat spoils the otherwise impressive show.

> They came on to the square through the small black door and marched between the lines of soldiers standing at attention: straight ahead, to the right, around two sides of the hollow square, to the left, and out into the middle where the gallows stood. Before each turn the beetle on the right glanced quickly at the beetle on the left; their traditional long, long antennae swerved sharply in the direction they were to turn and they did it to perfection. The mouse, of course, who had had no military training and who, at the moment, was crying so hard he could scarcely see where he was going, rather spoiled the precision and snap of the beetles.

If in class you read this passage aloud and invite students to give their ideas of what sort of person the narrator is, you probably will find that they see the very considerable limitations of the narrator. And you can then ask them if they think the narrator and the author hold identical views. Or you may want to read the next two sentences:

> At each corner [the mouse] fell slightly forward, and when he was jerked in the right direction his feet became tangled together. The beetles, however, without even looking at him, each time lifted him quickly into the air for a second until his feet were untangled.

The professionalism of the beetles can hardly be questioned, but surely their efficiency (and the implied indifference to the wretched mouse) appalls the reader, though not the narrator. Incidentally, in the penultimate paragraph the narrator again notices the mouse's feet: When the trap is sprung, the mouse's "feet flew up and curled into little balls like young fern-plants." The narrator's almost aesthetic perception of physical appearances is keen, making the imperception of brutality the more heartbreaking.

Thus far Bishop has been almost Swiftian in her irony, though Swift (who said his life was characterized by *saeva indignatio,* "savage indignation") is rarely so restrained. In her final paragraph Bishop becomes a little more direct (can one say "obvious"?), when she writes that the cat, concerned that the squirming and shrieking kitten may have experienced too much, nevertheless takes comfort in the thought the kitten has learned "an excellent moral lesson." Exactly what, you may want to ask students, *is* the lesson? That crime does not pay? Bishop is careful *not* to tell us what the mouse's offense is. No one in the crowd, apparently, knows what the condemned mouse has done that merits death, and certainly the impressively costumed frog who in an impressive voice reads the charge from an impressive-looking scroll gives no clue as to what the offender did that merits execution. In short, the "excellent moral lesson" that concludes a fable here is unstated, though perhaps we find ourselves saying that the story is about human blindness.

We hope that students will see in Bishop's verbal performance witty touches (the beetles in picturesque armor, the raccoon as the masked executioner), keen perception of detail (again, those tiny mouse feet curling "into little balls like young fern-plants"), and implicit in this unemotional voice the author's awareness of the horror.

Students who value Bishop might be advised to turn to her *Complete Poems, 1927–1979* (1983). Her *Collected Prose* (1984) and *Letters* (1994) are also stimulating—excellent sources for studying this important poet. Also rewarding: *Conversations with Elizabeth Bishop,* ed. George Monteiro (1996), and Gary Fountain, *Remembering Elizabeth Bishop: An Oral Biography* (1994).

Ursula K. Le Guin
The Ones Who Walk Away from Omelas (p. 1244)

When Thomas More called his book *Utopia,* he punned on the Greek "good place" *(eu topos)* and on "no place" *(ou topos).* Like all the rest of us, he knew that the fully happy society is "no place," if only because accidents, disease, and death are part of life. Le Guin's narrator gives us a fairly detailed description of an imagined happy society—Omelas is "bright-towered by the sea," the old celebrants in the festival wear "long stiff robes of mauve and grey," and the boys and girls are "naked in the bright air, with mud-stained feet and ankles and long, lithe arms"—but the narrator also is vague about many things that we would dearly like to know. For instance, although the narrator tells us that there is no king and there are no slaves in Omelas, the narrator also makes a confession, "I do not know the rules and laws of their society. . . ." The story includes other confessions of ignorance, and at one point the narrator, aware that the narrative thus far has been unconvincing and fairy-tale like (e.g., those bright towers by the sea), almost gives up, and urges the reader to imagine Omelas "as your own fancy bids."

Doubtless Le Guin is vague about important matters because she—like everyone else—cannot depict a convincing Utopia that can withstand scrutiny. But she is also vague for a more important reason: she is not earnestly writing a Utopian tale like, say, Edward Bellamy's *Looking Backward.* Rather, she is raising a moral problem, or, more exactly, she is amplifying a problem that William James had raised. Omelas need not be a convincing presentation of the perfectly happy life, and indeed the narrator makes Omelas most convincing when he (or she?) prefaces the information about the suffering child with these words: "Do you believe? Do you accept the festival, the city, the joy? No? Then let me describe one more thing." When we learn about the wretched child, Omelas becomes much more believable, for we are all aware that much of our happiness in fact depends on the suffering of others. These others may be the exploited workers whose painful labor allows us to eat and dress well; they may be the sick, whose ills make some physicians prosperous; they may be the aggrieved, whose lawsuits pay the college tuition for the children of lawyers; they may even be the suffering animals whose pain in medical laboratories may help to alleviate our own pain. In short, whoever we are, some of our happiness depends on the misfortunes of other creatures—and at times we are aware of this fact. Le Guin's happy city now becomes easily understandable: it is an image not of an ideal world but of our world.

Where a parable usually evokes a fairly clear moral and leaves us in little doubt about how we ought to act, this story leaves us puzzled. It heightens our awareness of a cruel fact of society, but it does not tell us how we can reform our society. Put another way, where does one go when one walks away from Omelas? Can we really envisage the possibility of a happy life that is not in any way based on suffering and injustice somewhere? Is the story therefore pointless, mere fantasy, mere escapism? Presumably Le Guin is simply seeking to make us think, so that we will learn to act in ways that minimize the suffering of others. It is inconceivable that life will ever be Utopian, but it is not inconceivable that injustice and human suffering may be reduced.

Topics for Critical Thinking and Writing

1. How convincing does the narrator think the picture of Omelas is? Why do you suppose that Le Guin did not offer details about the laws of the land? Does Omelas become more convincing when we learn about the child?
2. Characterize the narrator.
3. What is the point of walking away from Omelas? Can the walker go to a better society? If not, is the story pointless? (Put another way, the story is a fantasy, but is it also escapist fiction?)
4. If you were ever greatly bothered by an experience in which you realized that your happiness depended at least in part on the unhappiness of another, describe the situation, your response, and your present feelings.

WILLIAM FAULKNER
Barn Burning (p. 1249)

Against his vision of the ideals of the Confederacy, embodied in Major de Spain and Colonel Sartoris in much of Faulkner's writing, Faulkner sets his vision of a more widely held ideal—cunning and self-centeredness—embodied in the Snopes family. (Flem Snopes, the older brother in "Barn Burning," is a major character in *The Town, The Mansion,* and *The Hamlet;* Abner Snopes, the father in "Barn Burning," is a lesser character in *The Unvanquished* and in *The Hamlet.* But the boy, Colonel Sartoris Snopes, does not appear in the novels.)

It would be wrong, however, to see the Snopes family—and especially, here, Abner Snopes—as merely contemptible. Abner's single-mindedness, however unlovely and destructive, gives him a hero's aspect, for example when he walks resolutely on toward the great house and refuses to deviate by even a single step that would enable him to avoid stepping in the horse-dung. Abner Snopes has, we might say, something of the air of the tragic hero who, like Job confronted with what seems to be an assault on his integrity, will maintain his own ways even before God. He has, in Faulkner's words, a "ferocious conviction in the rightness of his own actions." Or, to quote again, a deep sense of the importance of "the preservation of integrity, else breath were not worth the breathing." This second passage, by the way, comes in the discussion of "the niggard blaze" that is part of Snopes's way of life. Coupled with the burning barns, it suggests that Snopes is a Promethean figure—not the Prometheus of the ancients, who gave fire to man out of pity, but a romantic Promethean figure who sets his blaze in defiance of authority.

As we read "Barn Burning" we are reminded of Alfred North Whitehead's comment that tragedy shows us "the remorseless working of things," an action that cannot be stopped, partly because the hero, insisting on asserting himself, is determined that it shall not be stopped. We can scarcely *like* Snopes, but we can scarcely fail to admire (especially in the older sense of "wonder at," "be awed by") him. Indeed, if we compare Major de Spain's justifiable but somewhat fussy anger over the rug ("You must realize you have ruined that rug") with Snopes's smoldering rage at any limitations imposed on him, we may feel that Snopes is by far the more vital figure. One notes, too, and cannot dismiss, Snopes's charge that Major de Spain's big white house has been built out of "sweat. Nigger sweat. Maybe it ain't white enough to suit him. Maybe he wants to mix some white sweat with it." We may feel that in large measure Snopes's ruthlessness proceeds from a sense of social inferiority, but we can scarcely deny that he offers a telling criticism of his social superiors.

Finally, a few words about Sarty, the boy. He too is a sort of hero, moved by the most painful kind of conflict—not good with evil but good with good, for he must choose between his sense of decency and his sense of loyalty to the family.

In his entry on "Barn Burning" in *A William Faulkner Encyclopedia* (1999), Charles A. Peek surveys the range of critical commentary. As he indicates, "Barn Burning" has usually been described as a story about Sarty's "coming of age." "Readings of this sort" says Peek, "emphasize the psychological and mythical implications of Sarty's conflict with his father. They tend to accept Sarty's final rebellion as ethically correct and to emphasize the evil—even demonic—aspects of Ab's behavior." More recent critics, however, have taken a different approach. As Peek explains, "they have sought to 'decenter' the story by emphasizing the social and economic sources of Ab's anger":

> While not excusing Ab's behavior, these readings tend to question the ideological sophistication and ethical correctness of Sarty's rebellion . . . . Critics interested in decentering the story have also emphasized how highly the narrator's negative rendering of Ab Snopes is colored by Sarty's anxiety and fear. (28–29)

For further discussion, consult *Faulkner and the Short Story: Faulkner and Yoknapatawpha, 1990,* ed. Evans Harrington and Ann J. Abadie (1992); Diane Brown Jones, *A Reader's Guide to the Short Stories of William Faulkner* (1994); and Hans H. Skei, *Reading Faulkner's Best Short Stories* (1999).

JAMES ALAN MCPHERSON
An Act of Prostitution (p. 1261)

Some students may—at least at first—be disturbed by some of the language, especially the racial epithets (e.g., "two-bit Jew shyster" in paragraph 9, "nigger" in paragraph 22), but they can easily understand that the characters are using these terms, not McPherson. And they can easily see that the really horrible "act of prostitution" is performed by the judge, not by Philomena Brown.

When the judge gets a serious case in court (the soldier, Irving Williams) he passes the buck, since he is not genuinely concerned with administering justice but only with satisfying his own ego by getting easy laughs from his audience. The Williams episode, unnecessary in terms of advancing the story, is important in terms of what it reveals about the judge and the doings of his court.

Laughter plays a large role in the story, so it is worth asking students *why* people laugh. Philomena is "always good for a laugh" (17 and 22), everyone will have "a good laugh" at Philomena's expense (26), people visit the court "to watch the fun" (46) "the entire court was laughing" (182), "there was here a roar of laughter from the court" (187), "Now everyone laughed again" (198). Again, *why* do people laugh? Laughter can be evoked by tickling, by anxiety, and by laughing gas (nitrous oxide), but most literary studies of laughter exclude such forces and concentrate on the relation between laughter and comedy. Many books—usually unfunny—have been written on the topic; for a fairly short guide to theories of laughter, we recommend D. H. Monro, *Argument of Laughter* (1951), old but still useful. And of course there is Henri Bergson's classic, *On Laughter* (1900), but Bergson is chiefly talking about the humor evoked by characters who act rigidly when life demands flexibility. His famous example concerns customs officers who heroically rescue passengers from a shipwreck and then, when they are ashore, ask, "Have you anything to declare?" This bit does indeed nicely illustrate his formula that the comic shows us the mechanical encrusted on the living. But the laughter evoked in McPherson's story is a bit different; it is the "sudden glory" that Hobbes famously spoke of, i.e., the spectator's sudden awareness of superiority, as when we see a fat man running after his wind-blown hat. The idea here is that *we* would never behave in so undignified a way.

A classic example is the business of someone slipping on a banana peel—again, the loss of control makes us laugh—*but* Bergson points out that we must not feel sympathy for the victim. There must be, in his words, "anesthesia of the heart." The archetype here is the cartoon cat that chases a mouse, smashes into the wall, sees stars, but a moment later is again chasing the mouse. We can laugh because we know it is only a cartoon cat, not something with feelings that can make a claim for our sympathy.

Now, why do the laughers in the judge's court (including the judge and the lawyers) not feel sympathy for Philomena? And here we get to some nasty business. She is fat, she is ill-educated, she is married to a "nigger," and she is a whore. In other words, so far as the judge and the others are concerned, she is scarcely a sentient human being; she is merely something ridiculous. The laughter that goes round the courtroom reminds us of what is called Homeric laughter, the laughter of the gods when they see the naked Mars and Venus, caught in Vulcan's net. Mars and Venus of course are not devoid of feelings, but at this moment their powerlessness makes them so ungodlike that the other gods cannot help but laugh at them.

McPherson's story of course is not a comic story—far from it—but we think (we may be sticking our heads out, or showing our own insensitivity) that a reader may indeed find an occasional passage funny. If we are correct, we are touching on an important issue. Take, for instance, the episode in which the judge asks a hangover defendant, "When was the last time you gave something to your wife?" The man says, "I help" (59), and the judge replies, "You help, all right. You help her raise her belly and her income every year." The pedant in us says, "Hey, a nice use of zeugma, where 'help' cleverly stands in the same grammatical relation to 'belly' as it does to 'income' but with a change in its meaning." (The most famous example in English of zeugma is Pope's line in *The Rape of the Lock*: "Or stain her honor, or her new brocade.") But if we smile at the judge's line, we are immediately ashamed of ourselves, or we should be. Or take what may be a clearer example: The judge says that when Philomena—whose girth has been emphasized—gets out of jail she should "keep off the streets. You're obstructing traffic." McPherson tells us that the line evoked "laughter from the entire courtroom"—and maybe it makes the reader smile a bit too. If so, we are guilty, at least a little, of the callousness exhibited by the others. We have acted indecently, committed an act of prostitution.

For students seeking a discussion of McPherson's literary career up to the mid-1990s, we recommend Herman Beavers, *Wrestling Angels into Song: The Fictions of Ernest J. Gaines and James Alan McPherson* (1995). Also stimulating is Jon Wallace, "The Politics of Style in Three Stories by James Alan McPherson," *Modern Fiction Studies* 34 (Spring 1988): 17–26. For a cogent account of McPherson's skills as a writer of stories, see ZZ Packer, "Mad Hope and Mavericks," *Poets & Writers* 30:1 (Jan./Feb. 2002): 54–56, which highlights his blend of "tragic and comic" elements.

Often we have found that students enjoy reading interviews with writers. You might direct them to Trent Masiki, "James Alan McPherson: Consistently Himself," *Poets & Writers* 29:2 (March/Apr. 2001): 34–39, where he describes his early literary success and place in the literary community. For an earlier interview, see Bob Shacochis and Dan Campion, "Interview with James Alan McPherson," *Iowa Journal of Literary Studies* 4:1 (1983): 6–33.

RALPH ELLISON
Battle Royal (p. 1272)

The term "battle royal" has two chief meanings: (1) a fight involving several or many contestants, and (2) a bitterly fought battle. Both meanings are relevant to this story, most obviously in the contest between the boys in the ring, and almost as obviously in the battle between blacks and whites.

The battle between blacks and whites in many ways is evident enough to all of the participants, but in two important ways it is not evident to some of them. First, the whites presumably did not perceive that the narrator's grandfather was a traitor and a spy; presumably they mistakenly accepted his feigned acquiescence as genuine submission, not realizing that in fact he was an enemy, maintaining his ideals in the only way available to him. Second, the narrator, who in his youth accepted the traditional answers, did not understand that a war was going on, or ought to be going on. In his immaturity he sought to please the whites, subjecting himself to all sorts of indignities—not only by fighting against blacks for the amusement of whites and grabbing for counterfeit coins on an electrified rug but also by giving a speech that he thinks is impressive but reduces him to a puppet mouthing ideas that lend support to his enemy. He is so unaware of his plight that even during the fisticuffs he wonders if his speech will impress his audience. (Ellison emphasizes the point a little later in various ways, for instance when the M.C. introduces the boy as someone who "knows more big words than a pocket-sized dictionary," and when the narrator tells us that he was swallowing his own blood while giving his speech to the amused audience.) As the narrator says at the beginning of the story, it took him a long time to realize that he must be himself—not the creature that white society wants him to be—and that as far as white society goes, a black is an invisible man, i.e., a person of no identity.

As long as he accepts the role the whites give him, he serves the purpose of whites. In fact, because he is verbally talented, he is extremely useful to whites; he will persuade other blacks to perceive themselves as the whites perceive them. As the school superintendent puts it, the boy will "lead his people in the proper paths." Thus the scholarship is used by the whites to strengthen their army by recruiting a man who betrays the blacks. If the narrator had not ultimately come to understand this, he would have become a traitor of a sort very different from his grandfather. Fortunately, however, the nightmarish experience of the battle and the subsequent speech are balanced by another sort of nightmare, a dream (presided over by his grandfather) in which the briefcase contains not a scholarship but a note: "Keep This Nigger-Boy Running." (The message is rooted in a horrible practical joke, in which a white plantation owner would send an illiterate African American to another plantation owner, with a letter supposedly recommending the bearer but which actually said, "Keep This Nigger-Boy Running." The second owner would say he could not offer a job, but would recommend that the bearer go to a third plantation, and so on.) The narrator's dream is as real as the battle, and more real than the scholarship, since the scholarship (though of course literally real) was not at all what the young man had thought it was.

"Battle Royal" became part of Ellison's novel, *Invisible Man* (1952). On this important book, see *New Essays on Invisible Man*, ed. Robert G. O'Meally (1988), and *Approaches to Teaching Ellison's Invisible Man*, ed. Susan Parr and Pancho Savery (1989). All students of modern and contemporary American and

African-American literatures should explore *The Collected Essays of Ralph Ellison,* ed. John F. Callahan (1995). Another essential resource is *Conversations with Ralph Ellison,* ed. Amritjit Singh and Maryemma Graham (1995).

GORDON PARKS
Ralph Ellison (photograph, p. 1273)

For centuries it has been said that the aim of portraiture is not to give an accurate representation of the face but to reveal the mind; or, in Horace's formulation in *Epistles* II, i, do both: *"Suspendit picta vultum mentemque tabella"* ("In painting, he shows both the face and the mind"). Or in the words of Chesterfield, writing to his son in 1747, "By portraits I do not mean the outlines and the coloring of the human figure, but the inside of the heart and mind of man." That the face does not reveal the personality we can easily verify by flipping through our high school yearbook, where we see familiar faces but not (for the most part) the *people* whom we knew. After all, as Prufrock tells us, we "prepare a face to meet the faces that [we] meet."

And yet we continue (perhaps correctly) to hold the view that the faces we create are indeed revealing. Eric Ambler, the English writer of thrillers, has a comment in *A Coffin for Dimitrios* (1939) that seems to us as shrewd as anything else that anyone has said about faces:

> A man's features, the bone structure and the tissue which covers it, are the product of a biological process; but his face he creates for himself. It is a statement of his habitual emotional attitude; the attitude which his desires need for their fulfillment and which his fears demand for their protection from prying eyes. He wears it like a devil mask; a device to evoke in others the emotion complementary to his own. If he is afraid, then he must be feared; if he desires, then he must be desired. It is a screen to his mind's nakedness. Only a few men, painters, have been able to see the mind through the face. (pp. 247–248)

What can we say of Gordon Parks's portrait of Ellison? First, it is a picture of a writer without any of the visible attributes of a writer. No book-lined study, no desk with a typewriter, no pen in hand. Ellison is shown out of what we would expect to be his usual element. In fact, he is isolated: he is out of doors, in a park, but he has no companion and there are not even any casual strollers in the distance. Further, judging from the bare trees and from Ellison's buttoned-up coat, the season is early or late winter, not the most hospitable time of year. He is seated, and seated portraits (in contrast to pictures of standing figures) usually suggest that the subject is comfortable, at ease, but here we get a different impression. The left arm is awkwardly bent, and the eyes look off to the viewer's left although the face is turned toward the viewer's right, suggesting tension. The bench on which Ellison sits, with its skeletal structure of narrow boards and twisting iron arms and legs, also suggests a wound-up mechanism. On the other hand, there Ellison is, smack in the middle of the frame, dominating the scene, his head highlighted against the sky. He says in effect, "All right, I'll sit here and let you take my picture, but I'm not going to let you show me as 'Eminent and beloved man of letters.'" What Parks has given us is very much Ellison the private man, the writer-as-observant-outsider.

A word about the photographer: Born in Fort Scott, Kansas, in 1912, Parks worked as a news correspondent before joining the staff at *Life* magazine as a photojournalist (1949–1970). In addition to his photography and journalism, he has written poetry and fiction, composed both popular songs and sonatas, and directed films. From September 10, 1997, to January 11, 1998, a major retrospective devoted to Parks's work was held at the Corcoran Gallery of Art, Washington, D.C.; it then moved on to a number of other museums across the nation. To accompany this exhibit, Bullfinch Press published a beautiful volume with 300 of Parks's best photographs: *Half-Past Autumn: A Retrospective* (1997). It features a wide range of his work, including portraits of Winston Churchill, Duke Ellington, Ingrid Bergman, Malcolm X, Eldridge Cleaver, and Muhammad Ali, along with his own narrative commentary.

You might also wish to consult Martin H. Bush, *The Photographs of Gordon Parks* (1983), the catalog for an exhibit held at various museums from April 1983 to August 1985. For an interview with Parks, see John Loengard, *Life Photographers: What They Saw* (1998).

BOOKER T. WASHINGTON
Atlanta Exposition Address (p. 1282)

Booker T. Washington is one of the most important figures in American and African-American history. He was born a slave in 1856 in Virginia, where racism was rampant and opportunities for education and advancement for a black child were almost nonexistent. But through hard work, determination, and good fortune, he rose from discrimination and poverty to a position of great renown and influence.

After graduating from Hampton Normal and Agricultural Institute in 1875 and serving as a member of its staff, Washington in 1881 took the lessons he had learned there to Tuskegee, Alabama, where he had been offered the job of heading up and building a new school for African Americans. Starting from scratch, Washington made Tuskegee Institute into a major institution, dedicated to moral uplift and industrial education. By 1915, the year of his death, the school that Washington established had an enrollment of 1,500 students, an outstanding 200-person faculty and staff, and an endowment of two million dollars.

It is often said that in his speeches, writings, and programs, Washington sacrificed political and civil rights—that he acquiesced in the ongoing racist and segregationist policies that the white South imposed on black people—but this is somewhat misleading. Washington did not assert that African Americans should never be allowed to vote or to enjoy fair and equal treatment. Rather, he stressed that black men and women should focus first on self-improvement, education in the basics (e.g., in personal hygiene), and training in the trades and industrial arts (bricklaying, carpentry, and agriculture, for instance). Once blacks possessed and displayed their "merit" (a key word for Washington), they would not need to battle and agitate for their rights—and such campaigns, in Washington's view, had in the past usually been counter-productive for and costly to black people. Instead, blacks would find, through their demonstrations of their worth and self-reliance, that Southerners and the American people as a whole would gladly welcome them into the national community.

Washington's most memorable expression of his views came in a speech, September 18, 1895, at the Atlanta Exposition, where he declared: "In all things that are purely social we can be separate as the fingers, yet one as the hand in all things essential to mutual progress." Whites throughout the country applauded Washington's words, hearing in them the implication that Washington and African Americans in general were content with the racial status quo. Washington knew that this would be their response, and he knew as well that this response would lead to stature, power, and influence for himself and financial support for his school and its affiliated institutions: he was telling whites what they wanted to hear. But, again, it is significant that Washington suggested only that blacks should postpone or suspend their campaign for their full measure of rights—which is different from saying that they should be content with where they were and should not move beyond that.

To the more militant and confrontational W. E. B. Du Bois (1868–1915) and other black leaders, however, Washington's approach was both dangerous and wrong. In their estimation, it encouraged whites to perpetuate racist ideas and practices that were, in fact, at odds with the clear guarantees of equality in the Declaration of Independence, the Constitution, and the amendments to the Constitution that had been passed and ratified in the aftermath of the Civil War. Du Bois argued powerfully that blacks should not defer their campaigns for social and political rights: these rights belonged to them; they were their due.

In our teaching of this selection, we have found that students are, at least initially, highly critical of Washington. To them, Washington is an arch compromiser, someone who coddles up to white authority and allows, for his own advantage, racism and segregation to remain in place, victimizing black people. But we try to remind students that the situation c. 1900, especially in the South, was very different from what it is today.

As the historian Howard N. Rabinowitz has noted, summing up the state of race relations in the late nineteenth and early twentieth centuries:

> Amid increased lynchings and antiblack political rhetoric, a coalition of Black Belt planters, elite townspeople, and agrarian radicals disfranchised blacks and passed state and local statutes that extended segregation to cover such new facilities as phone booths and water fountains, legalized long customary discriminatory practices in public accommodations, and eliminated whatever flexibility had survived in public conveyances. In *Plessy v. Ferguson* (1896), a

case that grew out of a Louisiana statute requiring segregation on the state's railroads, the U.S. Supreme Court held that such separation was constitutional as long as both races received equal treatment. That rarely occurred, but only in *Buchanan v. Warley* (1917), a decision that declared legally enforced residential segregation unconstitutional, was any form of segregation successfully challenged in court. A combination of white discrimination and, to a lesser extent, black choice produced widespread de facto segregation in southern housing. An occasional facility remained integrated into the twentieth century (normally where the lower classes of both races intermingled), and vestiges of exclusion persisted, but by the turn of the century the policy of separate but unequal treatment of the races had become firmly entrenched in the South. (*The Reader's Companion to American History*, ed. Eric Foner and John Garraty, 1991)

Did Washington's theory and practice reinforce racism or, rather, was it a realistic, pragmatic response to racism? Maybe Washington was a compromiser because he had no other choice. Perhaps, that is, he was a keen, savvy politician who worked as productively as he could within a very severe set of social, political, and economic constraints.

Washington's autobiography, *Up from Slavery* (1901), from which our selection is taken, is a fascinating work, a best-seller in its time and a complex and, indeed, elusive rhetorical performance. For background and context, see Louis R. Harlan, *Booker T. Washington: The Making of a Black Leader, 1856–1901* (1972), and *Booker T. Washington: The Wizard of Tuskegee, 1901–1915* (1983).

CHARLES KECK
The Booker T. Washington Memorial (photograph, p. 1284)

Traditionally sculpture has served one or more of several functions—votive, decorative, commemorative—but in the late nineteenth century and early twentieth centuries in the United States sculpture was chiefly commemorative (think of all the Civil War memorials). Clearly the *Booker T. Washington Memorial* is a commemorative monument; the very word "monument"—from *monere*, "to remind"—tells us what its function is.

In the text we quote (in the caption for the photograph of the monument) these words about Booker T. Washington, inscribed on the sides of the pedestal: "We shall prosper in proportion as we learn to dignify and glorify labor and put brains and skill into the common occupations of life."

The pedestal is also inscribed with three other quotations from Washington's writings: "He lifted the veil of ignorance from his people and pointed the way to progress through education and industry"; "There is no defense or security for any of us except in the highest intelligence and development of all"; and "I will let no man drag me down so low as to make me hate him." An inscription at the rear, by the donors, runs thus: "This monument is erected by contributions from Negroes in the United States as a loving tribute to the memory of their great leader and benefactor."

The larger-than-life monumental bronze statue (the figure is eight feet tall, and it stands on a granite base that also is eight feet tall), in the tradition of heroic sculpture, was of course intended to remind us of the achievements of a great man, in this case as a liberator of the black mind. But even in his lifetime his views were vigorously contested, notably by his slightly younger contemporary, W. E. B. Du Bois. This is not the place to go into Washington's strengths or weaknesses. He is in our text because he is in Ellison's story—you will recall that the narrator says, "I visualized myself as a potential Booker T. Washington," and he quotes from Washington's most famous speech, "The Atlanta Exposition Address" (1895). In this address, Washington urged blacks to "cast down your bucket where you are." The gist of his idea was that, at least for the nonce, blacks should put aside aspirations for social and political equality with whites; instead they should work for advances in education (especially in the trades and crafts) and they should develop the virtues of patience, thrift, and industry. When blacks had won wealth through this combination of training and virtue, Washington believed, whites would grant social acceptance.

Just as Washington's words have been questioned, so too the monument has been questioned, or "interrogated," to use a more fashionable word from today's critical vocabulary. That is, Keck's sculpture, which in its day was rightly regarded as a tribute to Washington, can now be read against the grain, deconstructed, and interpreted in a rather sinister fashion. In this view, Washington stands tall in the white man's clothes. With one hand in patriarchal fashion he frees the black man from superstition and ignorance, and with the other hand he makes a gesture that is intended to indicate a future available to the newly created black, but this gesture also smacks of self-congratulation, rather like the gesture of a stage magician who has just produced a beautiful lady out of a previously empty box. According to this view, which emphasizes the inscriptions, the black man who has not adopted the white man's ways apparently is helpless; black culture, including slave rebellions, personal relationships, and artistic creations, apparently count for nothing. What the freed black man must in effect do, in this view of Washington, is to adopt the white man's culture.

We are not at all happy with this interpretation. We hold a higher view of the sculpture and of Washington than this view can tolerate, but we do understand that works of art mean different things to different people. Today, it seems, in an age of deconstruction, seeing is disbelieving. This well-intentioned and ably executed monument apparently for some viewers sends a politically incorrect message.

Booker T. Washington's career was an extraordinary one, and he told his own story (with the aid of a ghostwriter) in the best-selling autobiography *Up from Slavery* (1901). There is a superb biography: Louis R. Harlan, *Booker T. Washington: The Making of a Black Leader, 1856–1901* (1972), and *Booker T. Washington: The Wizard of Tuskegee, 1901–1915* (1983).

W. E. B. DU BOIS
Of Our Spiritual Strivings (p. 1285)

When we teach Ellison and discuss his examination of Washington's ideas in *Invisible Man*, we often take the opportunity to highlight Du Bois's *The Souls of Black Folk* (1903), where he criticizes Washington's go-slow approach to racial progress.

The Souls of Black Folk is one of the major texts in the African-American tradition, but we do need to report that our students have said they find it tough going, in part because the historical context that Du Bois responds to so vividly feels very distant to them. For your advanced students, *The Souls of Black Folk* remains a book they should know about and explore; but for them and for others, an even better choice may be *Dusk of Dawn: An Essay Toward the Autobiography of a Race Concept* (1940), which includes autobiography, historical commentary, and work in other genres. We admire very much an excellent study of Du Bois's intellectual life and literary and historical work: Arnold Rampersad, *The Art and Imagination of W. E. B. Du Bois* (1976). Another important, richly detailed book on the subject is David L. Lewis, *W. E. B. Du Bois: Biography of a Race, 1868–1919* (1993).

ANONYMOUS
Birmingham Jail (p. 1299)

Many students are familiar with this song, and we have usually been able to recruit a student to sing it in class. The song reads well on the page, but it is better when sung, even when sung by a singer of no special talent, so we urge you to ask your students, the day before you assign the piece, if any of them will sing it—with a guitar—at the next meeting.

All three questions in the text (the first is about variants, the second is about the lack of explanation for the singer's plight, and the third is about why sad songs please the singer and the hearer) can lead to lively discussions in the classroom, but the third seems to us to be the most important, and the one that can get the widest variety of responses.

A. E. HOUSMAN
The Carpenter's Son (p. 1302)

We mention in our headnote that the poem enacts the Crucifixion in a late-nineteenth century guise, and to make certain that students see this connection—since they may not read the headnote—in a footnote we cite some Gospel references.

Perhaps the crucial lines in the poem are 19–20: "All the same's the luck we prove, / Though the midmost hangs for love." In the New Testament, the Greek words for *love* are *agape* and *philia*—not *eros*, which signifies sexual love. Jesus exhorts his hearers to love one another and to love God. God's love for fallen humankind motivated the Incarnation. In Paul's words, "But God commendeth his love toward us, in that, while yet we were sinners, Christ died for us" (Rom 5:8), i.e., died for our benefit. (The New Revised Standard Version is: "But God proves his love for us in that while we still were sinners Christ died for us.") The believer, Paul teaches, is moved not by mere human love but by Christ's gift of love. Having said this, we quickly add that Paul also bases his concept of love in several passages in the Hebrew Bible. For instance, in Galations 5:14 Paul says: ""For all the law is fulfilled in one word, even in this, Thou shalt love thy neighbor as thyself," i.e., Paul quotes Leviticus 19:18: "Thou shalt love thy neighbor as thyself."

Housman's poem works perfectly well as a tour de force, a transmutation of the story of the Crucifixion into a hanging in a rural English setting. The cross has become a gallows, but commentary on the Bible often called the cross a tree. Thus, whereas Adam and Eve brought sin into the world by eating fruit from the tree of knowledge, Christ was said to have brought the possibility of salvation by dying on the tree of the cross. Notice, too, in addition to the presence of two thieves, the anger of the mob, which reminds us of the scorn and anger that the Gospels speak of:

> Now, you see, they hang me high,
> And the people passing by
> Stop to shake their fists and curse;
> So 'tis come from ill to worse.

It is also worth calling attention to the wry line, "Had I but left ill alone," which plays on the familiar line about leaving well alone, i.e., the advice not to try to alter a state of affairs that is already satisfactory. (Cf. the commonplace, "If it ain't broke, don't fix it.") But what Jesus did, when he saw ill, was to mend it by the sacrifice on the cross.

Surely, then, the poem *is* about the Crucifixion. But given our knowledge of Housman's life, it seems reasonable to say that it is also about Housman's own fate, or at least a fate that he imagines, given his sexual orientation, his special kind of love. As we will see in the third and fourth poems that we reprint, Housman regards homosexuality as inborn, genetic, not something that one chooses but something comparable to the color of one's hair (the third poem) or even something that is the result of God's "bedevilment" (line 30 in "The laws of God, the laws of man"). For Housman, to be a homosexual was to be in an "ill" situation—not sick, as in the old psychoanalytic view of homosexuality, but something more like cursed, marked, bedeviled by God. The man who is a homosexual has had a bad break, bad luck—"All the same's the luck we prove, / Though the midmost hang for love." ("The luck we prove" is not easily paraphrased, but perhaps "the bad situation that we endure" comes near to the meaning.) But, again, all of this is presented within the form of a poem about Christ, with the evident ironies: Christ taught love but was scorned; he brought new life to mankind, but only at the cost of his own life.

A. E. HOUSMAN
Eight O'Clock (p. 1303)

A. E. Housman's "Eight O'Clock" is discussed by M. L. Rosenthal and A. J. M. Smith, *Exploring Poetry*, 2nd ed. (1973), pp. 84–85, and by Richard Wilbur, "Alfred Edward Housman," *Anniversary Lectures 1959* (Library of Congress), pp. 42–43. Wilbur points out that we learn almost nothing about the condemned man—not even what his crime was; we get only the last half-minute of his life. A clock strikes eight, the conventional hour for executions in England (before capital punishment was abolished); to the victim, and to the reader, it is a machine that strikes not merely hours but men. Note the ticking (i.e., the *k* sounds) in "clock collected," and the effect of the enjambment in the seventh line, where the clock collects its strength and (after a heavy pause) strikes the hour and ends the man's life.

The Library of Congress owns a notebook draft of the poem, in which lines 3–4 run thus:

> One, two, three, four, on jail and square and people
> They dingled down.

Wilbur points out that the deletion of the reference to the jail is a great improvement. "Suspense," he says, "requires that the reason for the man's intent listening should not be divulged until we come to the second stanza. Contrast requires too that the "morning town," as it is called in the first stanza, be simply presented as a crowded market place down to which the steeple clock almost gaily tosses its chiming quarters."

We are *not* saying that this poem has anything to do with homosexuality, but we do see it as connected with the rest of Housman's work, notably in its empathy for the victim. We get into the man's mind only in line 6: "He stood and counted them and cursed his luck." Again, as in "The Carpenter's Son," Housman introduces "luck," which in his world always means bad luck.

A. E. HOUSMAN
Oh who is that young sinner (p. 1303)

In our headnote we comment on the link between this poem and the imprisonment of Oscar Wilde. As we said in commenting on "The Carpenter's Son," with its talk of "luck" (line 19), Housman sees homosexuality as a matter of bad luck—this was long before the days of Gay Pride—or even as a matter of

God's "bedevilment" (line 16 in "The laws of God," though in fact Housman was an atheist from his early years). The form is a Kiplingesque ballad—"Danny Deever" (1890) comes to mind, so we quote the first four lines. (On p. 456 of this chapter in the manual we quote the entire poem.)

> "What are the bugles blowin' for?" said Files-on-Parade.
> "To turn you out, to turn you out," the Color-Sergeant said.
> "What makes you look so white, so white?" said Files-on-Parade.
> "I'm dreadin' what I've got to watch," the Color-Sergeant said.

What is the offense of this prisoner (Wilde, and but for the grace of God, Housman)? "The color of his hair," i.e., some innate quality, something he cannot have wished for or created for himself. Who created him thus? Well, the last line of the poem is, "He can curse the God that made him for the colour of his hair." Few people in Housman's day would have agreed that homosexuality was inborn, and indeed the causes of homosexuality are still hotly debated today, but Housman unambiguously says that it is not a matter of choice. It is something imposed on one.

It's interesting to discuss the speaker of the poem with students. The first line is spoken by some sort of innocent eye, "Oh who is that young sinner with the handcuffs on his wrists?" That is, the speaker sees a handcuffed man, and, law-abiding fellow that the speaker is, he assumes the man must be guilty of something or other, hence the prisoner is a sinner, but the speaker's tone is not especially hostile. Between the fourth and fifth lines he has learned what the offense is, and in the fifth line he says, "Oh they're taking him to prison for the colour of his hair."

And now, at the start of the second stanza, the reader is in for something of a shock:

> 'Tis shame to human nature, such a head of hair as his;
> In the good old time 'twas hanging for the colour that it is;
> Though hanging isn't bad enough and flaying would be fair
> For the nameless and abominable colour of his hair.

That is, once the speaker has learned what the offense is—presumably in the gap between the first and second stanzas—he expresses the horror and rage typical of the time, *not* horror and rage at the injustice of imprisoning a man for "the colour of his hair," but horror and rage at a man who dares to have such a head of hair, as though there were an alternative. There are alternatives, dying it or keeping his hat pulled down (i.e., remaining in the closet, from Housman's point of view), but society will have none of this: they have "pulled the beggar's hat off for the world to see and stare" (line 11). And now, having exposed the sinner, society right-eously is "haling him to justice for the colour of his hair." Notice, by the way, the phrase "nameless and abominable" in line 8. Wilde's lover, Alfred Douglas, in "Two Loves" writes, "I am the love that dare not speak its name"; and Leviticus 18:20 says that homosexual activity is described as an "abomination."

But if the speaker of the two central stanzas represents the mob of the day, the final stanza is somewhat ambivalent. The first three lines (beginning "Now 'tis oakum for his fingers and the treadmill for his feet") can be spoken with grim satisfaction, with the sense that the sinner is getting his just deserts, or they can be said with just a hint of pity entering into the words, but the last line almost takes us into the mind not of the man who in the first line wondered who the sinner was, or the man (or mob) who has been expressing indignation, but into the mind of the wretched prisoner:

> He can curse the God that made him for the colour of his hair.

That is (we labor the point, but we think it is important), here God is blamed, scarcely the view that the hostile observer, or the indignant crowd, would take. The next poem will also connect God with an individual who has the bad luck to be different from others.

Bibliographic note: Christopher Ricks, "A. E. Housman and 'the colour of his hair,'" *Essays in Criticism* 47 (1997): 240–255, has an interesting piece in which he points out that Locke, Macaulay, and Sir James Fitzjames Stephen in various treatises on tolerance gave as an analogy to discrimination against certain groups (e.g., Jews) the absurdity of discriminating against people with hair of a certain color. The essay displays Ricks's customary erudition and elegance, but it does not directly comment on the poem.

A. E. HOUSMAN
The laws of God, the laws of man (p. 1304)

Briefly, in our culture "the laws of man" are closely connected with "the laws of God." We hear about the Judeo-Christian tradition, and we have judges who post the Ten Commandments in the courtroom. It's probably fair to say—though we speak tentatively here, aware of our ignorance—that in ancient Greece there was little connection between these two kinds of law. On certain occasions a person made pious gestures, e.g., appropriate sacrifices to the gods, but the judicial system was not thought to be heaven-derived. With the triumph of Christianity, however, religion began to shape secular law. Housman says nothing here about homosexuality, but his speaker does say that God and others have decreed laws that ought to be for themselves, not for him. One can hardly avoid the thought that he is thinking of, among other things, the criminalization of homosexual activity. Further,

> . . . if my ways are not as theirs,
> Let them mind their own affairs.

He continues, perhaps mischievously toying with Jesus's command that we should not judge (Matthew 7:1):

> Their deeds I judge and much condemn,
> Yet when did I make laws for them?

His tone is genial:

> Please yourselves, say I, and they
> Need only look the other way.

Yet he knows that his tolerant way is not the way the world operates:

> But no, they will not; they must still
> Wrest their neighbour to their will,
> And make me dance as they desire
> With jail and gallows and hell-fire.

We note that again the laws of God and the laws of man come together (the hellfire of God, the gallows of society), and we note a bit later the blasphemous suggestion, in "bedevilment," that God may be a sort of devil. Of course "bedevilment" means only "to torment mercilessly"—an action bad enough to attribute to God—but since it contains the word "devil" Housman is being especially mischievous when he says that God may bedevil a man.

The tone changes a bit in the next line, "I, a stranger and afraid," where an admission of fear displaces the earlier jauntiness, though in a moment the speaker regains his self-confidence, or, better, his confidence that he knows what is what, even if he is powerless:

> I, a stranger and afraid
> In a world I never made.
> They will be master, right or wrong;
> Though both are foolish, both are strong.

What to do, then? There is no escape, no possible flight to another planet (the planets have classical names, but the classical world with its tolerance of homosexuality is finished), so one must try to obey the laws, that is—among other things—one must repress one's homosexuality, or at least keep it concealed, if one can.

Bibliographic note: For discussion of Housman's thoughts about homosexuality as they appear in certain poems, see Carol Efrati, "The Horses and the Reins," *Victorian Poetry* 34 (1996): 53–71.

Edgar Lee Masters
Judge Selah Lively (p. 1305)

This poem begins as an invitation to the reader ("Suppose you stood"), and at first it may seem to be describing a success story, about a hard-working youth who becomes an attorney. But by line 10, the poem has made clear its different course: the point is not the young man's triumph over obstacles but, rather, the mockery to which he was subjected. The townspeople did not support this fellow in his work but kept up a steady battery of insult and laughter. Perhaps, it should be said, part of the ridicule is connected to the kind of legal work that this attorney performed; he seems not to have been assigned very important or interesting or urgent cases but routine, low-level sorts of things. Still, our sympathies are nonetheless with the attorney. None of us would want to feel such derision directed toward ourselves, and we wonder, no doubt, about the kind of people who would behave in this cruel fashion.

The reversal comes in lines 12–13:

> And then you suppose
> You became the County Judge?

Here we feel the emerging bitterness of the former attorney who became a judge and held sway over the men who had mocked him. He terms them (with a sting in his voice) "the giants," and his recollection of their behavior toward him (they "sneered") dramatizes his intent to even the score. Notice that he singles out several of them by name, which perhaps implies that these men spoke to him in an especially barbed tone: he identifies them individually, apart from "all" the others whose behavior was similar. Surely, says the speaker—Judge Selah Lively is his name—it is "natural" that he would make them pay for their treatment of him.

It is a nicely pointed poem that, we think, makes the reader both pleased and uncomfortable. It's good that the Judge received the chance to wreak some revenge on his detractors and taunters. Wouldn't we do the same, and thus do we not agree with the judge's view that it is "natural" to act as he did when he had the opportunity at last to cut the giants down to size? But is this "natural" or not? Maybe so. Yet isn't such a form of vengeance a "natural" response that we are supposed to rise above? And how do we feel about the fact that a judge, who ought to be impartial, is using his position to settle some personal scores? Is this how the law ought to be administered? Is it reassuring to consider the possibility that not only Judge Lively but also perhaps other judges see their authority in the courtroom as enabling them to punish their enemies?

While this is troubling from one point of view, from another it is grimly reassuring. It may confirm for us what we have always suspected about the law: the law is not neutral at all, and hence one should not expect full, fair justice from its administrators. In court there may be a certain righting of wrongs, but this may accompany, rather than be directly related to, the deliberations about the specific case that is before the court. Judge Lively may not at all be focused on the making of a just decision in the case at hand but, instead, on getting some personal justice for bad treatment he received.

"Selah" is an intriguing choice of name. We recognized it as a Biblical word but were uncertain about its origin and meaning. According to the *HarperCollins Bible Dictionary* (rev. ed., 1996), "selah" is

> a word of uncertain derivation and unknown origin and meaning found in certain psalms in the Old Testament. . . . There has been much speculation about its meaning—a musical notation, a pause in singing for narration, instruction

on dynamics to the choir or to instrumental accompaniment—but there is no agreement among scholars about its function or significance. Absent new evidence, any attempt to define it must remain speculative. (p. 993)

This does not explain, however, why Masters chose the word for his Judge's name. Perhaps, as one of our students suggested, Masters simply wanted a Biblical association. Or, as another student said, maybe he wanted not only a word connected to the Bible but also a word connected to the Old Testament, where a harder, stricter vision of God (God as a judge who metes out tough justice) prevails than in the New Testament.

According to John E. Hallwas's note in *Spoon River Anthology: An Annotated Edition* (1992), this portrait is based on a real-life person, Judge Andrew N. Barrett (1863–1919), and the opening lines apparently do reflect the details of his life.

At one time, it was common for students to encounter selections from *Spoon River Anthology* in high school literature courses, but these days we find that the students we teach in college know little, if anything, about Masters. Yet he was a significant, even pioneering, figure as American literature developed during the first decades of the twentieth century.

As Herbert K. Russell observes in the *Concise Dictionary of American Literary Biography* (1987–1989), *Spoon River Anthology* "became an international popular and critical success and introduced with a flourish what has since come to be known as the Chicago Renaissance," whose notable writers included Masters, Carl Sandburg, Vachel Lindsay, and Theodore Dreiser. "It is safe to say," states Ernest Earnest in "Spoon River Revisited," *Western Humanities Review* 21 (Winter): 59–65, "that no other volume of poetry except *The Waste Land* (1922) made such an impact during the first quarter of this century."

The best discussion of Masters's book is a review-essay keyed to the *Annotated Edition* (cited above), written by John Hollander, in *The New Republic,* July 27, 1992. *Spoon River Anthology,* says Hollander,

> is one of those remarkable, seemingly *sui generis* American books, like William Carlos Williams's *Spring and All,* or John Dos Passos's *U.S.A.,* which seem to mark milestones in the long, strange course of our country's effort to understand itself. It creates a fictional community through the short dramatic monologues spoken by its deceased inhabitants, rather than by overt description. . . . Its author was a Chicago lawyer (he said the law and poetry were like "oil and water"), a political progressive, a literary figure (in the circle of Theodore Dreiser, Vachel Lindsay, and Carl Sandburg), a womanizer, and quite an uninspired poet, who in this unique format and under unique imaginative pressures excelled himself by producing a masterpiece.

Like Judge Selah Lively, Masters himself studied law, working in Chicago as an attorney for three decades and even serving for a few of these years as the partner of the famous trial lawyer, Clarence Darrow. Intent on becoming a literary success as well, Masters began publishing poems and other writings under a number of pseudonyms, concerned that publication under his own name might endanger his legal practice. Four books of poetry, a play, and a collection of essays preceded *Spoon River Anthology,* but none of them suggested that Masters had any special gift or talent. The breakthrough for him came when a publisher he knew, William Marion Reedy, encouraged him to write poetry about the people he had known when he was growing up in Illinois. The first of these poems appeared once again under a pseudonym, "Webster Ford," but for the publication of the completed book, Masters used his own name.

Scholars have also noted the influence of Masters's mother on the composition of *Spoon River Anthology;* she may have given him the specific idea of making the book consist of stories told from the grave. But it has been pointed out, too, that Masters was familiar with J. W. Mackail's *Selected Epigrams from the Greek Anthology* (published in 1913), which Reedy had given to him, and that his laconic, compressed form may have derived from the poems he read in his book. As Hollander explains,

> It is the little poems of the so-called *Greek Anthology* that Masters had most directly in mind, and particularly the sepulchral epigrams of Book VII. These are actual or (more usually) fictional epitaphs, sometimes of only one couplet, sometimes of greater length. Among them are the famous words of Simonides, quoted by Herodotus, for the Spartans killed at the battle of Thermopylae, as they might be put in the standard English epigrammatic meter:
>
> Tell them in Sparta, you who now pass by
> That here obedient to their laws we lie.

Because of its satiric exposure of the questionable morals of small-town America, including on sexual matters, *Spoon River Anthology* proved highly controversial—and in part for this very reason, it quickly became a best-seller; as the critic Stanley Edgar Hyman has noted, it was a "success de scandale—it was the sex-shocker, the Peyton Place of its day."

But it was not simply the disconcerting content of the poems that brought Masters's book to the attention of readers. It was also the style—the direct and unadorned capturing of a range of voices—that discerning critics and poets admired. "At last," remarked Ezra Pound, "America has discovered a poet. . . . At last the American West has produced a poet strong enough to weather the climate, capable of dealing with life directly, without circumlocution, without resonant meaningless phrases."

For further study, the best place to start is with the *Annotated Edition,* with its helpful introduction and notes. See also John T. Flanagan, *Edgar Lee Masters: The Spoon River Poet and His Critics* (1974); and James Hurt, "The Sources of the Spoon: Edgar Lee Masters and the *Spoon River Anthology,*" *Centennial Review* 24 (1980): 403–431. Also valuable is Herbert K. Russell, *Edgar Lee Masters: A Biography* (2001).

Claude McKay
If We Must Die (p. 1307)

In *Black Poets of the United States* (1962, 1973), the critic Jean Wagner states that McKay's "If We Must Die," though written in the specific context of American racism, has proven inspirational to people engaged in struggle and protest throughout the world: "Along with the will to resistance of black Americans that it expresses, it voices also the will of oppressed people of every age who, whatever their race and wherever their region, are fighting with their backs against the wall to win their freedom."

This point has been developed well by James R. Keller, in "'A Chafing Savage, Down the Decent Street': The Politics of Compromise in Claude McKay's Protest Sonnets," *African American Review* 28:3 (Fall 1994). "McKay's subversive efforts," Keller says,

> to expose America's hypocrisy in international affairs were appropriated and contained in ways the poet could not have anticipated. I refer specifically to the public reading of his poem "If We Must Die" by Winston Churchill during the war effort against Germany and Japan. . . . This 1919 poem in which McKay urged oppressed African Americans to rise up against their white persecutors, was employed two decades later by the dominant culture to rally support and, thereby, effect its own salvation in a war that the poet regarded as a blatant manifestation of idological fraud.

Keller notes, however, that McKay

> invites this misuse by his own exploitation of Henry V's famous "St. Crispin Day" speech (4.2.18–67). In Shakespeare's play, the embattled and worn English troops, hopelessly outnumbered by the French, are urged to fight bravely in the seemingly hopeless battle for nothing but dignity and honor. Their deaths are almost assured. McKay's reference to his "kinsmen . . . far outnumbered" is reminiscent of King Henry's promise that all men who fight heroically on St. Crispin Day will be his "brothers." That Henry V was a rallying point of English nationalism in their fight against Germany during World War II is evidenced by [Laurence] Olivier's film version, which was released in 1941 and which emphasized the unity of the British people.

There may be other echoes as well. "Inglorious" reminds us of, for example, the use of this somewhat unusual word in Andrew Marvell's "Horatian Ode":

> So restless Cromwell could not cease
> In the inglorious arts of peace,
> But through adventurous war
> Urgèd his active star.
>   *(lines 9–12)*

And perhaps, too, the use of the word in Thomas Gray's well-known "Elegy Written in a Country Churchyard":

Some village Hampden, that with dauntless breast
The little tyrant of his fields withstood,
Some mute inglorious Milton, here may rest,
Some Cromwell, guiltless of his country's blood.
(lines 57–60)

McKay is emphasizing that if death is the inescapable fate that "we" must face, then let this death be a noble one, not a scene of brute carnage.

We are not sure, but McKay may, further, be suggesting that the noble death of the men who fight back might possess the sacred splendor of the death of Jesus. Timothy Dwight (1752–1817) begins his poem "Love to the Church":

I love thy kingdom, Lord,
The house of thine abode,
The church our blest Redeemer saved
With his own precious blood.

This poem (there are many poems, hymns, and sermons where the phrase also is used) is included in *The Yale Book of American Verse*, published in 1912, a book that McKay might well have been familiar with.

There is at least one other possible or probable secular source (though with a religious grounding) for this same phrase—Whitman's prayer to the earth in his Civil War poem "Pensive on Her Dead Gazing, I Heard the Mother of All":

My dead absorb—my young men's beautiful bodies absorb—and their precious, precious, precious blood;
Which holding in trust for me, faithfully back again give me, many a year hence,
In unseen essence and odor of surface and grass, centuries hence;
In blowing airs from the fields, back again give me my darlings—give my immortal heroes.
(lines 11–14)

The year 1919 was a horrifying one for American race relations; more than seventy African Americans were lynched that year, and there were twenty-five race riots, many of them during the hot, oppressive summer months, which, because of the violence, became known as "the Red Summer." "If We Must Die" was one of a number of sonnets dealing with racial violence that McKay published in the July 1919 issue of the *Liberator*, a radical magazine founded by Max Eastman and his sister Crystal in March 1918 in order to publish John Reed's dispatches about the Russian Revolution, which Reed later collected under the title *Ten Days That Shook the World*.

The worst of the race riots occurred in Chicago in July 1919, when violence broke out between blacks and whites at a segregated beach. Black men and women were attacked and terrorized by white mobs, and blacks in turn battled with both whites and the police and state militia. By the time the riot had ended, after about a week of bloodshed and destruction, forty persons had been killed and hundreds more injured, and most of these casualties were African Americans.

For more context and analysis, see William M. Tuttle, Jr., *Chicago in The Red Summer of 1919* (1970).

The tone of the poem is desperate and defiant but doom-ridden. The speaker calls on his comrades to be strong, courageous; though they may be hunted down like animals, they will resist and fight back, to their last breath. Inspiring, true, in its historical context, and in the context of later episodes of strife and struggle. But the words themselves are, ultimately, hopeless in their message, and the claim that the other side will feel bound to honor the slain is unduly affirmative.

McKay's bitter, blazing absorption in brave but futile violence reminds us of the suicidal grandeur in Tennyson's "The Charge of the Light Brigade":

> Cannon to right of them,
> Cannon to left of them,
> Cannon in front of them
> Volley'd and thunder'd;
> Storm'd at with shot and shell,
> Boldly they rode and well,
> Into the jaws of Death,
> Into the mouth of hell
> Rode the six hundred.
> *(lines 18–26)*

For a good survey of McKay's life and career: Darryl Pinckney, "Claude McKay: Rebel Sojourner in the Harlem Renaissance," *The New York Review of Books,* Dec. 17, 1987. For a detailed biography, we recommend Wayne F. Cooper, *Claude McKay: Rebel Sojourner in the Harlem Renaissance: A Biography* (1987). Cooper also edited *Claude McKay: Selected Poetry and Prose, 1912–1948* (1973), and he included in it a forty-page biographical and critical essay.

JIMMY SANTIAGO BACA
Cloudy Day (p. 1308)

"Cloudy Day" was first published in Baca's *Immigrants in Our Own Land* (1979) and then reprinted in *Immigrants in Our Own Land and Selected Early Poems* (1990).

Born in Santa Fe, New Mexico, in 1952, Baca led a life of crime and drug-taking until he was arrested in his late teens and imprisoned for selling drugs. Illiterate when he entered the maximum-security system, he learned to read and discovered a deep interest in poetry and a vocation as a writer and teacher. Reading and writing saved him; as he explains in *Working in the Dark: Reflections on a Poet in the Barrio* (1992), "I was becoming what society told me I was—prone to drugs and alcohol, unable to control my own life, needing a master to order my affairs, unworthy of opportunity and justice—a senseless beast of labor. I drugged my pain and drowned my self-hatred in drink, seeking oblivion. I had no future, no plans, no destiny, no regard for my life; I was free falling into bottomless despair. Death seemed the only way out."

After his release from prison, Baca attended the University of New Mexico, receiving his B.A. in 1984. He has since conducted writing classes and led workshops for children and adults, and taught courses in grammar schools, high schools, colleges and universities, housing projects, and prisons. In *A Place to Stand: The Making of a Poet* (2001), Baca states: "I am a witness, not a victim. . . . My role as a witness is to give voice to the voiceless, hope to the hopeless, of which I am one."

Baca has won many prizes and awards and published a number of books, including (in addition to those cited above) *Black Mesa Poems* (1989) and *Healing Earthquakes: A Love Story in Poems* (2001).

Asked in an interview, published in *Callaloo* 17:1 (1994), about the origin of "Cloudy Day", Baca was terse:

Speaker: Tell us when you wrote this [poem].
JSB: Well, I remember I was standing outside, I guess it was about 1977 or 78, something like that.
Speaker: You were in prison?
JSB: Yeah, yeah.
Speaker: Was that written for a person?
JSB: It was written for me.

There are some good questions about style and structure that you can direct to the class. We have invited students to consider, for example, the changes in effect that would result from starting the poem with lines 24–29. Why is the memory placed in the middle and not at the beginning, where it might seem naturally to belong? And why the use of present tense ("It is windy today . . .")?

It is interesting also to discuss the impact of the "wind," and the way it causes the speaker to feel powerful enough to break the guardtower. Why is that?

Baca's poem might be understood, in part at least, as a tough-minded response (or, better, rebuttal) to the imagery of cooling and revivifying breezes that appear so often in the Romantic poets, as in, for example, this passage from Wordsworth:

I wander'd lonely as a cloud
That floats on high o'er vales and hills,

When all at once I saw a crowd,
A host of golden daffodils,
Beside the lake, beneath the trees,
Fluttering and dancing in the breeze. . . .

Or this, from Wordsworth's *The Recluse, Part First, Home at Grasmere*:

> He thought of clouds
> That sail on winds: of breezes that delight
> To play on water, or in endless chase
> Pursue each other through the yielding plain
> Of grass or corn, over and through and through,
> In billow after billow, evermore
> Disporting—nor unmindful was the boy
> Of sunbeams, shadows, butterflies and birds;
> Of fluttering sylphs and softly-gliding Fays,
> Genii, and winged angels that are Lords
> Without restraint of all which they behold.
> *(lines 24–35)*

Baca is working with and against this tradition, placing it in a harsh context, though in the final analysis his poem, too, ends in a scene of renewal and empowerment—though one marked, to be sure, by the conditional "as if": "I feel as if I have everything, everything."

The emergence of "you" near the end is puzzling. It feels abrupt—which may be part of the effect that Baca intends. And it feels vague, too, since we know nothing about the "you" being addressed. Yet this also may be in line with Baca's aims; if indeed the poem is one he wrote for himself, the significance of the "you" is the very personal (and shielded) connection between that person and Baca.

We have on occasion invited students to interpret this poem in the light of one of the following two quotations:

The human spirit will endure sickness; but a broken spirit—who can bear? *Proverbs 18:14*

Out of life's school of war.—What does not destroy me, makes me stronger. *Friedrich Nietzsche (1844–1900), in* Twilight of the Idols, *"Maxims and Arrows," section 8 (prepared for publication 1888, published 1889)*

Students interested in the subject of literature written by prisoners might consult *The Light from Another Country: Poetry from American Prisons*, Joseph Bruchac (1984), and *Prison Writing in Twentieth-Century America: A Collection of Poems, Stories, Essays* (1998). For historical background and context: H. Bruce Franklin, *The Victim as Criminal and Artist: Literature from the American Prison* (1978).

Susan Glaspell
Trifles (p. 1309)

Some students may know Glaspell's other version of this work, a short story entitled "A Jury of Her Peers." Some good class discussion can focus on the interchangeability of the titles. "Trifles" could have been called "A Jury of Her Peers," and vice versa. A peer is an equal, and the suggestion of the story's title is that Mrs. Wright is judged by a jury of her equals—Mrs. Hale and Mrs. Peters. A male jury would not constitute her equals because—at least in the context of the story and the play—males simply don't have the experiences of women and therefore can't judge them fairly.

Murder is the stuff of TV dramas, and this play concerns a murder, but it's worth asking students how the play differs from a whodunit. Discussion will soon establish that we learn, early in "Trifles," who performed the murder, and we even know, fairly early, *why* Minnie killed her husband. (The women know what is what because they correctly interpret "trifles," but the men are baffled since they are looking for obvious signs of anger.) Once we know who performed the murder, the interest shifts to the question of whether the women will cover up for Minnie.

The distinction between what the men and the women look for is paralleled in the distinction between the morality of the men and the women. The men stand for law and order, for dominance (they condescend to the women, and the murdered Wright can almost be taken as a symbol of male dominance), whereas the women stand for mutual support or nurturing. Students might be invited to discuss *why* the women protect Minnie. Is it because women are nurturing? Or because they feel guilt for their earlier neglect of Minnie? Or because, being women, they know what her sufferings must have been like and feel that she acted justly? All of the above?

The symbols will cause very little difficulty. (1) The "gloomy" kitchen suggests Minnie's life with her husband; (2) the bird suggests Minnie (she sang "like a bird," was lively, then became caged and was broken in spirit).

The title is a sort of symbol too, an ironic one, for the men think (in Mr. Hale's words) that "Women are used to worrying over trifles." The men in the play never come to know better, but the reader-viewer comes to understand that the trifles are significant and that the seemingly trivial women have outwitted the self-important men. The irony of the title is established by the ironic action of the play.

Does the play have a *theme*? In our experience, the first theme that students may propose is that "it's a man's world." There is something to this view, but (1) a woman kills her husband, and (2) other women help her to escape from the (male) legal establishment. Do we want to reverse the first suggestion, then, and say that (in this play) it is really a woman's world, that women run things? No, given the abuse that all of the women in the play take. Still, perhaps it is fair to suggest that one of the things the play implies is that overbearing male behavior gets what it deserves—at least sometimes. Of course, when put this way, the theme is ancient; it is at the root of the idea of *hubris*, which is said to govern much Greek tragedy. Glaspell gives it a very special twist by emphasizing the women's role in restoring justice to society.

For a thoughtful study of Glaspell's writings (she was a novelist and short-story writer as well as a playwright), see Veronia A. Makowsky, *Susan Glaspell's Century of American Women: A Critical Interpretation of Her Work* (1993). Also helpful are the critical commentaries in *Susan Glaspell: Essays on Her Theater and Fiction,* ed. Linda Ben-Zvi (1995). Students who would like further context and references should consult Mary E. Papke, *Susan Glaspell: A Research and Production Sourcebook* (1993).

APPENDIX C
NEW APPROACHES TO THE RESEARCH PAPER: LITERATURE, HISTORY, AND THE WORLD WIDE WEB

Mitsuye Yamada
The Question of Loyalty (p. 1344)

In our earlier discussion of a poem by Yamada ("To the Lady," in Chapter 24), we give some background information about the evacuation of Japanese and Japanese Americans from the west coast in the early 1940s.

The mood of the times demanded a single, unquestioning loyalty. This demand, however, was not engendered simply by World War II. It came out of the idea that the United States was a melting pot, a term first used, or at least popularized, by Israel Zangwill, in a play called *The Melting Pot* (1908): "America is God's crucible, the great Melting-Pot where all the races of Europe are melting and re-forming." At about the time that Zangwill wrote *The Melting Pot,* Theodore Roosevelt said,

> There is no room in this country for hyphenated Americans. . . . The one absolutely certain way of bringing this nation to ruin, of preventing all possibility of its continuing to be a nation at all, would be to permit it to become a tangle of squabbling nationalities. (1915)

Five years later Roosevelt was to say,

> There can be no fifty-fifty Americanism in this country. There is room here for only 100% Americanism, only for those who are Americans and nothing else.

It is our impression that most of the immigrants who came at the end of the nineteenth century, or in the early decades of the twentieth, turned their backs on the country of their origin and came here to be 100% Americans. Of course they retained many of their ways, and perhaps especially their foods, but they were fleeing poverty or political persecution; having made a living or even a good living here, they had little reason to look back with much affection. Further, in the days before World War II, it was difficult to maintain contact with the old country; ocean voyages took time and money, and long-distance telephone calls were almost unthinkable, except to report a death in the family. Today it is different; many middle-class immigrants, such as physicians and college professors, come here not because they are terribly oppressed but because they seek greater economic opportunity. They have no dislike of their native land; they keep in contact by telephone, and they fly back for frequent visits.

But even many immigrants who are relatively poor can maintain contact with their native lands.

Further, there are many people of this sort, partly because many people in the United States were born abroad. According to a recent report (*The New York Times,* August 30, 1995), the percentage of the country that is foreign-born is accelerating. In 1994 it was 8.7 percent, or 22.6 million people (about 4 million of whom are thought to have entered illegally). The figures for California and New York, the states with the highest proportions of foreign-born residents, are 25% and 16%.

You don't need to hear our ideas on why foreign-born people today can be Americans and can yet retain affectionate ties with their native lands. Yamada's poem takes us to an earlier era, when one could *not* be "doubly loyal" (line 14). It's obvious that she fully sympathizes with her mother, although she herself took a different course: "I was poor / at math. / I signed / my only ticket out." The wry joke about being poor at math—as though the mother has really posed a mathematical problem—conveys self-condemnation, and yet one wonders if she is not right when she says that signing was in fact a necessity, the "only ticket out."

DAVID MURA
An Argument: On 1942 (p. 1345)

Mura is a *sansei,* a third-generation Japanese American. Born in 1952, he did not experience internment in the relocation camps of 1942. The poem is rooted in the fairly widespread difference today between the attitude of, on the one hand, most of those who experienced the camps (chiefly *issei* [first-generation] and their American-born children, *nisei* [second-generation]), and on the other hand, many *sansei,* who were born after World War II and who cannot understand how their parents and grandparents allowed themselves to be so subjugated.

Mura's poem—in effect an argument between the poet and his mother—begins in the son's voice. Between the fourth and the fifth lines, however, the mother interrupts (or at least she does so in the son's imagination), and the poet reports her words: "—No, no, she tells me. Why bring it back? The camps are over." The mother wishes to forget the experience, or at least not to dwell on it, but her son, she says, is "like a terrier . . . gnawing a bone." For her, the experience was chiefly boring (line 9). (Of course one can say that she has repressed her memories of humiliation—but one can also entertain the possibility that for a child the experience was indeed chiefly boring.) For the son, who did not experience it but who now looks at it through the eyes of a mature Japanese American writing in the late 1980s, the thought of the indignity is galling.

What does a reader make of the conflict? Presumably the reader can hold both views, sharing the youth's sense of outrage but also understanding the mother's view—which, incidentally, is given the climactic final position: "David, it was so long ago . . . how useless it seems. . . ." In fact, it seems entirely possible that the poet himself holds both views. At least to our ear he voices them with equal effectiveness.

After we had written the preceding remarks we received the following comment from David Mura:

> The poem starts with an imaginary poem in my voice, a lament for the world that was destroyed by the internment order. I'm both attracted to and wary of the romantic cast to such a voice, and in the poem, my mother gives another version of the past, one which downplays the effect of the camps and argues against over-romanticizing both the past and past sufferings. In the end, I think there's a great deal of denial in my mother's version of the past, and yet, her version is a reality with which I must contend; after all, she was there, and I wasn't (of course, her presence at these events doesn't necessarily mean her interpretation of them can't be wrong). Both her version and my version exist in the poem as realities which the reader must confront. As with much of my work, I think of this poem as a political poem.

In both poetry and prose, Mura has examined race, ethnicity, and sexuality and has described his quest for self-knowledge and personal and familial identity. *A Male Grief: Notes on Pornography and Addiction* (1987) was his first book. Two years later he published *After We Lost Our Way* in the National Poetry Series and followed it with a second book of verse, *The Colors of Desire: Poems* (1995). He has also written *Turning Japanese: Memoirs of a Sansei* (1992) and *Where the Body Meets Memory: An Odyssey of Race, Sexuality, and Identity* (1996), which tells of his childhood in Chicago, his parents' recollections of the internment camps, and the impact of internment on several generations of Japanese Americans.

For another poem about the internment of Japanese Americans in 1942, see Mitsuye Yamada, "To the Lady," in Chapter 24.

Index of Authors and Titles

A & P, 96
About Men, 277
Act of Prostitution, An, 472
Address at the Dedication of the Gettysburg National Cemetery, 359
Aesop
   A Lion and Other Animals Go Hunting, 461
Aldrich, Thomas Bailey
   Unguarded Gates, The, 426
Alexie, Sherman
   On the Amtrak from Boston to New York City, 233
   Reservation Bues, 167
Alvarez, Julia
   Woman's Work, 296
American Flamingo, 181
Andre's Mother, 273
Angelou, Maya
   Graduation, 301
"A noiseless patient spider," 138
"An old pond," 129
Annunciation, 44
Anonymous (American and English)
   Birmingham Jail, 480
   Charlotte Perkins at a Suffrage Rally, 64
   Deep River, 136
   Father, Have Pity on Me, 440
   Hasidic Tales, 463
   Higamus, Hogamus, 286
   Judgment of Solomon, The, 21
   Marilyn Monroe, 63
   Mountain Climber, The, 219
   My Children, When at First I Liked the Whites, 440
   My God, How the Money Rolls In, 390
   Silver Swan, The, 80
   Western Wind, 255
   What Are Little Boys Made Of, 286
   Women at the Grave of Stonewall Jackson, 377
Antigone, 106
"anyone lived in a pretty how town," 123
Anzaldúa, Gloria
   To live in the Borderlands means you, 431
"Apparently with no surprise," 149
Araby, 304
Argument: On 1942, An, 497
Armas, José
   El Tonto del Barrio, 34
Arnold, Matthew
   Dover Beach, 201

"A slumber did my spirit seal," 194
At Chancellorsville, 380
Atlanta Exposition Address, 476
Auden, W. H.
    Funeral Blues, 157
    Musée des Beaux Arts, 178

Baca, Jimmy Santiago
    Cloudy Day, 491
    So Mexicans Are Taking Jobs from Americans, 432
Bait, The, 256
Bambara, Toni Cade
    Lesson, The, 215
Barbie Doll, 297
Barn Burning, 470
Basho
    An Old Pond, 129
"Batter my heart, three-personed God," 14
Battle Hymn of the Republic, 370
Battle Royal, 473
Beauty and Sadness, 174
"Because I could not stop for Death," 234
Before the Law, 465
Before the Mirror, 186
Behn, Aphra
    Song: Love Armed, 27
Berry, Wendell
    Stay Home, 231
Bible
    Judgment of Solomon, The, 21
    Parable of the Prodigal Son, 23
Bierce, Ambrose
    A Horseman in the Sky, 365
Birmingham Jail, 480
Bishop, Elizabeth
    Filling Station, 38
    Hanging of the Mouse, 467
Black Men and Public Space, 82
Blake, William
    Echoing Green, The, 311
    Garden of Love, The, 261
    Infant Joy, 309
    Infant Sorrow, 310
    London, 15
    Poison Tree, A, 262
    Sick Rose, The, 119
    Tyger, The, 42
Blue, 155
Boys and Girls, 284
Brodsky, Joseph
    Love Song, 269
Brontë, Emily
    Spellbound, 16
Brooks, Gwendolyn
    We Real Cool, 78
Brother, Can You Spare a Dime, 387
Browning, Robert
    My Last Duchess, 123
Bruchac, Joseph, III
    Ellis Island, 428
Brueghel's Two Monkeys, 188
Buffalo Bill's, 71
Bully, 40

Carpenter's Son, The, 480
Carver, Raymond
    Mine, 245
    Cathedral, 251
    Little Things, 245
    What We Talk about When We Talk about Love, 249
Casares, Oscar
    Yolanda, 91
Cash, Johnny
    Folsom Prison Blues, 159
Cask of Amontillado, The, 27
Cathedral, 251
Cat in the Rain, 237
Chekhov, Anton
    Misery, 87
Chesnut, Mary Boykin Miller
    November 28, 1861, 358
Child of the Americas, 430
Chinese Banquet, A, 271
Chivalry, 270
Chopin, Kate
    Désirée's Baby, 7
    Ripe Figs, 4

Index of Authors and Titles   501

Storm, The, 8
Story of an Hour, The, 6
Civil Disobedience, 453
Cloudy Day, 491
Cofer, Judith Ortiz
   I Fell in Love or My Hormones Awakened, 237
Collins, Billy
   Sonnet, 121
   The Names, 407
Come In, 38
Conflict of Interest, A, 458
Courting a Monk, 418
Crane, Stephen
   An Episode of War, 367
Cullen Countee
   Incident, 226
Cummings, E. E.
   anyone lived in a pretty how town, 123
   Buffalo Bill's, 71
   in Just-, 313

Daddy, 124
Davis, Jefferson
   Inaugural Address, 355
Daystar, 287
Dear Madam, 361
Death of the Ball Turret Gunner, 18
Declaration of Independence, The, 411
Deep River, 136
Design, 204
Désirée's Baby, 7
Dickinson, Emily
   Apparently with no surprise, 149
   Because I could not stop for Death, 234
   I felt a Funeral, in my Brain, 74
   I felt a Cleaving in my Mind, 74
   I got so I could hear his name—, 148
   I heard a Fly buzz—when I died, 141
   Papa above, 143
   Soul selects her own Society, The, 142

   Tell all the Truth but tell it slant, 150
   The Dust behind I strove to join, 74
   There's a certain Slant of light, 144
   These are the days when Birds come back, 143
   This World is not Conclusion, 146
   Those—dying, then, 149
   Wild Nights—Wild Nights, 112
Didion, Joan
   On Going Home, 214
Diving into the Wreck, 231
Dixie's Land, 369
Doll's House, A, 298
Doloff, Steven
   The Opposite Sex, 276
Donne, John
   Bait, The, 256
   Holy Sonnet XIV ("Batter my heart"), 14
   Valediction: Forbidding Mourning, A, 259
Dove, Rita
   Daystar, 287
Dover Beach, 201
Dover Bitch, The, 203
Du Bois, W. E. B.
   Of Our Spiritual Strivings, 480
   The Lesson for Americans, 363
Dunbar, Paul Laurence
   Blue, 155
Dupont's Round Fight, The 373
Dying words of Jackson, The, 375

Echoing Green, The, 311
Eight O'Clock, 482
XI. (from Twenty-One Love Poems), 267
Eliot, T. S.
   Love Song of J. Alfred Prufrock, The, 196
Ellis Island, 428
Ellison, Ralph
   Battle Royal, 473
El Tonto del Barrio, 34

Emmett, Daniel Decatur
   Dixie's Land, 369
Episode of War, An, 367
Erdrich, Louise
   Indian Boarding School: The Runaways, 125
Ehrlich, Gretel
   About Men, 277
Espada, Martin
   Bully, 40
Everyday Use, 417

Facing It, 398
Far Cry from Africa, A, 232
Father Death Blues, 163
Father, Have Pity on Me, 440
Faulkner, William
   Barn Burning, 470
   Rose for Emily, A, 239
Fences, 107
Filling Station, 38
fish cheeks, 84
Flanders, Jane
   Van Gogh's Bed, 169
Folsom Prison Blues, 159
For Allen Ginsberg, 43
For Malcolm, A Year After, 126
For the White Person Who Wants to Know How to Be My Friend, 433
Frog Prince, The, 267
Frost, Robert
   Come In, 38
   Design, 204
   Hardship of Accounting, The, 118
   Mending Wall, 193
   Pasture, The, 228
   Silken Tent, The, 265
   Stopping by Woods on a Snowy Evening, 192
   Telephone, The, 114
   Vanishing Red, The, 444
Funeral Blues, 157

Gallagher, Tess
   I Stop Writing the Poem, 294
Garden of Love, The, 261

Garrison, Deborah
   September Poem, 410
General Review of the Sex Situation, 287
Gerber, Michael
   What We Talk about When We Talk about Doughnuts, 254
Gershwin, Ira
   The Man That Got Away, 205
Gettysburg Address, 359
Gibbons, Orlando
   The Silver Swan, 80
Gilman, Charlotte Perkins
   The Yellow Wallpaper, 278
Ginsberg, Allen
   Father Death Blues, 163
Gioia, Dana
   Money, 117
Giovanni, Nikki
   Love in Place, 270
Glaspell, Susan
   Trifles, 494
Glass Menagerie, The, 110
Glück, Louise
   Gretel in Darkness, 315
   School Children, The, 314
Gogh, Vincent van
   The Starry Night, 176
   Van Gogh's Bed, 169
"Go, lovely rose," 118
Good Man Is Hard to Find, A, 93
Graduation, 301
Great Figure, The, 170
Gretel in Darkness, 315

Haggard, Merle
   Workin' Man Blues, 160
Hamlet, 315
Handy, W. C.
   St. Louis Blues, 151
Hanging, A, 455
Hanging of the Mouse, 467
Harburg, E. Y. (Yip)
   Brother, Can You Spare a Dime, 387
Hardship of Accounting, The, 118

Hardy, Thomas
   Neutral Tones, 132
   The Photograph, 139
Harlem, 12
Hasidic Tales, 463
Hawthorne, Nathaniel
   Young Goodman Brown, 302
Hayden, Robert,
   Those Winter Sundays, 288
Hayes, Alfred
   Joe Hill, 391
Hecht, Anthony
   The Dover Bitch, 203
Hemingway, Earnest
   Cat in the Rain, 237
Herrick, Robert
   To the Virgins, to Make Much of Time, 39
   Upon Julia's Clothes, 120
Higamus, Hogamous, 286
Holy Sonnet XIV (Batter my heart), 14
Homosexuality, 290
Hookups Starve the Soul, 84
Hooverville, 393
Hopkins, Gerald Manley
   Spring and Fall: To a Young Child, 312
Horseman in the Sky, A, 365
Housman, A. E.
   Carpenter's Son, 480
   Eight O'Clock, 482
   Laws of God, the Laws of Man, The, 484
   When I Was One-and-Twenty, 313
Howe, Julia Ward
   Battle Hymn of the Republic, 370
How to Live a Rational Life, 402
Hudgins, Andrew
   At Chancellorsville, 380
   The Wild Swans Skip School," 79
Hughes, Langston
   Harlem, 12
   One Friday Morning, 307
   Out of Work, 392
   Salvation, 83
   Theme for English B, 433
   Too Blue, 158
Hurston, Zora Neale
   A Conflict of Interest, 458
   Sweat, 241

"I am a child of the Americas," 430
I Ask My Mother to Sing, 18
Ibsen, Henrik
   A Doll's House, 298
I Fell in Love, Or My Hormones Awakened, 237
I felt a Funeral, in my Brain, 74
I felt a Cleaving in my Mind, 74
If We Must Die, 489
"I got so I could hear his name—," 148
"I heard a Fly buzz—when I died—," 141
In an Artist's Studio, 120
Inaugural Address, 355
Incident, 226
Indian Boarding School: The Runaways, 125
Indian's Welcome to the Pilgrim Fathers, The, 443
Infant Joy, 309
Infant Sorrow, 310
"in Just-," 313
Interviews, 382
"I saw in Louisiana a Live-Oak Growing," 264
I Stand Here Ironing, 385
I Stop Writing the Poem, 294
It's Hard Enough Being Me, 413
Ivins, Molly
   Short Story about the Vietnam War Memorial, A, 394

Jacobs, Lou
   What Qualties Does a Good Photograph Have? 53
Jarrell, Randall
   The Death of the Ball Turret Gunner, 18

Jefferson, Thomas
  The Declaration of Independence, 411
Jilting of Granny Weatherall, The, 32
Joe Hill, 391
John
  The Woman Taken in Adultery, 462
Johnson, Robert
  Walkin' Blues, 154
Joyce, James
  Araby, 304
Judge Selah Lively, 485
Judgment of Solomon, The, 21
Jump Cabling, 119

Kafka, Franz
  Before the Law, 465
Kaufman, Bel
  Sunday in the Park, 243
Keats, John
  Ode on a Grecian Urn, 197
  On First Looking into Chapman's Homer, 221
Kennedy, X. J.
  For Allen Ginsberg, 43
  Nude Descending the Staircase, 179
King, Jr., Martin Luther
  Letter from Birmingham Jail, 460
Kinsley, Michael
  How to Live a Rational Life, 402
Knight, Etheridge
  For Malcolm, A Year After, 126
Komunyakaa, Yusef
  Facing It, 398

Laguna Blues, 165
Lam, Andrew
  Who Will Light the Incense When Mother's Gone, 414
Lanier, Sidney
The Dying Words of Jackson, 375
Lazarus, Emma
  The New Colossus, 422
Leda, 49

Leda and the Swan (first version), 44
Leda and the Swan (second version), 44
Lee, Li-Young
  I Ask My Mother to Sing, 18
Le Guin, Ursula
  The Ones Who Walk Away from Omelas, 469
Lesson, The, 215
Lesson for Americans, The, 363
"Let me not to the marriage of true minds," 259
Letter from Birmingham Jail, 460
Lifshin, Lyn
  My Mother and the Bed, 40
Liggan, Martha
  Dear Madam, 361
Limited, 224
Lincoln, Abraham
  Gettysburg Address, 359
Lion and Other Animals Go Hunting, A, 461
Little Things, 245
London, 15
Love in Place, 270
"Love is not all: it is not meat nor drink," 265
Lover's Departure, A, 236
Love Song, 269
Love Song of J. Alfred Prufrock, The, 196
Luke
  The Parable of the Prodigal Son, 23
Luncheon on the Grass, 183
Lying in a Hammock at William Duffy's Farm in Pine Island, Minnesota, 135

Man That Got Away, The, 205
Man to Send Rain Clouds, The, 36
Man Who Was Almost a Man, The, 281
Mansfield, Katherine
  Miss Brill, 205
March into Virginia, The, 371

Marlowe, Christopher
   Come Live with Me and Be My Love, 256
Marvell, Andrew
   To His Coy Mistress, 260
Mason, Bobbie Ann
   Shiloh, 217
Masters, Edgar Lee
   Judge Selah Lively, 485
Maupassant, Guy de
   The Necklace, 28
McKay, Claude
   If We Must Die, 489
McNally, Terrence
   André's Mother, 273
McPherson, James Alan
   An Act of Prostitution, 472
Melville, Herman
   Dupont's Round Fight, The, 373
   The March into Virginia, 371
   Shiloh, 374
Mending Wall, 193
Millay, Edna St. Vincent
   Love Is Not All: It Is Not Meat nor Drink, 265
Milton, John
   When I Consider How My Light Is Spent, 193
Min, Katherine
   Courting a Monk, 418
Mine, 245
Mini Blues, 162
Misery, 87
Miss Brill, 205
Money, 117
Montesquieu, Charles de Secondat, Baron de la Brède
   Persian Letters, 214
Morales, Aurora Levins
   Child of the Americas, 430
Mountain-Climber, The, 219
Mourning Picture, 172
Moving Camp Too Far, 450
Munro, Alice
   Boys and Girls, 284

Mura, David
   An Argument: On 1942, 497
Musée des Beaux Arts, 178
Muske, Carol
   Chivalry, 270
My Children, When at First I Liked the Whites, 440
My God, How the Money Rolls In, 390
My Last Duchess, 123
"My mistress' eyes are nothing like the sun," 116
My Mother and the Bed, 40
My Papa's Waltz, 289

Names, The, 407
Naylor, Gloria
   The Two, 283
Necklace, The, 28
Neutral Tones, 132
New Colossus, The, 422
Noiseless patient spider, A, 138
northSun, Nila
   Moving Camp Too Far, 450
Novella, 266
November 28, 1861, 358
Nude Descending the Staircase, 179
Nymph's Reply to the Shepherd, The, 256

Oates, Joyce Carol
   Where Are You Going, Where Have You Been?, 103
O'Brien, Tim
   The Things They Carried, 395
O'Connor, Flannery
   Good Man Is Hard to Find, A, 93
   Revelation, 94
Ode on a Grecian Urn, 197
Of Our Spiritual Strivings, 480
O'Hara, Frank
   Homosexuality, 290
Old Pond, An, 129
Olds, Sharon
   Rites of Passage, 289
Oliver's Evolution, 101

Olsen, Tillie
   I Stand Here Ironing, 385
One Friday Morning, 307
Ones Who Walk Away from Omelas, The, 469
On First Looking into Chapman's Homer, 221
On Going Home, 214
On the Amtrak from Boston to New York City, 233
Opposite Sex, The, 276
Orwell, George
   Hanging, A, 455
Out of Work, 397
Ozymandias, 222

Pack, Robert
   The Frog Prince, 267
Paley, Grace
   Samuel, 86
"Papa above," 143
Pape, Greg
   American Flamingo, 181
Parable of the Prodigal Son, The, 23
Parker, Dorothy
   General Review of the Sex Situation, 287
Parker, Pat
   For the White Person Who Wants to Know How to Be My Friend, 433
Pastan, Linda
   Jump Cabling, 119
   Mini Blues, 162
Pasture, The, 228
Persian Letters, 214
Phillips, Carl
   Luncheon on the Grass, 183
Photograph, The, 139
Piercy, Marge
   Barbie Doll, 297
Plath, Sylvia
   Daddy, 124
Poe, Edgar Allan
   The Cask of Amontillado, 27
Poison Tree, A, 262

"Poor soul, the center of my sinful earth," 114
Porter, Katherine Anne
   The Jilting of Granny Weatherall, 32
Powder, 10
Prodigal Son, 23
Pygmalion, 97

Question of Loyalty, The, 496

Raleigh, Sir Walter
   Nymph's Reply to the Shepherd, 256
Raya, Anna Lisa
   It's Hard Enough Being Me, 413
Rebirth of Venus, The, 175
Reconciliation, 378
Red Wheelbarrow, The, 137
Reservation Blues, 167
Revelation, 94
Rich, Adrienne,
   Diving into the Wreck, 231
   Mourning Picture, 172
   Novella, 266
   XI. (from Twenty-One Love Poems), 267
Richard Cory, 430
Ripe Figs, 4
Rites of Passage, 289
Robinson, Edwin Arlington
   Richard Cory, 430
Roethke, Theodore
   My Papa's Waltz, 289
Rose, Wendy
   Three Thousand Dollar Death Song, 449
Rose for Emily, A, 239
Rossetti, Christina
   In an Artist's Studio, 120
   Uphill, 234
Rumor, The, 99

Sailing to Byzantium, 133
St. Louis Blues, 151

Salter, Mary Jo
   The Rebirth of Venus, 175
Salvation, 83
Samuel, 86
Sandburg, Carl
   Limited, 224
School Children, The, 314
Schwarz, Jonathan
   What We Talk about When We Talk about Doughnuts, 254
Secret Life of Walter Mitty, The, 25
September 11, 2001, 401
September Poem, 410
Sexton, Anne
   The Starry Night, 176
Shakespeare, William
   Hamlet, Prince of Denmark, 315
   Sonnet 29 (When, in disgrace with Fortune and men's eyes), 257
   Sonnet 73 (That time of year thou mayst in me behold), 13
   Sonnet 116 (Let me not to the marriage of true minds), 259
   Sonnet 130 (My mistress' eyes are nothing like the sun), 116
   Sonnet 146 (Poor soul, the center of my sinful earth), 114
Shelley, Percy Bysshe
   Ozymandias, 222
Shiloh, (Mason), 217
Shiloh (Melville), 374
Shōnagon, Sei
   A Lover's Departure, 236
Short Story about the Vietnam War Memorial, A, 394
Sick Rose, The, 119
Sigourney, Lydia Howard Huntley
   Indian's Welcome to the Pilgrim Fathers, The, 443
Silken Tent, The, 265
Silko, Leslie Marmon
   Man to Send Rain Clouds, 36
Silver Swan, The, 80
Singer, Isaac Bashevis
   Son from America, The, 308
Slumber Did My Spirit Seal, A, 194

Smith, Bessie,
   Thinking Blues, 152
So Mexicans Are Taking Jobs from Americans, 432
Son from America, The, 308
Song, Cathy
   Beauty and Sadness, 174
Song: Go, Lovely Rose, 118
Song: Love Armed, 27
Sonnet (by Billy Collins), 121
Sonnet 29 (When, in disgrace with Fortune and men's eyes), 257
Sonnet 73 (That time of year thou mayst in me behold), 13
Sonnet 116 (Let me not to the marriage of true minds), 259
Sonnet 130 (My mistress' eyes are nothing like the sun), 116
Sonnet 146 (Poor soul, the center of my sinful earth), 114
Sophocles
   Antigone, 106
Soul selects her own Society, The, 142
Spellbound, 16
Spring and Fall: To a Young Child, 312
Stafford, William
   Traveling Through the Dark, 227
Staples, Brent
   Black Men and Public Space, 82
Starry Night, The, 176
Stay Home, 231
Stimpson, Catharine R.,
   Staffing, 405
Stopping by Woods on a Snowy Evening, 192
Storm, The, 8
Story of an Hour, 6
Staffing, 405
Sunday in the Park, 243
Sweat, 241
Szymborska, Wislawa
   Brueghel's Two Monkeys, 188

Talk of the Town: September 11, 2001, 401

Tan, Amy
  fish cheeks, 84
  Two Kinds, 415
Telephone, The, 114
"Tell all the Truth but tell it slant," 150
Tennyson, Afred Lord
  Ulysses, 223
Terkel, Studs
  Interviews, 382
"That time of year thou mayst in me behold," 13
The Dust behind I strove to Join, 74
The laws of god, the laws of man, 484
Theme for English B, 433
"There's a certain Slant of light," 144
"These are the days when Birds come back," 143
"The Soul selects her own Society," 142
Things They Carried, The, 395
Thinking Blues, 152
This Is Just To Say, 50
"This World is not Conclusion," 146
Thoreau, Henry David
  from *Civil Disobedience*, 453
"Those—dying then," 149
Those Winter Sundays, 288
Three Thousand Dollar Death Song, 449
Thurber, James
  The Secret Life of Walter Mitty, 25
To His Coy Mistress, 260
To live in the Borderlands means you, 431
Tonto del Barrio, El, 34
Too Blue, 158
To the Lady, 434
To the Virgins, to Make Much of Time, 39
Tragedy of Hamlet, Prince of Denmark, The, 315
Traveling Through the Dark, 227
Trifles, 494
Tsui, Kitty
  A Chinese Banquet, 271

Two, The, 283
Two Kinds, 415
Tyger, The, 42

Ulysses, 223
Unguarded Gates, The, 426
Updike, John
  A & P, 96
  Before the Mirror, 186
  Oliver's Evolution, 101
  Pygmalion, 97
  Rumor, The, 99
  September 11, 2001, 401
Uphill, 234
Upon Julia's Clothes, 120

Valdez, Luis
  Los Vendidos, 437
Valediction Forbidding Mourning, A, 259
Vanderkam, Laura
  Hookups Starve the Soul, 84
Van Duyn, Mona
  Leda, 49
Van Gogh's Bed, 169
Vanishing Red, The, 444
Vendidos, Los, 437
Vigil Strange I Kept on the Field One Night, 378

Wagoner, David
  Hooverville, 393
Walcott, Derek
  A Far Cry from Africa, 232
Walker, Alice
  Everyday Use, 417
Walkin' Blues, 154
Waller, Edmund
  Song (Go, Lovely Rose), 118
Washington, Booker T.
  Atlanta Exhibition Address, 476
Welty, Eudora
  A Worn Path, 90
We real cool, 78
Western Wind, 255

Index of Authors and Titles 509

"Western wind, when will thou blow?" 255
What Are Little Boys Made Of, 286
What Qualties Does a Good Photograph Have? 53
What We Talk about When We Talk about Doughnuts, 254
What We Talk about When We Talk about Love, 249
"When I Consider How My Light Is Spent," 193
"When I heard at the close of the day how my name had been," 263
"When in disgrace with Fortune and men's eyes," 257
"When I was one-and-twenty," 313
Where Are You Going, Where Have You Been?, 103
Whitman, Walt
   I Saw in Louisiana a Live-Oak Growing, 264
   Noiseless patient spider, A, 138
   Reconciliation, 378
   Vigil Strange I Kept on the Field One Night, 378
   When I Heard at the Close of the Day, 263
Who Will Light the Incense When Mother's Gone, 414
Wild Swans Skip School, The, 79
Wild Nights—Wild Nights, 112
Wild Swans at Coole, The, 77
Williams, Tennessee
   The Glass Menagerie, 110
Williams, William Carlos
   The Great Figure, 170

The Red Wheelbarrow, 137
This Is Just To Say, 50
Wilson, August
   Fences, 107
Wolff, Tobias
   Powder, 10
Woman's Work, 296
Woman Taken in Adultery, The, 462
Wordsworth, William
   Slumber Did My Spirit Seal, A, 194
Workin' Man Blues, 160
Worn Path, A, 90
Wright, Charles
   Laguna Blues, 165
Wright, James
   Lying in a Hammock at William Duffy's Farm in Pine Island, Minnesota, 135
Wright, Richard
   Man Who Was Almost a Man, The, 281

Yamada, Mitsuye
   Question of Loyalty, The, 496
   To the Lady, 434
Yeats, William Butler
   Annunciation, 44
   Leda and the Swan (first version), 44
   Leda and the Swan (second version), 44
   Sailing to Byzantium, 133
   Wild Swans at Coole, 77
Yellow Wallpaper, The, 278
Yolanda, 91
Young Goodman Brown, 302

NOTES

NOTES

NOTES

NOTES

NOTES

NOTES